THE MATTER OF
BLACK
LIVES

THE MATTER OF BLACK LIVES

WRITING FROM
THE NEW YORKER

EDITED BY
JELANI COBB AND
DAVID REMNICK

ecco
An Imprint of HarperCollinsPublishers

HarperCollins books may be purchased for educational, business, or sales promotional use. For information, please email the Special Markets Department at SPsales@harpercollins.com.

Ecco® and HarperCollins® are trademarks of HarperCollins Publishers.

A hardcover edition of this book was published in 2021 by Ecco, an imprint of HarperCollins Publishers.

FIRST ECCO PAPERBACK EDITION PUBLISHED 2022

Designed by Renata De Oliveira

Library of Congress Cataloging-in-Publication Data has been applied for.

ISBN 978-0-06-301760-3 (pbk.)

22 23 24 25 26   LSC   10 9 8 7 6 5 4 3 2 1

All pieces in this collection were originally published in *The New Yorker*. The publication date is given at the beginning of each piece.

CONTENTS

FOREWORD

JELANI COBB

In 1962, subscribers to *The New Yorker* leafed through the pages of the new November 17th issue and, amid the cartoons and the bountiful holiday-season ads, they came upon a long, blistering piece of writing by James Baldwin, "Letter from a Region in My Mind." The tone, and also the subject, of Baldwin's prose was unusual, even shocking, for the magazine. As Ben Yagoda writes in "About Town," a history of the magazine, *The New Yorker* had, in its early decades, largely kept the subject of race at a distinct remove from its readers. (In doing this, it was similar to most other "mainstream" publications.) There were exceptions, including Rebecca West's masterly 1947 account of a lynching trial in South Carolina; Comment pieces by E. B. White gently criticizing discrimination; profiles by Joseph Mitchell, Whitney Balliett, and Bernard Taper; and short fiction by Nadine Gordimer. But, as Yagoda writes, between *The New Yorker's* founding, in 1925, and the beginning of the Second World War, even the cartoons and the advertisements all too often depicted Black Americans in the most stereotypical terms: "as servants, Pullman porters, and comic figures."

Baldwin's essay was, for many readers, a jolt, a concussive experience. It gave no comfort to what Baldwin called the "incredible, abysmal, and really cowardly obtuseness of white liberals." As an indictment of American bigotry and hypocrisy, tackling themes of violence, sex, history, and religion, the piece continues to resonate more than half a century later. *The New Yorker* had long employed the rubric "Letter from . . ."—Letter from London, Letter from Johannesburg—as a way to announce the far-flung locations of its correspondents. Baldwin's title indicated that he was writing, most of all, from his inner depths. (When he published the essay as a book, the following year, he called it "The Fire Next Time.")

"Letter from a Region in My Mind," which appeared before the March on Washington and the Civil Rights and Voting Rights Acts, helped to reorient the American discussion of race. The piece also helped to push the magazine, which reached a well-educated, if monochromatic, readership, toward deeper thinking and reporting about an essential American subject. And yet its appearance in the magazine was a matter of publishing happenstance. Like many freelance writers and artists, Baldwin habitually juggled multiple assignments and commitments. He had promised William Shawn, the editor of *The New Yorker*, a long report on his travels to the post-colonial states of Senegal, Sierra Leone, Liberia, Guinea, and Ghana. At the same time, he was working on a piece about his youth in Harlem for Norman Podhoretz, the editor of *Commentary*. (The multitasking did not stop there; Baldwin was also trying to finish his third novel, "Another Country.")

Somehow, the African trip, while important to Baldwin as a matter of personal experience, did not inspire successful writing. As his biographer David Leeming notes, Baldwin formed some tentative impressions of situations and of people whom he met there, but nothing seemed to cohere on the page. He was particularly reluctant to make any presumptions of kinship or shared experiences between Africans and Black Americans. The trip had the paradoxical effect of renewing Baldwin's interest in the autobiographical essay about Harlem and, by extension, Black life in America. He was also interested in finding a way to make sense of an encounter he'd had with Elijah Muhammad, the diminutive and enigmatic leader of the Chicago-based Nation of Islam. Baldwin wanted to write about the contrast between the Christian Church in which he was raised—his father was a preacher in Harlem—and the Nation of Islam, all in the greater context of the intolerably desperate conditions of Black life in the United States. And so, after giving up on the Africa piece, he concentrated on his American essay. But, instead of sending his manuscript to Podhoretz, he gave it to Shawn, at *The New Yorker*, which had a much bigger audience than *Commentary* and paid better. Podhoretz, who later became a godfather of the neoconservative movement, never forgave Baldwin, Shawn, or *The New Yorker*. (In 1963, Podhoretz published an essay of his own, called "My Negro Problem—and Ours," but that is another story.)

After publishing the Baldwin essay and sensing its resonance among readers, *The New Yorker*, like other publications, extended its coverage of race and devoted considerable space to the civil-rights movement. Shawn hired a young woman named Charlayne Hunter (now Hunter-Gault), an aspiring journalist who had generated national headlines when she and her classmate Hamilton Holmes integrated the University of Georgia. At first, she was an editorial assistant. In 1964, after she wrote about a riot in Bedford-Stuyvesant, she was promoted to staff writer, the first Black staff writer in *The New Yorker's* history. Calvin Trillin, who came to the magazine from *Time*, in 1963, and wrote about the drama in Georgia, began reporting consistently on the movement. Renata Adler wrote a long piece on the march from Selma to Montgomery. And, in 1968, Jervis Anderson, a Jamaican-born newspaper reporter, joined the staff and wrote numerous Talk of the Town pieces in addition to profiles of A. Philip Randolph, Bayard Rustin, and Ralph Ellison. His four-part portrait of Harlem in the first half of the twentieth century was eventually published as a book, "This Was Harlem." *The New Yorker* had hardly been transformed into *Ebony*, but it was no longer quite so pale.

THE FIRST PIECE I WROTE WHEN I ARRIVED AT *THE NEW YORKER*, IN 2012, was titled "Trayvon Martin and the Parameters of Hope," an exploration of the dynamics surrounding the shooting death of an unarmed seventeen-year-old Black boy in Sanford, Florida, in the context of the Obama Presidency. Martin's death, and the 2014 police shooting death of eighteen-year-old Michael Brown, in Ferguson, Missouri, launched what has come to be known as the Black Lives Matter movement.

In May, 2020, during the uprising that followed the murder of George Floyd, in Minneapolis, I found myself rereading Baldwin's essay. I don't think I was alone. His exploration of race seemed to me as vital, as ragingly alive, as when it was first published, more than half a century ago. And it helped make sense of what we were experiencing: the chaotic, angry, defiant tableaux in the streets of Minneapolis, Seattle, Los Angeles, New York, Philadelphia, Oakland, Atlanta, Chicago, Houston, Louisville, San Francisco, Indianapolis, Charleston, Detroit, Baltimore, and beyond represented a reckoning, a kind of American Spring, one long in the making. After his death, George Floyd's name had become a metaphor for the stacked inequities of the society that produced them. Race, to the degree that it represents anything coherent in the United States, is shorthand for a specific set of life probabilities. The inequalities between Black and white Americans are documented in radically varying rates of morbidity and infant mortality, and in wealth and employment. These disparities make it plain that, while race may be a biological fiction, its realities are painfully evident in what is likely to happen in our lives. The more than forty million people of African descent who live in the United States recognize this reality, but it has long been invisible, or of minimal concern, to most white Americans.

This seemed to be part of what Baldwin tried to reckon with in his "Letter." He wanted to make plain and inescapable that the legacy of racism—of slavery, Jim Crow, and the myriad structures of inequality that shape our lives today—defines, in large measure, the crisis of American life and the question of our common fate.

He was arguing for the *centrality* of the situation. One particularly searing, albeit gendered, line from Baldwin's "Letter" conveys the sentiment and even the national prospect with precision: the Negro, he wrote, is *"the* key figure in his country, and the American future is precisely as bright or as dark as his."

One of the earnest outgrowths of the spring and summer demonstrations of 2020 was the compiling of reading lists—endless lists, from slave narratives to novels to treatises on "white fragility," distributed by libraries, schools, even corporations. Better to have these lists than not, one supposed; it was a good thing to see at least some of these books get a wider audience, and Kelefa Sanneh wrote about some of them in a critical essay republished here. At *The New Yorker*, as at other publications, we thought hard about how to write about what the country was experiencing, what and whom we should publish in the future.

At the same time, we began to comb the archives to get a sense of how the political, cultural, and economic questions surrounding race and Black achievement have been portrayed in *The New Yorker* by writers as distinguished and as various as Toni Morrison and Hilton Als; Zadie Smith and Jamaica Kincaid; Henry Louis Gates, Jr., and Elizabeth Alexander—to name just a few. The result is this anthology.

Our hope is that we have assembled a collection, beginning with Baldwin's "Letter," that begins to suggest, through an array of writers, the depths of political thinking and argument connected to race in America; the range of cultural accomplishment; the variousness of personal experience. Race has exerted a profound, distorting effect on American life—all of it, not simply the portion labelled with the racial modifier "Black." But the very nature of the problem Baldwin highlighted insures that it is generally associated with only that sliver of the public. This is not an anthology about race. It is a collection about a broad, fascinating set of events and the people who are most commonly tasked with confronting it. The American future is precisely as bright or as dark as our capacity to grapple with this enduring concern. This collection is a chronicle of at least a part of our past and a lens to help envision a better American future.

PART I
REFLECTIONS

LETTER FROM
A REGION IN MY MIND

JAMES BALDWIN

November 17, 1962

Take up the White Man's burden—
Ye dare not stoop to less—
Nor call too loud on Freedom
To cloak your weariness;
By all ye cry or whisper,
By all ye leave or do,
The silent, sullen peoples
Shall weigh your Gods and you.

—Kipling

Down at the cross where my Saviour died,
Down where for cleansing from sin I cried,
There to my heart was the blood applied,
Singing glory to His name!

—Hymn

I underwent, during the summer that I became fourteen, a prolonged religious crisis. I use "religious" in the common, and arbitrary, sense, meaning that I then discovered God, His saints and
angels, and His blazing Hell. And since I had been born in a Christian nation, I accepted this Deity as the only one. I supposed Him
to exist only within the walls of a church—in fact, of *our* church—
and I also supposed that God and safety were synonymous. The

word "safety" brings us to the real meaning of the word "religious" as we use it. Therefore, to state it in another, more accurate way, I became, during my fourteenth year, for the first time in my life, afraid—afraid of the evil within me and afraid of the evil without. What I saw around me that summer in Harlem was what I had always seen; nothing had changed. But now, without any warning, the whores and pimps and racketeers on the Avenue had become a personal menace. It had not before occurred to me that I could become one of them, but now I realized that we had been produced by the same circumstances. Many of my comrades were clearly headed for the Avenue, and my father said that I was headed that way, too. My friends began to drink and smoke, and embarked—at first avid, then groaning—on their sexual careers. Girls, only slightly older than I was, who sang in the choir or taught Sunday school, the children of holy parents, underwent, before my eyes, their incredible metamorphosis, of which the most bewildering aspect was not their budding breasts or their rounding behinds but something deeper and more subtle, in their eyes, their heat, their odor, and the inflection of their voices. Like the strangers on the Avenue, they became, in the twinkling of an eye, unutterably different and fantastically *present*. Owing to the way I had been raised, the abrupt discomfort that all this aroused in me and the fact that I had no idea what my voice or my mind or my body was likely to do next caused me to consider myself one of the most depraved people on earth. Matters were not helped by the fact that these holy girls seemed rather to enjoy my terrified lapses, our grim, guilty, tormented experiments, which were at once as chill and joyless as the Russian steppes and hotter, by far, than all the fires of Hell.

Yet there was something deeper than these changes, and less definable, that frightened me. It was real in both the boys and the girls, but it was, somehow, more vivid in the boys. In the case of the girls, one watched them turning into matrons before they had become women. They began to manifest a curious and really rather terrifying single-mindedness. It is hard to say exactly how this was conveyed: something implacable in the set of the lips, something farseeing (seeing what?) in the eyes, some new and crushing determination in the walk, something peremptory in the voice. They did not tease us, the boys, any more; they reprimanded us sharply, saying, "You better be thinking about your soul!" For the girls also saw the evidence on the Avenue, knew what the price would be, for them, of one misstep, knew that they had to be protected and that we were the only protection there was. They understood that they must act as God's decoys, saving the souls of the boys for Jesus and binding the bodies of the boys in marriage. For this was the beginning of our burning time, and "It is better," said St. Paul—who elsewhere, with a most unusual and stunning exactness, described himself as a "wretched man"—"to marry than to burn." And I began to feel in the boys a curious, wary, bewildered despair, as though they were now settling in for the long, hard winter of life. I did not know then what it was that I was reacting to; I put it to myself that they were letting themselves go. In the same way that the girls were destined to gain as much weight as their mothers, the boys, it was clear, would rise no higher than their fathers. School began to reveal itself, therefore, as a child's game that one could not win, and boys dropped out of school and went to work. My father wanted me to do the same. I refused, even though I no longer had any illusions about what an education could do for me; I had already encountered too many college-graduate handymen. My friends were now "downtown," busy, as they put it, "fighting the man." They began to care less about the way they looked, the way they dressed, the things they did; presently, one found them in twos and threes and fours, in a hallway, sharing a jug of wine or a bottle of whiskey, talking, cursing, fighting, sometimes weeping: lost, and unable to say what it was that oppressed them, except that they knew it was "the man"—the white man. And there seemed to be no way whatever to remove this cloud that stood between them and the sun, between them and love and life and power, between them and whatever it was that they wanted. One did not have to be very bright to realize how little one could do to change one's situation; one did not have to be abnormally sensitive to be worn down to a cutting edge by the incessant and gratuitous humiliation and danger one encountered every working day, all day long. The humiliation did not apply merely to working days, or workers; I was thirteen and was crossing Fifth Avenue on my way to the Forty-second Street library, and the cop in the middle of the street muttered as I passed him, "Why don't you niggers stay uptown where you belong?" When I was ten, and didn't look, certainly, any older, two policemen amused themselves with me by frisking me, making comic (and terrifying) speculations concerning my ancestry and probable sexual prowess, and, for good measure, leaving me flat on my back in one of Harlem's empty lots. Just before and then during the Second World War, many of my friends fled into the service, all to be changed there, and rarely for the better, many to be ruined, and many to die. Others fled to other states and cities—that is, to other ghettos. Some went on wine or whiskey or the needle, and are still on it. And others, like me, fled into the church.

For the wages of sin were visible everywhere, in every wine-stained and urine-splashed hallway, in every clanging ambulance bell, in every scar on the faces of the pimps and their whores, in every helpless, newborn baby being brought into this danger, in every knife and pistol fight on the Avenue, and in every disastrous bulletin: a cousin, mother of six, suddenly gone mad, the children parcelled out here and there; an indestructible aunt rewarded for years of hard labor by a slow, agonizing death in a terrible small room; someone's bright son blown into eternity by his own hand; another turned robber and carried off to jail. It was a summer of dreadful speculations and discoveries, of which these were not the worst. Crime became real, for example—for the first time—not as *a* possibility but as *the* possibility. One would never defeat one's circumstances by working and saving one's pennies; one would never, by working, acquire that many pennies, and, besides, the social treatment accorded even the most successful Negroes proved that one needed, in order to be free, something more than a bank account. One needed a handle, a lever, a means of inspiring fear. It was absolutely clear that the police would whip you and take you in as long as they could get away with it, and that everyone else— housewives, taxi-drivers, elevator boys, dishwashers, bartenders, lawyers, judges, doctors, and grocers—would never, by the operation of any generous human feeling, cease to use you as an outlet for his frustrations and hostilities. Neither civilized reason nor Christian love would cause any of those people to treat you as they presumably wanted to be treated; only the fear of your power to retaliate would cause them to do that, or to seem to do it, which was (and is) good enough. There appears to be a vast amount of confusion on this point, but I do not know many Negroes who are eager to be "accepted" by white people, still less to be loved by them; they, the blacks, simply don't wish to be beaten over the head by the whites every instant of our brief passage on this planet. White people in this country will have quite enough to do in learning how to accept and love themselves and each other, and when they have achieved this—which will not be tomorrow and may very well be never—the Negro problem will no longer exist, for it will no longer be needed.

People more advantageously placed than we in Harlem were, and are, will no doubt find the psychology and the view of human nature sketched above dismal and shocking in the extreme. But the Negro's experience of the white world cannot possibly create in him any respect for the standards by which the white world claims to live. His own condition is overwhelming proof that white people do not live by these standards. Negro servants have been smuggling odds and ends out of white homes for generations, and white people have been delighted to have them do it, because it has assuaged a dim guilt and testified to the intrinsic superiority of white people. Even the most doltish and servile Negro could scarcely fail to be impressed by the disparity between his situation and that of the people for whom he worked; Negroes who were neither doltish nor servile did not feel that they were doing anything wrong when they robbed white people. In spite of the Puritan-Yankee equation of virtue with well-being, Negroes had excellent reasons for doubting that money was made or kept by any very striking adherence to the Christian virtues; it certainly did not work that way for black Christians. In any case, white people, who had robbed black people of their liberty and who profited by this theft every hour that they lived, had no moral ground on which to stand. They had the judges, the juries, the shotguns, the law—in a word, power. But it was a criminal power, to be feared but not respected, and to be outwitted in any way whatever. And those virtues preached but not practiced by the white world were merely another means of holding Negroes in subjection.

It turned out, then, that summer, that the moral barriers that I had supposed to exist between me and the dangers of a criminal career were so tenuous as to be nearly nonexistent. I certainly could not discover any principled reason for not becoming a criminal, and it is not my poor, God-fearing parents who are to be indicted for the lack but this society. I was icily determined—more determined, really, than I then knew—never to make my peace with the ghetto but to die and go to Hell before I would let any white man spit on me, before I would accept my "place" in this republic. I did not intend to allow the white people of this country to tell me who I was, and limit me that way, and polish me off that way. And yet, of course, at the same time, I *was* being spat on and defined and described and limited, and could have been polished off with no effort whatever. Every Negro boy—in my situation during those years, at least—who reaches this point realizes, at once, profoundly, because he wants to live, that he stands in great peril and must find, with speed, a "thing," a gimmick, to lift him out, to start him on his way.

And it does not matter what the gimmick is. It was this last realization that terrified me and—since it revealed that the door opened on so many dangers—helped to hurl me into the church. And, by an unforeseeable paradox, it was my career in the church that turned out, precisely, to be my gimmick.

For when I tried to assess my capabilities, I realized that I had almost none. In order to achieve the life I wanted, I had been dealt, it seemed to me, the worst possible hand. I could not become a prizefighter—many of us tried but very few succeeded. I could not sing. I could not dance. I had been well conditioned by the world in which I grew up, so I did not yet dare take the idea of becoming a writer seriously. The only other possibility seemed to involve my becoming one of the sordid people on the Avenue, who were not really as sordid as I then imagined but who frightened me terribly, both because I did not want to live that life and because of what they made me feel. Everything inflamed me, and that was bad enough, but I myself had also become a source of fire and temptation. I had been far too well raised, alas, to suppose that any of the extremely explicit overtures made to me that summer, sometimes by boys and girls but also, more alarmingly, by older men and women, had anything to do with my attractiveness. On the contrary, since the Harlem idea of seduction is, to put it mildly, blunt, whatever these people saw in me merely confirmed my sense of my depravity.

It is certainly sad that the awakening of one's senses should lead to such a merciless judgment of oneself—to say nothing of the time and anguish one spends in the effort to arrive at any other—but it is also inevitable that a literal attempt to mortify the flesh should be made among black people like those with whom I grew up. Negroes in this country—and Negroes do not, strictly or legally speaking, exist in any other—are taught really to despise themselves from the moment their eyes open on the world. This world is white and they are black. White people hold the power, which means that they are superior to blacks (intrinsically, that is: God decreed it so), and the world has innumerable ways of making this difference known and felt and feared. Long before the Negro child perceives this difference, and even longer before he understands it, he has begun to react to it, he has begun to be controlled by it. Every effort made by the child's elders to prepare him for a fate from which they cannot protect him causes him secretly, in terror, to begin to await, without knowing that he is doing so, his mysterious and inexorable punishment. He must be "good" not only in order to please his parents and not only to avoid being punished by them; behind their authority stands another, nameless and impersonal, infinitely harder to please, and bottomlessly cruel. And this filters into the child's consciousness through his parents' tone of voice as he is being exhorted, punished, or loved; in the sudden, uncontrollable note of fear heard in his mother's or his father's voice when he has strayed beyond some particular boundary. He does not know what the boundary is, and he can get no explanation of it, which is frightening enough, but the fear he hears in the voices of his elders is more frightening still. The fear that I heard in my father's voice, for example, when he realized that I really *believed* I could do anything a white boy could do, and had every intention of proving it, was not at all like the fear I heard when one of us was ill or had fallen down the stairs or strayed too far from the house. It was another fear, a fear that the child, in challenging the white world's assumptions, was putting himself in the path of destruction. A child cannot, thank Heaven, know how vast and how merciless is the nature of power, with what unbelievable cruelty people treat each other. He reacts to the fear in his parents' voices because his parents hold up the world for him and he has no protection without them. I defended myself, as I imagined, against the fear my father made me feel by remembering that he was very old-fashioned. Also, I prided myself on the fact that I already knew how to outwit him. To defend oneself against a fear is simply to insure that one will, one day, be conquered by it; fears must be faced. As for one's wits, it is just not true that one can live by them—not, that is, if one wishes really to live. That summer, in any case, all the fears with which I had grown up, and which were now a part of me and controlled my vision of the world, rose up like a wall between the world and me, and drove me into the church.

As I look back, everything I did seems curiously deliberate, though it certainly did not seem deliberate then. For example, I did not join the church of which my father was a member and in which he preached. My best friend in school, who attended a different church, had already "surrendered his life to the Lord," and he was very anxious about my soul's salvation. (I wasn't, but any human attention was better than none.) One Saturday afternoon, he took me to his church. There were no services that day, and the church was empty, except for some women cleaning and some other women praying. My friend took me into the back room to meet his pastor—a woman. There she sat, in her robes, smiling, an extremely proud and handsome woman, with Africa, Europe, and the America of the American Indian blended in her face. She was perhaps forty-five or fifty at this time, and in our world she was a very celebrated woman. My friend was about to introduce me when she looked at me and smiled and said, "Whose little boy are you?" Now this, unbelievably, was precisely the phrase used by pimps and racketeers on the Avenue when they suggested, both humorously and intensely, that I "hang out" with them. Perhaps part of the terror they had caused me to feel came from the fact that I unquestionably wanted to be *somebody's* little boy. I was so frightened, and at the mercy of so many conundrums, that inevitably, that summer, *someone* would have taken me over; one doesn't, in Harlem, long remain standing on any auction block. It was my good luck—perhaps—that I found myself in the church racket instead of some other, and surrendered to a spiritual seduction long before I came to any carnal knowledge. For when the pastor asked me, with that marvellous smile, "Whose little boy are you?" my heart replied at once, "Why, yours."

The summer wore on, and things got worse. I became more guilty and more frightened, and kept all this bottled up inside me, and naturally, inescapably, one night, when this woman had finished preaching, everything came roaring, screaming, crying out, and I fell to the ground before the altar. It was the strangest sensation I have ever had in my life—up to that time, or since. I had not known that it was going to happen, or that it could happen. One moment I was on my feet, singing and clapping and, at the same time, working out in my head the plot of a play I was working on then; the next moment, with no transition, no sensation of falling, I was on my back, with the lights beating down into my face and all the vertical saints above me. I did not know what I was doing down so low, or how I had got there. And the anguish that filled me cannot be described. It moved in me like one of those floods that devastate counties, tearing everything down, tearing children from their parents and lovers from each other, and making everything an unrecognizable waste. All I really remember is the pain, the unspeakable pain; it was as though I were yelling up to Heaven and Heaven would not hear me. And if Heaven would not hear me, if love could not descend from Heaven—to wash me, to make me clean—then utter disaster was my portion. Yes, it does indeed mean something—something unspeakable—to be born, in a white country, an Anglo-Teutonic, antisexual country, black. You very soon, without knowing it, give up all hope of communion. Black people, mainly, look down or look up but do not look at each other, not at you, and white people, mainly, look away. And the universe is simply a sounding drum; there is no way, no way whatever, so it seemed then and has sometimes seemed since, to get through a life, to love your wife and children, or your friends, or your mother and father, or to be loved. The universe, which is not merely the stars and the moon and the planets, flowers, grass, and trees, but *other people*, has evolved no terms for your existence, has made no room for you, and if love will not swing wide the gates, no other power will or can. And if one despairs—as who has not?—of human love, God's love alone is left. But God—and I felt this even then, so long ago, on that tremendous floor, unwillingly—is white. And if His love was so great, and if He loved all His children, why were we, the blacks, cast down so far? Why? In spite of all I said thereafter, I found no answer on the floor—not *that* answer, anyway—and I was on the floor all night. Over me, to bring me "through," the saints sang and rejoiced and prayed. And in the morning, when they raised me, they told me that I was "saved."

Well, indeed I was, in a way, for I was utterly drained and exhausted, and released, for the first time, from all my guilty torment. I was aware then only of my relief. For many years, I could not ask myself why human relief had to be achieved in a fashion at once so pagan and so desperate—in a fashion at once so unspeakably old and so unutterably new. And by the time I was able to ask myself this question, I was also able to see that the principles governing the rites and customs of the churches in which I grew up did not differ from the principles governing the rites and customs of other churches, white. The principles were Blindness, Loneliness, and Terror, the first principle necessarily and actively cultivated in order to deny the two others. I would love to believe that the principles were Faith, Hope, and Charity, but this is clearly not so for most Christians, or for what we call the Christian world.

I was saved. But at the same time, out of a deep, adolescent cunning I do not pretend to understand, I realized immediately that I could not remain in the church merely as another worshipper. I would have to give myself something to do, in order not to be too bored and find myself among all the wretched unsaved of the Avenue. And I don't doubt that I also intended to best my father on his own ground. Anyway, very shortly after I joined the church, I became a preacher—a Young Minister—and I remained in the pulpit for more than three years. My youth quickly made me a much bigger drawing card than my father. I pushed this advantage ruthlessly, for it was the most effective means I had found of breaking his hold over me. That was the most frightening time of my life, and quite the most dishonest, and the resulting hysteria lent great passion to my sermons—for a while. I relished the attention and the relative immunity from punishment that my new status gave me, and I relished, above all, the sudden right to privacy. It had to be recognized, after all, that I was still a schoolboy, with my schoolwork to do, and I was also expected to prepare at least one sermon a week. During what we may call my heyday, I preached much more often than that. This meant that there were hours and even whole days when I could not be interrupted—not even by my father. I had immobilized him. It took rather more time for me to realize that I had also immobilized myself, and had escaped from nothing whatever.

The church was very exciting. It took a long time for me to disengage myself from this excitement, and on the blindest, most visceral level, I never really have, and never will. There is no music like that music, no drama like the drama of the saints rejoicing, the sinners moaning, the tambourines racing, and all those voices coming together and crying holy unto the Lord. There is still, for me, no pathos quite like the pathos of those multicolored, worn, somehow triumphant and transfigured faces, speaking from the depths of a visible, tangible, continuing despair of the goodness of the Lord. I have never seen anything to equal the fire and excitement that sometimes, without warning, fill a church, causing the church, as Leadbelly and so many others have testified, to "rock." Nothing that has happened to me since equals the power and the glory that I sometimes felt when, in the middle of a sermon, I knew that I was somehow, by some miracle, really carrying, as they said, "the Word"—when the church and I were one. Their pain and their joy were mine, and mine were theirs—they surrendered their pain and joy to me, I surrendered mine to them—and their cries of "Amen!" and "Hallelujah!" and "Yes, Lord" and "Praise His name!"

and "Preach it, brother!" sustained and whipped on my solos until we all became equal, wringing wet, singing and dancing, in anguish and rejoicing, at the foot of the altar. It was, for a long time, in spite of—or, not inconceivably, because of—the shabbiness of my motives, my only sustenance, my meat and drink. I rushed home from school, to the church, to the altar, to be alone there, to commune with Jesus, my dearest Friend, who would never fail me, who knew all the secrets of my heart. Perhaps He did, but I didn't, and the bargain we struck, actually, down there at the foot of the cross, was that He would never let me find out.

He failed his bargain. He was a much better Man than I took Him for. It happened, as things do, imperceptibly, in many ways at once. I date it—the slow crumbling of my faith, the pulverization of my fortress—from the time, about a year after I had begun to preach, when I began to read again. I justified this desire by the fact that I was still in school, and I began, fatally, with Dostoevski. By this time, I was in a high school that was predominantly Jewish. This meant that I was surrounded by people who were, by definition, beyond any hope of salvation, who laughed at the tracts and leaflets I brought to school, and who pointed out that the Gospels had been written long after the death of Christ. This might not have been so distressing if it had not forced me to read the tracts and leaflets myself, for they were indeed, unless one believed their message already, impossible to believe. I remember feeling dimly that there was a kind of blackmail in it. People, I felt, ought to love the Lord *because* they loved Him, and not because they were afraid of going to Hell. I was forced, reluctantly, to realize that the Bible itself had been written by men, and translated by men out of languages I could not read, and I was already, without quite admitting it to myself, terribly involved with the effort of putting words on paper. Of course, I had the rebuttal ready: These men had all been operating under divine inspiration. *Had* they? *All* of them? And I also knew by now, alas, far more about divine inspiration than I dared admit, for I knew how I worked myself up into my own visions, and how frequently—indeed, incessantly—the visions God granted to me differed from the visions He granted to my father. I did not understand the dreams I had at night, but I knew that they were not holy. For that matter, I knew that my waking hours were far from holy. I spent most of my time in a state of repentance for things I had vividly desired to do but had not done. The fact that I was dealing with Jews brought the whole question of color, which I had been desperately avoiding, into the terrified center of my mind. I realized that the Bible had been written by white men. I knew that, according to many Christians, I was a descendant of Ham, who had been cursed, and that I was therefore predestined to be a slave. This had nothing to do with anything I was, or contained, or could become; my fate had been sealed forever, from the beginning of time. And it seemed, indeed, when one looked out over Christendom, that this was what Christendom effectively believed. It was certainly the way it behaved. I remembered the Italian priests and bishops blessing Italian boys who were on their way to Ethiopia.

Again, the Jewish boys in high school were troubling because I could find no point of connection between them and the Jewish pawnbrokers and landlords and grocery-store owners in Harlem. I knew that these people were Jews—God knows I was told it often enough—but I thought of them only as white. Jews, as such, until I got to high school, were all incarcerated in the Old Testament, and their names were Abraham, Moses, Daniel, Ezekiel, and Job, and Shadrach, Meshach, and Abednego. It was bewildering to find them so many miles and centuries out of Egypt, and so far from the fiery furnace. My best friend in high school was a Jew. He came to our house once, and afterward my father asked, as he asked about everyone, "Is he a Christian?"—by which he meant "Is he saved?" I really do not know whether my answer came out of innocence or venom, but I said, coldly, "No. He's Jewish." My father slammed me across the face with his great palm, and in that moment everything flooded back—all the hatred and all the fear, and the depth of a merciless resolve to kill my father rather than allow my father to kill me—and I knew that all those sermons and tears and all that repentance and rejoicing had changed nothing. I wondered if I was expected to be glad that a friend of mine, or anyone, was to be tormented forever in Hell, and I also thought, suddenly, of the Jews in another Christian nation, Germany. They were not so far from the fiery furnace after all, and my best friend might have been one of them. I told my father, "He's a better Christian than you are," and walked out of the house. The battle between us was in the open, but that was all right; it was almost a relief. A more deadly struggle had begun.

Being in the pulpit was like being in the theatre; I was behind the scenes and knew how the illusion was worked. I knew the other ministers and knew the quality of their lives. And I don't mean to suggest by this the "Elmer Gantry" sort of hypocrisy concerning sensuality; it was a deeper, deadlier, and more subtle hypocrisy than that, and a little honest sensuality, or a lot, would have been like water in an extremely bitter desert. I knew how to work on a congregation until the last dime was surrendered—it was not very hard to do—and I knew where the money for "the Lord's work" went. I knew, though I did not wish to know it, that I had no respect for the people with whom I worked. I could not have said it then, but I also knew that if I continued I would soon have no respect for myself. And the fact that I was "the young Brother Baldwin" increased my value with those same pimps and racketeers who had helped to stampede me into the church in the first place. They still saw the little boy they intended to take over. They were waiting for me to come to my senses and realize that I was in a very lucrative business. They knew that I did not yet realize this, and also that I had not yet begun to suspect where my own needs, *coming up* (they were very patient), could drive me. They themselves did know the score, and they knew that the odds were in their favor. And, really,

I knew it, too. I was even lonelier and more vulnerable than I had been before. And the blood of the Lamb had not cleansed me in any way whatever. I was just as black as I had been the day that I was born. Therefore, when I faced a congregation, it began to take all the strength I had not to stammer, not to curse, not to tell them to throw away their Bibles and get off their knees and go home and organize, for example, a rent strike. When I watched all the children, their copper, brown, and beige faces staring up at me as I taught Sunday school, I felt that I was committing a crime in talking about the gentle Jesus, in telling them to reconcile themselves to their misery on earth in order to gain the crown of eternal life. Were only Negroes to gain this crown? Was Heaven, then, to be merely another ghetto? Perhaps I might have been able to reconcile myself even to this if I had been able to believe that there was any loving-kindness to be found in the haven I represented. But I had been in the pulpit too long and I had seen too many monstrous things. I don't refer merely to the glaring fact that the minister eventually acquires houses and Cadillacs while the faithful continue to scrub floors and drop their dimes and quarters and dollars into the plate. I really mean that there was no love in the church. It was a mask for hatred and self-hatred and despair. The transfiguring power of the Holy Ghost ended when the service ended, and salvation stopped at the church door. When we were told to love everybody, I had thought that that meant *everybody*. But no. It applied only to those who believed as we did, and it did not apply to white people at all. I was told by a minister, for example, that I should never, on any public conveyance, under any circumstances, rise and give my seat to a white woman. White men never rose for Negro women. Well, that was true enough, in the main—I saw his point. But what was the point, the purpose, of *my* salvation if it did not permit me to behave with love toward others, no matter how they behaved toward me? What others did was their responsibility, for which they would answer when the judgment trumpet sounded.

But what *I* did was *my* responsibility, and I would have to answer, too—unless, of course, there was also in Heaven a special dispensation for the benighted black, who was not to be judged in the same way as other human beings, or angels. It probably occurred to me around this time that the vision people hold of the world to come is but a reflection, with predictable wishful distortions, of the world in which they live. And this did not apply only to Negroes, who were no more "simple" or "spontaneous" or "Christian" than anybody else—who were merely more oppressed. In the same way that we, for white people, were the descendants of Ham, and were cursed forever, white people were, for us, the descendants of Cain. And the passion with which we loved the Lord was a measure of how deeply we feared and distrusted and, in the end, hated almost all strangers, always, and avoided and despised ourselves.

But I cannot leave it at that; there is more to it than that. In spite of everything, there was in the life I fled a zest and a joy and a capacity for facing and surviving disaster that are very moving and very rare. Perhaps we were, all of us—pimps, whores, racketeers, church members, and children—bound together by the nature of our oppression, the specific and peculiar complex of risks we had to run; if so, within these limits we sometimes achieved with each other a freedom that was close to love. I remember, anyway, church suppers and outings, and, later, after I left the church, rent and waistline parties where rage and sorrow sat in the darkness and did not stir, and we ate and drank and talked and laughed and danced and forgot all about "the man." We had the liquor, the chicken, the music, and each other, and had no need to pretend to be what we were not. This is the freedom that one hears in some gospel songs, for example, and in jazz. In all jazz, and especially in the blues, there is something tart and ironic, authoritative and double-edged. White Americans seem to feel that happy songs are *happy* and *sad* songs are sad, and that, God help us, is exactly the way most white Americans sing them—sounding, in both cases, so helplessly, defenselessly fatuous that one dare not speculate on the temperature of the deep freeze from which issue their brave and sexless little voices. Only people who have been "down the line," as the song puts it, know what this music is about. I think it was Big Bill Broonzy who used to sing "I Feel So Good," a really joyful song about a man who is on his way to the railroad station to meet his girl. She's coming home. It is the singer's incredibly moving exuberance that makes one realize how leaden the time must have been while she was gone. There is no guarantee that she will stay this time, either, as the singer clearly knows, and, in fact, she has not yet actually arrived. Tonight, or tomorrow, or within the next five minutes, he may very well be sing- ing "Lonesome in My Bedroom," or insisting, "Ain't we, ain't we, going to make it all right? Well, if we don't today, we will tomor- row night." White Americans do not understand the depths out of which such an ironic tenacity comes, but they suspect that the force is sensual, and they are terrified of sensuality and do not any longer understand it. The word "sensual" is not intended to bring to mind quivering dusky maidens or priapic black studs. I am referring to something much simpler and much less fanciful. To be sensual, I think, is to respect and rejoice in the force of life, of life itself, and to be *present* in all that one does, from the effort of loving to the breaking of bread. It will be a great day for America, incidentally, when we begin to eat bread again, instead of the blasphemous and tasteless foam rubber that we have substituted for it. And I am not being frivolous now, either. Something very sinister happens to the people of a country when they begin to distrust their own reactions as deeply as they do here, and become as joyless as they have be- come. It is this individual uncertainty on the part of white American men and women, this inability to renew themselves at the fountain of their own lives, that makes the discussion, let alone elucidation, of any conundrum—that is, any reality—so supremely difficult. The person who distrusts himself has no touchstone for reality—for this touchstone can be only oneself. Such a person interposes between himself and reality nothing less than a labyrinth of attitudes. And these attitudes, furthermore, though the person is usually unaware of it (is unaware of so much!), are historical and public attitudes. They do not relate to the present any more than they relate to the person. Therefore, whatever white people do not know about Negroes reveals, precisely and inexorably, what they do not know about themselves.

White Christians have also forgotten several elementary historical details. They have forgotten that the religion that is now identified with their virtue and their power—"God is on our side," says Dr. Verwoerd—came out of a rocky piece of ground in what is now known as the Middle East before color was invented, and that in order for the Christian church to be established, Christ had to be put to death, by Rome, and that the real architect of the Christian church was not the disreputable, sun-baked Hebrew who gave it his name but the mercilessly fanatical and self-righteous St. Paul. The energy that was buried with the rise of the Christian nations must come back into the world; nothing can prevent it. Many of us, I think, both long to see this happen and are terrified of it, for though this transformation contains the hope of liberation, it also imposes a necessity for great change. But in order to deal with the untapped and dormant force of the previously subjugated, in order to survive as a human, moving, moral weight in the world, America and all the Western nations will be forced to reëxamine themselves and release themselves from many things that are now taken to be sacred, and to discard nearly all the assumptions that have been used to justify their lives and their anguish and their crimes so long.

"The white man's Heaven," sings a Black Muslim minister, "is the black man's Hell." One may object—possibly—that this puts the matter somewhat too simply, but the song is true, and it has been true for as long as white men have ruled the world. The Africans put it another way: When the white man came to Africa, the white man had the Bible and the African had the land, but now it is the white man who is being, reluctantly and bloodily, separated from the land, and the African who is still attempting to digest or to vomit up the Bible. The struggle, therefore, that now begins in the world is extremely complex, involving the historical role of Christianity in the realm of power—that is, politics—and in the realm of morals. In the realm of power, Christianity has operated with an unmitigated arrogance and cruelty—necessarily, since a religion ordinarily imposes on those who have discovered the true faith the spiritual duty of liberating the infidels. This particular true faith, moreover, is more deeply concerned about the soul than it is about the body, to which fact the flesh (and the corpses) of countless infidels bears witness. It goes without saying, then, that whoever questions the authority of the true faith also contests the right of the nations that hold this faith to rule over him—contests, in short, their title to his land. The spreading of the Gospel, regardless of the motives or the integrity or the heroism of some of the missionaries, was an absolutely indispensable justification for the planting of the flag. Priests and nuns and schoolteachers helped to protect and sanctify the power that was so ruthlessly being used by people who were indeed seeking a city, but not one in the heavens, and one to be made, very definitely, by captive hands. The Christian church itself—again, as distinguished from some of its ministers— sanctified and rejoiced in the conquests of the flag, and encouraged, if it did not formulate, the belief that conquest, with the resulting relative well-being of the Western populations, was proof of the favor of God. God had come a long way from the desert—but then so had Allah, though in a very different direction. God, going north, and rising on the wings of power, had become white, and Allah, out of power, and on the dark side of Heaven, had become— for all practical purposes, anyway—black. Thus, in the realm of morals the role of Christianity has been, at best, ambivalent. Even leaving out of account the remarkable arrogance that assumed that the ways and morals of others were inferior to those of Christians, and that they therefore had every right, and could use any means, to change them, the collision between cultures—and the schizophrenia in the mind of Christendom—had rendered the domain of morals as chartless as the sea once was, and as treacherous as the sea still is. It is not too much to say that whoever wishes to become a truly moral human being (and let us not ask whether or not this is possible; I think we must *believe* that it is possible) must first divorce himself from all the prohibitions, crimes, and hypocrisies of the Christian church. If the concept of God has any validity or any use, it can only be to make us larger, freer, and more loving. If God cannot do this, then it is time we got rid of Him.

I HAD HEARD A GREAT DEAL, LONG BEFORE I FINALLY MET HIM, OF THE Honorable Elijah Muhammad, and of the Nation of Islam movement, of which he is the leader. I paid very little attention to what I heard, because the burden of his message did not strike me as being very original; I had been hearing variations of it all my life. I sometimes found myself in Harlem on Saturday nights, and I stood in the crowds, at 125th Street and Seventh Avenue, and listened to the Muslim speakers. But I had heard hundreds of such speeches—or so it seemed to me at first. Anyway, I have long had a very definite tendency to tune out the moment I come anywhere near either a pulpit or a soapbox. What these men were saying about white people I had often heard before. And I dismissed the Nation of Islam's demand for a separate black economy in America, which I had also heard before, as willful, and even mischievous, nonsense. Then two things caused me to begin to listen to the speeches, and one was the behavior of the police. After all, I had seen men dragged from their platforms on this very corner for saying less virulent things, and I had seen many crowds dispersed by policemen, with clubs or on horseback. But the policemen were doing nothing now. Obviously, this was not because they had become more human but because they were under orders and because they were afraid. And indeed they were, and I was delighted to see it. There they stood, in twos and threes and fours, in their Cub Scout uniforms and with their Cub Scout faces, totally unprepared, as is the way with American he-men, for anything that could not be settled with a club or a fist or a gun. I might have pitied them if I had not found myself in their hands so often and discovered, through ugly experience, what they were like when *they* held the power and what they were like when *you* held the power. The behavior of the crowd, its silent intensity, was the other thing that forced me to reassess the speakers and their message. I sometimes think, with despair, that Americans will swallow whole any political speech whatever—we've been doing very little else, these last, bad years—so it may not mean anything to say that this sense of integrity, after what Harlem, especially, has been through in the way of demagogues, was a very startling change. Still, the speakers had an air of utter dedication, and the people looked toward them with a kind of intelligence of hope on their faces—not as though they were being consoled or drugged but as though they were being jolted.

Power was the subject of the speeches I heard. We were offered, as Nation of Islam doctrine, historical and divine proof that all white people are cursed, and are devils, and are about to be brought down. This has been revealed by Allah Himself to His prophet, the Honorable Elijah Muhammad. The white man's rule will be ended forever in ten or fifteen years (and it must be conceded that all present signs would seem to bear witness to the accuracy of the prophet's statement). The crowd seemed to swallow this theology with no effort—all crowds do swallow theology this way, I gather, in both sides of Jerusalem, in Istanbul, and in Rome—and, as theology goes, it was no more indigestible than the more familiar brand asserting that there is a curse on the sons of Ham. No more, and no less, and it had been designed for the same purpose; namely, the sanctification of power. But very little time was spent on theology, for one did not need to prove to a Harlem audience that all white men were devils. They were merely glad to have, at last, divine corroboration of their experience, to hear—and it was a tremendous thing to hear—that they had been lied to for all these years and generations, and that their captivity was ending, for God was black. Why were they *hearing* it now, since this was not the first time it had been said? I had heard it many times, from various prophets, during all the years that I was growing up. Elijah Muhammad himself has now been carrying the same message for more than thirty years; he is not an overnight sensation, and we owe his ministry, I am told, to the fact that when he was a child of six or so, his father was lynched before his eyes. (So much for states' rights.) And now, suddenly, people who have never before been able to hear this message hear it, and believe it, and are changed. Elijah Muhammad has been able to do what generations of welfare workers and committees and resolutions and reports and housing projects and playgrounds have failed to do: to heal and redeem drunkards and junkies, to convert people who have come out of prison and to keep them out, to make men chaste and women virtuous, and to invest both the male and the female with a pride and a serenity that hang about them like an unfailing light. He has done all these things, which our Christian church has spectacularly failed to do. How has Elijah managed it?

Well, in a way—and I have no wish to minimize his peculiar role and his peculiar achievement—it is not he who has done it but time. Time catches up with kingdoms and crushes them, gets its teeth into doctrines and rends them; time reveals the foundations on which any kingdom rests, and eats at those foundations, and it destroys doctrines by proving them to be untrue. In those days, not so very long ago, when the priests of that church which stands in Rome gave God's blessing to Italian boys being sent out to ravage a defenseless black country—which until that event, incidentally, had not considered itself to be black—it was not possible to believe in a black God. To entertain such a belief would have been to entertain madness. But time has passed, and in that time the Christian world has revealed itself as morally bankrupt and politically unstable. The Tunisians were quite right in 1956—and it was a very significant moment in Western (and African) history—when they countered the French justification for remaining in North Africa with the question "Are the *French* ready for self-government?" Again, the terms "civilized" and "Christian" begin to have a very strange ring, particularly in the ears of those who have been judged to be neither civilized nor Christian, when a Christian nation surrenders to a foul and violent orgy, as Germany did during the Third Reich. For the crime of their ancestry, millions of people in the middle of the twentieth century, and in the heart of Europe—God's citadel— were sent to a death so calculated, so hideous, and so prolonged that no age before this enlightened one had been able to imagine it, much less achieve and record it. Furthermore, those beneath the Western heel, unlike those within the West, are aware that Germany's current role in Europe is to act as a bulwark against the "uncivilized" hordes, and since power is what the powerless want, they understand very well what we of the West want to keep, and are not deluded by our talk of a freedom that we have never been willing to share with them. From my own point of view, the fact of the Third Reich alone makes obsolete forever any question of Christian superiority, except in technological terms. White people were, and are, astounded by the holocaust in Germany. They did not know that they could act that way. But I very much doubt whether black people were astounded—at least, in the same way. For my part, the fate of the Jews, and the world's indifference to it, frightened me very much. I could not but feel, in those sorrowful years, that this human indifference, concerning which I knew so much already, would be my portion on the day that the United States decided to murder its Negroes systematically instead of little by little and catch-as-catch-can. I was, of course, authoritatively assured that what had happened to the Jews in Germany could not happen to the Negroes in America, but I thought, bleakly, that the German Jews had probably believed similar counsellors, and, again, I could not share the white man's vision of himself for the very good reason that white men in America do not behave toward black men the way they behave toward each other. When a white man faces a black man, especially if the black man is helpless, terrible things are revealed. I know. I have been carried into precinct basements often enough, and I have seen and heard and endured the secrets of desperate white men and women, which they knew were safe with me, because even if I should speak, no one would believe me. And they would not believe me precisely because they would know that what I said was true.

The treatment accorded the Negro during the Second World War marks, for me, a turning point in the Negro's relation to America. To put it briefly, and somewhat too simply, a certain hope died, a certain respect for white Americans faded. One began to pity them, or to hate them. You must put yourself in the skin of a man who is wearing the uniform of his country, is a candidate for death in its defense, and who is called a "nigger" by his comrades-in-arms and his officers; who is almost always given the hardest, ugliest, most menial work to do; who knows that the white G.I. has informed the Europeans that he is subhuman (so much for the American male's sexual security); who does not dance at the U.S.O. the night white soldiers dance there, and does not drink in the same bars white soldiers drink in; and who watches German prisoners of war being treated by Americans with more human dignity than he has ever received at their hands. And who, at the same time, as a human being, is far freer in a strange land than he has ever been at home. *Home!* The very word begins to have a despairing and diabolical ring. You must consider what happens to this citizen, after all he has endured, when he returns—home: starch, in his shoes, for a job, for a place to live; ride, in his skin, on segregated buses; see, with his eyes, the signs saying "White" and "Colored," and especially the signs that say "White Ladies" and "Colored *Women*"; look into the eyes of his wife; look into the eyes of his son; listen, with his ears, to political speeches, North and South; imagine yourself being told to "wait." And all this is happening in the richest and freest country in the world, and in the middle of the twentieth century. The subtle and deadly change of heart that might occur in you would be involved with the realization that a civilization is not destroyed by wicked people; it is not necessary that people be wicked but only that they be spineless. I and two Negro acquaintances, all of us well past thirty, and looking it, were in the bar of Chicago's O'Hare Airport several months ago, and the bartender refused to serve us, because, he said, we looked too young. It took a vast amount of patience not to strangle him, and great insistence and some luck to get the manager, who defended his bartender on the ground that he was "new" and had not yet, presumably, learned how to distinguish between a Negro boy of twenty and a Negro "boy" of thirty-seven. Well, we were served, finally, of course, but by this time no amount of Scotch would have helped us. The bar was very crowded, and our altercation had been extremely noisy; not one customer in the bar had done anything to help us. When it was over, and the three of us stood at the bar trembling with rage and frustration, and drinking—and trapped, now, in the airport, for we had deliberately come early in order to have a few drinks and to eat—a young white man standing near us asked if we were students. I suppose he thought that this was the only possible explanation for our putting up a fight. I told him that he hadn't wanted to talk to us earlier and we didn't want to talk to him now. The reply visibly hurt his feelings, and this, in turn, caused me to despise him. But when one of us, a Korean War veteran, told this young man that the fight we had been having in the bar had been his fight, too, the young man said, "I lost my conscience a long time ago," and turned and walked out. I know that one would rather not think so, but this young man is typical. So, on the basis of the evidence, had everyone else in the bar lost *his* conscience. A few years ago, I would have hated these people with all my heart. Now I pitied them, pitied them in order not to despise them. And this is not the happiest way to feel toward one's countrymen.

But, in the end, it is the threat of universal extinction hanging over all the world today that changes, totally and forever, the nature of reality and brings into devastating question the true meaning of man's history. We human beings now have the power to exterminate ourselves; this seems to be the entire sum of our achievement. We have taken this journey and arrived at this place in God's name. This, then, is the best that God (the white God) can do. If that is so, then it is time to replace Him—replace Him with what? And this void, this despair, this torment is felt everywhere in the West, from the streets of Stockholm to the churches of New Orleans and the sidewalks of Harlem.

God is black. All black men belong to Islam; they have been chosen. And Islam shall rule the world. The dream, the sentiment is old; only the color is new. And it is this dream, this sweet possibility, that thousands of oppressed black men and women in this country now carry away with them after the Muslim minister has spoken, through the dark, noisome ghetto streets, into the hovels where so many have perished. The white God has not delivered them; perhaps the black God will.

While I was in Chicago last summer, the Honorable Elijah Muhammad invited me to have dinner at his home. This is a stately mansion on Chicago's South Side, and it is the headquarters of the Nation of Islam movement. I had not gone to Chicago to meet Elijah Muhammad—he was not in my thoughts at all—but the moment I received the invitation, it occurred to me that I ought to have expected it. In a way, I owe the invitation to the incredible, abysmal, and really cowardly obtuseness of white liberals. Whether in private debate or in public, any attempt I made to explain how the Black Muslim movement came about, and how it has achieved such force, was met with a blankness that revealed the little connection that the liberals' attitudes have with their perceptions or their lives, or even their knowledge—revealed, in fact, that they could deal with the Negro as a symbol or a victim but had no sense of him as a man. When Malcolm X, who is considered the movement's second-in-command, and heir apparent, points out that the cry of "violence" was not raised, for example, when the Israelis fought to regain Israel, and, indeed, is raised only when black men indicate that they will fight for *their* rights, he is speaking the truth. The conquests of England, every single one of them bloody, are part of what Americans have in mind when they speak of England's glory. In the United States, violence and heroism have been made synonymous except when it comes to blacks, and the only way to defeat Malcolm's point is to concede it and then ask oneself why this is so. Malcolm's statement is not answered by references to the triumphs of the N.A.A.C.P., the more particularly since very few liberals have any notion of how long, how costly, and how heartbreaking a task it is to gather the evidence that one can carry into court, or how long such court battles take. Neither is it answered by references to the student sit-in movement, if only because not all Negroes are students and not all of them live in the South. I, in any case, certainly refuse to be put in the position of denying the truth of Malcolm's statements simply because I disagree with his conclusions, or in order to pacify the liberal conscience. Things are as bad as the Muslims say they are—in fact, they are worse, and the Muslims do not help matters—but there *is* no reason that black men should be expected to be more patient, more forbearing, more farseeing than whites; indeed, quite the contrary. The real reason that nonviolence is considered to be a virtue in Negroes—I am not speaking now of its tactical value, another matter altogether—is that white men do not want their lives, their self-image, or their property threatened. One wishes they would say so more often. At the end of a television program on which Malcolm X and I both appeared, Malcolm was stopped by a white member of the audience who said, "I have a thousand dollars and an acre of land. What's going to happen to me?" I admired the directness of the man's question, but I didn't hear Malcolm's reply, because I was trying to explain to someone else that the situation of the Irish a hundred years ago and the situation of the Negro today cannot very usefully be compared. Negroes were brought here in chains long before the Irish ever thought of leaving Ireland; what manner of consolation is it to be told that emigrants arriving here—voluntarily—long after you did have risen far above you? In the hall, as I was waiting for the elevator, someone shook my hand and said, "Goodbye, Mr. James Baldwin. We'll soon be addressing you as Mr. James X." And I thought, for an awful moment, My God, if this goes on much longer, you probably will. Elijah Muhammad had seen this show, I think, or another one, and he had been told about me. Therefore, late on a hot Sunday afternoon, I presented myself at his door.

I was frightened, because I had, in effect, been summoned into a royal presence. I was frightened for another reason, too. I knew the tension in me between love and power, between pain and rage, and the curious, the grinding way I remained extended between these poles—perpetually attempting to choose the better rather than the worse. But this choice was a choice in terms of a personal, a private better (I was, after all, a writer); what was its relevance in terms of a social worse? Here was the South Side—a million in captivity—stretching from this doorstep as far as the eye could see. And they didn't even read; depressed populations don't have the time or energy to spare. The affluent populations, which should have been their help, didn't, as far as could be discovered, read, either—they merely bought books and devoured them, but not in order to learn: in order to learn new attitudes. Also, I knew that once I had entered the house, I couldn't smoke or drink, and I felt guilty about the cigarettes in my pocket, as I had felt years ago when my friend first took me into his church. I was half an hour late, having got lost on the way here, and I felt as deserving of a scolding as a schoolboy.

The young man who came to the door—he was about thirty, perhaps, with a handsome, smiling face—didn't seem to find my lateness offensive, and led me into a large room. On one side of the room sat half a dozen women, all in white; they were much occupied with a beautiful baby, who seemed to belong to the youngest of the women. On the other side of the room sat seven or eight men, young, dressed in dark suits, very much at ease, and very imposing. The sunlight came into the room with the peacefulness one remembers from rooms in one's early childhood—a sunlight encountered later only in one's dreams. I remember being astounded by the quietness, the ease, the peace, the taste. I was introduced, they greeted me with a genuine cordiality and respect—and the respect increased my fright, for it meant that they expected something of me that I knew in my heart, for their sakes, I could not give—and we sat down. Elijah Muhammad was not in the room. Conversation was slow, but not as stiff as I had feared it would be. They kept it going, for I simply did not know which subjects I could acceptably bring up. They knew more about me, and had read more of what I had written, than I had expected, and I wondered what they made of it all, what they took my usefulness to be. The women were carrying on their own conversation, in low tones; I gathered that they were not expected to take part in male conversations. A few women kept coming in and out of the room, apparently making preparations for dinner. We, the men, did not plunge deeply into any subject, for, clearly, we were all waiting for the appearance of Elijah. Presently, the men, one by one, left the room and returned. Then I was asked if I would like to wash, and I, too, walked down the hall to the bathroom. Shortly after I came back, we stood up, and Elijah entered.

I do not know what I had expected to see. I had read some of his speeches, and had heard fragments of others on the radio and on television, so I associated him with ferocity. But, no—the man who came into the room was small and slender, really very delicately put together, with a thin face, large, warm eyes, and a most winning smile. Something came into the room with him—his disciples' joy at seeing him, his joy at seeing them. It was the kind of encounter one watches with a smile simply because it is so rare that people enjoy one another. He teased the women, like a father, with no hint of that ugly and unctuous flirtatiousness I knew so well from other churches, and they responded like that, with great freedom and yet from a great and loving distance. He had seen me when he came into the room, I knew, though he had not looked my way. I had the feeling, as he talked and laughed with the others, whom I could only think of as his children, that he was sizing me up, deciding something. Now he turned toward me, to welcome me, with that marvellous smile, and carried me back nearly twenty-four years, to that moment when the pastor had smiled at me and said, "Whose little boy are you?" I did not respond now as I had responded then, because there are some things (not many, alas!) that one cannot do twice. But I knew what he made me feel, how I was drawn toward his peculiar authority, how his smile promised to take the burden of my life off my shoulders. *Take your burdens to the Lord and leave them there.* The central quality in Elijah's face is pain, and his smile is a witness to it—pain so old and deep and black that it becomes personal and particular only when he smiles. One wonders what he would sound like if he could sing. He turned to me, with that smile, and said something like "I've got a lot to say to *you*, but we'll wait until we sit *down*." And I laughed. He made me think of my father and me as we might have been if we had been friends.

In the dining room, there were two long tables; the men sat at one and the women at the other. Elijah was at the head of our table, and I was seated at his left. I can scarcely remember what we ate, except that it was plentiful, sane, and simple—so sane and simple that it made me feel extremely decadent, and I think that I drank, therefore, two glasses of milk. Elijah mentioned having seen me on television and said that it seemed to him that I was not yet brainwashed and was trying to become myself. He said this in a curiously unnerving way, his eyes looking into mine and one hand half hiding his lips, as though he were trying to conceal bad teeth. But his teeth were not bad. Then I remembered hearing that he had spent time in prison. I suppose that I *would* like to become myself, whatever that may mean, but I knew that Elijah's meaning and mine were not the same. I said yes, I was trying to be me, but I did not know how to say more than that, and so I waited.

Whenever Elijah spoke, a kind of chorus arose from the table, saying "Yes, that's right." This began to set my teeth on edge. And Elijah himself had a further, unnerving habit, which was to ricochet his questions and comments off someone else on their way to you. Now, turning to the man on his right, he began to speak of the white devils with whom I had last appeared on TV: What had they made *him* (me) feel? I could not answer this and was not absolutely certain that I was expected to. The people referred to had certainly made me feel exasperated and useless, but I did not think of them as devils. Elijah went on about the crimes of white people, to this endless chorus of "Yes, that's right." Someone at the table said, "The white man sure *is* a devil. He proves that by his own actions." I looked around. It was a very young man who had said this, scarcely more than a boy—very dark and sober, very bitter. Elijah began to speak of the Christian religion, of Christians, in this same soft, joking way. I began to see that Elijah's power came from his single-mindedness. There is nothing calculated about him; he means every word he says. The real reason, according to Elijah, that I failed to realize that the white man was a devil was that I had been too long exposed to white teaching and had never received true instruction. "The so-called American Negro" is the only reason Allah has permitted the United States to endure so long; the white man's time was up in 1913, but it is the will of Allah that this lost black nation, the black men of this country, be redeemed from their white masters and returned to the true faith, which is Islam. Until this is done—and it will be accomplished very soon—the total destruction of the white man is being delayed. Elijah's mission is to return "the so-called Negro" to Islam, to separate the chosen of Allah from this doomed nation. Furthermore, the white man knows his history, knows himself to be a devil, and knows that his time is running out, and all his technology, psychology, science, and "tricknology" are being expended in the effort to prevent black men from hearing the truth. This truth is that at the very beginning of time there was not one white face to be found in all the universe. Black men ruled the earth and the black man was perfect. This is the truth concerning the era that white men now refer to as pre-historic. They want black men to believe that they, like white men, once lived in caves and swung from trees and ate their meat raw and did not have the power of speech. But this is not true. Black men were never in such a condition. Allah allowed the Devil, through his scientists, to carry on infernal experiments, which resulted, finally, in the creation of the devil known as the white man, and later, even more disastrously, in the creation of the white woman. And it was decreed that these monstrous creatures should rule the earth for a certain number of years—I forget how many thousand, but, in any case, their rule now is ending, and Allah, who had never approved of the creation of the white man in the first place (who knows him, in fact, to be not a man at all but a devil), is anxious to restore the rule of peace that the rise of the white man totally destroyed. There is thus, by definition, no virtue in white people, and since they are another creation entirely and can no more, by breeding, become black than a cat, by breeding, can become a horse, there is no hope for them.

There is nothing new in this merciless formulation except the explicitness of its symbols and the candor of its hatred. Its emotional tone is as familiar to me as my own skin; it is but another way of saying that *sinners shall be bound in Hell a thousand years.* That sinners have always, for American Negroes, been white is a truth we needn't labor, and every American Negro, therefore, risks having the gates of paranoia close on him. In a society that is entirely hostile, and, by its nature, seems determined to cut you down—that has cut down so many in the past and cuts down so many every day—it begins to be almost impossible to distinguish a real from a fancied injury. One can very quickly cease to attempt this distinction, and, what is worse, one usually ceases to attempt it without realizing that one has done so. All doormen, for example, and all policemen have by now, for me, become exactly the same, and my style with them is designed simply to intimidate them before they can intimidate me. No doubt I am guilty of some injustice here, but it is irreducible, since I cannot risk assuming that the humanity of these people is more real to them than their uniforms. Most Negroes cannot risk assuming that the humanity of white people is more real to them than their color. And this leads, imperceptibly but inevitably, to a state of mind in which, having long ago learned to expect the worst, one finds it very easy to believe the worst. The brutality with which Negroes are treated in this country simply cannot be overstated, however unwilling white men may be to hear it. In the beginning—and neither can this be overstated—a Negro just cannot *believe* that white people are treating him as they do; he does not know what he has done to merit it. And when he realizes that the treatment accorded him has nothing to do with anything he has done, that the attempt of white people to destroy him—for that is what it is—is utterly gratuitous, it is not hard for him to think of white people as devils. For the horrors of the American Negro's life there has been almost no language. The privacy of his experience, which is only beginning to be recognized in language, and which is denied or ignored in official and popular speech—hence the Negro idiom—lends credibility to any system that pretends to clarify

it. And, in fact, the truth about the black man, as a historical entity and as a human being, *has* been hidden from him, deliberately
and cruelly; the power of the white world is threatened whenever a
black man refuses to accept the white world's definitions. So every
attempt is made to cut that black man down—not only was made
yesterday but is made today. Who, then, is to say with authority
where the root of so much anguish and evil lies? Why, then, is it
not possible that all things began with the black man and that he
was perfect—especially since this is precisely the claim that white
people have put forward for themselves all these years? Furthermore, it is now absolutely clear that white people are a minority in
the world—so severe a minority that they now look rather more
like an invention—and that they cannot possibly hope to rule it any
longer. If this is so, why is it not also possible that they achieved
their original dominance by stealth and cunning and bloodshed
and in opposition to the will of Heaven, and not, as they claim, by
Heaven's will? And if *this* is so, then the sword they have used so
long against others can now, without mercy, be used against them.
Heavenly witnesses are a tricky lot, to be used by whoever is closest to Heaven at the time. And legend and theology, which are
designed to sanctify our fears, crimes, and aspirations, also reveal
them for what they are.

I said, at last, in answer to some other ricocheted question, "I left
the church twenty years ago and I haven't joined anything since." It
was my way of saying that I did not intend to join their movement,
either.

"And what are you now?" Elijah asked.

I was in something of a bind, for I really could not say—could
not allow myself to be stampeded into saying—that I was a Christian. "I? Now? Nothing." This was not enough. "I'm a writer. I like
doing things alone." I heard myself saying this. Elijah smiled at me.
"I don't, anyway," I said, finally, "think about it a great deal."

Elijah said, to his right, "I think he ought to think about it *all* the deal," and with this the table agreed. But there was nothing malicious or condemnatory in it. I had the stifling feeling that *they* knew I belonged to them but knew that I did not know it yet, that I remained unready, and that they were simply waiting, patiently, and with assurance, for me to discover the truth for myself. For where else, after all, could I go? I was black, and therefore a part of Islam, and would be saved from the holocaust awaiting the white world whether I would or no. My weak, deluded scruples could avail nothing against the iron word of the prophet.

I felt that I was back in my father's house—as, indeed, in a way, I was—and I told Elijah that *I* did not care if white and black people married, and that I had many white friends. I would have no choice, if it came to it, but to perish with them, for (I said to myself, but not to Elijah), "I love a few people and they love me and some of them are white, and isn't love more important than color?"

Elijah looked at me with great kindness and affection, great pity, as though he were reading my heart, and indicated, skeptically, that I *might* have white friends, or think I did, and they might be trying to be decent—now—but their time was up. It was almost as though he were saying, "They had their chance, man, and they goofed!"

And I looked around the table. I certainly had no evidence to give them that would outweigh Elijah's authority or the evidence of their own lives or the reality of the streets outside. Yes, I knew two or three people, white, whom I would trust with my life, and I knew a few others, white, who were struggling as hard as they knew how, and with great effort and sweat and risk, to make the world more human. But how could I say this? One cannot argue with anyone's experience or decision or belief. All my evidence would be thrown out of court as irrelevant to the main body of the case, for I could cite only exceptions. The South Side proved the justice of the indictment; the state of the world proved the justice of the indictment. Everything else, stretching back throughout recorded time, was merely a history of those exceptions who had tried to change the world and had failed. Was this true? *Had* they failed? How much depended on the point of view! For it would seem that a certain category of exceptions never failed to make the world worse—that category, precisely, for whom power is more real than love. And yet power *is* real, and many things, including, very often, love, cannot be achieved without it. In the eeriest way possible, I suddenly had a glimpse of what white people must go through at a dinner table when they are trying to prove that Negroes are not subhuman. I had almost said, after all, "Well, take my friend Mary," and very nearly descended to a catalogue of those virtues that gave Mary the right to be alive. And in what hope? That Elijah and the others would nod their heads solemnly and say, at last, "Well, *she's* all right—but the *others!*"

And I looked again at the young faces around the table, and looked back at Elijah, who was saying that no people in history had ever been respected who had not owned their land. And the table said, "Yes, that's right." I could not deny the truth of this statement. For everyone else has, *is*, a nation, with a specific location and a flag—even, these days, the Jew. It is only "the so-called American Negro" who remains trapped, disinherited, and despised, in a nation that has kept him in bondage for nearly four hundred years and is still unable to recognize him as a human being. And the Black Muslims, along with many people who are not Muslims, no longer wish for a recognition so grudging and (should it ever be achieved) so tardy. Again, it cannot be denied that this point of view is abundantly justified by American Negro history. It is galling indeed to have stood so long, hat in hand, waiting for Americans to grow up enough to realize that you do not threaten them. On the other hand, how is the American Negro now to form himself into a separate nation? For this—and not only from the Muslim point of view—would seem to be his only hope of not perishing in the American backwater and being entirely and forever forgotten, as though he had never existed at all and his travail had been for nothing.

Elijah's intensity and the bitter isolation and disaffection of these young men and the despair of the streets outside had caused me to glimpse dimly what may now seem to be a fantasy, although, in an age so fantastical, I would hesitate to say precisely what a fantasy is. Let us say that the Muslims were to achieve the possession of the six or seven states that they claim are owed to Negroes by the United States as "back payment" for slave labor. Clearly, the United States would never surrender this territory, on any terms whatever, unless it found it impossible, for whatever reason, to hold it—unless, that is, the United States were to be reduced as a world power, exactly the way, and at the same degree of speed, that England has been forced to relinquish her Empire. (It is simply not true— and the state of her ex-colonies proves this—that England "always meant to go.") If the states were Southern states—and the Muslims seem to favor this—then the borders of a hostile Latin America would be raised, in effect, to, say, Maryland. Of the American borders on the sea, one would face toward a powerless Europe and the other toward an untrustworthy and nonwhite East, and on the North, after Canada, there would be only Alaska, which is a Russian border. The effect of this would be that the white people of the United States and Canada would find themselves marooned on a hostile continent, with the rest of the white world probably unwilling and certainly unable to come to their aid. All this is not, to my mind, the most imminent of possibilities, but if I were a Muslim, this is the possibility that I would find myself holding in the center of my mind, and driving toward. And if I were a Muslim, I would not hesitate to utilize—or, indeed, to exacerbate—the social and spiritual discontent that reigns here, for, at the very worst, I would merely have contributed to the destruction of a house I hated, and it would not matter if I perished, too. One has been perishing here so long!

And what were they thinking around the table? "I've come," said Elijah, "to give you something which can never be taken away from you." How solemn the table became then, and how great a light rose in the dark faces! This is the message that has spread through streets and tenements and prisons, through the narcotics wards, and past the filth and sadism of mental hospitals to a people from whom everything has been taken away, including, most crucially, their sense of their own worth. People cannot live without this sense; they will do anything whatever to regain it. This is why the most dangerous creation of any society is that man who has nothing to lose. You do not need ten such men—one will do. And Elijah, I should imagine, has had nothing to lose since the day he saw his father's blood rush out—rush down, and splash, so the legend has it, down through the leaves of a tree, on him. But neither did the other men around the table have anything to lose. "Return to your true religion," Elijah has written. "Throw off the chains of the slavemaster, the devil, and return to the fold. Stop drinking his alcohol, using his dope—protect your women—and forsake the filthy swine." I remembered my buddies of years ago, in the hallways, with their wine and their whiskey and their tears; in hallways still, frozen on the needle; and my brother saying to me once, "If Harlem didn't have so many churches and junkies, there'd be blood flowing in the streets." *Protect your women*: a difficult thing to do in a civilization sexually so pathetic that the white man's masculinity depends on a denial of the masculinity of the blacks. *Protect your women*: in a civilization that emasculates the male and abuses the female, and in which, moreover, the male is forced to depend on the female's breadwinning power. *Protect your women*: in the teeth of the white man's boast "We figure we're doing you folks a favor by pumping some white blood into your kids," and while facing the Southern shotgun and the Northern billy. Years ago, we used to say, "*Yes*, I'm black, goddammit, and I'm beautiful!"—in defiance, into the void. But now—now—African kings and heroes have come into the world, out of the past, the past that can now be put to the uses of power. And black has *become* a beautiful color—not because it is loved but because it is feared. And this urgency on the part of American Negroes is *not to be forgotten!* As they watch black men elsewhere rise, the promise held out, at last, that they may walk the earth with the authority with which white men walk, protected by the power that white men shall have no longer, is enough, and more than enough, to empty prisons and pull God down from Heaven. It has happened before, many times, before color was invented, and the hope of Heaven has always been a metaphor for the achievement of this particular state of grace. The song says, "I know my robe's going to fit me well. I tried it on at the gates of Hell."

It was time to leave, and we stood in the large living room, saying good night, with everything curiously and heavily unresolved. I could not help feeling that I had failed a test, in their eyes and in my own, or that I had failed to heed a warning. Elijah and I shook hands, and he asked me where I was going. Wherever it was, I would be driven there—"Because, when we invite someone here," he said, "we take the responsibility of protecting him from the white devils until he gets wherever it is he's going." I was, in fact, going to have a drink with several white devils on the other side of town. I confess that for a fraction of a second I hesitated to give the address—the kind of address that in Chicago, as in all American cities, identified itself as a white address by virtue of its location. But I did give it, and Elijah and I walked out onto the steps, and one of the young men vanished to get the car. It was very strange to stand with Elijah for those few moments, facing those vivid, violent, so problematical streets. I felt very close to him, and really wished to be able to love and honor him as a witness, an ally, and a father. I felt that I knew something of his pain and his fury, and, yes, even his beauty. Yet precisely because of the reality and the nature of those streets—because of what he conceived as his responsibility and what I took to be mine—we would always be strangers, and possibly, one day, enemies. The car arrived—a gleaming, metallic, grossly American blue—and Elijah and I shook hands and said good night once more. He walked into his mansion and shut the door.

The driver and I started on our way through dark, murmuring—and, at this hour, strangely beautiful—Chicago, along the lake. We returned to the discussion of the land. How were we—Negroes—to get this land? I asked this of the dark boy who had said earlier, at the table, that the white man's actions proved him to be a devil. He spoke to me first of the Muslim temples that were being built, or were about to be built, in various parts of the United States, of the strength of the Muslim following, and of the amount of money that is annually at the disposal of Negroes—something like twenty billion dollars. "That alone shows you how strong we are," he said. But, I persisted, cautiously, and in somewhat different terms, this twenty billion dollars, or whatever it is, depends on the total economy of the United States. What happens when the Negro is no longer a part of this economy? Leaving aside the fact that in order for this to happen the economy of the United States will itself have had to undergo radical and certainly disastrous changes, the American Negro's spending power will obviously no longer be the same. On what, then, will the economy of this separate nation be based? The boy gave me a rather strange look. I said hurriedly, "I'm not saying it *can't* be done—I just want to know *how* it's to be done." I was thinking, In order for this to happen, your entire frame of reference will have to change, and you will be forced to surrender many things that you now scarcely know you have. I didn't feel that the things I had in mind, such as the pseudo-elegant heap of tin in which we were riding, had any very great value. But life would be very different without them, and I wondered if he had thought of this.

How can one, however, dream of power in any other terms than in the symbols of power? The boy could see that freedom depended on the possession of land; he was persuaded that, in one way or another, Negroes must achieve this possession. In the meantime, he could walk the streets and fear nothing, because there were millions like him, coming soon, now, to power. He was held together, in short, by a dream—though it is just as well to remember that some dreams come true—and was united with his "brothers" on the basis of their color. Perhaps one cannot ask for more. People always seem to band together according to a principle that has nothing to do with love, a principle that releases them from personal responsibility.

Yet I could have hoped that the Muslim movement had been able to inculcate in the demoralized Negro population a truer and more individual sense of its own worth, so that Negroes in the Northern ghettos could begin, in concrete terms, and at whatever price, to change their situation. But in order to change a situation one has first to see it for what it is: in the present case, to accept the fact, whatever one does with it thereafter, that the Negro has been formed by this nation, for better or for worse, and does not belong to any other—not to Africa, and certainly not to Islam. The paradox—and a fearful paradox it is—is that the American Negro can have no future anywhere, on any continent, as long as he is unwilling to accept his past. To accept one's past—one's history—is not the same thing as drowning in it; it is learning how to use it. An invented past can never be used; it cracks and crumbles under the pressures of life like clay in a season of drought. How can the American Negro's past be used? The unprecedented price demanded—and at this embattled hour of the world's history—is the transcendence of the realities of color, of nations, and of altars.

"Anyway," the boy said suddenly, after a very long silence, "things won't ever again be the way they used to be. I know that."

And so we arrived in enemy territory, and they set me down at the enemy's door.

NO ONE SEEMS TO KNOW WHERE THE NATION OF ISLAM GETS ITS money. A vast amount, of course, is contributed by Negroes, but there are rumors to the effect that people like the Birchites and certain Texas oil millionaires look with favor on the movement. I have no way of knowing whether there is any truth to the rumors, though since these people make such a point of keeping the races separate, I wouldn't be surprised if for this smoke there was some fire. In any case, during a recent Muslim rally, George Lincoln Rockwell, the chief of the American Nazi party, made a point of contributing about twenty dollars to the cause, and he and Malcolm X decided that, racially speaking, anyway, they were in complete agreement. The glorification of one race and the consequent debasement of another—or others—always has been and always will be a recipe for murder. There is no way around this. If one is permitted to treat any group of people with special disfavor because of their race or the color of their skin, there is no limit to what one will force them to endure, and, since the entire race has been mysteriously indicted, no reason not to attempt to destroy it root and branch. This is precisely what the Nazis attempted. Their only originality lay in the means they used. It is scarcely worthwhile to attempt remembering how many times the sun has looked down on the slaughter of the innocents. I am very much concerned that American Negroes achieve their freedom here in the United States. But I am also concerned for their dignity, for the health of their souls, and must oppose any attempt that Negroes may make to do to others what has been done to them. I think I know—we see it around us every day—the spiritual wasteland to which that road leads. It is so simple a fact and one that is so hard, apparently, to grasp: *Whoever debases others is debasing himself.* That is not a mystical statement but a most realistic one, which is proved by the eyes of any Alabama sheriff—and I would not like to see Negroes ever arrive at so wretched a condition.

Now, it is extremely unlikely that Negroes will ever rise to power in the United States, because they are only approximately a ninth of this nation. They are not in the position of the Africans, who are attempting to reclaim their land and break the colonial yoke and recover from the colonial experience. The Negro situation is dangerous in a different way, both for the Negro qua Negro and for the country of which he forms so troubled and troubling a part. The American Negro is a unique creation; he has no counterpart anywhere, and no predecessors. The Muslims react to this fact by referring to the Negro as "the so-called American Negro" and substituting for the names inherited from slavery the letter "X." It is a fact that every American Negro hears a name that originally belonged to the white man whose chattel he was. I am called Baldwin because I was either sold by my African tribe or kidnapped out of it into the hands of a white Christian named Baldwin, who forced me to kneel at the foot of the cross. I am, then, both visibly and legally the descendant of slaves in a white, Protestant country, and this is what it means to be an American Negro, this is who he is—a kidnapped pagan, who was sold like an animal and treated like one, who was once defined by the American Constitution as "three-fifths" of a man, and who, according to the Dred Scott decision, had no rights that a white man was bound to respect. And today, a hundred years after his technical emancipation, he remains—with the possible exception of the American Indian—the most despised creature in his country. Now, there is simply no possibility of a real change in the Negro's situation without the most radical and far-reaching changes in the American political and social structure. And it is clear that white Americans are not simply unwilling to effect these changes; they are, in the main, so slothful have they become, unable even to envision them. It must be added that the Negro himself no longer believes in the good faith of white Americans—if, indeed, he ever could have. What the Negro *has* discovered, and on an international level, is that power to intimidate which he has always had privately but hitherto could manipulate only privately—for private ends often, for limited ends always. And therefore when the country speaks of a "new" Negro, which it has been doing every hour on the hour for decades, it is not really referring to a change in the Negro, which, in any case, it is quite incapable of assessing, but only to a new difficulty in keeping him in his place, to the fact that it encounters him (again! again!) barring yet another door to its spiritual and social ease. This is probably, hard and odd as it may sound, the most important thing that one human being can do for another—it is certainly *one* of the most important things; hence the torment and necessity of love—and this is the enormous contribution that the Negro has made to this otherwise shapeless and undiscovered country. Consequently, white Americans are in nothing more deluded than in supposing that Negroes could ever have imagined that white people would "give" them anything. It is rare indeed that people give. Most people guard and keep; they suppose that it is they themselves and what they identify with themselves that they are guarding and keeping, whereas what they are actually guarding and keeping is their system of reality and what they assume themselves to be. One can give nothing whatever without giving oneself—that is to say, risking oneself. If one cannot risk oneself, then one is simply incapable of giving. And, after all, one can give freedom only by setting someone free. This, in the case of the Negro, the American republic has never become sufficiently mature to do. White Americans have contented themselves with gestures that are now described as "tokenism." For hard example, white Americans congratulate themselves on the 1954 Supreme Court decision outlawing segregation in the schools; they suppose, in spite of the mountain of evidence that has since accumulated to the contrary, that this was proof of a change of heart—or, as they like to say, progress. Perhaps. It all depends on how one reads the word "progress." Most of the Negroes I know do not believe that this immense concession would ever have been made if it had not been for the competition of the Cold War, and the fact that Africa was clearly liberating herself and therefore had, for political reasons, to be wooed by the descendants of her former masters. Had it been a matter of love or justice, the 1954 decision would surely have occurred sooner; were it not for the realities of power in this difficult era, it might very well not have occurred yet. This seems an extremely harsh way of stating the case—ungrateful, as it were—but the evidence that supports this way of stating it is not easily refuted. I myself do not think that it can be refuted at all. In any event, the sloppy and fatuous nature of American good will can never be relied upon to deal with hard problems. These have been dealt with, when they have been dealt with at all, out of necessity—and in political terms, anyway, necessity means concessions made in order to stay on top. I think this is a fact, which it serves no purpose to deny, *but, whether it is a fact or not, this is what the black populations of the world, including black Americans, really believe.* The word "independence" in Africa and the word "integration" here are almost equally meaningless; that is, Europe has not yet left Africa, and black men here are not yet free. And both of these last statements are undeniable facts, related facts, containing the gravest implications for us all. The Negroes of this country may never be able to rise to power, but they are very well placed indeed to precipitate chaos and ring down the curtain on the American dream.

This has everything to do, of course, with the nature of that dream and with the fact that we Americans, of whatever color, do not dare examine it and are far from having made it a reality. There are too many things we do not wish to know about ourselves. People are not, for example, terribly anxious to be equal (equal, after all, to what and to whom?) but they love the idea of being superior. And this human truth has an especially grinding force here, where identity is almost impossible to achieve and people are perpetually attempting to find their feet on the shifting sands of status. (Consider the history of labor in a country in which, spiritually speaking, there are no workers, only candidates for the hand of the boss's daughter.) Furthermore, I have met only a very few people—and most of these were not Americans—who had any real desire to be free. Freedom is hard to bear. It can be objected that I am speaking of political freedom in spiritual terms, but the political institutions of any nation are always menaced and are ultimately controlled by the spiritual state of that nation. We are controlled here by our confusion, far more than we know, and the American dream has therefore become something much more closely resembling a nightmare, on the private, domestic, and international levels. Privately, we cannot stand our lives and dare not examine them; domestically, we take no responsibility for (and no pride in) what goes on in our country; and, internationally, for many millions of people, we are an unmitigated disaster. Whoever doubts this last statement has only to open his ears, his heart, his mind, to the testimony of—for example— any Cuban peasant or any Spanish poet, and ask himself what *he* would feel about us if *he* were the victim of our performance in pre-Castro Cuba or in Spain. We defend our curious role in Spain by referring to the Russian menace and the necessity of protecting the free world. It has not occurred to us that we have simply been mesmerized by Russia, and that the only real advantage Russia has in what we think of as a struggle between the East and the West is the moral history of the Western world. Russia's secret weapon is the bewilderment and despair and hunger of millions of people of whose existence we are scarcely aware. The Russian Communists are not in the least concerned about these people. But our ignorance and indecision have had the effect, if not of delivering them into Russian hands, of plunging them very deeply in the Russian shadow, for which effect—and it is hard to blame them—the most articulate among them, and the most oppressed as well, distrust us all the more. Our power and our fear of change help bind these people to their misery and bewilderment, and insofar as they find this state intolerable we are intolerably menaced. For if they find their state intolerable, but are too heavily oppressed to change it, they are simply pawns in the hands of larger powers, which, in such a context, are always unscrupulous, and when, eventually, they do change their situation—as in Cuba—we are menaced more than ever, by the vacuum that succeeds all violent upheavals. We should certainly know by now that it is one thing to overthrow a dictator or repel an invader and quite another thing really to achieve a revolution. Time and time and time again, the people discover that they have merely betrayed themselves into the hands of yet another Pharaoh, who, since he was necessary to put the broken country together, will not let them go. Perhaps, people being the conundrums that they are, and having so little desire to shoulder the burden of their lives, this is what will always happen. But at the bottom of my heart I do not believe this. I think that people can be better than that, and I know that people can be better than they are. We are capable of bearing a great burden, once we discover that the burden is reality and arrive where reality is. Anyway, the point here is that we are living in an age of revolution, whether we will or no, and that America is the only Western nation with both the power and, as I hope to suggest, the experience that may help to make these revolutions real and minimize the human damage. Any attempt we make to oppose these outbursts of energy is tantamount to signing our death warrant.

Behind what we think of as the Russian menace lies what we do not wish to face, and what white Americans do not face when they regard a Negro: reality—the fact that life is tragic. Life is tragic simply because the earth turns and the sun inexorably rises and sets, and one day, for each of us, the sun will go down for the last, last time. Perhaps the whole root of our trouble, the human trouble, is that we will sacrifice all the beauty of our lives, will imprison ourselves in totems, taboos, crosses, blood sacrifices, steeples, mosques, races, armies, flags, nations, in order to deny the fact of death, which is the only fact we have. It seems to me that one ought to rejoice in the *fact* of death—ought to decide, indeed, to *earn* one's death by confronting with passion the conundrum of life. One is responsible to life: It is the small beacon in that terrifying darkness from which we come and to which we shall return. One must negotiate this passage as nobly as possible, for the sake of those who are coming after us. But white Americans do not believe in death, and this is why the darkness of my skin so intimidates them. And this is also why the presence of the Negro in this country can bring about its destruction. It is the responsibility of free men to trust and to celebrate what is constant—birth, struggle, and death are constant, and so is love, though we may not always think so—and to apprehend the nature of change, to be able and willing to change. I speak of change not on the surface but in the depths—change in the sense of renewal. But renewal becomes impossible if one supposes things to be constant that are not—safety, for example, or money, or power. One clings then to chimeras, by which one can only be betrayed, and the entire hope—the entire possibility—of freedom disappears. And by destruction I mean precisely the abdication by Americans of any effort really to be free. The Negro can precipitate this abdication because white Americans have never, in all their long history, been able to look on him as a man like themselves. This point need not be labored; it is proved over and over again by the Negro's continuing position here, and his indescribable struggle to defeat the stratagems that white Americans have used, and use, to deny him his humanity. America could have used in other ways the energy that both groups have expended in this conflict. America, of all the Western nations, has been best placed to prove the uselessness and the obsolescence of the concept of color. But it has not dared to accept this opportunity, or even to conceive of it as an opportunity. White Americans have thought of it as their shame, and have envied those more civilized and elegant European nations that were untroubled by the presence of black men on their shores. This is because white Americans have supposed "Europe" and "civilization" to be synonyms—which they are not—and have been distrustful of other standards and other sources of vitality, especially those produced in America itself, and have attempted to behave in all matters as though what was east for Europe was also east for them. What it comes to is that if we, who can scarcely be considered a white nation, persist in thinking of ourselves as one, we condemn ourselves, with the truly white nations, to sterility and decay, whereas if we could accept ourselves *as we are*, we might bring new life to the Western achievements, and transform them. The price of this transformation is the unconditional freedom of the Negro; it is not too much to say that he, who has been so long rejected, must now be embraced, and at no matter what psychic or social risk. He is *the* key figure in his country, and the American future is precisely as bright or as dark as his. And the Negro recognizes this, in a negative way. Hence the question: Do I really *want* to be integrated into a burning house?

White Americans find it as difficult as white people elsewhere do to divest themselves of the notion that they are in possession of some intrinsic value that black people need, or want. And this assumption—which, for example, makes the solution to the Negro problem depend on the speed with which Negroes accept and adopt white standards—is revealed in all kinds of striking ways, from Bobby Kennedy's assurance that a Negro can become President in forty years to the unfortunate tone of warm congratulation with which so many liberals address their Negro equals. It is the Negro, of course, who is presumed to have become equal—an achievement that not only proves the comforting fact that perseverance has no color but also overwhelmingly corroborates the white man's sense of his own value. Alas, this value can scarcely be corroborated in any other way; there is certainly little enough in the white man's public or private life that one should desire to imitate. White men, at the bottom of their hearts, know this. Therefore, a vast amount of the energy that goes into what we call the Negro problem is produced

by the white man's profound desire not to be judged by those who
are not white, not to be seen as he is, and at the same time a vast
amount of the white anguish is rooted in the white man's equally
profound need to be seen as he is, to be released from the tyranny
of his mirror. All of us know, whether or not we are able to admit it,
that mirrors can only lie, that death by drowning is all that awaits
one there. It is for this reason that love is so desperately sought and
so cunningly avoided. Love takes off the masks that we fear we
cannot live without and know we cannot live within. I use the word
"love" here not merely in the personal sense but as a state of being,
or a state of grace—not in the infantile American sense of being
made happy but in the tough and universal sense of quest and daring and growth. And I submit, then, that the racial tensions that
menace Americans today have little to do with real antipathy—on
the contrary, indeed—and are involved only symbolically with color.
These tensions are rooted in the very same depths as those from
which love springs, or murder. The white man's unadmitted—and
apparently, to him, unspeakable—private fears and longings are
projected onto the Negro. The only way he can be released from
the Negro's tyrannical power over him is to consent, in effect, to become black himself, to become a part of that suffering and dancing
country that he now watches wistfully from the heights of his lonely
power and, armed with spiritual traveller's checks, visits surrepti-
tiously after dark. How can one respect, let alone adopt, the values
of a people who do not, on any level whatever, live the way they
say they do, or the way they say they should? I cannot accept the
proposition that the four-hundred-year travail of the American Negro should result merely in his attainment of the present level of the
American civilization. I am far from convinced that being released
from the African witch doctor was worthwhile if I am now—in
order to support the moral contradictions and the spiritual aridity
of my life—expected to become dependent on the American psychiatrist. It is a bargain I refuse. The only thing white people have

that black people need, or should want, is power—and no one holds power forever. White people cannot, in the generality, be taken as models of how to live. Rather, the white man is himself in sore need of new standards, which will release him from his confusion and place him once again in fruitful communion with the depths of his own being. And I repeat: The price of the liberation of the white people is the liberation of the blacks—the total liberation, in the cities, in the towns, before the law, and in the mind. Why, for example—especially knowing the family as I do—I should *want* to marry your sister is a great mystery to me. But your sister and I have every right to marry if we wish to, and no one has the right to stop us. If she cannot raise me to her level, perhaps I can raise her to mine.

In short, we, the black and the white, deeply need each other here if we are really to become a nation—if we are really, that is, to achieve our identity, our maturity, as men and women. To create one nation has proved to be a hideously difficult task; there is certainly no need now to create two, one black and one white. But white men with far more political power than that possessed by the Nation of Islam movement have been advocating exactly this, in effect, for generations. If this sentiment is honored when it falls from the lips of Senator Byrd, then there is no reason it should not be honored when it falls from the lips of Malcolm X. And any Congressional committee wishing to investigate the latter must also be willing to investigate the former. They are expressing exactly the same sentiments and represent exactly the same danger. There is absolutely no reason to suppose that white people are better equipped to frame the laws by which I am to be governed than I am. It is entirely unacceptable that I should have no voice in the political affairs of my own country, for I am not a ward of America; I am one of the first Americans to arrive on these shores.

This past, the Negro's past, of rope, fire, torture, castration, infanticide, rape; death and humiliation; fear by day and night, fear as deep as the marrow of the bone; doubt that he was worthy of life, since everyone around him denied it; sorrow for his women, for his kinfolk, for his children, who needed his protection, and whom he could not protect; rage, hatred, and murder, hatred for white men so deep that it often turned against him and his own, and made all love, and trust, all joy impossible—this past, this endless struggle to achieve and reveal and confirm a human identity, human author- ity, yet contains, for all its horror, something very beautiful. I do not mean to be sentimental about suffering—enough is certainly as good as a feast—but people who cannot suffer can never grow up, can never discover who they are. That man who is forced each day to snatch his manhood, his identity, out of the fire of human cruelty that rages to destroy it knows, if he survives his effort, and even if he does not survive it, something about himself and human life that no school on earth—and, indeed, no church—can teach. He achieves his own authority, and that is unshakable. This is be- cause, in order to save his life, he is forced to look beneath appear- ances, to take nothing for granted, to hear the meaning behind the words. If one is continually surviving the worst that life can bring, one eventually ceases to be controlled by a fear of what life can bring; whatever it brings must be borne. And at this level of expe- rience one's bitterness begins to be palatable, and hatred becomes too heavy a sack to carry. The apprehension of life here so briefly and inadequately sketched has been the experience of generations of Negroes, and it helps to explain how they have endured and how they have been able to produce children of kindergarten age who can walk through mobs to get to school. It demands great force and great cunning continually to assault the mighty and indiffer- ent fortress of white supremacy, as Negroes in this country have done so long. It demands great spiritual resilience not to hate the hater whose foot is on your neck, and an even greater miracle of perception and charity not to teach your child to hate. The Negro boys and girls who are facing mobs today come out of a long line of improbable aristocrats—the only genuine aristocrats this country has produced. I say "this country" because their frame of reference was totally American. They were hewing out of the mountain of white supremacy the stone of their individuality. I have great respect for that unsung army of black men and women who trudged down back lanes and entered back doors, saying "Yes, sir" and "No, Ma'am" in order to acquire a new roof for the schoolhouse, new books, a new chemistry lab, more beds for the dormitories, more dormitories. They did not like saying "Yes, sir" and "No, Ma'am," but the country was in no hurry to educate Negroes, these black men and women knew that the job had to be done, and they put their pride in their pockets in order to do it. It is very hard to believe that they were in any way inferior to the white men and women who opened those back doors. It is very hard to believe that those men and women, raising their children, eating their greens, crying their curses, weeping their tears, singing their songs, making their love, as the sun rose, as the sun set, were in any way inferior to the white men and women who crept over to share these splendors after the sun went down. But we must avoid the European error; we must not suppose that, because the situation, the ways, the perceptions of black people so radically differed from those of whites, they were racially superior. I am proud of these people not because of their color but because of their intelligence and their spiritual force and their beauty. The country should be proud of them, too, but, alas, not many people in this country even know of their existence. And the reason for this ignorance is that a knowledge of the role these people played—and play—in American life would reveal more about America to Americans than Americans wish to know.

The American Negro has the great advantage of having never believed that collection of myths to which white Americans cling: that their ancestors were all freedom-loving heroes, that they were born in the greatest country the world has ever seen, or that Americans are invincible in battle and wise in peace, that Americans have always dealt honorably with Mexicans and Indians and all other neighbors or inferiors, that American men are the world's most direct and virile, that American women are pure. Negroes know far more about white Americans than that; it can almost be said, in fact, that they know about white Americans what parents—or, anyway, mothers—know about their children, and that they very often regard white Americans that way. And perhaps this attitude, held in spite of what they know and have endured, helps to explain why Negroes, on the whole, and until lately, have allowed themselves to feel so little hatred. The tendency has really been, insofar as this was possible, to dismiss white people as the slightly mad victims of their own brainwashing. One watched the lives they led. One could not be fooled about that; one watched the things they did and the excuses that they gave themselves, and if a white man was really in trouble, deep trouble, it was to the Negro's door that he came. And one felt that if one had had that white man's worldly advantages, one would never have become as bewildered and as joyless and as thoughtlessly cruel as he. The Negro came to the white man for a roof or for five dollars or for a letter to the judge; the white man came to the Negro for love. But he was not often able to give what he came seeking. The price was too high; he had too much to lose. And the Negro knew this, too. When one knows this about a man, it is impossible for one to hate him, but unless he becomes a man—becomes equal—it is also impossible for one to love him. Ultimately, one tends to avoid him, for the universal characteristic of children is to assume that they have a monopoly on trouble, and therefore a monopoly on *you*. (Ask any Negro what he knows about the white people with whom he works. And then ask the white people with whom he works what they know about *him*.)

How can the American Negro past be used? It is entirely possible that this dishonored past will rise up soon to smite all of us. There are some wars, for example (if anyone on the globe is still mad enough to go to war) that the American Negro will not support, however many of his people may be coerced—and there is a limit to the number of people any government can put in prison, and a rigid limit indeed to the practicality of such a course. A bill is coming in that I fear America is not prepared to pay. "The problem of the twentieth century," wrote W. E. B. Du Bois around sixty years ago, "is the problem of the color line." A fearful and delicate problem, which compromises, when it does not corrupt, all the American efforts to build a better world—here, there, or anywhere. It is for this reason that everything white Americans think they believe in must now be reëxamined. What one would not like to see again is the consolidation of peoples on the basis of their color. But as long as we in the West place on color the value that we do, we make it impossible for the great unwashed to consolidate themselves according to any other principle. Color is not a human or a personal reality; it is a political reality. But this is a distinction so extremely hard to make that the West has not been able to make it yet. And at the center of this dreadful storm, this vast confusion, stand the black people of this nation, who must now share the fate of a nation that has never accepted them, to which they were brought in chains. Well, if this is so, one has no choice but to do all in one's power to change that fate, and at no matter what risk—eviction, imprisonment, torture, death. For the sake of one's children, in order to minimize the bill that *they* must pay, one must be careful not to take refuge in any delusion—and the value placed on the color of the skin is always and everywhere and forever a delusion. I know that what I am asking is impossible. But in our time, as in every time, the impossible is the least that one can demand—and one is, after all, emboldened by the spectacle of human history in general, and American Negro history in particular, for it testifies to nothing less than the perpetual achievement of the impossible.

When I was very young, and was dealing with my buddies in those wine- and urine-stained hallways, something in me wondered, *What will happen to all that beauty?* For black people, though

I am aware that some of us, black and white, do not know it yet, are very beautiful. And when I sat at Elijah's table and watched the baby, the women, and the men, and we talked about God's—or Allah's—vengeance, I wondered, when that vengeance was achieved, *What will happen to all that beauty then?* I could also see that the intransigence and ignorance of the white world might make that vengeance inevitable—a vengeance that does not really depend on, and cannot really be executed by, any person or organization, and that cannot be prevented by any police force or army: historical vengeance, a cosmic vengeance, based on the law that we recognize when we say, "Whatever goes up must come down." And here we are, at the center of the arc, trapped in the gaudiest, most valuable, and most improbable water wheel the world has ever seen. Everything now, we must assume, is in our hands; we have no right to assume otherwise. If we—and now I mean the relatively conscious whites and the relatively conscious blacks, who must, like lovers, insist on, or create, the consciousness of the others—do not falter in our duty now, we may be able, handful that we are, to end the racial nightmare, and achieve our country, and change the history of the world. If we do not now dare everything, the fulfillment of that prophecy, re-created from the Bible in song by a slave, is upon us: *God gave Noah the rainbow sign, No more water, the fire next time!*

THE COLOR FETISH

TONI MORRISON

September 14, 2017

O f constant fascination for me are the ways in which literature employs skin color to reveal character or drive narrative—especially if the fictional main character is white (which is almost always the case). Whether it is the horror of one drop of the mystical "black" blood, or signs of innate white superiority, or of deranged and excessive sexual power, the framing and the meaning of color are often the deciding factors. For the horror that the "one-drop" rule excites, there is no better guide than William Faulkner. What else haunts "The Sound and the Fury" or "Absalom, Absalom!"? Between the marital outrages, incest, and miscegenation, the latter (an old but useful term for "the mixing of races") is obviously the more abhorrent. In much American literature, when plot requires a family crisis, nothing is more disgusting than mutual sexual congress between the races. It is the mutual aspect of these encounters that is rendered shocking, illegal, and repulsive. Unlike the rape of slaves, human choice or, God forbid, love receives wholesale condemnation. And for Faulkner they lead to murder.

In Chapter 4 of "Absalom, Absalom!," Mr. Compson explains to Quentin what drove Henry Sutpen to kill his half-brother Charles Bon:

> And yet, four years later, Henry had to kill Bon to
> keep them from marrying. . . .
> Yes, granted that, even to the unworldly Henry, let
> alone the more traveled father, the existence of the eighth

part negro mistress and the sixteenth part negro son, granted even the morganatic ceremony . . . was reason enough. . . .

Much later in the novel Quentin imagines this exchange between Henry and Charles:

—So it's the miscegenation, not the incest which you can't bear. . . .
Henry doesn't answer.
—And he sent me no word? . . . He did not have to do this, Henry. He didn't need to tell you I am a nigger to stop me. . . .
—You are my brother.
—No I'm not. I'm the nigger that's going to sleep with your sister. Unless you stop me, Henry.

Equally, if not more, fascinating is Ernest Hemingway's employment of colorism. His use of this wholly available device moves through several modes of colorism—from despicable blacks, to sad but sympathetic ones, to extreme black-fuelled eroticism. None of these categories is outside the writer's world or his or her imaginative prowess, but how that world is articulated is what interests me. Colorism is so very available—it is the ultimate narrative shortcut.

Note Hemingway's employment of colorism in "To Have and Have Not" ("The Tradesman's Return"). When Harry Morgan, a rum smuggler and the novel's main character, speaks directly to the only black character in the boat, he calls him by his name, Wesley. But when Hemingway's narrator addresses the reader he says (writes) "nigger." Here, the two men, who are in Morgan's boat, have both been shot up after a run-in with Cuban officials:

> . . . and he said to the nigger, "Where the hell are we?"
> The nigger raised himself up to look. . . .
> "I'm going to make you comfortable, Wesley," he
> said. . . .
> "I can't even move," the nigger said. . . .
> He gave the Negro a cup of water. . . .
> The nigger tried to move to reach a sack, then groaned
> and lay back.
> "Do you hurt that bad, Wesley?"
> "Oh, God," the nigger said.

Why the actual name of his companion isn't enough to drive, explain, or describe their venture is not clear—unless the author intends to pinpoint the narrator's compassion for a black man, a compassion that might endear this bootlegger to readers.

Now compare that rendering of a black man as constantly complaining, weak, and in need of his (more seriously injured) white boss's help with another of Hemingway's manipulations of racial tropes—this time for erotic, highly desirable effect.

In "The Garden of Eden," the male character, called "the young man" first and David later, is on an extended honeymoon on the Côte d'Azur with his new bride, called alternately "the girl" and Catherine. They lounge, swim, eat, and make love over and over. Their conversation is mostly inconsequential chatter or confessions, but running through it is a dominating theme of physical blackness as profoundly beautiful, exciting, and sexually compelling:

> ". . . you're my good lovely husband and my brother
> too . . . when we go to Africa I'll be your African girl too."
> "It's too early to go to Africa now. It's the big rains and
> afterwards the grass is too high and it's very cold."
> "Then where should we go?"

"We can go to Spain but . . . It's too early for the Basque coast. It's still cold and rainy. It rains everywhere there now."

"Isn't there a hot part where we could swim the way we do here?"

"You can't swim in Spain the way we do here. You'd get arrested."

"What a bore. Let's wait to go there then because I want us to get darker."

"Why do you want to be so dark?"

". . . Doesn't it make you excited to have me getting so dark?"

"Uh-huh. I love it."

This strange brew of incest, black skin, and sexuality is so unlike Hemingway's separation of "Cubans" from "niggers" in "To Have and Have Not." Although in that novel both in fact refer to Cubans (people born in Cuba), the latter is deprived of nationality and a home.

There is a perfectly good reason for the part colorism plays in literature. It was the law. Even a casual examination of the "so-called" color laws makes the case for the emphasis on color as indicator of what is legal and what is not. The legislative acts of Virginia to enforce slavery and to control blacks (collected by June Purcell Guild as "Black Laws of Virginia") are, as the foreword notes, representative of laws that "permeated the life of the eighteenth and nineteenth century Negro, whether slave or free; and by implication, the fabric of life for the white majority." For example, a statute of 1705 stated that "Popish recusants, convicts, Negroes, mulattoes, and Indian servants, and others not being Christians, shall be incapable to be witnesses in any cases whatsoever."

According to a criminal code of 1847, "Any white person assembling with slaves or free Negroes for purpose of instructing them to read or write . . . shall be confined in jail not exceeding six months and fined not exceeding $100.00."

Much later, under Jim Crow, the General Code of the City of Birmingham of 1944 prohibited any negro and white, in any public space, from playing together in "any game with cards, dice, dominoes or checkers."

Those laws are archaic and, in a way, silly. And while they are no longer enforced or enforceable, they have laid the carpet on which many writers have danced to great effect.

The cultural mechanics of becoming American are clearly understood. A citizen of Italy or Russia immigrates to the United States. She keeps much or some of the language and customs of her home country. But if she wishes to be American—to be known as such and to actually belong—she must become a thing unimaginable in her home country: she must become white. It may be comfortable for her or uncomfortable, but it lasts and has advantages, as well as certain freedoms.

Africans and their descendants never had that choice, as so much literature illustrates. I became interested in the portrayal of blacks by culture rather than skin color: when color alone was their bête noire, when it was incidental, and when it was unknowable, or deliberately withheld. The latter offered me an interesting opportunity to ignore the fetish of color, as well as a certain freedom accompanied by some very careful writing. In some novels, I theatricalized the point by not only refusing to rest on racial signs but also alerting the reader to my strategy. In "Paradise," the opening sentences launch the ploy: "They shoot the white girl first. With the rest they can take their time." This is meant to be an explosion of racial identification, which is subsequently withheld throughout descriptions of the community of women in the convent where the attack takes place. Does the reader search for her, the white girl? Or does he or she lose interest in the search? Abandon it to concentrate on the substance of the novel? Some readers have told me of their guess, but only one of them was ever correct. Her focus was on behavior—something she identified as a gesture or assumption no black girl would make or have—no matter where she came from or whatever her past. This raceless community neighbors one with exactly the opposite priority—race purity is everything to its members. Anyone who isn't "eight rock," the deepest level of a coal mine, is excluded from his or her town. In other works, such as "The Bluest Eye," the consequences of the color fetish are the theme: its severely destructive force.

I tried again in "Home" to create a work in which color was erased but could be easily assumed if the reader paid close attention to the codes, the restrictions black people routinely suffered: where one sits on a bus, where one urinates, and so on. But I was so very successful in forcing the reader to ignore color that it made my editor nervous. So, reluctantly, I layered in references that verified the race of Frank Money, the main character. I believe it was a mistake that defied my purpose.

In "God Help the Child," color is both a curse and a blessing, a hammer and a golden ring. Although neither, the hammer nor the ring, helped make the character a sympathetic human being. Only caring unselfishly for somebody else would accomplish true maturity.

There are so many opportunities to reveal race in literature—whether one is conscious of it or not. But writing non-colorist literature about black people is a task I have found both liberating and hard.

How much tension or interest would Ernest Hemingway have lost if he had simply used Wesley's given name? How much fascination and shock would be dampened if Faulkner had limited the book's central concern to incest rather than the theatrical "one-drop" curse?

Some readers coming for the first time to "A Mercy," which takes place two years before the Salem witch trials, may assume that only blacks were slaves. But so too might be a Native American, or a white homosexual couple, like the characters in my novel. The white mistress in "A Mercy," though not enslaved, was purchased in an arranged marriage.

I first tried this technique of racial erasure in a short story titled "Recitatif." It began as a screenplay that I was asked to write for two actresses—one black, one white. But since in the writing I didn't know which actress would play which part, I eliminated color altogether, using social class as the marker. The actresses didn't like my play at all. Later, I converted the material into a short story—which, by the way, does exactly the opposite of my plan. (The characters are divided by race, but all racial codes have been deliberately removed.) Instead of relating to plot and character development, most readers insist on searching for what I have refused them. My effort may not be admired by, or interesting to, other black authors. After decades of struggle to write powerful narratives portraying decidedly black characters, they may wonder if I am engaged in literary whitewashing. I am not. And I am not asking to be joined in this endeavor. But I am determined to defang cheap racism, annihilate and discredit the routine, easy, available color fetish, which is reminiscent of slavery itself.

BLACK LIKE THEM

MALCOLM GLADWELL

April 29, 1996

My cousin Rosie and her husband, Noel, live in a two-bedroom bungalow on Argyle Avenue, in Uniondale, on the west end of Long Island. When they came to America, twelve years ago, they lived in a basement apartment a dozen or so blocks away, next to their church. At the time, they were both taking classes at the New York Institute of Technology, which was right nearby. But after they graduated, and Rosie got a job managing a fast-food place and Noel got a job in asbestos removal, they managed to save a little money and bought the house on Argyle Avenue.

From the outside, their home looks fairly plain. It's in a part of Uniondale that has a lot of tract housing from just after the war, and most of the houses are alike—squat and square, with aluminum siding, maybe a dormer window in the attic, and a small patch of lawn out front. But there is a beautiful park down the street, the public schools are supposed to be good, and Rosie and Noel have built a new garage and renovated the basement. Now that Noel has started his own business, as an environmental engineer, he has his office down there—Suite 2B, it says on his stationery—and every morning he puts on his tie and goes down the stairs to make calls and work on the computer. If Noel's business takes off, Rosie says, she would like to move to a bigger house, in Garden City, which is one town over. She says this even though Garden City is mostly white. In fact, when she told one of her girlfriends, a black American, about this idea, her friend said that she was crazy—that Garden City was no place for a black person. But that is just the point.

Rosie and Noel are from Jamaica. They don't consider themselves black at all.

This doesn't mean that my cousins haven't sometimes been lumped together with American blacks. Noel had a job once removing asbestos at Kennedy Airport, and his boss there called him "nigger" and cut his hours. But Noel didn't take it personally. That boss, he says, didn't like women or Jews, either, or people with college degrees—or even himself, for that matter. Another time, Noel found out that a white guy working next to him in the same job and with the same qualifications was making ten thousand dollars a year more than he was. He quit the next day. Noel knows that racism is out there. It's just that he doesn't quite understand—or accept—the categories on which it depends.

To a West Indian, black is a literal description: you are black if your skin is black. Noel's father, for example, is black. But his mother had a white father, and she herself was fair-skinned and could pass. As for Rosie, her mother and my mother, who are twins, thought of themselves while they were growing up as "middle-class brown," which is to say that they are about the same shade as Colin Powell. That's because our maternal grandfather was part Jewish, in addition to all kinds of other things, and Grandma, though she was a good deal darker than he was, had enough Scottish blood in her to have been born with straight hair. Rosie's mother married another brown Jamaican, and that makes Rosie a light chocolate. As for my mother, she married an Englishman, making everything that much more complicated, since by the racial categories of my own heritage I am one thing and by the racial categories of America I am another. Once, when Rosie and Noel came to visit me while I was living in Washington, D.C., Noel asked me to show him "where the black people lived," and I was confused for a moment until I realized that he was using "black" in the American sense, and so was asking in the same way that someone visiting Manhattan might ask where Chinatown was. That the people he wanted to see were in many cases racially indistinguishable from him didn't matter. The facts of his genealogy, of his nationality, of his status as an immigrant made him, in his own eyes, different.

This question of who West Indians are and how they define themselves may seem trivial, like racial hairsplitting. But it is not trivial. In the past twenty years, the number of West Indians in America has exploded. There are now half a million in the New York area alone and, despite their recent arrival, they make substantially more money than American blacks. They live in better neighborhoods. Their families are stronger. In the New York area, in fact, West Indians fare about as well as Chinese and Korean immigrants. That is why the Caribbean invasion and the issue of West Indian identity have become such controversial issues. What does it say about the nature of racism that another group of blacks, who have the same legacy of slavery as their American counterparts and are physically indistinguishable from them, can come here and succeed as well as the Chinese and the Koreans do? Is overcoming racism as simple as doing what Noel does, which is to dismiss it, to hold himself above it, to brave it and move on?

These are difficult questions, not merely for what they imply about American blacks but for the ways in which they appear to contradict conventional views of what prejudice is. Racism, after all, is supposed to be indiscriminate. For example, sociologists have observed that the more blacks there are in a community the more negative the whites' attitudes will be. Blacks in Denver have a far easier time than blacks in, say, Cleveland. Lynchings in the South at the turn of this century, to give another example, were far more common in counties where there was a large black population than in areas where whites were in the majority. Prejudice is the crudest of weapons, a reaction against blacks in the aggregate that grows as the perception of black threat grows. If that is the case, however, the addition of hundreds of thousands of new black immigrants to the New York area should have made things worse for people like Rosie and Noel, not better. And, if racism is so indiscriminate in its application, why is one group of blacks flourishing and the other not?

The implication of West Indian success is that racism does not really exist at all—at least, not in the form that we have assumed it does. The implication is that the key factor in understanding racial prejudice is not the behavior and attitudes of whites but the behavior and attitudes of blacks—not white discrimination but black culture. It implies that when the conservatives in Congress say the responsibility for ending urban poverty lies not with collective action but with the poor themselves they are right.

I think of this sometimes when I go with Rosie and Noel to their church, which is in Hempstead, just a mile away. It was once a white church, but in the past decade or so it has been taken over by immigrants from the Caribbean. They have so swelled its membership that the church has bought much of the surrounding property and is about to add a hundred seats to its sanctuary. The pastor, though, is white, and when the band up front is playing and the congregation is in full West Indian form the pastor sometimes seems out of place, as if he cannot move in time with the music. I always wonder how long the white minister at Rosie and Noel's church will last—whether there won't be some kind of groundswell among the congregation to replace him with one of their own. But Noel tells me the issue has never really come up. Noel says, in fact, that he's happier with a white minister, for the same reasons that he's happy with his neighborhood, where the people across the way are Polish and another neighbor is Hispanic and still another is a black American. He doesn't want to be shut off from everyone else, isolated within the narrow confines of his race. He wants to be part of the world, and when he says these things it is awfully tempting to credit that attitude with what he and Rosie have accomplished.

Is this confidence, this optimism, this equanimity all that separates the poorest of American blacks from a house on Argyle Avenue?

IN 1994, PHILIP KASINITZ, A SOCIOLOGIST AT MANHATTAN'S HUNTER College, and Jan Rosenberg, who teaches at Long Island University, conducted a study of the Red Hook area of Brooklyn, a neighborhood of around thirteen or fourteen thousand which lies between the waterfront and the Gowanus Expressway. Red Hook has a large public-housing project at its center, and around the project, in the streets that line the waterfront, are several hundred thriving blue-collar businesses—warehouses, shipping companies, small manufacturers, and contractors. The object of the study was to resolve what Kasinitz and Rosenberg saw as the paradox of Red Hook: despite Red Hook's seemingly fortuitous conjunction of unskilled labor and blue-collar jobs, very few of the Puerto Ricans and African-Americans from the neighborhood ever found work in the bustling economy of their own back yard.

After dozens of interviews with local employers, the two researchers uncovered a persistent pattern of what they call positive discrimination. It was not that the employers did not like blacks and Hispanics. It was that they had developed an elaborate mechanism for distinguishing between those they felt were "good" blacks and those they felt were "bad" blacks, between those they judged to be "good" Hispanics and those they considered "bad" Hispanics. "Good" meant that you came from outside the neighborhood, because employers identified locals with the crime and dissipation they saw on the streets around them. "Good" also meant that you were an immigrant, because employers felt that being an immigrant implied a loyalty and a willingness to work and learn not found among the native-born. In Red Hook, the good Hispanics are Mexican and South American, not Puerto Rican. And the good blacks are West Indian.

The Harvard sociologist Mary C. Waters conducted a similar study, in 1993, which looked at a food-service company in Manhattan where West Indian workers have steadily displaced African-Americans in the past few years. The transcripts of her interviews with the company managers make fascinating reading, providing an intimate view of the perceptions that govern the urban work-place. Listen to one forty-year-old white male manager on the sub-ject of West Indians:

> They tend more to shy away from doing all of the illegal things because they have such strict rules down in their countries and jails. And they're nothing like here. So like, they're like really paranoid to do something wrong. They seem to be very, very self-conscious of it. No matter what they have to do, if they have to try and work three jobs, they do. They won't go into drugs or anything like that.

Or listen to this, from a fifty-three-year-old white female man-ager:

> I work closely with this one girl who's from Trinidad. And she told me when she first came here to live with her sister and cousin, she had two children. And she said I'm here four years and we've reached our goals. And what was your goal? For her two children to each have their own bedroom. Now she has a three bedroom apartment and she said that's one of the goals she was shooting for. . . . If that was an American, they would say, I reached my goal. I bought a Cadillac.

This idea of the West Indian as a kind of superior black is not a new one. When the first wave of Caribbean immigrants came to New York and Boston, in the early nineteen-hundreds, other blacks dubbed them Jewmaicans, in derisive reference to the emphasis they placed on hard work and education. In the nineteen-eighties, the economist Thomas Sowell gave the idea a serious intellectual imprimatur by arguing that the West Indian advantage was a historical legacy of Caribbean slave culture. According to Sowell, in the American South slaveowners tended to hire managers who were married, in order to limit the problems created by sexual relations between overseers and slave women. But the West Indies were a hardship post, without a large and settled white population. There the overseers tended to be bachelors, and, with white women scarce, there was far more commingling of the races. The resulting large group of coloreds soon formed a kind of proto-middle class, performing various kinds of skilled and sophisticated tasks that there were not enough whites around to do, as there were in the American South. They were carpenters, masons, plumbers, and small businessmen, many years in advance of their American counterparts, developing skills that required education and initiative.

My mother and Rosie's mother came from this colored class. Their parents were schoolteachers in a tiny village buried in the hills of central Jamaica. My grandmother's and grandfather's salaries combined put them, at best, on the lower rungs of the middle class. But their expectations went well beyond that. In my grandfather's library were Dickens and Maupassant. My mother and her sister were pushed to win scholarships to a proper English-style boarding school at the other end of the island; and later, when my mother graduated, it was taken for granted that she would attend university in England, even though the cost of tuition and passage meant that my grandmother had to borrow a small fortune from the Chinese grocer down the road.

My grandparents had ambitions for their children, but it was a special kind of ambition, born of a certainty that American blacks did not have—that their values were the same as those of society as a whole, and that hard work and talent could actually be rewarded. In my mother's first year at boarding school, she looked up "Negro" in the eleventh edition of the Encyclopædia Britannica. "In certain . . . characteristics . . . the negro would appear to stand on a lower evolutionary plane than the white man," she read. And the entry continued:

> The mental constitution of the negro is very similar to that of a child, normally good-natured and cheerful, but subject to sudden fits of emotion and passion during which he is capable of performing acts of singular atrocity, impressionable, vain, but often exhibiting in the capacity of servant a dog-like fidelity which has stood the supreme test.

All black people of my mother's generation—and of generations before and since—have necessarily faced a moment like this, when they are confronted for the first time with the allegation of their inferiority. But, at least in my mother's case, her school was integrated, and that meant she knew black girls who were more intelligent than white girls, and she knew how she measured against the world around her. At least she lived in a country that had blacks and browns in every position of authority, so her personal experience gave the lie to what she read in the encyclopedia. This, I think, is what Noel means when he says that he cannot quite appreciate what it is that weighs black Americans down, because he encountered the debilitating effects of racism late, when he was much stronger. He came of age in a country where he belonged to the majority.

When I was growing up, my mother sometimes read to my brothers and me from the work of Louise Bennett, the great Jamaican poet of my mother's generation. The poem I remember best is about two women—one black and one white—in a hair salon, the black woman getting her hair straightened and, next to her, the white woman getting her hair curled:

same time me mind start 'tink
'bout me and de white woman
how me tek out me natural perm
and she put in false one

There is no anger or resentment here, only irony and playfulness—
the two races captured in a shared moment of absurdity. Then comes
the twist. The black woman is paying less to look white than the
white woman is to look black:

de two a we da tek a risk
what rain or shine will bring
but fe har risk is t're poun'
fi me onle five shillin'

In the nineteen-twenties, the garment trade in New York was
first integrated by West Indian women, because, the legend goes,
they would see the sign on the door saying "No blacks need apply"
and simply walk on in. When I look back on Bennett's poem, I
think I understand how they found the courage to do that.

IT IS TEMPTING TO USE THE WEST INDIAN STORY AS EVIDENCE THAT
discrimination doesn't really exist—as proof that the only thing
inner-city African-Americans have to do to be welcomed as warmly
as West Indians in places like Red Hook is to make the necessary cultural adjustments. If West Indians are different, as they
clearly are, then it is easy to imagine that those differences are the
reason for their success—that their refusal to be bowed is what lets
them walk on by the signs that prohibit them or move to neighborhoods that black Americans would shy away from. It also seems
hard to see how the West Indian story is in any way consistent with
the idea of racism as an indiscriminate, pernicious threat aimed at
all black people.

But here is where things become more difficult, and where what seems obvious about West Indian achievement turns out not to be obvious at all. One of the striking things in the Red Hook study, for example, is the emphasis that the employers appeared to place on hiring outsiders—Irish or Russian or Mexican or West Indian immigrants from places far from Red Hook. The reason for this was not, the researchers argue, that the employers had any great familiarity with the cultures of those immigrants. They had none, and that was the point. They were drawn to the unfamiliar because what was familiar to them—the projects of Red Hook—was anathema. The Columbia University anthropologist Katherine Newman makes the same observation in a recent study of two fast-food restaurants in Harlem. She compared the hundreds of people who applied for jobs at those restaurants with the few people who were actually hired, and found, among other things, that how far an applicant lived from the job site made a huge difference. Of those applicants who lived less than two miles from the restaurant, ten per cent were hired. Of those who lived more than two miles from the restaurant, nearly forty per cent were hired. As Newman puts it, employers preferred the ghetto they didn't know to the ghetto they did.

Neither study describes a workplace where individual attitudes make a big difference, or where the clunky and impersonal prejudices that characterize traditional racism have been discarded. They sound like places where old-style racism and appreciation of immigrant values are somehow bound up together. Listen to another white manager who was interviewed by Mary Waters:

> Island blacks who come over, they're immigrant. They may not have such a good life where they are so they gonna try to strive to better themselves and I think there's a lot of American blacks out there who feel we owe them. And enough is enough already. You know, this is something

that happened to their ancestors, not now. I mean, we've done so much for the black people in America now that it's time that they got off their butts.

Here, then, are the two competing ideas about racism side by side: the manager issues a blanket condemnation of American blacks even as he holds West Indians up as a cultural ideal. The example of West Indians as "good" blacks makes the old blanket prejudice against American blacks all the easier to express. The manager can tell black Americans to get off their butts without fear of sounding, in his own ears, like a racist, because he has simultaneously celebrated island blacks for their work ethic. The success of West Indians is not proof that discrimination against American blacks does not exist. Rather, it is the means by which discrimination against American blacks is given one last, vicious twist: I am not so shallow as to despise you for the color of your skin, because I have found people your color that I like. Now I can despise you for who you are.

This is racism's newest mutation—multicultural racism, where one ethnic group can be played off against another. But it is wrong to call West Indians the victors in this competition, in anything but the narrowest sense. In American history, immigrants have always profited from assimilation: as they have adopted the language and customs of this country, they have sped their passage into the mainstream. The new racism means that West Indians are the first group of people for whom that has not been true. Their advantage depends on their remaining outsiders, on remaining unfamiliar, on being distinct by custom, culture, and language from the American blacks they would otherwise resemble. There is already some evidence that the considerable economic and social advantages that West Indians hold over American blacks begin to dissipate by the second generation, when the island accent has faded, and those in positions of power who draw distinctions between good blacks and bad blacks begin to lump West Indians with everyone else. For

West Indians, assimilation is tantamount to suicide. This is a cruel fate for any immigrant group, but it is especially so for West Indians, whose history and literature are already redolent with the themes of dispossession and loss, with the long search for identity and belonging. In the nineteen-twenties, Marcus Garvey sought community in the idea of Africa. Bob Marley, the Jamaican reggae singer, yearned for Zion. In "Rites of Passage" the Barbadian poet Edward Kamau Brathwaite writes:

> Where, then, is the nigger's
> home?
>
> In Paris Brixton Kingston
> Rome?
>
> Here?
> Or in Heaven?

America might have been home. But it is not: not Red Hook, anyway; not Harlem; not even Argyle Avenue.

There is also no small measure of guilt here, for West Indians cannot escape the fact that their success has come, to some extent, at the expense of American blacks, and that as they have noisily differentiated themselves from African-Americans—promoting the stereotype of themselves as the good blacks—they have made it easier for whites to join in. It does not help matters that the same kinds of distinctions between good and bad blacks which govern the immigrant experience here have always lurked just below the surface of life in the West Indies as well. It was the infusion of white blood that gave the colored class its status in the Caribbean, and the members of this class have never forgotten that, nor have they failed, in a thousand subtle ways, to distance themselves from those around them who experienced a darker and less privileged past.

In my mother's house, in Harewood, the family often passed around a pencilled drawing of two of my great-grandparents; she was part Jewish, and he was part Scottish. The other side—the African side—was never mentioned. My grandmother was the ringleader in this. She prized my grandfather's light skin, but she also suffered as a result of this standard. "She's nice, you know, but she's too dark," her mother-in-law would say of her. The most telling story of all, though, is the story of one of my mother's relatives, whom I'll call Aunt Joan, who was as fair as my great-grandmother was. Aunt Joan married what in Jamaica is called an Injun—a man with a dark complexion that is redeemed from pure Africanness by straight, fine black hair. She had two daughters by him—handsome girls with dark complexions. But he died young, and one day, while she was travelling on a train to visit her daughter, she met and took an interest in a light-skinned man in the same railway car. What happened next is something that Aunt Joan told only my mother, years later, with the greatest of shame. When she got off the train, she walked right by her daughter, disowning her own flesh and blood, because she did not want a man so light-skinned and desirable to know that she had borne a daughter so dark.

My mother, in the nineteen-sixties, wrote a book about her experiences. It was entitled "Brown Face, Big Master," the brown face referring to her and the big master, in the Jamaican dialect, referring to God. Sons, of course, are hardly objective on the achievements of their mothers, but there is one passage in the book that I find unforgettable, because it is such an eloquent testimony to the moral precariousness of the Jamaican colored class—to the mixture of confusion and guilt that attends its position as beneficiary of racism's distinctions. The passage describes a time just after my mother and father were married, when they were living in London and my eldest brother was still a baby. They were looking for an apartment, and after a long search my father found one in a London suburb. On the day after they moved in, however, the landlady ordered them out. "You didn't tell me your wife was colored," she told my father, in a rage.

In her book my mother describes her long struggle to make sense of this humiliation, to reconcile her experience with her faith. In the end, she was forced to acknowledge that anger was not an option—that as a Jamaican "middle-class brown," and a descendant of Aunt Joan, she could hardly reproach another for the impulse to divide good black from bad black:

> I complained to God in so many words: "Here I
> was, the wounded representative of the negro race in our
> struggle to be accounted free and equal with the dominat-
> ing whites!" And God was amused; my prayer did not ring
> true with Him. I would try again. And then God said,
> "Have you not done the same thing? Remember this one
> and that one, people whom you have slighted or avoided
> or treated less considerately than others because they were
> different superficially, and you were ashamed to be iden-
> tified with them. Have you not been glad that you are
> not more colored than you are? Grateful that you are not
> black?" My anger and hate against the landlady melted. I
> was no better than she was, nor worse for that matter. . . .
> We were both guilty of the sin of self-regard, the pride
> and the exclusiveness by which we cut some people off
> from ourselves.

I GREW UP IN CANADA, IN A LITTLE FARMING TOWN AN HOUR AND A half outside of Toronto. My father teaches mathematics at a nearby university, and my mother is a therapist. For many years, she was the only black person in town, but I cannot remember wondering or worrying, or even thinking, about this fact. Back then, color meant only good things. It meant my cousins in Jamaica. It meant the graduate students from Africa and India my father would bring home from the university. My own color was not something I ever thought much about, either, because it seemed such a stray fact. Blacks knew what I was. They could discern the hint of Africa beneath my fair skin. But it was a kind of secret—something that they would ask me about quietly when no one else was around. ("Where you from?" an older black man once asked me. "Ontario," I said, not thinking. "No," he replied. "Where you *from*?" And then I understood and told him, and he nodded as if he had already known. "We was speculatin' about your heritage," he said.) But whites never guessed, and even after I informed them it never seemed to make a difference. Why would it? In a town that is ninety-nine per cent white, one modest alleged splash of color hardly amounts to a threat.

But things changed when I left for Toronto to attend college. This was during the early nineteen-eighties, when West Indians were immigrating to Canada in droves, and Toronto had become second only to New York as the Jamaican expatriates' capital in North America. At school, in the dining hall, I was served by Jamaicans. The infamous Jane-Finch projects, in northern Toronto, were considered the Jamaican projects. The drug trade then taking off was said to be the Jamaican drug trade. In the popular imagination, Jamaicans were—and are—welfare queens and gun-toting gangsters and dissolute youths. In Ontario, blacks accused of crimes are released by the police eighteen per cent of the time; whites are released twenty-nine per cent of the time. In drug-trafficking and importing cases, blacks are twenty-seven times as likely as whites to be jailed before their trial takes place, and twenty times as likely to be imprisoned on drug-possession charges.

After I had moved to the United States, I puzzled over this seeming contradiction—how West Indians celebrated in New York for their industry and drive could represent, just five hundred miles northwest, crime and dissipation. Didn't Torontonians see what was special and different in West Indian culture? But that was a naïve question. The West Indians were the first significant brush with blackness that white, smug, comfortable Torontonians had ever had. They had no bad blacks to contrast with the newcomers, no African-Americans to serve as a safety valve for their prejudices, no way to perform America's crude racial triage.

Not long ago, I sat in a coffee shop with someone I knew vaguely from college, who, like me, had moved to New York from Toronto. He began to speak of the threat that he felt Toronto now faced. It was the Jamaicans, he said. They were a bad seed. He was, of course, oblivious of my background. I said nothing, though, and he launched into a long explanation of how, in slave times, Jamaica was the island where all the most troublesome and obstreperous slaves were sent, and how that accounted for their particularly nasty disposition today.

I have told that story many times since, usually as a joke, because it was funny in an appalling way—particularly when I informed him much, much later that my mother was Jamaican. I tell the story that way because otherwise it is too painful. There must be people in Toronto just like Rosie and Noel, with the same attitudes and aspirations, who want to live in a neighborhood as nice as Argyle Avenue, who want to build a new garage and renovate their basement and set up their own business downstairs. But it is not completely up to them, is it? What has happened to Jamaicans in Toronto is proof that what has happened to Jamaicans here is not the end of racism, or even the beginning of the end of racism, but an accident of history and geography. In America, there is someone else to despise. In Canada, there is not. In the new racism, as in the old, somebody always has to be the nigger.

BARACK X

JELANI COBB

October 7, 2012

I.

It's mid-March in Harlem and the streets are an improvised urban bazaar. Young men hawk umbrellas, vintage vinyl, and knit caps. The aromas of curry and fried plantains waft out from the Caribbean spot, and just ahead of me is a teen-ager so slight that I scarcely notice him at first. There's a perfectly calibrated swagger in his stride. He's swaddled in an oversized black leather jacket, his jeans cinched five inches below the waist, his footwear immaculate. I've nearly passed him before I notice something that makes me pause for a second and then snap a picture with my cell phone: stitched onto the back of the jacket, in dimensions broader than his back, is the seal of the President of the United States. He is standing on Malcolm X Boulevard, and a generation ago that jacket would've been emblazoned with a defiant X in homage to a man who defined radical black dissent. There are a dozen questions I could ask him—whether there are metal detectors in his school or when was the last time he was frisked by the N.Y.P.D., whether he sees his future as an amorphous blob of curtailed possibilities or if he has real plans. But I don't have to ask how the most revered symbol of the American establishment came to adorn his jacket.

In the halcyon days after Barack Obama's inauguration, newspapers ran stories marvelling at an Obama effect that seemed to lift black students beyond the achievement gap. Some openly hoped that his election would inspire increased numbers of black law-school applicants, the way that "C.S.I." spawned a generation of forensic-science majors. In a poll taken just after the inauguration, some seventy per cent of respondents said that they expected his tenure to bring an improvement in race relations. Obama himself played to this dynamic early on, saying that in a crowded field of talented Democratic contenders the rationale for his campaign was that his election would tell every child in this country that anything was possible. And for a brief moment, it seemed that might actually be true.

Nearly four years later, the fickle-hearted arbiters of cool have migrated onward, finding new cultural pastures to stake out. There are no A-list rappers crafting themes in Obama's honor, no catchy call-and-response phrases on par with "fired up and ready to go." Yet here on Lenox Avenue is an Obama testimony in clashing motifs that underscores the complexity of the President's current undertaking. A handful of men have been elected President and then become a symbol for an era, but very few beyond the current occupant of 1600 Pennsylvania Avenue have made the opposite transition. And it is for this reason that 2012 seems like so much anticlimax: a symbol ran for President four years ago; today a man is seeking to hold onto that position.

Prior to 2008, the distinctions between a black leader and a leader who is black were largely semantic. There had been black leaders of largely white enterprises—Richard Parsons, Condi Rice, Ken Chenault—but they were seen as inspired anomalies, envoys dispatched to the broadened frontiers of possibility. In the days leading up to the 2008 election, it was common to hear African-Americans ask whether white America was "ready" for a black President. I tended to wonder if *black* America was. To the extent that the public thinks of our Presidents, it tends toward a kind of cultural shorthand. We think of Teddy Roosevelt as a trust-buster despite the fact that Taft moved more aggressively against the nascent corporate order than he did. J.F.K.'s reputation as a civil-rights stalwart is all but immunized against his record of foot-dragging on racial matters. Beyond wonks and history grad students there aren't many Americans who hedge Reagan's standing as an avatar of small government with his multiple tax increases. We tend toward a glossy, forgiving view of historic Presidencies. For African-Americans in particular, however, Obama presented a dilemma—he is both a figure of history, a representative of a centuries-long struggle to have our humanity recognized, and a contemporary elected official sent to Washington to address specific problems and policies. It is a balancing act that few of us were prepared for, nor ever thought we would need to be.

At a casual glance it seems contradictory that African-American unemployment remains double white unemployment but that the President retains a ninety per cent approval rate among black people. But that fails to recognize many of us who remember that blacks were disproportionately unemployed under Bush, Clinton, Bush, and Reagan. The black community understood better than anyone else how intractable this problem was. Obama would not be measured by whether he fixed the problem; he would be measured by how credibly and diligently he attempted to.

In black America—where people have been voting for Presidential candidates who didn't share their racial background since even before the Fifteenth Amendment—the 2008 election wasn't seen as the star-spangled "Kumbaya" it was billed as elsewhere. White rejoicing at Obama's racial landmark seemed tone deaf, unduly self-congratulatory. White voters had simply done something black voters had been doing for at least the previous hundred and thirty-four years. For this reason and others like it, there was a tendency among blacks to see Obama as an extension of black achievement—but not necessarily a barometer of changing white attitudes. The hyperbolic talk of a post-racial society suggested that white voters, or at least a highly visible segment of them, tended to see the election in precisely the opposite terms.

2.

The more onerous aspects of Jim Crow conspired to obscure a reality key to understanding Barack Obama's complicated relationship to black America: simply put, the colored section was far more democratic than the ostensibly free segments of America because virtually *any* tincture of black ancestry was sufficient to gain admission. The boundaries of whiteness required vigilant policing and scrutiny, but black people were far more catholic in our self-perception.

In response, America conjured a usable mythology, one in which the product of interracial unions were uniformly doomed to suffer disproportionate woe. Fiction, folklore, and films like "Imitation of Life" cinched the concept of the tragic mulatto in American popular imagination. But the concept didn't square with our own lived experience. There was nothing tragic about the trajectories of Frederick Douglass, Booker T. Washington, Mordecai Johnson, or any other biracial black person—aside from the burden of racial inequality they shouldered along with anyone else of African descent. The activist Walter White used his nearly white skin as a kind of camouflage that allowed him to investigate lynchings for the N.A.A.C.P. in the nineteen-twenties. Obama understood this history well enough to stand nearly outside of it. In 2008, Barack Obama authored a new archetype—a biracial man who was not so much tragic as ironic. Unlike the maligned mulattoes of old, Obama wasn't passing for white—he was passing for mixed. For those with an eye to this history it was a masterful performance, a riff as adroit as anything conjured by Dizzy Gillespie or Sonny Rollins.

Early on, observers noted Obama's Ebonic lapses when speaking to black audiences and saw in them a sly attempt to pander to African-American voters. But they had it precisely backward: to black audiences, his ability to speak in pulpit inflections one moment and concave Midwestern tones the next made him seem *more* black, not less. We saw him as no different than any African-American lawyer who speaks black English at home and another, entirely more formal language, in his professional environment.

Not surprisingly this has translated into confusion over who the President of the United States is. A 2010 Pew poll showed that fifty-three per cent of whites see the President as biracial while only a quarter see him as black. At the same time, fifty-five per cent of African-Americans see Obama as black while a third see him as mixed race. What the poll failed to ask, however, was whether African-Americans see those two categories as mutually exclusive. Slavery, coercion, and the randomness of social exchange conspired to ensure that virtually all of black America is biracial in some regard. Walter White had blonde hair, fair skin, and blue eyes—yet was black enough to serve as the N.A.A.C.P.'s chief executive for twenty-four years. What was known but left unsaid is that Obama was at least as black as any of the other forty million of us and biracial in the same sense that Douglass, Washington, and White were.

This is not a simple equation: Obama received more white support than John Kerry or Al Gore, both of whom have *two* white parents. Yet there was a notable *hmph* of dissatisfaction, in 2010, when Obama noted that he identified as black on the census. What it meant was that a quorum of white voters were not going to let "Dreams from my Father," the South Side of Chicago, and Obama's own census form prevent them from debiting some aspect of identity and remaking him as *meta*black.

A sharp politician looking to maximize his surface area with voters would see no upside in further clarifying this state of affairs. As the actor Vin Diesel found some years back, the guiding principle was that as long as people were intrigued about where you fit in the racial taxonomy, they'd remain fundamentally intrigued by you. In an undertaking as vast and unwieldy as the United States, any President is required to simultaneously be many things—ideologically, socially, politically—but not until November 4, 2008, was any of them required to be many things racially.

The received wisdom holds that Obama has been reluctant to deal explicitly with race for fear of igniting the ire of his white detractors. But this is only part of the equation—the ground is nearly as fraught for his dealings with his white supporters, particularly those who took him as validation for the counterfeit belief that we were beyond the racial dramas of old. By the time of the 2008 election Obama had become a sort of racial O-negative, a fragile position he could maintain only so long as circumstance coöperated. (Circumstance, as Skip Gates, Shirley Sherrod, and especially Trayvon Martin could attest, chose not to.) All this meant that black America knew that, contrary to the New York *Times* headline following the election, "the racial barrier" had not fallen with Obama's election; it had become a selectively permeable membrane, though that in itself was reason enough to do the Electric Slide in the streets.

The post-racial myth is the logical outgrowth of an older mythology that the black struggle for freedom was anchored in a moral crusade to redeem America at large. The truth of the matter is that Martin Luther King, Jr., was more of a backroom operator than that. The idea of redemption stemmed from a moral sales pitch proffered by King, a transaction in which whites would confront the awful contours of American history and be granted exemption from its implications. Black people had a more tangible yield in mind: removing the dusty boot of Jim Crow from our necks. If fashioning spiritual redemption as a form of higher patriotism was enough to end abominations like the waterlogged obscenity that was Emmett Till's body, then so be it. But the deeper truth is that black people were more concerned with saving our own necks than saving America's soul.

For this reason, white claims to have "marched with Dr. King" eventually became an unintentional punch-line, a disclaimer for whatever racially obtuse commentary followed that preface. The joke, however, was on us. Few could conceive that forty years after King's death, the nation would elect a black President—an event deeply rooted in the civil-rights ethos, a bolder redemption, a stronger immunization against the claims of history. And, as with the claims to have marched with Dr. King, the very fact of Obama's election has been a disclaimer against the racism that came after it.

3.

I pointed out earlier that a majority of people polled felt that race relations would improve under Obama, but a more honest statement would be that there is no such thing as "race relations." There is only the relative presence or absence of racism and beyond that the fuzzy euphemisms that are just a notch better than inflammatory code words (welfare, crime) in our stilted racial dialogue. Good race relations meant that hundreds of thousands of diverse Americans could huddle together against the arctic cold on the National Mall to celebrate the inauguration of Barack Obama. Racism, however, meant that those black celebrants would disproportionately face police brutality, foreclosure, health disparities, and unemployment after the festivities were over.

The faulty gospel of good race relations means that in his dealings with black America, Obama has to abide by the old guideline of ethics: avoid not only a conflict of interest but the *appearance* of a conflict of interest. And by all appearances Obama's Administration over-learned this lesson. It was a backhanded compliment that the same polls show that fifty-seven per cent of whites think he's paid "about enough" attention to black issues.

The net result of this awkward act is that Obama's Presidency appears like a type of infidelity: married to America at large but conducting an affair with black people. As such, he speaks to us most often in veiled dispatches and surreptitious winks. Our most intimate recognition occurs behind closed doors.

It is this theme that his black critics seized upon even before he'd won the election. In 2008, at the point where enthusiasm for Obama had nearly morphed into messianic fervor, a group of black protesters at a Florida rally hoisted a banner that asked "What about the black community, Obama?" At first glance the visual was jarring, discordant. It seemed like a question for which the answer could be presumed—certainly by that segment of America that viewed his election as an antidote for the previous three centuries of racial history. But the banner was a response in very specific terms to Obama's tepid remarks on the acquittal of the police officers who had gunned down Sean Bell, an unarmed black man, on the eve of his wedding. It spoke to a broader suspicion that a candidate, even a black one, who would scarcely talk about black concerns (until his pastor's radioactive sermons gave him no choice), could not be trusted to address those same concerns when elected.

In the days before he lost his perspective amid a froth of personal animus toward Obama, Cornel West made this point repeatedly. Following Obama's speech at the Democratic Convention, which coincided with the forty-fifth anniversary of the "I Have a Dream" speech, West lit into Obama for referring to Dr. King only obliquely as a "young preacher from Georgia."

Fredrick Harris, a professor of political science at Columbia University, has argued that Obama's allergy to race is so severe as to invalidate the idea that we've seen a black Presidency:

> Obama's defenders have repeatedly said he must be a
> president for all Americans, not just African Americans,
> and Obama himself has made similar statements. But

this argument is disingenuous. When other important constituencies ask the president to support their policy initiatives—say, Jewish groups on Middle East matters, or the LGBT community on "don't ask, don't tell" and marriage equality, or women's groups on reproductive rights—can you imagine him responding that he can't address their particular interests because, as president, he has to be concerned with all people?

So on racial inequality, why do black voters have to take a back seat?

When a reporter for BET asked the president in 2009, during the debate over the stimulus bill, if he would do something to specifically address high unemployment among blacks and Latinos, Obama responded that "every step we are taking is designed to help all people" and reiterated that "my general approach is that if the economy is strong, that will lift all boats." But what of those who have no boats to begin with?

If these criticisms haven't put a dent in Obama's approval ratings, it's not because black people disagreed—it's because they ultimately place the blame for this state of affairs elsewhere. We, too, witnessed a nation ripped at its seams in 2009: when a President tried to provide citizens with affordable health care, we saw Glenn Beck achieve a demagogic cachet that made Father Coughlin look like a Henry Wallace liberal. We remember circumstances of the first-generation black mayors of major cities and the ways in which they inherited declining tax revenues, industrial bases, and white flight but were nonetheless given all the blame for the misery of the urban black poor. It also has to be understood that African-American perspectives on Obama have been filtered, first and foremost, through an abiding concern for his safety. During the 2008 primaries, I encountered black voters who spoke of voting against

Obama because they didn't believe a black man could be elected President and live through his entire term.

At every turn at which black people might have evaluated him more harshly on his political choices, Obama's most irrational foes forced African-Americans to consider him as a proxy for our own contused personal experiences. To be clear, eighty per cent of blacks feel that Obama has paid about enough attention to black concerns—that's twenty-three percentage points *more* than whites who feel this way. But "about enough" doesn't really mean about enough; it means we understand that he's paid as much attention as he could while performing the racial high-wire act required of a black man leading a nation populated by two hundred million whites. The question was not whether he'd paid enough attention to our concerns, it was whether you would prefer circumstances in which he could reasonably pay more.

Nothing better defined the precise nature of his circumstances than that triumphal moment of birtherism, in which a sitting President was forced to prove his own citizenship. Viewed through the lens of black history, that moment appeared as Dred Scott remixed, the means by which a President is racially profiled. That humiliation resounded with every black person who's ever felt that their qualifications were questioned despite years of education, hard work, and sacrifice. It made perfect sense that Donald Trump would follow up the question of Obama's citizenship with one casting doubts on his academic performance at Columbia. He was trafficking in the greatest hits of white entitlement. For black people, the implications of this were clear: if the most powerful man in the world could be played like that because he's black, what hope was there for the rest of us?

Cornel West himself unintentionally made the most cogent defense of Obama when he criticized the 2008 race speech. After rightfully citing it for the false evenhandedness with which it treated racial conflict, West offered that it was the best speech that could be given "in a racially immature society." There is a thematic bond that connects a broad swath of our contemporary politics, a bratty truculence that gives context to the rebranded nativism of birthers, to Rep. Joe Wilson's Tourette's-like outburst during a State of the Union address, to Beck's fevered dissociative ramblings, and the Muslim-socialist-fascist axis imagined by the unhinged. That immaturity found its most honest expression in a 2011 poll in which eleven per cent of white respondents said they felt that *they* are now the primary victims of racism. It is not hard to imagine that some future historian will refer to the Obama era, or at least the first four years of it, as the Age of Tantrums. Twenty years ago, in the midst of the culture wars, establishment critics assailed multiculturalism as an assault on the fabric of common citizenship. How ironic that it would be a black man—who rose to prominence in 2006 by asserting that "there's no white America or black America but the United States of America"—whose Presidency would ignite the balkanization they warned of.

There is an obvious downside to this familiarity with the obstacles implicit within a black Presidency. Obama at times tends toward insouciance regarding black voters who, epidermal affiliations aside, nonetheless represent roughly a quarter of his electorate and the single largest and most reliable voting block in the Democratic Party. That casual arrogance was on display when he warned the Congressional Black Caucus (already wavering in their support for him) to "stop complaining," during a speech in 2011. There are moments where even amid the racial minefield his Presidency inhabits, he appears to have been let off easy; black America has settled for a brother who feels our pain, rather than evaluated how effectively he's alleviated it. Yet even this frustration yields layers of complexity.

It's also worth noting that despite the gossamer-thin margin separating them in this election, the Romney campaign did not, until relatively late in the game, resort to the kinds of coded racial appeals that were a cornerstone of Presidential politics. And when it did, the campaign's loose talk about Obama undoing welfare reform and its head nod at birtherism seemed half-hearted and desperate, not an integral part of the strategy. Indeed, Romney's most inflammatory statement—his reference to a parasitic forty-seven per cent of the population—suggested bigoted attitudes that ran along class lines, not epidermal ones. It's possible that Romney, perhaps inspired by his father's example, has no stomach for such racial measures. Or that the blowback would alienate more voters than those tactics would win over. It's also possible that the Southern Strategy wouldn't fly today because it would ruin our national high. We like ourselves now in the way the blissfully un-self-aware people often do. Even slick, encrypted racism might inspire a kind of historical reflux, remind us of the terrible limbic appeal of bigotry, and put us collectively in a bad head space. Things have changed, just not the things that many of us suspected on Election Day.

Malcolm X occupied a similar crossroads in American history, a point at which a vast chunk of history had fallen away and a new vista of possibilities emerged. His criticism of integration inspired a view of him as the antithesis of the movement associated with King. A more subtle reading of him suggested that he was a herald who saw more starkly than many the unpaved places in the road ahead. The demise of segregation was as stunning to his generation as the election of Barack Obama was to this one. The troubles and complexities that would follow both those events were seemingly cloaked by momentous victories—encrypted, as it were, by the tides of change.

The Obama Presidency has thus far validated both our hopes and our fears and given duelling legitimacy to optimism and cynicism simultaneously. It has pitted the audacity of hope against the recalcitrance of memory. If his election validated the ideals of King, what has happened since then lends credence to Malcolm X. What remains clear is that whether it's a function of defiance or affirmation, Obama has already been inducted into a narrative black America tells itself, one in which we are the central characters and we are the primary deed-holders to our own triumphs. Whether or not he is reëlected is secondary to this concern. The more enduring question is whether black people will maintain a broader faith in America because a black man has been elected President, or despite it.

NOW IS THE TIME TO TALK ABOUT WHAT WE ARE ACTUALLY TALKING ABOUT

CHIMAMANDA NGOZI ADICHIE

December 2, 2016

America has always been aspirational to me. Even when I chafed at its hypocrisies, it somehow always seemed sure, a nation that knew what it was doing, refreshingly free of that anything-can-happen existential uncertainty so familiar to developing nations. But no longer. The election of Donald Trump has flattened the poetry in America's founding philosophy: the country born from an idea of freedom is to be governed by an unstable, stubbornly uninformed, authoritarian demagogue. And in response to this there are people living in visceral fear, people anxiously trying to discern policy from bluster, and people kowtowing as though to a new king. Things that were recently pushed to the corners of America's political space—overt racism, glaring misogyny, anti-intellectualism—are once again creeping to the center.

Now is the time to resist the slightest extension in the boundaries of what is right and just. Now is the time to speak up and to wear as a badge of honor the opprobrium of bigots. Now is the time to confront the weak core at the heart of America's addiction to optimism; it allows too little room for resilience, and too much for fragility. Hazy visions of "healing" and "not becoming the hate we hate" sound dangerously like appeasement. The responsibility to forge unity belongs not to the denigrated but to the denigrators.

The premise for empathy has to be equal humanity; it is an injustice to demand that the maligned identify with those who question their humanity.

America loves winners, but victory does not absolve. Victory, especially a slender one decided by a few thousand votes in a handful of states, does not guarantee respect. Nobody automatically deserves deference on ascending to the leadership of any country. American journalists know this only too well when reporting on foreign leaders—their default mode with Africans, for instance, is nearly always barely concealed disdain. President Obama endured disrespect from all quarters. By far the most egregious insult directed toward him, the racist movement tamely termed "birtherism," was championed by Trump.

Yet, a day after the election, I heard a journalist on the radio speak of the vitriol *between* Obama and Trump. No, the vitriol was Trump's. Now is the time to burn false equivalencies forever. Pretending that both sides of an issue are equal when they are not is not "balanced" journalism; it is a fairy tale—and, unlike most fairy tales, a disingenuous one.

Now is the time to refuse the blurring of memory. Each mention of "gridlock" under Obama must be wrought in truth: that "gridlock" was a deliberate and systematic refusal of the Republican Congress to work with him. Now is the time to call things what they actually are, because language can illuminate truth as much as it can obfuscate it. Now is the time to forge new words. "Alt-right" is benign. "White-supremacist right" is more accurate.

Now is the time to talk about what we are actually talking about. "Climate contrarian" obfuscates. "Climate-change denier" does not. And because climate change is scientific fact, not opinion, this matters.

Now is the time to discard that carefulness that too closely resembles a lack of conviction. The election is not a "simple racism story," because no racism story is ever a "simple" racism story, in which grinning evil people wearing white burn crosses in yards. A racism story is complicated, but it is still a racism story, and it is worth parsing. Now is not the time to tiptoe around historical references. Recalling Nazism is not extreme; it is the astute response of those who know that history gives both context and warning.

Now is the time to recalibrate the default assumptions of American political discourse. Identity politics is not the sole preserve of minority voters. This election is a reminder that identity politics in America is a white invention: it was the basis of segregation. The denial of civil rights to black Americans had at its core the idea that a black American should not be allowed to vote because that black American was not white. The endless questioning, before the election of Obama, about America's "readiness" for a black President was a reaction to white identity politics. Yet "identity politics" has come to be associated with minorities, and often with a patronizing undercurrent, as though to refer to nonwhite people motivated by an irrational herd instinct. White Americans have practiced identity politics since the inception of America, but it is now laid bare, impossible to evade.

Now is the time for the media, on the left and right, to educate and inform. To be nimble and alert, clear-eyed and skeptical, active rather than reactive. To make clear choices about what truly matters.

Now is the time to put the idea of the "liberal bubble" to rest. The reality of American tribalism is that different groups all live in bubbles. Now is the time to acknowledge the ways in which Democrats have condescended to the white working class—and to acknowledge that Trump condescends to it by selling it fantasies. Now is the time to remember that there are working-class Americans who are not white and who have suffered the same deprivations and are equally worthy of news profiles. Now is the time to remember that "women" does not equal white women. "Women" must mean all women.

Now is the time to elevate the art of questioning. Is the only valid resentment in America that of white males? If we are to be sympathetic to the idea that economic anxieties lead to questionable decisions, does this apply to all groups? Who exactly are the élite?

Now is the time to frame the questions differently. If everything remained the same, and Hillary Clinton were a man, would she still engender an overheated, outsized hostility? Would a woman who behaved exactly like Trump be elected? Now is the time to stop suggesting that sexism was absent in the election because white women did not overwhelmingly vote for Clinton. Misogyny is not the sole preserve of men.

The case for women is not that they are inherently better or more moral. It is that they are half of humanity and should have the same opportunities—and be judged according to the same standards—as the other half. Clinton was expected to be perfect, according to contradictory standards, in an election that became a referendum on her likability.

Now is the time to ask why America is far behind many other countries (see: Rwanda) in its representation of women in politics. Now is the time to explore mainstream attitudes toward women's ambition, to ponder to what extent the ordinary political calculations that all politicians make translate as moral failures when we see them in women. Clinton's careful calibration was read as deviousness. But would a male politician who is carefully calibrated—Mitt Romney, for example—merely read as carefully calibrated?

Now is the time to be precise about the meanings of words. Trump saying "They let you do it" about assaulting women does not imply consent, because consent is what happens before an act.

Now is the time to remember that, in a wave of dark populism sweeping the West, there are alternative forms. Bernie Sanders's message did not scapegoat the vulnerable. Obama rode a populist wave before his first election, one marked by a remarkable inclusiveness. Now is the time to counter lies with facts, repeatedly and unflaggingly, while also proclaiming the greater truths: of our equal humanity, of decency, of compassion. Every precious ideal must be reiterated, every obvious argument made, because an ugly idea left unchallenged begins to turn the color of normal. It does not have to be like this.

THE COLOR OF INJUSTICE

KELEFA SANNEH

August 19, 2019

Sixteen years ago, in 2003, the student newspaper at Florida Agricultural and Mechanical University, a historically black institution in Tallahassee, published a lively column about white people. "I don't hate whites," the author, a senior named Ibram Rogers, wrote. "How can you hate a group of people for being who they are?" He explained that "Europeans" had been "socialized to be aggressive people," and "raised to be racist." His theory was that white people were fending off racial extinction, using "psychological brainwashing" and "the AIDS virus." Perhaps the most incendiary line appeared at the end, after the author's byline and e-mail address: "Ibram Rogers' column will appear every Wednesday."

As it turned out, that final claim, like a few of the claims that preceded it, was not quite accurate. The column caused a stir, and Rogers was summoned to see the editor of the local newspaper, the Tallahassee *Democrat*, where he was an intern. The editor demanded that Rogers discontinue his column, and Rogers agreed under protest, though he resolved to continue his examination of race in America, which became his life's work. He eventually earned a Ph.D. in African-American studies from Temple, and gained a reputation in the field, along with some new names. He changed his middle name from Henry to Xolani, which is Zulu for "be peaceful," after learning the history of Prince Henry the Navigator, a fifteenth-century Portuguese explorer who helped pioneer the African slave trade. And at his wedding, in 2013, he and his wife, Sadiqa, told their guests that they had chosen a new last name: Kendi, which means "the loved one" in the Kenyan language of Meru. In 2016, as Ibram X. Kendi, he published "Stamped from the Beginning," a voluminous, sober-minded book that aimed to present "the definitive history of racist ideas in America."

In the thirteen years since his abortive college-newspaper column, Kendi had become ever more convinced that racism, not race, was the central force in American history, and so he reached back to 1635 to show how malleable racism could be. The preachers who justified slavery used racist arguments, he wrote, but so did many of the abolitionists—the ubiquity of racism meant that no one was immune to its seductive power, including black people. In his view, the pioneering black sociologist W. E. B. Du Bois was propping up racist ideas in 1897, when he condemned "the immorality, crime, and laziness among the Negroes." So, too, was Barack Obama, when, as a Presidential candidate in 2008, he decried "the erosion of black families." Although Obama noted that this erosion was partly due to "a lack of economic opportunity," he also made an appeal to black self-reliance, saying that members of the African-American community needed to face "our own complicity in our condition." Kendi saw statements like these as reflections of a persistent but delusional idea that something is wrong with black people. The only thing wrong, he maintained, was racism, and the country's failure to confront and defeat it.

"Stamped from the Beginning" was an unreservedly militant book that received a surprisingly warm reception. Amid a series of police shootings of African-Americans during President Obama's second term, "Black lives matter" became a rallying cry and then a movement, and helped push racism to the front of the progressive conversation. By the time Obama left office, in 2017, polls showed record-high support among Democrats for "special treatment" to help African-Americans, and for the idea that "racial discrimination" is the main obstacle to racial parity. A prominent cohort of writers, led by Ta-Nehisi Coates, was calling for a serious reckoning with racism, and with the way racist policies had worked to depress black earnings and constrain black life. In this climate, Kendi's book was celebrated as a well-timed contribution to a national conversation. It won a National Book Award and transformed Kendi into a leading public intellectual. His scholarly project has been institutionalized: Kendi is now the founding director of the Antiracist Research & Policy Center at American University, in Washington, D.C.

In modern American political discourse, racism connotes hatred, and just about everyone claims to oppose it. But many on the contemporary left have pursued a more active opposition, galvanized by the rise of Donald Trump, who has been eager to denounce black politicians but reluctant to denounce white racists. In many liberal circles, a movement has gathered force: a crusade against racism and other isms. It is a fierce movement, and sometimes a frivolous one, aiming the power of its outrage at excessive prison sentences, tasteless Halloween costumes, and many offenses in between. This movement seems to have been particularly transformative among white liberals, who are now, by some measures, more concerned about racism than African-Americans are. One survey found that white people who voted for Hillary Clinton felt warmer toward black people than toward their fellow-whites.

Most white people in America are not liberals, of course, and so the campaign against racism has often taken the form of an intrawhite conflict. One of the most prominent combatants is Robin DiAngelo, a white workplace-diversity trainer, available to help organizations teach their employees to be more sensitive to race. Last year, DiAngelo published "White Fragility: Why It's So Hard for White People to Talk About Racism," a reflection on her career and her cause. "White identity is inherently racist," she writes. "I strive to be 'less white.'" She cites Kendi as an authority, even if she sometimes seems closer in spirit to Ibram Rogers, the undergraduate. But, then, Kendi himself is in an instructive mood: his new work presents itself as a how-to book, although, in a little more than two hundred absorbing pages, it's also a manifesto and, from time to time, a memoir. It is titled "How to Be an Antiracist," and in it Kendi explains how he became one, which means explaining how he used to be (as he currently sees it) a racist. Kendi is convinced that racism can be objectively identified, and therefore fought, and one day vanquished. He argues that we should stop thinking of "racist" as a pejorative, and start thinking of it as a simple description, so that we can join him in the difficult work of becoming antiracists. "One either endorses the idea of a racial hierarchy as a racist or racial equality as an antiracist," Kendi writes, adding that it isn't possible to be simply "not racist." He thinks that all of us must choose a side; in fact, he thinks that we are already choosing, all the time.

THE MODERN BATTLE AGAINST RACISM, AS MANY PEOPLE HAVE OB-served, is driven by a kind of sacred fervor, and in "How to Be an Antiracist" Kendi makes this link explicit. "I cannot disconnect my parents' religious strivings to be Christian from my secular strivings to be an antiracist," he writes. Indeed, Christianity and antiracism were intimately connected for his parents. They were inspired by Tom Skinner, a fiery black evangelist who preached the gospel of "Jesus Christ the Radical," and by James H. Cone, one of the originators of black-liberation theology. Kendi's parents taught him black pride, and he took these lessons seriously. As Kendi tells it, his parents' belief in black pride led them to embrace black self-reliance, a doctrine that urged black people to overcome the legacy of racism by working hard and doing well. Kendi bitterly recalls a speech he gave at an oratory contest in high school, decrying the bad habits of black youth. "They think it's okay not to think," he said. "They think it's okay to be those who are most feared in society." Kendi won the competition, but he now regards the speech as shamefully racist, because it blamed black people for their own failures. "I was a dupe, a chump," he writes. He argues that the idea of black underachievement lends support for anti-black policies, which in turn help perpetuate the conditions that inspire speeches like his.

By the time he got to college, Kendi was outspokenly problack: he "pledged to date only Dark women," as a personal protest against standards of beauty that favor lighter skin. His infamous newspaper column was actually a fairly mild representation of his collegiate beliefs, which included a dalliance with the notion that white people were literally aliens, and a conviction that racist whites and treacherous blacks had formed a sinister partnership—"A team of 'them niggers' and White folks." But as he studied African-American history he came to believe that the basic story was even simpler than he had thought. American history, he discovered, was "a battle between racists and antiracists."

In "Stamped from the Beginning," Kendi divided the racists into two kinds, segregationists and assimilationists. Historically, segregationists argued that black people were inherently defective or dangerous, and needed to be kept under control. Assimilationists sounded kinder: they often fought against black oppression, but they also argued that black people needed to change their behavior—their culture—in order to catch up to white people and assimilate into white society. In 1834, the American Anti-Slavery Society issued a pamphlet of admonishment:

> We have noticed with sorrow, that some of the colored people are purchasers of lottery tickets, and confess ourselves shocked to learn that some persons, who are situated to do much good, and whose example might be most salutary, engage in games of chance for money and for strong drink.

Sometimes these lectures were intended as a political strategy, on the theory that civil rights would be easier to win if black

Americans were perceived to be working hard. And sometimes, especially in the twentieth century, they were intended as acknowledgments of the limits of politics. In Kendi's view, though, talk of failures in culture or conduct supposes that black people are somehow to blame for the effects of racism—as if they could have chosen, instead, to be unaffected by it. He thinks that it is both unfair and impractical to suggest that black communities must somehow heal themselves before the government can intervene. Ranging across the centuries, "Stamped" identified segregationists, assimilationists, and antiracists with a confident clarity that was also the book's greatest weakness, because it reduced complicated lives to a series of pass-fail tests. Kendi noted with satisfaction that when Du Bois was in his sixties he concluded that black people would never "break down prejudice" through virtuous comportment—thus becoming, at last, an antiracist.

Kendi's position has radical implications: in ruling out criticism of black culture or black behavior, it stipulates that any problems must be either fictional or the result of contemporary discrimination. If you reject "assimilationism," then you can't suggest, as Obama did, that centuries of racism have eroded the black nuclear family. You might try to show, instead, that black men are often shut out of the labor market, which makes them less likely to marry. Or you might conclude that the nuclear family is merely one cultural ideal among others, and not one to be universally preferred.

In the case of education, Kendi's commitment to antiracist thinking leads him to dispute the existence of an "achievement gap" between white and black students. Black students may, on average, get lower scores on standardized tests, and drop out of high school at higher rates. But such metrics, he argues in "How to Be an Antiracist," are themselves racist, devised to "degrade" and "exclude" black students; he suggests that a "low-testing" black student and a "high-testing" white student may simply be demonstrating "different kinds of achievement rather than different levels of achievement." This celebration of difference comes to an end when it is time to judge the educational systems themselves. Kendi claims that "chronic underfunding of Black schools" does create "diminished"—and not merely "different"—"opportunities for learning." Throughout the book, the idea is to judge unfair policies, while refusing to judge, as a group, the people who are subjected to them. Kendi believes that "individual Blacks have suffered trauma" in America, but he rejects the "racist" idea that "Blacks are a traumatized people."

In successive chapters of "How to Be an Antiracist," Kendi explains that there are many forms of racism: there is class racism, which conflates blackness with poverty, as well as gender racism, queer racism, and something called "space racism," which is less exciting than it sounds—it has to do with the way people associate black neighborhoods, or spaces, with violence. "'Racist' and 'antiracist,'" Kendi writes, "are like peelable name tags that are placed and replaced based on what someone is doing or not doing, supporting or expressing in each moment." This suggests that people can change, as Kendi did, and as Du Bois did. But it also suggests that nonracist identity is contingent and unstable: we are all constantly peeling and resticking those nametags.

The result is to complicate the seemingly straightforward definitions Kendi offers in "How to Be an Antiracist." For instance, he says that a policy can be either racist or antiracist; it is racist if it "produces or sustains racial inequity," and a person is racist if he or she supports such a policy. But it may take many years to determine whether a policy produces or sustains racial inequity. For instance, some cities, including New York, generally forbid employers to ask job seekers about their criminal history, or to check their credit scores. These measures are designed in part to help African-American applicants, who may be more likely to have a criminal record, or to have poor credit. But some studies suggest that such prohibitions make black men, in general, less likely to be hired, perhaps because employers fall back on cruder generalizations. Are these laws and their supporters racist? In Kendi's framework, the only possible answer is: wait and see.

Kendi's definition of racism is decidedly unsentimental. If the word "racist" is capacious enough to describe both proud slaveholders and Barack Obama, and if it nevertheless must constantly be recalibrated in light of new policy research, then it may start to lose the emotional resonance that gives it power in the first place. There are a few moments in the book, though, when Kendi uses the word in a more colloquial, less rigorous sense. In the third grade, he had a white teacher who was, Kendi thought, quicker to call on white students, and quicker to punish nonwhite ones. One day, after seeing a shy black girl ignored, Kendi staged an impromptu sit-in at chapel. Years later, he says that the teacher was one of a number of "racist White people over the years who interrupted my peace with their sirens." In a moment like this, "racist" seems less like a sticker and more like a tattoo: the word stings because it seems to convey something distasteful and profound about the person it describes. Even for the exponent of a new definition of racism, older ones are not easily banished.

IT IS NO CRITICISM OF KENDI'S BOOK TO SAY THAT ITS TITLE IS MISLEADing: he offers a provocative new way to think about race in America, but little practical advice. He wants readers to become politically active—to work to change public policy, and to "focus on power instead of people." DiAngelo, the author of "White Fragility," is unapologetically interested in people, particularly white people. She is perhaps the country's most visible expert in anti-bias training, a practice that is also an industry, and from all appearances a prospering one. (Last year, anti-bias training was in the headlines when Starbucks closed its American stores for a day to conduct a company-wide lesson in "racial bias and discrimination.") DiAngelo has been helping to lead workplace seminars since the nineties, and she has encountered some resistance. "When we try to talk openly and honestly about race," she writes, "we are so often met with silence, defensiveness, argumentation, certitude, and other forms of pushback." To explain this phenomenon, she coined the phrase "white fragility."

DiAngelo holds a Ph.D. in multicultural education, but her most important credential is all the time she has spent in conference rooms. Where Kendi insists that racism can cloud anyone's judgment, DiAngelo sees white people as singularly responsible. "Only whites have the collective social and institutional power and privilege over people of color," she writes. She is unimpressed by white participants who swear they "treat everyone the same," since that's not possible. And she is alert to acts of racial transgression, as when a white woman uses what DiAngelo considers a "stereotypical" voice while telling an anecdote about an African-American. She thanks the woman for her "insight," and then asks her to "consider not telling that story in that way again." When the woman tries to defend herself, DiAngelo interrupts, speaking in the friendly but steely voice of administrative authority. "I am offering you a teachable moment," she says.

Despite her sensitivity to racial power dynamics and to the reality of racial harassment, DiAngelo seems to have little interest in other workplace power dynamics, which might explain why she's so surprised that many of the employees who attend her sessions aren't happier to see her. DiAngelo is devoted to "challenging injustice," but her corporate clients doubtless have their own priorities, and in any case it's not clear what the effect of these seminars is. A group of social scientists has come up with the concept of "implicit bias," which many trainers aim to diagnose and treat, even though there is scant evidence that implicit bias reliably affects behavior. DiAngelo mentions implicit bias, but, even more than Kendi, she is engaged in something that resembles a spiritual practice. In the sanctuaries she creates, one of the rules is that white people, especially white women, should not cry. It attracts too much attention, and it may upset nonwhite participants, by evoking the "long historical backdrop of black men being tortured and murdered because of a white woman's distress." If DiAngelo herself can't resist, she performs a ritual of abnegation. "I try to cry quietly so that I don't take up more space," she writes, "and if people rush to comfort me, I do not accept the comfort."

If there is scripture in DiAngelo's world, it is the testimony of "people of color," a term that usefully reduces all of humanity to two categories: white and other. Since white people are presumed to have "institutional power," and therefore institutional responsibility, people of color function in this world as sages, speaking truths that white people must cherish, and not challenge. DiAngelo has sometimes received "feedback from people of color on my racist patterns and assumptions," which she first found uncomfortable but eventually, as she grew more enlightened, came to find encouraging. "There is no way for me to avoid enacting problematic patterns," DiAngelo writes, "so if a person of color trusts me enough to take the risk and tell me, then I am doing well."

Once, when she offended a black client by referring to another black woman's hair, DiAngelo discussed the incident with another white person (so as not to burden any other people of color), and then apologized to the offended party. She was forgiven her trespasses, but says she was prepared not to be. When you get feedback, especially from a person of color, what's most important is to be grateful, and to try to do better. "Racism is complex," she writes, "and I don't have to understand every nuance of the feedback to validate that feedback."

Unlike Kendi, who boldly defines racism, DiAngelo is endlessly deferential—for her, racism is basically whatever any person of color thinks it is. In the story she tells about the world, she and her fellow white people have all the power, and therefore all the responsibility to do the gruelling but transformative spiritual work she calls for. The story makes white people seem like flawed, complicated characters; by comparison, people of color seem good, wise, and perhaps rather simple. This narrative may be appealing to its target audience, but it doesn't seem to offer much to anyone else. At least, that's my interpretation, and perhaps DiAngelo will be grateful to hear it. After all, I am what she would call a person of color, and whatever I write surely counts as "feedback." Maybe that means she is, indeed, doing well.

PART OF WHAT MAKES DIANGELO'S PROJECT SURREAL IS THE DIFFER-ence in scale between the historical injustices she invokes and the contemporary slights she addresses: on one side, the indescribable horror of lynching; on the other, careless crying. Kendi is less concerned about manners, and he strives to stay grounded in the brute facts of racial oppression. But his latest book, too, grows surreal at times, as he tries to reconcile the reality of black life in America with his own refusal to generalize.

"To be an antiracist is to realize there is no such thing as Black behavior," he writes. He did not always grasp this. As a boy in Queens, Kendi found his life shaped by a fear of victimization. "I avoided making eye contact, as if my classmates were wolves," he writes. "I avoided stepping on new sneakers like they were land mines." In South Jamaica, his neighborhood, there was a local bully named Smurf, who pulled a gun on Kendi, and once, with Kendi watching, beat a boy unconscious on a city bus in order to steal his Walkman. This sounds terrifying, but Kendi now claims that his fears were delusional. "I believed violence was stalking me," he writes, "but in truth I was being stalked inside my own head by racist ideas." He thinks that prominent African-Americans can be unduly influenced by their rough childhoods. "We don't write about all those days we were not faced with guns in our ribs," he writes, at which point his antiracist project sounds less like a form of truthtelling and more like a kind of propaganda.

Crime poses a conceptual problem for Kendi. As most people know, African-Americans are greatly overrepresented among both victims and perpetrators of violent crime in America—indeed, this fact provides stark evidence of the country's stubborn racial inequality. But Kendi's approach disallows talk of criminality as a particular "problem" in black neighborhoods; he suggests that white neighborhoods have their own dangers, including crooked bankers (they "might steal your life savings") and suburban traffic accidents; he even insists that there are a "disproportionate number of White males who engage in mass shootings," although mass shootings account for a tiny percentage of gun deaths, and white people are not disproportionately likely to commit them. By the end of the section, the bully named Smurf seems less like a real person and more like a spectre: the personification of old racist ideas, come to life in the imagination of a fretful future scholar in Queens.

As it happens, there actually is a notorious tough guy named Smurf who grew up in Kendi's neighborhood around the same time. He came to be known as Bang 'Em Smurf, a sometime rapper who, during the two-thousands, was an ally turned antagonist of 50 Cent, the hip-hop star. Not long ago, Bang 'Em Smurf self-published a memoir-cum-manifesto of his own, a seemingly unedited collection of fragments that provides a glimpse of the world that Kendi writes about. Smurf is evidently happy to think of himself as one of the "wolves" who roamed the neighborhood: his book is called "Wisdom of a Wolf," and in it he recounts how he started stealing after his own bicycle was stolen, and explains the formative effect of seeing his mother stabbed when he was four or five. (According to Smurf, she fought back and won the fight.)

Smurf doesn't mention a bookish militant named Ibram, but he does offer his own assessment of the neighborhood: "Where we are from Jamaica Queens the average youth doesn't have hope or inspiration to live." Smurf no longer lives there: in 2004, he was convicted of illegal-weapon possession, and after serving his sentence he was deported to Trinidad and Tobago, where he was born. But he is sure that things have grown only more difficult for young people in neighborhoods like Jamaica. Unlike Kendi, Smurf thinks that something is wrong there. "Most of these youth come from poverty," he writes. "There is Lack of love and discipline in the household." Smurf thinks that these families could and should do better, which means that, by Kendi's definition, he is an assimilationist—and probably a space racist, too.

Kendi thinks that calls for racial uplift are doomed to failure, because they can never change enough minds, black or white, to alter either behavior or policy. They are prayer disguised as politics. But his approach demands a fair amount of faith, too, given that it requires a great part of the country to undergo a revolution in thought that took Kendi decades of study to achieve. Where DiAngelo says she is not sure that the country is making any progress toward reducing racism, Kendi thinks an antiracist world is possible. "Racism is not even six hundred years old," he writes, tracing its origin to the fifteenth-century explorations of his former namesake Prince Henry. "It's a cancer that we've caught early." But the cure, he thinks, will start with policies, not ideas. He suggests that, just as ideologies of racial difference emerged after the slave trade in order to justify it, antiracist ideologies will emerge once we are bold enough to enact an antiracist agenda: criminal-justice reform, more money for black schools and black teachers, a program to fight residential segregation.

"Once they clearly benefit," Kendi writes, "most Americans will support and become the defenders of the antiracist policies they once feared." This is an inspiring prediction, although Kendi's own scholarship provides less reason for optimism. But, if he is right, becoming an antiracist might entail a realization that our national conversation about race is largely beside the point. If it is possible, as Kendi insists, to change "racist policy" without first changing "racist minds," then perhaps we needn't worry quite so much about who thinks what, and why. Kendi wants us to see not only that there is nothing wrong with black people but that there is likewise nothing wrong with white people. "There is nothing right or wrong with any racial groups," he writes. This is the bittersweet message hidden in his book: that, in the grand racial drama of America, every group is already doing the best it can.

PART II
PERSONAL HISTORIES

QUILTS

ANDREA LEE

July 11, 1983

I never cared about patchwork quilts until I spent a week with my
Aunt Lucy, in Ahoskie, North Carolina, not long ago. When I
was fifteen, my mother threw out a quilt that her mother had made,
and I was glad of it, because the quilt was so ragged it was unmend-
able, and at night, lying under it, you could slide your whole foot
into the tears in the brittle old fabric. The quilt—a faded yellow-
and-maroon calico—had been assigned to my room in wintertime
and made, I felt, an unhappy contrast with the psychedelic mobile
I had hanging from my overhead light, and with the posters of Jim
Morrison and Douglas Fairbanks that I had taped up on my walls.
A few years later, when I was at college and had discovered the
expensive charm of Appalachian crafts, I scolded my mother for
having thrown out a piece of Americana. But I didn't really care.
Similarly, I was envious when friends in Boston and New York began spending hundreds of dollars to transform their apartments
into rustic retreats, with quilts hanging on the walls or, in some
cases, billowing in a vaguely Arabic manner from the ceilings. But
the quilts themselves didn't move me, although I was taken with
their names: Rising Sun, Brown Goose, Children of Israel, Churn
Dash, Chips and Whetstones. It was only when I woke up after
Norfolk on the overnight bus from New York to the Carolinas
that I discovered in myself a pressing desire for a patchwork quilt.
Ahoskie, in Hertford County, is a town of about five thousand
that lies near the Chowan River, not far from the Great Dismal
Swamp, in the flat terrain of forest and farmland which makes up

the eastern borderland of Virginia and North Carolina. If you don't have a car, it's easiest to take the bus there. (In fact, the bus driver will let you out at Aunt Lucy's house, on Highway 13, if you tell him where to stop.) I was half awake, leaning back in the bus seat and staring out at the early-morning mist steaming in the sunlight over the fields of corn, tobacco, and soybeans and at the old frame houses that sagged as if they were melting into the fields, when the idea of owning a quilt simply presented itself to me, as if it had jumped in off the highway.

I told Aunt Lucy about it after dinner that night, and nagged her until she brought out two old quilts of her own to show me. They were appliquéd quilts (quilts in which a cutout design is sewn to a cloth ground, as opposed to pieced quilts, which are made of many fabrics sewn together)—the most beautiful I'd seen outside a museum. One of them, which her own aunt had made late in the last century, was stitched in a stylized pattern of red and green called Baskets, and the other was a fan pattern. "I made this one myself, around about 1935," Aunt Lucy said of the fan quilt. "I put in pieces of some of my favorite dresses." A kind of lust came over me when I saw the two quilts, and I began to beg Aunt Lucy in a shameless way to give me one of them, but I knew that such a gift wouldn't be fair, or likely. Although Aunt Lucy is childless, she has close relatives who should inherit the quilts. (I am not directly related to her. She is the sister of my mother's sister-in-law, and we have known each other through years of visits exchanged between Ahoskie and my family's house in Philadelphia.) Aunt Lucy is a widow in her early seventies who looks about fifty, with a girlishly pretty, rather wistful pink-cheeked face and a plaintive, gentle voice that conceals an iron streak of practicality and tenacity. She lives in a neat brick ranch house among fields—now rented out to tenants—which her husband left her, and examines events and objects that come her way with the unsentimental eye of one for whom there are but two categories of things in the world: the useful and the useless. Beyond this, she has the near-ferocious air of independence, the pride in solitary achievement that I have seen in other widows who labor alone against the encroachments of old age to maintain a house, a farm, a way of life. Once, when I was reading "Walden," she borrowed the book from me and read several pages.

"Is this about a man who goes off to live away from other people?" she asked.

"Yes," I said. "What do you think of it?"

"It sounds sensible," she said.

Aunt Lucy was a Rooks before she married Uncle Sherman Hall. She and her surviving brother and sister are the descendants of Sally Rooks, a plantation owner's daughter from nearby Gates County, who in the seventeen-nineties had four children by Jacob Brady, a slave. Manumitted at birth, the children of Sally Rooks and Jacob Brady took the name Rooks, and became prosperous artisans and farmers, marrying into other free Negro families that, long before the Civil War, made up a sizable percentage of the population of Virginia and North Carolina. (The historian John Hope Franklin, of Duke University, has pointed out that the 1790 census for North Carolina shows over five thousand free Negroes in the state, the heaviest concentration of them living in the coastal and Piedmont counties, near Ahoskie.) Like the descendants of many of the old free Negro families in the Ahoskie area—the Chavises, the Archers, the Weavers, the Bentons, the Halls—the members of the Rooks family have so much English, Irish, and American Indian blood that in most of them it is difficult to see any signs of African ancestry. It is a curious thing to visit Ahoskie and hear a gray-eyed, white-skinned person describe himself as a black American.

The abundance of these venerable families of mixed blood is one of the peculiarities of this ancient region. The Chowan was first explored in 1585, by Ralph Lane. In the marshy wilderness, Negroes, whites, and Indians mingled early, and a tradition of liberalism and individualism, unusual in the Old South, allowed those born of the union of master and slave or indentured servant to live, in many cases, as free men and women. William Byrd, in his "History of the Dividing Line Betwixt Virginia and Carolina Run in the Year of Our Lord 1728," describes encountering in the Dismal Swamp "a Family of Mulattoes that call'd themselves free." The lists of members of the Revolutionary militia for the Gates and Hertford Counties area, around Ahoskie, include a substantial minority of free black soldiers, and their descendants are alive in the countryside today. Families like the Rookses live on land that has been theirs for generations, among fields that inevitably hold old family graveyards, fenced in or bricked in among the corn and the tobacco. Marriages among their own kind have made a dense web of reiterated kinships which reaches back into the eighteenth century and has helped to solidify this group of part-white families into what is almost an intermediate caste between black and white (although the boundaries of twentieth-century segregation make no official distinction between the light-skinned descendant of free-issue family and the darker-skinned grandchild of slaves). Change came late to this ingrown society: it is only in the last twenty or thirty years that many children of these families have started marrying outside the traditional boundaries, and have begun leaving the coastal farmlands, to settle in cities all over the country. Aunt Lucy's nephews and their children—the latest generations of the Rooks family—live in Los Angeles and New York.

IN 1962, WHEN I WAS NINE, I SPENT A SUMMER IN AHOSKIE. EVERY MORNing, Aunt Lucy would braid my hair, and then I would spend much of my time performing aerial stunts in a large chinaberry tree in the company of an exquisitely pretty, round-faced little neighbor girl named Mitzi. Tiring of that, we would hold endless, exhausting races through the cornfields near Aunt Lucy's house—races that were thrilling because we ran in separate rows, and you could tell your invisible opponent's progress only by the slight shiver of the dense corn leaves: the ending was always a surprise. I met a few old women who pinched my chin and declared that I favored my great-grandmother, who had been a Benton from Gates County. And I kidded around with Aunt Lucy's husband, Uncle Sherman, a wry-tongued jokester under whose hands every kind of land, every business prospered. Uncle Sherman swore that he would teach me to talk like a Tarheel. "Brang uh chyar," he would say, in a broad drawl, for "Bring it here." The first time I heard it, I mistakenly brought him a chair, and he nearly collapsed with laughter.

That summer, I developed a mania for whittling, and my ambition was to carve a miniature basket out of a peach pit—a difficult feat even for an experienced whittler. I had seen a peach-pit basket once; it had been shown me by an old woman, a cousin of my grandmother's, who also came from this part of the country. At that time in my life, I weighted my dungaree pockets with talismans and lucky pieces of all sorts—horse chestnuts, broken bits of jewelry, quartz pebbles—and the tiny basket, blackened and shiny from the handling of a score of children over the years, fascinated me. I passed the long, light evenings of June and July—evenings when, after the despotic sun had vanished, the fields and ditches almost audibly exhaled coolness, like a long-repressed sigh—sitting on the back steps of Aunt Lucy's house stabbing my thumb with a penknife as I ruined peach pit after peach pit, my stomach gurgling from the number of peaches I'd eaten.

On my recent visit to Ahoskie—the first in many years—I felt the same inexplicable yearning for a quilt that I had felt for a carved peach pit. I couldn't have Aunt Lucy's quilts, and I was incapable of making one of my own, being, as Colette's mother once remarked of her, "like a boy with a needle," so I determined that I would find a wonderful quilt and buy it. Once I had told Aunt Lucy, and the information had been diffused in the slow but inexorable way in which news spreads in the country, things began to happen. First, Dessie Rooks, Aunt Lucy's sister-in-law and neighbor down the road, offered to take me to see Julia James, over in the town of Co-field. Miss Julia (she is a "Miss" out of respect, the way most elderly ladies are in this part of the world) was a Hall before she married, and, at ninety, she is well known for her quilts.

Early on the morning that Miss Dessie was to drive me to Co-field, Colice Hall, who is a cousin of Uncle Sherman's, came by on his motorbike to cultivate his half of a big vegetable garden that he shares with Aunt Lucy. Colice lives, with his wife, in a small pale-green house down the highway. He is about the same age as Aunt Lucy, with the same oddly youthful appearance. He is wiry, has freckles and very high cheekbones, wears thick, black-rimmed glasses, and has a way of rocking rapidly on his heels as he talks, like an impudent twelve-year-old. Colice's eyes have been weak all his life. As a young man, he farmed his family's land; then, after he married, he worked at a basket factory in town. Now he's retired. Most mornings, he pulls into the gravel driveway behind Aunt Lucy's house and calls through the screen door in a high, screechy voice, "Lu-cy!"

Aunt Lucy usually calls back, "Hoo-oo! Colice!" Then they begin their morning conversation, which goes something like this:

"How you this morning?"

"Pretty good. How you?"

"Pretty good. Nothing extra."

On my first day there, Aunt Lucy introduced me to Colice, and he looked so bashful that Aunt Lucy said, "Colice! You're shy!"

Colice, twisting his hands in his pockets, gave me a swift, small grin, showing tobacco-brown teeth. "No, sir!" he said, with the bravado of a very young adolescent. "I'm not shy! I don't usually run from the ladies—I run to them!"

Aunt Lucy told him that I lived in New York, and he looked pleased. Twelve years ago, he told us, he had visited the city with his cousins Sherman and Winfield Hall. "We was only there one day," he said. "We drove real slow all over the city—saw the Empire

State, the Statue of Liberty, and Yankee Stadium. We saw all the street lights in town turn off that night—we only slept but one hour." He ended with a low whistle and shake of his head, so that I could better understand the delicious extravagance of that excursion: the three country-dwellers, who were normally asleep by nine or ten o'clock, riding slowly through the city dawn as the lights blinked out on Broadway.

On June mornings at Aunt Lucy's place, it is so misty that you can't see the dark pinewoods beyond the fields. Bobwhites call steadily, and the sun appears and disappears in the haze. When I was visiting, the corn was already five feet tall—a restless green barrier standing around the house on three sides, filling the nights with slight, continuous shivering sound, like that of moving water. The house itself had changed little since I carved peach pits on the back steps. Set close to the highway, it was still cool and dim in the daytime, with a big Victorian sofa and a grandfather clock in the living room, hooked rugs in the master bedroom, a ruffly pastel bedspread and pink throw rugs in the guest room, and, throughout, ornate prints of floral arrangements which revealed a streak of girlish romanticism in Aunt Lucy. There were several pictures of Uncle Sherman and a wonderful photograph of Aunt Lucy and her sister Mabel, taken in the twenties, when they were known as the prettiest girls in Gates County: they are sitting in a field, with their curls blowing across their flushed faces, and behind them is an immense, shiny Buick. The television room had a bookshelf holding a couple of Bibles, a copy of "Etiquette," by Emily Post, "Wuthering Heights," a *Yearbook of Agriculture* for 1940, and a book called "Two from Galilee." In the garage were the neatly arranged tools, buckets, and mud-caked rubber boots of a serious gardener. There was also a sink, for washing hands, and, on an oilcloth-covered table beside the sink, a few vegetables, in limbo between the garden and the kitchen: beet greens soaking in a pail of water, tiny greenish summer squash, big, sprouting seed potatoes.

Before the trip to Cofield, as I sat on the back porch eating a breakfast of biscuits, eggs, and country sausages which Aunt Lucy had left for me (she eats when she rises, at dawn), I watched her and Colice in the garden and listened to them talk.

"Pick that squash now, Colice," Aunt Lucy said in her sweet, frail voice, "because it'll be past its prime tomorrow."

"I got all my squash," said Colice.

"Oh Colice, go to grass!" said Aunt Lucy. "You leave half your vegetables to rot." She pushed leaves aside with a stick she was holding, to show Colice squash still on the vine. Then she laid down her stick and stood up facing the cornfield. "Look at that corn," she said. "Isn't it rank! Won't it be pretty when it silks out!"

Colice and Aunt Lucy looked very small in the big, lush garden, where, besides squash, they had planted pole beans, string beans, tomatoes, collard greens, beets, peppers, potatoes, and roasting ears. Aunt Lucy was wearing a green cotton hat that tilted up at the front like a child's sunbonnet, accentuating the expression of grave innocence on her pretty face. Colice's hat was a jaunty light-blue mesh cap, decorated with an insignia of crossed golf clubs, one pink and one blue. He and Aunt Lucy seemed alike as they worked together—not, particularly, in the look of their faces (although there is a blurred resemblance between most of the members of the old mixed-blood families) but in the way they moved and spoke, in the comfortable kind of accommodation each made for the other. They might have been old siblings or a couple married for fifty years; they are probably, in some obscure fashion, related by blood. "I reckon everyone in the area is kin," Colice told me once.

When Dessie Rooks drove up, Aunt Lucy hurried over to the car with the news that the man who cut her grass had found a copperhead that morning. "Ooh, I was like to die," she said. "There's one thing that I hate, and that's a snake."

"The corn has been right snaky this year," said Miss Dessie. She is a handsome woman of Aunt Lucy's age—brown-skinned, with an almost majestically slow way of talking. "Did you hear what happened over by Sam James' tenants' place?" she asked. "They came home and found a moccasin sleeping across the stove."

Aunt Lucy gave a plaintive little yelp, and Colice chuckled dryly. As I got into the car, Aunt Lucy said to Miss Dessie, "Please help this child to find a quilt. She is crazy about them."

"Julia James will have a quilt," said Miss Dessie.

During the drive down Highway 13, Miss Dessie pointed out something that other people had proudly pointed out to me on my past trips to North Carolina: that the land stretching to the skyline along the nine-mile stretch of highway that joins Ahoskie and the small town of Winton is entirely owned by blacks—specifically, by the old free-issue families—and has been for generations. She indicated land boundaries and identified for me the frame farmhouses and the newer, suburban-style homes of her relatives and neighbors. Occasionally, when I asked about a dilapidated house or a shack, she would say, "Honey, I don't know—probably tenants." Ahoskie society seems as rigidly divided into castes as Edith Wharton's old New York was, with the prosperous descendants of the free-issue families forming a stratum distinct both from whites and from the poorer, usually darker-skinned blacks, who are often tenants or field workers. Aunt Lucy and Miss Dessie are generally aware of the identity of the tenants in the tumbledown houses, but they speak of them with innocent professions of ignorance, as if the tenants belonged to a different planet; similarly, they address white acquaintances in tones that are not quite deferential but suggest that the whites breathe different air.

When Miss Dessie speaks of the people she "knows," she goes into minute genealogical detail, and her stories, like many stories I have heard out in the country, are seasoned with violence. In her slow, matter-of-fact voice, she told me about a nephew of hers who was killed in a tobacco-barn explosion; a farmer who had a stroke, fell into his hog pen, and was devoured by his hogs; a young boy who was struck by lightning as he ran in the fields with other children. Miss Dessie's calm in the face of natural cataclysm and human tragedy seems to stem from the same deep-rooted practicality that I see in Aunt Lucy, who accommodates the caprices of nature and fate in the same way that she accommodates the shortsightedness of Colice Hall in looking for squash.

Before Miss Dessie married, she was a Chavis, and at one point on the ride to Cofield she stopped at the Pleasant Plains Baptist Church, to show me the grave of her husband and the plot beside it where she will lie. The handsome brick church, first organized in 1851, as the Free Colored Baptist Church, lies across the highway from farmland owned by the Chavis family; and from Miss Dessie's future grave site—which she contemplates with the grand equanimity with which she regards all the rest of the world—you can see across cornfields to the old green-roofed white farmhouse where she was born, some seventy years ago. "After Dad died, I bought the others out of the property and sold the farm to my niece, because I thought it should stay in the family," she told me. "One of her nephews lives there on the property now. They have rented out the tobacco and pecan allotment, but they still grow corn and soybeans."

When we were back on the highway, Miss Dessie and I started talking about restaurants and fast-food places in Ahoskie—the fried chicken at the Golden Skillet, the fried trout, catfish, and hush puppies at O'Connor's, the new McRib sandwich at McDonald's. Miss Dessie had never tasted a McRib sandwich and was eager to do so. She and Aunt Lucy have little nostalgia for old-fashioned cooking or old-fashioned ways, and eagerly embrace anything—like a McRib—that speaks to them of modernity. It was the forward-thinking side of the two ladies that made them laugh rather pityingly at my interest in quilts. When I complained to Miss Dessie about the number of trailers that had sprung up around the old wooden farmhouses in the area, she told me calmly that trailers made nice houses if they were properly tied down against the wind. "In a trailer, everything's convenient to your hand, like on a ship," she said. In the same calm voice—the voice of one who does not yearn after the past—she told me more about her family's land. "Farming is different these days," she said, slowing down as a huge lumber truck laden with stripped pine trunks roared past. "It isn't the way it used to be. You can't get by with twenty acres—or fifty acres—anymore. You need machinery, and one piece of machinery will cost you maybe fifty thousand dollars. Our children aren't interested. Most of them have gone to the cities, and who can blame them? They'll make more money there than here. Nowadays, Negroes are selling their land and the whites are buying it, and it's a pity. The way I see it, after I'm gone my family's land will probably be sold."

BY THE TIME WE GOT TO JULIA JAMES' HOUSE—HAVING PASSED A huge Perdue Chicken billboard in the middle of a tobacco field; a Continental Grain Company warehouse; several signs advertising night crawlers and crickets for sale; and the Cofield store (a one-story red tarpaper structure with two men, a black and a white, seated comfortably on straight-backed chairs on the front porch)—I was dreamily repeating to myself a list of quilt names I knew: Spider Web, Corn and Beans, Goose Tracks, Broken Dishes, Log Cabin, Grandmother's Fan. Miss Julia James did indeed have quilts, or, at least, quilt tops—the completed patchwork patterns of pieced fabric which need only to be hand-stitched to cotton or wool padding and to the breadths of yard goods that make up the quilt back. In her small bedroom, a red-and-white sheet of pieced rectangles was stretched on a pine frame and attached all around with loops of white string; a pair of scissors, a needle, and a spool of white thread lay on top. Miss Julia is a tall elderly lady with a very straight spine and with white hair drawn back in two braids into a bun. She wore a print dress with a yellowish apron fastened over it, and a pair of flat leather slippers, one with the toe cut out to ease pressure on a bunion. She is very deaf, and Miss Dessie had to shout my name and a family identification, which is essential in this part of the world: "I said, she's Lucy Rooks' sister's niece, and her great-grandmother was a Benton from over in Corapeake!"

Miss Julia's house was a small turquoise-painted cement-block house set in the midst of a group of four or five modest, low houses of brick, tarpaper, or clapboard which bordered on a short paved road off the highway. The house lay behind a privet hedge, and a screened side porch held magnificent geraniums, begonias, and coleus plants, and also a large freezer, a wringer-washer, and hanging bunches of dried peppers and mint. The living room had a yellow linoleum floor and was furnished with a braided rag rug, a brown vinyl sofa, a color television, a set of blue fibre-glass curtains in a brocade print, and many photographs of children and grandchildren. When Miss Julia led us into her bedroom, dislodged several boxes from her closet, and began to pull quilt tops out of a large paper bag, I felt my chest squeeze tight with anticipation. But the big pieced squares she pulled out were strangely disappointing to me, for a reason I could not at first discern. She spread the first quilt top over her high double bed and stood back with the stiff, self-consciously modest bearing of an artist aware of her own merit. The design was a sort of modified Double Wedding Ring. (In a Double Wedding Ring, pieced patches form an interlocking series of circles on a solid background.) But the pieces of fabric that had been sewn into the curving pattern were made of stretch polyester in boldly patterned prints. I looked closer at one patch and saw that the print was of little smile faces. "That polyester holds the colors beautifully," Miss Dessie said, in her slow, deep voice. "Most everything I do now is in polyester," said Miss Julia, who had a loud, firm, decisive voice. "It's easy for me to get the remnants." She pulled out quilt top after quilt top, and Miss Dessie and I spread them on the bed. Miss Julia had been rather unbending toward us at first, but now the sight of her own work seemed to excite her, and she gave an occasional rattly laugh, peering at me with bright little eyes. There was a Blazing Star design (small, diamond-shaped patches making up a large eight-pointed star), and nine or ten patterns I couldn't identify. All of them were exquisitely hand-stitched and showed a strong, spirited sense of design, and all but two were—maddeningly to me—made of polyester. I picked out the two cotton quilts—a Log Cabin (narrow strips of fabric joined to form a complex system of rectangles) and an ambitious appliquéd piece depicting rows of women in sunbonnets and fan-shaped skirts. Handsome as they were, even these two were pieced in fabrics too modern for my taste. "I see you like cotton," Miss Julia said, giving me a sharp glance. "I don't get much of it, because people don't wear much of it these days."

She told me she could have the two tops I'd chosen quilted for me by the fall. "I used to be faster, but my eyes are bad," she said. "I used to know one or two ladies who could come together and do this work in a few days, but they have passed. No one quilts anymore. They use them big stitches, and I don't like that—that's not quilting."

She showed us the thick, unglamorous comforters she had made for winter warmth over the years; composed of two sides of coarse cotton or wool, they were "tacked"—attached every few inches with a single knotted stitch of heavy thread—rather than quilted. Although Miss Julia appeared to look down on tacking as inferior to quilting, these comforters were the only examples she had of her finished work; the quilts that had earned her local fame over sixty or seventy years of needlework had all been sold, or given to family members. Caught up in the excitement of showing her work, Miss Julia began showing us everything, emptying her closet to display her best clothes: elaborate nylon dresses that showed little sign of wear; a floor-length pale-blue, mock-fur bathrobe. Outside, she kept on showing us things—her grape arbor; the butter beans in her enormous garden; the wild barn kittens curled in the shade of a Ford Pinto parked in the dust beside the house; the rank-smelling maze of small pens and cages that held rabbits, ducks, geese, hogs, and chickens, and ran right back to the rubbish heap at the edge of the woods; and, finally, her brother—a shy, astoundingly handsome old man named Edgar Hall, who gave us a wordless grin. It was past noon and the sun was shining hard and hot on the group of small houses along the road when we got in the car to leave.

In the car, Miss Dessie asked me if I was happy with my quilts, and I said that I liked them but that they were not exactly what I had wanted. "You should have taken the polyester," she said. "It's bright and washable and makes a right nice quilt."

On the drive back to Aunt Lucy's house, Miss Dessie pointed out the sprawling, rather elegant white farmhouse with three green gables where Julia James had grown up, in the midst of peanut and tobacco fields, as Julia Hall, the daughter of the old and prosperous mixed-blood family of Halls, who own large tracts of land in the county. (Miss Julia's sister still lives in the house.) Later, Miss Dessie identified for me the various family graveyards that dot the fields along Highway 13: Reynolds, Reid, Chavis, Hall. Some of the small clusters of Victorian-style limestone grave markers (more recent graves are generally in churchyards) were neatly fenced in and decorated with flowers; others were half hidden in underbrush or among crops. "Sometimes," Miss Dessie told me, rolling up her window and turning on the air-conditioner, "people get tired of those old plots if they're in the middle of a field, and just plow them right under."

EARLY ONE MORNING A FEW DAYS AFTER THE TRIP TO COFIELD, I WENT out target shooting with Aunt Lucy's neighbor Samuel James and his granddaughter Tammy. We drove to clearing in a cornfield on one of the farms that James, a retired farmer and bail bondsman, rents out to tenants, and we shot through the morning mists with a pistol and a .22 at a piece of paper nailed to a stick. I liked the smell of gun smoke on the damp air, the sharp recoil of the pistol and the rifle, and the fact that I could hit the marks on the target. Tammy, who is fourteen and has a pert flip of hair over her eyes, squealed at the noise each time she fired, but she shot accurately; Sam James, of course, hit everything with contemptuous ease. "It's good for a woman to know how to shoot," he told us. "You might have to shoot a snake—or a man."

Sam James, like Aunt Lucy, like Julia James, like so many members of the old, inbred mixed-blood families of Ahoskie, looks, to put it bluntly, like a white person: it is an exercise in absurdity to watch him—with his light complexion, gray eyes, and long, dour, handsome, windburned face, striding across his property in boots, a pale-blue cord suit, and a bow tie, and greeting his tenants and criticizing some little lapse in the feeding of hogs or the upkeep of a road—and then to realize that this quintessential Southern landowner had to attend segregated schools as a child. Outsiders often ask why Sam James and others like him didn't in their youth simply travel far away and melt into the white world. The answer might be that this would have meant severing connections to the Chowan area which went back to the beginning of the state itself. Beyond that, the life that the old light-skinned, free-issue families made for themselves before and after the Civil War and during the period of segregation was (based though it might have been on inbreeding and a certain amount of prejudice against the darker-skinned descendants of emancipated slaves) a good and a comfortable one—at least, in Ahoskie. Now that a younger generation of these families, moving in a world freer of official restraints and filled with novel attractions, is leaving the farms and—horror of horrors—marrying whites or dark-skinned blacks whom nobody "knows," it seems that the Ahoskie group, symbolized for me by Aunt Lucy and Sam James, a group tied to the land and set firmly in their own enclave between black and white, might be about to disappear.

When Sam James, Tammy, and I had finished shooting and were heading back down the highway in Sam James' big, glossy pickup truck, I asked Tammy, who is in the eighth grade at the Ahoskie Middle School, whether she wanted to live in Ahoskie all her life.

She shook her head briskly. "No, sir!" she said. "I'm going to go live in the city and be a psychiatrist."

"Well, who's going to take care of me when I'm old and feeble?" asked Sam James.

"Oh, Grandpa!" said Tammy. "I don't want to be no bed nurse for you. But I'll make lots of money and bring it back here."

"Now you're talking! Now you're talking!" Sam James said in a satisfied voice.

After sunset that day, I went, as the two of them had suggested, across the highway from Aunt Lucy's house to visit old Mrs. Chavis, who is Tammy's great-grandmother and Sam James' mother-in-law, and who was famous for quilts in her day. I found Mrs. Chavis, whom everyone calls Miss Madgie, sitting on the front porch of her small white house watching the traffic go by on the darkening highway from behind a screen of wisteria vine as thick as an arm. Miss Madgie is ninety-one, plump and pink, and prone to fits of chuckling; rosy streaks of her scalp are visible through thinning white hair she pulls back into a tiny bun. She had quilts to show me—chiefly crazy quilts, pieced of a mixture of cotton and acrylic, and fancifully embroidered with family names and private symbols—but none to sell. "I don't quilt in the summer," she told me. "I work in my garden—crooks my fingers up, and then I can't stitch for nothing." She was flattered by my interest in her quilts, but, like most people I had spoken to in Ahoskie, she was also amused by that interest. "Young people usu'ly aren't interested in old things and old-time ways," she said. "I have a grandniece, though, who is like you. She lives up in Philadelphia, and she came here with a tape machine, a recorder, and she asked me to talk about my old home place. I was born Madgie Keene, on a farm on this same road, and I told her about the house and Mama and Daddy, and she took it all down on that machine!" The recollection amused Miss Madgie so much that she shut her eyes and shook with laughter, and it was some time before we folded up the quilts that she had shown me.

THE NEXT NIGHT—MY LAST IN AHOSKIE—I WENT, WITH THERESA AR-cher, over to the weekly auction in Roxobel. Theresa (who is close to my own age, so I don't call her Miss Theresa) is another of Aunt Lucy's neighbors across the road. She and her husband, Kenneth, who is in the mortuary-vault business, live in a new brick ranch house on the former site of a decrepit house that was occupied by Aunt Lucy and Uncle Sherman's tenants. When I visited Ahoskie as child, the house and the large, untidy family who lived there (with litters of cats so starved that they devoured string beans) seemed to me the ultimate in fascinating raffishness. The Archer family is completely respectable, but a tinge of eccentricity seems to have lingered in the soil of the place. Whenever people on this stretch of Highway 13 hear of one of Theresa's ideas or creations, they say "Well, if that isn't exactly like Theresa!" in admiring and wondering tones. It isn't that they consider her outlandish—it's just that she does things no one else would think of. For example, she took the revolving drum from a large old-fashioned washing machine, set it on her front porch, and planted geraniums in it; also, in her large garden, which, like all gardens in Ahoskie, forms a constant topic of reflection and conversation through the summer, she grows an odd kind of beet that sometimes turns orange when you cook it. Theresa, who is a good-looking woman with a narrow face and has a lively, quirky glint in her eyes, gives a sharp, crowing laugh of triumph when she speaks of her new ideas and projects. She was born near Ahoskie, into a family that worked on truck farms, and she is now a teacher of English and history at Ahoskie High School. Theresa is a poet as well as a teacher, and is the author of a dark-red privately published book titled "The Flaming Depths." "The Flaming Depths" is dedicated to Theresa's sister, Mrs. Prunetta Johns, and in the foreword the late Henry D. Cooper, who was the principal of a local high school, observes, "The uncompromising aim of our gifted local poetess is to express her ideas, and set them forth in their appropriate moods. She will not be a slave to rhyme, or even to meter, if either of these masters attempts to restrict her freedom. . . . Her heart must be relieved of what she has to say, and no tiny unsaid portion can be left behind." Theresa's poetry is highly lyrical, and sometimes has gleams of the same quirkiness one notes in her eyes.

I drove to the Roxobel auction with Theresa, Kenneth, and Thomasine, Kenneth's grown daughter by a previous marriage. Roxobel is a tiny town deep in the country southwest of Ahoskie, and the auctions regularly held there are important social events for people from small towns scattered through the corn and tobacco fields of the Chowan region. "You'll find what you want here," Theresa told me, with one of her vigorous nods, as we pulled into the auction-house parking lot, which was jammed with the long, shiny cars and big, new four-wheel-drive vehicles that seem to have taken over from the legendary dusty pickup truck—at least, in this area of the rural South. "They always have quilts," she added.

The auction house, a low red wooden building with a corrugated-metal roof, was set near a cornfield. Inside, it consisted of several enormous rooms with rough pine beams and plywood walls. In the middle of the central room was a high wooden platform, where the auctioneer stood with two assistants. The rooms were crowded with things to be sold. Near the front door was a jumble of new living-room furniture, including perhaps ten chairs and couches upholstered in a garish plasticized plaid, and on this furniture men—black and white—were sitting peacefully, smoking cigars and cigarettes, talking among themselves, and giving an occasional guffaw. It looked like a club meeting: all the men seemed to be wearing mesh caps that bore printed logos for farm machinery, pesticides, or fertilizers. One stooped old man had a cap with a handprinted sign sewn onto it that read "THE FISH MASTER."

The air was hot and smoky in the main room, except in the paths of several powerful steel fans, which flattened your clothes against your body if you passed nearby. There were a lot of small children, who all seemed to be drinking Cokes and eating roasted peanuts; the floor was thick with shells. There were also a lot of big, bumbling flies that collided with the people, who were strolling up and down, looking at the heaped furniture, rugs, china, and boxes full of miscellaneous junk that represented the odd, often pathetic accumulations of whole lifetimes. The contents of a dozen farmhouses were there. I recognized the mixture of old, rangy pine furniture, scarred and repainted over fifty years, and newer, veneered additions from Sears and the Ahoskie Department Store.

"Look at this!" cried Thomasine, holding up a small china donkey she had found in a box. "Buy it for me, please?" she said to her father.

"Have to bid for the whole lot," said Kenneth, who is imperturbable. Kenneth is one of the Archers from Archertown, a clan renowned in Hertford County for their blond hair and blue eyes and their gentle persistence in defining themselves as black.

"Kenny, there's good things in this box," said Theresa, studying a brightly painted china rooster with her sharp, restless gaze. "Look—it says 'Made in Italy'!"

I wandered over to a corner filled with books. One box held, among others, Taine's "Notes on England," Cecil Beaton's "Diaries," "The Letters of Richard Wagner," and "Byron, Shelley, and Their Pisan Circle." I glanced at the chapter headings in a volume called "Stories of Authors' Loves," published in 1902 and kept in damp storage for some time after that; they included "Brave-Hearted Thackeray," "The Pitiful Passion of Poor John Keats,"

"The Variously-Estimated Byron and His Life of Unrest," and "The Heart-Hunger of Margaret Fuller." The earwiggy look of the books gave me, for an instant, a mournful vision of a deserted library in one of the white-painted Greek Revival houses that one sees in outlying sections of the town of Ahoskie—a library where only the lowland dews entered and sat long, and where one might, like Aunt Lucy's neighbor, find a snake lying across the furniture.

The auctioneer, a round-faced man with three perfectly symmetrical curls pasted down on his forehead, began the bidding in a discreet, flat, nasal tone. "Got a dollar bill . . . Give me two dollars. . . . Bid three in the back. . . . Want to bid four for the old mailbox."

After the rusty mailbox came a heap of bathroom rugs in fluorescent oranges and pinks, a flintlock rifle, a gold watch, a large cassette holder painted with a lurid rendering of Gene Simmons, of Kiss. Bidding never became intense; the crowd moved around the room in the wake of the two stout assistants who displayed the items, but its whole consciousness, like that of *le tout Paris* at a spectacle, was bent on seeing and being seen, flirting, greeting friends and neighbors. As usual, I was impressed by the calm interaction of black and white: one would never have seen such a mixed gathering in Boston or Philadelphia. Groups of teen-age boys and girls eyed each other, advanced, retreated, sent oblique messages, dissolved into giggles, in the classic choreography of early courtship, while young mothers in shorts and shifts chatted with each other over boxes of vinegar cruets and worn-out hair dryers, pausing now and then to retrieve their small, Coke-drinking offspring. Everyone stared at a beautiful young woman with a Farrah Fawcett haircut who strolled up and down the aisles with a discontented expression. A plump black man about seventy years old left the crowd and went up to a young white man who was wearing a red baseball cap turned around backward. "Young man, it seems like I know you and I don't know you," he said. "What's your name?"

"Riddick," answered the young man, who was very broad across the chest, and whose mouth remained a bit open after he finished speaking.

"Oh, I grew up with a whole lot of Riddicks," the old man said, nodding with a pleased look, as if a stray part of the universe had just fallen into place. "You favor them."

I walked over to the far end of the central auction room and found a couple of quilts heaped on the foot of a laminated-wood Colonial-style bunk bed. They were recently made quilts, hand-sewn—one in the Blazing Star pattern and the other in a pattern I couldn't identify. They were carefully done, but with the same unhappy choice of fabric I had found in Julia James' quilts. One had patches printed in a Fred Flintstone design.

A little woman sitting on another bunk bed, across the aisle—a woman whose sharp-featured, olive-skinned face showed the mixture of black, Indian, and white blood that is common in the Chowan region—spoke up suddenly. "I've got quilts," she said. "I've got drawers full of them at home—old ones and new ones. How much would you pay?"

My heart began to pound as I told her and got her phone number. My excitement was, I realized with some embarrassment, that of the genuine fanatic. I would have to wait until my next trip to Ahoskie, but it was not at all unpleasant to picture myself on yet another wild-goose chase over the countryside that my great-grandmother had known, and, perhaps, stumbling on a treasure: Arabic Lattice in deliciously faded blue-and-red calico, smelling faintly of camphor; a Double Wedding Ring, more modern, perhaps, but in cotton patches that drew out all the various bright and sombre tints of the Carolina farmland.

AFTER ABOUT AN HOUR, WE LEFT THE AUCTION, COMING OUT OF THE hot lights and close air into an evening where a band of deep-lavender cloud had spread itself across the sky. Below the cloud, a clear strip of pinkish light made the pines and the corn along the roadside look entirely black. Two grain silos with pointed tops were silhouetted against the sky. The crickets were loud, and the air was almost dizzyingly fresh. In the parking lot, a handsome young black man, wearing jeans and a sleeveless white undershirt that stood out startlingly in the pinkish dusk, was leaning against the door of a nineteen-thirties pickup truck—carefully restored and painted a dove gray—talking to a young black woman in curlers who sat behind the wheel.

As we drove back to Ahoskie, a thin crescent moon rose above the woods, fields, farmhouses, and trailers. The car windows were down, and the cool air rushing in was printed with the smell of whatever we were passing—hogs, corn, chickens, pinewoods—so that one could have drawn a picture of the country landscape with one's eyes closed. Kenny had turned on the radio, and we drove to the beat of disco songs I had heard in New York. It was curious music to hear while driving down a deserted country road where house lights were scattered miles and miles apart. We stopped beside a field so that Theresa could dig up some crape myrtle for her front yard, and I sat in the fragrant darkness talking to Thomasine. She is twenty-two, with a strong, compact figure, curly hair, and a beautiful, broad-cheekboned face, with a masklike expression that she presents to strangers like me. I felt worlds removed from her. Many young people have left Ahoskie, but Thomasine doesn't much care for that idea. She works in town at McDonald's; before that she spent her days stitching pockets in the Blue Bell jeans factory.

I asked her what she did for fun, and she said there wasn't much to do.

"We go to the auction, we visit friends, and for something special we drive to Greensboro or Norfolk, or maybe Virginia Beach," she said, lighting a cigarette. "Once, I went to Philadelphia."

I asked her if she would like to move to the city, and she said she supposed she'd spend her whole life around Hertford County. "I'd go crazy in the city," she said, fondling a little box of china ornaments she had bought at the auction. "Too many people there."

As we drove on, Theresa began teasing me about my interest in quilts. "You're peculiar," she said, with a laugh. "I'd rather sleep under a blanket or under one of those nice Sears comforters. We all grew up with quilts, and they wore out, and it wasn't anything special. What are you going to do with a quilt when you get it, anyway—hang it on a wall?"

The whole family, including the imperturbable Kenny, laughed at me indulgently.

"Instead of a quilt, you should get a nice wall hanging," Theresa said. "Now, I have a nice wall hanging bought in Charleston. It shows Jesus and a lamb, and it's on a kind of velvety material."

Thomasine interrupted her to point out to me Ahoskie's new, twenty-four-hour store and the drive-in theatre. "That nasty place," said Theresa, shaking her head as we passed the theatre, which was showing two sex films. "If you want to see common women acting sassy on the screen, *that* is where to go."

When I got back to Aunt Lucy's house, she was sitting in the television room drowsing in front of a Western. She sniffed sharply as I came in. "You've been out at that auction with all those back-country people," she said. "Your clothes smell like snuff. Did you find a quilt?"

"No," I said, hoping she might take pity on me and give me one of her beauties, but she only straightened up and looked at me with the unexpected severity that her mild round face could hold. "You're in too much of hurry," she said. "That's the trouble with everyone nowadays. People get in such a strut—they don't know how to take their time to visit, they can't be patient. You've been here a week. Maybe if you come back and stay for longer time, you might find what you're looking for. Or maybe—but don't count on it—I might let you have one of mine." She yawned, and buttoned the top of her housedress. "Things like that take a lot of looking. But you had fun, didn't you?"

"Oh, yes, I had fun," I said.

I went to bed that night and dreamed that the countryside was stitched up in patches.

PUTTING MYSELF TOGETHER

JAMAICA KINCAID

February 20, 1995

Last Halloween, my daughter—her name is Annie; she is ten years old—decided that the scary person she wanted to impersonate was the Countess Dracula, and so, without even knowing whether there ever was such a creature, I set out to make her a costume. I bought yards of gray and black lace, some black satin ribbon, and black thread. I stitched the black and gray lace together by hand to make a cape, and ran the black satin ribbon through a hem I had made along the neckline. The cape pleased her very much: I could see that from the way she twisted and turned while standing in front of the looking glass. Underneath the cape she wore an old black dress of mine that I had grown too fat to fit into any longer. She painted her face white, then blackened the area around her eyes with a pencil made for that purpose, drew long lines of red from the corner of her mouth to under her chin with my lipstick, and colored her lips with lipstick of another shade.

She also wore a hat—a black hat, made of corded velvet, that was flat and round, like a dinner plate. It had a tassel in the center—a piece of the corded velvet that had been deliberately unravelled by its maker. There was an elastic band that ran from one side to the other and was worn under the chin or tucked under the hairline in back, for anchoring the hat on the head. My daughter wore the band tucked under a bun I had made of her hair in the back. She did not scare anyone; she looked very beautiful. My daughter lives in a small village in a small state, and, when she stepped out to trick-or-treat, the neighbors greeted her with enthusiasm. Her hat, especially, was admired.

That hat was one I used to wear all the time. I bought it at a store that sold old clothes, but I cannot remember if it was a store called Early Halloween and owned by a woman named Joyce, or a store called Harriet Love and owned by a woman named Harriet Love, or a store whose name I can't remember but which was owned by a woman named Enid. This was many years ago; I must have been twenty-five when I bought it, because I remember wearing it on my twenty-sixth birthday. I was born in 1949. My twenty-sixth birthday was the birthday when I felt old and used up—I had left home when I was sixteen, and ten years in a young life is a long time—and someone had taken me to dinner at a restaurant called the SoHo Charcuterie. While eating some absurd combination of food (or so it then struck me; no doubt it would seem quite ordinary now), I wondered aloud whether, at my advanced age, I would ever have any new relationships to look forward to.

I LIVED IN NEW YORK. IT WAS NOT THE FORBIDDING PLACE THEN THAT it has become to me now. I was not afraid in those days. I used to tell perfect strangers how they should behave in public—that is, if I saw them misbehaving in public. My hat was firmly strapped in place. I was invulnerable. And if, for my interference, they threatened to kill me, I would inform them that killing me was not a proper response. None of them killed me; they only threatened to do so.

I had found a place to live near Bellevue Hospital, in a small apartment above a restaurant. The exhaust fan of the restaurant was just outside the window that I slept next to, on a lumpy rollout bed. The noise the exhaust fan made felt like such an injustice that I went to the owner of the restaurant to ask if he could be more considerate and close his restaurant earlier in the evening. The restaurant was owned by a family who came from somewhere in Asia.

He did not say yes, he did not say no; everything went on just as it had done before.

I had no money. In the middle of the night, the landlord would call me up to demand the back months' rent. After a while, I did not answer the phone so late at night. I looked for a job, but I was not qualified to do anything respectable. On Sunday afternoons, I worked in a place where people rented bicycles. I changed my name, and started telling people I knew that I was a writer. This declaration went without comment. In this apartment, I slept with a man who used to buy me dinner. I liked fish of every kind, but I never ate much, no matter how hungry I had been when I sat down. When I went out with him, it was only to eat fish. Most of what we did together was inside the apartment, and that was soon over. In the middle of kissing me and doing other things, he would ask me to tell him of the other people I had kissed, but the list was so short then that he soon lost interest in kissing me and doing the other things. If only he had waited—for the list would become long and varied. So long and varied that if I met him today I would not be able to identify his face or any other part of him.

Soon I moved to an apartment on West Twenty-second Street. It was on the third floor; the walk up was tiring, but perhaps was good for me. The apartment was at the front of the building; it had two rooms and a small kitchen, which could hold no more than two people at once. The bathroom had a porcelain bathtub, and I used to lie in it and give myself coffee enemas. I don't remember who recommended such a thing to me; I do remember that once the coffee was too hot and I burned my bottom all the way up inside.

I slept on the floor in one of the rooms, because I could not afford a bed. I slept at first on newspapers and then on an old mattress I found on the street; someone gave me sheets, though I no longer remember who. I know that I slept more comfortably on the mattress than I did on the newspapers. The other room was empty except for a large old office desk, an old typewriter, and books that were piled on the floor. I was hungry; I could not afford to eat much real food. In the refrigerator I kept yogurt, a tin of brewer's yeast, orange juice, powdered skim milk, and many different kinds of vitamins; in the freezer compartment I kept slices of bananas. It was the refrigerator of someone who lived alone.

Below me lived a man who talked to himself: he had been in a war, and after that he never worked again—only talked to himself. On the ground floor, a man and a woman lived in the apartment they'd had since they were married, sometime in the nineteen-twenties. How the landlord wished them dead, for they paid a low rent. At first, the landlord had no luck at all: then the husband died, and the wife was very sad. I know she was very sad because she told me so. I don't know what became of her; I lost interest. Nothing happened to me as a result of all this.

In the New York days of my twenties, the streets were wide and open and always sunny, not narrow and closed and dark, the way they are now when I walk down the same streets. When I lived in the house on Twenty-second Street, I used to get up late in the morning—so late that the morning was by then quite stale, on the brink of being another time of day altogether. Then I would parade around the apartment without my clothes on, and I would bathe and, if it was the right day of the week, take my enema. I would have a small meal of something liquid, for I still would not and could not satisfy my appetite—any of my appetites. And then, finally, I would put on some clothes. This was not done carelessly.

I was very thin, because I had no money to eat properly, and because what little money I had I used to buy clothes. Being very thin, however, I looked good in clothes. I loved the way I looked all dressed up. I bought hats, I bought shoes, I bought stockings and garter belts to hold them up, I bought handbags, I bought suits, I bought blouses, I bought dresses, I bought skirts, and I bought jackets that did not match the skirts. I used to spend hours happily buying clothes to wear. Of course, I could not afford to buy my clothes in an actual store, a department store. Instead, they came from used-clothing stores, and they were clothes of a special kind, stylish clothes from a long-ago time—twenty or thirty or forty years earlier. They were clothes worn by people who were alive when I had not been; by people who were far more prosperous than I could imagine being. As a result, it took me a long time to get dressed, for I could not easily decide what combination of people, inconceivably older and more prosperous than I was, I wished to impersonate that day. It was sometimes hours after I started the process of getting dressed that I finally left my house and set off into the world.

My world at that time was a restaurant, someone else's apartment, or any other place where I had agreed to meet a friend; the location was almost never chosen by me. One rainy day in spring, I left my house after my elaborate dressing ritual, and when I was two blocks away from my house and two blocks away from the subway a wind came and blew my hat off my head. My hat, the one made of black corded velvet, landed in the gutter. When I picked it up, it was wet and dirty. That was a moment in my life when I could not take much more of sad realities: I turned around and walked home, and when I got there I took off my clothes and lay down on my bed. When my friends called to inquire why they would not be seeing me that day, I only repeated, again and again, the words "Because my hat fell into the gutter."

THE DAY THAT THE WIND BLEW MY HAT INTO THE GUTTER, MY HAIR was not in its natural state, which would have been black and long and thick and tightly curled. I had left it tightly curled but I had made it short and blond. Had I worn this hat with my hair in its natural state, I would have been wearing it with sincerity, with good intentions; I would have meant the hat to be a hat. But this was not so at all. With my hair in its natural state, such a hat—a style of hat that had been popular when my mother was a young woman—would not have appealed to me. For, really, it was impractical for a modern woman, suitable only as a costume. To wear such a hat, I needed to transform my hair. And should I say that transforming my hair was a way of transforming myself? I had no consciousness of such things then.

I did not know then that I had embarked on something called self-invention, the making of a type of person that did not exist in the place where I was born—a place far away from New York and with a climate quite unlike the one that existed in New York. I wanted to be a writer; I was a person with opinions, and I wanted them to matter to other people. I can admit that about myself as I was then; I cannot admit it about myself as I am now. It was just when I had despaired of ever becoming a writer that I applied for a secretarial position at the magazine *Mademoiselle*. I was twenty-four years old. To my job interview I wore a very short skirt, a nylon blouse under which I wore no brassiere, red shoes with very high heels and white anklets, and no hat to cover my short-cropped blond hair. *Mademoiselle* did not hire me. The people I talked to there had been so kind and sweet toward me, both on the phone and in person, that it took me a very long time to understand that they would never hire me. I wondered if it was my shoes and the anklets, or perhaps my hair. I was speaking of these things to a friend, wondering out loud why had I not been offered a job at *Mademoiselle* when the people there seemed to like me so much, and he said, But how could I have applied to a place like that—didn't I know that they never hired black girls? And I thought, But how was I to know that I was a black girl? I never pass myself in a corridor and say, I am a black girl. I never see myself coming toward me as I come round a bend and say, There is that black girl coming toward me. How was I really to know such a thing?

THIS LIFE WENT ON, THIS LIFE OF BEING YOUNG AND IN NEW YORK. I wondered if I would be young forever; I wondered if I would live in New York forever. Neither prospect gave me pleasure. What did I yearn for? In the New York of my youth, the evenings were too long, no matter what the time of year was. What I did with some people I knew was to drink. What I did with other people was to go and buy drugs from a man who kept a Physicians' Desk Reference on a table in his very pleasant living room. We would sit on his comfortable sofa and order drugs. He would present us with a tray of tablets, small and in many colors—it reminded me of going to a shop in my childhood, where I would stand behind a counter and gaze at the jars full of sweets, sweets I was too poor to afford more than one or two of. In this man's pleasant living room, we would gaze upon his tray of colorful tablets, and we would decide which ones to buy on the basis of our attraction to the colors, and then look up the results they were expected to give in the Physicians' Desk Reference. On a day we were not visiting him, he was taken away by the police, and I have not heard of him since.

There were other ways of filling those long evenings. The list of the people who kissed me and did other things with me became so long that now I cannot remember the names on it. And though I remember many faces, I cannot say with certainty whose face I allowed to kiss me and do other things to me, and whose face I stood with in the dark before we shook hands and said good night. It was always in the dark, at night. There was a reason for that, perhaps practical, perhaps not; to give a reason now, I would have to make it up. Sometimes I meet people who say to me that they knew me well very long ago, and I can only wonder, How well could that have been? Sometimes I meet people who tell me they knew me in those days and they mention an event. I can remember the event, but I cannot remember them. At least, I don't recognize their faces; perhaps I would recognize other parts of them. But even the act of recollection is exhausting. My youth was exhausting, it was dangerous, and it is a miracle that I grew out of it unscathed.

Really, the list of those who went in and out of my bed was

not so long; it was only a long list when compared with the sad facts regarding a part of my upbringing. I was brought up to marry one man and to have children with this one man, and this one man would be the only man to go in and out of my bed. It was understood that this one man would go in and out of the bed of many other women and have many children with them, which is not to say that he would have been a father to them any more than he would have been a husband to me. The person I had become, the person I had made myself into, did not place an obligation on anyone I allowed into my bed. But this was not without its snags and inconveniences. So many people are not as pleasing to look at in the light of the sun as they are to look at by the light of a lamp. It would happen that some of them left their smell with me, and it took the smell of many others to get rid of the one smell. It would happen that I would wake up, my throat raw from hours of gasping, my tongue sore from being fastened between my teeth, suppressing cries of ecstasy or boredom.

One year, I created a Halloween costume for myself by buying a dozen and a half bananas made of plastic (the sort used in some homes as a centerpiece for the dining table), stringing them together so that they made a skirt of sorts, and then tying the whole thing around my waist. I wore nothing underneath, had nothing to cover the rest of my body except an old fur coat that I had bought in an old-fur-coat store for thirty dollars. When I arrived at the party, of course, I removed the coat. The hair on the other parts of my body was not the same color as the hair on my head. I wore no hat to conceal this; it was not a detail that concerned me. And the evening passed, joining the other long evenings that were so exhausting to fill. What did I want? Did I know? I was twenty-five, I was twenty-six, I was twenty-seven, I was twenty-eight. At thirty, I was married.

AMERICAN INFERNO

DANIELLE ALLEN

July 24, 2017

We, who are in prison, had to answer for our sins and our lives were taken from us. Our bodies became the property of the state of California. We are reduced to numbers and stripped of our identity. To the state of California I am not Michael Alexander Allen but I am K-10033. When they want to know anything about me they do not type my last name in the computer but it is my number that is inputted. My number is my name. . . . Dante was not in hell due to a fatal sin but somewhere in his life he strayed onto the path of error, away from his true self. I, K-10033, strayed away from my true self: Michael Alexander Allen.

What sets the course of a life? Three years before my beloved cousin's murder—before the weeping, before the raging, before the heated self-recriminations and icy reckonings—I awoke with the most glorious sense of anticipation I've ever felt. It was June 29, 2006, the day that Michael was going to be freed. Outside my vacation condo in Hollywood, I climbed into the old white BMW I'd bought from my mother and headed to my aunt's small stucco home, in South Central. On the corner, a fortified drug house stood like a sentry, but her pale cottage seemed serene, aglow in the morning sun. Poverty never looks quite as bad in the City of Angels as it does elsewhere.

Aunt Karen, my father's youngest sister, then drove a crew of us to collect Michael from the California Rehabilitation Center–Norco, which lies on a dusty stretch of Riverside County. Michael, the youngest of her three kids, was born when I was eight years old. I had grown up with him. The baby of a sprawling family, he was also *my* baby, a child of magnetizing energy and good humor. We had lost him eleven years earlier, when he was arrested, at fifteen, for an attempted carjacking. Now we'd get him back. It felt like a resurrection.

At the parking lot for Tower 8, a white van drove up to deposit the prisoners being released. Michael stepped out, saw us, and smiled. His broad, toothy grin took up half his face, a bright flash of white against his dark skin. He had a little bob in his step, the same natural spring he'd had as a child. His late adolescence and early adulthood had been spent in captivity, yet he bounded toward us like a fawn.

The homecoming party was in the driveway of my aunt's house, next to the postage stamp of a lawn. Uncles and friends, cousins and second cousins, and cousins who knows how many times removed pulled folding chairs up to folding tables, which were covered with paper tablecloths and laden with fried chicken and sweet tea. The merriment continued all afternoon, and seemed to attract some attention from the neighbors. More than once, a glamorous-looking woman drove past, slowly, in a low-slung two-door gold Mercedes sports car. Michael feasted and played Football Manager with the nephews and nieces who had been born while he was in prison.

After the party, we had little time to waste. That summer, I was telecommuting to my job as the dean of the humanities at the University of Chicago. Michael, for his part, was intent on making something of himself. He had spent some time as a firefighter when he was at Norco, and he was ready to rebuild his life. Making that happen, managing his reëntry in the months to come, was my job. Not mine alone, but mine consistently, day after day, as the cousin on duty, the one with resources, the one who had been to college and who had become a professional.

The plans we had were not the plans we had hoped to have. Michael should have been paroled to a fire camp or to a fire station in Riverside County, where we had family who were ready to take him in. He could have lived there and gone to school and kept on beating back wildfires. But the rule was that you had to be paroled to the county where your offense was committed—crime-ridden Los Angeles County, in his case. So we developed the best alternatives we could. We made task lists, and moved through them efficiently. We met the parole officer, opened a bank account, and went to the library, where Michael got a card and started learning how to use a computer. (Google hadn't existed when he went to prison.) At the D.M.V., he took a test and got his driver's license.

Then, under the scorching sun of the deadliest California heat wave in nearly sixty years, we returned each day to the cool library and scoured Web sites for jobs. We focussed on large chains, which would have room for advancement, and sent out a lot of applications. Most of the time, Michael never got a reply. Then he caught a break: Sears invited him to a job interview. One morning in late July, he donned a new pair of khaki trousers and a button-down shirt, and we headed to Hollywood, to Santa Monica and Western. It was the perfect opportunity—but also, to me, a fraught one. A man who had been imprisoned for more than a decade would have to make the case that he ought to be hired. We had practiced bits and pieces of his story, but never the whole thing. In fact, I never heard Michael recount his own tale from start to finish.

I wonder now whether this was because the full version would have led me to ask questions that Michael did not want to answer. He had so much to give—stories, reflection, engagement—that somehow none of us ever noticed just how much he was withholding. He could love everybody on the terms on which they needed to be loved, give everybody what they needed to receive; and so, in the end, none of us really knew him. I've come to realize that he didn't quite know himself, either.

THE TROUBLE BEGAN IN PREADOLESCENCE. HIS MOTHER GOT MARRIED to a man who had kept from her the fact that he had a criminal record, and who soon became abusive. Karen took her children to Mississippi and then to southern Georgia. There, a few months shy of twelve, Michael stole a jar of coins, amounting to something under ten dollars, from a white family across the street. He was starting to want things, impatiently, and he was also naïve, a California kid transplanted to the Deep South. Only out of naïveté could he have thought to steal from a white family in southern Georgia.

Rather than telling Karen and asking for the money back, the family pressed charges. It was Michael's first encounter with the law, and he went to court with his mother. Karen had by then filed for divorce and bought plane tickets to California. The judge told her the charges would be dropped so long as they got on the plane and never came back.

In the fall of 1991, Michael and his family moved to Claremont, where my father, William, taught, and where my mother, Susan, worked as a college librarian. For my cousins, my parents' house was a second home, screened with laurel bushes, framed by pink-blossomed crêpe myrtles, and shaded by a spreading loquat tree in front.

William and Karen—children of a Florida fisherman who became a charismatic Baptist preacher—were close, but their courses in life were not. My father, with the encouragement of a grade-school teacher, was academically ambitious, and he turned into a pipe-smoking, NPR-listening professor, a political scientist who chaired the U.S. Commission on Civil Rights. He spent much of his days amid heaps of paper in a book-filled study, orchestral harmonies from the radio perfumed by the tweedy, comforting smell of pipe tobacco. Karen's story was different; she worked for a time as a certified nursing assistant, but bringing up three young kids while working full time was a struggle. Her ex-husband wasn't the first abusive man she had been involved with, and plans for furthering her education were often derailed.

Now, with my brother and me away at college, my parents helped Karen find an apartment a few blocks away. Michael took piano lessons from a stern, diminutive woman who had been my own teacher and who taught us how to sit up straight, "like the Queen of England." Michael earned money gardening for her, but resented the hectoring lessons about life that she delivered as he weeded.

He was becoming something of a rule breaker in Claremont. He and his new friend Adam were caught stealing chocolate-chip cookies from the school cafeteria, and sometimes had to be separated after making noise in class. Michael was also caught shoplifting at a nearby mall. Luckily, the store owner delivered Michael to my father, not to the police. But Michael's pattern of petty theft worried his mother, and my father; the weeding job was meant to deal with his need for money.

Then, in early 1993, a fire swept through the family's apartment complex, and they moved again, to the L.A. neighborhood of Inglewood. Although the area was scarred from the ravages of the previous year's riots, the move meant that Karen could be closer to her new job, at an organization called Homeless Health Care Los Angeles. It also meant that Michael started a new school year in yet another district.

We know something about his experiences as a student, because the State of California surveyed its youth during the 1993–94 school year. Forty per cent of ninth graders reported being in a physical fight; nearly sixty per cent reported seeing someone at school with a weapon. Gangs filled in for family; almost one in five ninth graders reported belonging to one at some point. Michael, then just shy of fourteen, seems to have flirted with the Queen

Street Bloods, who were active on the west side of Inglewood; later, he started hanging with a friend from the Crips, a rival gang.

Michael was testing out a new world. But in that summer of 1993 he would also return to his old one, riding a bus back to Claremont to hang out with Adam. During one of those visits, Adam's parents were looking after the next-door neighbor's house, and the two boys let themselves in and took a radio and some other items. The neighbor reported a burglary, and when Karen realized who was responsible she hauled Michael to the police station. The boys returned everything. They were given a two-year juvenile probation, which entailed a curfew but no court date.

The narrative so far is familiar. A kid from a troubled home, trapped in poverty, without a stable world of adults coördinating care for him, starts pilfering, mostly out of an impatience to have things. In Michael's first fourteen years, his story includes not a single incidence of violence, aside from the usual wrestling matches with siblings. It could have had any number of possible endings. But events unfold along a single track. As we make decisions, and decisions are made for us, we shed the lives that might have been. In Michael's fifteenth year, his life accelerated, like a cylinder in one of those pneumatic tubes, whisking off your deposit at a drive-through bank. To understand how that acceleration could happen, though, another story is needed.

•

Like Dante I am forced to descend lower into hell
to achieve a full awakening. I am forced into depression,
scarred by obscenities, war after war, but each war that I
survive I am a step closer to a full awakening of self. My
hell is no longer demonstrating what I am capable of doing
in order to survive. It has become what I can tolerate and
withstand in order to live.

CONSIDER THE VISIBLE SURFACE OF LOS ANGELES. UNDERPASSES, BRIDGES, alleyways, delivery trucks, service entrances, corner stores, mailboxes, water towers, exhaust vents, and the streets—in the nineties, at least, all were covered with graffiti. Few can read that graffiti. I couldn't then, and have only now begun to learn how to decipher it. But it's a language that represents a world. It records deaths and transactions, benefactions and trespasses, favors done and owed, vendettas pursued. Laws and punishments. If you can't read that graffiti, you have no conception of the parallel universe, all around you, that is fundamentally at war with the legally recognized state. It's a regime with its own rules and penalties—in effect, a parastate. Michael grew up there.

Behind that parastate's economy and criminal-justice system lies the war on drugs. In the eighties, as the state sought to break the global drug-supply chain by rounding up low-level peddlers and deterring them with outsized penalties, the wholesalers established their own system of deterrence for gang members who served as retailers. If you didn't do what you were supposed to do, you were shot. Maybe in the knee first. If you riled the gang system again, you or someone you loved might be killed. The drug business, dependent on a well-established witness-suppression program, operates a far more powerful system of deterrence, with far swifter punishment, than any lawful state could ever devise.

In these years, the Los Angeles County Sheriff's Department created its first gang database. In 1988, after a much publicized drive-by shooting of a bystander, near U.C.L.A., the Los Angeles Police Department used the database to round up no fewer than fourteen hundred African-American youths and detain them in the parking lot of the L.A. Coliseum. More than eighteen thousand people were jailed in six months. Between 1982 and 1995, the African-American prison population in California grew from 12,470 to 42,296; the Latino prison population soared from 9,006 to 46,080. Los Angeles was a city ready to explode when the four police officers who had been caught on video beating Rodney King were acquitted.

When Michael stole the jar of coins in Georgia, and the judge dropped the charges, you might say that Michael met the "forgiving world." The same happened when he shoplifted, and when he stole the radio in Claremont, in 1993. But, back in the City of Angels, Michael met the unforgiving world. Nearly half the black men in Los Angeles between the ages of twenty-one and twenty-four were officially identified as gang members, and this simple fact of classification, accurate or not, affected that community profoundly. The angels had turned their backs.

The summer before Michael's junior year, in 1995, he began looking for a job. His cousin Marc—my younger brother—had worked in a grocery store as a bag boy throughout high school, and Michael wanted a similar gig. But, at fifteen, he needed a work permit, and nobody in his mother's social network could help. He again began to roam the streets, and stayed out past his curfew. In math class, his grades plunged from straight A's to an F. Karen had conferences with Michael and his teachers, who told him that he was smarter than this. He countered, "I don't want to be smarter than this." On those warm summer days, he spent as much time as he could out-of-doors. Sometimes he would stand in front of the house of a kid he'd come to know. Karen spotted him once, lean and muscled, standing shirtless in khaki trousers—gangbanging gear. Although he was only four blocks away from her apartment, it felt like a different neighborhood.

Karen's last day with her boy was Friday, September 15th. Michael didn't have school. He went to work with his mother and hung out in her office. Then she took him to the Los Angeles Public Library, where she planned to meet him when she got off work, to take him shopping. But Michael was gone when she returned. The next time she saw him, he was in handcuffs.

WHERE WERE YOU WHEN YOU WERE FIFTEEN? WHEN I CLOSE MY EYES, I can still see a bedroom with a brass bed topped with a blue-and-white striped Laura Ashley comforter. There were matching valences on my windows, and I had a wooden rolltop desk, with a drawer that locked and held my secrets, including dirty letters that I couldn't at the time translate from a German boy with whom I'd had a minor romance at summer music camp.

I grew up in a college town where everyone knew my parents. They had made a critical decision, early in the lives of their two children, not to move until we had graduated from high school. I was a faculty brat, an insecure and often lonely child; the only time I ever got grounded was when my mother caught me sneaking a ride to French class with a friend. I was younger than most of my classmates at Claremont High School, and, although my friends all had their driver's licenses by the start of our junior year and I didn't, I wasn't allowed to ride in their cars. Eight years later, in L.A., my fifteen-year-old cousin, who also didn't yet have a driver's license, was arrested, for the first time, for an attempted carjacking.

It was September 17, 1995, a cool and foggy Sunday morning. Larry Smith, a lanky forty-four-year-old, was buffing the dashboard of his blue Cadillac Coupe de Ville in the alley behind his apartment, on Rosecrans Avenue. The street was lined with drab stucco apartment buildings, whose uncovered staircases led down to carports below. Michael appeared holding a chrome Lorcin .380, a cheap pistol prone to malfunction. An older friend, Devonn, a member of the Rollin 60s Crips, was apparently on lookout, but not visible to Smith as he worked in his car. (Both names have been changed.) Michael approached Smith, told him not to move, and demanded his watch. Smith handed it over.

Then Michael asked for his wallet. When he found that it was empty, he tossed it back into the car. Then, as the police report recounted, Michael "tapped Smith's left knee with the gun and said he was going to take the car." According to Smith, Michael kept the gun pointed at the ground. Smith lunged for the weapon. They wrestled. Michael punched him. Smith gained control of the gun and shot Michael through the neck.

As Michael lay bleeding on the ground, Smith hollered to his wife to call 911. When the police arrived, they collected evidence and looked for witnesses, although no one had anything to say. Meanwhile, paramedics took Michael to a hospital, where he was treated for a "through and through" bullet wound that had narrowly missed his spine.

A police officer accompanying Michael in the ambulance reported that, "during transport, Allen made a spontaneous statement that he was robbing a man when he got shot." At the hospital, Michael was read his Miranda rights and additional juvenile admonishments in the presence of a second officer. According to the police report, he waived his rights and said again that he had tried to rob the man, using a gun that he claimed he had found about two and a half weeks earlier. He also confessed that he had robbed three people during the previous two days on the same block, and that he had robbed someone a week earlier, about ten blocks away. The police had no reports for two of the four robberies he confessed to; in the two that had been reported, Michael had taken twenty dollars from one victim and two dollars from another. In other words, on his way to the hospital, and upon admission, with no adults present other than the officers, a wounded fifteen-year-old talked a blue streak.

By the time Karen got to Michael's bedside, he had wrapped up his confession. The only thing he didn't mention was Devonn's involvement. Did Devonn suggest the crime, or provide the gun? We have no way of knowing. I don't believe that Michael was prepared, that morning, to be violent; he had a gun, but refrained from using it. Still, I was far away, a graduate student in England. Along the banks of the River Cam, I shared poems with friends and debated crime and punishment in ancient Athens. I had gravitated toward the subject upon being struck by how a sophisticated, democratic society had made next to no use of imprisonment. When the news of Michael's arrest came, it was stupefying. My brain raced in endless loops. *How could it be? How could it be?* I now have a sense of an answer. But there were harder questions ahead.

•

> I'm trapped in a hell with whom society decrees to be
> the worst of living and better off dead. Robbers, rapists,
> child molesters, carjackers, murderers, and dope fiends
> who would spend their mother's monthly rent for a quick
> fix. And here I am, amongst them. As much as the mere
> thought disgusts me, I am one of them. Just another
> number, not deserving of a second chance.

BEFORE HIS ARREST, MICHAEL DID NOT HAVE A CRIMINAL RECORD. That day, he gained one with a vengeance. For the watch and the wallet, Michael was charged with robbery; for the car, attempted carjacking. Both charges were "enhanced" because of the gun. He was also charged with the two earlier robberies. Four felonies, two from one incident, and all in one week.

Eighteen months earlier, in March, 1994, California's Three Strikes and You're Out law, the nation's first, had gone into effect. Once you were convicted of your third felony, it meant twenty-five years to life, or a plea deal. If Michael pursued a jury trial, convictions on at least three of his four charges would trigger the law. Worse, this was happening at the high point of L.A.'s panic about carjackings. In Los Angeles County alone, the number of carjackings had nearly doubled between 1991 and 1992, from 3,600 to 6,297. In 1993, the state legislature had unanimously passed a bill that made carjacking an offense for which sixteen-year-olds could be tried as adults. Two years later, the bar was lowered to fourteen. A Los Angeles *Times* article titled "Wave of Fear," which ran the year before Michael's arrest, quoted then Senator Joseph Biden saying, "Name me a person in L.A. who has a fender-bender and doesn't fear an imminent carjacking. Yes, it's still remote, but you're in the statistical pool now. It's like AIDS. Everyone's in the pool now."

California's legislators had given up on the idea of rehabilitation in prison, even for juveniles. This is a point that critics of the penal system make all the time. Here is what they don't say: legislators had also given up on retribution. Anger drives retribution. When the punishment fits the crime, retribution is achieved, and anger is sated; it softens. This is what makes it anger, not hatred, a distinction recognized by philosophers all the way back to antiquity. Retribution limits how much punishment you can impose.

The legislators who voted to try as adults sixteen-year-olds, and then fourteen-year-olds, were not interested in retribution. They had become deterrence theorists. They were designing sentences not for people but for a thing: the aggregate level of crime. They wanted to reduce that level, regardless of what constituted justice for any individual involved. The target of Michael's sentence was not a bright fifteen-year-old boy with a mild proclivity for theft but the thousands of carjackings that occurred in Los Angeles. Deterrence dehumanizes. It directs at the individual the full hatred that society understandably has for an aggregate phenomenon. But no individual should bear that kind of responsibility.

On February 5, 1996, four and a half months after Michael's last night at home, he sat in court, in an orange jumpsuit and handcuffs, as the judge told him to choose whether to stand trial and face a possible conviction of twenty-five years to life or to plead guilty and take a reduced sentence. The judge didn't say how much the sentence would be reduced, but he did say, "Please take the plea."

Michael could not choose. Now sixteen, he asked his mother to decide. Karen went outside the courtroom and prayed. "God told me," she says, "that he would only get seven years, versus risking a trial of twenty-five years to life. I made the decision." So Michael pleaded guilty. A few months later, he learned that his "earliest possible release date" was June 29, 2006. According to Karen, the only time Michael cried in court was when he got sentenced.

When you're sixteen, the farthest back you can remember is about thirteen years, to the age of three. Michael's sentence was almost equivalent, in psychological terms, to the whole of his life. It stretched past what was for him the limit of knowable time. The mind cannot fasten onto this sort of temporality; we are unable to give it concrete meaning in relation to our own lives. The imagination wanders into white space. For Michael, it was, he later wrote, "a mountain of time" to climb. It would be a steep one. The moment he turned seventeen, he was transferred to adult prison.

"How could it have happened?" is the question everyone asks. Where were the lawyers? What did your family do? I think back to the stolen radio. Michael came from a family who believed that if you did something wrong you admitted it, you fixed it, and you suffered the consequences. Michael was guilty of the attempted carjacking; he was going to have to suffer the consequences. Our family trusted in the fairness of the criminal-justice system. At each turn, we learned too late that this system was no longer what we thought it was, that its grip was mercilessly tightening, that our son would be but one among many millions soon lost in its vise.

When we read that the point of the Three Strikes law is to lock up repeat offenders, we do not think of the fifteen-year-old who has just been arrested for the first time. An underground nuclear test is conducted, and the land above craters only much later. This, I think, describes the effect of the Three Strikes law and the slow, constant escalation of penal severity. An explosion occurred underground. The people standing on the surface conducted their lives as usual. They figured out what was really going on only after the earth had collapsed beneath them.

THE YEARS BETWEEN THE AGES OF FIFTEEN AND TWENTY-SIX ARE punctuated by familiar milestones: high school, driver's license, college, first love, first job, first serious relationship, perhaps marriage, possibly a child. For those who pass adolescence in prison, some of these rites disappear; the ones that occur take on a distorted shape. And extra milestones get added. First long-term separation from family. First racial melee. First time in solitary, formally known as "administrative segregation." First time sodomized.

Between his arrest and his sentencing, Michael was mainly in Central, the juvenile prison, where only parents and legal guardians could visit. When Michael and I reconnected properly, in the late nineties, he was making his way through Chino—a notoriously tough prison—before landing in Norco. Its full name was the California Rehabilitation Center-Norco, but little rehabilitation was on offer. There was the obligatory library, but no classes past the G.E.D. level. In the nineties, college and university classes were scrapped because of budget cuts, and the state and federal governments ceased providing prisoners access to Pell Grants for correspondence courses. Higher education, once seen as an antidote to recidivism, had come to be seen as a privilege that inmates hadn't earned.

After I started teaching at the University of Chicago, in 1998, Michael and I began talking regularly on the phone. Once he was at Norco, I began to visit him, too, every other week in the summer and during the Christmas holidays. Michael would call at least once a week, sometimes more, except when the prison was on lockdown owing to outbreaks of violence. Then weeks might pass without a word. I was a good phone partner, because I could afford the astronomical collect-call charges. Every call began with a reminder, a robotic voice saying, "This is the California Department

of Corrections. Will you accept the charges?" And then, every fifteen seconds, as if we could forget, there was another interruption:
"This call has originated from a California state prison."

Michael, who had already completed his G.E.D., desperately
wanted to go to college, and I understood his desire to learn. I believed in education; I believed in Michael. So I researched how Michael might be able to get a college degree. On November 8, 2001,
Michael sent me his application to Indiana University's Program in
General Studies, and I mailed it with a check nine days later. He
would aim for a bachelor's degree. The day he was admitted was as
exhilarating as the day I received my fat envelope from Princeton,
thirteen years earlier.

There was a catch, however. No hardcover books were allowed
into the prison. Michael could enroll only in classes for which the
textbooks had soft covers. I made a round of phone calls. The remaining choices for introductory classes were Intro to Ethics and
Intro to Writing and Study of Literature. Michael chose the second, Lit 141. I paid the fees and ordered the books.

New Year's came and so did the Bible, the Odyssey, the Inferno, "The Canterbury Tales," and "Persian Letters." But there was
no shortage of distractions, and Michael had trouble completing
the assignments. At one point, suspected of participating in a "racial melee," he was transferred to Chino and placed in solitary, until
an investigation absolved him. A year later, he repeated the class.
This time he churned out one essay after another, with readings
that were full of insight and personal connection to ancient texts.
He was finding his voice. "I don't take kindly to seeing myself in
Hell but Dante's writing makes it impossible to just read without
visualization," he wrote in one essay. "It is the life I live in Prison
which to me is Hell. . . . I think of Dante's use of ice as nothing but
a mere deception. Ice within itself is enticing to the burning soul.
Ice can get so cold that it burns flesh. And it's parallel to any sin
committed on earth."

Along the way, Michael fell in love. I remember his words on the phone: "I've met someone, Danielle. She's beautiful." And I remember my sense of confusion. Met someone? How? Where? I was thinking of the female guards whom I'd got to know in the course of my visits. But in a fumbling way we came to understand each other. Michael had fallen in love with a fellow-inmate who had implants or hormone-induced breasts, and who dressed and lived as Bree. (I've changed the name.) She was, he said, unquestionably the most beautiful woman in the prison. He hadn't told his mother, and he made me promise not to say anything. He knew Karen would be upset and he feared she would judge him, as he trusted I would not.

Like freedom, desire was dizzying to Michael. A month later, he mailed me a piece of writing unlike anything he had ever sent me. "The world has change and brothas far from the same," he rapped, and continued:

Am I losing my mind
No; I think I found it
Realizing greatness in one's self is very astounding
and truth be told, I recognize a King
cause when I look in the mirror all I see is me
And us, so please trust, we can't be touch
standing together forever is a necessary must.

Soon afterward, he sent me Bree's annual prison shot. She was posed as a woman, lying on the floor like a sports pinup, made up and in colorful clothing. Why did he love her? He loved her because she was the most beautiful woman he had ever seen. He loved her because, of all the men in prison, she had chosen him—and that was a gift of surpassing value. But it was also a gift that came to blind him. When he was finally released from prison, I failed to grasp that he was not yet free.

UPSTAIRS, IN THE SEARS PERSONNEL DEPARTMENT, EVERYTHING WAS beige and brightly lit. I settled into a metal chair and waited while Michael had his interview, in an office down the hall. I did a lot of waiting that summer, but I never questioned why I was there. My brother and I had long ago formed a tight circle with Aunt Karen's three kids—Nicholas, Roslyn, and Michael, each born about two years apart—and, as the oldest, I was always the one in charge. As I waited, I typically spent my time thinking about my task lists, about what had to be done next. Forty-five minutes into this particular wait, the door opened and I learned that the managers had offered Michael a job as an inventory clerk.

It felt as if time had begun. I could imagine a future, even a happy ending. There was still school and housing to be arranged, but we were steadily assembling the pieces of a possible life, as if doing a jigsaw puzzle. The goal was for Michael to work full time and to enroll in one of California's famed community colleges. No one in his immediate family had a degree, but I was in my element—pretty much my deepest expertise was in going to school.

Los Angeles Valley College, in Valley Glen, was the obvious place, a decent school with good general-education courses and— our goal—a fire-technology program. The subway's Red Line had stops at Santa Monica and Vermont, about a mile from the Sears, and in North Hollywood, not too far from campus. We battled our way through the thicket of federal financial-aid forms, visited the tutoring center, and hungrily collected flyers posting apartments for rent.

We needed a place cheap enough to manage on Michael's wages. Together, we searched the listings, drove by addresses, and made calls and appointments. We landed on a promising place on Ethel Avenue, in Valley Glen, a few blocks north of the college. The advertisement was for a studio apartment in a converted garage behind a modest home. Once again, Michael practiced telling his story, and we scheduled a visit.

The home was impeccable, a white bungalow circled by a white iron fence. Alongside the fence stood some small shrubs, neatly tended, and rosebushes spraying white flowers. I went up to the house by myself. Two women met me at the door, a mother, perhaps in her sixties, and her daughter. Dressed in linen trousers and a black T-shirt, I introduced myself. I was a professor, I told them, and I was helping my cousin, who had recently been released from prison. He had just enrolled at Los Angeles Valley College and been hired at Sears. I would be paying his deposit and guaranteeing his rent. He'd been sentenced as a young person and this was his second chance. Were they willing to meet him and hear him out?

They agreed, and I sat outside while Michael spoke to his prospective landlords. He could charm anyone with that bouncing gait and electric grin. Finally, the three emerged, in good spirits, and the women took us around to the back to see the studio. It was clean and peaceful, and equipped with a hot plate and an electric heater. I could imagine being comfortable there. And it was walking distance from the school.

Michael said he wanted it; we all shook hands in the gaze of the late-afternoon sun. I was moved by the trust and the generosity of these two women, and I still am. Driving back to South Central, my mood was all melody. I imagined Michael felt the same. Little more than a month out and here he was, with a driver's license, a bank account, a library card, and a job. He was enrolled in college, with a clean, safe, comfortable place to live. This was a starter set for a life, enabling him to defy the pattern of parolees.

I dropped him off in South Central and headed back to Hollywood, expecting to sleep soundly for the first time in a while. But that night Michael called. He wasn't sure he should take the apartment. I felt a stone drop to the bottom of a well.

Why not? I asked.

He couldn't explain, he said. He just didn't feel quite right about it.

I told him to sleep on it, and when we talked in the morning he told me he wanted the apartment after all. Relieved, I headed off to collect a cashier's check for the security deposit, and Michael headed off under yet another cloudless sky to his job at Sears. At midday, he called me again: Had I taken the check over yet? He said that he had changed his mind again.

"Michael, what on earth are you talking about?"

He told me that he wasn't sure what it would be like if his associates came by.

The word surprised me, but I didn't ask him what he meant by "associates." The purpose of the word, somehow, was to insist on his privacy, and it brought me up short. I paused, didn't ask questions. I told him to think about it some more. Disagreement was rare for us.

He called me a few hours later. He said he would take the apartment and asked me to pick him up after work. Then, just before I did so, he called again. "I've made up my mind," he said. "I don't want the apartment."

My memory of the conversation is hazy, but it's likely we exchanged some sharp words. His plan, it emerged, was to live with his mother and to ride the bus the nine miles from there to Sears and the ten miles from there to Los Angeles Valley College, and then the twenty-two miles home—through the worst of Los Angeles traffic. It was madness, but there was nothing I could do. It was well into August. School would start soon. I would have incoming students to welcome, new faculty to orient, budgets to plan. I bought him more khakis and button-down shirts, spent as much time with him as I could. A few weeks later, I headed back to Chicago.

•

The root of sin is lust and the desire to satisfy that lust. . . . Lust only creates wanting and wanting creates greed and greed burns Flesh. It is lust that causes us to believe we have to have something at all cost. This is my suffering, this is my hell. 24 hours all night. There is no day. My soul in its entirety is in darkness.

THE JIGSAW PUZZLE SOON FELL APART, AND COLLEGE WAS THE FIRST piece to go. The commute was just too much; I doubt Michael made it through even two weeks of classes. The job, meanwhile, lasted until November, when I got a nearly hysterical call. Michael said he couldn't do it. He was drowning. He wasn't going to make it. When I left L.A., I had promised him that if he ever needed me I would be there. After the call, I went straight to the airport, and arrived in L.A. just in time to take him to dinner.

Michael was teary and despondent. After work, he said, some of his Latino co-workers had called him a nigger. He fought them in the parking lot, and walked away from the job. Never told his bosses or co-workers that he was quitting—just didn't return. So now he was back to square one. Worse than that, really, since he'd proved himself unreliable to an employer. He was mostly spending his time at home, playing video games with his nephews. He no longer saw a future for himself.

I mainly tried to listen; I didn't have much to offer. I could promise to get him into an apartment, if he could get another job. But I was no longer in a position to stay and help him find one. I had too many obligations in Chicago. November was tenure-review time, with mounds of papers to read and unending cycles of meetings that the dean, in particular, was not supposed to miss. My professional reputation was at stake. Michael would have to make the next push for himself.

When I visited L.A. just before the winter break, it seemed as if Michael had made that push. He had found an apartment, he told me, and was ready to put down a deposit. Could I come and see it? The place was on the fourth floor of a vintage Craftsman-style building overlooking the 101 freeway. It was big and spacious, with gleaming wood floors. As I wound through the rooms, Michael began telling me about how he and Bree wanted to move in.

I had no idea he was still seeing Bree, let alone making plans to move in together. My face must have conveyed surprise, though I tried not to react too strongly. (Learning how to suppress visible emotion is an occupational demand of being a dean.) I told him that I wanted to know what the job situation was. Had he lined up a new gig? What did Bree do—did she have a job? Our voices echoed in the empty apartment. Michael leaned against a window-sill, the sky and the freeway shining behind him.

There was something shamefaced in him as he answered. No, he didn't have a job. Bree was into hair styling, but, no, she didn't have one, either. What, exactly, were they thinking? Michael didn't have much of an answer. Plainly, the plan involved taking advantage of me to some degree.

In that moment, I encountered a different Michael from the one I knew. I saw something calculating, something I'd never seen before. I didn't ask to talk to Bree, who I'd come to realize was the woman in the gold Mercedes crawling past our homecoming party. All I was able to say was that I couldn't possibly pay the deposit—plus some number of months' rent, plus co-sign a lease—when neither of them had a job.

Michael's face tensed. He said he understood.

This was the day I understood that the idea that I could stand my baby cousin up on his own two feet was a fantasy; it had always had too much of me in it. From this point on, Michael ceased confiding in me. Our phone conversations never burrowed below the surface. I no longer knew how to help.

Michael spent more and more time with Bree, whose possessiveness was violent. According to Karen, Bree cut Michael three times between December and May, and each time Michael tried to pass the injuries off as the result of someone attempting to rob him.

He had also begun to suspect Bree of cheating. Late one night, he sneaked under her window, in the hope—he told me later—that catching her in the act would give him an easy out from the relationship. That night, he got into a fight with a lover of Bree's, and the police were called. Michael went straight to prison for a parole violation, and remained there for around a year.

It was a catastrophic defeat. Despite the fact that we wrote each other letters, I somehow obliterated from my memory all traces of Michael's second stint in prison. When he got out again, just months before the 2008 stock-market crash, he returned to what we hoped would be the comfort of his mother's house. Just a short time later, though, he began living with Bree.

In the months before Michael's parole violation, Karen and Bree had waged a battle rooted in a strong mutual dislike. Now Bree sought a formal treaty. She called Karen to say that Michael would be living with her, and that she didn't want any conflict. This was hard for Karen. She knew that her son's relationship was violent. As Karen understood it, Bree had been in prison for attempting to kill a boyfriend, and the only time she had seen Michael get physical with anyone was when he fought Bree on her pin-neat front lawn. Bree had been going down the street, breaking car windows and throwing things at Karen's house. Michael had gone outside to warn her away. The two came to blows. Through a window, Karen saw Michael knock Bree out. That night, Karen added to her prayers the hope that the Lord would liberate Michael from his misery.

By December, Michael's world had fully contracted. While living at Bree's house, he became known on the street as Big Mike. That winter, he revealed to his sister a gun, hidden in a towel, in Bree's Mercedes. By the spring, he was running drugs, including at least one trip to Texas. Later, the detectives investigating his murder found PCP in his room.

In June, 2009, I got married, in New Jersey, where I had re-

cently accepted an appointment at a distinguished research institute. Michael came to the wedding—his first airplane flight since
his release. He was handsome in a beige jacket and crimson shirt,
with matching crimson alligator-skin shoes. But there was so much
I couldn't see: I couldn't make out the demons chasing Michael as
he greeted the other guests at the door to the chapel.

FIVE WEEKS AFTER THAT CHAMPAGNE-FILLED WEDDING DAY, MY
father called me from Maryland with the news: Michael had been
discovered in a car in South Los Angeles, dead from multiple gunshots. I was in England, and I remember my father's voice, the careful, clipped speech of a retired professor, crackling as if through the
first transatlantic cables. Heading to the airport, I knew that the
police were looking for a woman, and that Bree had disappeared.
Two weeks later, she was charged with his murder.

She had, evidently, shot Michael in her kitchen. There had been
one witness, a middle-school-age boy. He hadn't seen anything,
but he had heard voices and gunshots. With the help of relatives,
Bree cleaned Michael up nicely. She then bundled him in a blanket,
put him in his little hatchback, and drove him to the street corner where he was found. Three accessories—all members of Bree's
family—were also charged. Eventually, Bree pleaded no contest to
voluntary manslaughter, and was sentenced to twenty-two years in
prison. Having by now undergone gender-reassignment surgery,
she was sent to a women's prison.

Michael and Bree had first met and become lovers when they
were both inmates at Norco, which she had entered at the age of
twenty-five. Bree was a little more than two years older than Michael. She was just his height and just his weight, a transgender
woman still early in the process of transitioning. As far as the public record reveals, she'd been convicted for assault with a firearm.

I thought back to Michael's homecoming in 2006, to Bree cruis-
ing by in her chariot, coming for to carry Michael home. We all

had thought the relationship ended when Bree left prison a year ahead of Michael, and we believed that Michael's home was with us. What Michael himself thought or wanted that homecoming day, I will never know. He hadn't invited Bree to the picnic. Yet she came and would stay.

When Michael contemplated renting that tidy little studio apartment on Ethel Avenue, with its white fence and pearly roses, it was voluptuous Bree in her tight clothes and gold Mercedes whom he was visualizing having to introduce to those kindly landladies. How would it have gone if he had taken this "associate" home with him? When he spent those twenty-four hours dithering over whether to rent the apartment, I see now that his real choice was whether to repudiate the first and only love of his life. He chose Bree, and it would prove to be his life's defining decision.

•

There are those who await to fulfill their destiny. I see in them a sincere and apologetic heart for their ill misdeeds. They are the one who will change the world positively or positively change someone's world. Hell cannot hold the latter of the two opposites but in time will only spit them back out into society to do what is right. The hell that I live in cannot hold Dante. Hell can test and try one's self but it cannot hold Dante and it will not hold me. In the *Inferno*, the dead are trapped forever. Surely, the biggest and most important difference in the Inferno and my hell called prison, is that I have a way out.

BETHLEHEM TEMPLE, KAREN'S PARISH, MOUNTED A FUNERAL SERVICE like those from my childhood, when I visited my grandfather the Baptist preacher. There were soul-busting songs and unpainted, teetotalling women; women in hats, with fans, on the verge of fainting. Karen had to be held, and the preacher lifted the roof off. We wept enough to make our own riverside. *Oh, we'll wait till Jesus comes / Down by the riverside.*

The service was followed by a brief lunch back at Karen's house, and then it was onward to a second service, at the church that Michael belonged to. The street had turned out for this service, bringing its jive step. The place was filled with people we didn't recognize. The detectives were here, too, working. They hadn't yet solved the murder of the man they knew as Big Mike, and were watching to see who showed up. The pastor had nothing to say about Michael; instead, he spent the eulogy giving himself credit for the worldly success of this or that parishioner, before descending into an anti-Semitic rant about moneylenders and lawyers.

Where was Michael in all of these remarks? He wasn't there. Not in those words, or, in fact, in his casket. We'd had a viewing a few days earlier. I'd been taken aback, seeing him, his still face so sombre in repose, with a slightly grayish tinge. In the satin-lined casket, he was dressed in the very suit he'd worn to my wedding, a month earlier. I was struck by his solidity. I had never noticed how much he had bulked up. In the casket, there was no smile. The light was gone, and with it, I suppose, the lightness. Later, much later, writing this, I've had to face the fact that on that day I was looking at Big Mike, not at little Michael. The hardest part of my effort to understand what happened to my cousin has been learning when and how Big Mike replaced Michael.

After the service, we went back to Aunt Karen's house to celebrate what we called Michael's homegoing, his passage to the promised land. Next to that postage stamp of a lawn, we gathered around folding chairs pulled up to folding tables, laden with fried chicken and sweet tea, to commemorate the baby of the family. We had lost him at fifteen to jail; we regained him eleven years later. At twenty-nine, he was lost to us again, gone for good. My cousin's

idea of hell was to be reduced to a number; now he became a statistic, joined to the nearly two hundred thousand black Americans
who have died violently in the years since his arrest on Rosecrans
Avenue.

In my heart's locket, five gangly brown-skinned kids, cousins,
will be forever at play beneath a pair of crêpe-myrtle trees bathed in
June sunshine. Michael and I loved to climb trees. An arm here, a
leg there, juts out from the trees' floral sundress, a delicate skein of
pink and purple blooms. When we found unbloomed buds on the
dichondra lawn, we would gently press at their nubs until the skins
slit and fragile, crinkled blossoms emerged whole. Meanwhile, inside the house, through the living-room picture window, the adults,
beloved, pass their time in glancing, distracted talk.

THE YELLOW HOUSE

SARAH BROOM

August 24, 2015

In early spring, before the Jane magnolia tree bloomed, I set off to close the distance between the me of now and the me of then. When I made the drive to New Orleans from upstate New York, where I live now, I began as I had dozens of times before, from various starting points, cradling a longing to see what, if anything, had changed. These returns always seem necessary, as if I were a rubber band, stretched to its breaking point.

In the ten years since Hurricane Katrina, what has plagued me most is the unfinished business of it all. Why is my brother Carl still babysitting ruins, sitting on the empty plot where our childhood home used to be? Why is my seventy-four-year-old mother, Ivory Mae, still unmoored, living in St. Rose, Louisiana, at Grandmother's house? We call it Grandmother's even though she died ten years ago. Her house, the only one remaining in our family, is a squat three-bedroom in a subdivision just off the River Road, which snakes seventy miles along the Mississippi, where plantation houses sit alongside grain mills and petrochemical refineries.

On the evening of the second day, I arrive in New Orleans. I call Carl, who tells me to find him at the Yellow House, where we grew up. It was demolished a year after the water. None of us was there to see it go. When it came down, all seven of my siblings who lived in New Orleans were displaced. There are twelve of us in all, and I am the baby.

I exit the interstate in New Orleans East, fifteen miles from the French Quarter, at Chef Menteur, a highway named for a deceitful

Choctaw Indian chief or an early colonial governor, depending on whom you ask.

There is no welcome sign here, nothing to signify the New Orleans of most people's imagination. The East, where nearly twenty per cent of the city lives, lies in the shadow of more mythologized sections of New Orleans: the French Quarter, the Garden District, and even the Lower Ninth Ward, which became the drowned and abandoned symbol of the storm's destructive power. The totems—architecturally significant houses, second-line parades, and historical markers—are nearly nonexistent.

The East comprises more than half of New Orleans's geography, though it is mostly water: Lake Pontchartrain on one side, the Mississippi River on the other. To the west, the Industrial Canal, dredged in 1923 to make a commercial route between the lake and the river, is a watery bifurcation that divides the East from the rest of the city.

CHEF MENTEUR SLASHES THROUGH THE EAST, CUTTING SOME LONG streets off at their ends, creating impromptu culs-de-sac where sometimes only five houses exist. Chef severs a street called America, and splits Wilson Avenue, where I grew up, separating us from a mile-long line of handsome brick houses and from Jefferson Davis, my elementary school, which in 1993 was renamed for Ernest (Dutch) Morial, the city's first black mayor, but is now an empty field.

My sister Karen was struck by a car and dragged down the ruthless highway when she was nine years old and trying to get to third grade. She survived with skin grafts that formed islets on her arms and legs, and with faith in God.

For the past ten years, the only inhabitants of our side of Wilson Avenue have been our neighbor Rachelle and her two children, who live in a cream-colored shotgun house. Next door was our house, a narrow camelback shotgun, with a second floor in the back that did not run the length of the house.

When I pull into the drive, I see Carl at the back of the lot, seated at a trestle table with several men. Carl sits here at least five times a week, when he is not fishing, or working his maintenance job at NASA, or tending his own house. In the past, I have arrived unannounced to find him sitting on an ice chest, a skinny man with socks pulled up to his kneecaps, a gold picture frame around his front tooth, searching the view.

This time, a light-skinned man named Mark is here, smoking a cigar. Another, Arsenio, rushes out to buy Popeyes chicken. Carl's son, a three-year-old whom we call Mr. Carl for how grown he acts, is here, too. Carl, six feet four, with a loping walk, stands and beckons me over. The top of my head kisses his armpit. "Welcome back, li'l sis," he says. Carl is fifty-two, my older brother by sixteen years.

Certain things have changed since I was last here, four months ago. The table rests on the concrete foundation that used to hold the house's den. Carl has painted the slab black. His Mardi Gras trailer and matching boil pots, large enough for several thirty-five-pound sacks of crawfish, have been painted orange and blue with streaks of yellow.

Carl asks if during my stay I'll "see what's happening with that Road Home." Louisiana's Road Home program, designed to return the displaced to permanent housing, has thus far led my family nowhere. The federally funded program has awarded nine billion dollars in grants to Louisiana residents to rebuild their homes and protect their property against storm damage in the future. But we fear losing the land. An unkempt lot could be reported as a public nuisance. If accused, we could be subject to legal proceedings and, worse, private shame for not attending to the only thing our mother has left. "This is still our land," Carl says.

I stay until the chicken arrives. Then the sun sets and the mosquitoes become too much.

Mom is calling by now anyway, happy to know that I have found

Carl, less happy that we are on the lot. "Looks like nothing was ever there," she has said. But when she feels like remembering she says, "That house was my beginnings."

MY MOTHER BOUGHT THE YELLOW HOUSE IN 1961, FOR THIRTY-TWO hundred dollars. She was nineteen years old, mother to three, and already widowed. Her husband, Webb, an Army recruit, had been run over by a car near Fort Hood, in Texas, the year before.

Until the sixties, people called the land east of the Industrial Canal Gentilly or the Ninth Ward or the East. Then a development firm, New Orleans East, Inc., led by two Texas oilmen, Clint Murchison and Toddie Lee Wynne, bought thirty-two thousand acres of it. The area was to be a "city within a city," rising from swamplands, self-contained, with a population of two hundred and fifty thousand.

To my mother, who grew up on Roman Street, uptown, around the corner from Rex's Carnival den, New Orleans East was the country. When she first saw the house on Wilson, she thought little of it. A wooden house with a screened-in porch and two bedrooms, it was already sinking in the back.

For fifty dollars a load, a dump truck arrived with gravel and rocks and stones. No one was exempt from the work, even though my brothers were toddlers. Ivory Mae pushed wheelbarrows over planks laid down by Simon Broom, her second husband and my father.

She set out to make a garden that ran for a hundred and sixty feet along the side of the house, and planted camellias, magnolias, and mimosas—rain trees, they called them, for the way their pink flowers fell in drifts. She planted gladiolus and pink geraniums, as she had seen her mother, Amelia, do on Roman Street. Simon planted two cedar trees in front near the ditch that marked Wilson Avenue. Nothing had yet been paved.

They hung narrow black house numbers near the front door

in a crooked vertical line. This is where we—the three children Simon Broom brought with him from his first marriage, the three my mother already had, and the six they made together—grew up.

IN AUGUST, 2005, MY FAMILY SCATTERED. I LIVED IN A TOWN HOUSE IN Harlem, two doors away from my older sister Lynette. She had come to New York at nineteen for fashion school, but was making a living as a makeup artist. I worked at a national magazine. On the day we heard the hurricane warnings, Lynette and I were swinging out at the Charlie Parker Jazz Festival, in Marcus Garvey Park. While I was tapping my foot, my mother was evacuating with my sister Karen and her two children.

My brother Troy left his carpentry job early and was making his way to them. The confusion lent them time: everyone packed a single bag. My mother called the nursing home where Grandmother was an Alzheimer's patient, after realizing that there wouldn't be enough time to get her. The nursing home promised a speedy evacuation.

My brother Eddie called from the highway, on his way to Missouri, to say what everyone already knew: Get out. Ivory Mae and the others headed to a cousin's house in Hattiesburg, Mississippi. What was normally a two-hour drive became five. My sister Valeria drove east with her two daughters and their children. When she finally stopped driving, she was in Ozark, Alabama.

CARL AND MY BROTHER MICHAEL SAT OUTSIDE THE YELLOW HOUSE that day, grilling.

"You gotta realize," Carl told me later, "it's August, it's beautiful, a Sunday. I cut all the grass, weed-eated and everything, had it looking pretty."

He went on, "It got to be dark, eight or eight-thirty, still no rain or nothing." He packed up his ice chest and said goodbye to Michael, who left to meet his girlfriend at their house, on Charbonnet

Street, in the Lower Ninth Ward. It was already too late; he knew they wouldn't be travelling far. They made their way to a friend's elevated apartment in the Lafitte Projects, in the Treme, where they slept outside on balconies.

Carl took Chef Menteur to his one-story house, just off Paris Road, in the East. Mindy and Tiger, his Pekinese dogs, greeted him at the door. The telephone was ringing. "Mama and them kept calling, saying, 'Boy, get out of the house,'" he told me. He sat in his recliner and fell asleep so that the TV was watching him.

A little later, he woke and made small preparations. He had lived through Hurricane Betsy, in 1965. He knew what to do. He pulled the attic steps down and placed his hatchet and ice chest near them. He went back to bed.

"About three, four o'clock in the morning, the dogs in the bed scratching, licking on me," he said. "It's dark, you could hear it storming outside, sound like a freight train derailing. I put my feet down. Water."

He put Mindy and Tiger on the attic steps. "Stuff crashing, stuff flying. I can't see nothing, but I know the house.

"I go in the icebox, take the water out. Five minutes later it come off the ground. Floating. I got to go up now myself. I got pajamas on. I took a pair of jeans—I still got them jeans, my Katrina jeans." He climbed into the attic to wait. "I got my light on my head," he said. "That water coming higher and higher."

After five hours, it stopped.

MY MOTHER CALLED ME FROM HATTIESBURG. SHE SAID, "WATER IS coming into the house. We're calling for help." The phone cut out right as she was speaking. For the next three days, those two lines kept replaying in my head—during half-sleep and at my job, where I pretended to have it together.

Water is. We are. Calling. Help.

CARL SPENT THE NIGHT IN THE ATTIC. IN THE MORNING, THE WATER started rising again. He figured that the levees had collapsed or been blown up.

He took up his axe.

"I said, 'I got to get through this attic now.' Never panic—you can never panic. I'm cutting through that sucker. Once I got my head out, I looked around."

Men who were stranded on rooftops several houses down called out. It was beaming on the roof, but suffocating in the attic. He and the other men stayed up talking until about midnight. Someone told stories about alligators in the water, but Carl didn't know if that was the truth or just exhaustion speaking.

Back in the attic, the dogs ran wild, never sleeping.

After three days, Carl and another man started swimming. They reached an apartment complex that housed the elderly. "We stayed there a couple of hours. One dude had food and was grilling and smoking cigarettes." Carl was hungry, but if he ate he would have to use the bathroom.

Days passed in this way, as Carl travelled between his roof and the apartment complex. From the roof, he could see the staging area on the interstate where boats dropped the rescued. "We knew they was eventually coming to get us, but you go to getting mad anyway," he said.

On his seventh day on the roof, rescuers arrived: "White guys from Texas on big old airboats." Carl was deposited on the interstate, and he set off toward the Convention Center, where people were taking refuge, using his shoelaces as leashes for the dogs.

Carl stayed on the perimeter of the Convention Center, watching the clamor from a distance. After days of observing the growing and agitated crowd, Carl and a few friends started walking toward the interstate. At the base of the Orleans Avenue ramp, close to where he normally spent Mardi Gras, he found a boat with paddles.

The men rowed down Orleans to Broad Street. That night, they stayed in the boat, tethered to the huge metal roll-up gates of the Regional Transit Authority parking lot, stranded cars and buses just inside. "Just like we were fishing somewhere," Carl said.

The next morning, they made their way to the freeway bridge at Tulane and Broad, joining a long queue of boats. Inmates from the Orleans Parish Prison, in orange jumpsuits, were being evacuated by helicopter. Afterward, Carl headed to the top of the bridge with his dogs and climbed into a helicopter. "I'm home free now. I'm there now," he said when he saw Louis Armstrong International Airport, a few miles from Grandmother's house.

Inside the airport, people lay on stretchers and on luggage carts. Carl ate his first solid meal—red beans and rice—before he and the dogs walked a mile down Airline Highway to a cousin's house on the River Road. The cousin drove him the final mile to Grandmother's house, where the lights had never gone out.

TO FEEL LESS HELPLESS, I HAD FLOWN TO VACAVILLE, CALIFORNIA, where my brother Byron lives. My mother and her crew had eventually made their way there, in the days after the storm. When Carl finally called, after two weeks, we let out a collective sigh: *Cuuuuurrrrrl.*

It rained more than usual in the days after Carl got to Grandmother's house. He imagined water topping the levees nearby and stayed up all night watching. Even after the rain quit, the water could still do something, he knew.

His stomach hurt constantly and he suffered from headaches, but his physical ailments, he told himself, were due to the water. It just needed to run through him.

WE HEARD FROM MICHAEL A FEW DAYS AFTER CARL ARRIVED AT Grandmother's house. He had made it to San Antonio.

Three weeks later, Grandmother was still lost. Only a hundred and twenty of the nursing home's three hundred and seventy patients got out before the storm hit. A second group left three days later, on September 1st. By then, thirteen patients had died. Eventually, a cousin found Grandmother's name online: Amelia Williams, Briarcliff Health Center, Tyler, Texas. She had fallen ill; her organs were failing. Ivory Mae flew to Texas, arriving just hours before her mother died.

In late September, a month after the storm, my family gathered in St. Rose to bury Grandmother. We wanted to memorialize her in the *Times-Picayune*, but no one answered the phone at the newspaper.

A few days after the funeral, we drove to see the Yellow House. At the checkpoint on Chef Menteur, Carl flashed his NASA employee badge. "I'm legal," he said to the officer. At the house, my mother stayed in the car, hand cradling the side of her face, a surgical mask over her nose and mouth, while we poked our heads through its blown-out windows. The house had split in two—we could see straight through to the lavender-walled room that was once Lynette's and my childhood bedroom. The walls of the narrow house bulged toward us as if it were threatening to spill its guts. No one made a sound.

We went on to visit Carl's destroyed house. He was desperate to recover his weed-eater. My mother begged him, "Just leave it, Carl—I'll get you another one," but her voice was muffled by the mask.

As we looked on from below, Carl loped around the roof, his movements wild yet measured. We formed a semicircle, as if poised to catch him. We were there, it is apparent now, as witnesses to what he had come through. To help him retrieve, in some way, the memory.

IN MAY, 2006, WHEN LESS THAN HALF OF THE NEW ORLEANIANS DIS-placed by the storm had returned, a letter was delivered to the Yellow

House announcing its intended demolition. Our house was one of almost two thousand on the Red Danger List. These houses bore bright-red stickers no larger than a child's hand.

The notice read, in part, "Dear Ms. Bloom: This serves as your official notification that the City of New Orleans intends to demolish and remove the home/property and/or remnants of the home/property located at 4121 Wilson Avenue. . . . this is the only notification you will receive. Sincerely, Law Department–Demolition Task Force."

That June, the house was demolished without our knowing it. Everyone in my family had been displaced—to Texas, Alabama, California, and Mississippi—and Carl was in the hospital, undergoing surgery for twisted intestines. The only person to see the house razed was our next-door neighbor, Rachelle, who took a Polaroid that she lost and never found. "That land clean as a whistle now," my mother said. "Looks like nothing was ever there."

When the Yellow House fell down, so did, in a way, the view I had of my father. In the summer of 1980, six months after I was born, he died in its small bathroom, of a brain aneurysm. My mother discovered him on the toilet, blood draining from his ear. He had built the house's second story, where the boys ruled. He was a man prone to beginning but not to finishing, and so what I knew of his labors were the temporary stairs that remained in place and the upstairs closet that was meant to contain a bathroom, where I used to hide as a child. From the window there, I looked down on my brothers—Byron and Troy and Carl, sometimes Michael or Darryl or Eddie—while they slept or lifted weights or polished sneakers or ironed creases into their jeans. Sometimes I stayed in the closet for hours while the boys were away, peering down at nothing, stuffed between shoeboxes, hats, and suits.

THESE TRIPS HOME RECALL FOR ME THE LULL OF THOSE DAYS. IT IS partly this: I have no friends to visit, and few outside of my family to call. Most of the people I grew up with are either in prison or buried in the cemetery. This was true before August 29, 2005. Now there is even less to find. Still, I follow the traces, driving alone through a pockmarked New Orleans East.

In my teen-age years, I yearned to belong to the "real" New Orleans, twenty minutes away. My brothers and sisters found jobs there, and so did I, working in ice-cream shops and cafés on the Riverwalk and on Jackson Square. Those of us who worked in the French Quarter and lived elsewhere recognized one another by our stained uniforms, which could feel like marks of dishonor as we walked to catch buses home.

In the eighties, the oil bust set into motion a disinvestment from which the East never recovered. The New Orleans East firm pulled out. The Plaza Shopping Center, which had drawn customers from all over, travelling there on the newly built interstate, lost three of its four flagship stores. White flight happened, and the Red Barn, which had blared country music, became the Ebony Barn. The skating rink closed down and so did the movie theatres. New Orleans East came to be seen as a no man's land, and crime soared.

These events gave new meaning to a proclamation made in a pamphlet commissioned by the developers in boom times: "If ever the future can be studied from the past, New Orleans, augmented by its last remaining section, is surely destined for a tomorrow that neither the facile pen of the journalist nor the measured phrases of a lawyer can express. Posterity will certainly look upon it one day and say, 'What hath God wrought.'"

MY MOTHER AND I MAKE THE TRIP TO THE ROAD HOME OFFICE, WHERE even the caseworker is surprised that we're still in limbo. It's too late, he says—they're closing down the program. I plead and insist: my mother was sixty-four when the process began; she's seventy-four now.

As long as we owned the land, my mother could sell it to Road

Home in exchange for a grant that would allow her to buy another home. But the program had become an endless loop, bungled and exhausting, seemingly designed to wear you out. My mother tried to make it go. So did my brother Eddie, who has a big job at an oil plant where daily he makes things go.

Because we children were all part owners of the Yellow House, we had to transfer our stakes to my mother. The law firm contracted by Road Home to close the file suddenly changed. Its requests for materials were unclear. My mother would call me in New York, speaking in vague avoidance: "Those people said they need another paper or something." Without the means to hire lawyers, very little advanced.

Days before I arrived, my mother called the law firm and was told that her case had been closed for nonresponsiveness. They had made a single unanswered call.

I tell all of this to the caseworker. My mother stays silent, peeking at the man as if from behind a veil. We take all the required steps to reopen the case. The caseworker promises that he'll do his best—he seems hopeful—but we've heard nothing since then about the status of our case, which is really the question of whether my mother will ever live in her own house again.

Recently, the city notified us that our property would be sold for nonpayment of back taxes if we did not appeal within sixty days. My mother called me, upset, saying, "You know I'm not all that business-minded." All I could think was to call the Road Home number and leave another message. "Please tell us what to do," I said.

UNTIL WE KNOW, WE TEND THE PROPERTY. WE ARE CUTTING GRASS FOR the look of it. From above, where the survey images are taken, this would not show.

As usual, people stop by the spot where they know Carl will be. Everyone is dressed up as if going somewhere. Mr. Carl's mom wears a pink visor and matching pants with a gold-and-pink pocket-book resting on one leg. Mr. Carl sits on the other.

"You never came to our Yellow House?" I ask.

She shakes her head.

Michael says, "They got a tree right here, a tree right there," referring to the cedar trees that once framed the front door.

She strains to see.

AFTER A WHILE, THE SUN WANED AND CARL CLIMBED ON THE MOWER. He drove a bit and then asked if I wanted to cut the grass. He sat at the trestle table, where the front of the house had been, and yelled directions. "Push that clutch in!" he called. The mower stuttered and quit.

Someone yelled, "Go 'head, cut that grass!"

At the back of the lot, the view opened up in a way I had never seen. I imagined the time before the houses, when this was marshland, and the time long after that, when my sister Deborah had her wedding reception here. That morning, my father cut the grass to submerge his nerves, and then all of my brothers set up the tables and chairs before my mother laid out the lace tablecloths that she had sewn.

Cutting grass could seem so simple an act, but Carl was drawing a line around what belonged to us. As long as we had the ground, and as long as we kept him company, we were not homeless, which was Carl's definition of tragedy. What will happen when the case is resolved, our house replaced by another house on another lot? Will we ever shake the precarious nature of finding home? I think of all the sentinels, like Carl, who still tend to the remains of what used to be and who have not found a place on earth where they might settle down. I count myself as one.

THE EVENING OF MY LAST DAY IN NEW ORLEANS, THE FAMILY GATH-ered at Grandmother's house. I packed my car with acquired things, mostly plants my mother has grown, things that don't have a chance of surviving northern temperatures. I took them anyway. They remind me of a photograph I love: my mother standing on her land, between the two shotgun houses, a hoe in one hand, a pulled weed in the other, hair a bit wild, her arms open, as if saying, "Ta-da!"

I drove away before sunrise the next morning, as if possessed, completing the fourteen-hundred-mile stretch to New York without stopping for the night, feeling that everything and absolutely nothing was behind me.

TEST CASE

VINSON CUNNINGHAM

March 9, 2020

A little more than half a century ago, New York City attempted an experiment in a handful of its public schools. In the thirteen years since Brown v. Board of Education, the city's public schools had become *more* segregated. Many black parents decided that hope for their children rested in self-determination rather than in waiting for integration. Under pressure from grassroots groups, Mayor John Lindsay, a liberal Republican, approved a plan to create three locally governed school districts, in which community-elected boards would assume a degree of control over personnel and curriculum.

One of the school districts was in Brownsville, a Brooklyn neighborhood that had once been Jewish and middle class but was, by the late sixties, mainly black and poor. Starting in the fall of 1967, the new Ocean Hill–Brownsville district deëmphasized traditional grading, added curricular units on black identity and culture, and, in predominantly Puerto Rican schools, adopted bilingual teaching. The new arrangement was popular with parents, and was supported by a surprisingly heterogeneous coalition that included Black Power separatists and the liberal Ford Foundation. It was opposed by the United Federation of Teachers, which was largely white and Jewish; the union's leader, Albert Shanker, considered the community-control effort to be a veiled attempt at union-busting. Near the end of the school year, the district's governing board dismissed thirteen teachers and six administrators—nearly all of whom were white, and critical of the new arrangement.

Rhody McCoy, the district's administrator, said that "the community lost confidence in them." The union insisted that the dismissals were illegal. Local teachers went on strike. In September, 1968, the strike went citywide.

Gary Simons, the son of a housepainter and a homemaker, had just been hired as a teacher at P.S. 140, an elementary school in the Bronx, his home borough. When the strike reached the Bronx, he was living with a roommate about a half hour north of the school, in the upper-middle-class neighborhood of Riverdale. As the days passed, he noticed that teachers in Riverdale and other rich areas were convening in synagogues, churches, and community centers, continuing to educate their students, albeit unofficially. In the South Bronx, the schools were simply closed.

"That bothered me," Simons said recently. I'd gone to see him in New Milford, Connecticut, where he has lived for a decade, a late-in-life refugee from the city. Simons has a wide face and a John Bolton–like mustache; he had recently had surgery to remove cataracts from both of his cloudy-day-colored eyes. His house is full of glass-enclosed wooden bookcases, in which he keeps a growing collection of hardback first editions of the books he considers to be the most important in the world. The walls are packed with pictures, many of alumni of Prep for Prep, the educational nonprofit that he founded ten years after the strikes. Prep, as its alumni call it, conducts an annual citywide talent search for high-achieving students of color, then administers a battery of exams and interviews. The kids who are accepted by the program agree to spend the summers before and after sixth grade in classes five days a week, and to attend classes on Wednesday evenings and all day on Saturdays during the intervening school year. In exchange, the program secures spots for them at New York's most selective private schools. (The organization's Prep 9 program sends high-school freshmen to boarding schools in the Northeast, such as Deerfield Academy and Choate Rosemary Hall.)

Simons speaks in a nasal and faintly sibilant Bronx lilt, allowing his vowels to accommodate extra syllables mid-thought; sometimes he ascends to a high, gravelly whine when remembering surprise, or confusion, or anger. Back in 1968, he told me, a few teachers at P.S. 140 decided to break the strike early. "I probably was the only white teacher from the school that went in," Simons said. Among the union's black members, the strike was widely seen as a racist backlash against a brief moment of black empowerment. When the strike ended, in November, Simons said, he was "sort of persona non grata." He and another teacher were assigned to a first-grade class with thirty students. Three of the kids, he quickly noticed, were far ahead of the others academically—almost disruptively so. The teachers eventually put them in a separate reading group. "And then, when we got to a certain point with the three of them," Simons said, his face brightening with the memory, "it was very clear that one was much abler than the other two."

When Simons was young, his father would sometimes come home with armfuls of flowers from the garden of a house he'd spent the day painting on Long Island. On the acre behind his home in Connecticut, Simons tends to a bevy of flowers and bushes and impressively large trees. Now, as he spoke about that talented first grader, he looked a little like a horticulturalist recalling a prize pack of seed. By the spring of 1969, Simons was going regularly to the boy's house to tutor him. The kid sped through the lessons for advanced second graders, and was ready for third-grade reading, but, in the summer, Simons had to return to his own studies, at Columbia Teachers College. When school started again, in the fall, the three advanced students were given reading that was several levels below where they'd left off, on the assumption that low-income kids inevitably slid backward over the summer. Simons was furious—he resolved to make extra efforts on behalf of his especially gifted students. One year, when he was teaching third grade, a "group of about six parents marched themselves into the principal's office and insisted that I be able to take the kids on to fourth grade," he said. A few years later, he shepherded a fifth-grade class to the end of elementary school, and then contacted several prep schools on the students' behalf, assuring the admissions and financial-aid officers that the children would fit right in at their exclusive institutions. Among these students was a son of Puerto Rican immigrants named Frankie Cruz, who would go to Calhoun and Hotchkiss and later become a poster boy for Prep. Simons's lucky discovery of him is something like the program's founding myth.

Simons knew that there were bright but understimulated kids all over the city. Maybe, he thought, he could place more of them at schools worthy of their talents—new lilies in the old soil of élite education. In 1978, he secured funds from Columbia and from a Sears in the Bronx, hired a few teachers, and got space for classes at the Trinity School, on the Upper West Side. Trinity's headmaster, Robin Lester, became an evangelist for Simons's mission. "I used to call him St. Gary," Lester told me. Most of Lester's peers didn't see a fresh influx of minority talent as a top priority, but a few younger admissions officials and school heads, shaped politically by the civil-rights movement, were immediately on board. The plan that Simons had outlined for Prep for Prep echoed the approach of A Better Chance, a national organization that was founded in 1963 to help poor black students and now focusses on ethnic diversity without attention to income. (Notable alums include the recent Presidential candidate Deval Patrick and the singer-songwriter Tracy Chapman.) These administrators were part of a vanguard that would eventually establish diversity of this sort—the simple fact of more nonwhite faces in a room—as a preoccupation of their profession.

Simons knew nothing about management, or what it would take to raise money from wealthy people for an annual budget. "To me, a board was a piece of wood," he said. But he had strong opinions about what the kids should learn. He also "had a work ethic to beat the band," according to Dominic Michel, who worked as a deputy to Simons for many years. Simons held staff meetings that stretched into the evening, and he assigned his students piles of homework. When he described the course of study to the admissions director at the Ethical Culture Fieldston School, she said, "Gary, if by the end of the first summer there are four or five kids still standing, pin a badge on each one of them and quit while you're ahead."

I WAS ACCEPTED BY PREP IN THE SPRING OF 1996, AT THE AGE OF ELEVEN, and my life has, in many ways, ordered itself around this early and somewhat arbitrary triumph: when I was a kid, I did well on a test.

I was a soft and oversensitive only child, afraid of failure. During my first week of classes, I would sit at home, in my makeshift study at the dining-room table, holding my head in my hands, overawed by the amount of work I was being asked to do. The kids I met at Prep were bright and hyperverbal; even the ostensibly cool among them had an obvious nerdiness that they had stopped hiding now that they were away from their normal schools. Rounds of Magic: The Gathering, a role-playing card game, turned gladiatorial at lunch; Tamagotchis—small electronic Japanese toys on which you'd tend to a digital creature—were passed around like samizdat pamphlets. We were a hundred or so of a kind, all humming with the seductive feeling of having been called out from a crowd. Grouped into small units of about ten, and placed under the charge of high-school-age and college-age advisers who'd gone through the program before us, we quickly developed fellow-feeling. What we had most in common were noodgy, hard-driving parents, the type of people who'd push their children to attend supplemental schooling for a year and a half.

Some of my new friends had horror stories about their schools. They talked about walking through metal detectors and sitting through fights in classrooms where there were more than thirty or forty students. That wasn't my experience. I'd been attending a

Catholic boys' school in Harlem, where all the students were black or Latino, except for one white kid named Alex, who always looked bewildered. We wore slacks and ties and memorized the names of the books of the Bible. I had to write weekly essays for a class called Literature, Speech, and Writing and recite them aloud. The sweet, stern woman who taught the class judged our performances, on composition and delivery, and gave chocolate to those who did best. When I was in trouble—I was often in trouble—I'd have to stay after school and write some bland penitential sentence a hundred times, until my wrist was sore and the meat of my hand was numb. This was called JUG, for Justice Under God.

At Prep, the only G whose justice we feared was Gary. On many Friday afternoons, at lunch, in the Trinity cafeteria, Simons would stand before us, his mustache hiding his mouth, and rattle off a fresh list of kids who had left or been dropped from the program, because they couldn't keep up. Even more powerful than the fear of dismissal was a kind of wonder at our exotically well-resourced surroundings. Trinity's science labs had smooth tables and deep sinks, Bunsen burners and goggles, powerful microscopes we used to scrutinize slides of our own cells. There was an Olympic-size pool in the basement and turf on the fenced-in roof, both open to us at recess. We were being prepared academically, but we were also being made to understand anew what a school could be.

Our instructors gave us a foretaste of the eccentric and informal adults we would meet at the prep schools where we would later be placed. I studied Latin with a wisecracking Englishman who made constant, morbid fun of Caecilius, the Pompeian nobleman who was our textbook's protagonist. ("*Caecilius est in horto*," we'd recite. "And now," the teacher would say, pantomiming horror at an exploding volcano, "*Caecilius mortuus est.*") The literature curriculum moved swiftly through lighter fare, such as Conrad Richter's "The Light in the Forest" and Maia Wojciechowska's "Shadow of a Bull," to potentially age-inappropriate stuff, like Richard Wright's "Black

Boy." I read the latter under the close attention of kids in their second Prep summer, who told us younger ones the pages where we could find the hanging of a kitten and loose bits of racial-sexual reverie.

If you were having trouble in class, you were supposed to ask for a meeting with a teacher. For no reason I can determine, apart from my mother over my shoulder in the dining room—sometimes she'd sit at the computer and transcribe my essays as I spoke them aloud, like a prepubescent Milton—I learned to love the program, and made it through.

Two decades later, on a July afternoon, I visited Trinity again, where a new batch of Prep kids was missing out on a lovely day. Bluish light streamed into the classrooms as if to tease the suckers within. The typical Prep contingent has about a hundred and twenty-five students. They are bused from all over the city to wherever Prep's courses are being held—usually Trinity—and divided into classes according to math aptitude. Every first-year kid takes a period of literature, a period of intensive writing instruction, a period of history, a period of laboratory science, and one or two periods of math. Most also take Latin. I peeked in on a second-summer literature class, where students were talking about Odysseus and his lonely though by no means solitary ramble around the ancient world's mythical-physical map. The teacher wanted to know what the students thought about his character—what it meant when he asked for and accepted help, and whether his virtues in any way mitigated his obvious, trip-extending flaws. Kids piped up one by one, each adding to the class's group portrait of the wave-tossed, homesick man. I recognized the approach: Prep's teachers often use literature to teach something akin to ethics, and to illustrate the values that might be useful in succeeding at, say, a challenging new school. Elsewhere, in a long-standing Prep class called Problems and Issues in Modern American Society, students discussed the carceral state and its effects on black communities.

I saw love and care reflected by each detail in the room: the bright backpacks, the pressed clothes, the manners and the syntax that had been hammered into place by parents anxious about how their children might be seen in the world. (My mother hunted slang and unconjugated verbs as if they were big game.) Like the parents in Brownsville, they had noticed something amiss in the system that was supposed to steward their kids, and they had made a bid for control. I knew how radically these efforts might change one's life: my wife and most of my best friends are Prep alums; much of what I have that is good I can trace back to the program. The change isn't only personal. No matter the context, certain privileges accompany being thought smart: teachers kindle your ego; people listen when you talk. And, at a mostly white private school, in a society eager for signs of success, each plucked-out black or brown kid carries an unspoken message. With every new way of seeing comes, subtly, a new way to be seen.

THERE WERE CRITICISMS OF PREP'S METHODS FROM THE BEGINNING. People asked Simons whether it was wrong, in a system marred by disparity, to focus on students already advantaged by their intelligence. This concern made him livid, he told me. "It is precisely these kids who are losing the most, because of the difference between what they're achieving and what their potential is," he said. Simons regarded human intelligence as a special substance that, if left untapped, would sour, and he believed that this was happening all over the country. "He thought, in some cases, that we were producing very gifted criminals," Lester, the Trinity headmaster, told me. Simons studied at Teachers College under Abe Tannenbaum, a pioneer in the identification and teaching of "gifted and talented" children. Each Prep applicant takes an I.Q. test—I remember solving puzzles in a wood-panelled room on the Upper West Side, stressed about my speed. When I spoke with Simons in Connecticut, he frequently, and with obvious relish, launched into tangents about various kinds of I.Q. tests, and about how a stellar writing sample could, in rare cases, trump test scores.

By the time I went through the program, in the mid-nineties, Simons had more or less acclimated to life as a nonprofit executive—and Prep, bolstered by a highly motivated board of directors, was easily raising the money to cover its yearly budget, which had grown to several million dollars. *New York* had put the program on its cover in 1985, along with the headline "The Best Prep School in Town." In 1986, Simons created the Lilac Ball, an annual ceremony for Prep students who have been accepted to college. The event doubled as a large fund-raising gala, and quickly became a fixture on New York's philanthropic circuit.

Simons had also developed what he believed to be his best idea yet: a so-called summer advisory system, which employed older Prep students as mentors to guide younger kids through the first summer, making life easier for newbies and insuring a loyal and motivated body of alumni. To lead the effort, Simons tapped Frankie Cruz, who was about to graduate from Hotchkiss. Cruz headed up the summer advisory system during his college years—he attended Princeton—and then went to work for Prep full time.

By showing how much demand there was among private-school admissions officers for exceptional students of color, Simons established a template. Oliver Scholars was created in 1984, to prepare "high-achieving Black and Latino students from underserved New York City communities for success at top independent schools and prestigious colleges." The Posse Foundation, which recruits talented high schoolers and sends them in small groups to a number of selective colleges and universities, was founded in 1989. An economy was growing, and its chief product, smart black and brown kids, was increasingly visible, if still decidedly outnumbered, on élite campuses. But Simons was restless. He'd envisaged Prep as a simple series of chutes out of poverty and the working class. Now he saw how to make it something more. Each year, Prep kids were being voted class president or head of student government at their schools. "I began to realize that although, initially, my intention was to give these kids a chance because I thought it was just outrageous how the deck was stacked against them," he told me, "these kids were also potentially, like, *national treasures*. And not to have their potential developed is a loss to everyone else." He decided that Prep would become a "leadership development" organization. "I realized that this was a way to raise a lot more money, on the basis that the larger society stood to gain," he said.

In the mid-nineties, Simons called Charles Guerrero, a Prep alum who grew up in the Bronx, went to Harvard, and then moved to San Francisco, in part to start a theatre company with a group of his friends from back East. "Prep had a reputation at the time— sometimes deservedly so—that they only pushed people toward business and law, and if you did something a bit weirder you'd be off their radar," Guerrero told me. Simons, known for having favorites, supported Guerrero's adventure in art. Later, Guerrero became one of Prep's longest-serving employees. He's now the director of admissions at his alma mater, the Ethical Culture Fieldston School.

Simons asked Guerrero to look over his plan for a new leadership curriculum. "I thought it'd be five or six pages, so I said sure," Guerrero told me. Soon, a stack of more than a hundred typewritten pages arrived in the mail. Simons laid out a three-part course of study—which included reading assignments, classroom sessions, movie screenings, and hours-long role-playing simulations—that would identify the "attributes," "ethics," and "tactics" of leaders, focussing on the difficulties inherent in a pluralistic democracy. This curriculum, called Aspects of Leadership, began with a few specially selected students but soon became mandatory for high-school-age Prep kids. For many years, the classes were held at an estate in the village of Wappingers Falls, New York, where kids would stay for three nights at a time, during winter and spring breaks. (Now, to save money, they're held in the city, and have no overnight component.)

The curriculum was an extension of what Simons called the "Prep ethos," which he'd been trying to impart informally all along. In the early days, when the program was still serving a fairly small number of kids, he'd sit them down in a hallway after a long Saturday of grinding work and give motivational speeches, to remind them of the rewards that awaited if they just kept going. One of the signature classes at Prep, on ethics and personal responsibility, is called Invictus, named for the William Ernest Henley poem: "I am the master of my fate, / I am the captain of my soul."

"One thing that I didn't always articulate—but, if you think about it, it's built into the whole fabric—is that I have always been appalled at the whole ethos of victimization," Simons told me. "Because, if you get people to subscribe to it, it's like squeezing all the air out of the balloon. You're taking away the psychic energy that could propel them." When he talked to prospective parents, he made this point again and again. "One of the things we're going to be doing is telling your kids every which way from Sunday that they can do it," he recalled saying to parents. "That whatever obstacles remain"—racial, social, economic—"They can overcome them. If the message you're giving your kid is directly contrary to that, it's too much cognitive dissonance for an eleven-year-old to be asked to deal with."

For some, this emphasis on the individual ability of a handful of students is a fundamental flaw in the program's design. Nikole Hannah-Jones, the *Times* journalist who created the 1619 Project—which marked the four-hundredth anniversary of black people's arrival in the Americas with a multifaceted argument about the persistent effects of slavery and its aftermath—is writing a book about school segregation. She told me that programs like Prep obscure the system's deep inequalities. "They allow us to say, 'If kids really wanted an education, if they wanted to work hard, they could get it. Look at this program! They can apply for this program!'" she said. "And it allows us to sustain all the other inequality and feel O.K. about it, because we've given this very small avenue to this small number of kids who 'wanted it.'"

One summer day, I visited an N.Y.U. building on the eastern edge of Washington Square Park, where an Aspects of Leadership session was taking place. In recent years, Prep has added an extra day to the retreats, called Day 4, during which students design and lead their own lessons. A group of maybe a dozen high schoolers were standing side by side in a wide hallway, participating in an exercise meant to illustrate the workings of privilege. "Take a step forward if your parents own their home," the girl who was leading the exercise shouted out. "Take a step back if your parents don't speak English as a first language." When the exercise was over, the person farthest ahead was Mike O'Leary, a peppy visual artist who helps run Prep's leadership programming and who was the only white person in the room. I couldn't help but imagine Simons rolling his eyes.

PREP WAS BUILT ATOP A FAULT LINE OF AMERICAN EDUCATION. IN 1778, shortly before he became the governor of Virginia, Thomas Jefferson drafted A Bill for the More General Diffusion of Knowledge. In Jefferson's vision, all the free boys and girls in the state would spend three tuition-free years learning "reading, writing, and common arithmetick" and becoming "acquainted with Græcian, Roman, English, and American history." Of the boys in each district whose parents were "too poor to give them further education, some one of the best and most promising genius and disposition" would go on to grammar school. The others—along with all the girls and the nonwhite children—would be left behind. Jefferson's bill gave rise to the Act to Establish Public Schools, which the state passed but largely ignored. It was not until the "common school" movement gathered momentum, in the eighteen-thirties and forties, that public education began, gradually, to take hold. The movement's ideals were most famously promulgated by the Massachusetts reformer Horace Mann, who believed that education could be "the great equalizer of the conditions of men."

When Teachers College was established, in 1887, it created an experimental school, and named it for Horace Mann. It is now a notoriously exclusive preparatory school that sits on a grassy campus overlooking Van Cortlandt Park, in Riverdale. This is where I was placed, by Prep for Prep, in the fall of 1997. Thanks in large part to R. Inslee (Inky) Clark, the school's Waspy, charismatic headmaster from 1970 to 1991, it had become a much more racially diverse school than it had been just a generation before. In the late sixties, Clark had been the director of admissions at Yale, and had helped establish relatively meritocratic admissions standards there, welcoming a stream of Jewish students and then, increasingly, students of color. He also helped initiate coeducation. Clark signed an agreement with Simons, reserving spots in each seventh-grade class for Prep students. (Several years ago, the *Times* and this magazine reported that Clark, who died in 1999, had presided over a widespread culture of sexual abuse of students. The athletic field at Horace Mann that bore his name when I was there has been renamed Alumni Field.)

Nine other Prep students arrived at Horace Mann with me. There were other black and brown kids already on campus, most of them also from Prep or similar programs. In the cafeteria, a group of tables we collectively called the Middle Table was informally reserved for the darker skinned; we often pushed the tables together and used them to anchor marathon games of spades and rounds of the dozens. We were theatre kids and singers, athletes and library shut-ins, student politicians and social outcasts and "loungies" (vaguely political punks who hung out in the student lounge). I straddled worlds, trying and failing at sports, eventually settling for being the manager of the football team; I sang in the glee club and in the boys' ensemble, flitting around the city in a blazer and khakis, harmonizing under Christmas trees in office lobbies. I performed in musicals, too. One year, I played the villain in "Carousel," a seafaring baritone named Jigger. A very kind white English teacher pulled me aside to make sure that I wasn't worried about the unfortunate rhyme.

At meetings of the Union, Horace Mann's multicultural club, we watched standup specials and satirical movies like Spike Lee's "Bamboozled" and puzzled over how our favorite artists had turned the country's lousy realities into something joyful. Alongside my friends, from a jarring double vantage of privilege and its lack, I came to know America better, and began honing my responses to it. I also left America for the first time: during my junior year, my Japanese teacher led a trip to Tokyo, where I spent a few days with a host family, at whose table I ate profusely, terrified to offend, and spoke stilted Japanese in nervous bursts. The next summer, I went with the glee club on a tour of the Baltics, where we sang Verdi's Requiem in huge churches in Tallinn, Helsinki, and St. Petersburg. I knew, without ever being explicitly told, that this kind of rare experience was just as much the point of prep school as what I learned in any of my classes.

One night, during an after-school concert in the Horace Mann cafeteria, a rumor crept through the crowd. It was the winter of 2000, and we'd all been following the story of Amadou Diallo, a young Guinean immigrant who had been shot and killed—forty-one shots, nineteen bullet wounds—by four New York City police officers; they had supposedly mistaken him for a rapist on the loose. An older boy named Damien, also a Prep kid, a football player with a high, flutelike voice—who, later that year, would be elected student-body president—pulled me outside, into the cold, and broke the news: the cops had been acquitted. We cursed and shouted for a while, then just stood there, backs against the wooden fence that ringed the athletic field, shaking our heads.

My friends were my world, and I realize now that I never thought to hope for more than that. Recently, I had dinner with one of them, a classmate at Prep and at Horace Mann named Chris, who is now a private-school teacher and administrator. The *Times* had just published the first installment of the 1619 Project, and, on a WhatsApp group chat that my high-school friends and I have maintained for years, Chris said that a project like that would have changed our lives if it had come out when we were younger. At dinner, over Chinese food, I asked him what he'd meant. Had we needed our lives to be changed? Was high school tougher for us than it was for others? If I was angry then, or had a chip on my shoulder—a thing I was told more than once; I must have learned the phrase around that time—who could really say why? But, even as I asked these questions, one after another in a quick, strained bunch, I wondered why I suddenly wasn't sure I wanted to hear his answers. Chris raised his brow, looking compassionate but also ready to laugh, and asked me about Halloween during our senior year. I had dressed up by wearing my usual dark-gray hoodie but with a sign strung from my neck that said "The Black Kid Who Stole Your Bike." "You were obviously working through something," he said.

WHEN I TALKED WITH SIMONS ABOUT THE ARGUMENTS AGAINST PREP when it began, he said people had told him that Prep kids were "going to have lots of problems socially. They're not going to know who they are. You're going to mess with their minds and their sense of identity and blah, blah, blah, blah. I was getting that from a whole lot of liberals. They were a bigger problem, initially, than conservatives."

In January, 2019, a video showing two students wearing blackface and acting like monkeys surfaced at the Poly Prep Country Day School, in Brooklyn. A demonstration ensued; one of the protesters was the daughter of Diahann Billings-Burford, a Prep alum who started at Poly Prep in the mid-eighties, and later served as New York's first chief service officer, overseeing volunteer programs, during Michael Bloomberg's administration. (Bloomberg has been a major donor to Prep and is a onetime trustee.) Billings-Burford is now the C.E.O. of the Ross Initiative in Sports for Equality. "The kids reached a point where they said, 'This is not O.K.,'" she told me. "They were, like, 'This is our school, and if you valued us you wouldn't ask us to feel like this.'" On Martin Luther King, Jr., Day that year, a multiracial group of students wore all black and boycotted classes.

The incident reminded Billings-Burford of her time at Poly Prep. Late in 1986, a young black man named Michael Griffith died after he was beaten by a mob of white men in Howard Beach, Queens. "Some of our white friends were, like, 'You don't understand, it was just where he was, it wasn't a race thing,'" she recalled. "There wasn't a space to discuss these issues." She later became the head of the student government, and, against the wishes of the school's administration, she led a group of students in creating Umoja, Poly Prep's first black-student group.

Jackson Collins, another Prep alum, now serves as the program's associate executive director. He's also the author of a doctoral dissertation about the experiences of students of color in private schools. He surveyed more than five hundred Prep students and measured their happiness according to three variables: "sense of belonging," "emotional wellbeing," and "racial coping self-efficacy and competence"—i.e., how someone reacts in a moment of racial tension. Among older generations, Collins has found, avoidance is a common tactic, but, he told me, "students and their families are much more candid now, much more outspoken."

A few months before the Poly Prep incident, Prep for Prep, which was celebrating its fortieth anniversary, held a symposium at the Schomburg Center for Research in Black Culture, in Harlem. Alumni and staff walked through the building's atrium in neat suits, vibrant dresses, and polished shoes; bronze light fell from high windows. People hugged and shouted at one another and flagged down favorite teachers they hadn't seen in a while. The symposium featured panels on education and on electoral politics, and during the Q. & A. portions people got into good-natured arguments and tossed out earnest ideas. Should we form a Prep PAC to support political candidates who share our values? Should we start a school of our own?

Prep's current chief executive is Aileen Hefferren, who was the program's operations director and, later, its fund-raising chief before succeeding Simons, in 2002. She has the efficient mien of a newly elected congressperson—speaking quickly and affably, calling dates and figures frictionlessly to mind, swerving purposefully between budgetary and programming specifics and the program's guiding ideals. For the final session at Schomburg, she spoke with Leslie-Bernard Joseph, then the chair of Prep's alumni council. (He is now the C.E.O. of the Coney Island Prep charter-school network.) During the Q. & A. that followed, a tall young alum wearing a floral shirt and a skeptical look stood up. "I want to know," he began, "whether you feel that there needs to be an ideological shift from a white-supremacist, élitist mentality that Prep is at minimum participating in, if not encouraging or propagating." The crowd quieted, and he went on. Many of the Prep kids he knew and had mentored had a "fraught relationship" with "this Prep identity," he said, "given Prep's relationship with white-supremacy norms."

Joseph, who is black—and who looked, to me, as if he sensed the peril inherent in the question—spoke before Hefferren, who is white, could. "There is an answer you want, an answer Aileen believes, and an answer Aileen can give," he said, suggesting that, rather than making her offer any of those, he would field the question. Then he steered his answer toward a pitch to his fellow-alumni: those who are active in fund-raising and charitable giving can bring about the changes they want to see, he said.

I later tracked down the young questioner. His name is Anthony White. He went through Prep 9, attended Choate Rosemary Hall and Georgetown, and got jobs in finance—first at Barclays, then at Credit Suisse, which has a long-standing relationship with Prep. (A number of Credit Suisse employees have served on Prep's board and have been major donors to the program; the bank frequently hires alums as interns, and many go on to work there.) White told me that he had no love for banking but that the money was more than anybody in his family had ever earned, and that he used it partly to provide financial security for his mother and younger sister. He'd worked as a Prep adviser in the summers and, since finishing college, had continued to mentor Prep students. Many of them, he said, felt torn between their genuine interests and what they felt Prep expected of them.

"A lot of people I know are unhappy with what they think Prep wants their lives to be," he said. "The mission itself is élitist. And when you have a mission that's élitist, and then you use these institutions that are élitist, it's difficult for children or teen-agers to even have a healthy self-esteem. A lot of them want to figure out how they can decide their identities outside of these rarefied spaces."

White had always wanted to be a musician. As he talked to these students, he realized that he couldn't advise them in good conscience if he wasn't living his values. He quit his job at Credit Suisse and used some of his savings to start recording music as well as a one-man podcast about pop culture and current events called "The Black Sublime Podcast." He now works as a server at a restaurant in Greenwich Village.

"My real question to Aileen," he explained, "was: How are you going to protect the psychologies of these kids?"

A FEW YEARS AGO, THE SOCIOLOGIST ANTHONY ABRAHAM JACK conducted a study of the experiences of undergraduates of color from low-income backgrounds who attend élite private colleges.

Drawing from nationwide data and his own research, he found that half of these students are graduates of private day schools, boarding schools, or college-preparatory high schools. The study became the basis for his book "The Privileged Poor: How Elite Colleges Are Failing Disadvantaged Students." Class mobility via élite education is not usually an up-from-nothing story. What is more common, in the relatively rare instances of mobility which our society currently provides, is a series of institutional incursions, which lend a kind of jerry-rigged privilege to a chosen few.

Ed Boland worked in Yale's admissions office before becoming Prep's head of external affairs. (He left Prep in 2018.) He first heard about Prep, he told me, during the admissions season of 1989. Everybody had a vague sense of what a prospective Yale student looked like, he said. "They've got grades like this, and scores like this, and attended a summer camp in Maine with a Native American name, and worked at a soup kitchen in France, and had internships at their father's bank," he said. "These experiences are how we have shaped our leadership class for a very long time." He went on, "But, on this particular afternoon in '89, there was this whole crop of kids who had the same kind of Park Avenue pedigree, but with outer-borough addresses. This was not, I hate to say it, your typical 'scholarship kid.' These kids were every bit as strong, and every bit as credentialled—and I'm not just talking grades and scores. The whole package was very Park Avenue." Prep had helped its students not only do well at demanding schools but also signify a kind of social standing. "Prep for Prep is like a stimulus package for an individual," Jack told me. My friends often joke that, instead of a rich parent or a working social safety net, we had Prep.

In 2002, I left New York City for Vermont, to attend Middlebury. There, I learned what a Wasp was. I met kids who had gone to East Coast boarding schools and their analogues in the Midwest and San Francisco. They wore Patagonia fleeces and drank entire glasses of milk at meals. They carried Nalgenes full of water which never seemed to empty. They were friendlier than I knew what to do with.

I also met black kids from other states—North Carolina, Washington, Massachusetts—who belonged to the suburban middle class. We couldn't read one another: they came from families richer than mine, but my education had been tonier. Many of the black Middlebury students who came from New York had attended segregated public high schools in Harlem and the outer boroughs. A few had applied to Middlebury directly, but most had come through programs like the Posse Foundation. (Equality, I was learning, depends so much on mediation, at every step along the way.) These other New Yorkers mostly seemed smarter than I was, but they had not spent the previous several years being initiated into upper-crust education and its folkways. In my early days on campus, I was told more than once, by basically nice white classmates, how much different my speaking voice was from those of the other kids from New York they'd met. What this meant, I knew, was that I sounded, to their ears, sort of white, and that the others didn't.

The academic work wasn't any harder than it had been at Horace Mann, but, by my sophomore year, something in my approach to it had unscrewed itself, fallen loose. I was still diligent about art—singing and doing my best in plays and beginning, tentatively, to write—but, that spring, I stopped going to class, and let late essays pile up. After a flunked semester, I was sent home to New York for a probationary term: I would take classes at Hunter College, part of the City University system; if I earned a B average, I could return to Middlebury. I went home, got the B's, and headed back north. Then I found out mid-semester that I was going to be a father, and I promptly flunked out again.

Twenty years old, frazzled, living with my mother, and in terrifying need of a job, I landed a low-level position at a hospital. On the day I was supposed to start, I couldn't will myself to go. Maybe I was feeling squeamish about the blood and shit that my interviewer, a kind-looking black woman, had taken pains to inform me, in a don't-act-surprised-when-you-show-up tone of voice, would be a constant part of the job. Or perhaps it was the way that she'd said, with something like suspicion, but also with something like concern, "Do you think you're maybe overqualified? I'm surprised you want this job." As if, really, she meant to say, "It looks like you're on a much different path from this one. Keep going."

My daughter was born in the fall of 2005, when I should've been a college senior. I got another job interview, at a well-known education nonprofit in Harlem. The interviewer was tall and heavyset and wore a T-shirt bearing the nonprofit's name in bright letters. As he looked at my résumé, he dragged his eyebrow upward, squinching his forehead into folds. In the summers between school years at Middlebury, I'd worked as a teaching assistant at Prep. "I'm sure that was really nice," he said. "Lotta smart kids." I knew where this was headed. "But, you know, real classrooms—classrooms like ours—aren't really like that. Have you ever broken up a fight? Had a kid curse at you?"

It is an odd feeling to watch yourself be seen—or, worse, read. I was being interpreted, reasonably but not totally accurately, according to the schools I'd gone to and the kinds of jobs I'd had. I didn't feel like a member of the class to which my education said I was someday supposed to belong. I felt like what I was: young, black, jobless, an unmarried father. I wanted to tell those interviewers that I was afraid.

Then Prep stepped back into my life. Luck. A stimulus package. I got a job at the program's headquarters, a brownstone on West Seventy-first Street, shuffling papers in the basement. The job required focus, bureaucratic speed, and an ability to communicate regularly and clearly with a Prep administrator whom I'd known since I was a kid. I was not good at this job. Piles of paper turned my desk into a model skyline. Information went unfiled, spreadsheets unfilled. Whatever I'd learned at school, it hadn't been this.

So Prep recommended me as a tutor for the teen-age son of a black investment banker who was on Prep's board of directors. The banker paid me directly, by the hour, and I sent him occasional e-mail updates on his son's progress. We read plays and short stories and articles from the sports pages, and ran through long sets of simple algebra. The kid didn't like to concentrate; I could relate. One day, I got a call from his stepmother, who was from Chicago. She was supporting a young Illinois senator who was preparing to run for President. His campaign was setting up a fund-raising office in New York, and they'd need an assistant. I knew that I was stumbling into another unmerited adventure. Without having finished college, I rode the first Obama campaign all the way to Washington, D.C., where I worked at the Democratic National Committee, raising money, and then at the White House, where I helped recruit minor functionaries to work at Cabinet agencies. On Friday evenings, I'd throw clothes into a duffel and catch a BoltBus home to hang out with my daughter—and to spend most of each Saturday on the Upper East Side, pecking away at a degree from Hunter College.

I had run up student-loan debt at Middlebury, and I was paying my way through Hunter credit by credit, up front and in cash. Some semesters, out of fatigue or because I was flat broke, I gave up school entirely. Once or twice, I convinced myself that I should quit, that I'd made a fine beginning for myself—unreasonably fine, given the circumstances—as a college dropout. But something about the difficulty of this arrangement, and its maddening slowness, helped me focus. At Hunter, what I learned, I learned well, and in a hungry way I hadn't really experienced since high school. It was the first time since fifth grade that I'd attended a public school. I wasn't advancing anyone's notion of diversity. My classmates were New Yorkers, and therefore from everywhere. Everybody had at least one job, and lots of them had two or three. Nobody strolled across a quad to class—Hunter has no grass—and everybody was always on the train. Many of my teachers were adjuncts, shuttling between one city campus and another; they managed, mostly, to project total sincerity about the subjects at hand. Nobody complained when, lacking a babysitter, I sometimes brought my kid to class. Nothing depended on my presence. I didn't signify.

One professor, a white woman with graying hair who wore a series of rumpled shirts, wept while recounting the events of the twenty-fourth book of the Iliad. By the time she finished, my eyes were puddling, too. I studied the Hebrew Bible with an instructor in his seventies who tape-recorded each of his digressive lectures, intent on one day turning them into a book. A garrulous Southerner taught me early American literature: Winthrop, Edwards, Mather. A fastidious graduate student with a sideline in editing technical manuals taught a seminar on Japanese cinema and another class focussed solely on Kurosawa; I took both, and now, rereading my essays for those classes, I can see that I was starting to learn how to make my close readings bearable as prose. When I finally graduated, at a huge, happily impersonal ceremony at Radio City Music Hall—Chuck Schumer was the featured speaker—I was living in New York again, writing speeches for minor executives at an N.G.O., a few months away from turning thirty. "Twelve Years an Undergraduate," I joked with my friends.

GARY SIMONS STEPPED DOWN AS PREP'S DIRECTOR SHORTLY BEFORE I first left for Middlebury, in 2002. His ouster registered as an earthquake among the alumni, who regarded him both as a father figure and as a remote, eccentric guru. Simons had long presented himself as a kind of educator-saint, and his air of extra-professional intensity had started to wear thin with the board. He had insisted on involvement in every aspect of Prep's operations—including maintaining personal relationships with students, which the board found inappropriate but Simons felt was intrinsic to his work. Although Simons was in tune with the individualism of the age, his shambly persona, tendency to micromanage, and allergy to compromise put him out of step with the era's technocratic drift.

"By the end," Peter Bordonaro, the longtime director of Prep 9, told me, "he was sort of impossible to deal with." A stocky seventy-five-year-old with a dark mustache, Bordonaro, who left the program six years ago, has a philosophical air but speaks with the blunt diction of a lifelong teacher. He is a beloved figure among Prep alumni. We met on a cool day not long after Christmas, at a diner in the West Village. He told me that he's tried not to obsess over Prep since he left, and that he was working on a memoir of his time in Vietnam. He recalled a day, in 1999, when Simons charged into his office and presented him with a memo titled "Prep for Prep in 2000." In it were ten brief—brief for Simons—ideas on how Prep should adjust to a new millennium. One was a plan to focus on young Latino immigrants. "He wanted to find the kids, give them a year of English-language training, and then have them start the preparatory component," Bordonaro said. These days, I noted, a program like that would register as a fairly unsubtle rebuke of the Trump Administration. Would that play well at private schools? "And the fund-raising—Prep's always had to avoid seeming partisan," Bordonaro said.

After leaving Prep, Simons almost immediately started a new nonprofit, Leadership Enterprise for a Diverse America, which, among other things, searches the country for exceptional high-school students in under-resourced communities and helps them gain admission to prestigious colleges. The program is not restricted to students of color; typically, about a tenth of the kids are white. (Simons stepped down from LEDA after just a couple of years, because of medical problems.)

Hefferren was, in some ways, an obvious choice to replace Simons at Prep. She knew the program well and had an extensive background in fund-raising. The educational landscape in New York was shifting: the year that Hefferren took over Prep, Bloomberg was elected mayor, and assumed unprecedented control of the school system. He closed schools, opened smaller ones, and implemented a program of "school choice," in which city residents could apply to attend middle and high schools across the city. He also encouraged the growth of charter schools. Nominally public entities, charters are often run and partially financed by private boards of directors; they can hire non-union teachers and can recruit from a broader pool of students than traditional public schools can. They can also, crucially, craft their own curricula. Some of the donor money that once flowed to Prep began drifting toward those institutions. Philanthropists tend to swim in tight schools, often under the influence of a small group of paid charitable advisers. Ed Boland told me, "Now we often hear, 'I'm very attracted to how successful your program has been, but I'd rather support public schools.'" Prep's budget is now thirteen million dollars; its partner schools offer more than thirty-five million dollars in financial aid to Prep students annually.

This past fall, Leslie-Bernard Joseph—whom I'd seen talk, a year before, with Hefferren at the Schomburg Center—received Prep's annual Alumni Prize. He accepted the award at a private ceremony for generous donors, and took the opportunity to make an announcement. "Prep cannot say with integrity that it fulfills its mission until it has diverse executive leadership that reflects the communities it serves and represents," he said. "What got us here will not get us through." He said that he wanted the five thousand dollars that came with the prize to be used to help fund the search for a new chief executive.

Hefferren, approaching her twenty-fifth anniversary with Prep, had, in fact, already submitted her resignation to the board. Less than a month after the donor ceremony, she announced that she would step down in the summer of 2020. The time had come for "Prep's next chapter," she said, in a statement, and for her "to explore life outside of Prep." I spoke with her shortly after her announcement, and asked what that next chapter might be. She reiterated the value of Prep's current mission. "Not so long ago, people were thinking about, you know, have we reached a post-racial society," she said. "And I think that in the last couple of years people are saying, 'Now, more than ever, Prep for Prep's work is vital.'" The board's search for a new chief executive, led by the firm Spencer Stuart, is under way.

In January, I called Joseph at his office in Brooklyn, to ask what he thought of Prep's future. He'd said in his speech that "Prep's mission has never been about just getting us into private school," and I asked him to elaborate. "We got really good at this one thing, and that became who we are," he said. "Companies that get really good at one thing tend to fall off the face of the earth when they don't change with the times." Maybe the organization could begin to branch out—by, say, selling Prep's curriculum to failing school districts and helping them to implement it. Prep, he seemed to be saying, was too small: the organization needed to help more kids, even if it did so in different ways. Perhaps it could reach beyond New York, and perhaps it could reach those who aren't scooped up in its talent search. It's not enough to promote a "talented tenth," Joseph said, referring to W. E. B. DuBois's notion that "the Negro race, like all races, is going to be saved by its exceptional men." He added, "Our success alone does not open any doors."

FORTY YEARS AFTER THE 1968 STRIKE, THE MIDDLE SCHOOL WHERE IT began, J.H.S. 271, was closed by Bloomberg, for poor performance. The building is now home to three separate schools, including the Ocean Hill Collegiate Charter School. During Bloomberg's tenure, New York's graduation rates improved, but segregation deepened— the city's public schools are as segregated now as they were un- der John Lindsay. In the interim, millions of black children have passed through the system, some served well enough, others hardly at all, none of them ever able to simply assume that the education offered to them by their government would prepare them for the wider world. (A school-desegregation plan that includes a proposal to abolish "gifted" education is being considered under New York's current mayor, the liberal Democrat Bill de Blasio.)

We are all embedded within systems, but each life—each child—is an unrepeatable anecdote. According to the adults I knew when I was a kid, the worst thing in the world was to be a "statistic," subsumed into a mass of low expectations and bad outcomes determined by color and class and sustained by a bureaucracy that was, at best, inept and, at worst, intractably racist. Education, then, was triage; escape was a higher-order concern than reform. Parents murmured about how So-and-So had got her daughter into Such-and-Such school, and had spirited the kid away from a school system whose failures symbolized—and, in many ways, flowed out of—a larger set of brutal social facts.

Before her announcement, I asked Hefferren whether Prep, by its nature, helps to keep broader inequalities intact. "We're going to help create principals, superintendents, education commissioners—people who are going to really change that system," she said. Among Prep graduates, education is the second-most-popular field of work. Is it their—is it our—responsibility to change the system now? Are we succeeding? When I spoke with Nikole Hannah-Jones, she criticized Prep's philosophical orientation, but also told me that she does not begrudge the choice some black parents make to send their kids to such programs. "The onus of fixing the system" should not fall on them, she said.

I thought of conversations I'd had over the years with all the Prep alums I know, about what the program had and hadn't done. One friend, a fellow Horace Mann graduate and a son of Nigerian immigrants, who now lives in Amsterdam and is perpetually astonished at the thick web of public services there, told me, over dinner near his home, "If Gary Simons had devoted his life to single-handedly turning around the whole system, he'd have died

(a) sooner and (b) without having changed that much." And here we were, two kids from nothing much, gently arguing over dinner at a bistro across the ocean from where we grew up. Another alum pointed out to me, at a birthday party, that her son was only a generation removed from the material want she had known, and two generations from the Haiti her parents had left. Yes, it would be good for well-off people to send their kids to public schools, she thought. But, no, she couldn't afford for the "experiment" to start with her son.

To be educated is to be subject to a series of experiments. When Simons was planning the lessons for Aspects of Leadership, he considered adding a section focussed specifically on politics, which would have been reserved for the students who had taken most ardently to the curriculum. These superbly trained young people could go on, he thought, to fix the society-wide problems that had made Prep necessary. The course was never implemented at Prep, but Simons later incorporated it into LEDA. Simons remains a close observer of national politics: on an e-mail list and a blog that he updates more than once a day, he regularly shares thoughts in support of his preferred 2020 Presidential candidate, the unusually bookish thirty-eight-year-old Pete Buttigieg, a graduate of Harvard and Oxford.

In January, I attended an open forum of Prep alumni, held by the search committee that will choose the program's new chief executive later this year. There was a nervous mood in the room, less about the future leader than about the existential issues that the change represented. What, exactly, made Prep different from other similar programs? And now that private schools, on their own, without nonprofit intervention, seek out nonwhite students, starting in kindergarten—often from affluent families—what exactly was the program's role?

Prep has more than three thousand alums now, many of whom

are in their forties and early fifties, with their own children to ago-
nize over. One of them, a father of two, spoke up. "All of us have
to make that decision," he said. "Am I going to send my kids to the
same place I went to?" It was one in a series of rhetorical questions.
The representative from the search committee wrote it down.

PART III
THE POLITICAL SCENE

REACHING FOR THE MOON

JERVIS ANDERSON

December 9, 1972

One morning in June of 1925, when A. Philip Randolph was two months past his thirty-sixth birthday, he was walking up Seventh Avenue, from an apartment that he and his wife had recently taken, at 314 West 133rd Street, on his way to the office of the *Messenger*, the monthly magazine of black politics and culture. Randolph and a close friend, Chandler Owen, had started the magazine in 1917, and for several years it had been what one writer described as "one of the ornaments of its age." But by 1925 the *Messenger*'s brand of politics—Socialist and radical—was in decline, and the magazine, which had never been financially secure, had lost the prominence and a good deal of the status it once enjoyed. As he made his way to work that morning, he was stopped at the corner of 135th Street and Seventh Avenue by a man who doffed a panama hat, introduced himself as Ashley L. Totten, and asked to have a word with Randolph. Totten was a well-built man of medium height, with a strong, handsome face and a decisive manner. A native of Christiansted, St. Croix, Totten had been living in Harlem since 1915 and had been working most of the time as a Pullman sleeping-car porter, out of the New York Central District. Aggressive and outspoken, he had, by 1925, developed a reputation among New York porters as a "firebrand." Totten told Randolph that he had been reading the *Messenger* for several years and had been a regular listener at the Sunday-evening soapbox forums that Randolph and Owen once conducted on the corner of Lenox

Avenue and 135th Street. What he had on his mind was this: Would Randolph consider coming to a social club known as the Pullman Porters Athletic Association and speaking to the members on the subject of trade unionism and collective bargaining? Randolph said he would be glad to.

The meeting was not an accident. Totten had been thinking for several months of approaching Randolph, and, in fact, was on his way to the *Messenger* office, on Seventh Avenue, when he ran into the editor. His invitation to Randolph grew out of widening unrest among sleeping-car porters in New York and other cities over their working conditions and, specifically, over the functioning of the Pullman Company's Plan of Employee Representation—a glorified company union, which Pullman had presented to the porters five years earlier.

Every previous effort by Pullman porters to organize themselves had been crushed by the company, and the ringleaders had been fired. The company simply fixed its wage rates and working conditions, and employees were free either to accept or, if they disliked the terms, to quit. As Totten and his disgruntled colleagues thought about their need to organize a labor union, it occurred to them that there was no better man to undertake the task than Randolph. He had some formidable liabilities, to be sure: his impeccable dress, his "Harvard" accent, and his highly cultivated manners were scarcely compatible with the popular conception of a labor leader or a champion of the workingman's cause. But he also possessed assets that were remarkably expedient to their purpose. Totten knew from reading the *Messenger* and from listening to Randolph's soapbox speeches that no one in Harlem had a deeper understanding of the need for labor unionism or a greater concern for the problems of workers. Randolph was one of the best public speakers that Harlem had ever heard. He also had a magazine, a ready-made platform for a new labor organization. And, most important, he wasn't a Pullman porter. Randolph's preëminent credential was that he could not be picked off by the Pullman Company.

A few weeks after Randolph addressed the Porters Athletic Association, W. H. Des Verney—one of the older and more prosperous New York porters—invited Randolph to a secret meeting at his home, on West 131st Street. Four other porters were there: Totten and Lancaster; Thomas T. Patterson, a tall, courtly, ascetic-looking Jamaican; and R. R. Matthews, a part-time Christian Science reader, who was an inveterate pro-unionist. During the meeting, Totten and Des Verney put it squarely to Randolph: Would he organize the porters? Randolph said that, flattered though he was by the request, he had no further interest in organizing anything. Nevertheless, he would not close the door entirely. He would like to give the idea some more thought, and in the meantime he would prepare a series of articles for his magazine calling public attention to the plight of the Pullman porters.

BY THE EARLY NINETEEN-TWENTIES, THE PULLMAN COMPANY HAD BE-come one of the country's industrial giants and its largest private employer of black labor. Among his neighbors, the porter of the early nineteen-twenties was regarded, on the whole, as a model of solid black citizenship. He had a secure job; he mixed with white people, including many of wealth and distinction; he usually owned his own home, even if he had to take in boarders to pay off the mortgage; he was a pillar of the local church; he saved to send his children to college; he voted the Republican ticket; he subscribed to the American way of life, and, as far as people could tell, he was never unfaithful to his wife. In his community, the porter was not, to be sure, on the same social level as the black middle-class professional—or, at least, so it seemed to the black middle-class professional, who saw the porter as something of a joke. But many people who lacked professional credentials—and who held a less exalted estimate of their own social status—saw the porter as an example of what black men could make of their lives within the limits of their situation.

For several years, however, the majority of the porters had not been as happy in the Pullman service as everyone seemed to feel. A few of them had stopped smiling, not only at their situation but also at the passengers. Such men meant business; they wanted to change both their working conditions and the way the public regarded them. In 1915, when the porter's minimum monthly wage was twenty-seven dollars and fifty cents, the chairman of the United States Commission on Industrial Relations asked the company's general manager, L. S. Hungerford, who was testifying before the commission, "Do you consider twenty-seven dollars and fifty cents a month sufficient for a man who is required to discharge all the duties you have detailed here and to follow all the rules referred to?" Hungerford replied, "All I can say is that you can get all the men you require to do the work."

But that was not the sum of the porter's exploitation. The basic work month consisted of almost four hundred hours or eleven thousand miles, whichever was logged first. No overtime was paid until a porter exceeded one of these figures, and then it was paid only at the rate of sixty cents for every extra hundred miles or twenty-five cents an hour over four hundred hours. Out of his salary and tips, moreover, a porter paid for his own meals and bought his own uniforms and equipment for the first ten years—down to the polish he used to shine the passengers' shoes. And if he ran out of polish on the job he was reported by the white conductor and penalized. A porter was also expected to work many hours or log hundreds of miles a month without pay. It worked this way: A porter scheduled to leave New York at 12:30 A.M. on a train for Washington, D.C., say, was required to report for duty at 7:30 P.M. He spent the next few hours preparing the train for departure and receiving passengers. His paid time, however, did not begin until 12:30, when the train pulled out. And if, at 12:30, there were no passengers, the porter was required to deadhead into Washington, in the hope that there would be passengers coming back.

Then there were times when the porter had to "double out," whether he liked it or not. That is, when he returned from a long run—which may have lasted as much as a week—he could be ordered out on the very next train, without a rest period and at a lower rate of pay. This, of course, gave him no time to shower, shave, change his clothes, or see his family. But if while he was doubling out he was found untidy, unclean, or asleep, he was docked, suspended, or fired. A porter could also be ordered to run "in charge." On such runs, he performed not only his own duties but also those of the conductor. If he was "lucky" enough to run in charge for a month, he received ten dollars above his basic salary. This, of course, was a considerable saving to the company, for a conductor's salary in, say, 1925 was a hundred and fifty dollars a month. "Then, too, there was this thing of George," one porter recalls. "No matter who you were, or how old, most everybody wanted to call you George. It meant that you were just George Pullman's boy—same as in slave days, when if the owner was called Jones the slave was called Jones. It got so you were scared to go into the office to pick up your check, for fear some little sixteen-year-old office boy would yell out 'George.'"

AFTER LOOKING INTO THE HISTORY OF THE PORTERS' WORKING CONDI-tions, Randolph wrote two articles—"The Case of the Pullman Porter" and "Pullman Porters Need Own Union"—which appeared in the *Messenger* in July and August, 1925. They aroused so much interest among the porters in New York that Totten renewed his pressure on Randolph to take on the job of organizing a union. This time, Randolph agreed. An organizing committee was set up, with Randolph as general organizer, W. H. Des Verney as assistant general organizer for the Eastern zone, and Roy Lancaster as secretary-treasurer. Lancaster also became the business manager of the *Messenger*, which Randolph agreed to transform into the voice of the new union.

The Brotherhood of Sleeping Car Porters was inaugurated on the night of August 25, 1925, in the auditorium of the Imperial Lodge of Elks, at 160 West 129th Street. Five hundred people met there that night, and the *Amsterdam News* called the gathering "the greatest labor mass meeting ever held of, for and by Negro working men."

Randolph also told the porters that the Brotherhood would be demanding recognition of the union and the abolition of the Employee Representation Plan; an end to tipping, and a minimum monthly wage of a hundred and fifty dollars; a basic work month of two hundred and forty hours, compensation for deadheading, and an adjustment of doubling out; conductors' pay for conductors' work; and, "not the least . . . is that of being treated like men."

The following day more than two hundred porters came to the *Messenger*'s office—now also the headquarters of the Brotherhood—to join the union. The initial enthusiasm was so great that within two months the Brotherhood said it had a majority of the nine hundred or so porters in New York. But now the message had to be spread. Pullman porters in cities all across the country had to be organized. There seemed no way, at first, for this to be done, because the Brotherhood had no money to conduct a national membership drive. The parent organization in New York took in just enough dues (fifty cents per man per month) to keep itself alive. Randolph turned to his connections among white Socialists and liberals in New York, and the Garland Fund, a supporter of liberal causes, came through with a grant of ten thousand dollars.

By the end of 1926, divisions of the Brotherhood had been set up in New York, Chicago, St. Louis, Kansas City, Seattle, Minneapolis, St. Paul, Omaha, Wichita, Oakland, Los Angeles, Denver, Portland, Washington, D.C., Boston, Detroit, and Buffalo. It had been, and it continued to be, a grueling effort.

Across the country, hundreds of porters were fired as Pullman—through a system of company spies—uncovered their membership in the union. In Oakland, the company retired Dad Moore [, the seventy-year-old porter who had volunteered to organize the local division of the Brotherhood,] from his job as caretaker of the two old sleeping cars in which porters slept. The Brotherhood would have gone under but for the handful of secret union members who defied Pullman's wishes. "I am going to stand by the ship, no matter what happen," Moore wrote in May, 1926, when he was having a hard time raising money for rent. "The sea is ruff and the wind are high but I'll stay with her until she make the harbor." A month later, he wrote [to another organizer], "I will not stop until the flag of the Brotherhood fly high in the breeze of victory. . . . If the ship sink I will be on head end, with such men as yourself . . . and Mr. Randolph."

THE PULLMAN COMPANY HAD NO MORE FORMIDABLE ALLIES IN THE black community than the "Big Negroes," the Negro church, and the Negro press. Dean Kelly Miller, of Howard University, came out against Negro unionism, arguing in the *American Mercury*, in November, 1925, that the best interests of black workers would be served by standing with capital. Most of the prominent black churches outside New York and Boston denied their platforms to Brotherhood speakers, and their ministers preached openly against the union.

The black press was almost solid in its opposition to Randolph and the Brotherhood, the most notable exceptions being the New York *Amsterdam News*, the Chicago *Bee*, the Kansas City *Call* and, briefly, the Pittsburgh *Courier*. To counteract the influence of the *Messenger* as the mouthpiece of the organized porters, the Pullman Company subsidized the publication among loyalists of a journal called the Pullman *Porter-Messenger*. This journal, in its May, 1926, issue, called Randolph a "Lamp Post orator" and the members of

his union "poor, disloyal, yellowed, spotted out, ungrateful, unde-
sirable, beggars for a job, not wanted, exiled, abandoned, set, slipping around here and there under cover Wormy Pullman fruit . . ."

Randolph, an estimable propagandist himself but lacking Pullman's access to publicity, had to rely on his circulars to the porters,
almost all of which were reprinted in the *Messenger*. And in the
March, 1926, issue, fearing that Pullman's all-out offensive might
shatter the foundation of his following among the porters, he threw
himself upon their mercy:

> When I enlisted in the cause, I knew that slander
> would attempt to blacken my character with infamy; I
> knew that among the wicked, corrupt and unenlightened,
> my pleadings would be received with disdain and
> reproach; that persecution would assail me on every side;
> that the dagger of the assassin would gleam behind my
> back; that the arm of arrogant power would be raised
> to crush me to the earth; that I would be branded
> as a disturber of the peace, as a madman, fanatic, an
> incendiary, a Communist, Anarchist and whatnot; that
> the heel of friendship would be lifted against me, that
> love be turned into hatred, confidence into suspicion,
> respect into derision: that my worldly interests would
> be jeoparded. I knew that the base and servile would
> accuse me of being actuated with the hope of reward.
> But brethren, I am undaunted and unafraid. The only
> reward I seek is that your cause secures full and complete
> vindication.

This appeal had the effect of arresting the slow erosion of the
porters' support, and with the signing into law, on May 20, 1926,
of the Railway Labor Act—protecting the right of railroad workers
to organize—dues and membership began to climb again.

THE RAILWAY LABOR ACT PROVIDED FOR "THE PROMPT DISPOSITION" of all disputes between railroad carriers and their employees. To avoid "any interruption to commerce or to the operation of any carrier," the act called upon the two sides in any dispute to meet in joint conference to "make and maintain agreements" on rates of pay, rules, and working conditions. Employee and employer representatives were to be designated without "interference, influence, or coercion," and any dispute that could not be resolved in conference was to be submitted to a federal Board of Mediation. The leaders of the Brotherhood were joyful. The Railway Labor Act seemed a clear affirmation of the porters' right to independent self-organization. It would be merely a matter of time, they felt—the time it would take to exhaust the due process of the act—before their union was recognized as the bona-fide bargaining agent of the porters.

Randolph set the process in motion on September 20th, when he wrote to E. F. Carry, the president of the Pullman Company, calling attention to the provisions of the Railway Labor Act, informing him that porters had "designated and authorised" the Brotherhood to bargain with the company on their behalf, and requesting a conference with Pullman's representatives.

No reply came from the Pullman Company, but that in itself was no reason for alarm. The Railway Labor Act required Randolph to write again if no reply was received after ten days, and on September 30th he sent another letter to Carry. Well aware by now of the contempt in which they were held by the Pullman Company, Randolph and his colleagues probably expected no reply. On October 15th, Randolph notified the Board of Mediation, in a letter, that he had not heard from Pullman and that a dispute existed between the Brotherhood and Pullman, and requested the Board's intervention.

The Mediation Board assigned Edwin P. Morrow, a former governor of Kentucky, to investigate the dispute, and a preliminary inquiry was set for December 8, 1926, in Chicago. The Brotherhood retained Donald R. Richberg, a prominent Chicago labor lawyer—later active in the New Deal—to prepare its brief. Because Richberg, representing the big railroad unions, had helped to write the bill that became the Railway Labor Act, Randolph assured his membership that their case was in capable hands, since Richberg knew more about the act "than any living man in America."

When Morrow opened the preliminary inquiry, in December, the Brotherhood claimed a membership of 5,763—or, based on its estimate of 10,875 porters in the Pullman service, slightly more than fifty-three per cent. Of these, the union said, 4,203 had authorized it, in a referendum held in May, June, and July, 1926, to be their representative. But Pullman had its own figures. By "actual nose count," it employed 12,354 porters, the company replied. Furthermore, it claimed, in an Employee Representation Plan election that it had recently conducted, eighty-five per cent of the porters had voted to be represented by the company's plan. Therefore, it argued, the Brotherhood "does not now, and never has represented a majority" of Pullman porters. Morrow then adjourned the inquiry, instructing the disputants to await word of its resumption.

The Brotherhood had been totally unprepared for Pullman's claim that eighty-five per cent of the porters had voted in the company-union election. There was no doubt in the minds of the Brotherhood's leaders that the porters had been intimidated into voting for the company's plan, since those very porters had authorized the Brotherhood to be their representative. Such coercion was a clear violation of the Railway Labor Act, and evidence of it would have to be gathered and submitted to Morrow when he reconvened the inquiry. As evidence of coercion, Randolph collected nine hundred affidavits from the porters, swearing that the Pullman management had forced them to vote against their will. A porter in Chicago, who was asked by a superintendent why he did not vote, asked in return, "Does a man have to vote in this plan?" The superintendent replied, "You do not have to go on the new train; you do not have to work for the Pullman Company unless you want to; and you do not have to live unless you want to."

By June of 1927, the porters' enthusiasm had waned again. [Milton] Webster, [the leader of the Brotherhood's Chicago division,] had written to inform Randolph of "considerable uneasiness" among the men. And Randolph, who was contending with a similar uneasiness among the porters in New York, replied, "I know just what you are up against."

He may even have begun to lose faith in the Railway Labor Act, for on June 9th, when he still had heard nothing definite from Morrow, he seems to have been shaken. Taking a friendly and amicable tone, he wrote a fifteen-page letter to Carry, in which he assured him that "the Brotherhood is building a new porter, upstanding, responsible, efficient, with initiative and constructive, practical intelligence, who will work to build up a bigger and better Pullman industry to serve the nation," and went on, "You will find the Brotherhood ever ready fully to coöperate with you frankly, intelligently, loyally and honorably to achieve this end mutually beneficial to the property and human and business elements of the Pullman industry."

The letter was a tactical blunder from which it would take Randolph years to recover. Shortly after the letter from Randolph had been received, the company's general manager, L. S. Hungerford, wrote to Morrow:

> When the Railway Labor Act was passed . . . there was in effect, and now is in operation an agreement between the Pullman Company and its porters and maids. This agreement fully meets all the requirements of the law. . . . No dispute, and therefore no situation requiring mediation, exists between the Pullman Company and its employees of the classes mentioned. . . . In these circumstances, and because of the existence of the

agreement . . . the Company cannot properly confer [with the Brotherhood].

Thus, when Morrow finally got around to reconvening the Mediation Board's inquiry, in July, he could not have been surprised to learn that the Pullman Company refused to send a representative. In any case, the company left Morrow no alternative—or so it seemed—but to inform the parties that "efforts to bring about an amicable adjustment through mediation of the dispute . . . have been unsuccessful." The dispute, he said, was now a matter for arbitration. Randolph was ready and eager to go along. He had no choice, for he had nothing yet to show the porters. But Pullman was now firmly in control. Not only was it free of any urgent need to appeal to the good offices of the federal government but it also knew something that Randolph and the Brotherhood either did not know or had forgotten: though arbitration was provided for under the Railway Labor Act, it was not mandatory. Therefore, the company simply reiterated to Morrow, "As no dispute existed . . . which required mediation, and the status not having changed, it follows that there is now no dispute and therefore no cause for arbitration." As of July 12, 1928, the case was retired and John Marrinan, the Board secretary, informed both sides that the Mediation Board had "exhausted its efforts under the law," and that "nothing can be accomplished in the further handling of this case."

Six days after the Pullman Company refused to enter into arbitration, Randolph told the porters, in a press release, "The fight has just begun." Pullman's refusal to arbitrate was "a challenge to the manhood of every Pullman Porter," he wrote. And, in a letter, he said, "We are now in the fight to the finish and propose to go the limit to beat the company into submission. . . ." Those were brave words—partly meant to revive hope among the porters, and partly presenting an accurate description of his determination. In speaking thus, Randolph was pinning his hopes on the last resort that remained to the Brotherhood under the Railway Labor Act. The act provided that the powers of the Mediation Board could again be invoked in the event of "any interruption to commerce or to the operation of any carrier." In other words, the Brotherhood could now call a strike, or, in the words of its leaders, create an "emergency."

After the union announced such an intention, it began to re-gain members. But the precariousness of the Brotherhood's situation dictated a strategy so delicate—even innocuous—that it was almost bound to fail. Knowing that the porters were afraid of losing their jobs—since the Pullman Company did not hesitate to replace them—and fearing another large-scale desertion by its membership, the union could not demand from them a firm commitment to strike. Thus, if the "emergency" was to be created, it would have to be created not by calling a strike but by simply indicating the Brotherhood's ability and readiness to call a strike.

In any event, by the beginning of June, 1928, the Brotherhood announced that 6,013 out of 10,994 porters (possibly its own estimate of the total) had voted to walk off the sleeping cars whenever the word was given. With the results of its poll, the Brotherhood now went back to the Mediation Board.

On the morning of June 4th, Morrow, the Mediation Board's chief investigator, called Randolph in to give the Brotherhood's arguments and state the facts. The meeting was purely a formality, however, for by then Morrow's mind was already partly made up. In March, after reading newspaper reports that the union was voting to strike, Colonel Samuel E. Winslow, the chairman of the Mediation Board, had dispatched Morrow to Chicago to look into the truth of the reports. Morrow had talked with Pullman officials and had then informed Winslow:

The following is a fair statement of their [Pullman's] position. They do not believe that any *real* strike is threatened by Randolph or those associated with him. They do not believe that Randolph can induce any considerable number of their employees to leave the service, but is taking a *fake* strike vote in order to induce the board to believe that large numbers of porters will go out of the service.

By the time of the formal conference, in June, the chairman of the Mediation Board had long been satisfied that the porters' union was incapable of causing a genuine emergency. Nor, by then, could Morrow himself—who had not even thought it necessary to consult the Brotherhood—have had much of an open mind on the question. Morrow said he would check the strike ballots to see whether they were authentic. Moreover, he added, it wasn't sufficient for Randolph to threaten an emergency; he would have to give the date on which the emergency would occur. Randolph's hand was forced. Setting a strike date was not part of his strategy, but now that Morrow had asked, he came up with Friday, June 8th.

On June 5th, the day after hearing Randolph, Morrow called in the Pullman Company, whose representative repeated, in substance, what the company had told him in March: the Brotherhood was incapable of disrupting the Pullman sleeping-car service.

It was not surprising, therefore, that on June 6th—a day after his meeting with the Pullman representatives, and two days before the strike date Randolph had given him—Morrow instructed John Marrinan, secretary of the Mediation Board, to send Randolph a letter that said, in part:

> After . . . full consideration [of] the presentations made by both parties and in view of the facts and circumstances surrounding the situation, it is the judgment of the Board that at this time the emergency . . . does not exist.

Randolph, on the contrary, believed that the union was ready and able to cripple the New York yards. On a visit to Kansas City, he found Totten "in a little hole in a Negro business building" collecting knives, clubs, sawed-off shotguns, and boxes of matches. Alarmed, Randolph asked Totten what he was going to do with "the ammunition." Totten replied that he wasn't going to let any strikebreakers into the Pullman yards, whereupon Randolph begged him "to dispense with the hardware." In Chicago, Webster said he expected eighty-five per cent of the porters in his district to respond to the union's call, and, out in Oakland, Moore expected ninety per cent.

Violence was averted, along with the strike itself, when William Green, the president of the American Federation of Labor, who admired Randolph and had been giving his personal support to the Brotherhood's fight, advised the union to call off the strike. Green had met Randolph in 1926, when Randolph had unsuccessfully approached the American Federation of Labor to seek affiliation. Green remained sympathetic toward the porters' cause, however, and not only had developed a personal admiration for Randolph but had been raising his voice in support of the Brotherhood's fight ever since. Now, however, Green told Randolph that the union was still not strong enough to carry off a strike against a powerful corporation like Pullman.

In July, the Mediation Board formally retired the case, after which Randolph wrote them his opinion of their conduct: "May I say that your decision is not calculated to increase the respect of Negro American citizens for the spirit of fair-play of Government agencies where their interests are involved." Still, it all meant that the Brotherhood had failed again. After almost three years of nursing the porters' hopes, it had no tangible gains to show them. And, having exhausted the procedures of the Railway Labor Act, had no idea where to turn next. Heavy with a sense that he had let the porters down, and that his faith and theirs had been betrayed by the

Board of Mediation, Randolph said that the moment of calling off the strike was "next to the saddest" of his life.

THE PULLMAN COMPANY, IN THE WAKE OF ITS VICTORY, WAS FIRING OR suspending every porter who—as far as it could be ascertained—had voted to strike. Over the next two or three years, the Brotherhood lost almost all of its membership. Porters who did not desert the union because of disappointment or to escape reprisals, simply dropped out because, as a result of the Depression, they were unemployed. By 1932, the union's membership, which had risen to almost seven thousand in the early months of 1928, dropped to seven hundred and seventy-one. Almost every divisional office was deep in debt, and the offices in Denver, Omaha, Cincinnati, Louisville, Pittsburgh, Columbus, Norfolk, Albany, and Buffalo had to be closed.

With the May-June issue of 1928, the *Messenger* had folded. The disappointed porters had stopped reading it, and, with the union's dwindling membership, there had not been enough money to keep it going. It had also lost its readership among white liberals and radicals as well as the black middle class. According to C. L. Dellums, "the public couldn't take the *Messenger* anymore. Too much Brotherhood in it."

Dad Moore, who had pledged to "fite to the Finish" and to stick with the Brotherhood "until Deth carry me to my last Restin Place," had died in January, 1930.

By 1933, as far as the public could tell—and as far as the majority of porters were concerned—the Brotherhood was dead. In fact, its obituary had been written two years earlier, when the labor historians Sterling D. Spero and Abram L. Harris said in "The Black Worker," their study of "The Negro and the Labor Movement," "The hope that this movement would become the center and rallying point of Negro labor as a whole is now dead."

THOUGH THE BROTHERHOOD WAS PROBABLY THE SHAKIEST RAIL-road union in America during the early nineteen-thirties, it was not the only one that had been thwarted by company unions, nor was it the only one that had been retarded by the failure of the Railway Labor Act to guarantee the right to collective bargaining. As the Brotherhood had found, the Railway Labor Act, while it provided for the arbitration of disputes, did not have enough teeth in it even to compel management to come to the arbitration table—let alone to abide by the results of arbitration. In 1933, seven years after the act was signed, workers in a hundred and forty-seven of the two hundred and thirty-three largest railroad enterprises were still formally represented by company unions or plans of employee representation. The American Federation of Labor had become disenchanted with the act, and, as Green had told Randolph, was waiting for a favorable opportunity to press for amendment. That opportunity came in 1932 when, with the support of the majority of organized labor, Franklin D. Roosevelt was elected President.

After the election, Donald Richberg, who by now was general counsel of the railroad unions, called a group of labor executives together in Washington to discuss possible legislation "to strengthen the right of self-organization and the power of collective bargaining as already provided in the Railway Labor Act." And not long after that the President appointed Richberg to a committee to draft legislation for a national recovery program. Thus, as the representative of the railroad-union interests, Richberg was largely responsible for one of the most important sections of the National Industry Recovery Bill, which the committee drafted. That was Section 7a, stating that "employees shall have the right to organize and bargain collectively through representatives of their own choosing, and shall be free from the interference, restraint, or coercion of employers of labor, or their agents, in the designation of such representatives or in self-organization," and that "no employee and no one seeking employment shall be required as a condition of employment to join any company union or to refrain from joining, organizing, or assisting a labor organization of his own choosing." These provisions became law in the National Industrial Recovery Act, passed in June, 1933. This act constituted one of the most impressive victories that railroad unions—and the labor movement in general—had ever won.

Reënergized by Roosevelt's legislative revolution, the labor movement—including the Brotherhood of Sleeping Car Porters—launched the most vigorous organizational campaign in its history. New unions were founded and shattered memberships rebuilt. By mid-1933, porters were flocking back to the Brotherhood as Randolph, waving the promises of the National Industrial Recovery Act and the Emergency Railroad Transportation Act, assured them that victory was near—that the Brotherhood had finally "licked" the Pullman Company.

Randolph now wrote to the company again, saying, "As duly authorized representatives of the majority of the porters and maids [the Brotherhood of Sleeping Car Porters requests a] conference to negotiate an agreement on wages and rules governing working conditions . . . in conformity with the principles promulgated by the Railway Labor Act, the Railway Emergency Act and the general program . . . outlined under the National Recovery Act." Once again, as with every letter he had written to Pullman since September, 1926, he got no reply. Randolph then took the next logical step, calling upon Joseph B. Eastman, the Federal Coördinator of Transportation, to intervene and enforce the Emergency Railroad Transportation Act. But Randolph now learned from Eastman something that Pullman must have known all along: by the terms of the Transportation Act, the Pullman Company was not a railroad but a common carrier; thus the emergency legislation applied neither to the Pullman Company nor its sleeping-car porters.

However, Eastman offered to coöperate with any effort the Brotherhood cared to make to seek changes in the emergency railroad legislation. Encouraged by Eastman's promise, Randolph wrote letters to President Roosevelt and to friends of the Brotherhood on Capitol Hill protesting the exclusion of the Pullman Company and its sleeping-car porters and dining-car employees from the provisions of the railroad legislation. And at the fifty-third annual convention of the A.F.L., in Washington, in 1933, he called upon the Federation to urge President Roosevelt "to issue an Executive Order interpreting the Emergency Railroad Transportation act, 1933, to include within its scope sleeping-car companies, thereby correcting a situation that results in the Pullman Company's occupying a favored status."

Embarrassed by Randolph's demands, railroad-labor executives joined officials within the Administration to support the Brotherhood's efforts to rectify the inequities, and early in 1934 the Senate Interstate Commerce Committee opened hearings, with a view to amending the Emergency Railroad Transportation Act and the Railway Labor Act. During the hearings, twenty-one railroad unions urged that the acts be changed to include "sleeping-car and express companies." Despite Pullman's argument that it was more "an innkeeper" than a railroad enterprise—and thus had been properly exempted from the emergency legislation—the Transportation Act and the Railway Labor Act were amended to include sleeping-car companies and their employees.

Suspecting that it was about to lose the long battle against Randolph's union, the Pullman Company suddenly started laying off hundreds of porters whose loyalty to the company was in doubt, desiring to lessen the number of porters who were now trooping back to the Brotherhood. And still hoping, within the letter of the new law, to frustrate its intent, the company handpicked a few loyal porters and authorized them to form an "independent" union, the Pullman Porters and Maids Protective Association, as a legal alternative to the Brotherhood. The Protective Association was in fact a glorified company union—controlled by porters who were controlled by Pullman. Randolph had a few other words for it: "A mushroom sprung forth full growth out of the fertile soil of Pullman gold."

On November 13, 1934, Randolph wrote to the president of the Pullman Company again, requesting a conference, and, for the first time, he received a reply. But it was not the one he had hoped for. The Brotherhood was not "the duly authorized representative" of the porters, F. L. Simmons, the Company's supervisor of industrial relations, wrote. Therefore, "there is no occasion for a conference with you." Randolph then wrote to the Board of Mediation, pointing out that the Brotherhood was the porters' authorized representative under the amended railroad acts. Almost immediately, the Pullman Porters and Maids Protective Association entered a similar claim in its own behalf. To resolve the conflicting claims, the Board of Mediation ordered a secret ballot, and from May 27 to June 22, 1935—ten years since the Brotherhood began its fight for recognition—porters in sixty-six Pullman districts around the country voted.

Victory for the Brotherhood was by no means just around the corner, but it was nearer than ever before. And, sensing this, Randolph wrote to Walter White, executive secretary of the N.A.A.C.P., just before the balloting:

> This is the first time that Negro workers have had the opportunity to vote as a national group in an election under federal supervision, for their economic rights. It is an extraordinary occasion. It is the result of 10 years of militant, determined and courageous fighting by a small band of black workers against one of the most powerful corporations in the world.

When the ballots were counted, on the night of June 27th, in Chicago, 89 were void, 1,422 had been cast for the Pullman Porters and Maids Protective Association, and 5,931 for the Brotherhood of Sleeping Car Porters. Randolph sent White an exultant telegram: "FIRST VICTORY OF NEGRO WORKERS OVER GREAT INDUSTRIAL CORPORATION." And on July 1st the Mediation Board finally certified the Brotherhood as "duly designated and authorized to represent the porters and maids of the Pullman Company."

AT 10 A.M. ON JULY 29, 1935, RANDOLPH, WEBSTER, SMITH, BRADLEY, Dellums, and two working porters—Thomas T. Patterson and Clarence Kendrick—walked into Room 412 of the Pullman headquarters, on East Adams Street, in Chicago. It was their finest moment in ten years. They had forced the Pullman Company to do what one of the union's detractors had said the company would never do: sit down around the same table with "a bunch of black porters."

Anyway, it would take them two years to negotiate an agreement with Pullman. Webster said later, "The Pullman Company was messing around, handing it to us line by line. We couldn't get a full paragraph. We had about a thousand sheets of paper with two lines . . ." McLaurin said that Pullman "just could not conceive of Negroes' sitting across the table talking to them as equals," and added, "It took months and months to get past that stumbling block."

It was not until April 1, 1937—three days after the Supreme Court had upheld the Constitutionality of the amended Railway Labor Act—that the Pullman Company started bargaining in good faith. And it was not until August 25th—the twelfth anniversary of the founding of the Brotherhood—that E. F. Carry told the mediator and the Brotherhood's negotiators, "Gentlemen, the Pullman Company is ready to sign." The agreement, the first ever signed between a union of black workers and a major American corporation, called for a reduction in the work month from nearly four hundred hours to two hundred and forty, and a wage increase of one and a quarter million dollars. Almost overnight, Randolph became the most popular black political figure in America. The Brotherhood had been made a full-fledged member of the A.F.L. a year earlier, when, anticipating its victory, Green had awarded it an international charter. Shortly after the victory, New York's Mayor Fiorello LaGuardia received a delegation of porters at City Hall and praised Randolph as "one of the foremost progressive labor leaders in America." And a few years later, as Murray Kempton has observed, the Brotherhood would "achieve for the Negro a place in society" that the Pullman porter had never before known.

SAINT PAULI

KATHRYN SCHULZ

April 17, 2017

The wager was ten dollars. It was 1944, and the law students of Howard University were discussing how best to bring an end to Jim Crow. In the half century since Plessy v. Ferguson, lawyers had been chipping away at segregation by questioning the "equal" part of the "separate but equal" doctrine—arguing that, say, a specific black school was not truly equivalent to its white counterpart. Fed up with the limited and incremental results, one student in the class proposed a radical alternative: why not challenge the "separate" part instead?

That student's name was Pauli Murray. Her law-school peers were accustomed to being startled by her—she was the only woman among them and first in the class—but that day they laughed out loud. Her idea was both impractical and reckless, they told her; any challenge to Plessy would result in the Supreme Court affirming it instead. Undeterred, Murray told them they were wrong. Then, with the whole class as her witness, she made a bet with her professor, a man named Spottswood Robinson: ten bucks said Plessy would be overturned within twenty-five years.

Murray was right. Plessy was overturned in a decade—and, when it was, Robinson owed her a lot more than ten dollars. In her final law-school paper, Murray had formalized the idea she'd hatched in class that day, arguing that segregation violated the Thirteenth and Fourteenth Amendments of the United States Constitution. Some years later, when Robinson joined with Thurgood Marshall and others to try to end Jim Crow, he remembered

Murray's paper, fished it out of his files, and presented it to his colleagues—the team that, in 1954, successfully argued Brown v. Board of Education.

By the time Murray learned of her contribution, she was nearing fifty, two-thirds of the way through a life as remarkable for its range as for its influence. A poet, writer, activist, labor organizer, legal theorist, and Episcopal priest, Murray palled around in her youth with Langston Hughes, joined James Baldwin at the MacDowell Colony the first year it admitted African-Americans, maintained a twenty-three-year friendship with Eleanor Roosevelt, and helped Betty Friedan found the National Organization for Women. Along the way, she articulated the intellectual foundations of two of the most important social-justice movements of the twentieth century: first, when she made her argument for overturning Plessy, and, later, when she co-wrote a law-review article subsequently used by a rising star at the A.C.L.U.—one Ruth Bader Ginsburg—to convince the Supreme Court that the Equal Protection Clause applies to women.

This was Murray's lifelong fate: to be both ahead of her time and behind the scenes. Two decades before the civil-rights movement of the nineteen-sixties, Murray was arrested for refusing to move to the back of a bus in Richmond, Virginia; organized sit-ins that successfully desegregated restaurants in Washington, D.C.; and, anticipating the Freedom Summer, urged her Howard classmates to head south to fight for civil rights and wondered how to "attract young white graduates of the great universities to come down and join with us." And, four decades before another legal scholar, Kimberlé Williams Crenshaw, coined the term "intersectionality," Murray insisted on the indivisibility of her identity and experience as an African-American, a worker, and a woman.

Despite all this, Murray's name is not well known today, especially among white Americans. The past few years, however, have seen a burst of interest in her life and work. She's been sainted by the Episcopal Church, had a residential college named after her at Yale, where she was the first African-American to earn a doctorate of jurisprudence, and had her childhood home designated a National Historic Landmark by the Department of the Interior. Last year, Patricia Bell-Scott published "The Firebrand and the First Lady" (Knopf), an account of Murray's relationship with Eleanor Roosevelt, and next month sees the publication of "Jane Crow: The Life of Pauli Murray" (Oxford), by the Barnard historian Rosalind Rosenberg.

All this attention has not come about by chance. Historical figures aren't human flotsam, swirling into public awareness at random intervals. Instead, they are almost always borne back to us on the current of our own times. In Murray's case, it's not simply that her public struggles on behalf of women, minorities, and the working class suddenly seem more relevant than ever. It's that her private struggles—documented for the first time in all their fullness by Rosenberg—have recently become our public ones.

PAULI MURRAY WAS BORN ANNA PAULINE MURRAY, ON NOVEMBER 20, 1910. It was the year that the National Urban League was founded, and the year after the creation of the N.A.A.C.P.; "my life and development paralleled the existence of the two major continuous civil rights organizations in the United States," she observed in a posthumously published memoir, "Song in a Weary Throat." Given Murray's later achievements, that way of placing herself in context makes sense. But it also reflects the gap in her life where autobiography would normally begin. "The most significant fact of my childhood," Murray once said, "was that I was an orphan."

When Murray was three years old, her mother suffered a massive cerebral hemorrhage on the family staircase and died on the spot. Pauli's father, left alone with his grief and six children under the age of ten, sent her to live with a maternal aunt, Pauline Fitzgerald, after whom she was named. Three years later, ravaged by anxiety, poverty, and illness, Pauli's father was committed to the Crownsville State Hospital for the Negro Insane—where, in 1922, a white guard taunted him with racist epithets, dragged him to the basement, and beat him to death with a baseball bat. Pauli, then twelve years old, travelled alone to Baltimore for the funeral, where she acquired her second and final memory of her father: laid out in an open casket, his skull "split open like a melon and sewed together loosely with jagged stitches."

Fortunately for Murray, she had, by then, a strong, if complicated, sense of family elsewhere. She lived with her Aunt Pauline in Durham, North Carolina, at the home of her maternal grandparents, Cornelia and Robert Fitzgerald. Cornelia was born in bondage; her mother was a part-Cherokee slave named Harriet, her father the owner's son and Harriet's frequent rapist. Robert, by contrast, was raised in Pennsylvania, attended anti-slavery meetings with Harriet Tubman and Frederick Douglass, and fought for the Union in the Civil War. Together, they formed part of a large and close-knit family whose members ranged from Episcopalians to Quakers, impoverished to wealthy, fair-skinned and blue-eyed to dark-skinned and curly-haired. When they all got together, Murray wrote, it looked "like a United Nations in miniature."

Amid all this, Murray grew up, in her own words, "a thin, wiry, ravenous child," exceedingly willful yet eager to please. She taught herself to read by the age of five, and, from then on, devoured both books and food indiscriminately: biscuits, molasses, macaroni and cheese, pancakes, beefsteaks, "The Bobbsey Twins," Zane Grey, "Dying Testimonies of the Saved and Unsaved," Chambers's Encyclopedia, the collected works of Paul Laurence Dunbar, "Up from Slavery." In school, she vexed her teachers with her pinball energy, but impressed them with her aptitude and ambition. By the time she graduated, at fifteen, she was the editor-in-chief of the school newspaper, the president of the literary society, class secretary, a member of the debate club, the top student, and a forward on the basketball team.

With that résumé, Murray could have easily earned a spot at the North Carolina College for Negroes, but she declined to go, because, to date, her whole life had been constrained by segregation. Around the time of her birth, North Carolina had begun rolling back the gains of Reconstruction and using Jim Crow laws to viciously restrict the lives of African-Americans. From the moment Murray understood the system, she actively resisted it. Even as a child, she walked everywhere rather than ride in segregated street-cars, and boycotted movie theatres rather than sit in the balconies reserved for African-Americans. Since the age of ten, she had been looking north. When the time came to pick a college, she set her sights on Columbia, and insisted that Pauline take her up to visit.

IT WAS IN NEW YORK THAT MURRAY REALIZED HER LIFE WAS CON-strained by more factors than race. Columbia, she learned, did not accept women; Barnard did, but she couldn't afford the tuition. She could attend Hunter College for free if she became a New York City resident—but not with her current transcript, because black high schools in North Carolina ended at eleventh grade and didn't offer all the classes she needed to matriculate. Dismayed but determined, Murray petitioned her family to let her live with a cousin in Queens, then enrolled in Richmond Hill High School, the only African-American among four thousand students.

Two years later, Murray entered Hunter—which, at the time, was a women's college, a fact that Murray initially resented as another form of segregation but soon came to appreciate. Not long afterward, she swapped her cousin's place in Queens for a room at the Harlem Y.W.C.A. In Harlem, Murray befriended Langston Hughes, met W. E. B. Du Bois, attended lectures by the civil-rights activist Mary McLeod Bethune, and paid twenty-five cents at the Apollo Theatre to hear the likes of Duke Ellington and Cab Calloway. Eighteen, enrolled in college, living in New York, planning to become a writer—she was, it seemed, living the life she'd always dreamed of.

Then came October 29, 1929. Murray, who was supporting herself by waitressing, lost, in quick succession, most of her customers, most of her tips, and her job. She looked for work, but everyone was looking for work. By the end of her sophomore year, in the reverse of today's joke about college, she had lost fifteen pounds and was suffering from malnutrition. She took time off from school, took odd jobs, took shared rooms in tenement buildings. She graduated in 1933—possibly the worst year in U.S. history to enter the job market. Nationwide, the unemployment rate was twenty-five per cent. In Harlem, it was greater than fifty.

For the next five years, Murray drifted in and out of jobs— among them, a stint at the W.P.A.'s Workers Education Project and the National Urban League—and in and out of poverty. She learned about the labor movement, stood in her first picket line, joined a faction of the Communist Party U.S.A., then resigned a year later because "she found party discipline irksome." Meanwhile, her relatives in North Carolina were pressuring her to return home. In 1938, worried about their health and lacking any job prospects, she decided to apply to the graduate program in sociology at the University of North Carolina—which, like the rest of the university, did not accept African-Americans.

Murray knew that, but she also knew her own history. Two of her slave-owning relatives had attended the school, another had served on its board of trustees, and yet another had created a permanent scholarship for its students. Surely, Murray reasoned, she had a right to be among them. On December 8, 1938, she mailed off her application. Six days later, she got a reply. "Dear Miss Murray," it read, "I write to state that . . . members of your race are not admitted to the University."

Thanks to an accident of timing, that letter made Murray briefly famous. Two days earlier, in the first serious blow to segregation, the Supreme Court had ruled that graduate programs at public universities had to admit qualified African-Americans if the state had no equivalent black institution. Determined not to integrate, yet bound by that decision and facing intense public scrutiny after news broke of Murray's application, the North Carolina legislature promised to set up a graduate school at the North Carolina College for Negroes. Instead, it slashed that college's budget by a third, then adjourned for two years.

Murray hoped to sue, and asked the N.A.A.C.P. to represent her, but lawyers there felt her status as a New York resident would imperil the case. Murray countered that any university that accepted out-of-state white students should have to accept out-of-state black ones, too, but she couldn't persuade them. Nor was she ever admitted to U.N.C. Soon enough, though, she did get into two other notable American institutions: jail and law school.

IN MARCH OF 1940, MURRAY BOARDED A SOUTHBOUND BUS IN NEW York, reluctantly. She had brought along a good friend and was looking forward to spending Easter with her family in Durham, but, of all the segregated institutions in the South, she hated the bus the most. The intimacy of the space, she wrote, "permitted the public humiliation of black people to be carried out in the presence of privileged white spectators, who witnessed our shame in silence or indifference."

Murray and her friend changed buses in Richmond, Virginia. Since the available seats in the back were broken, they sat down closer toward the front. Some time earlier, they had discussed Gandhi and nonviolent resistance, and so, without premeditation, when the bus driver asked them to move they politely refused. The driver called the cops, a confrontation ensued, and they were thrown in jail.

This time, the N.A.A.C.P. *was* interested; lawyers there hoped to use the arrest to challenge the constitutionality of segregated interstate travel. But the state of Virginia, steering clear of that powder keg, charged Murray and her friend only with disorderly conduct. They were found guilty, fined forty-three dollars they didn't have, and sent back to jail. When Murray was released some days later, she swore she'd never set foot in Virginia again.

That vow did not last six months. Back in New York, the Workers Defense League asked Murray to help raise money on behalf of an imprisoned Virginia sharecropper named Odell Waller. Waller had been sentenced to death for shooting the white man whose land he farmed: in self-defense, he claimed; in cold blood, according to the all-white jury that convicted him. His case, which became something of a cause célèbre, helped cement the friendship between Murray and Eleanor Roosevelt, who had grown interested in Waller's plight. (As Bell-Scott documents, that friendship had begun two years earlier, after Murray wrote an angry letter to F.D.R., accusing him of caring more about Fascism abroad than white supremacy at home. Eleanor responded, unperturbed, and later invited her to tea—the first of countless such visits, and the beginning of a productively contentious, mutually joyful decades-long relationship.)

To Murray's dismay, the Workers Defense League asked her to begin her fund-raising efforts in Richmond. While there, she gave a speech that reduced the audience to tears—an audience that, by chance, included Thurgood Marshall and the Howard law professor Leon Ransom. Later that day, Murray ran into the two men in town; Ransom, who had admired her speech, suggested that she apply to Howard. Murray replied that she would if she could afford it. Ransom told her that if she got in he'd see to it that she got a scholarship.

Murray applied. Marshall wrote her a recommendation. Ransom kept his word. By the time Odell Waller's final appeal was denied and he died in the electric chair, she had enrolled at Howard, with "the single-minded intention of destroying Jim Crow."

AT HOWARD, MURRAY'S RACE CEASED TO BE AN ISSUE, BUT HER GEN-der abruptly became one. Everyone else was male—all the faculty, all her classmates. On the first day, one of her professors announced to his class that he didn't know why a woman would want to go to law school, a comment that both humiliated Murray and guaranteed, as she recalled, "that I would become the top student." She termed this form of degradation "Jane Crow," and spent much of the rest of her life working to end it.

Her initial efforts were dispiriting. Upon earning her J.D. from Howard, Murray applied to Harvard for graduate work—only to get the Jane Crow version of the letter she'd once received from U.N.C.: "You are not of the sex entitled to be admitted to Harvard Law School." Murray, outraged, wrote a memorable rejoinder:

> Gentlemen, I would gladly change my sex to meet
> your requirements, but since the way to such change has
> not been revealed to me, I have no recourse but to appeal
> to you to change your minds on this subject. Are you to
> tell me that one is as difficult as the other?

Apparently so. Neither Murray's own efforts nor F.D.R.'s intercession persuaded Harvard. She went to Berkeley instead, then returned to New York to find work.

This proved challenging. At the time, only around a hundred African-American women practiced law in the entire United States, and very few firms were inclined to hire them. For several years, Murray scraped by on low-paying jobs; then, in 1948, the women's division of the Methodist Church approached her with a problem. They opposed segregation and wanted to know, for all thirty-one states where the Church had parishes, when they were legally obliged to adhere to it and when it was merely custom. If they paid her for her time, they wondered, would she write up an explanation of segregation laws in America?

What the Methodist Church had in mind was basically a pamphlet. What Murray produced was a seven-hundred-and-forty-six-page book, "States' Laws on Race and Color," that exposed both the extent and the insanity of American segregation. The A.C.L.U. distributed copies to law libraries, black colleges, and human-rights organizations. Thurgood Marshall, who kept stacks of it around the N.A.A.C.P. offices, called it "the bible" of Brown v. Board of Education. In this way, to Murray's immense gratification, the book ultimately helped render itself obsolete.

Completing this project left Murray low on work again, until, in 1956, she was hired by the New York law firm of Paul, Weiss, Rifkind, Wharton & Garrison. It was a storied place, lucrative and relatively progressive, but Murray never felt entirely at home there, partly because, of its sixty-some attorneys, she was the only African-American and one of just three women. (Two soon left, although a fourth briefly appeared: Ruth Bader Ginsburg, a summer associate with whom Murray crossed paths.) In 1960, frustrated both by her isolation and by corporate litigation, she took an overseas job at the recently opened Ghana School of Law. When she arrived, she learned that, back home, a group of students had staged a sit-in at a Woolworth's lunch counter in North Carolina. It was the first time Murray had ever left her country. Now, five thousand miles away, the modern civil-rights movement was beginning.

When Murray returned (sooner than expected, since Ghana's nascent democracy soon slid toward dictatorship), the civil-rights movement was in full swing. The women's movement, however, was just beginning. For the next ten years, Murray spent much of her time trying to advance it in every way she could, from arguing sex-discrimination cases to serving on President Kennedy's newly created Presidential Commission on the Status of Women.

In 1965, frustrated with how little progress she and others were making, she proposed, during a speech in New York, that women organize a march on Washington. That suggestion was covered with raised eyebrows in the press and earned Murray a phone call from Betty Friedan, by then the most famous feminist in the country. Murray told Friedan that she believed the time had come to organize an N.A.A.C.P. for women. In June of 1966, during a conference on women's rights in Washington, D.C., Murray and a dozen or so others convened in Friedan's hotel room and launched the National Organization for Women.

In retrospect, Murray was a curious figure to help found such an organization. All her life, she had encountered and combatted sex discrimination; all her life, she had been hailed as the first woman to integrate such-and-such a venue, hold such-and-such a role, achieve such-and-such a distinction. Yet, when she told the Harvard Law School faculty that she would gladly change her sex if someone would show her how, she wasn't just making a point. She was telling the truth. Although few people knew it during her lifetime, Murray, the passionate advocate for women's rights, identified as a man.

IN 1930, WHEN MURRAY WAS TWENTY YEARS OLD AND LIVING IN HARlem, she met a young man named William Wynn. Billy, as he was known, was also twenty, and also impoverished, uprooted, and lonely. After a brief courtship, the two married in secret, then spent an awkward two-day honeymoon at a cheap hotel. Almost immediately, Murray realized she had made "a dreadful mistake." Emotionally, the marriage didn't outlast the weekend; some years later, they had it annulled.

This entire adventure occupies two paragraphs in Murray's autobiography—the only paragraphs, in four hundred and thirty-five pages, in which she addresses her love life at all. That elision, which proves to be enormous, is obligingly corrected by Rosenberg,

who documents Murray's lifelong struggle with gender identity
and her sexual attraction to women. (Following Murray's own cue,
Rosenberg uses female pronouns to refer to her subject, as have I.)
The result is two strikingly different takes on one life: a scholarly
and methodical biography that is built, occasionally too obviously,
from one hundred and thirty-five boxes of archival material; and a
swift and gripping memoir that is inspiring to read and selectively
but staggeringly insincere.

"Why is it when men try to make love to me, something in
me fights?" Murray wrote in her diary after ending her marriage.
In pursuit of an answer, she went to the New York Public Library
and read her way through its holdings on so-called sexual devi-
ance. She identified most with Havelock Ellis's work on "pseudo-
hermaphrodites," his term for people who saw themselves as
members of the opposite gender from the one assigned to them at
birth. Through Ellis, Murray became convinced that she had either
"secreted male genitals" or an excess of testosterone. She wondered,
as Rosenberg put it, "why someone who believed she was internally
male could not become more so by taking male hormones" and, for
two decades, tried to find a way to do so.

Although this biological framework was new to Murray, the
awareness of being different was not. From early childhood, she had
seemed like, in the words of her wonderfully unfazed Aunt Pauline, a "little boy-girl." She favored boy's clothes and boy's chores,
evinced no attraction to her male peers, and, at fifteen, adopted the
nickname Paul. She later auditioned others, including Pete and
Dude, then began using Pauli while at Hunter and never referred
to herself as Anna again.

Sometimes, Murray seemed to regard herself as a mixture of
genders. "Maybe two got fused into one with parts of each sex,"
she mused at one point, "male head and brain (?), female-ish body,
mixed emotional characteristics." More often, though, she identified as fundamentally male: "one of nature's experiments; a girl who

should have been a boy." That description also helped her make sense of her desires, which she didn't like to characterize as lesbian. Instead, she regarded her "very natural falling in love with the female sex" as a manifestation of her inner maleness.

Rosenberg mostly takes Murray at her word, though she also adds a new one: transgender. Such retroactive labelling can be troubling, but the choice seems appropriate here, given how explicitly Murray identified as male, and how much her quest for medical intervention mirrors one variety of trans experience today. Still, Murray's disinclination to identify as a lesbian rested partly on a misprision of what lesbianism means. By way of explaining why she believed she was a heterosexual man, Murray noted that she didn't like to go to bars, wanted a monogamous relationship, and was attracted exclusively to "extremely feminine" women. All of that is less a convincing case for her convoluted heterosexuality than for her culture's harsh assessment of the possibilities of lesbianism.

According to Rosenberg, Murray had just two significant romantic relationships in her life, both with white women. The first, a brief one, was with a counsellor at a W.P.A. camp that Murray attended in 1934. The second, with a woman named Irene Barlow, whom she met at Paul, Weiss, lasted nearly a quarter of a century. Rosenberg describes Barlow as Murray's "life partner," although the pair never lived in the same house, only occasionally lived in the same city, and left behind no correspondence, since Murray, otherwise a pack rat, destroyed Barlow's letters. She says little about the relationship in her memoir, and only when Barlow is dying, of a brain tumor in 1973, does she even describe her as "my closest friend."

By leaving her gender identity and romantic history out of her autobiography, Murray necessarily leaves out something else as well: the lifetime of emotional distress they caused. From the time she was nineteen, Murray suffered breakdowns almost annually, some of them culminating in hospitalizations, all of them triggered either by feeling as if she were a man or by having feelings for a woman.

Aside from making her miserable, those breakdowns, like her race and her perceived gender, hindered her professional life. "This conflict rises up to knock me down at every apex I reach in my career," she confessed to her diary. To a doctor, she wrote, "Anything you can do to help me will be gratefully appreciated, because my life is somewhat unbearable in its present phase."

Such help was not forthcoming. Well into middle age, Murray tried without success to obtain hormone therapy—a treatment that scarcely existed before the mid-nineteen-sixties, and even then was seldom made available to women who identified as men. When she did manage to persuade medical professionals to take her seriously, the results were disappointing. In 1938, she prevailed on a doctor to test her endocrine levels, only to learn that her female-hormone results were regular, while her male ones were low, even for a woman. Later, while undergoing an appendectomy, she asked the surgeon to check her abdominal cavity and reproductive system for evidence of male genitalia. He did so and, to her dismay, reported afterward that she was "normal."

WHEN MURRAY DIED, IN 1985, SHE HAD NEARLY COMPLETED THE AUTO-biography that omits this entire history. That omission is not, of course, entirely surprising. Murray had lived long enough to know about the Stonewall riots and the election and assassination of Harvey Milk, but not long enough to see a black President embrace gay rights, the Supreme Court invoke the precedent of Loving v. Virginia to rule that lesbian and gay couples can marry, or her home state of North Carolina play a starring role in the turbulent rise of the transgender movement. Still, Murray's silence about her gender and sexuality is striking, because she otherwise spent a lifetime insisting that her identity, like her nation, must be fully integrated. She hated, she wrote, "to be fragmented into Negro at one time, woman at another, or worker at another."

Yet every movement to which Murray ever belonged vivisected her in exactly those ways. On the weekend of the 1963 March on Washington for Jobs and Freedom—often regarded as the high-water mark of the civil-rights movement—the labor activist A. Philip Randolph gave a speech at the National Press Club, an all-male organization that, during events, confined women in attendance to the balcony. (Murray, who had never forgotten the segregated movie theatres of her childhood, was outraged.) Worse, no women were included in that weekend's meeting between movement leaders and President Kennedy, and none were in the major speaking lineup for the march—not Fannie Lou Hamer, not Diane Nash, not Rosa Parks, not Ella Baker.

As the civil-rights movement was sidelining women, the women's movement was sidelining minorities and poor people. After stepping away from NOW to serve on the Equal Employment Opportunity Commission, Murray returned and discovered that, in Rosenberg's words, her "NAACP for women had become an NAACP for professional, white women." As a black activist who increasingly believed true equality was contingent on economic justice, Murray was left both angry and saddened. She was also left—together with millions of people like her—without an obvious home in the social-justice movement.

It might have been this frustration that prompted Murray's next move. Then, too, it might have been Irene Barlow's death, her own advancing age, or the same restlessness that she had displayed since childhood. Or it might have been, as she later came to believe, something that had simmered in her for a lifetime. Whatever it was, it came as a shock to everyone when, having achieved the most stable and lucrative job of her life—a tenured professorship at Brandeis, in the American Studies department she herself helped pioneer—Murray resigned her post and entered New York's General Theological Seminary to become an Episcopal priest.

In classic Murray fashion, the position she sought was officially unavailable to her: the Episcopal Church did not ordain women. For once, though, Murray's timing was perfect. While she was in divinity school, the Church's General Convention voted to change that policy, effective January 1, 1977—three weeks after she would complete her course work. On January 8th, in a ceremony in the National Cathedral, Murray became the first African-American woman to be vested as an Episcopal priest. A month later, she administered her first Eucharist at the Chapel of the Cross—the little church in North Carolina where, more than a century earlier, a priest had baptized her grandmother Cornelia, then still a baby, and still a slave.

It was the last of Murray's many firsts. She was by then nearing seventy, just a few years from the mandatory retirement age for Episcopal priests. Never having received a permanent call, she took a few part-time positions and did a smattering of supply preaching, for twenty-five dollars a sermon. She held four advanced degrees, had friends on the Supreme Court and in the White House, had spent six decades sharing her life and mind with some of the nation's most powerful individuals and institutions. Yet she died as she lived, a stone's throw from penury.

It is easy to wonder, in the context of the rest of Murray's life, if she joined the priesthood chiefly because she was told she couldn't. There was a very fine line in her between ambition and self-sabotage; highly motivated by barriers, she often struggled most after toppling them. It's impossible to know what goals she might have formed for herself in the absence of so many impediments, or what else she might have achieved.

Murray herself felt she didn't accomplish all that she might have in a more egalitarian society. "If anyone should ask a Negro woman in America what has been her greatest achievement," she wrote in 1970, "her honest answer would be, 'I survived!'" But, characteristically, she broke that low and tragic barrier, too, making her own life harder so that, eventually, other people's lives would be easier. Perhaps, in the end, she was drawn to the Church simply because of the claim made in Galatians, the one denied by it and by every other community she ever found, the one she spent her whole life trying to affirm: that, for purposes of human worth, "there is neither Jew nor Greek, there is neither slave nor free, there is neither male nor female."

LETTER FROM JACKSON

CALVIN TRILLIN

August 29, 1964

I happened to fly from Atlanta to Jackson on the same plane as Martin Luther King, who was about to begin his tour of Mississippi with some speeches and meetings in Greenwood. He was accompanied by four of his aides in the Southern Christian Leadership Conference—Andrew Young, C. T. Vivian, Bernard Lee, and Dorothy Cotton—and except that all of them are Negroes and that the men were wearing buttons in their lapels that said, "S.C.L.C. Freedom Now," the group might have been thought to consist of a corporation executive off to make a sales-conference speech accompanied by efficient, neatly dressed young assistants brought along to handle arrangements and take care of the paperwork. As the plane left Atlanta, Young began going through a number of file folders, making notes on a legal-sized yellow pad and occasionally passing them up to King, who paused in his reading of the *Times* and the news magazines now and then to consult with Young or Mrs. Cotton. Lee opened "The Souls of Black Folk," by W. E. B. DuBois, and Mrs. Cotton brought out a copy of "Southern Politics," by V. O. Key, which she read when she wasn't talking with King. Across the aisle from King, there happened to be sitting a stocky, nice-looking young white man with a short haircut and wearing Ivy League clothes. He looked as if he might have been a responsible member of a highly regarded college fraternity six or eight years ago and was now an equally responsible member of the Junior Chamber of Commerce of a Southern city that prided itself on its progress.

About halfway between Atlanta and Montgomery, the plane's first stop, he leaned across the aisle and politely said to King, in a thick drawl, "Excuse me. I heard them calling you Dr. King. Are you Martin Luther King?"

"Yes, I am," said King, just as politely.

"I wonder if I could ask you two questions," the young man said, and Young, Vivian, and Lee, all of whom were sitting behind King, leaned forward to hear the conversation. "I happen to be a Southerner, but I also happen to consider myself a Christian. I wonder, do you feel you're teaching Christian love?"

"Yes, that's my basic approach," King said. "I think love is the most durable element in the world, and my whole approach is based on that."

"Do you think the people you preach to have a feeling of love?" the young man asked.

"Well, I'm not talking about weak love," King explained. "I'm talking about love with justice. Weak love can be sentimental and empty. I'm talking about the love that is strong, so that you love your fellow-men enough to lead them to justice."

"Do you think that's the same love Jesus taught?" the young man asked.

"Yes, I do."

"Even though you incite one man against another?"

"You have to remember that Christ was crucified by people who were against him," said King, still in a polite, careful tone. "Do you think there's love in the South now? Do you think white people in the South love Negroes?"

"I anticipated that," said the young man. "There hasn't always been love. I admit we've made some mistakes."

"Uh-huh. Well, let me tell you some of the things that have happened to us. We were slaves for two hundred and fifty years. We endured one hundred years of segregation. We have been brutalized and lynched. Can't you understand that the Negro is bound to have some resentment? But I preach that despite this resentment we should organize militantly but non-violently. If we organize non-violently, we can show the injustice. I don't think you'd be talking to me now if we hadn't had some success in making people face the issue."

"I happen to be a Christian," the young man repeated.

"Do you think segregation is Christian?" asked King.

"I was anticipating that," the young man said. "I don't have any flat answer. I'm questioning your methods as causing more harm than good."

"Uh-huh. Well, what do you suggest we need?" King was able to say "Uh-huh" in a way that implied he had registered a remark for what it was worth and decided not to bring up its more obvious weaknesses, but he and the young man did seem genuinely interested in each other's views.

"I think we need respect and good will," said the young man.

"How do you propose to get that?" King asked.

The young man hesitated for a moment and then said, "I don't know. I just don't agree that it does any good to incite people. I know there's resentment, and you're able to capitalize on this resentment and create friction and incite discord. And you know this."

"I don't think we're inciting discord but exposing discord," King said.

"Well, let me ask you this," said the young man. "Are you concerned that certain people—well, let's come out with political labels—that this plays into the hands of the Communists?"

"I think segregation and discrimination play into the hands of the Communists much more than the efforts to end them," said King.

"But it's certainly been playing into the Communists' hands since you and the others—as you put it—started exposing what was there. There's certainly more attention given to it."

"Don't you think that if we don't solve this the Communists will have more to gain?"

"I think much more progress was made between the two races before the last few years, when you and other people started inciting trouble between the two races."

"What is this progress?" asked King. "Where was the lunch-counter desegregation? Where was the civil-rights law?"

"In good relations," the young man answered.

"Good white relations," interrupted Vivian, who apparently felt unable to keep out of the argument any longer.

"Well, I just wanted to ask those questions," said the young man. He seemed ready to end the discussion.

"Uh-huh," said King. "Well, I'd like to be loved by everyone, but we can't always wait for love. Maybe you ought to read my writings. I've done quite a bit of writing on non-violence."

"Well, I think you are causing violence," the young man said.

"Would you condemn the robbed man for possessing the money to be robbed?" asked King. "Would you condemn Christ for having a commitment to truth that drove men to crucify him? Would you condemn Socrates for having the views that forced the hemlock on him? Society must condemn the robber, not the man he robs."

"I don't want to discuss our philosophical differences," said the young man. "I just wanted to ask you those questions."

"Uh-huh. Well, I'm sorry you don't think I'm a Christian."

"I didn't say that."

"Well, I'm sorry that you don't think that what I preach is Christian, and I'm sorry you don't think segregation is un-Christian."

King turned back to his paper for a few moments, as if the conversation had ended—without progress but with no animosity—and then he looked up and said to the young man, "What do you think of the new civil-rights law? Do you think that's a good law?"

"Well, I haven't read it, but I think parts of it just carry on the trend toward federal dictatorship."

"You sound like a good Goldwater-ite," said King, with a slight smile. "Are you going to vote for Goldwater?"

"Yes, I expect I will," the young man said.

"It's too bad you're going to back a loser, because I'm afraid we're going to hand him a decisive defeat in November." King's tone was light; he might have been joking with a long-time neighbor who had always been a member of the opposing political party.

"I've voted for losers before," said the young man.

King turned back to his reading, and Vivian said, "What do you mean by federal dictatorship?"

The white man didn't seem anxious to take on a fresh adversary, but he replied, "I think everything should be done at the lowest level of government."

"How about all the federal hospitals? The roads?" said Vivian. "You say you want the federal government to stay out of everything unless it has to do it. That's why you have those hospitals and roads in Georgia, because Georgia was too poor to pay for them. Do you know how much more Mississippi takes from the federal government per person than it puts in? You didn't start talking about federal dictatorship until it came to race—"

"Are you asking me a question or making a speech?" said the young man.

"Both," Vivian said.

King looked up from his paper and smiled across at the young man. "We're all preachers, you see," he explained, and then turned to discuss something with Mrs. Cotton as the young man was making a point to Vivian.

"You must be talking about Toynbee's book," said Vivian, and he launched into a rapid-fire series of questions about Toynbee's theories on race.

"There's no need to debate this," the young man said finally, and he began to look out the window. At Montgomery, he walked off the plane.

"What do you think of that?" King asked, shaking his head, as the white man left. "Such a young man, too. Those are the people who are rallying to Goldwater. You can't get to him. His mind has been cold so long there's nothing that can get to him."

The young man returned to the plane before it left Montgomery, but, with a quick, embarrassed smile, he walked past King and the others and settled in a rear seat.

Lunch was served between Montgomery and Meridian, and afterward Lee went to sleep and Young crossed the aisle to talk with Vivian about arrangements for that night. "I called the Justice Department today, and they said they think we should go back to Jackson after the meeting," he said.

"I don't like to have Dr. King on the road at night," Vivian replied.

"Apparently, Greenwood is the kind of place now where a mob might form," said Young. "They came right into the Negro neighborhood a few months ago to get the kids at the S.N.C.C. office."

"I never know if the Justice Department knows something it's not telling us," said Vivian. "But I hate to be on the road."

"Even with a state-patrol escort?"

"That state patrol isn't a patrol," Vivian said.

"I hear they were pretty good with the congressmen who went down there," said Young.

"Well, maybe so."

"Well, let's see what the mood is when we get there," Young said in conclusion. He walked across the aisle, lowered the back of his seat, and soon went to sleep. In front of him, King was engrossed in a news magazine.

LETTER FROM SELMA

RENATA ADLER

April 10, 1965

MARCH 27

The thirty thousand people who at one point or another took part in this week's march from the Brown Chapel African Methodist Episcopal Church in Selma, Alabama, to the statehouse in Montgomery were giving highly dramatic expression to a principle that could be articulated only in the vaguest terms. They were a varied lot: local Negroes, Northern clergymen, members of labor unions, delegates from state and city governments, entertainers, mothers pushing baby carriages, members of civil-rights groups more or less at odds with one another, isolated, shaggy marchers with an air of simple vagrancy, doctors, lawyers, teachers, children, college students, and a preponderance of what one marcher described as "ordinary, garden-variety civilians from just about everywhere." They were insulated in front by soldiers and television camera crews, overhead and underfoot by helicopters and Army demolition teams, at the sides and rear by more members of the press and military, and overall by agents of the F.B.I. Most of them were aware that protection along a route of more than fifty miles of hostile country could not be absolute (on the night before the march, a student who had come here from Boston University was slashed across the cheek with a razor blade), yet few of the thirty-two hundred marchers who set out on Sunday morning seemed to have a strong consciousness of risk. They did not have a sharply defined sense of purpose, either. President Johnson's speech about voting rights and Judge Johnson's granting of permission for the march to take place had made the march itself ceremonial—almost redundant. The immediate aims of the abortive earlier marches had been realized: the national conscience had been aroused and federal intervention had been secured. In a sense, the government of Alabama was now in rebellion, and the marchers, with the sanction and protection of the federal government, were demonstrating against a rebellious state. It was unclear what such a demonstration could hope to achieve. Few segregationists could be converted by it, the national commitment to civil rights would hardly be increased by it, there was certainly an element of danger in it, and for the local citizenry it might have a long and ugly aftermath. The marchers, who had five days and four nights in which to talk, tended for the most part to avoid discussions of principle, apparently in the hope that their good will, their sense of solidarity, and the sheer pageantry of the occasion would resolve matters at some symbolic level and yield a clear statement of practical purpose before the march came to an end.

From this point of view, the first few hours of Sunday morning in Selma were far from satisfying. Broad Street, the town's main thoroughfare, was deserted and indifferent. At the Negro First Baptist Church, on the corner of Sylvan Street and Jefferson Davis Avenue, denim-clad veterans of earlier marches stood wearily aloof from recruits, who ate watery scrambled eggs, drank watery coffee, and simply milled about. On Sylvan Street itself, an unpaved red sand road dividing identical rows of brick houses known as the George Washington Carver Development, crowds were gathering, some facing the entrance to the Brown Chapel Church, others on the steps of the church facing out. Inside the church, more people were milling, while a few tried to sleep on benches or on the floor. For several hours, nothing happened. The church service that was to begin the march was scheduled to take place at ten o'clock, but veterans advised newcomers—in the first of several bitter, self-mocking jokes that became current on the Selma-Montgomery road—that this was C.P.T., Colored People Time, and the service actually began more than an hour behind schedule. In a field behind the housing development, the Reverend Andrew Young, executive director of Dr. Martin Luther King's Southern Christian Leadership Conference (S.C.L.C., referred to by some of the marchers as Slick), which sponsored the march, was giving marshals and night security guards last-minute instructions in the tactics of non-violence. "Keep women and children in the middle," he said. "If there's a shot, stand up and make the others kneel down. Don't be lagging around, or you're going to get hurt. Don't rely on the troopers, either. If you're beaten on, crouch and put your hands over the back of your head. Don't put up your arm to ward off a blow. If you fall, fall right down and look dead. Get to know the people in your unit, so you can tell if somebody's missing or if there's somebody there who shouldn't be there. And listen! If you can't be non-violent, let me know now." A young man in the standard denim overalls of the Student Nonviolent Coordinating Committee (S.N.C.C., otherwise known as Snick) murmured, "Man, you've got it all so *structured*. There seems to be a certain anxiety here about *structure*." Everyone laughed, a bit nervously, and the marshals went to the front of the church.

The crowd there was growing, still arrayed in two lines, one facing in, the other facing out. There were National Guardsmen and local policemen, on foot and in jeeps and cars, along the sides of Sylvan Street and around its corners, at Jefferson Davis and Alabama Avenues. The marchers themselves appeared to have dressed for all kinds of weather and occasions—in denims, cassocks, tweed coats, ponchos, boots, sneakers, Shetland sweaters, silk dresses, college sweatshirts, sports shirts, khaki slacks, fur-collared coats, pea jackets, and trenchcoats. As they waited, they sang innumerable, increasingly dispirited choruses of "We Shall Overcome," "Ain't

Gonna Let Nobody Turn Me 'Round," and other songs of the movement. There was a moment of excitement when Dr. King and other speakers assembled on the steps, but a succession of long, rhetorical, and, to a certain extent (when press helicopters buzzed too low or when the microphone went dead), inaudible speeches put a damper on that. An enthusiastic lady, of a sort that often afflicts banquets and church suppers, sang several hymns of many stanzas, with little melody and much vibrato. Exhaust fumes from a television truck parked to the right of the steps began to choke some of the marchers, and they walked away, coughing. Speakers praised one another extravagantly in monotonous political-convention cadences ("the man who . . ."). An irreverent, irritated voice with a Bronx accent shouted, "Would you mind please talking a little louder!" Several members of the crowd sat down in the street, and the march assumed the first of its many moods—that of tedium.

Then Dr. King began to speak, and suddenly, for no apparent reason, several Army jeeps drove straight through the center of the crowd. ("Didn't realize we were interrupting," said one of the drivers, smiling. He had a D.D., for Dixie Division, emblem on his uniform.) The startled crowd, divided in half for a moment, became aware of its size. Dr. King's speech came to an end. The marshals quickly arranged the crowd in columns, six abreast—women and children in the middle—and the procession set out down Sylvan Street. It was about one o'clock. On Alabama Avenue, the marchers turned right, passing lines of silent white citizens on the sidewalks. On Broad Street, which is also U.S. Route 80 to Montgomery, they turned left, and as segregationist loudspeakers along the way blared "Bye, Bye, Blackbird" and the white onlookers began to jeer, the marchers approached and crossed the Edmund Pettus Bridge. And the march entered another mood—jubilation.

The day was sunny and cool. The flat road, an amalgam of asphalt and the local sand, looked pink. The people in the line linked arms, and the procession was long enough to permit the marchers to sing five different civil-rights songs simultaneously without confusion; the vanguard could not hear what the rear guard was singing. Occasionally, various leaders of the movement broke out of the line to join interviewers from the television networks, which took turns using a camera truck that preceded the line of march. For the first few miles, the highway was flanked by billboards ("Keep Selma Beautiful, Cover It with Dodge"), smaller signs (Rotary, Kiwanis, Lions, Citizens Council), diners, and gas stations. Little clusters of white onlookers appeared at various points along the road, some shouting threats and insults, others silently waving Confederate flags, and still others taking pictures of the marchers, presumably as a warning that their faces would not be forgotten when the march was over. The procession filled the two left lanes of the four-lane highway, but in the two right lanes traffic was proceeding almost normally. A black Volkswagen passed the marchers several times; on its doors and fenders were signs, lettered in whitewash: "MARTIN LUTHER KINK," "WALK, COON," "COONESVILLE, U.S.A.," and "RENT YOUR PRIEST SUIT HERE." Several small children at the roadside waved toy rifles and popguns and chanted "Nigger lover!," "White nigger!," "Half-breed!," and other epithets. A man in front of a roadside diner thumbed his nose for the entire twenty minutes it took the procession to pass him, and a well-dressed matron briefly stopped her Chrysler, got out, stuck out her tongue, climbed in again, slammed the door, and drove off.

By sunset of the first day, the caravan was more than seven miles from Selma, and most of the marchers returned by a special train to town, where some of them left for their home communities and others were put up for the night in the Negro development on Sylvan Street. Two hundred and eighty Negroes, representing Alabama counties (a hundred and forty-eight from Dallas County, eighty-nine from Perry, twenty-three from Marengo, and twenty from Wilcox), and twenty whites, from all over the country, who had been chosen to make the entire journey to Montgomery (the court permitted no more than three hundred marchers on the twenty-mile stretch of Route 80 midway between Selma and Montgomery, where it is only a two-lane highway) turned off Route 80 onto a tarred road leading to the David Hall farm—their campsite for the night. Four large tents had already been pitched in a field. As the marchers lined up for supper (three tons of spaghetti), which was served to them on paper plates, from brand-new garbage pails, night fell. Groups of National Guardsmen who surrounded the farm lighted campfires. "It looks like Camelot," said one of the younger whites.

BY THE TIME DAWN CAME, THE CAMPERS WERE A THOROUGHLY CHILLED and bleary-eyed group. The oatmeal served at breakfast gave rise to a certain amount of mirth ("Tastes like fermented library paste," said one of the clergymen), and the news that the National Guardsmen had burned thirteen fence posts, two shovel handles, and an outhouse belonging to a neighboring church in order to keep warm during the night cheered everyone considerably.

The procession set out promptly at 8 a.m. The distance to the next campsite—Rosa Steele's farm—was seventeen miles. Again the day was sunny, and as the air grew warmer some of the more sunburned members of the group donned berets or Stetsons or tied scarves or handkerchiefs around their heads. To the white onlookers who clustered beside the road, the three hundred marchers must have seemed a faintly piratical band. At the head of the line were Dr. and Mrs. King, wearing green caps with earmuffs and reading newspapers as they walked. Not far behind them was a pale-green wagon (known to the marchers as the Green Dragon) with Mississippi license plates, in which rode doctors wearing armbands of the M.C.H.R. (the Medical Committee for Human Rights). Farther back were some of the younger civil-rights leaders: Hosea Williams, S.C.L.C. director of the march and veteran of the bitter struggle for public accommodations in Savannah, Georgia; the Reverend

James Bevel, formerly of S.N.C.C., now S.C.L.C. project director for Alabama (Mr. Bevel was wearing the many-colored yarmulke that has become almost his trademark—"A link," he says, "to our Old Testament heritage"); John Lewis, chairman of S.N.C.C.; and the Reverend Andrew Young.

Around two o'clock, as the middle ranks of marchers passed an intersection just outside Lowndes County, a female bystander apparently could stand it no longer. "They're carrying the flag upside down!" she screamed to the nearest trooper. "Isn't there a law against that? Can't you arrest them? Look at them so-called white men with church collars that they bought for fifty cents! And them devirginated nuns! I'm a Catholic myself, but it turns my stomach to see them. They said there was thousands yesterday, but there wasn't near a thousand. Them niggers and them girls! I've watched the whole thing three times, and there isn't a intelligent-looking one in the bunch. I feel sorry for the black folks. If they want to vote, why don't they just go out and register? Oh, honey, look! There goes a big one. Go home, scum! Go home, scum!" The procession began to sing a not very hearty version of "A Great Camp Meeting in the Promised Land."

Not all the bystanders along the road were white. At the boundary of Lowndes County (with a population of fifteen thousand, eighty per cent of them Negroes, not one of whom had been registered to vote by March 1, 1965), John Maxwell, a Negro worker in a Lowndes County cotton-gin mill (at a salary of six dollars for a twelve-hour day), appeared at an intersection.

"Why don't you register to vote?" a reporter from the *Harvard Crimson* asked Mr. Maxwell.

"They'd put us off the place if I tried," Mr. Maxwell said.

In the town of Trickem, at the Nolan Elementary School—a small white shack on brick stilts, which had asbestos shingles, a corrugated-iron roof, six broken windows, and a broken wood floor patched with automobile license plates—a group of old people and barefoot children rushed out to embrace Dr. King. They had been waiting four hours.

"Will you march with us?" Dr. King asked an old man with a cane.

"I'll walk one step, anyway," said the man. "Because I know for every one step I'll take you'll take two."

AGAIN THE NIGHT WAS COLD AND DAMP. AT THE ENTRANCE TO THE field, there was so much mud that boards and reeds had been scattered to provide traction for cars. Most of the marchers went to sleep in their four tents soon after supper, but at Steele's Service Station, across the highway, a crowd of Negroes from the neighborhood had gathered. Some of them were dancing to music from a jukebox, and a few of the more energetic marchers, white and black, joined them.

"This is getting to be too much like a holiday," said a veteran of one if the earlier marches. "It doesn't tell the truth of what happened."

At about ten o'clock, the last of the marchers crossed the highway back to camp. Shortly afterward, a fleet of cars drove up to the service station and a group of white boys got out. Two of the boys were from Georgia, two were from Texas, one was from Tennessee, one was from Oklahoma, one was from Monroeville, Alabama, and one was from Selma. The Reverend Arthur E. Matott, a white minister from Perth Amboy, New Jersey, who was a member of the night patrol, saw them and walked across the highway to where they were standing. "Can I help you fellows?" Mr. Matott asked.

"We're just curious," the boy from Monroeville said. "Came out to see what it was like."

"How long are you planning to stay?" said Mr. Matott.

"Until we get ready to leave," the boy said.

A Negro member of the night patrol quietly joined Mr. Matott.

"I cut classes," said the boy from Tennessee. "Sort of impulsive. You hear all these stories. I wondered why you were marching."

"Well, you might say we're marching to get to know each other and to ease a little of the hate around here," Mr. Matott said.

"You don't need to march for that," said one of the boys from Texas. "You're making it worse. The hate was being lessened and lessened by itself throughout the years."

"Was it?" asked the Negro member of the guard.

"It was," the Texas boy said.

"We never had much trouble in Nashville." said the boy from Tennessee. "Where you have no conflict, it's hard to conceive . . ."

"Why don't you-all go and liberate the Indian reservations, or something?" said the boy from Monroeville. "The Negroes around here are happy."

"I don't think they are," said Mr. Matott.

"I've lived in the South all my life, and I know that they are," the boy from Georgia said.

"I'm not happy," said the Negro guard.

"Well, just wait awhile," said the boy from Monroeville.

AT MIDNIGHT IN THE CAMP, CHARLES MAULDIN, AGED SEVENTEEN, THE head of the Dallas County Student Union and a student at Selma's Hudson High School, which is Negro, was awakened in the security tent by several guards, who ushered in a rather frightened-looking Negro boy.

"What's going on?" asked Charles.

The boy replied that he was trying to found a Negro student movement in Lowndes County.

"That's fine," said Charles.

"The principal's dead set against it," the boy said.

"Then stay underground until you've got everybody organized," Charles said. "Then if he throws one out he'll have to throw you all out."

"You with Snick or S.C.L.C., or what?" the boy asked.

"I'm not with anything," Charles said. "I'm with them all. I used to just go to dances in Selma on Saturday nights and not belong to anything. Then I met John Love, who was Snick project director down here, and I felt how he just sees himself in every Negro. Then I joined the movement."

"What about your folks?" the boy asked.

"My father's a truck driver, and at first they were against it, but now they don't push me and they don't hold me back," Charles said.

"Who've you had personal run-ins with?" the boy asked.

"I haven't had personal run-ins with anybody," Charles said. "I've been in jail three times, but never more than a few hours. They needed room to put other people in. Last week, I got let out, so I just had to march and get beaten on. In January, we had a march of little kids—we called it the Tots March—but we were afraid they might get frightened, so we joined them, and some of us got put in jail. Nothing personal about it."

"Some of us think that for the march we might be better off staying in school," the boy said.

"Well, I think if you stay in school you're saying that you're satisfied," Charles said. "We had a hundred of our teachers marching partway with us. At first, I was against the march, but then I realized that although we're probably going to get the voting bill, we still don't have a lot of other things. It's dramatic, and it's an experience, so I came. I thought of a lot of terrible things that could happen, because we're committed to non-violence, and I'm responsible for the kids from the Selma school. But then I thought, If they killed everyone on this march, it would be nothing compared to the number of people they've killed in the last three hundred years."

"You really believe in non-violence?" the boy asked Charles.

"I do," Charles said. "I used to think of it as just a tactic, but now I believe in it all the way. Now I'd just like to be tested."

"Weren't you tested enough when you were beaten on?" the boy asked.

"No, I mean an individual test, by myself," Charles said. "It's easy to talk about non-violence, but in a lot of cases you've got to be tested, and re-inspire yourself."

WEDNESDAY, THE FOURTH AND LAST FULL DAY OF MARCHING, WAS sunny again, and the marchers set out in good spirits. In the morning, a minister who had rashly dropped out at a gas station to make a telephone call was punched by the owner, and a freelance newspaper photographer was struck on the ear by a passerby. (Although he required three stitches, he was heartened by the fact that a Montgomery policeman had come, with a flying tackle, to his rescue.) There seemed, however, to be fewer segregationists by the side of the road than usual—perhaps because the Montgomery *Advertiser* had been running a two-page advertisement, prepared by the City Commissioner's Committee on Community Affairs, imploring citizens to be moderate and ignore the march. The coverage of the march in the Southern press had consistently amused the marchers. "Civil Righters Led by Communists" had been the headline in the Birmingham weekly *Independent;* the Selma *Times-Journal,* whose coverage of the march was relatively accurate, had editorialized about President Johnson, under the heading "A Modern Mussolini Speaks, 'We Shall Overcome,'" "No man in any generation . . . has ever held so much power in the palm of his hand, and that includes Caesar, Alexander, Genghis Khan, Napoleon, and Franklin D. Roosevelt"; and the Wednesday *Advertiser*'s sole front-page item concerning the march was a one-column, twenty-one-line account, lower right, of the Alabama legislature's resolution condemning the demonstrators for being "sexually promiscuous." ("It is well known that the white Southern segregationist is obsessed with fornication," said John Lewis, chairman of S.N.C.C. "And that is why there are so many shades of Negro.")

By noon, most of the marchers were sunburned or just plain weatherburned. Two Negroes scrawled the word "Vote" in sunburn cream on their foreheads and were photographed planting an American flag, Iwo Jima fashion, by the side of the road. Flags of all sorts, including state flags and church flags, had materialized in the hands of marchers. One of the few segregationists watching the procession stopped his jeering for a moment when he saw the American flag, and raised his hand in a salute.

In the early afternoon, Dr. King and his wife, who had dropped out for a day in order for him to go to Cleveland to receive an award, rejoined the procession. The singing began again. Marching behind Dr. King was his friend the Reverend Morris H. Tynes, of Chicago, who teased Dr. King continuously. "Moses, can you let your people rest for a minute?" Mr. Tynes said. "Can you just let the homiletic smoke from your cigarette drift out of your mouth and engulf the multitude and let them rest?" Dr. King smiled. Some of the other marchers, who had tended to speak of Dr. King half in joking and half in reverent tones (most of them referred to him conversationally as "De Lawd") laughed out loud.

A Volkswagen bus full of marchers from Chicago ran out of gas just short of the procession. "Now, we all believe in non-violence," one of the passengers said to the driver, "but if you don't get this thing moving pretty soon . . ."

"Are you members of some sort of group?" asked a reporter, looking inside the bus.

"No," said the driver. "We're just individuals."

At last, on the outskirts of Montgomery, the marchers reached their fourth campsite—the Catholic City of St. Jude, consisting of a church, a hospital, and a school built in a style that might be called Contemporary Romanesque. The four tents were pitched by the time they arrived, and they marched onto the grounds singing "We Have Overcome." They also added two new verses to the song—"All the way from Selma" and "Our feet are soaked." Inside the gates of St. Jude's, they were greeted by a crowd of Montgomery Negroes singing the national anthem.

"*What* do you *want?*" the marchers chanted.

This time, the response from the onlookers was immediate and loud: "*Freedom!*"

"*When* do you *want* it?"

"*Now!*"

"How *much* of it?"

"*All* of it!"

ON ITS FOURTH NIGHT, THE MARCH BEGAN TO LOOK FIRST LIKE A football rally, then like a carnival and a hootenanny, and finally like something dangerously close to a hysterical mob. Perhaps because of a new feeling of confidence, the security check at the main gate had been practically abandoned. Thousands of marchers poured in from Selma and Montgomery, some of them carrying luggage, and no one had time to examine its contents. The campsite was cold and almost completely dark, and a bomb or a rifle shot would have left everyone helpless. Word got out that the doctors on the march had treated several cases of strep throat, two of pneumonia, one of advanced pulmonary tuberculosis, and one of epilepsy, and because of the number and variety of sick and handicapped who had made the march a macabre new joke began to go the rounds: "What has five hundred and ninety-nine legs, five hundred and ninety-eight eyes, an indeterminate number of germs, and walks singing? The march from Selma."

An entertainment had been scheduled for nine o'clock that night, but it was several hours late getting started, and in the meantime the crowd of thousands churned about in the mud and chanted.

A minister, who had been seeking for several hours to clear the platform, wept with chagrin. "Betcha old Sheriff Clark and his troopers could clear it!" someone shouted.

Finally, the entertainment got under way, and the situation improved. Tony Perkins and a few others spoke with well-considered brevity. The crowd clapped along with the singers as they sang folk songs and songs of the movement, and it laughed at the comedians, including Dick Gregory, Nipsey Russell, Mike Nichols, and Elaine May. ("I can't afford to call up the National Guard," said Mike Nichols, impersonating Governor Wallace. "Why not?" said Elaine May, impersonating a telegraph operator. "It only costs a dime.")

At 2 a.m., the entertainment and speeches were over, and the performers left for a Montgomery hotel, which was surrounded for the remainder of the night by shouting segregationists. Most of the crowd drifted off the field and headed for Montgomery, and the tents were left at last to the marchers. Suddenly security tightened up. At one point, the Reverend Andrew Young himself was asked for his credentials. The hours before dawn passed without incident.

ON THURSDAY MORNING, THE MARCH EXPANDED, PULLED ITSELF TO-gether, and turned at once serious and gay. It finally seemed that the whole nation was marching to Montgomery. Signs from every conceivable place and representing every conceivable religious denomination, philosophical viewpoint, labor union, and walk of life assembled at St. Jude's and lined up in orderly fashion. A Magic Marker pen passed from hand to hand, and new signs went up: "The Peace Corps Knows Integration Works," "So Does Canada," "American Indians" (carried by Fran Poafpybitty, a Comanche from Indiahoma, Oklahoma), "Freedom" in Greek letters (carried by a Negro girl), "Out of Vietnam into Selma" in Korean (carried by a white girl), "The Awe and Wonder of Human Dignity We Want to Maintain" (on a sandwich board worn by a succession of people), and, on two sticks tied together, with a blue silk scarf above it, a sign reading simply "Boston." A young white man in a gray flannel suit hurried back and forth among the platoons of marchers; on his attaché case was written "D. J. Bittner, Night Security."

Near the tents, Ivanhoe Donaldson and Frank Surocco (the first a Negro project director for S.N.C.C. in Atlanta, the second a white boy, also from S.N.C.C.) were distributing orange plastic jackets to the original three hundred marchers. The jackets, of the sort worn by construction workers, had been bought for eighty-nine cents apiece in Atlanta, and jackets just like them had been worn throughout the march by the marshals, but for the marchers the orange jacket had become a singular status symbol. There was some dispute about who was entitled to wear one. There was also a dispute about the order of march.

Finally, after another session of virtually inaudible speeches, the parade was ready to go. "Make way for the originals!" the marshals shouted, forming a cordon to hold back the other marchers and the press. Behind the three hundred came Martin Luther King, Ralph Bunche, A. Philip Randolph, the Reverend Ralph Abernathy, the Reverend Fred L. Shuttlesworth, Charles G. Gomillion, the Reverend F. D. Reese, and other civil-rights leaders; behind them came the grandfather of Jimmie Lee Jackson, the Negro boy who had been shot in nearby Perry County, and the Reverend Orloff Miller, a friend of the Reverend James Reeb's, who had been beaten with Reeb on the night of Reeb's murder; and behind them came a crowd of what turned out to be more than thirty thousand people. "We're not just down here for show," said Mr. Miller. "A lot of our people are staying here to help. But the show itself is important. When civil rights drops out of the headlines, the country forgets."

Stationed, like an advance man, hundreds of yards out in front of the procession as it made its way through the Negro section of Montgomery and, ultimately, past a hundred and four intersections was Charles Mauldin, dressed in his Hudson High sweatshirt and blue jeans and an orange jacket, and waving a little American flag and a megaphone. One pocket of his denims was split, and the fatigue in his gentle, intelligent face made him seem considerably younger than his seventeen years. "Come and march with us!" he

shouted to Negro bystanders. "You can't make your witness standing on the corner. Come and march with us. We're going downtown. There's nothing to be afraid of. Come and march with us!"

At the intersection of Montgomery Street and Dexter Avenue
(the avenue leading to the capitol), Charles Mauldin turned and
looked around. "They're still coming out of St. Jude's," a reporter
told him. And when the vanguard of the march reached the capitol
steps, they were *still* coming out of St. Jude's.

Charles and the rest of the orange-jacketed three hundred
stood below. Behind them, the procession was gradually drawing
together and to a halt. Ahead, a few green-clad, helmeted officers
of the Alabama Game and Fish Service and some state officials
blocked the capitol steps, at the top of which, covering the bronze
star that marks the spot where Jefferson Davis was inaugurated
President of the Confederacy, was a plywood shield constructed
at the order of Governor Wallace—"To keep that s.o.b. King from
desecrating the Cradle of the Confederacy," according to a spokesman for the Governor. Martin Luther King had managed to draw
a larger crowd than the leader of the Confederacy a hundred years
before.

Onto a raised platform—erected by the marchers for the
occasion—in a plaza between the crowd and the steps climbed a
group of entertainers that included, at one point or another, Joan
Baez; the Chad Mitchell Trio; Peter, Paul, and Mary; and Harry
Belafonte. As Alabamians peered from the statehouse windows,
Negro and white performers put their arms around each other's
shoulders and began to sing. Although the songs were familiar and
the front rank of the three hundred mouthed a few of the words,
none of the crowd really sang along. Then Len Chandler, a young
Negro folk singer who had marched most of the way, appeared on
the platform. He was dressed peculiarly, as he had been on the
road—in a yellow helmet, a flaglike blue cape with white stars on it,
and denims—and the crowd at once joined him in singing:

"You've got to move when the spirit say move,
Move when the spirit say move.
When the spirit say move, you've got to move, oh, Lord,
You got to move when the spirit say move."

Joan Baez, wearing a purple velvet dress and a large bronze crucifix, even broke into a rather reverent Frug.

After an invocation by a rabbi and speeches by the Reverend Andrew Young and the Reverend Ralph Abernathy, the crowd turned away from the Confederate and Alabama State flags flying from the capitol, faced its own American flags, and sang the national anthem. Then there was the succession of speeches, most of them eloquent, some of them pacific ("Friends of freedom," said Whitney Young, of the Urban League), others militant ("Fellow Freedom Fighters," said John Lewis, of S.N.C.C.), and nearly all of them filled with taunts of Governor Wallace as the list of grievances, intimidations, and brutalities committed by the state piled up.

"This march has become a rescue operation," Charles Mauldin said quietly to a friend as the speeches continued. "Most of those Negroes along the way have joined us, and although this Wallace-baiting sounds like a little boy whose big brother has come home and who is standing outside a bully's window just to jeer, these Negroes are never going to be quite so afraid of the bully again. When the bill goes through, they're going to vote, and the white men down here are going to think twice before they try to stop them. Big brothers have come down from the North and everywhere, and they've shown that they're ready and willing to come down again. I don't think they're going to have to."

Near the end of the ceremony, Rosa Parks, the "Mother of the Movement," who had set off Dr. King's first demonstration when she was jailed for refusing to yield her seat to a white man on a bus in Montgomery, received the most enthusiastic cheers of all. "Tell it! Tell! Tell!" some of the marchers shouted. "Speak! Speak!"

Finally, after an extravagant introduction by Mr. Abernathy, who referred to Dr. King as "conceived by God" ("This personality cult is getting out of hand," said a college student, and, to judge by the apathetic reception of Mr. Abernathy's words, the crowd agreed), Dr. King himself spoke. There were some enthusiastic yells of "Speak! Speak!" and "Yessir! Yessir!" from the older members of the audience when Dr. King's speech began, but at first the younger members were subdued. Gradually, the whole crowd began to be stirred. By the time he reached his refrains—"Let us march on the ballot boxes. . . . We're on the move now. . . . How long? Not long"—and the final, ringing "Glory, glory, hallelujah!," the crowd was with him all the way.

The director of the march, Hosea Williams, of S.C.L.C., said some concluding words, remarking that there should be no lingering in Montgomery that night and exhorting the crowd to leave quietly and with dignity. There was a last rendition of "We Shall Overcome." Within ten minutes, Dexter Avenue was cleared of all but the press and the troopers.

A FEW HOURS LATER, THE DELEGATION AND ITS PETITION WERE TURNED away by Governor Wallace. At the airport, where there had been some difficulty during the preceding days (an uncanny number of suitcases belonging to marchers were mislaid by the airlines), new flights had been scheduled to get the marchers out of Montgomery. Still, many marchers had to wait at the airport all night long. They rested on the floor, and on the lawn outside, and as often as the police cleared then away they reappeared and fell asleep again. Word came that Mrs. Viola Liuzzo had been shot. Some of the marchers went back to Selma at once. Others boarded planes for home. At the Montgomery airport exit was a permanent official sign reading "Glad You Could Come. Hurry Back."

THE CHARMER

HENRY LOUIS GATES, JR.

April 29, 1996

The drive to Louis Farrakhan's house, on South Woodlawn Avenue, took me through the heart of black Chicago—past campaign billboards for a hot city-council race, past signs for Harold the Fried Chicken King and Tony's Vienna Beef Hotdogs. Much of the area is flecked with housing projects and abandoned lots, but when you turn the corner at Woodlawn and Forty-ninth Street things abruptly look different. You can see why the late Elijah Muhammad, who led the Nation of Islam—the Black Muslims—for almost four decades, built his house in this little pocket of opulence. It's a street of large brick houses, enshrining the vision of black-bourgeois respectability, and even grandeur, that has always been at the nostalgic heart of the Nation of Islam's creed. The neighborhood, known as South Kenwood, is integrated and professional. In 1985, Farrakhan bought Elijah Muhammad's house—a yellow brick neo-Mediterranean structure—and he has lived there ever since; the creed and the neighborhood remain intact.

It was a warm spring morning the week after Easter, and everything was peaceful, quiet, orderly, which somehow made matters all the more unsettling. I wasn't expecting the Death Star, exactly, but wouldn't have been surprised to see a formidable security detail: the Fruit of Islam patrolling the roof and gates with automatic weapons; perhaps a few attack dogs roaming the grounds. In fact, the only security measure in evidence was a rather elegant wrought-iron fence. After I spent a minute or so fumbling around, trying to find a hinge, a baby-faced young man with close-cropped hair and gleaming black combat boots came over and flicked the gate open. Together, we walked up a short, curved driveway, past two marble lions flanking the front door, and into the house that Elijah Muhammad built.

People in the Nation of Islam refer to the house as the Palace, and it does have an undeniable, vaguely Orientalist splendor. There is a large center hall, two stories high, filled with well-tended tropical plants, some reaching up between ten and twenty feet. Sunlight floods in from a huge dome of leaded glass; at its center, Arabic characters spell out "Allahu Akbar," or "God Is Great." To the right is a large and vibrant triptych: the Nation's founder, Wallace D. Fard; his prophet, Elijah Muhammad (with a set of gold keys in his hands); and Elijah's successor as the head of the Nation, a very youthful-looking Louis Farrakhan. The walls are spanking white, the floors are tiled in white and gray marble. A C-shaped sofa is upholstered in white fabric and covered with clear vinyl—the same stuff my mother put on to protect *her* good furniture, back in Piedmont, West Virginia.

Farrakhan's wife, Khadijah, came down to check on me, and to make sure everything was tidy now that company had arrived. Khadijah Farrakhan has a soft brown face and a warm smile. I had a bad cold that day, and she offered me some advice on how to unblock my ears, which still hadn't recovered from the flight to Chicago. "Open your mouth wide, and shift your jaw from side to side," she said, helpfully demonstrating the motion. We stood facing each other, our mouths contorted like those of a pair of groupers.

That is about when America's great black Satan himself came gliding into the room. Farrakhan was resplendent in a three-button suit of chocolate-brown silk, a brown-and-beige bow tie, and a matching pocket square. Only then did I notice that my own trousers did not match my suit jacket. Moments later, I referred to his wife as "Mrs. Muhammad," and there was glint of amusement in his eyes. The truth is, I was having a bad case of nerves that morning.

For good reason. After I criticized Farrakhan in print three years ago, a few of his more impetuous followers had shared with me their fervent hope for my death. Now that I was face to face with Farrakhan, I did feel, in fact, pretty deathly. "I'm a wounded warrior," I admitted.

Farrakhan, relaxed and gracious, made sure I was supplied with hot tea and honey. "Get the battlefield ready," he said, laughing. For the rest of a long day, we sat together at his big dining-room table, and it became clear that Farrakhan is a man of enormous intelligence, curiosity, and charm. He can also be deeply strange. It all depends on the moment and the subject. When he talks about the need for personal responsibility or of his fondness for Johnny Mathis and Frank Sinatra, he sounds as jovial and bourgeois as Bill Cosby; when he is warning of the wicked machinations of Jewish financiers, he seems as odd and obsessed as Pat Robertson.

Not long after we began talking, Farrakhan told me about an epiphany he had recently about the waning of white cultural supremacy. Farrakhan takes moments of revelation very seriously; one of his most profound occurred, he has said, while he was aboard a giant spacecraft. This particular revelation, less marvellously, took place at a Lionel Ritchie concert. There Farrakhan saw a beautiful young blond woman and her little daughter, who both clearly idolized this black performer. And when Ritchie told the mostly white crowd to raise their hands in the air almost everyone joined in. Farrakhan saw this as something not only amazing but telling.

"I see something happening in America," he said. "You go into white folks' homes, you see Michael Jackson on the wall, you see Michael Jordan on the wall, you see Hank Aaron on the wall. Their children are being influenced by black faces. And I say to myself: 'Where is this leading?' And what I see is that white supremacy is being challenged in so many subtle and overt ways, and gradually children are losing that thing about being superior."

The myths of black superiority are also going by the wayside.

Someone might believe that a white cannot play the horn, he said, "then Kenny G. blows that all away." (Joe Lovano, maybe, but Kenny G.?) It used to be that white people listened to the blues but could never sing it. Now, though, "white people are experiencing that out of which the blues came," he said. "White people are suffering. Now you drive your streets and you see a white person with stringy hair sitting by the side of the road plucking his guitar, like we used to do in the South. Now *they're* doing that." What people must do is "outgrow the narrowness of their own nationalistic feelings," Farrakhan declared. "When we outgrow the color thing, outgrow the race and the ethnic thing, outgrow the religious thing to see the oneness of God and the oneness of humanity, then we can begin to approach our divinity."

I scratched my head: we'd gone from Kenny G. to God in a matter of seconds; "the blue-eyed devils"—Elijah Muhammad's favorite designation for white folk—are learning the blues, and we're mightily impressed.

It turns out that there is in Farrakhan's discourse a strain that sounds awfully like liberal universalism; there is also, of course, its brutal opposite. The two tendencies, in all their forms, are constantly in tension. Pundits like to imagine that Farrakhan is a kind of radio program: the incendiary Louis Farrakhan Show. In fact, Farrakhan is more like a radio station: what you hear depends on when you tune in. His talk ranges from far-fetched conspiracy theories to Dan Quayle–like calls for family values. Farrakhan really does believe that a cabal of Jews secretly controls the world; he also suspects, I learned later in our conversation, that one of his own grandparents was a Portuguese Jew. Apologists and detractors alike feel free to decide which represents the "real" Farrakhan. The result may score debating points, but it has little to do with the man who lives at South Woodlawn and Forty-ninth Street.

Much is made of Farrakhan's capacity to strike fear into the hearts of white liberals. And it does seem that for many of them

Farrakhan represents their worst nightmare: the Nat Turner figure, crying out for racial vengeance. As Adolph Reed, Jr., writes of Farrakhan, "he has become uniquely notorious because his inflammatory nationalist persona has helped to center public discussion of Afro-American politics on the only issue (except affirmative action, of course) about which most whites ever show much concern: What do blacks think of whites?"

A subject that receives far less attention is the fear that Farrakhan inspires in blacks. The truth is that blacks—across the economic and ideological spectrum—often feel astonishingly vulnerable to charges of inauthenticity, of disloyalty to the race. I know that I do, despite my vigorous efforts to deconstruct that vocabulary of reproach. Farrakhan's sway over blacks—the answering chord his rhetoric finds—attests to the enduring strength of our own feelings of guilt, our own anxieties of having been false to our people, of having sinned against our innermost identity. He denounces the fallen in our midst, invokes the wrath of heaven against us: and his outlandish vitriol occasions both terror and a curious exhilaration.

FARRAKHAN IS A DISTINCTIVE FIGURE WITH A DISTINCTIVE MESSAGE, but it is a message that has a context and a history. In the summer of 1930, a door-to-door salesman appeared in the Detroit ghetto selling raincoats and silks. In those days, he was known as Wallace D. Fard; later, in the literature of the Nation of Islam, his name would be given an Arabic form—Farrad Muhammad. Some say that Fard was a white man, and others believe he was an Arab; Farrakhan has said that Fard's mother was "from the Caucasus."

Fard told his customers in the early thirties that he carried silks of the same kind that Africans were still using. He seemed to know a great deal about Africa, and soon he was holding meetings about African history at the homes of various customers. For black people at that time, this was news they could use. He had, for instance, all sorts of dietary tips: he pointed out foods that were bad for black people, explaining that the people of their native land never touched them and were always in good health. Before long, Fard moved toward religious expostulations. If the diet that your African ancestors followed was best for you, so was their religion. As time went by, the numbers of people who wanted to attend Fard's meetings grew to the point where his followers rented a hall and called it the Temple of Islam. And so, while inner-city Detroit struggled through the Great Depression, a new religion was born.

Fard taught that although the world was still dominated by "the blue-eyed devils," they were only temporary interlopers. Fard himself had been sent to awaken the consciousness of the Black Nation, the earth's "Original Man." Those who sought to join Fard could send him their current surnames—their "slave names," that is— and receive their true Islamic surnames by return mail. In time, Fard began to refer to himself as the Supreme Ruler of the Universe. And then, in June of 1934, he mysteriously vanished, never to be seen again.

After the vanishing, Fard' s fiery chief minister, Elijah Muhammad, (né Poole), declared Fard to have been an incarnation of Allah, thus elevating himself to the status of Prophet, or Messenger— Muhammad's title in the Koran. Fard's birthday, February 26th, became a holiday, Saviour's Day, and the organizational—and doctrinal—basis for the Nation of Islam was established.

"I must create a system, or be enslav'd by another man's," William Blake wrote in "Jerusalem." In that spirit, Elijah Muhammad's creed offered a unique creation myth, Leviticus-like strictures on diet and behavior, and a strong component of prophecy. In the world according to Elijah Muhammad, blacks were descended from the tribe of Shabazz, which "came with the earth," when an explosion separated the earth and the moon sixty-six trillion years ago. White people, by contrast, came into existence less than seven thousand years ago, the result of the genetic experiments of a wicked scientist named Yakub. Whites were drained not only of color but of humanity: "The human beast—the serpent, the dragon, the devil, and Satan—all mean one and the same; the people or race known as the white or Caucasian race, sometimes called the European race." Black Muslim theology features no afterlife; what it offers is the promise that the reign of the blue-eyed devils is nearing its end. One could be sure of this because of a particularly splendid element of Elijah's cosmogony: the whole of history was written ahead of time, by twenty-four black scientists, under the supervision of a twenty-fifth.

Not all doctrine pertained to such lofty matters. Elijah Muhammad also published several books on "How to Eat to Live." Tobacco and alcohol were forbidden and so were corn bread and pork. Small navy beans were permissible; lima and pinto beans were not. The Messenger instituted for members a regime of two or more temple meetings a week. Men would be expected to do some proselytizing—or "fishing for the dead," as it was known. A woman's behavior was strictly circumscribed: she was not to let herself be alone in a room with any man who wasn't her husband; her dress had to be modest.

The idiosyncrasies of the Nation of Islam should not blind one to Elijah Muhammad's organizational genius. Fard was not the only black Messiah to have achieved prominence in the thirties, or the most influential, but his was the only legacy that has thrived. Similarly, the esoteric details of Black Muslim doctrine should not obscure the real sense of absence that Elijah Muhammad addressed. Louis Farrakhan told me that the Nation of Islam might be understood as a kind of Reformation movement within the black church—a church that had grown all too accommodating to American racism. It's true that, despite the prominence of such groups as the Southern Christian Leadership Conference during the civil-rights movement, most black churches were extremely conservative when came to race matters. Dexter Avenue Baptist Church achieved legendary status because of the leadership of

Martin Luther King, Jr., and yet that same church had fired King's predecessor, Vernon Johns, for protesting racism with too much zeal. Muhammad's fierce militancy and his inversion of reigning notions of racial inferiority should be seen in relation to the failures of the black churches—especially when it came to providing a moral language in which to address the political sins of state-sponsored racial inequality.

LOUIS FARRAKHAN, FOR HIS PART, REMAINS FIRMLY TETHERED TO THE tradition of Christian homiletics. I asked him something that my father wanted to know: How did a good Episcopalian boy like Farrakhan, born Louis Eugene Walcott, end up leaving the true church?

Farrakhan laughed, and said I should tell my father that he never really left. "I thought I did," he said, "but my love is there, my roots are the church." And that's true: references to the Koran in his speeches are perfunctory, with passages from the Old and New Testaments taking pride of place.

"We were from St. Cyprian's"—an Episcopal church in the Roxbury section of Boston, where he grew up—"And I was in the choir," he went on to tell me. He still refers to Nathan Wright, the minister when he was growing up, as "Father Wright." Roxbury retains its hold on him in other ways, too. He spent his formative years in a bustling working-class neighborhood, which was populated by immigrants from the West Indies and boasted flourishing black-owned businesses and a thriving musical scene. It has been suggested that this experience of a tight-knit, prosperous, all-black community may undergird Farrakhan's conservative social views.

Born in 1933, Gene, as he was known, was the younger of two sons of Mae Clark, who was from Barbados. Gene was named after his father, a very light-skinned man from Jamaica; he was a philanderer, whom the family seldom saw—an exceptional circumstance in what was largely a community of intact families. Nathan Wright tells me the mother was "a little old-fashioned and a disciplinarian," even "a bit too strict." Mae Clark stressed education and paid for private music lessons for both her sons. Gene played the violin.

"When I was a young boy, hardly anybody in my all-black school could not read," Farrakhan recalled. "By the time I left the eighth grade, I knew every country on this earth, every capital. I knew their lakes and rivers, I knew what those countries produced for wealth." An honor student in high school, Gene studied, among other subjects, Latin and German, calculus and medieval history. He was also a star on the track team.

A couple of decades later, an accomplished scholar, musician, and athlete like Gene Walcott would have been given the financial aid to go to one élite university or another. In fact, in his high-school yearbook Walcott wrote that he wanted to attend the Juilliard School of Music. Instead, 1950 he went off to a teachers college for blacks in Winston-Salem, North Carolina, on an athletic scholarship. It was there, in the South, that he first experienced the full impact of racism. Once, stopping over in Washington on the way down, Farrakhan decided to take in a movie, only to be told that tickets were not sold to Negroes. "A very close friend of mine had just been killed in Korea, and I walked down the street with a twenty-dollar bill in one hand, my wallet in the other, and at that point I was very, very angry with America," he said. "I started writing a calypso song called 'Why America Is No Democracy.'"

Within a few years, Gene Walcott had dropped out of college and taken up a career as a calypso singer, styling himself the Charmer. Among those charmed, he would recount years later, were many women: "I wouldn't go to bed with them. They wanted to give me money. . . . I told them, 'You're out of your damn mind.' They said, 'I think you're a faggot.' And I said, 'I *know* what I am. *You'll* never find out.'"

At about the same time as the Charmer was making a name for himself in Boston, Malcolm X was making the rounds as a Black

Muslim preacher. "A friend of mine tried to get me to go to the temple," Farrakhan told me "He said, 'You know, Gene, the white man is the Devil.' And I looked at him and said, 'If I go home to-night and my wife is in bed with a black man, *she* has committed adultery. And if I pick up a gun and kill them, *I* have committed murder. Where's the Devil in that?' He couldn't give me an answer. So I went on about my business—I wasn't about to join the Muslims." Still, Farrakhan described himself as having grown disillusioned with the Episcopal Church: "I couldn't understand why Jesus would preach so much love and why there was so much hate demonstrated by white Christians against black Christians."

In 1955, Walcott was playing the Blue Angel night club in Chicago, and he ran into some old friends who had got involved with the Nation of Islam. Walcott agreed to go to hear Elijah Muhammad preach at the mosque, and when he did he liked what he heard. That night, he went back to his hotel and started copying out the standard form letter to register as a Muslim:

> Dear Saviour Allah, Our Deliverer: I have attended
> the Teachings of Islam, two or three times, as taught
> by one of your ministers, I believe in it. I bear witness
> that there is no God but Thee. And, that Muhammad
> is Thy Servant and Apostle. I desire reclaim my Own.
> Please give me my Original name. My slave name is as
> follows . . .

"I wouldn't call it a conversion experience, because I wasn't thoroughly convinced," Farrakhan said. In any case, he never received a reply. Then, just a few months later, when he heard Malcolm X preach, back on the East Coast, sympathy turned into something like conviction. "I'd never heard any man talk like that," Farrakhan went on, brightening now. "*Then* I was convinced that this was where I wanted to be."

While Farrakhan was telling story, one of his daughters—a cheerful young woman in a sari-like dress—came by with a real-estate brochure. She wanted to show her father a picture of a three-story brownstone that she and her husband were hoping to buy; Farrakhan expressed his approval. By that point, I'd already met his son Nasir, a handsome, self-possessed young man who was interested in filmmaking, and another daughter who, Farrakhan boasted, was attending law school. Farrakhan plainly was a man who was enormously proud of his children and seemed to enjoy a relaxed and affectionate relationship with them. A bit later, we were visited by a pregnant granddaughter, in her early twenties, who tapped her belly and beamed. "I'm going to be a great-grandfather again," Farrakhan said, in the tone of a happy patriarch.

Farrakhan may have grown up without a father himself, but he speaks often of his mother and her brothers. Indeed, his early interest in the Black Muslims was only a new twist on an established family tradition. Most of Farrakhan's relatives were already followers of the most widely influential black nationalist of the century—Marcus Garvey, whose Universal Negro Improvement Association achieved fame and notoriety in the early twenties. Even so, the reaction of Gene's mother to his decision to join the Muslims was less than effusive. "She was a very reserved, strong woman," Farrakhan said, "and she said, 'It's very interesting.' She didn't say nay or yea."

Before long, her son emerged as Minister Louis X, of the Boston Temple. He had been trained well by Malcolm in public speaking, and he also brought his own particular gifts to the task. He recorded a song entitled "A White Man's Heaven Is a Black Man's Hell," which was a hit in Black Muslim circles, and he swiftly established himself as one of the most promising members of the ministry. He wrote—and performed in—a play entitled "Orgena" ("A Negro" spelled backward), a satire about assimilated blacks. He also wrote "The Trial," in which a black prosecutor (usually played by Louis) tries the White Man for his myriad sins, and at the conclusion a black jury finds the defendant guilty and sentences him to death. Audiences responded with clamorous ovations.

But the Black Muslims would soon be appearing on a far larger stage, for Elijah Muhammad was discovering that even ostensibly hostile exposure in the mass media could serve him well. In the summer of 1959, Mike Wallace and Louis Lomax produced a television documentary on the Black Muslims, a group that then numbered less than thirty thousand. The Nation seemed to arouse alarm in white audiences, but that alarm only deepened its appeal to its natural constituency. The religious scholar C. Eric Lincoln, who in 1961 conducted a landmark study of the Nation of Islam, points out that weeks after the documentary appeared Muhammad's following doubled in size.

Malcolm X was the public, charismatic face of the Nation of Islam in these years, while Louis, eight years his junior, proved his best student. Close as they were, however, there were occasional flareups between them, especially as a rift between Malcolm and Elijah was gradually making itself felt. C. Eric Lincoln recalls a signal incident in the early sixties: "Alex Haley and Louie and I were all seated with Malcolm in a Muslim restaurant down in Harlem, and Lou, who is very irreverent and outspoken, suddenly said to Malcolm, 'Malcolm, why don't you stop all this "Mister Muhammad" shit and go out and lead your *own* movement? Man, you could—' And before he could get the words out of his mouth, Malcolm had shot up like an onion in the rain. His face was contorted, he was so angry. And he was reaching for Lou, and Alex Haley stepped between them. Malcolm said, 'Lou, we've been friends a long time. But don't you ever say that to me!'"

In 1964, however, Malcolm finally did break with the Nation of Islam, telling newspapers that he had been disillusioned by discovering that Elijah Muhammad had fathered children with his young secretaries. (Since the facts of Muhammad's philandering had long been an open secret among the Muslim élite, Malcolm's claim to have been shocked by such revelations struck his brethren as spurious and vengeful, aimed solely at causing embarrassment.) And Louis proved himself staunchly loyal to the Nation of Islam, denouncing in thunderous tones the Judas in its midst.

In a column that appeared in December of that year in *Muhammad Speaks*, the Nation of Islam's weekly newspaper, Louis wrote some now notorious words: "The die is set, and Malcolm shall not escape . . . Such a man as Malcolm is worthy of death." Malcolm was assassinated in Harlem on February 21, 1965. Farrakhan has been dogged by speculation that he was somehow involved in the killing. One of the men convicted of the murder said that, once Malcolm had been denounced as a traitor, he simply understood it to be his duty to take him out. In recent years, Farrakhan has admitted his responsibility in helping to create the poisonous atmosphere in which the killing took place; still, he denies any more direct involvement.

Just as Fard's disappearance had propelled Elijah Muhammad into preëminence, Farrakhan was now left to fill the void left by Malcolm. By the end of the year, Farrakhan had assumed Malcolm's old position as minister of the Harlem Mosque No. 7 and as Elijah Muhammad's National Representative. Yet for some the aura of regicide would never fade. Eldridge Cleaver, who considers the assassination of Malcolm one of the crimes of the century against black people, speaks about the succession bitterly: "It was the old show-business adage: 'The show must go on.' And so, with Malcolm not being present, where was the best clone they could find? Farrakhan gravitated to the top of the heap as the slimeball, scheming, renegade bandwagoner that he is. He was able to get that position because, unlike any of the others around him, he was able to sing Malcolm's song."

In recent years, Malcolm has been retrieved by the mainstream as a palatable culture hero, whose path to enlightenment can be contrasted with Farrakhan's blinkered vision. The civil-rights activist

Julian Bond says, "Malcolm grew. Farrakhan never did." It's hard to speak conclusively about Malcolm, since he was assassinated so soon after he announced his universalist creed, but the fact remains that, his conversion to Sunni Islam aside, he never really relinquished black nationalism. Like Malcolm, Farrakhan says that we must learn to move beyond color, and transcend all the divisions of humanity; like Malcolm, he asks the black community to develop its own self-reliance in the meantime. So the supposed contrast between the two men can seem more convenient than convincing.

It's equally difficult to recapture a sense of the enmity that existed between black radicals and the civil-rights mainstream in the sixties. Malcolm and Martin Luther King (whom Malcolm used to refer to as the Reverend Dr. Chicken Wing) have in some measure been melded through martyrdom. But the Muslims' rhetoric was far from conciliatory. "I was a Muslim then," Farrakhan said to me. "I wasn't for integration—I was a separatist. I thought Dr. King wasn't going in the right direction." But he also spoke of these tensions as part of a historical pattern. "In all the years of our progress in our century, there have always been these two poles. The masses are hearing the arguments like a tennis match, and all the time there is a level of consciousness coming up." This was also true during the civil-rights era, when Malcolm X and the nationalists were squaring off against Dr. King and the integrationists.

"The argument was healthy," Farrakhan went on. "You can see it now, when you are getting old and about to die. We've tried socialism, some have tried Communism, we've tried nationalism, we've tried Americanism, we've tried integration. But in all these experiments we've become wiser, and what I see today is that there is and was good in every step that we made, and now what we need is not a thesis and an antithesis—what we need is a synthesis of the best ideas of this hundred years of struggle. And that's why in my maturity or my process of maturing I fell in love with Dr. King."

In the sixties and seventies, the Nation of Islam also began to attract followers for its level of discipline, its political savvy, and its emphasis on self-help. The eminent African-American novelist Leon Forrest served as managing editor of *Muhammad Speaks* in the early seventies, when many of its editors and writers were, like him, non-Muslims. He recalls that Elijah Muhammad was so politically agile that he ordered the paper not to write anything bad about Richard Nixon, hoping to profit from Nixon's proposal to set up enterprise zones in the inner city. That model of economic self-reliance was altogether consonant with the preachings of the Messenger. "The base of Elijah's movement and personality was steeped in a real deep conservatism," Forrest says. "Any number of whites who knew I worked for the Nation of Islam would say, 'You know, I really admire the Muslims.' And it was because it represents all the old American values of thrift and hard work, discipline, respect for the family and the women. Keep to yourself. Build small businesses. All the old American values, really. And then Elijah put in a little radical stuff here and there. But when you think about all the in-your-face, ready-to-duke-it-out vision people have of the Muslims, how many white people did they kill?"

AS ELIJAH MUHAMMAD'S HEALTH DECLINED, IN THE EARLY SEVENTIES, many people believed that he was grooming Farrakhan to be his successor. And yet when Muhammad lay dying, in 1975, he designated not Farrakhan but, rather, his own son, Wallace Deen Muhammad. It was a bizarre choice. Wallace—or Warith, as he then renamed himself—had sided with Malcolm X against his father in the sixties, and had even been excommunicated for several years. He had also been taking very seriously his studies of Sunni Islam, and the teachings of his father had struck him as essentially heretical. Now that he was at last at the helm of his father's movement, he renounced the doctrines of Yakub, of racial demonology, of the divinity of Fard, even of his own father's status as prophet. He also set about divesting himself of Nation properties; soon an estate thought to be worth as much as a hundred million dollars had gone the way of the original Black Muslim doctrine.

By 1977, Louis Farrakhan had had enough. He announced that he was breaking with Warith's organization in order to reëstablish the Nation of Islam according to the original tenets of the Messenger. Carrying on the tradition of *Muhammad Speaks*, Farrakhan started up *The Final Call*, in which Elijah Muhammad's credo would be faithfully reproduced in every issue. Farrakhan also revived the creation myth of Yakub.

As a literary critic, I've long been impressed by Elijah Muhammad as a man who invented his own mythology. I asked Farrakhan whether he really believed the story of Yakub—or was it better understood as a metaphor?

"It is not, in our judgment, metaphorical," Farrakhan replied stolidly. "The reason it seems like an invention—and I know you meant that in the best sense—is that it was not heard before. And, rather than credit it as a revelation, intellectually we give it a name that allows us to deal with it. Personally, I believe that Yakub is not a mythical figure—he is a very real scientist."

Nevertheless, Farrakhan does seem to have quietly downgraded Elijah Muhammad's cherished demonology. Muhammad was asked, a few years before his death, whether he would really label *all* white people "blue-eyed devils." His reply was "Whether they are actually blue-eyed or not, if they are actually one of the members of that race they are devils." But now Farrakhan said, "If you saw a picture of Master Farrad Muhammad"—that is, Wallace Fard, the founder—"He looked like a white man." He went on to say that many of his own relatives, including his father and his grandfather, were fair-skinned, so how could he hate people because of the color of their skin?

While the burden of slavery and history and societal structure cannot be ignored, he argued, black men and women must accept responsibility, "more so than in any other time in our history," for their failures. "It's so easy to put it on the white man," he said. "As long as we can beat up on white people and make the world think that everything that went wrong in the world is due to them and we had nothing to do with this, then we rob ourselves of the impetus, the motivation, and the inspiration for personal change and for accepting personal responsibility. I say to black audiences today, 'There was a time when you could blame the white man and there was a time you could say the white man is a devil, but, with the way we're raising hell today and the way we're inflicting evil and pain on each other, you can't say that anymore.'"

IN THE LATE SEVENTIES AND EARLY EIGHTIES, FARRAKHAN WAS BUSY trying to shore up the ranks of the Nation of Islam, both economically and ideologically, but the nation at large was barely aware of his existence. Then came 1984, Jesse Jackson's campaign for the Presidency, and Farrakhan's decision to break with Elijah Muhammad's principled abstention from politics.

Inspired by Jackson's campaign, Farrakhan registered to vote and volunteered the Nation's Fruit of Islam to provide security for Jackson. According to Farrakhan, Jackson's bid alarmed Jews, who distrusted his attitude toward Israel, and sought to derail the campaign by using Farrakhan's extremist rhetoric against Jackson. The wildly menacing statements, the apocalyptic imagery of race warfare, and all the other staples of Black Muslim oratory played well at Mosque Maryam, in Chicago, but were less warmly received on network television. Farrakhan complained that Jews controlled the media, and then raised his voice even more when he was attacked as a "black Hitler." Around the same time, Jackson got himself in trouble when a black reporter quoted him referring to New York City as "Hymietown." Farrakhan thereupon made things worse for Jackson by urging the black community to ostracize the reporter, and adding that one day traitors like him would be killed. Then came the press conference at which, in reply to a question about the Hitler comparison, Farrakhan said that any man who is talked about forty years after his death is a great man but that Hitler was wickedly great. (It's clear, in context, that Farrakhan meant "great" in the same spirit in which *Time* named Hitler Man of the Year for 1938.) "The next day, in the Chicago *Sun-Times*, in the New York *Post*: 'JACKSON PAL HAILS HITLER,'" Farrakhan recalled. "I took umbrage at being compared with Hitler. I haven't even been arrested for spitting on the sidewalk or doing anything violent to anyone. And now you're going to call me a Hitler, like I'm planning to do something evil to Jewish people?"

Four months later, Farrakhan made a radio broadcast during which he talked about Israelis' "using God's name to shield your dirty religion." Now he said, "Fine. I said that. They said I said 'gutter,' but it was 'dirty.' I had no reference whatsoever in my mind to Judaism. However, anybody who distilled that could say, and rightly so, that I was talking about Judaism. So the headline the next day was 'FARRAKHAN CALLS JUDAISM A GUTTER RELIGION.'"

It is true that the two things nearly everybody knows about Farrakhan—that he extolled Hitler as a great man and deplored Judaism as a "gutter religion"—are, strictly speaking, false. That point may not speak well of the accuracy of some of our leading media, but it hardly absolves him of the larger charge of anti-Semitism. And, for all his talk of reconciliation, Farrakhan refuses to budge. "It doesn't make any difference what I say, how I explain myself," he said. "I have never got away from 'Judaism is a gutter religion,' 'Hitler is a great man.'" He shrugged. "I'm a *man*—I'm not afraid of white folk. And so if they got the nerve to say that about me I got nerve enough to defend myself and to drop an accusation on them that I believe be true. So the fight was on—me and the Jews." He spread his arms, holding up two clenched fists, like a pugilist.

If the public consternation over the Black Muslims in the late nineteen-fifties magnified Elijah Muhammad's influence, the controversy in the wake of the Jackson campaign performed a similar service for Farrakhan. David Jackson, of the Chicago *Tribune*, notes that Farrakhan's 1983 Christmas address attracted a small handful of listeners on folding chairs, whereas today he routinely commands audiences of ten thousand and more. The commentator Roger Wilkins says of Farrakhan's Jewish critics, "I'm not saying they're wrong to strike back—I'm never going tell the guy whom somebody slams the stomach, 'Well, here's what you must do now.' But, once they struck back, he became a national figure. These attacks don't hurt him in his base; they enhance him, because he has told his people that though he is not anti-Semitic, there's this free-floating Zionist plot that is directed at him. So when the Anti-Defamation League attacks him all he has to do is turn to his people and say 'See?' Then, of course, one of the messages is 'They are attacking me because I am supporting you and your interests.'"

LOUIS FARRAKHAN WILL SAY, UP AND DOWN, THAT HE REVERES THE Jewish people. Listen to him: "Personally, I don't know what this argument has served. Jewish people are the world leaders, in my opinion. They are some of the most brilliant people on this planet. The Jews are some of the greatest scientists, the greatest thinkers, the greatest writers, the greatest theologians, the greatest in music, the greatest in business. And people hate them sometimes because of envy, and because the Jews succeed in spite of the hatred of their Gentile brethren, or anybody else's hatred. I admire that, as God is my witness."

Farrakhan has a theological explanation for Jewish preëminence. His theory that the Jews have had many prophets in their midst and so have been the greatest recipients of divine revelation, and that this elevated wisdom has translated itself into achievement of all kinds. "When you have a people who receive revelation," he says, "they can do very good things or they can become very base, evil, and use the revelation for wicked purposes."

For many years, Farrakhan has been saying that there is a small group of Jews who meet (variously) in a Park Avenue apartment or in Hollywood to plan the course of the nation. I had to ask, "Do you think that there's a cabal—that there's a central planning group within the Jewish community?"

"I do believe that," Farrakhan replied. "I believe that there are very, very wise Jews who plan good and there are very wise Jews who plan evil." He added, "I am not hateful. I am deeply respectful of the Jewish people, man. I know they are great, but I also know that there are some scoundrels among them. And those scoundrels have to be condemned by them. And if they don't condemn the scoundrels—well, that's all right. I will."

I began to focus on Farrakhan's reddish-ochre complexion and his silky, wavy hair—what we called "Jesus moss" when I was growing up. "Do you know anything about your white ancestry?" I asked him.

Farrakhan explained that his father was very light-skinned and had straight hair, and that his mother had told him his father's parentage was, in fact, white Portuguese. Then he said, "I'm going to tell you something. You really want to know what think? I think they were members of the Jewish community." This sounds like a fantastical joke, but it is highly probable, given what we know about migration to the West Indies. Orlando Patterson, a historical sociologist at Harvard, who has made a study of merchant populations in the islands, confirms that nearly all people of Iberian descent in Jamaica and Barbados, even today, are of Sephardic Jewish ancestry.

"I believe that in my blood, and not in a bad way," Farrakhan said. "Because when I was a little boy I used to love listening to the Jewish cantors in Boston. They had a program, and every week I would listen. I was struck by the cantor, and I've always loved the way they sing or recite the Torah." Farrakhan is always happy to elaborate on his admiration for Jewish musicians. "When my mom put that violin in my hand and I fell in love with that instrument, I never was thinking Jew, Gentile, anything like that," he said. "But all my heroes were Jewish. The greatest was Jascha Heifetz, and I loved him then and I love him now. I was driving my car when it came over the news that Vladimir Horowitz, the pianist, had passed. I pulled my car over to the side of the road and I said a prayer for his soul." He went on, "If in my lineage there are Jews, I would hope that in the end, before my life is over, I not only will have rendered a service to my own beloved community of black people but will also have rendered a service to the Jewish community." What he seemed to have in mind was not what most people would consider a service: he was evidently referring to the notorious book "The Secret Relationship Between Blacks and Jews," published by the Nation of Islam, the implicit assumption of which is that a Jewish predilection for evil is visible throughout the centuries.

"You read 'The Secret Relationship Between Blacks and Jews,'" Farrakhan said.

"And critiqued it," I put in.

"And critiqued it," he said, nodding. "I didn't order anybody to research this. They wanted to defend me, so they went to research it. We are making the point that the Jewish people were involved in slavery, and seventy-five per cent of the Jews owned slaves." He gave me a level look. "You have a relationship with Jews of scholarship and brilliance, whom you can admire and have a lovely friendship with," he said. "I know there are Jews like that and I could have a wonderful friendship with them. I'm hoping and I believe that in the future it will develop. Sometimes, Dr. Gates, when you are new in the neighborhood, you get in a fight and you bloody the guy's nose, and he bloodies your nose, and before you know it you end up being the best of friends. But you're not friends without mutual respect."

Farrakhan took a deep breath and continued, "But my point is

I don't like our relationship with Jews. I think it's a weak relationship. I think it's a paternalistic relationship. I don't like a relationship where they are the agent or the manager and we are the talent alone. We bring a lot to the table, but we get so little from the table. The I.R.S. puts the principal in jail and the accountant gets away with the money. This is wrong. There is so much injustice here."

What is one to make of all this? Farrakhan isn't feigning admiration for Jews as distraction from his hate-mongering. Rather, his love and his loathing flow from the same ideas. There's a sense in which Farrakhan doesn't want his followers to battle Jews, but, rather, wants them to *be* Jews. Yet when he describes Jews as "world leaders" it is a double-edged compliment. There is no sense in being gladdened when he extolls Jewish wisdom and troubled only when he warns of Jewish evil: both sentiments are sincere, and both are aspects of a single unhealthy obsession.

In speeches he has made over the past several years, Farrakhan stresses the fact that he is condemning only some Jews—the scoundrelly ones. But the question begged is one of relevance: What makes a scoundrel's ethnicity or religion of central concern to Farrakhan or his audiences? Farrakhan protests that he didn't say all Jews, he said *some* Jews, but the protest misses the point. Partitive anti-Semitism remains anti-Semitism.

Consider, even, the figure that Farrakhan often returns to: that seventy-five per cent of the Jews in the South owned slaves. He returns to it because, he says, no one has refuted it. It is a fact—the result of an 1830 survey—and not something just concocted. But facts, as Ronald Reagan once said, are stupid things. The historian Harold Brackman points out that in 1830 only a third of America's Jews lived in the South. Those Southern Jews tended to be middle-class urban dwellers, with small numbers of domestic servants; by contrast, Jewish representation among the plantation owners who held most of the slaves was minuscule. Furthermore, in 1830 black slaveowners outnumbered Jewish slaveowners by fifteen to one.

But the real question is why the results of this 1830 survey should be of such concern to a constituency that you might think had more pressing matters to contend with: mounting poverty, crime, AIDS. Farrakhan arouses the indignation of inner-city audiences when he speaks of an exploitative relationship between Jewish agents and black talent. You may cringe, but when you scan his flock you see that there's something bleakly comic about it, too. They're struggling to make ends meet. Agents? Accountants? What is Louis Farrakhan talking about? And why?

"Whenever our interests seemed diametrically opposed," Farrakhan told me, "Jews followed what they felt was in their best interest." And he cited Jewish opposition to Jackson's candidacy, and Jewish opposition to affirmative action. But, since most whites opposed Jackson and most whites are hostile to affirmative action, one might think that the more interesting fact that Jews are disproportionately represented among those whites who did support Jackson, and who favor measures like affirmative action. Blacks, Farrakhan has said, must pursue their self-interest. But hurling invective at liberal allies doesn't sound like prudent self-interest to me. Even if Farrakhan's discourse on the Jews can't be reduced purely to a matter of fear and loathing, it doesn't bespeak sweet reason, either.

THE TRULY PARANOID HEART OF FARRAKHAN'S WORLD VIEW HAS been revealed in recent speeches in which he has talked about a centuries-old conspiracy of international bankers—with names like Rothschild and Warburg—who have captured control over the central banks in many countries, and who incite wars to increase the indebtedness of others and maximize their own wealth. The Federal Reserve, the I.R.S., the F.B.I., and the Anti-Defamation League were all founded in 1913, Farrakhan says (actually, the I.R.S. was founded in 1862 and the F.B.I. in 1908, but never mind), and then he poses the favorite rhetorical question of all paranoid historians: "Is that a coincidence?"

What do you do with a religious demagogue who promulgates the theory that Jewish financiers have manipulated world events for centuries? Well, if you're a Republican contender for the Presidency, and the demagogue's name is Pat Robertson, you genuflect. It turns out that Farrakhan's conspiracy theory of Jewish cabals is essentially identical to Robertson's. "Rest assured, there is a behind-the-scenes Establishment in this nation, as in every other," Robertson writes in "The New World Order," his recent best-selling book. "It has enormous power. It has controlled the economic and foreign policy objectives of the United States for the past seventy years, whether the man sitting in the White House is a Democrat or a Republican, a liberal or a conservative, a moderate or an extremist." Robertson goes on to inveigh against the tentacular Rothschilds and Warburgs. Michael Lind, who has analyzed Robertson's conspiracy theories at length, suggests that not since the days of Father Coughlin has the grassroots right been as overtly anti-Semitic as it is now.

And Farrakhan? He, too, believes all this conspiracy stuff, and thinks he's just telling it like it is. He must realize that such talk goes down well with inner-city audiences hungry for secret histories that explain how things went wrong. He turns mainstream criticism to his advantage, winning ovations by representing himself as the persecuted truth-teller. But turnabout isn't always fair play: and the fact that Farrakhan is a black American only makes his deafness to historical context all the more dismaying. Within his own lifetime, one of every three Jews on the face of the earth died at the hands of a regime suffused by the same language about nefarious Jewish influence. Ultimately, Farrakhan's anti-Semitism has the characteristics of a psychological obsession, and once in a while he shows signs of recognizing this. "I would prefer that this whole conflict would go away, in truth," he said to me. His voice sounded husky, and little tired. "But it's like I'm locked now in a struggle. It's like both of us got a hold on each other, and each of us is filled with electricity. I can't let them go, and they can't let me go."

FARRAKHAN'S PECULIAR MIXTURE OF INSIGHT AND DELUSION WOULD be a matter of mainly academic interest if it weren't for his enormous populist appeal among black Americans—an appeal that was clearly demonstrated in last fall's Million Man March. That occasion has been widely seen as an illustration both of Farrakhan's strengths and of his weaknesses. "If only somebody else had convened it," the liberal-minded are prone to say. But nobody else—not Colin Powell, not Jesse Jackson—could have. Some of the most heartfelt tributes to the event's success are also the most grudging. There's little doubt, after all, that the Farrakhan phenomenon owes much to a vacuum of radical black leadership. (Jesse Jackson has emerged over the past decade as the leading spokesman of the American left, I submit, rather than of black America.) "We have the worst leadership in the black community since slavery," Eldridge Cleaver maintains. "Farrakhan saw that vacuum, saw nothing motivating the people, no vision being projected to the people, and he came up with the defining event for a generation of people, this Million Man March."

Timing had a lot to do with the event's success, of course. As Roger Wilkins likes to say, Newt Gingrich was one of the main organizers of the march. "If the white middle class feels it's losing ground, the black working class and unskilled working class are being slaughtered—hit by a blitzkrieg that no one notices," Wilkins points out. "And their plight is not on anyone's agenda anymore. Farrakhan supplies an answer, and an emotional discharge."

Farrakhan's people have won some real credibility in the black community. "It's as if Malcolm was having a march on Washington," Robert Moses, the civil-rights activist and education reformer, says. And Wilkins says, "Nobody else can go into the prisons and save souls to the degree that they have." "Nobody else is able to put as many neat and clean young people on the streets of the inner city as they are. You think about the fellows who are selling their papers as opposed to those fellows you see standing around the liquor stores. Their men have this enviable sense of discipline, orderliness, and human purpose." (The Nation of Islam continues to have very conservative sexual politics, and Farrakhan is vehemently anti-abortion, but he has also inveighed against domestic violence, and—in a sharp break from tradition—even named a woman to be a nation of Islam minister.) Hugh Price, the president of the National Urban League, calls the march "the largest family-values rally in the history of the United States." Indeed, another sign of its success was the number of mainstream civil-rights leaders who were present. Whatever their discomfort with Farrakhan's extremist rhetoric, they calculated that their absence might well imperil their legitimacy with the black public.

Attendance or non-attendance was a delicate decision. General Colin Powell was prominent among those blacks who decided that they could not afford to appear. When I asked Farrakhan if he would consider supporting a future Powell Presidential bid, he said, "I don't want to support anybody because he's black—I think have outgrown the need to support somebody because of the color of his skin. What is in the best interest of our people is really in the best interest of the country. So if General Powell had an agenda that is good for the totality of our people—the American people first—and in that package is something that can lift our people, he's got our support."

Farrakhan's level of support among black Americans is vigorously debated. If you gauge his followers by the number who regularly attend mosques affiliated with the Nation of Islam and eschew lima beans and corn bread, they are not very numerous. Estimates range from twenty thousand to ten times that. On the other hand, if you go by the number of people who consider him a legitimate voice of black protest, the ranks are much larger. (In a recent poll, more than half the blacks surveyed reported a favorable impression of him.) The march was inspired by the Muslims but not populated by them. Farrakhan knows that the men who came to the march were not his religious followers. They tended to be middle class and college-educated and Christian. Farrakhan is convinced that those men came "to a march called by a man who is considered radical, extremist, anti-Semitic, anti-white" because of a yearning "to connect with the masses."

Not everyone, to be sure, was quite so deeply impressed. "This was an opportunity for the black middle class to feel this symbolic connection, but what were the solutions that were proposed, except atonement?" Angela Davis asks. Julian Bond says bluntly, "You know, that Negro didn't even vote until 1984. He's the leader in the sense that he can gather people to him, but they don't go anyplace when they leave him." And Jesse Jackson, who addressed the marchers, now views the march as fatally flawed by its failure to reach out to Capitol Hill. "The 1963 March on Washington was connected to public policy—public accommodations," he says, and notes that the result was the signing into law of the Civil Rights Act the following year. By contrast, he argues, the Million Man March had "essentially a religious theme—atonement—disconnected from public policy," so it brought no political dividends in its aftermath. "On the very next day—the very next day, *the very next day*—there was the welfare bill," he said, referring to the House and Senate conferences to work out a final draft of a bill excusing the federal government from a degree of responsibility toward the poor. "The next day was the vote on the unfair sentence guidelines. The next day was the Medicare bill," another hostile measure. "The big debates in Congress took place between that Wednesday and Thursday. And so those who were taking away our rights and attacking us did not see any connection between the gathering and public policy." The lesson he draws is straightforward: "The march was essentially disconnected from our political leadership. Any mass action must be connected to the public-policy leaders."

Some critics express a sense that the mass mobilization may itself be a relic of a bygone era. It was an arena where Farrakhan was able to stake a claim for mass black leadership, in part because of the near-sacralization of the 1963 precursor; but its continued political viability has not been demonstrated. Indeed, the growing fragmentation of black leadership—the irrelevance of the old-fashioned notion of a "head nigger in charge"—is one sign that an élite now exists in black America that does enjoy an unmediated relation to power. Privately, many black leaders say that Farrakhan's moment has passed. Such remarks inevitably carry an air of wishful thinking. White liberal allies sometimes worry that pressure is required to keep black leaders from being "soft on Farrakhan"; in reality, no love is lost among those who would compete for the hearts and souls of black America. At the helm of the mainstream black-advocacy groups are men and women who may say conciliatory things about the Nation of Islam, but their jaws are tense and their smiles are tight. They reassure themselves that Farrakhan is bound to remain a marginal phenomenon because of his extremism. Yet the organic leaders of the disenfranchised are seldom moderate in tone; and since, from all indications, the underclass is continuing to expand, Farrakhan's natural power base will only increase.

In the months following the march, Farrakhan dropped out of public view, and he spoke of having suffered from depression, in part because he was still being misrepresented by the press. This response highlights Farrakhan's paradoxical relation to the wider public—that of a pariah who wants to be embraced. "Both Malcolm and Farrakhan had a very tough ideology but at the same time wanted a degree of public acceptance in the white community," Ron Walters, a political scientist and an adviser to Jackson, says. "To me, that's a tremendous contradiction. I don't know whether it's a personality thing or just what happens to you when you reach a certain level of prominence—that you do want sort of universal acceptance."

Such acceptance has been elusive so far. A few weeks before the Million Man March, Farrakhan gave an interview to make it clear that when he referred to Jewish "bloodsuckers" he didn't mean Jews in particular—he meant all nonblack shopkeepers in the inner city, some of them Jewish but these days more often Koreans or Arabs. He must have found it galling when many newspapers wrested his remarks out of context, leaving the impression that he had merely repeated the original accusation: Farrakhan calls Jews bloodsuckers. Farrakhan's image also suffered when, early last year, the Chicago *Tribune* published an investigative series, by David Jackson and William Gaines, revealing financial disarray among Nation-owned businesses. Farrakhan's calls for economic self-sufficiency, it appeared, were not matched by his organization's performance.

Farrakhan hurt himself yet again, with his so-called World Friendship Tour, in January and February. He claims that his decision to make this trip to Third World capitals was a matter of divine inspiration, but it isn't hard to imagine human motivations as well. Public figures who feel that they have been badly used by the local papers often find that solace awaits them in admiring throngs overseas: call it the Jerry Lewis syndrome. Besides, how better to shore up your position as the leader of black America than by being received as such by foreign potentates?

The domestic fallout, however, has lingered. Even many of those who supported Farrakhan were chagrined to find him holding friendly meetings with some of the world's worst dictators: Nigeria's Sani Abacha, Libya's Muammar Qaddafi, Zaire's Mobutu, and Sudan's Omar al-Bashir. Ron Walters observes, "He gave all those people who wanted an opportunity not to have to deal with him the golden reason. The tremendous political capital of the march had been dissipated." Black nationalists were among those who were the most horrified. Molefi Kete Asante, the Afrocentric scholar, says, "What Farrakhan did, in my judgment, was to take the legitimacy of the march and put it in his back pocket, and march around to these terrible governments, as if somehow he were the leader of a million black people. That upset me."

It is a sore subject with Farrakhan. Sure, he met with dictators, he said to me, but when you are dealing with atonement, sin, and reconciliation you don't travel to the blameless. "It's all right for Jesse to sit down with George Wallace in Alabama and for them to pray together—and there's applause," he went on. "But I can't go sit down with my brother who is a sinner? Nixon died a hero, but I cannot forgive a black man?" There was a surge of anger in his voice. "That's the damnable thing that I hate about this whole damned thing," he said. "If I go to a black man to retrieve him, all of a sudden I'm cavorting with a damned dictator, but Jesus could sit down with the sinners and you give him honor and credit. And Reagan can sit down with Gorbachev, and he gets honor and credit. He sits with the evil empire, but I can't sit with my own brother. To hell with you for that. That's why I am not a politician."

"Has the tour compromised the achievement of the march?" I asked him.

He sounded subdued when he said, "If it lost momentum, I believe it's only temporary."

FARRAKHAN LAYS MUCH *STRESS* ON THE IMAGERY OF DIALOGUE AND conciliation these days. Certainly the Farrakhan I met was a model of civility and courtesy. I was reminded of Eric Lincoln's account of the last couple of visits he had paid to Farrakhan at his home: "Louie insisted on getting down on his hands and knees on the floor to take my shoes off. You know, I'm overweight and it's a difficult task to get shoes and socks off. And so Louis said, 'I will do that.' And I said, 'No, no.' And Louis said, 'No, I want to do it.' He took my shoes off and rubbed my feet to get the blood circulating."

If the Farrakhan phenomenon remains disquieting, the man himself seems oddly, jarringly vulnerable. I met someone who was eager, even hungry, for conversation; someone of great intelligence who seemed intellectually lonely. In fiery speeches before packed auditoriums, Farrakhan speaks of plots against his life, and does so in alarmingly messianic tones. ("I don't care nothing about my life," he told his audience on Saviour's Day in 1995, his voice breaking. "It's *your* life that I want to save!") To me he spoke of mortality in a quieter mode. He spoke movingly of watching the funeral of Yitzhak Rabin—about the tragedy of a wise and tempered elder statesman assassinated by a callow extremist. He spoke about having a growing appreciation for compromise, about coming to see the value in the positions of his ideological antagonists within the civil-rights tradition. And he told me about a fight of his own, against prostate cancer, over the past several years.

"At first, it was frightening to me—how could I have cancer? I've eaten well, I've tried to live clean. Then I fasted and I prayed and I went into the desert, and after a month I went and had an M.R.I. and one of those rectal ultrasounds, and all they could find was a little scar." He paused, and added quietly, "But then it came back." He looks in splendid health: he is sixty-three, and his skin remains soft and almost unlined. He recently made a health-and-exercise video, which shows him going through an arduous regimen of weight-training. And he *is* remarkably fit. He has undergone seed-implantation radiation-therapy for his cancer, and remains optimistic about the results. "I've never had to take a pain pill, and I hope and pray that God will bless me ultimately to overcome it. At least, all accounts up to date, the P.S.A."—the blood-screening test for prostate cancer—"has been normal. And so I'm going on with my life, but warning all of us that this is such a hell of a killer of our people. And when you reach your early forties, many of us won't like somebody poking around in our rectum, but we have to encourage our young men and our middle-aged brothers, and the population as a whole, to do that for themselves, because all we have is our health."

We all know that the world isn't divided between saints and sinners. And yet the private Farrakhan's very humanness—those traits of kindness, concern, humor—makes his paranoia all the more disconcerting. He rails against the way the mainstream has demonized him, and yet he refuses to renounce the anti-Semitic conspiracy theories that have made him anathema: to him, it would be like denying the law of gravity. And so he is trapped, immobilized by his contradictory desires. His ongoing calls for dialogue are seemingly heartfelt; he genuinely wants seat at the table, craves the legitimation of power. Yet he will not engage in the compromises and concessions that true dialogue requires. He cannot afford to. This is a man whose political identity is constituted by antagonism to the self-image of America. To moderate his stance of unyielding opposition would be to destroy the edifice he has spent his life constructing. Moreover, Farrakhan knows that there are people around him whose militancy puts his to shame. Some of them are former lieutenants of his in the Nation of Islam, such as Khalid Muhammad, whom Farrakhan suspended after judging him to have been *too* intemperate in his public pronouncements. Others have established an independent base of support, such as Silas Muhammad, another Elijah loyalist who split with the organization, and whose sect is now based in Atlanta. For leaders whose appeal is based on intransigence, outrage, and wrath, there is always the danger of being outflanked by those even more intransigent, more outrageous, more wrathful. This, in part, is why Farrakhan could not truly atone even at his own day of atonement.

IN THE END, HOWEVER, IT ISN'T FARRAKHAN BUT FARRAKHAN'S FOLlowing that demands explanation. We might start by admitting the moral authority that black nationalism commands even among those blacks who ostensibly disapprove of it. In the village where

I grew up, there was a Holiness Church, where people spoke in tongues and fell down in religious ecstasy. It was not my church; my family and I shunned the Pentecostal fervor. And yet, on some level, we believed it to be the real thing, realer than our own, more temperate Episcopal services. It was the place to go if you really needed something—if you got desperately sick, say—because the Holy Ghost lived there. (There are Reform Jews who admit to a similar attitude toward their Hasidic brethren.) In this same vein, the assimilated black American, who lives in Scarsdale and drives a Lexus, responds to Farrakhan and Farrakhanism as a presence at once threatening and exhilarating, dismaying and cathartic. Though blackness isn't exactly a religion, it has become invested with a quasi-religious structure. Black nationalism is a tradition extending at least back to Martin R. Delany, in the nineteenth century. Cross it with the black messianic tradition—which spawned the legendary likes of Father Divine, Daddy Grace, and Prophet Jones—and you have the Nation of Islam.

Hard as it is to take stock of the organization's membership, it's harder to take stock of Farrakhan's place in the mind of black America. For his dominion is, in a sense, a dominion of metaphor, which to say that it is at once factitious and factual. The political theorist Benedict Anderson has defined nations as "imagined communities," and the black nation is even more imaginary than most. We know that thirty-six million sepia Americans do not a collective make, but in our minds we sometimes insist upon it.

The Million Man March had all the hallmarks a watershed event, yet a march is not a movement. I asked Farrakhan at one point what the country would look like if, by magic, he could turn his hopes into reality. The answer he gave me was long and meandering, but it centered on things like "revamping the educational system" to make it less Eurocentric—proposals of the sort debated by the New York State Board of Regents, rather than something that was radically transformative in any obvious way.

That was, in a sense, the most dismaying response I'd heard all day. Farrakhan is a man of visions. Just weeks before the march, he told congregants in a Washington, D.C., church about the "Mother Wheel"—a heavily armed spaceship the size of a city, which will rain destruction upon white America but save those who embrace the Nation of Islam. ("Ezekiel saw the wheel, way up in the middle of the air," in the words of the old spiritual.) What gave me pause was the realization that such visions coexist in Farrakhan's mind with a real poverty of—well, vision, which is to say a broader conception of the human future.

Farrakhan is a man of unhealthy fixations, but the reciprocal fixation on Farrakhan that you find in the so-called mainstream is a sign of our own impoverished political culture. Thirteen decades have passed since Emancipation, and half of our black men between twenty-four and thirty-five are without full-time employment. One black man graduates from college for every hundred who go to jail. Almost half of black children live in poverty. People say that Farrakhan is now the leading voice of black rage in America. One day, America will realize it got off easy.

MOURNING FOR WHITENESS

TONI MORRISON

November 21, 2016

This is a serious project. All immigrants to the United States know (and knew) that if they want to become real, authentic Americans they must reduce their fealty to their native country and regard it as secondary, subordinate, in order to emphasize their whiteness. Unlike any nation in Europe, the United States holds whiteness as the unifying force. Here, for many people, the definition of "Americanness" is color.

Under slave laws, the necessity for color rankings was obvious, but in America today, post-civil-rights legislation, white people's conviction of their natural superiority is being lost. Rapidly lost. There are "people of color" everywhere, threatening to erase this long-understood definition of America. And what then? Another black President? A predominantly black Senate? Three black Supreme Court Justices? The threat is frightening.

In order to limit the possibility of this untenable change, and restore whiteness to its former status as a marker of national identity, a number of white Americans are sacrificing themselves. They have begun *to do things they clearly don't really want to be doing*, and, to do so, they are (1) abandoning their sense of human dignity and (2) risking the appearance of cowardice. Much as they may hate their behavior, and know full well how craven it is, they are willing to kill small children attending Sunday school and slaughter churchgoers who invite a white boy to pray. Embarrassing as the obvious display of cowardice must be, they are willing to set fire to churches, and to start firing in them while the members are at prayer. And, shameful as such demonstrations of weakness are, they are willing to shoot black children in the street.

To keep alive the perception of white superiority, these white Americans tuck their heads under cone-shaped hats and American flags and deny themselves the dignity of face-to-face confrontation, training their guns on the unarmed, the innocent, the scared, on subjects who are running away, exposing their unthreatening backs to bullets. Surely, shooting a fleeing man in the back hurts the presumption of white strength? The sad plight of grown white men, crouching beneath their (better) selves, to slaughter the innocent during traffic stops, to push black women's faces into the dirt, to handcuff black children. Only the frightened would do that. Right?

These sacrifices, made by supposedly tough white men, who are prepared to abandon their humanity out of fear of black men and women, suggest the true horror of lost status.

It may be hard to feel pity for the men who are making these bizarre sacrifices in the name of white power and supremacy. Personal debasement is not easy for white people (especially for white men), but to retain the conviction of their superiority to others—especially to black people—they are willing to risk contempt, and to be reviled by the mature, the sophisticated, and the strong. If it weren't so ignorant and pitiful, one could mourn this collapse of dignity in service to an evil cause.

The comfort of being "naturally better than," of not having to struggle or demand civil treatment, is hard to give up. The confidence that you will not be watched in a department store, that you are the preferred customer in high-end restaurants—these social inflections, belonging to whiteness, are greedily relished.

So scary are the consequences of a collapse of white privilege that many Americans have flocked to a political platform that supports and translates violence against the defenseless as strength. These people are not so much angry as terrified, with the kind of terror that makes knees tremble.

On Election Day, how eagerly so many white voters—both the poorly educated and the well educated—embraced the shame and fear sowed by Donald Trump. The candidate whose company has been sued by the Justice Department for not renting apartments to black people. The candidate who questioned whether Barack Obama was born in the United States, and who seemed to condone the beating of a Black Lives Matter protester at a campaign rally. The candidate who kept black workers off the floors of his casinos. The candidate who is beloved by David Duke and endorsed by the Ku Klux Klan.

William Faulkner understood this better than almost any other American writer. In "Absalom, Absalom," incest is less of a taboo for an upper-class Southern family than acknowledging the one drop of black blood that would clearly soil the family line. Rather than lose its "whiteness" (once again), the family chooses murder.

THE SOUTHERN STRATEGIST

JELANI COBB

May 14, 2018

At first glance, the crowds of people congregating on a block of Mulberry Street, a stretch of squat brick buildings near downtown Memphis, on the morning of April 4th, might have been there for a variety of reasons. The street venders selling T-shirts and posters and the jumbotron set up near a parking lot suggested the start of a music festival; delegations of men and women dressed in their union best pointed to a labor rally. But the plaintive notes of gospel music drifting from speakers and the black bunting draped over a balcony of the building at the center of the activities indicated a more sombre occasion. The space behind the bunting had begun as an overlook, became a crime scene, and is now a historic site. The hundreds of people, most but by no means all of them black, were gathering at the Lorraine Motel and the National Civil Rights Museum, to mark the moment when, fifty years earlier, Martin Luther King, Jr., was assassinated as he stood on the balcony outside Room 306. The past five years have been a season of semicentennials: 2013, 2014, and 2015 brought anniversaries of the triumphs of the March on Washington, the Civil Rights Act, and the Voting Rights Act. This year recalls losses: King's death and, with it, the hopes of a signal phase of the civil-rights struggle.

Speeches, some of them from associates of King's, went on all day. James Lawson, who, at eighty-nine, is nearly as dynamic as he was when he helped organize the Freedom Rides of 1961, spoke about the landmark strike of black sanitation workers, called in Memphis in early 1968 to protest unsafe work conditions and unequal pay. It was Lawson who had invited King to Memphis, to lend his support. (A sanitation worker at the commemoration who had travelled with a group from New York City told me that it was important to reclaim King's connections to organized labor.) Jesse Jackson, who was with King when he was shot, movingly recounted the final moments of his life. Gina Belafonte, the daughter of King's close friend Harry Belafonte, runs Sankofa, an organization that connects the arts with activism, and she spoke about the imperatives of culture in the service of social change. But the day was warm, and, by the afternoon, the crowd was beginning to grow restless. As with any rite that is repeated at regular intervals, even for an event so consequential, the speeches began to seem rote. The comparisons between the past and the present and the inevitable declarations that we still have "so far to go," which tend to reinforce how creative and distinctive those monumental events of the past were, sometimes raised the dispiriting question of whether anything being done in the present would warrant such celebration in the future.

All this added to the anticipation surrounding one of the final speakers of the day. The Reverend Dr. William Barber, a pastor of Greenleaf Christian Church, in Goldsboro, North Carolina, has become, in the past few years, an indispensable figure in the civil-rights landscape, and, perhaps, the individual most capable of crafting a broad-based political counterpoint to the divisiveness of Trumpism. Charismatic, tireless, eloquent, and yet resistant to an excessive nostalgia for the glory days of the movement, he has presence. At around five o'clock, he came out on the balcony. A tall, heavyset, handsome man with the kind of face that people describe as being "of indeterminate age"—he is fifty-four—Barber was dressed in a black suit, a magenta shirt with a clergyman's collar, and a white clerical stole that read, "Jesus Was a Poor Man." He has an ursine bearing, and moves methodically, which gave the applause a moment to build.

Allotted just five minutes to speak, Barber began by addressing not King's victories but the burdens that he bore. "The weight of these years, by the time he got to Memphis, to stand with black men who were organizing a garbage strike, were heavy," Barber said. "By the time he got to Memphis, he had racists, moderates, politicians, a President, and even jealous criticism from black leaders, who used his position against the Vietnam War as an excuse to diminish his status in the eyes of liberal white America, while raising their own. And then the bullet rang. And his body fell." But what was more important than mourning King's suffering, Barber said, was honoring the work that he undertook in the last months of his life: confronting racism, to be sure, but also militarism and poverty.

Barber speaks in a resonant baritone, with precise phrasing, but he is a true thespian of the pulpit: his eyes widen in mock surprise or squint in faux confusion at an act of outrage or injustice. Sometimes, after making a point, he whirls around, looking over his shoulder as if to see whether anyone has overheard him. From the balcony, he boomed, "We don't need a commemoration, we need a *reconsecration*." He had blown past the five-minute mark, but the crowd was with him. He warned, "The Bible says woe unto those who love the tombs of the prophets." The duty of the living, he said, is not simply to recall the martyrs of the movement but to continue their work. "We've got to hold up the banner until every person has health care, we've got to hold it up until every child is lifted in love, we've got to hold it up until every job is a living-wage job, until every person in poverty has guaranteed subsistence." He finished to loud and sustained applause. Shortly afterward, at a minute past six, the time that King was shot, an enormous bell in the motel courtyard rang thirty-nine times—once for each year of King's life—and the crowd on Mulberry Street began to disperse.

BARBER HAD OFFERED THE MOST CONCRETE ANSWER THAT DAY TO the question King asked in the title of his last book, "Where Do

We Go from Here?," and he wasn't speaking rhetorically. For the past three years, Barber and the Reverend Liz Theoharis, a co-director of the Kairos Center, at Union Theological Seminary, in New York, who stood next to him as he spoke in Memphis, have led an effort to revive King's most radical project: the 1968 Poor People's Campaign. At the commemoration, Jesse Jackson spoke about how King, after shepherding the movement to the Civil Rights Act and the Voting Rights Act, had begun to wonder if he had achieved enough. Despite the pivotal new laws, he knew that the structures of racism, inequality, and injustice had hardly crumbled. So he proposed to broaden the movement's targets from the race-specific concerns of fighting Jim Crow to an assault on the plight of the impoverished across racial lines.

The Poor People's Campaign demanded full employment, a guaranteed basic income, and access to capital for small and minority businesses. King's decision to support the Memphis strike was a way of recognizing labor struggles as part of the movement. The campaign called on people across the country to travel to Washington, D.C., where, for six weeks over the summer, protesters occupied tents on the National Mall, in a camp called Resurrection City. The idea had roots in both the 1963 March on Washington and the 1932 Bonus Army marches of First World War veterans who, left destitute by the Great Depression, set up a camp in the capital and insisted that their pensions be paid early. The centerpiece of the 1968 campaign was a mule-cart procession of people from Marks, Mississippi, the poorest town in the poorest county of the poorest state in the country.

Barber and Theoharis met in 2013, at the opening of the Kairos Center, where he was one of the speakers. (The center advocates a grassroots approach to ending poverty, in which poor people are the key elements of leadership.) At the time, he was launching his Moral Monday movement in North Carolina, enlisting a broad-based alliance of Christians, Muslims, Jews, nonbelievers, blacks,

Latinos, poor whites, feminists, environmentalists, and others to protest the conservative agenda of the state legislature. Theoharis, an ordained Presbyterian minister, had spent twenty-five years doing organizing and social-justice work among domestic workers and Native Americans, and advocating for the rights of the homeless. The new project is called the Poor People's Campaign: A National Call for Moral Revival. This time, the demands include federal and state living-wage laws, equity in education, an end to mass incarceration, a single-payer health-care system, and the protection of the right to vote.

Beginning on Mother's Day and continuing until June 23rd—the last full day of the 1968 campaign—thousands of people in some forty states are expected to commit acts of civil disobedience and protest against policies enacted at the federal and, especially, the state level, that have disproportionately affected poor people. "If you have bad voting laws in your state," Barber told me, "that's not done in Congress, that's something done at the local level." The movement is largely intended to be an independent undertaking of community groups, but it is aided by Theoharis's indefatigable organizing efforts and Barber's ability to project his charisma from the pulpit and the TV screen—he is a regular presence on CNN and, in particular, MSNBC.

On the left, Barber tends to inspire unsolicited testimonials. Last winter, I found myself seated in front of Senator Elizabeth Warren, of Massachusetts, on a train from New York to Boston. We started talking, and I mentioned that I was writing a story about Barber. She said that she had participated in an event with him years earlier, and had followed his work since. She was impressed by his intelligence and his commitment. "He's the real thing," she said. A few weeks later, at a restaurant in Cambridge, Cornel West used the same words when he saw that I had a copy of Barber's book "The Third Reconstruction," which is partly a memoir of his activism and partly an elucidation of his ideas for the movement that he is attempting to build. "That brother is the real thing," West told me. Theoharis has also heard the phrase applied to Barber. "He has really given his life and all that is in it to the struggle," she said. "And I don't think that happens every time. I don't think that, in this society, that actually is heralded, or valued, or upheld as what you're supposed to do. But he embodies this."

His work has been made more difficult by the fact that he suffers from ankylosing spondylitis, an arthritic condition that causes him chronic pain, and forces him to lean forward when he stands, as if he were poring over a book, or speaking to a child. Last year, on an icy night in Boston, I watched as he arrived in an S.U.V. at Trinity Church, on Copley Square, where he was scheduled to speak. He had been resting, fully reclined, in the passenger seat, but, in a ritual that came to be familiar to me, he hoisted himself up, swung his legs out the door, shifted his weight onto a cane, stood, and slowly made his way across the pavement and up the church steps. I asked him how he copes with his condition, given the schedule that he keeps. He chuckled, and told me that once, when he was visiting an encampment of homeless people, a woman offered him her chair, one of her few possessions. He was moved by the gesture. "I first had to put my own struggle in perspective," he said. "I had to turn my ankylosing into a testimony, in this sense: every time I'm fighting for health care, I'm reminded I have it. How many people are there that have this disease but don't have health care? It gives you a sense of deep—not just sympathy but empathy, right?" He reminded me that Harriet Tubman suffered from epilepsy, and that Franklin Roosevelt commanded the country for thirteen years, through the Depression and global war, despite having been stricken with polio—and that all the heroes of the Bible had some physical or mental challenge. As Barber sees it, the challenges that he confronts are shared by many who are called to serve; it would be indecent to complain.

BARBER'S CAREER HAS VEERED BETWEEN THE POLITICAL AND THE RELI-
gious, but the two paths often intersect: he argues politics from
a theological perspective, while his sermons are informed by the
lessons of the streets. When he mentions "the good book," he is
as likely to be referring to Howard Zinn's progressive primer "A
People's History of the United States" as he is to the one that contains the Old and New Testaments. He learned both traditions at
home.

Barber was born on August 30, 1963, in Indianapolis. His mother,
Eleanor, a government clerk, had gone into labor forty-eight hours
earlier, on the day of the March on Washington, he likes to point
out. His father, for whom he was named, was an ordained minister
in the predominantly white Disciples of Christ denomination, who
held degrees in physics and social work as well as in theology. Like
millions of African-Americans in the first half of the twentieth
century, Barber's father had left the South—North Carolina, in his
case—as part of the Great Migration to Northern and Midwestern
cities. He met Eleanor in Indiana, and they settled there.

Despite having achieved a middle-class stability that was infinitely more difficult to maintain in the South, in 1968, the couple
heeded the call of E. V. Wilkins, a high-school principal and family friend who asked them to help him with a school-integration
movement that he was attempting to build in Roper, a small town
in the eastern part of North Carolina, near where Barber's father
had grown up. When Barber was in second grade, his parents enrolled him as one of the first black students in the local elementary
school. He told me jokingly, "My first foray into activist work was
not of my choice." It was a family undertaking: his mother worked
in the high-school office, and his father taught science. Eleanor,
who is now eighty-five, still works at the school.

In "The Third Reconstruction," Barber writes that his father
could have secured a prestigious position as the pastor of a large

urban church, but that coming home to Roper "was a vow of poverty" for him. He was respected in clerical circles—when he wasn't teaching, he travelled the state as an itinerant preacher—but he was such an uncompromising and fervent critic of racism that some black congregations were hesitant to host him. As a child, Barber accompanied his father on his travels. He learned that the concerns of religion could hardly be distinct from those of earthly matters, like racial injustice. He remembers visiting a friend of his father's, a bishop, who had run afoul of some local whites, and praying together in the man's yard that he might be kept safe. As night fell, the friend went inside and placed shotguns by the windows. "What's that for?" Barber asked. His father answered, "That's an extra precaution in case the prayers don't work."

In 1978, at the age of fifteen, Barber was elected president of the local N.A.A.C.P. Youth Council. Three years later, he enrolled in North Carolina Central University, a historically black institution in Durham. In his senior year, he met a first-year nursing student, Rebecca McLean, when she joined a march he had organized to support Jesse Jackson's 1984 Presidential bid. They married three years later and had five children; she works as a psychiatric nurse. Barber is hesitant to talk about his family, because death threats are still an occupational hazard for civil-rights leaders. "I believe he is doing what the Church as a whole, all of us, are called to do," Rebecca Barber told me. "And that is do justice, love mercy, and walk humbly with God." That sense of abiding purpose, she said, has allowed her not to dwell on the threats, which, in recent years, have grown in number.

INITIALLY, BARBER RESISTED ENTERING THE CLERGY; HE WANTED TO BE A civil-rights lawyer. "I had developed a distaste for the Church," he told me. "I always believed in God, but I was struggling with the Church piece of it." He chose Central in part because there was no religious-course requirement. But in his senior year he had a crisis

of conscience over the question of what he could do with his life versus what he was called to do with it. In March of 1985, he discussed
his dilemma with his father, who urged him to distinguish between
the failings of the Church and the perfection of God. Three weeks
later, Barber preached his first sermon, on the Good Samaritan.
The Samaritan, he noted, was not concerned about how to get into
Heaven, the focus of too much of religion, in his opinion. Instead,
"he chose to go down into the ditch, he chose to go down to where
people were hurting." After graduating, Barber enrolled at Duke
University, to earn a master's degree in divinity. His father died in
1988, but Barber still often mentions him when talking about his
understanding of Christianity.

At Duke, Barber studied with C. Eric Lincoln, the acclaimed
scholar of the black church whose work explored the ways that race
had shaped American Christianity—rendering the religion, for
example, entirely capable of reconciling fidelity to its creed with
slavery and racism. He also read the works of Reinhold Niebuhr,
whose concept of Christian realism led Barber toward a practical
theology, a way of faith that is rooted in the struggles of common
people and seeks justice and mercy against unfavorable odds. His
studies gave him an intellectual scaffolding that was no less important than what he had learned from his father about the moral
and practical obligations of faith. Later, he met the theologians
Paul Tillich and James Cone, whose thinking also became a major influence on him. His approach to faith, however, put him at
odds with the Moral Majority version of evangelicalism that was
ascendant in the nineteen-eighties. He told me on the phone one
evening that those Christians "say so much about areas where the
Bible says very little"—abortion, homosexuality—"And speak so
little about the issues where the Bible says so much," like poverty,
empathy, and justice.

Meanwhile, Barber's belief in the possibility of an alliance of
poor people across racial lines was beginning to take shape. The

idea may seem radical, particularly in the era of Donald Trump, but it isn't novel; it had a long history even when King proposed it. A number of such alliances formed during Reconstruction, in a grand, if short-lived, experiment in inclusive populism. In North Carolina, the Fusion movement came together to protest the Democratic Party's monetary policy, which hurt both black and white small farmers, and for a time it created one of the most progressive governments in the state's history. In 1894, a Fusion-Republican alliance won every state office up for election, and it sent George Henry White, a black Republican, to the U.S. House of Representatives in 1896. It all came to an end just two years later, with the Wilmington race riots, in which an estimated two thousand white men attacked black residents, burned black businesses, and unseated Fusionist officials, replacing them with white Democrats, in what was essentially a coup d'état. The movement of resurgent white nationalists, unironically referred to as "redemption," had triumphed in North Carolina. Nevertheless, the inspiration of the Fusionists has stayed with Barber throughout his career.

AFTER DUKE, BARBER WAS HIRED AS THE CHAIR OF THE NORTH CAROlina State Human Relations Commission, in Durham. He travelled around the state investigating instances of discrimination in housing and employment. He was committed to the work, but, in the summer of 1993, when he was thirty, Greenleaf Christian Church, in Goldsboro, part of the Disciples of Christ denomination, asked him to be its pastor, and he decided to accept the offer. A month later, he awoke unable to move. Ankylosing spondylitis causes joints and vertebrae in the spine to fuse; Barber's neck, hips, and the base of his spine had essentially frozen in place. He had played football in high school, and the pain and stiffness in his back that signalled the onset of the disease had been misdiagnosed as a bad disk. There is no cure for ankylosing spondylitis, but therapy and medication can alleviate some of its symptoms.

He spent nearly three months in the hospital, and began an intensive, painful process of regaining mobility. He sank into a depression, and encouraged Greenleaf to find an able-bodied pastor, a request that the church rejected. With the assistance of a walker, he was eventually able to take a few tentative steps. He continued to preach at Greenleaf, mastering a technique of swinging the walker behind him in the pulpit and bracing himself against it. One morning in 2005, he managed to walk to the bathroom unassisted. Later that day, he bought a white wooden cane for the blind, which he painted black. He still uses it; battered and weathered, it is a testament to his twelve years of trial and endurance.

In Goldsboro, a city of some thirty thousand, he threw himself into local issues, securing funding to build a community day-care center and housing for low-income families and seniors. He had remained active with the N.A.A.C.P., and in 2005 he was elected president of the North Carolina State Conference, which had a history of front-line activism and outsized personalities. Ella Baker, whose work was key to the successes of the Southern Christian Leadership Conference, had organized branches of the N.A.A.C.P. in North Carolina in the nineteen-forties. Barber remembers his father speaking about Baker's work whenever the topic of political organizing came up. "She was a hero in my family," he said. Robert F. Williams, the president of the Union County branch, was known for his defense of two young boys falsely accused of rape in the infamous 1958 "kissing case." The next year, he urged blacks to take up arms in self-defense, a suggestion that alarmed not only the chief of police, Jesse Helms, Sr., the father of the future Republican United States senator, but also Roy Wilkins, the organization's staid, pacifist national president, who suspended him for six months. In 1961, facing a false kidnapping charge, he and his wife fled the country for several years, first to Cuba and then to China; the charges were eventually dropped. He became a legendary figure, and was widely credited with anticipating Malcolm X's

statements about the right to self-defense. "Some choose to only focus on Williams's decision to have armed guards," Barber told me,
but that overshadowed his contributions, such as his willingness
to defend the poorest African-Americans, even those whom other
blacks considered "not high enough on the social ladder."

Barber pushed to return the state conference to its dynamic
roots. He steered it into a battle in Wake County, where a school
board had gutted guidelines promoting racial diversity in classrooms. The organization set about organizing protests and mobilizing voters. The following year, every member of the board who had
tried to resegregate the schools was voted out. Barber also built a
coalition of social-justice organizations, N.A.A.C.P. chapters, and
youth groups from around the state called Historic Thousands on
Jones Street, named for the street where the North Carolina General Assembly meets. The idea was to influence legislators' priorities
around fourteen key issues, including criminal justice, health care,
immigrants' rights, and voting rights.

UNLIKE MOST OF THE SOUTH, WHICH RELIABLY GIVES REPUBLICAN CAN-
didates big majorities, North Carolina is a purple state. But when
Barack Obama managed a slim win there in the 2008 Presidential election—becoming the first Democrat to carry the state since
Jimmy Carter—conservatives worried that North Carolina could
become a beachhead for Democrats and progressives in the region.
Two years later, after the Supreme Court's Citizens United decision allowed a massive infusion of campaign cash from the retail
heir James Arthur Pope—the Raleigh *News & Observer* once called
Pope "the Knight of the Right"—Republicans took control of both
houses of the legislature, for the first time in more than a century.
They immediately redrew voting districts, eliminated the earned-
income tax credit, introduced a bill that would allow residents to
carry firearms in public parks and restaurants, cut funding to pre-
kindergarten education, and engineered a voter-I.D. bill that would

have made it disproportionately difficult for African-Americans to vote. (In 2016, the Fourth Circuit Court of Appeals struck down the voter-I.D. law, saying that it targeted black voters "with almost surgical precision," and earlier this year it declared the redistricting map unconstitutional.)

In 2012, a Republican, Pat McCrory, was elected governor, displacing Beverly Purdue, a Democrat. The McCrory-era legislature passed restrictions on abortion, loosened environmental regulations, and refused Medicaid expansion under the Affordable Care Act, in a state where twenty per cent of the residents lacked health insurance. McCrory also signed a law preventing transgender individuals from using the bathroom that conforms to their gender identity. Conservatives in the state exulted in their ability to fulfill their agenda—and to raise the funds to do so—but there was a boomerang effect: they encouraged a diverse group of dissenters to recognize a common cause.

On April 29, 2013, a Monday, Barber led a group of some seventy-five people, including members of the Historic Thousands coalition, to the state legislature, to protest what Barber has said was the legislature's attempt to persecute minorities and the disadvantaged. As he once put it, "We said if they were going to crucify the poor, the sick, the children, the unemployed, the immigrants, the L.G.B.T., and the women, and then on top of that crucify voting rights, then every crucifixion, as Billy Kyles"—a Tennessee civil-rights leader—"would say, needs a witness." The protesters disrupted the legislature's deliberations and confronted Thom Tillis, the Republican speaker of the House. Police arrested Barber and sixteen others. This was the start of Moral Mondays.

The group returned the following week, and nearly twice as many people were arrested. By the end of the term, fourteen weeks later, more than a thousand protesters had been arrested. The Moral Monday demonstrations continued for four years, with tens of thousands of participants. The protests are largely credited with helping Roy Cooper, a Democrat, narrowly defeat McCrory in the 2016 gubernatorial race.

BARBER HAS A PARTICULAR DISDAIN FOR POLITICIANS WHO USE RACIAL rhetoric and voter suppression in order to win elections, but whose agenda is broadly damaging to poor whites as well as blacks. "They get elected using racial gerrymandering, then enact policies that affect everybody," he said. He sees the current political polarization as a result of a deception that has driven a good deal of American politics since at least the 1968 Presidential election, when Richard Nixon exploited the resentment of white Southerners in an attempt to draw them into a Republican coalition. The so-called Southern Strategy was, in many respects, the antithesis of King's campaign. "Poverty has been so racialized," Barber told me, "that most people don't even know that, in raw numbers, the majority of poor people are white."

Marian Wright Edelman, the founder of the Children's Defense Fund, which was an outgrowth of the original Poor People's Campaign, also sees a cyclical history of racial division at play. The country "sold poor white men on their skin and denied them basic opportunities," she said. "Their resentment flares up every half century. And you have to constantly fight it back." Demagogic politicians, economic malaise, and racism, she told me, often lead people to "vote against their own interests." The duelling populism of Senator Bernie Sanders and Donald Trump during the 2016 campaign—inclusiveness versus tribalism—was another replay of this conflict. Sanders told me that he thinks Barber "is doing some of the most important work in the country." More precisely, he and Barber share the same theory of social change: "What he understands is that real change never takes place from the top on down," Sanders said. "It is always from the bottom on up, and that's what he is trying to do and what he understands and what he preaches."

I spoke to Barber by phone one night and asked if the prospect of rekindling a Fusion-style alliance is, at this moment, far-fetched. He responded, as he often does, with a story. He met Jonathan Wilson-Hartgrove, an evangelical minister, twenty years ago. Wilson-Hartgrove had once been a Senate page for Strom Thurmond, of South Carolina, who ran for President in 1948 on a platform of segregation, despite having fathered a child with a black domestic worker employed in his family's home. But, in 1998, Wilson-Hartgrove heard Barber speak at an event organized by the state's Human Relations Commission, in Raleigh, and invited him to visit his all-white Southern Baptist church, in Stokes County. The area was known as a stronghold of the Ku Klux Klan. Barber visited anyway, and the two men developed a friendship that pushed Wilson-Hartgrove to question the racial assumptions he had grown up with, and the ways that they were connected to conservative theology. Eventually, he collaborated with Barber on "The Third Reconstruction." In the afterword to the book, he wrote, "I can trust a man who embraces his enemy and then trusts him to tell his story." Later that night, Barber texted me images from recent Poor People's Campaign rallies in Appalachia, with hundreds of people, most of them white, in the audience.

MORAL MONDAYS BROUGHT BARBER TO THE ATTENTION OF BOTH progressives and Democratic Party officials—the model of large-scale protests against legislative assaults on civil rights was followed in Georgia, Alabama, and Missouri—but it was not until the summer of 2016, when he spoke in a prime-time slot at the Democratic National Convention, in Philadelphia, that he became a nationally recognizable figure. He touched on now familiar themes: the common ground of the disenfranchised and the attenuated brand of morality that has been marketed by religious conservatives. "I worry," Barber said, "about the way that faith is cynically used by some to serve hate, fear, racism, and greed." His message harked back to the politics of King in 1968 and to a kind of liberation theology: "Pay people what they deserve. Share your food with the hungry. Do this and then your nation shall be called a repairer of the breach." This last phrase was a reference to the Book of Isaiah and an admonition to leaders who abuse their authority and deprive the poor. (The reference was strategic: since 2015, Barber has also led an organization called Repairers of the Breach, which seeks to reclaim the notion of morality for progressive activism.) He concluded with an extended riff on the heartlessness of Republican policies and those who would "harden the heart" of American democracy, and called on the assembled Democrats to be "the moral defibrillators of our time," a phrase that brought them to their feet. "We must shock this nation with the power of love, we must shock this nation with the power of mercy," he said. "We can't give up on the heart of our democracy, not now, not ever!" The speech was so rousing and so well received that a headline on an article by Janell Ross in the Washington *Post* read, "THE REV. WILLIAM BARBER DROPPED THE MIC."

The activist contingent in the N.A.A.C.P. hoped that Barber would become the organization's national president, but, instead, the following year, he stepped down from the North Carolina conference (he is still on the national board of directors). There doesn't seem to have been a great deal of acrimony surrounding the departure, although Barber's independent streak and his growing national profile—he had not consulted with the organization before he spoke in Philadelphia—had apparently provoked some discord in the upper ranks. Jotaka Eaddy, who served as a senior adviser to several presidents of the N.A.A.C.P., including Ben Jealous, told me that Barber's departure was "in alignment with his world view." He left, she said, "to create space for someone else to lead, and he focussed on where he was being naturally pulled." Barber told me, "I left after twelve years—that's four years longer than the President of the United States serves." He turned to his work with Repairers of the Breach and to the idea of rebuilding King's coalition.

Barber had already begun talking with Liz Theoharis about creating a national platform to address the intersecting effects of poverty. They then started a Moral Revival tour, which eventually led to a series of discussions including people such as Roz Pelles, the executive director of Repairers of the Breach; Traci Blackmon, the executive minister of justice for the United Church of Christ, and a pastor of a church in Florissant, Missouri; Alan McSurely, an attorney and organizer now based in North Carolina, who had worked with the original Poor People's Campaign; and the civil-rights historian Timothy Tyson, who wrote a biography of Robert F. Williams. McSurely, who is eighty-one, had advised Barber on the Moral Monday movement, and serves on the steering committee for the new project. This working group set the agenda, and Barber and Theoharis began travelling across the country, speaking and leading workshops on organizing and civil-disobedience training. Barber has created a structure that allows him to oversee Greenleaf and the Repairers of the Breach despite his constant travels. He begins each day on conference calls with the officers of the Repairers and then with the leadership of the church. "I don't believe a pastor should be doing everything," he told me. "I believe in power-sharing."

Barber won't discuss the particulars of any of the actions planned for the campaign, since a number of them will involve civil disobedience, but, he told me, "I can say we intend to nonviolently confront our government and its policies and we will refuse to give up our constitutional right to protest." The campaign has attracted the support of organizations such as the Service Employees International Union, the Fight for $15, and the United Food and Commercial Workers International Union, but Barber considers the grassroots network the crucial part of what the group has accomplished. "Our movement is a national call for moral revival," he told me. "Sometimes people will only think of something as national because you have the presence of national organizations. Our focus has been to go to the people first, in the states, on the ground, and build a network of coördinating committees." The campaign approached the larger community organizations only after it had support from local people affected by issues of poverty.

AFTER KING'S DEATH, THE 1968 POOR PEOPLE'S CAMPAIGN FOUNDERED, dogged by federal surveillance and the infiltration efforts of J. Edgar Hoover. It also strained under the logistical demands of delivering thousands of people who, by definition, lacked resources to take care of themselves, to the nation's capital. The assassination of Robert F. Kennedy, on June 5th, deprived the campaign of one of its most important allies. The number of people in Resurrection City dwindled from three thousand to about five hundred. On June 24th, the police forcibly removed the last occupiers, and later that day, the mayor, fearing a repeat of the unrest in the capital that followed King's death, called in the National Guard (thirty-six years earlier, the Army had been called in to evict the Bonus Marchers). The Poor People's Campaign was over before it had achieved any of its objectives. The movement's most ambitious undertaking became its most conspicuous failure.

The Moral Monday movement captured the imagination of activists across the country, and achieved tangible results in North Carolina, but it remains to be seen whether its tactics can succeed nationwide. Marian Wright Edelman is sanguine about the prospects of the new initiative. Barber, whom she described as "brilliant," is in a position to help finish the work that was begun fifty years ago, she told me. When I asked Barber how he hoped to translate protest into progress, he said, "The civil disobedience is just one part of the plan." A second phase of the campaign will focus on voter registration, building a broader network, and creating a detailed list of policy demands, which will be released late in the summer. "We surely want to influence the 2018 midterm elections and the 2020 Presidential election," Theoharis told me. But they do not plan to endorse candidates or to cast their lot with either of the major political parties. They want to change the political conversation around poverty, to create a climate in which it is impossible for any candidate or party to continue ignoring the subject. In this they have as much in common with the Occupy Movement as with the original Poor People's Campaign. Barber and Theoharis seem to see history as a guide, not a script.

THREE WEEKS AFTER THE COMMEMORATION IN MEMPHIS, BARBER spoke at the Performing Arts Center in Montgomery, Alabama, for the opening of the National Memorial for Peace and Justice, a monument to the more than forty-four hundred African-Americans who were lynched between the end of Reconstruction and the beginning of the modern civil-rights movement. At the site, a project of the Equal Justice Initiative, led by Bryan Stevenson, hundreds of metal markers list the locations of lynchings and the names of the people who died there. The impact is traumatic, and not simply in a historical sense. Barber told me, "We should be traumatized by the idea that something like this can be seen as normal, and think about the wrongs we've become accustomed to today."

He had spent the previous two days discussing the Poor People's Campaign with Apache activists in Arizona and with representatives of the U.F.C.W. in Las Vegas. But, despite the long journey, in Montgomery, before an audience of about a thousand, he delivered the best speech I have heard him give. It was a sprawling oration, citing the historian Nell Painter, the Constitution, the crusading journalist Ida B. Wells-Barnett, the lyrics to "Strange Fruit," and the speech that King delivered in Montgomery, in 1965, at the end of the march from Selma. That speech, which Barber encouraged the audience to listen to in its entirety, contains King's recitation of the history of populism and the ways that racism disadvantaged both black and white poor people—the points that Barber has been reiterating across the country. (Segregation, King said, was "a simple thing to keep the poor white masses working for near-starvation wages in the years that followed the Civil War.")

Barber touched on his usual themes of inequality and the mistaken priorities of the Church, but the audience erupted in applause when he turned to the monument itself, declaring that "Jesus was lynched—an innocent victim of mob hysteria." He again charged his listeners with avoiding the hypocrisy of commemorating the victims of the past while failing to build a movement to address the present. We must pay homage, he said, "to all those who continued to fight, even after they saw the bodies swinging from trees. But there are all kinds of things swinging in the air today"—hunger, police violence, and the hundreds of thousands of deaths each year linked to poverty-related causes. He was interrupted six times by standing ovations, and the crowd was on its feet and applauding long after he'd stopped speaking.

As he walked off the stage, I detected, just for a moment, a rare note of fatigue. Barber is, it occurred to me, relentless, not tireless; determined, not indefatigable. He is driven by a fugitive hope that an ancestral breach might finally be cemented. Backstage, organizers praised him for the speech, but he didn't linger. He had a nine-hour drive ahead of him, to North Carolina, where he would tend to his church and, after a brief respite, head out on the road again.

PART IV
LIFE AND LETTERS

PHILLIS WHEATLEY ON TRIAL

HENRY LOUIS GATES, JR.

January 20, 2003

It was the primal scene of African-American letters. Sometime
before October 8, 1772, Phillis Wheatley, a slim African slave
in her late teens who was a published poet, met with eighteen of
the most influential thinkers and politicians of the Massachusetts
Colony. The panel had been assembled to verify the authorship of
her poems and to answer a much larger question: Was a Negro
capable of producing literature? The details of the meeting have
been lost to history, but I've often imagined how it all might have
happened. Phillis walks into a room—perhaps in Boston's Town
Hall, the Old Colony House—and stands before these New England illuminati with a manuscript consisting of twenty-odd
poems that she claims to have written. She is on trial, and so is
her race.

Wheatley's poems had been appearing in periodicals and
newspapers in New England and Britain since she was fourteen.
One of her adolescent works, "On Being Brought from Africa to
America," displays her typical subject matter and the hallmarks
of her early style—religious piety wrapped in heroic couplets.
The eight-line poem has been widely anthologized in collections of African-American literature in this century, most recently in James G. Basker's "Amazing Grace: An Anthology of
Poems About Slavery, 1660–1810" (Yale; $45). It is a modest and
not particularly sophisticated paean to her Christian education,
and expresses a forgiving, even grateful attitude toward human
trafficking:

'Twas mercy brought me from my *Pagan* land,
Taught my benighted soul to understand
That there's a God, that there's a *Saviour* too:
Once I redemption neither sought nor knew.
Some view our sable race with scornful eye,
"Their colour is a diabolic die."
Remember, *Christians*, *Negros*, black as *Cain*,
May be refin'd, and join th' angelic train.

She had arrived in Boston on July 11, 1761, on board the Phillis, a slaver that was returning from Senegal, Sierra Leone, and the Isles de Los, off the coast of Guinea. Most likely a native Wolof speaker from the Senegambian coast, she was "a slender, frail, female child," naked except for a kilt made from "a quantity of dirty carpet," as a descendant of her owners wrote in 1834. She had lost her front teeth, and so was thought to be about seven or eight years old. Susanna Wheatley, the wife of a prosperous tailor and merchant, John Wheatley, acquired her as a house servant, and named her after the slave ship.

John and Susanna Wheatley had teen-aged twins, Nathaniel and Mary, who were living at home when Phillis arrived. Phillis spoke no English, and Mary, apparently with her mother's encouragement, began to teach her to read, tutoring her in English, Latin, and the Bible. By 1765, Wheatley had written her first poem; in 1767, when she was thirteen or fourteen, the Newport *Mercury* published a poem that Susanna Wheatley submitted on her behalf. In 1770, when she was about seventeen, an elegy she wrote on the death of the Reverend George Whitefield, a popular English preacher who was a leader of the evangelical movement in England and America, was published in newspapers in Boston, Newport, New York, and Philadelphia. Whitefield had been the personal chaplain of an English philanthropist, Selina Hastings, the Countess of Huntingdon. Wheatley shrewdly apostrophized the Countess in the Whitefield elegy and sent her a letter of condolence with the poem enclosed. With the poem's publication in London, in 1771, Wheatley suddenly had a wide readership on both sides of the Atlantic.

As her literary reputation grew, however, so did doubts about her authenticity, and the Wheatleys, attempting to publish her manuscript, were unable to elicit the number of book orders that printers in those days required. Eighteenth-century philosophers like David Hume believed that blacks were a different species, and there was widespread incredulity at the idea of a black litterateur. It was John Wheatley who assembled the illustrious group of interrogators, hoping that they would support Phillis's claim of authorship, and that the opinion of the general public would follow.

Picture the eighteen men gathered in a semicircle. At the center was, no doubt, His Excellency Thomas Hutchinson, the governor of Massachusetts. Hutchinson, a Colonial historian and a royal official, was born into a wealthy merchant family in Boston. He entered Harvard College at the age of twelve, where, because of his family's social position, he was ranked third in his class. (Even back then, grade inflation loomed on the Charles.) Following the Boston Tea Party, he went to London, "for consultations," and never returned.

Andrew Oliver, the colony's lieutenant governor, would have been seated on one side of Hutchinson. Oliver imprudently allowed himself to be publicly identified as a supporter of the Stamp Act of 1765, prompting angry crowds to ransack his house and uproot his garden. When, in 1774, Oliver had a stroke and died, commentators assumed that it was related to the political turmoil.

Quite a few men of the cloth were present. The Reverend Mather Byles was the minister of the Hollis Street Congregational Church, in Boston; he was the grandson of Increase Mather and the nephew of Cotton Mather. As a young man, he had corresponded with Alexander Pope and Isaac Watts, and in 1744 he had published a book of verse, "Poems on Several Occasions." Like Hutchinson and Oliver, Byles was a Tory loyalist, and he lost his pulpit when Massachusetts finally rebelled. He was sentenced to banishment, later commuted to house arrest, for his loyalist views. (Byles called the sentry stationed just outside the house his "Observe-a-Tory.")

Others of the Wheatley witnesses, though, were to become prominent figures in the newly founded republic. Among them was John Hancock, the head of the House of Hancock, which had grown rich by trading in whale oil and real estate. Hancock was later the president of the Second Continental Congress and the first governor of the Commonwealth of Massachusetts.

Nearly all the men present were Harvard graduates and a majority were slaveholders. One, Thomas Hubbard, had been a dealer in slaves; another, the Reverend Charles Chauncy, had attacked the Great Awakening, an evangelical movement that threatened the established religious order, because it allowed "women and girls; yea Negroes . . . to do the business of preachers." The group that Wheatley faced was not exactly an association for the advancement of colored people.

There is no transcript of what took place in that room. Was Wheatley given scansion tests? Quizzed on the Latin subjunctive? Asked to recite the Psalms? We'll never know. Whatever the nature of the exam, she passed it, and earned the letter of support that she and her master had hoped for:

> We whose Names are under-written, do assure the
> World, that the Poems specified in the following Page, were
> (as we verily believe) written by Phillis, a young Negro Girl,
> who was but a few Years since, brought an uncultivated
> Barbarian from *Africa*, and has ever since been, and now is,
> under the Disadvantage of serving as a Slave in a Family
> in this Town. She has been examined by some of the best
> Judges, and is thought qualified to write them.

Even after the validation of the esteemed Bostonians, no American publisher was willing to take on Wheatley's manuscript, and so Susanna Wheatley turned to English friends for help. The publishing climate in England was more receptive to black authors. The Countess of Huntingdon, though a slaveholder herself (she had inherited slaves in Georgia), had already, in 1772, shepherded into print one of the earliest slave narratives, by James Gronniosaw. Vincent Carretta, a leading scholar of eighteenth-century black transatlantic literature and an expert on Wheatley, has observed that the British market for black literature may have been indirectly created by a court ruling, in 1772, that made it illegal for slaves who had come to England to be forcibly returned to the colonies. Although the ruling stopped short of outlawing slavery in England, it encouraged an atmosphere of sympathy toward blacks.

Through the captain of the commercial ship that John Wheatley used for trade with England, Susanna engaged a London publisher, Archibald Bell, to bring out the manuscript. The Countess agreed to let Wheatley dedicate the book to her. An engraving of Wheatley appeared as the book's frontispiece, at the Countess's request.

"Poems on Various Subjects, Religious and Moral, by Phillis Wheatley, Negro Servant to Mr. John Wheatley of Boston" was published in September, 1773. Five advertisements that ran in the London *Morning Post & Daily Advertiser* the month before pointed to the statement of the Boston panel as proof that Wheatley was the "real Author." The book's publication represented a significant moment in black literary achievement. Various black authors had published individual poems, but even these instances were rare. Jupiter Hammon, a slave from Long Island, had published the first of several poems in 1760. Francis Williams, a Jamaican who is said to have studied at Cambridge University, had caused a minor sensation when it was posthumously revealed that he had written an ode in Latin in 1759. Wheatley's book was widely reviewed and discussed in England and in America, where it became available in 1774. Voltaire wrote to a correspondent that Phillis Wheatley had proved blacks could write poetry.

While Phillis was in London, where she had been sent with Nathaniel Wheatley in the spring of 1773 to oversee the book's publication, she met the Earl of Dartmouth, who gave her five guineas to buy the works of Alexander Pope; Granville Sharp, the scholar and anti-slavery activist, who took her to the Tower of London; and Brook Watson, a future Lord Mayor of London, who gave her a folio edition of "Paradise Lost." Benjamin Franklin paid her a visit, which he mentions in a letter to his nephew Jonathan Williams, Sr. "Upon your Recommendation I went to see the black Poetess and offer'd her any Services I could do her," he wrote. "And I have heard nothing since of her." On the strength of this seemingly perfunctory visit, Wheatley decided to dedicate her second volume of poetry to Franklin. Even an audience with King George was arranged, although she had to cancel it when Susanna Wheatley suddenly fell ill and needed her care.

Within a month of the book's publication and Phillis's return to America, the Wheatleys freed her. (English reviewers, using Wheatley's book as a point of departure, had condemned the hypocrisy of a colony that insisted on liberty and equality when it came to its relationship to England but did not extend those principles to its own population.) Freedom meant that she became fully responsible for her literary career, and for her finances. In mid-October, she wrote a letter to David Wooster, the customs collector in New Haven, alerting him that a shipment of her books would soon arrive from England, and urging him to canvass among his friends for orders. "Use your interest with Gentlemen & Ladies of your acquaintance to subscribe also, for the more subscribers there are, the more it will be for my advantage as I am to have half the Sale of the Books." She continued, "This I am the more solicitous for, as I am now upon my own footing and whatever I get by this is entirely mine, & it is the Chief I have to depend upon. I must also request you would desire the Printers in New Haven, not to reprint that Book, as it will be a great hurt to me, preventing any further Benefit that I might receive from the Sale of my Copies from England."

In the spring of 1774, the British occupied Boston. Susanna Wheatley died the same year, and when John Wheatley fled the city, Phillis moved to Providence, where John Wheatley's daughter, Mary, and her husband lived. With the outbreak of war, in April of 1775, Phillis's prospects dimmed considerably. A number of the people who had signed the attestation were dead, and the others who had earlier supported her, both Tories and Patriots, were more concerned with winning the war than with the African prodigy. But Wheatley lost no opportunity to cultivate powerful friends, and on October 26, 1775, she wrote to General George Washington at his headquarters in Cambridge, aligning herself with the Revolutionary cause:

SIR

I Have taken the freedom to address your Excellency in the enclosed poem, and entreat your acceptance, though I am not insensible of its inaccuracies. Your being appointed by the Grand Continental Congress to be Generalissimo of the armies of North America, together with the fame of your virtues, excite sensations not easy to suppress. Your generosity, therefore, I presume, will pardon the attempt. Wishing your Excellency all possible success in the great cause you are so generously engaged in, I am,

Your Excellency's most obedient humble servant,

PHILLIS WHEATLEY

The accompanying poem was nothing if not flattering:

One century scarce perform'd its destined round,
When Gallic powers Columbia's fury found;
And so may you, whoever dares disgrace
The land of freedom's heaven-defended race! . . .

Proceed, great chief, with virtue on thy side,
Thy ev'ry action let the goddess guide.
A crown, a mansion, and a throne that shine,
With gold unfading, WASHINGTON! be thine.

On February 28, 1776, Washington responded:

Miss Phillis,

Your favor of the 26th of October did not reach my
hands, till the middle of December. Time enough, you
will say, to have given an answer ere this. Granted. But a
variety of important occurrences, continually interposing
to distract the mind and withdraw the attention, I hope
will apologize for the delay, and plead my excuse for the
seeming but not real neglect. I thank you most sincerely for
your polite notice of me, in the elegant lines you enclosed;
and however undeserving I may be of such encomium and
panegyric, the style and manner exhibit a striking proof of
your poetical talents; in honor of which, and as a tribute
justly due to you, I would have published the poem, had
I not been apprehensive, that, while I only meant to give
the world this new instance of your genius, I might have
incurred the imputation of vanity. This, and nothing else,
determined me not to give it place in the public prints.

If you should ever come to Cambridge, or near
headquarters, I shall be happy to see a person so favored
by the Muses, and to whom nature has been so liberal and
beneficent in her dispensations. I am, with great respect,
your obedient humble servant.

GEORGE WASHINGTON

In the event, Washington overcame his fear of the imputation
of vanity and, by means of an intermediary, secured publication of
Wheatley's pentametric praise in the *Virginia Gazette*, in March of
1776.

By late 1776, Wheatley had moved back to Boston. In 1778, she
married a black man named John Peters. Peters was a small-time
grocer and a some-time lawyer about whom very little is known—
only that he successfully applied for the right to sell spirits in his
store, and that a Wheatley relative remembered him as someone
who affected the airs of a gentleman. Meanwhile, the poet continued her efforts to publish a second volume. In 1779, she advertised
six times in the Boston *Evening Post & General Advertiser*, mentioning that she intended to dedicate the book to Benjamin Franklin. The advertisements failed to generate the necessary number of
subscribers, and the book was never published.

Wheatley's freedom had enslaved her to a life of hardship.
Peters abandoned her soon after she gave birth to their third child
(the first two died in infancy). She placed her last advertisement
in the September, 1784, issue of *The Boston Magazine* and died in
December, at the age of thirty, poor and alone. Her baby died with
her. Peters is thought to have sold the only copy of the second manuscript. A few years ago, one of the poems surfaced at Christie's,
and sold for nearly seventy thousand dollars, but the full manuscript has never been recovered.

TO HER BLACK CONTEMPORARIES, WHEATLEY WAS A HEROINE. JUPI-
ter Hammon published a laudatory poem entitled "An Address
to Miss Phillis Wheatley Ethiopian Poetess, in Boston," in 1778.
Hammon's poem echoed and approved of the sentiments expressed
in "On Being Brought from Africa to America": "Thou hast left
the heathen shore, / Thro' mercy of the Lord, / Among the heathen live no more, / Come magnify thy God." Wheatley encouraged the work of other black artists, such as Hammon and Scipio
Moorhead, a well-known painter to whom she dedicated a poem.
In letters to her best friend, Obour Tanner, a black woman she
had met in Providence, Wheatley argued for the inherent right of
blacks to be free. She corresponded with the English philanthropist
John Thornton, a wealthy merchant and a friend of the Countess of
Huntingdon. She used her fame and her acquaintance with political figures to complain bitterly about the human costs of the slave
trade, as in a famous poem called "To the Right Honourable William, Earl of Dartmouth":

> I, young in life, by seeming cruel fate
> Was snatch'd from *Afric's* fancy'd happy seat:
> What pangs excruciating must molest,
> What sorrows labour in my parent's breast?
> Steel'd was that soul and by no misery mov'd
> That from a father seiz'd his babe belov'd:
> Such, such my case. And can I then but pray
> Others may never feel tyrannic sway?

And there is a letter Wheatley wrote about the evils of slavery to the Reverend Samson Occom, a Mohegan Indian minister
in the Countess's circle. The letter was published several months
after her manumission. It appeared in *The Connecticut Gazette* on
March 11, 1774, and reads, in part:

In every human Breast, God has implanted a
Principle, which we call Love of Freedom; it is impatient
of Oppression, and pants for Deliverance; and by the
Leave of our Modern Egyptians I will assert, that the
same Principle lives in us.

In the half century following her death, Wheatley remained
something of an icon in the abolitionist movement, and was frequently
cited as proof of Africans' innate intellectual equality with whites.

At the same time, her popularity among the abolitionists brought
her some formidable detractors. In "Notes on the State of Virginia,"
which was published in America in 1787, Thomas Jefferson dismissed Wheatley's poetry as undeserving of the name:

Misery is often the parent of the most affecting
touches in poetry. Among the blacks is misery enough,
God knows, but no poetry. Love is the peculiar oestrum
of the poet. Their love is ardent, but it kindles the senses
only, not the imagination. Religion, indeed, has produced
a Phillis Wheatley; but it could not produce a poet. The
compositions composed under her name are below the
dignity of criticism.

Phillis had plenty of experience—"Misery enough"—and, thanks
to the Wheatleys, training in spelling and composition. What she
lacked, Jefferson wrote, was an animating intellect. "Epictetus,
Terence, and Phaedrus, were slaves. But they were of the race of
whites. It is not [the blacks'] condition then, but nature, which has
produced the distinction." The authentication of Wheatley's authorship in 1772 missed the point, in Jefferson's view. The issue
wasn't whether she was the genuine author but whether what she
produced was genuine poetry.

The emergence, in the mid-eighteen-forties, of fugitive-slave authors, such as Frederick Douglass, rendered Wheatley's stylized rhymes passé. Under the leadership of William Lloyd Garrison, the abolitionist movement was assuming an urgency and a stridency consonant with the angry realism of Douglass's voice. Wheatley disappeared from view, and when she reappeared, in the late nineteenth century, it was as a version of what Jefferson had made of her—a symbol of artificiality, of spiritless and rote convention. Unlike Douglass, who was embraced by the black literary community, she was a pariah, reviled for "On Being Brought from Africa to America," even though the poem belongs among her juvenilia. In 1887, Edward Wilmot Blyden, one of the fathers of black nationalism, wrote about her contemptuously, and the tone was set for the century to come.

"One looks in vain for some outburst or even complaint against the bondage of her people, for some agonizing cry about her native land," James Weldon Johnson wrote about "On Being Brought from Africa to America," in 1922. Instead, one finds a "smug contentment at her own escape therefrom." Wallace Thurman, in 1928, called her "a third-rate imitation" of Alexander Pope: "Phillis in her day was a museum figure who would have caused more of a sensation if some contemporary Barnum had exploited her." Another black critic described her as "a clever imitator, nothing more."

By the nineteen-sixties, criticism of Wheatley had risen to a high pitch of disdain. Amiri Baraka, a founder of the Black Arts movement, wrote in 1962 that Wheatley's "pleasant imitations of eighteenth-century English poetry are far and, finally, ludicrous departures from the huge black voices that splintered southern nights with their *hollers, chants, arwhoolies,* and *ballits*." In "Images of the Negro in American Literature" (1966), Seymour Gross wrote, "This Negro poetess so well fits the Uncle Tom syndrome. . . . She is pious, grateful, retiring, and civil." A few years later, the critic Addison Gayle, Jr., issued his own bill of indictment: Wheatley, he wrote, was the first among black writers "to accept the images and symbols of degradation passed down from the South's most intellectual lights and the first to speak with a sensibility finely tuned by close approximation to [her] oppressors." She had, in sum, "surrendered the right to self-definition to others." Phillis Wheatley, who had once been cast as the great paragon of Negro achievement, was now given a new role: race traitor.

The examples could be multiplied, as versions of the Jeffersonian critique have been taken up by successive generations of black writers and critics. Too black to be taken seriously by white critics in the eighteenth century, Wheatley was now considered too white to interest black critics in the twentieth. She was an impostor, a fraud, an avatar of inauthenticity. It's striking that Jefferson and Amiri Baraka, two figures in American letters who agreed on little else, could concur in the terms of their condemnation of Phillis Wheatley.

For Wheatley's critics, her sacrifices, her courage, her humiliations, her trials could never be enough. And so things came full circle: the sorts of racist suspicions and anxieties that first greeted Wheatley's writing were now directed at forms of black expression that failed the new test of cultural affirmation. The critics of the black Arts movement and after were convening their own interrogators, and they were a rather more hostile group than met that day in 1772. We can almost imagine Wheatley being frogmarched through another hall in the nineteen-sixties or seventies, surrounded by dashiki-clad figures of "the Revolution": "What is Ogun's relation to Esu?" "What are the seven principles of Kwanzaa?" "Santeria is derived from which African culture?" And, finally, "Where you gonna be when the revolution comes, *sista*?"

If Wheatley stood for anything, of course, it was the creed that culture did, or could, belong equally to everyone. That's an ideal that has been arraigned, interrogated, and prosecuted with unremitting zeal, but it remains worth defending. The republic of letters that Wheatley so yearned to join—one that might embrace the writing of both Jefferson and his African-American descendants— was based on common expression, not common experience. What would happen, then, if we ceased to stereotype Wheatley, to cast her in this role or that, but, instead, *read* her, with all the resourcefulness that she herself brought to her craft? That's the only way to let Phillis Wheatley take the stand.

A SOCIETY OF ONE

CLAUDIA ROTH PIERPONT

February 17, 1997

In the spring of 1938, Zora Neale Hurston informed readers of the *Saturday Review of Literature* that Mr. Richard Wright's first published book, "Uncle Tom's Children," was made up of four novellas set in a Dismal Swamp of race hatred, in which not a single act of understanding or sympathy occurred, and in which the white man was generally shot dead. "There is lavish killing here," she wrote, "perhaps enough to satisfy all male black readers." Hurston, who had swept onto the Harlem scene a decade before, was one of the very few black women in a position to write for the pallidly conventional *Saturday Review*. Wright, the troubling newcomer, had already challenged her authority to speak for their race. Reviewing Hurston's novel "Their Eyes Were Watching God" in the *New Masses* the previous fall, he had dismissed her prose for its "facile sensuality"—a problem in Negro writing that he traced to the first black American female to earn literary fame, the slave Phillis Wheatley. Worse, he accused Hurston of cynically perpetuating a minstrel tradition meant to make white audiences laugh. It says something about the social complexity of the next few years that it was Wright who became a Book-of-the-Month Club favorite, while Hurston's work went out of print and she nearly starved. For the first time in America, a substantial white audience preferred to be shot at.

Black anger had come out of hiding, out of the ruins of the Harlem Renaissance and its splendid illusions of justice willingly offered up to art. That famed outpouring of novels and poems and

plays of the twenties, anxiously demonstrating the Negro's humanity and cultural citizenship, counted for nothing against the
bludgeoning facts of the Depression, the Scottsboro trials, and
the first-ever riot in Harlem itself, in 1935. The advent of Richard
Wright was a political event as much as a literary one. In American
fiction, after all, there was nothing new in the image of the black
man as an inarticulate savage for whom rape and murder were a
nearly inevitable means of expression. Southern literature was filled
with Negro portraits not so different from that of Bigger Thomas,
the hero of Wright's 1940 bombshell, "Native Son." In the making
of a revolution, all that had shifted was the author's color and the
blame.

As for Hurston, the most brazenly impious of the Harlem literary avant-garde—she called them "the niggerati"—she had never
fit happily within any political group. And she still doesn't. In this
respect, she was the unlikeliest possible candidate for canonization
by the black- and women's-studies departments. Nevertheless, since
Alice Walker's "In Search of Zora Neale Hurston" appeared in *Ms.*
in 1975, interest in this neglected ancestress has developed a seemingly unstoppable momentum. All her major work has been republished (most recently by the Library of America), she is the subject
of conferences and doctoral dissertations, and the movie rights to
"Their Eyes Were Watching God"—which has sold more than a
million copies since 1990—have been bought by Oprah Winfrey
and Quincy Jones. Yet, despite the almost sanctified status she has
achieved, Hurston's social views are as obstreperous today as they
were sixty years ago. For anyone who looks at her difficult life and
extraordinary legacy straight on, it is nearly impossible to get this
disarming conjure artist to represent any cause except the freedom
to write what she wanted.

Hurston was at the height of her powers in 1937, when she
first fell seriously out of step with the times. She had written a love
story—"Their Eyes Were Watching God"—and become a counter-

revolutionary. Against the tide of racial anger, she wrote about sex and talk and work and music and life's unpoisoned pleasures, suggesting that these things existed even for people of color, even in America; and she was judged superficial. By implication, merely feminine. In Wright's account, her novel contained "no theme, no message, no thought." By depicting a Southern small-town world in which blacks enjoyed their own rich cultural traditions, and were able to assume responsibility for their own lives, Hurston appeared a blithely reassuring supporter of the status quo.

The "minstrel" charge was finally aimed less at Hurston's subjects, however, than at her language. Black dialect was at the heart of her work, and that was a dangerous business. Disowned by the founders of the Harlem Renaissance for its association with the shambling, watermelon-eating mockeries of American stage convention, dialect remained an irresistible if highly self-conscious resource for writers, from Langston Hughes and Sterling Brown to Wright himself (whose use of the idiom Hurston gleefully dismissed as tone deaf). But the feat of rescuing the dignity of the speakers from decades of humiliation required a rare and potentially treacherous combination of gifts: a delicate ear and a generous sympathy, a hellbent humor and a determined imperviousness to shame. All this Hurston brought to "Their Eyes Were Watching God"—a book that, despite its slender, private grace, aspires to the force of a national epic, akin to works by Mark Twain or Alessandro Manzoni, offering a people their own language freshly caught on paper and raised to the heights of poetry.

"It's sort of duskin' down dark," observes the otherwise unexceptional Mrs. Sumpkins, checking the sky and issuing the local evening variant of rosy-fingered dawn. "He's uh whirlwind among breezes," one front-porch sage notes of the town's mayor; another adds, "He's got uh throne in de seat of his pants." The simplest men and women of all-black Eatonville have this wealth of images easy at their lips. This is dialect not as a broken attempt at higher correctness but as an extravagant game of image and sound. It is a record of the unique explosion that occurred when African people with an intensely musical and oral culture came up hard against the King James Bible and the sweet-talking American South, under conditions that denied them all outlet for their visions and gifts except the transformation of the English language into song.

HURSTON WAS BORN TO A FAMILY OF SHARECROPPERS IN TINY NOTA-sulga, Alabama, in 1891—about ten years before any date she ever admitted to. Both her biographer, Robert E. Hemenway, and her admirer Alice Walker, who put up a tombstone in 1973 to mark Hurston's Florida grave (inscribed "'A Genius of the South' 1901–1960 Novelist, Folklorist, Anthropologist"), got this basic fact as wrong as their honored subject would have wished. Hurston was a woman used to getting away with things: her second marriage license lists her date of birth as 1910. Still, the ruse stemmed not from ordinary feminine vanity but from her desire for an education and her shame at how long it took her to get it. The lie apparently began when she entered high school, in 1917, at twenty-six.

She had been very young when the family moved to Eatonville, Florida, the first incorporated black town in America (by 1914 there would be some thirty of them throughout the South), in search of the jobs and the relief from racism that such a place promised. In many ways, they found precisely what they wanted: John Hurston became a preacher at the Zion Hope Baptist Church and served three terms as mayor. His daughter's depictions of this self-ruled colored Eden have become legend, and in recent years have seemed to hold out a ruefully tempting alternative to the ordeals of integration. The benefits of the self-segregated life have been attested to by the fact that Eatonville produced Hurston herself: a black writer uniquely whole-souled and self-possessed and imbued with (in Alice Walker's phrase) "racial health."

Her mother taught her to read before she started school, and encouraged her to "jump at de sun." Her father routinely smacked her back down and warned her not to act white; the child he adored was her docile older sister. One must go to Hurston's autobiographical novel, "Jonah's Gourd Vine," for a portrait of this highly charismatic but morally weak man, whose compulsive philandering eventually destroyed all he'd built. The death of Zora's mother, in 1904, began a period she would later seek to obliterate from the record of her life. Although her actual autobiography, "Dust Tracks on a Road," is infamously evasive and sketchy (burying a decade does not encourage specificity), it does acknowledge her having been shunted among her brothers' families with the lure of school ever giving way to cleaning house and minding children. And all the while, she recalls, "I had a way of life inside me and I wanted it with a want that was twisting me."

Working at every kind of job—maid, waitress, manicurist—she managed to finish high school by June, 1918, and went on to Howard University, where she published her first story, in the literary-club magazine, in 1921. Harlem was just then on the verge of vogue, and the Howard club was headed by Alain Locke, founding prince of the Renaissance, a black aristocrat out of Harvard on the lookout for writers with a sense of the "folk." It was what everybody would soon be looking for. The first date that Hurston offers in the story of her life is January, 1925, when she arrived in New York City with no job, no friends, and a dollar and fifty cents in her pocket—a somewhat melodramatic account meant to lower the lights behind her rising glory.

One story had already been accepted by *Opportunity*, the premier magazine of "New Negro" writing. That May, at the first *Opportunity* banquet, she received two awards—one for fiction and one for drama—from such judges as Fannie Hurst, a best-selling, four-handkerchief novelist, and Eugene O'Neill. Hurston's flamboyant entrance at a party following the ceremonies, sailing a scarf over her shoulder and crying out the title of her play—"'Color

Struck'!"—made a greater impression than her work would do for years. This was the new, public Zora, all bravado and laughter, happily startling her audience with the truth of its own preoccupations.

That night, she attached herself to Fannie Hurst, for whom she was soon working as a secretary and then, when it turned out that she couldn't type or keep anything in order, as a kind of rental exotic, complete with outlandish stories and a turban. (Her new boss once tried to pass her off in a segregated restaurant as an African princess.) Hurston's Harlem circle was loudly scornful of the part she was willing to play. For her, though, it was experience: it was not washing floors, it was going somewhere. And the somewhere still hadn't changed. At the banquet she had also met Annie Nathan Meyer, a founder of Barnard College. In the fall of 1925, this ever-masquerading, newly glamorous Scott-within-Zelda of Lenox Avenue enrolled in school again—she had completed less than two years at Howard, and had finagled a scholarship out of Meyer—and discovered anthropology.

Hurston dived headlong into this new field of intellectual possibility, which had been conceived principally by her teacher, Franz Boas, a German-Jewish immigrant who'd founded the department at Columbia. (Like all his students, Hurston called him Papa Franz, and he teased that of course she was his daughter, "just one of my missteps.") The bedrock of Boas's frankly political theorizing was the adaptability and mutability of the races. Believing that culture and learning have as much influence on human development as heredity, he set out to prove how close the members of the family of man might really be. Probably no one except her mother influenced Hurston more.

Boas's fervent belief in the historic importance of African cultures had already had tremendous impact on W. E. B. Du Bois, and Hurston was similarly inspired by the sense of importance that Boas gave to Southern black culture, not just as a source of entertaining stories but as the transmitted legacy of Africa—and as an independent cultural achievement, in need of preservation and study. Boas literally turned Hurston around: he sent her back down South to put on paper the things that she'd always taken for granted. Furthermore, his sanction gave her confidence in the value of those things—the old familiar talk and byways—which was crucial to the sense of "racial health" and "easy self-acceptance" that so many relish in her work today. It seems safe to say that no black woman in America was ever simply allotted such strengths, no matter how strong she was or how uniformly black her home town. They had to be won, and every victory was precarious.

AS A CHILD, HURSTON INFORMS US IN HER AUTOBIOGRAPHY, SHE WAS confused by the talk of Negro equality and Negro superiority which she heard in the town all around her: "If it was so honorable and glorious to be black, why was it the yellow-skinned people among us had so much prestige?" Even in first grade, she saw the disparity: "The light-skinned children were always the angels, fairies and queens of school plays." She was not a light-skinned child, although her racial heritage was mixed. If the peculiarities of a segregated childhood spared her the harshest brunt of white racism, the crippling consciousness of color in the black community and in the black soul was a subject she knew well and could not leave alone.

Such color-consciousness has a long history in African-American writing, starting with the first novel written by a black American, William Wells Brown's 1853 "Clotel" (a fantasy about Thomas Jefferson's gorgeous mulatto daughter), which takes color prejudice "among the negroes themselves" as its premise. By 1929, the heroine of Wallace Thurman's bitterly funny novel "The Blacker the Berry . . ." was drenching her face with peroxide before going off to dance in Harlem's Renaissance Casino. But there is no more disconcertingly morbid document of this phenomenon than Hurston's prize-winning "Color Struck." This brief, almost surreal play tracks a talented and very dark-skinned woman's decline into self-destructive madness, a result of her inability to believe that any man could love a woman so black. Although the intended lesson of "Color Struck" seems clear in the retelling, the play's fevered, hallucinatory vehemence suggests a far more complex response to color than Hurston's champions today can comfortably allow—a response not entirely under the author's control.

It would be wrong to say that whites did not figure prominently in Hurston's early life, despite their scarcity. It was precisely because of that scarcity that she took hold of racism not at its source but as it reverberated through the black community. Whites around Eatonville were not the murderous tyrants of Richard Wright's Deep South childhood, but they exerted, perhaps, an equally powerful force—as tantalizing, world-withholding gods, and as a higher court (however unlikely) of personal justice.

There is a fairy-tale aspect to the whites who pass through her autobiography: The "white man of many acres and things" who chanced upon her birth and cut her umbilical cord with his knife; the strangers who would drive past her house and give her rides out toward the horizon. (She had to walk back, and was invariably punished for her boldness.) Most important was a pair of white ladies who visited her school and were so impressed by her reading aloud—it was the myth of Persephone, crossing between realms of dark and light, which, she recalls, she read exceptionally well because it "exalted" her—that they made her a present of a hundred new pennies and the first real books she ever owned.

Hurston's autobiography won an award for race relations, in 1943, and put her on the cover of the *Saturday Review*. The book has since been reviled by the very people who rescued her fiction from oblivion, and for the same reason that the fiction was once consigned there: a sense that she was putting on a song and dance for whites. In fact, there is nothing in "Dust Tracks on a Road" that is inconsistent with the romantic images of white judges and jurors and plantation owners which form a fundamental part of

Hurston's most deeply admired work. The heroine of "Their Eyes Were Watching God" ends up on trial for the murder—in self-defense—of the man she loved. (Having been infected by a rabid dog, he lost his senses and came at her with a gun.) The black folks who knew the couple have sided against her at the trial, hoping to see her hanged. It is the whites—the judge and jury and a group of women gathered for curiosity's sake—who see into the anguished depths of a black woman's love, and acknowledge her dignity and her innocence.

Does this reflect honest human complexity or racial confusion? In what world, if any, was Hurston ever at home? While at Barnard, she apparently told the anthropologist Melville Herskovits that, as he put it, she was "more white than Negro in her ancestry." On her first trip back South to gather evidence of her native culture she could not be understood because of her Barnard intonations. She couldn't gain people's confidence; the locals claimed to have no idea what she wanted. When Hurston returned to New York, she and Boas agreed that a white person could have discovered as much.

So she learned, in effect, to pass for black. In the fall of 1927, in need of a patron, she offered her services to Mrs. R. Osgood Mason, a wealthy white widow bent on saving Western culture from rigor mortis through her support of Negro artistic primitivism. For more than three years, Mrs. Mason paid for Hurston to make forays to the South to collect Negro folk material. Hurston's findings were not always as splendidly invigorating nor her attitude as positive as they later appeared. "I have changed my mind about the place," she wrote despairingly from Eatonville, in an unpublished letter of 1932. "They steal everything here, even greens out of a garden." But she became increasingly accomplished at ferreting out what she had been hired to find, and the results (if not always objectively reliable) have proved invaluable. Alan Lomax, who worked with Hurston on a seminal 1935 Library of Congress folk-music-recording expedition, wrote of her unique ability to win over the locals, since she "talks their language and can out-nigger any of them."

The fruits of her field work appeared in various forms throughout the early thirties: stories, plays, musical revues, academic articles. Her research is almost as evident in the 1934 novel "Jonah's Gourd Vine" as in her book of folklore, "Mules and Men," which appeared the following year. Now routinely saluted as the first history of black American folklore by a black author, "Mules and Men" was faulted by black critics of its own time for its adamant exclusion of certain elements of the Southern Negro experience: exploitation, terror, misery, and bitterness.

By this time, however, Hurston had won enough recognition to go off on a Guggenheim grant to study voodoo practices in the Caribbean. It was not a happy trip. The anecdotal study she produced—"Tell My Horse," published in 1938—is tetchy and belligerent, its author disgusted by the virulent racism of light-skinned mulattoes toward blacks in Jamaica, and as distinctly put out by the unreliability and habitual lying she experienced among the Haitians. In any case, this particular trip had been prompted less by an interest in research than by a need to escape from New York, where she'd left the man she thought of as the love of her life—a still mysterious figure who belongs less to her biography than to her art. In a period of seven weeks, in Haiti, in the fall of 1936, she wrote "Their Eyes Were Watching God," a novel meant to "embalm all the tenderness of my passion for him."

IN HER AUTOBIOGRAPHY, HURSTON QUICKLY DISMISSES HER FIRST MARriage and entirely neglects to mention her second; each lasted only a matter of months. She wed her longtime Howard University boyfriend in May, 1927, and bailed out that August. (Apparently unruffled, Hurston wrote her friends that her husband had been an obstacle, and had held her back.) In 1939, her marriage to a twenty-three-year-old W.P.A. playground worker dissolved with her claims that he drank and his claims that she'd failed to pay for his college education and had threatened him with voodoo. "The great difficulty lies in trying to transpose last night's moment to a day which has no knowledge of it," she writes in "Dust Tracks on a Road." She concludes, "I have come to know by experience that work is the nearest thing to happiness that I can find."

Those admirers who wish Hurston to be a model feminist as well as a racial symbol have seized on the issue of a woman's historic choice between love and work, and have claimed that Hurston instinctively took the less travelled path. On the basis of Hurston's public insouciance, Alice Walker describes, with delicious offhand aplomb, "the way she tended to marry or not marry men, but enjoyed them anyway, while never missing a beat in her work." No sweat, no tears—one for the girls. It is true that Hurston was never financially supported by a man—or by anyone except Mrs. Mason. Hemenway, her biographer, writes that it was precisely because of her desire to avoid "such encroachment" on her freedom that her marriages failed.

Without doubt, Hurston was a woman of strong character, and she went through life mostly alone. She burned sorrow and fear like fuel, to keep herself going. She made a point of not needing what she could not have: whites who avoided her company suffered their own loss; she claimed not to have "ever really wanted" her father's affection. Other needs were just as unwelcome. About love, she knew the way it could make a woman take "second place in her own life." Repeatedly, she fought the pull.

There is little insouciance in the way Hurston writes of the man she calls P.M.P. in "Dust Tracks on a Road." He was "tall, dark brown, magnificently built," with "a fine mind and that intrigued me. . . . He stood on his own feet so firmly that he reared back." In fact, he was her "perfect" love—although he was only twenty-five or so to her forty, and he resented her career. It is hard to know whether his youth or his resentment or his perfection was the central problem. Resolved to "fight myself free from my obsession," she took little experimental trips away from him to see if she could stand it. When she found she couldn't, she left him for good.

Her diligent biographer, who located the man decades later, reports that he had never known exactly what had happened. She'd simply packed her bags and gone off to the Caribbean. Once there, of course, she wrote a book in which a woman who has spent her life searching for passion finally finds it, lets herself go within its embrace, and learns that her lover is honest and true, and that she is not being played for a fool—despite the familiar fact that he is only twenty-five or so and she is forty. (He tells her, "God made it so you spent yo' ole age first wid somebody else, and saved up yo' young girl days to spend wid me.") And then, in the midst of love's perfection, the woman is forced—not out of anger or betrayal but by a hurricane and a mad dog and a higher fate—to shoot him dead, and return to a state of enlightened solitude.

"THEIR EYES WERE WATCHING GOD" BROUGHT A HEARTBEAT AND breath to all Hurston's years of research. Raising a folk culture to the heights of art, it fulfilled the Harlem Renaissance dream just a few years after it had been abandoned; Alain Locke himself complained that the novel failed to come to grips with the challenges of "social document fiction." The recent incarnation of Hurston's lyric drama as a black feminist textbook is touched with many ironies, not the least of which is the need to consider it as a social document. The paramount ironies, however, are two: the heroine is not quite black, and becomes even less black as the story goes on; and the author offers perhaps the most serious Lawrentian vision ever penned by a woman of sexual love as the fundamental spring and power of life itself.

The heroine of "Eyes," Janie Crawford, is raised by her grandmother, who grew up in "slavery time," and who looks on in horror as black women give up their precious freedom for chains they forge themselves. "Dis love! Dat's just whut's got us uh pullin' and uh haulin' and sweatin' and doin' from can't see in de mornin' till can't see at night." But no one can give a woman what she will not claim. Nanny's immovable goal to see Janie "school out" meets its match in the teenager's bursting sexuality. Apprehensive, Nanny marries her off to a man with a house and sixty acres and a pone of fat on the back of his neck. "But Nanny, Ah wants to want him sometimes. Ah don't want him to do all de wantin'," Janie complains, and she walks off one day down the road, tossing her apron onto a bush.

It isn't exactly Nora slamming the door. There's another man in a buggy waiting for Janie, and another unhappy marriage—this time to a bully who won't let her join in the dazzling talk, the wildly spiralling stories, the earnest games of an Eatonville that Hurston raises up now like a darktown Camelot. After his death, a full twenty years later, she is rather enjoying the first freedom of widowhood when a tall, laughing man enters the general store and asks her to play checkers: "She looked him over and got little thrills from every one of his good points. Those full, lazy eyes with the lashes curling sharply away like drawn scimitars. The lean, over-padded shoulders and narrow waist. Even nice!"

It's the checkers almost as much as the sex. After Nanny, this man, who is called Tea Cake ("Tea Cake! So you sweet as all dat?"), is the staunchest feminist in the novel. He pushes Janie to play the games, talk the talk, "have de nerve tuh say whut you mean." They get married and set off together to work in the Everglades, picking beans side by side all day and rolling dice and dancing to piano blues at night. Hurston isn't unaware of the harsh background to these lives—trucks come chugging through the mud carrying migrant workers, "people ugly from ignorance and broken from being poor"—but she's willing to leave further study to the Wrights and the Steinbecks. Her concern is with the flame that won't go out, the making of laughter out of nothing, the rhythm, the intensity of feeling that transcends it all.

DURING THE NINETEEN-SEVENTIES, WHEN "THEIR EYES WERE WATCHING God" was being rediscovered with high excitement, Janie Crawford was granted the status of "earliest . . . heroic black woman in the Afro-American literary tradition." But many impatient questions have since been asked about this new icon. Why doesn't Janie speak up sooner? Why can't she go off alone? Why is she always waiting for some man to show her the way? Apologies have been made for the difficulties of giving power and daring to a female character in 1936, but then Scarlett O'Hara didn't fare too badly with the general public that year. The fact is that Janie was not made to suit independent-minded female specifications of any era. She is not a stand-in for her author but a creation meant to live out other possibilities, which are permitted her in large part because—unlike her author—she has no ambition except to live, and because she is beautiful.

"I got an overwhelming complex about my looks before I was grown," Hurston wrote her friend and editor Burroughs Mitchell in 1947, but went on to declare that she had triumphed over it. "I don't care how homely I am now. I know that it doesn't really matter, and so my relations with others are easier." Despite the possible exaggerations of a moment, this vibrantly attractive woman was well acquainted with what might be called the aesthetic burdens of race ("as ugly as Cinderella's sisters" is a phrase meaning Negro, Hurston reported to Mrs. Mason), and she spared her romantic heroine every one of them.

Janie recalls of an early photograph, "Ah couldn't recognize dat dark chile as me," and by the middle of the book neither can we. By then, we've heard a good deal about her breasts and buttocks and so extraordinarily much about her "great rope of black hair"—a standard feature of the gorgeous literary mulatto—that one critic wrote that it seemed to be a separate character. But it is only when Janie and Tea Cake get to the Everglades and confront the singularly racist Mrs. Turner, eager to "class off" with other white-featured blacks ("Ah ain't got no flat nose and liver lips. Ah'm uh featured woman"), that we hear of Janie's "coffee-and-cream complexion" and "Caucasian characteristics." The transformation is both touching and embarrassing—something like George Eliot's suddenly making Dorothea sublimely beautiful in the Roman-museum scene of "Middlemarch." It's as though the author could no longer withhold from her beloved creation the ultimate reward: Dorothea starts to look like a Madonna, and Janie starts to look white.

With Hurston, though, pride always rushes back in after a fall. These alternating emotional axes are what make her so unclassifiable, so easily susceptible to widely different readings, all of which she may intend. For Janie never acts white, or even seems to care whether she looks that way. She is sincerely mystified by Mrs. Turner's tirades. "We'se uh mingled people," she responds, seeming to rebuke her author's own reflexive notions of beauty, too. "How come you so against black?"

Although Janie spends much of the book struggling to gain the right to speak her mind, she is not particularly notable for her eloquence. There is, however, a great deal of poetry of observation running through her head, which we hear not as her thoughts, precisely, but in the way the story is told. Those who analyze "narrative strategies" have pulped small forests trying to define Hurston's way of slipping in and out of a storytelling voice that sometimes belongs to Janie and sometimes doesn't and, by design, isn't always clear. (As in "Mrs. Dalloway," the effect is of a woman's sensual dispersal through the world.) Janie's panting teen-age sexuality is rendered in a self-consciously hyper-adolescent prose of kissing bees and creaming blossoms—prose that Wright seized on for its "facile sensuality" and that Hurston's admirers now quote with dismaying regularity as an example of her literary art. But Hurston at her best is simple, light, lucid, nearly offhand, or else just as simply, Biblically passionate. Janie wakes to see the sun rise: "He peeped up over the door sill of the world and made a little foolishness with red." (There is an archaic sense of power in Hurston's sexing of all things: "Havoc was there with her mouth wide open.") As for Tea Cake, even as Janie tries to push his image away he "seemed to be crushing scent out of the world with his footsteps," Hurston writes. "Crushing aromatic herbs with every step he took. Spices hung about him. He was a glance from God."

This is a sermon from the woman's church of Eros. And, like the sermons in which Hurston was schooled—like her entire book, as it winds in and out of this realization of sexual grace—her message lives in its music. At her truest as a writer, Hurston was a musician. The delightfully quotable sayings that she "discovered" on her field trips (many of which recur as plucked examples in "Mules and Men" and her other books) are embedded in this single volume like folk tunes in Dvořák or Chopin: seamlessly, with beauties of invention often indistinguishable from beauties of discovery. The rhythms of talk in her poetry and the substance of poetry in her talk fuse into a radiant suspension. "He done taught me de maiden language all over," Janie says of Tea Cake, and there may be some truth to the tribute: Hurston had never written this way before, and she never rose to it again. It seems likely that without the intensity of her feelings for "P.M.P." this famously independent woman would not have written the novel that is her highest achievement and her lasting legacy. It perhaps complicates the issue of a woman's life and work that the love she tore herself away from so that she could be free, and free to write, turned out to have been the Muse.

HURSTON'S ABILITY TO WRITE FICTION SEEMS TO HAVE DRIED UP AFTER the commercial failure of "Their Eyes Were Watching God," which sank without a trace soon after publication. Her next novel, "Moses, Man of the Mountain," published in 1939, seems a failed reprise of the Bible-based all-Negro Broadway hit "Green Pastures," with the story of Exodus as its blackface subject. ("Oh, er—Moses, did you ask about them Hebrews while you was knocking around in Egypt?") Gone is the miraculous ear. Gone, too, are her great humor and heart. "Moses" is a weary book, heavy with accumulated resentments. Hurston's disillusionment is fully evident in her mordant, angry journalism of the nineteen-forties, in which she witheringly commends the Southern custom of whites favoring their own "pet Negroes" (and their eager pets returning the favor) as a functioning racial system, and rails against the substandard Negro colleges she calls "begging joints." The title of one article—"Negroes Without Self-Pity"—speaks for itself.

This was her life's theme, and she sounded it all the louder as two new novels were rejected, her poverty went from bohemian to chronic, and her health gave way. She bought a houseboat and spent much of the mid-forties sailing Florida rivers: individualism, her refuge from racism, had lapsed into nearly total isolation. She returned to New York in 1946, looking for work, and wound up in the campaign office of the Republican congressional candidate running against Adam Clayton Powell. When her side lost, she was stranded for a terrible winter in a room on 124th Street, in a different sort of isolation. She didn't ask for help, and she didn't get any. She felt herself slipping, surrounded by racists and haters, the whole city "a basement to Hell."

It was just after this that she wrote her last published novel, "Seraph on the Suwanee." The story of a white Southern woman and her family, it contains no prominent black characters. Among Hurston's supporters, Alice Walker has called it "reactionary, static, shockingly misguided and timid," and Mary Helen Washington has called it "vacuous as a soap opera." Everyone agrees that Hurston had fallen into the common trap of believing that a real writer must be "universal"—that is to say, must write about whites—and that she had simply strayed too far from the sources that fed her. In fact the book is poisonously fascinating, and suggests, rather, that she came too close.

The story of beautiful, golden-haired Arvay Henson, who believes herself ugly and unworthy of love, contains many echoes of Hurston's earlier work, but its most striking counterpart is the long-ago play "Color Struck." The works set a beginning and an end to years of struggle with their shared essential theme—the destructive power of fear and bitterness in a woman's tortured psyche. Arvay is born to a poor-white "cracker" family; in a refraction of Hurston's own history, a preference for her older sister "had done something to Arvay's soul across the years." She falls in love with a magnificent fallen aristocrat, who rapes her—for Arvay this is an act of ecstatic, binding possession—and marries her. Tormented by her failure to live up to his perfection, she comes to hate him almost as much as she hates herself.

The book is a choking mixture of cynicism and compulsion. Hurston was desperate for a success, and hoped for a movie sale—hence, no doubt, the formulaic rape and the book's mawkish ending, in which Arvay learns to sing happily in her marital chains. But to reach this peace Arvay must admit, after years of pretense, that she is not really proud of her own miserably poor and uneducated family, that poverty and ignorance lend them neither moral superiority nor charm, and that she is, in fact, shamed and disgusted by them. Arvay's last attempt to go home to her own people results in her burning down the house in which she was raised.

The book was sharply criticized because Hurston's white Southerners speak no differently from the Eatonville blacks of her earlier work. The inflections, the rhythms, the actual expressions that had been declared examples of a distinctive black culture were all now simply transferred to white mouths. The incongruous effects, as in her "Moses" book, point to a failure of technique, an aural exhaustion. But in a letter to her editor Hurston gave an even more dispiriting explanation for what she'd done. "I think that it should be pointed out that what is known as Negro dialect in the South is no such thing," she wrote, in a repudiation nearly as sweeping as Arvay's, at once laying waste to her professional past and her extraordinary personal achievement. The qualities of Southern speech—black and white alike, she claimed—were a relic of the Elizabethan past preserved by Southern whites in their own closed and static society. "They did *not* get it from the Negroes. The Africans coming to America got it from them."

The novel's publication, in the fall of 1948, was swallowed up in a court case that tested all Hurston's capacity for resisting bitterness. That September, in New York, an emotionally disturbed ten-year-old boy accused her of sexual molestation. The Children's Society filed charges, and Hurston was arrested and indicted. Although the case was eventually thrown out, a court employee spilled the news to one of the city's black newspapers—the white papers were presumably not interested—and the lurid story made headlines. Hurston contemplated suicide, but slowly came back to herself on a long sailing trip.

She never returned to New York. For the rest of her life, she lived in Florida, on scant money and whatever dignity she was able to salvage. In Miami, she worked as a maid. Later, she moved to a cabin up the coast that rented for five dollars a week, where she grew much of her own food. She labored over several books, none considered publishable. Her radical independence was more than ever reflected in her politics: fervently anti-Communist, officially Republican, resisting anything that smacked of special pleading. When Brown v. Board of Education was decided, in 1954, she was furious—and wrote furiously—over the implication that blacks could learn only when seated next to whites, or that anyone white should be forced to sit beside anyone black. It was plain "insulting." Although there was some hard wisdom in her conclusion—"The next ten years would be better spent in appointing truant officers and looking after conditions in the homes from which the children come"—her defiant segregationist position was happily taken up by whites of the same persuasion. Her reputation as a traitor to her people overshadowed and outlasted her reasoning, her works, and her life.

Hurston died in January, 1960, in the Saint Lucie County welfare home, in Fort Pierce, Florida, four days before the first sit-in took place, at a Woolworth lunch counter in Greensboro, North Carolina. She was buried in an unmarked grave in a segregated cemetery in Fort Pierce. All her books were out of print. In 1971, in one of the first important reconsiderations of writers of the Harlem Renaissance, the critic Darwin Turner wrote that Hurston's relative anonymity was understandable, for, despite her skills, she had never been more than a "wandering minstrel." He went on to say that it was "eccentric but perhaps appropriate"—one must pause over the choice of words—for her "to return to Florida to take a job as a cook and maid for a white family and to die in poverty." There was a certain justice in these actions, he declared, in that "she had returned to the level of life which she proposed for her people."

THE GLEAMING TWO-VOLUME LIBRARY OF AMERICA EDITION OF HURston's "Novels & Stories" and "Folklore, Memoirs, & Other Writings" makes for a different kind of justice. These books bring Hurston a long way from the smudged photocopies that used to circulate, like samizdat, at academic conventions, and usher her into the national literary canon in highly respectable hardback. She is the fourth African-American to be published in this august series, and the fifth woman, and the first writer who happens to be both. Although the Hurston revival may have been driven in part by her official double-victim status—a possibility that many will take as a sign that her literary status has been inflated—"Their Eyes Were Watching God" can stand unsupported in any company. Harold Bloom has written of Hurston as continuing in the line of the Wife of Bath and Falstaff and Whitman, as a figure of outrageous vitality, fulfilling the Nietzschean charge that we try to live as though it were always morning.

Outside of fiction, this kind of strength is mainly a matter of determination. For many who have embodied it in literature—Nietzsche, Whitman, Lawrence, Hurston—it is a passionate dream of health (dreamed while the simply healthy are sound asleep) which stirs a rare insistence and bravado. "Sometimes, I feel discriminated against, but it does not make me angry," Hurston wrote in 1928. "It merely astonishes me. How *can* any deny themselves the pleasure of my company!" In the venerable African-American game of "the dozens," the players hurl monstrous insults back and forth as they try to rip each other apart with words. (Hurston and Wright both call up the game, and quote the same now rather quaint chant of abuse: "Yo' mama don't wear no DRAWS, Ah seen her when she took 'em OFF"). The near-Darwinian purpose was to get so strong that, no matter what you heard about whomever you loved, you would not let on that you cared to do anything but laugh. It's a game that Richard Wright must have lost every time. But Zora Neale Hurston was the champ.

It is important not to blink at what she had to face and how it made her feel. Envy, fury, confusion, desire to escape: there is no wonder in it. We know too well the world she came from. It is the world she rebuilt out of words and the extraordinary song of the words themselves—about love and picking beans and fighting through hurricanes—that have given us something entirely new. And who is to say that this is not a political achievement? Early in "Their Eyes Were Watching God" Hurston describes a gathering of the folks of Eatonville on their porches at sundown: "It was the time to hear things and talk. These sitters had been tongueless, earless, eyeless conveniences all day long. Mules and other brutes had occupied their skins. But now, the sun and the bossman were gone, so the skins felt powerful and human. They became lords of sounds and lesser things. They passed notions through their mouths. They sat in judgment."

The powerless become lords of sounds, the dispossessed rule all creation with their tongues. Language is not a small victory. It was out of this last, irreducible possession that the Jews made a counter-world of words, the Irish vanquished England, and Russian poetry bloomed thick over Stalin's burial grounds. And in a single book one woman managed to suggest what another such heroic tradition, rising out of American slavery, might have been—a literature as profound and original as the spirituals. There is the sense of a long, ghostly procession behind Hurston: what might have existed if only more of the words and stories had been written down decades earlier, if only Phillis Wheatley had not tried to write like Alexander Pope, if only literate slaves and their generations of children had not felt pressed to prove their claim to the sworn civilities. She had to try to make up for all of this, and more. If out of broken bits of talk and memory she pieced together something that may once have existed, out of will and desire she added what never was. Hurston created a myth that has been gratefully mistaken for history, and in which she herself plays a mythic role—a myth about a time and place fair enough, funny enough, unbitter enough, glad enough to have produced a woman black and truly free.

HUGHES AT COLUMBIA

CHARLAYNE HUNTER-GAULT

December 30, 1967

On a miserably wet evening seven months after the death of Langston Hughes, we sat, almost comfortably (except for our damp feet), in the cavernous Wollman Auditorium, at Columbia University, and listened to the low, bemused voice of Hughes on tape as, against a taped musical background, it sent his "Weary Blues" floating over a group of people who had assembled to pay tribute to him. The program, "A Langston Hughes Memorial Evening," was sponsored by The Forum, which is, in the words of its nineteen-year-old president, Bruce Kanze, "a student organization that brings to the University interesting people whom the University itself would never consider bringing, to discuss issues and topics that are important."

A few minutes after eight, when nearly every seat was filled, three men walked onto the stage: Leon Bibb, the actor and singer; Jonathan Kozol, author of "Death at an Early Age"; and Professor James P. Shenton, of Columbia. ("He teaches a course on Reconstruction—the closest thing to a course on Negro history at Columbia," Mr. Kanze told us later.) They were soon joined by Miss Viveca Lindfors, the actress, who was wearing a pale-gray fur coat but removed it as she was sitting down, and gracefully placed it over her mini-exposed knees.

Professor Shenton, who had to leave early, was introduced, and hurried to the microphone. "I am here partly as a way of saying for Columbia that we owe some apologies," he said solemnly. "For a while, there lived a poet down the street from Columbia, and Columbia never took the time to find out what he was about." The Professor paused for a few seconds, and then continued, "For a while, there lived a poet down the street from Columbia, who even attended Columbia for a while, and yet he never received an honorary degree from here. When we buried him, *then* we gave him a memorial. But, after all, that's the experience of the black man down the street from Columbia."

Professor Shenton left the platform, and Mr. Kozol, a slim young man wearing rimless glasses, came to the microphone. In 1965, he was discharged from a ghetto school in Boston, in part because he read Langston Hughes' poem "Ballad of the Landlord" to his class:

Landlord, landlord,
My roof has sprung a leak.
Don't you 'member I told you about it
Way last week?

Landlord, landlord,
These steps is broken down.
When you come up yourself
It's a wonder you don't fall down.

Ten bucks you say I owe you?
Ten bucks you say is due?
Well, that's ten bucks more'n I'll pay you
Till you fix this house up new.

What? You gonna get eviction orders?
You gonna cut off my heat?
You gonna take my furniture and
Throw it in the street?

Um-huh! You talking high and mighty.
Talk on—till you get through.

You ain't gonna be able to say a word
If I land my fist on you.

Police! Police!
Come and get this man!
He's trying to ruin the government
and overturn the land!

Copper's whistle!
Patrol bell!
Arrest.

Precinct station.
Iron cell.
Headlines in press:

> MAN THREATENS LANDLORD
>
> TENANT HELD NO BAIL
>
> JUDGE GIVES NEGRO 90 DAYS IN COUNTY JAIL

Mr. Kozol said that he might have avoided some of the trouble that eventually led to his firing if he had chosen to "restrict his reading and reference materials to the list of approved publications"— poetry, for instance, to be read from officially approved selections called "Memory Gems." He gave the Hughes audience a sample:

"Dare to be right! Dare to be true:
The failings of others can never save you.
Stand by your conscience, your honor, your faith;
Stand like a hero, and battle till death."

And another:

"There is beauty in the sunshine
An' clouds that roam the sky;

There is beauty in the Heavens,
An' the stars that shine on high."

Later, Mr. Kozol read from a paper that had been handed in by one of his fourth-grade students after he had asked the class to write about the kinds of things *they* saw around them:

"In my school I see dirty boards and I see papers on
the floor. I see an old browken window with a sign on it
saying, Do not unlock this window are browken. And I
see cracks in the walls and I see old books with ink poured
all over them and I see old painting hanging on the walls.
I see old alfurbet letter hanging on one nail on the wall.
I see a dirty fire exit, I see a old closet with supplys for
the class. I see pigons flying all over the school. I see old
freght trains throgh the fence of the school yard. . . ."

The young teacher spoke at length about his experiences in this school, and then read a few paragraphs from a description of Africa in a book called "Our Neighbors Near and Far":

"Yumbu and Minko are a black boy and a black girl
who live in this jungle village. Their skins are of so dark a
brown color that they look almost black. Their noses are
large and flat. Their lips are thick. Their eyes are black and
shining, and their hair is so curly that it seems like wool.
They are Negroes and they belong to the black race."

Two children in another area of the world were described this way:

"Two Swiss children live in a farmhouse on the edge
of town. . . . These children are handsome. Their eyes are

blue. Their hair is golden yellow. Their white skins are clear, and their cheeks are as red as ripe, red apples."

Mr. Kozol said that he had never met Langston Hughes but that a short while after his much publicized firing he had received a new collection of Hughes' "Simple" stories from the poet, with these words written on the flyleaf: "I wish the rent / Was heaven sent."

Leon Bibb, in his turn, rose and thanked Mr. Hughes, whom he called Lang, first by reading the James Weldon Johnson poem "O Black and Unknown Bards" and then by giving a poignant rendering of Mr. Hughes' poem "The Negro Speaks of Rivers" and the spiritual "I've Been 'Buked and I've Been Scorned." He wound up by saying, "Lang had the foresight to stand on his own words."

Soon Hughes' own words were being read by Miss Lindfors, who remained seated, and whose Swedish accent was lost in translation as she read from "The Panther and the Lash," a recent Hughes collection, brought out by Knopf. She read about the "Junior Addict":

". . . Yes. easier to get dope
than to get a job—
daytime or nighttime job,
teen-age, pre-draft,
pre-lifetime job.

"Quick, sunrise, come!
Sunrise out of Africa,
Quick, come!
Sunrise, please come!
Come! Come!"

And she read about the "Dream Deferred." And she read "Impasse":

"I could tell you,
If I wanted to,
What makes me
What I am.

"But I don't
Really want to—
And you don't
Give a damn."

Miss Lindfors also read the poem whose first line is "That Justice is a blind goddess" and the poem about "Birmingham Sunday"—September 15, 1963, when four little Negro girls were killed in Sunday school by a bomb thrown from outside the church. Miss Lindfors read several more poems—some bitterly humorous ones, and the one that asks, "What color / Is the face / Of war?," and one called "Peace," and, finally, "Down Where I Am":

"Too many years
Beatin' at the door—
I done beat my
Both fists sore.

"Too many years
Tryin' to get up there—
Done broke my ankles down,
Got nowhere.

"Too many years
Climbin' that hill,
'Bout out of breath.
I got my fill.

"I'm gonna plant my feet
On solid ground.

If you want to see me,
Come down."

The memorial to Langston Hughes ended as it had begun, with Langston Hughes' low, bemused voice—this time telling about how he came from the Midwest to Columbia to go to school, and caused great consternation when he presented himself at Hartley Hall. That was in 1921, and no one of African descent, he says, had ever lived in a dormitory at Columbia. "There are many barriers people try to break down," he told an audience (which had also been a Columbia audience) when the tape was made, in 1964. "I try to do it with poetry."

KING OF CATS

HENRY LOUIS GATES, JR.

April 8, 1996

In the late seventies, I used to take the train from New Haven to New York on Saturdays, to spend afternoons with Albert Murray at Books & Company, on Madison Avenue. We would roam—often joined by the artist Romare Bearden—through fiction, criticism, philosophy, music. Murray always seemed to wind up fingering densely printed paperbacks by Joyce, Mann, Proust, or Faulkner; Bearden, typically, would pick up a copy of something daunting like Rilke's "Letters on Cézanne" and then insist that I read it on the train home that night.

In those days, Murray was writing Count Basie's autobiography—a project that he didn't finish until 1985. ("For years," he has remarked more than once, "when I wrote the word 'I,' it meant Basie.") But he had already published most of the books that would secure his reputation as a cultural critic—perhaps most notably, his début collection, "The Omni-Americans" (1970), which brought together his ferocious attacks on black separatism, on protest literature, and on what he called "the social science-fiction monster." Commanding as he could be on the page, Murray was an equally impressive figure in the flesh: a lithe and dapper man with an astonishing gift of verbal fluency, by turns grandiloquent and earthy. I loved to listen to his voice—grave but insinuating, with more than a hint of a jazz singer's rasp. Murray had been a schoolmate of the novelist Ralph Ellison at the Tuskegee Institute, and the friendship of the two men over the years seemed a focal point of black literary culture in the ensuing decades. Ellison's one novel, "Invisible Man,"

was among the few unequivocal masterpieces of American literature in the postwar era, satirizing with equal aplomb Garveyites,
Communists, and white racists in both their Southern-agrarian
and their Northern-liberal guises. Murray's works of critique and
cultural exploration seemed wholly in the same spirit. Both men
were militant integrationists, and they shared an almost messianic
view of the importance of art. In their ardent belief that Negro
culture was a constitutive part of American culture, they had defied an entrenched literary mainstream, which preferred to regard
black culture as so much exotica—amusing, perhaps, but eminently
dispensable. Now they were also defying a new black vanguard,
which regarded authentic black culture as separate from the rest of
American culture—something that was created, and could be appreciated, in splendid isolation. While many of their peers liked to
speak of wrath and resistance, Murray and Ellison liked to speak of
complexity and craft, and for that reason they championed the art
of Romare Bearden.

In terms of both critical regard and artistic fecundity, these
were good days for Bearden, a large, light-skinned man with a basketball roundness to his head. (I could never get over how much
he looked like Nikita Khrushchev.) He, like Murray, was working
at the height of his powers—he was completing his famous "Jazz"
series of collages—and his stature and influence were greater than
those which any other African-American artist had so far enjoyed.
The collages combined the visual conventions of black American
folk culture with the techniques of modernism—fulfilling what
Murray called "the vernacular imperative" to transmute tradition
into art.

After a couple of hours at the bookstore, we'd go next door to
the Madison Cafe, where Romie, as Murray called him, always
ordered the same item: the largest fruit salad that I had ever seen
in public. He claimed that he chose the fruit salad because he was
watching his weight, but I was convinced that he chose it in order

to devour the colors, like an artist dipping his brush into his palette. He'd start laying the ground with the off-white of the apples and the bananas, and follow them with the pinkish orange of the grapefruit, the red of strawberries, the speckled green of kiwifruit; the blueberries and purple grapes he'd save for last. While Romie was consuming his colors, Murray would talk almost non-stop, his marvellous ternary sentences punctuated only by the occasional bite of a B.L.T. or a tuna fish on rye. Murray was then, as now, a man with definite preoccupations, and among the touchstones of his conversation were terms like "discipline," "craft," "tradition," "the aesthetic," and "the Negro idiom." And names like Thomas Mann, André Malraux, Kenneth Burke, and Lord Raglan. There was also another name—a name that never weighed more heavily than when it was unspoken—which sometimes took longer to come up.

"Heard from Ralph lately?" Bearden would almost whisper as the waitress brought the check.

"Still grieving, I guess," Murray would rasp back, shaking his head slowly. He was referring to the fire, about a decade earlier, that had destroyed Ellison's Massachusetts farmhouse and, with it, many months of revisions on his long-awaited second novel. "That fire was a terrible thing." Then Murray, who was so rarely at a loss for words, would fall silent.

Later, when Bearden and I were alone in his Canal Street loft, he'd return to the subject in hushed tones: "Ralph is mad at Al. No one seems to know why. And it's killing Al. He's not sure what he did."

THE RIFT, OR WHATEVER IT AMOUNTED TO, USED TO VEX AND PUZZLE me. It was a great mistake to regard Murray simply as Ellison's sidekick, the way many people did, but he was without question the most fervent and articulate champion of Ellison's art. The two were, in a sense, part of a single project: few figures on the scene shared as many presuppositions and preoccupations as they did.

Theirs was a sect far too small for schismatics. At the very least, the rift made things awkward for would-be postulants like me.

When "The Omni-Americans" came out, in 1970, I was in college, majoring in history but pursuing extracurricular studies in how to be black. Those were days when the Black Power movement smoldered, when militancy was the mode and rage de rigueur. Just two years before, the poets Larry Neal and Amiri Baraka had edited "Black Fire," the book that launched the so-called Black Arts movement—in effect, the cultural wing of the Black Power movement. Maybe it was hard to hold a pen with a clenched fist, but you did what you could: the revolution wasn't about niceties of style anyway. On the occasions when Ralph Ellison, an avatar of elegance, was invited to college campuses, blacks invariably denounced him for his failure to involve himself in the civil-rights struggle, for his evident disdain of the posturings of Black Power. For me, though, the era was epitomized by a reading that the poet Nikki Giovanni gave in a university lecture hall, to a standing-room-only crowd—a sea of colorful dashikis and planetary Afros. Her words seemed incandescent with racial rage, and each poem was greeted with a Black Power salute. "Right on! Right on!" we shouted, in the deepest voices we could manage, each time Giovanni made another grand claim about the blackness of blackness. Those were days when violence (or, anyway, talk of violence) had acquired a Fanonist glamour; when the black bourgeoisie—kulaks of color, nothing more—was reviled as an obstacle on the road to revolution; when the arts were seen as merely an instrumentality for a larger cause.

Such was the milieu in which Murray published "The Omni-Americans," and you couldn't imagine a more foolhardy act. This was a book in which the very language of the black nationalists was subjected to a strip search. Ever since Malcolm X, for instance, the epithet "house Negro" had been a staple of militant invective; yet here was Murray arguing that if only we got our history straight we'd realize that those house Negroes were practically race patriots.

("The house slave seems to have brought infinitely more tactical information from the big house to the cabins than any information about subversive plans he ever took back.") And while radicals mocked their bourgeois brethren as "black Anglo-Saxons," Murray defiantly declared, "Not only is it the so-called middle class Negro who challenges the status quo in schools, housing, voting practices, and so on, he is also the one who is most likely to challenge total social structures and value systems." Celebrated chroniclers of black America, including Claude Brown, Gordon Parks, and James Baldwin, were shown by Murray to be tainted by the ethnographic fallacy, the pretense that one writer's peculiar experiences can represent a social genus. "This whole thing about somebody revealing what it is really like to be black has long since gotten out of hand anyway," he wrote. "Does anybody actually believe that, say, Mary McCarthy reveals what it is really like to be a U.S. white woman, or even a Vassar girl?" But he reserved his heaviest artillery for the whole social-science approach to black life, whether in the hands of the psychologist Kenneth Clark (of Brown v. Board of Education fame) or in those of the novelist Richard Wright, who had spent too much time reading his sociologist friends. What was needed wasn't more sociological inquiry, Murray declared; what was needed was cultural creativity, nourished by the folkways and traditions of black America but transcending them. And the work of literature that best met that challenge, he said, was Ellison's "Invisible Man."

The contrarian held his own simply by matching outrage with outrage—by writing a book that was so pissed-off, jaw-jutting, and unapologetic that it demanded to be taken seriously. Nobody had to tell this veteran about black fire: in Murray the bullies of blackness had met their most formidable opponent. And a great many blacks—who, suborned by "solidarity," had trained themselves to suppress any heretical thoughts—found Murray's book oddly thrilling: it had the transgressive frisson of samizdat under Stalinism. You'd read it greedily, though you just might want to switch dust jackets with "The Wretched of the Earth" before wandering around with it in public. "Very early on, he was saying stuff that could get him killed," the African-American novelist David Bradley says. "And he did not seem to care." The power of his example lingers. "One February, I had just delivered the usual black-history line, and I was beginning to feel that I was selling snake oil," Bradley recalls. "And right here was this man who has said this stuff. And I'm thinking, Well, *he* ain't dead yet."

As if to remove any doubts, Murray has just published two books simultaneously, both with Pantheon. One, "The Seven League Boots," is his third novel, and completes a trilogy about a bright young fellow named Scooter, his fictional alter ego; the other, "The Blue Devils of Nada," is a collection of critical essays, analyzing some favorite artists (Ellington, Hemingway, Bearden) and expatiating upon some favorite tenets (the "blues idiom" as an aesthetic substrate, the essentially fluid nature of American culture). Both are books that will be discussed and debated for years to come; both are vintage Murray.

THE MOST OUTRAGEOUS THEORIST OF AMERICAN CULTURE LIVES, AS he has lived for three decades, in a modest apartment in Lenox Terrace, in Harlem. When I visit him there, everything is pretty much as I remembered it. The public rooms look like yet another Harlem branch of the New York Public Library. Legal pads and magnifying glasses perch beside his two or three favorite chairs, along with numerous ball-point pens, his weapons of choice. His shelves record a lifetime of enthusiasms; James, Tolstoy, Hemingway, Proust, and Faulkner are among the authors most heavily represented. Close at hand are volumes by favored explicants, such as Joseph Campbell, Kenneth Burke, Carl Jung, Rudolph Arnheim, Bruno Bettelheim, Constance Rourke. On his writing desk sits a more intimate canon. There's Thomas Mann's four-volume "Joseph and his Brothers"—the saga, after all, of a slave who gains the power to decide the fate of a people. There's André Malraux's "Man's Fate," which represented for Ellison and Murray a more rarefied mode of engagé writing than anything their compeers had to offer. There's Joel Chandler Harris's "The Complete Tales of Uncle Remus," a mother lode of African-American folklore. One wall is filled with his famously compendious collection of jazz recordings; a matte-black CD-player was a gift from his protégé Wynton Marsalis. You will not, however, see the sort of framed awards that festooned Ellison's apartment. "I have received few of those honors," he says, pulling on his arthritic right leg. "No American Academy, few honorary degrees."

A quarter of a century has passed since Murray's literary début, and time has mellowed him not at all. His arthritis may have worsened over the past few years, and there is always an aluminum walker close by, but as he talks he sprouts wings. Murray likes to elaborate on his points and elaborate on his elaborations, until you find that you have circumnavigated the globe and raced through the whole of post-Homeric literary history—and this is what he calls "vamping till ready." In his conversation, outrages alternate with insights, and often the insights are the outrages. Every literary culture has its superego and its id; Albert Murray has the odd distinction of being both. The contradictions of human nature are, fittingly, a favorite topic of Murray's. He talks about how Thomas Jefferson was a slaveholder but how he also helped to establish a country whose founding creed was liberty. "Every time I think about it," he says, "I want to wake him up and give him ten more slaves." He's less indulgent of the conflicting impulses of Malcolm X. Dr. King's strategy of nonviolence was "one of the most magnificent things that anybody ever invented in the civil-rights movement," he maintains. "And this guy came up and started thumbing his nose at it, and, to my utter amazement, he's treated as if he were a civil-rights leader. He didn't lead anything. He was in Selma laughing at these guys. God *damn*, nigger!"

Albert Murray is a teacher by temperament, and as he explains a point he'll often say that he wants to be sure to "work it into your consciousness." The twentieth century has worked a great deal into Murray's consciousness. He was fifteen when the Scottsboro trial began, twenty-two when Marian Anderson sang at the Lincoln Memorial. He joined the Air Force when it was segregated and rejoined shortly after it had been desegregated. He was in his late thirties when Brown v. Board of Education was decided, when the conflict in Korea was concluded, when Rosa Parks was arrested. He was in his forties when the Civil Rights Act was passed, when S.N.C.C. was founded, when John F. Kennedy was killed. And he was in his fifties when the Black Panther Party was formed, when King was shot, when Black Power was proclaimed. Such are the lineaments of public history—the sort of grainy national drama that newsreels used to record. For him, though, the figures of history are as vivid as drinking companions, and, on the whole, no more sacrosanct.

He is equally unabashed about taking on contemporary figures of veneration, even in the presence of a venerator. Thus, about the novelist Toni Morrison, we agree to disagree. "I do think it's tainted with do-goodism," he says of her Nobel Prize, rejecting what he considers the special pleading of contemporary feminism. "I think it's redressing wrongs. You don't have to condescend to no goddam Jane Austen. Or the Brontës, or George Eliot and George Sand. These chicks are tough. You think you'll get your fastball by Jane Austen? So we don't need special pleading for anything. And the same goes for blackness." He bridles at the phenomenon of Terry McMillan, the best-selling author of "Waiting to Exhale"—or, more precisely, at the nature of the attention she has received. "I think it's a mistake to try to read some profound political significance into everything, like as soon as a Negro writes it's got to be some civil-rights thing," he says. "It's just Jackie Collins stuff."

At times, his pans somehow edge into panegyrics, the result

being what might be called a backhanded insult. About Maya Angelou's much discussed Inaugural poem he says, "It's like the reaction to 'Porgy and Bess.' Man, you put a bunch of brown-skinned
people onstage, with footlights and curtains, and they make *anything* work. White people have no resistance to Negro performers:
they charm the pants off anything. Black people make you listen
up. They're singing 'Old Man River'—'Tote that barge, lift that
bale'? What the fuck is that? Everybody responded like 'This is
great.' That type of fantastic charm means that black performers
can redeem almost any type of pop fare."

Since discipline and craft are his bywords, however, he distrusts staged spontaneity. "He plays the same note that he perfected
twenty-five years ago, and he acts like he's got to sweat to get the
note out of the goddam guitar," Murray says of the contemporary
blues musician B. B. King. "He's got to shake his head and frown,
and it's just going to be the same goddam note he already played
twenty-five years ago." Murray himself doesn't mind returning to
notes he played twenty-five years ago—his nonfiction books explore
the same set of issues, and can be read as chapters of a single ongoing opus. Indeed, from all accounts the fashioning of this particular
cultural hero began long before the start of his writing career.

IN MURRAY'S CASE, HEROISM WAS A MATTER BOTH OF CIRCUMSTANCE
and of will. Certainly he has long been an avid student of the subject. Lord Raglan's classic "The Hero: A Study in Tradition, Myth,
and Drama" (1936) is among the books most frequently cited in
his writing, and it remains a part of his personal canon. Moreover,
the mythic patterns that Lord Raglan parsed turn out to have had
resonances for Murray beyond the strictly literary. According to
Raglan's exhaustively researched generalizations, the hero is high-
born, but "the circumstances of his conception are unusual," and he
is "spirited away" to be "reared by foster-parents in a far country."
Then, "on reaching manhood," he "returns or goes to his future

kingdom," confronts and defeats the king, or a dragon, or some such, and starts being heroic in earnest. So it was, more or less, with Oedipus, Theseus, Romulus, Joseph, Moses, Siegfried, Arthur, Robin Hood, and—oh, yes—Albert Murray.

Murray was born in 1916 and grew up in Magazine Point, a hamlet not far from Mobile, Alabama. His mother was a housewife, and his father, Murray says, was a "common laborer," who sometimes helped lay railroad tracks as a cross-tie cutter and at other times harvested timber in the Turpentine woods. "As far as the Murrays were concerned, it was a fantastic thing that I finished the ninth grade," he recalls, "or that I could read the newspaper." But he had already decided that he was bound for college. Everyone in the village knew that there was something special about him. And he knew it, too.

He had known it ever since an all-night wake—he was around eleven at the time—when he had fallen asleep in the living room, his head cradled in his mother's lap. At one point, he surfaced to hear himself being discussed, but, with a child's cunning, he pretended he was still asleep.

"Tell me something," a relative was saying. "Is it true that Miss Graham is really his mama?"

"She's the one brought him into the world," Mrs. Murray replied. "But I'm his mama. She gave him to me when he was no bigger than a minute, and he was so little I had to put him on a pillow to take him home. I didn't think he was going to make it. I laid him out for God to take him two or three times. And I said, 'Lord, this child is here for something, so I'm going to feed this child and he's going to make it.'" It was a moment that Al Murray likens to finding out the truth about Santa Claus.

Murray's birth parents were, as he slowly learned, well educated and securely middle class—people who belonged to an entirely different social stratum from that of his adoptive parents. His natural father, John Young, came from a well-established family in town.

His natural mother had been attending Tuskegee as a boarding student and working part time for John Young's aunt and uncle, who were in the real-estate business. When she learned that a close encounter with John Young had left her pregnant, she had to leave town—"Because of the disgrace," Murray explains. As luck would have it, a cousin of hers knew a married woman who, unable to bear a child of her own, was interested in adopting one. Murray doesn't have to be prodded to make the fairy-tale connection. "It's just like the prince left among the paupers," he says cheerfully. (In "The Omni-Americans" he wrote, apropos of the 1965 Moynihan report on the breakdown of the black-family structure, "How many epic heroes issue from conventional families?")

As a freshman at the Tuskegee Institute—the ancestral kingdom he was fated to enter—Murray became aware of a junior whose reading habits were alarmingly similar to his. He was a music major from Oklahoma named Ralph Waldo Ellison, and what first impressed Murray about him was his wardrobe. "Joe College, right out of *Esquire*—he had fine contrasting slacks, gray tweed jacket. He would be wearing bow ties and two-tone shoes," Murray recalls. "In those days, when you checked out a book from the library you had a little slip in the back where you would write your name, and then they would stamp the due date." Consequently, when Murray took out a book by, say, T. S. Eliot or Robinson Jeffers, he could see who had previously borrowed the book. Time and again, it was that music major with the two-tone shoes.

Ellison left Tuskegee for New York before completing his senior year: his absence was meant to be temporary, a means of saving some money, but he never went back. Murray earned his B.A. at Tuskegee in 1939, and stayed on to teach. In 1941, he married Mozelle Menefee, who was a student there. He spent the last two years of the Second World War on active duty in the Air Force. "I was just hoping I'd live long enough for Thomas Mann to finish the last volume of 'Joseph and His Brothers,'" he says. Two years after his discharge, he moved to New York, where, on the G.I. bill, he got a master's degree in literature from New York University. It was also in New York that the friendship between him and Ellison took off. Ellison read passages to Murray from a manuscript that would turn into "Invisible Man." The two men explored the streets and the sounds of Harlem together; over meals and over drinks, they hashed out ideas about improvisation, the blues, and literary modernism. Even then, Murray had a reputation as a "great explainer."

The prominent black religious and literary scholar Nathan A. Scott, who was a graduate student in New York in the forties and had become a friend of Ellison's, tells about being in the Gotham Book Mart one day and noticing another black man there. "I was somewhat surprised to find this slight, dark man there, because I'd never bumped into a Negro there," Scott recounts. "And some young white chap came in and they knew each other and immediately plunged into a spirited conversation, and at a certain point I overheard this chap say to the black man, 'Well, what are you working on these days?' To which the black chap replied, 'Oh, I am doing an essay in self-definition.'" (And Scott laughs loudly.) Later, at a dinner at Ellison's apartment, Ellison introduced Scott to his friend Albert Murray: "Immediately, I thought, By God, here is the chap who was doing that essay in self-definition! Inwardly, I laughed all over again."

If it was clear that the young man was interested in trying to write, it wasn't so clear what the results were. In the early fifties, Saul Bellow and Ralph Ellison shared a house in Dutchess County, and Bellow recalls seeing Murray from time to time down in the city. "I think he agreed with Ralph, in simply assuming that they were deeply installed in the whole American picture," Bellow says. He adds that Ellison talked about Murray's writing in those days, but that he himself never saw any of it. In 1952, Ellison published "Invisible Man." The book was a best-seller for several months, and garnered some of the most enthusiastic critical responses anyone could remember. It was soon a classroom staple, the subject of books and dissertations. It was read and reread. Ellison, in short, had become an immortal. And Murray? With a wife and a daughter to support, he was pursuing a more conventional career—in the Air Force, which he rejoined in 1951.

AS A MILITARY OFFICER, MURRAY TAUGHT COURSES IN GEOPOLITICS IN the Air Force R.O.T.C. program at Tuskegee, where he was based for much of the fifties, and he oversaw the administration of large-scale technical operations both in North Africa and in the United States. While his military career has remained oddly isolated from his creative work—a matter of regret, in the opinion of some of his friends—the experience would leave him impatient with the pretensions of the by-any-means-necessary brigade. He says, in that distinctively Murrayesque tone of zestful exasperation, "Let's talk about 'the fire next time.' You know damn well they can put out the fire by Wednesday."

When Murray retired from the military, in 1962, he moved to New York, and soon his articles began to appear in periodicals (*Life*, *The New Leader*) and collections ("Anger, and Beyond"). In 1964, Ellison wrote a letter about his old friend to one Jacob Cohen, who was planning to start a magazine. "Actually I find it very difficult to write about him," the letter began. "I suppose because I have known him since our days at Tuskegee, and because our contacts since that time have been so constant and our assumptions about so many matters in such close agreement that I really don't have the proper sense of perspective." Ellison went on to say of Murray, "He has the imagination which allows him to project himself into the centers of power, and he uses his imagination to deal with serious problems seriously and as though he were a responsible participant in the affairs of our nation and our time." The following year, a panel of book critics, authors, and editors found "Invisible

Man" to be the most widely admired novel published since the Second World War. Meanwhile, Albert Murray, then two years out of the Air Force, was scarcely known outside the circle of his acquaintances.

However asymmetric the public stature of the pair, people who spent time with Murray and Ellison in those days were impressed by the ease and intimacy of their friendship. In the late sixties, Willie Morris, then the editor of *Harper's*, eagerly sought their company: they provided him with a refreshing contrast to what he found a suffocating literary climate. He recalls, "In every way, they were like brothers—you know, soul brothers and fellow-writers—but Ellison's star was so bright, and Al was just really getting started." Soul brothers they may have been; they were also brothers-in-arms. When Murray rose to do battle with the rising ranks of black nationalism, he knew he shared a foxhole with Ralph Ellison, and there must have been comfort in that.

IT MAY SEEM IRONIC THAT THE PERSON WHO FIRST URGED "THE OMNI-Americans" on me was Larry Neal, one of the Black Arts founders. But Neal was a man of far greater subtlety than the movement he spawned, and he understood Albert Murray's larger enterprise— the one that he shared with Ellison—better than most. People who may not read Murray but like the *idea* of him reflexively label him an "integrationist"; seldom do they take in the term's full complexity. In Murray's hands, integration wasn't an act of accommodation but an act of introjection. Indeed, at the heart of Murray and Ellison's joint enterprise was perhaps the most breathtaking act of cultural chutzpah this land had witnessed since Columbus blithely claimed it all for Isabella.

In its bluntest form, their assertion was that the truest Americans were black Americans. For much of what was truly distinctive about America's "national character" was rooted in the improvisatory prehistory of the blues. The very sound of American English "is derived from the timbre of the African voice and the listening habits of the African ear," Ellison maintained. "If there is such a thing as a Yale accent, there is a Negro wail in it." This is the lesson that the protagonist of Ellison's novel learns while working at a paint factory: the whitest white is made by adding a drop of black. For generations, the word "American" had tacitly connoted "white." Murray inverted the cultural assumptions and the verbal conventions: in his discourse, "American," roughly speaking, means "black." So, even as the clenched-fist crowd was scrambling for cultural crumbs, Murray was declaring the entire harvest board of American civilization to be his birthright. In a sense, Murray was the ultimate black nationalist. And the fact that people so easily mistook his vision for its opposite proved how radical it was.

But why stop with matters American? What did the European savants of Existentialism understand about *la condition humaine* that Ma Rainey did not? In later works, most notably "Stomping the Blues" (1976), Murray took the blues to places undreamed-of by its originators. It has long been a commonplace that the achievements of black music have far outstripped those of black literature—that no black writer has produced work of an aesthetic complexity comparable to Duke Ellington's, Count Basie's, or Charlie Parker's. This much, for Murray, was a point of departure: he sought to process the blues into a self-conscious aesthetic, to translate the deep structure of the black vernacular into prose. Arguably, LeRoi Jones attempted something similar in his celebrated "Blues People" (1963), but there sociology gained the upper hand over art. (Ellison, writing in *The New York Review of Books*, complained that Jones's approach was enough to "give even the blues the blues.") To Murray, the blues stood in opposition to all such reductionism. "What it all represents is an attitude toward the nature of human experience (and the alternatives of human adjustment) that is both elemental and comprehensive," he wrote in "Stomping the Blues," and he continued:

It is a statement about confronting the complexities
inherent in the human situation and about improvising
or experimenting or riffing or otherwise playing with (or
even gambling with) such possibilities as are also inherent
in the obstacles, the disjunctures, and the jeopardy. It is
also a statement about perseverance and about resilience
and thus also about the maintenance of equilibrium
despite precarious circumstances and about achieving
elegance in the very process of coping with the rudiments
of subsistence.

Though Murray's salvific conception of the blues may seem fantastical, it represented precisely the alternative that Larry Neal and
others were searching for. In truth, you could no more capture the
sublimity of music in earthbound prose than you could trap the
moon's silvery reflection in a barrel of rainwater, but there was heroism, surely, in the effort.

Nor was it only literature that could be revivified by jazz and
the blues. That was where Bearden came in, and that was why his
friendship with Murray had to be understood also as an artistic alliance. Bearden's mixed-media works could serve as a cultural paradigm for the kind of bricolage and hybridity that Murray favored.

In recent stanzas entitled "Omni-Albert Murray" the young
African-American poet Elizabeth Alexander writes, "In my mind
and in his I think a painting is a poem / A tambourine's a hip shake
and train whistle a guitar." Certainly Murray proved an authoritative exponent of Bearden's works, the titles of which were frequently
of his devising. The literary scholar Robert O'Meally remembers being with Bearden and Murray in Books & Company when the two
were trying to decide on a name for whatever picture Bearden had
brought along that day. O'Meally recalls, "It might be that Al Murray's eye was caught by the figure of a woman in one corner of the
image. And he'd say, 'Who's that?' And Bearden would be looking

embarrassed, because the woman in question had been an old girl-friend of his. Maybe Bearden would say, 'Oh, she's just a woman I once knew from North Carolina.' And then Murray would say, 'I've got it. Let's call it "Red-Headed Woman from North Carolina."' Or, 'I know, call it "Red-Headed Woman from North Carolina with Rooster."' And Bearden would go and write that on the back of his painting."

Murray stood ready to assist in other ways, too. When, in 1978, I asked Bearden if he would conduct a seminar on Afro-American art at Yale, where I was teaching, his immediate response was "Why don't you ask Al?" But this particular appointment called for an artist, and Bearden finally did accept, though with genuine reluctance and vehement protestations of pedagogic incompetence. So reluctant was he that I was astonished by the remarkably well-organized and cogent weekly lectures he had prepared—always neatly double-spaced and fifty minutes in duration, the precise length of the academic lecturer's hour. Comprehension soon dawned. Bearden, taking matters into his own hands, had found a way to bring Murray along to New Haven: the critic had ghost-written Professor Bearden's erudite lectures.

BUT DID MURRAY HAVE DEBTS OF HIS OWN TO ACKNOWLEDGE—IN PAR-ticular, to his Tuskegee schoolmate? The very similarity of their preoccupations proved a source of friction. Now it was Murray—here, there, and everywhere—spreading the glad word about the literary theorist Kenneth Burke, about Lord Raglan, about the luminous blending of craft and metaphysics represented by André Malraux and by Thomas Mann. Ellison's claim, at least to Kenneth Burke and Lord Raglan, seems clear: they were part of the swirl of ideas at Bennington College in the early fifties, when Ellison was living nearby and socializing with the faculty. One writer who had been friendly with both Murray and Ellison since the forties assures me that he has no doubt as to who was the exegete and who the originator: "This is not to say that Al was simply some sort of epigone. But *all* the fundamental ideas that are part of 'The Omni-Americans' came from Ellison. Al made his own music out of those ideas, but *I* know where they came from. The course of thought that Murray began to follow in the sixties was a result of Ralph's influence, I think there is no doubt about this at all."

That has become something of a consensus view. In a recent appreciation of Murray, the jazz critic Gene Seymour writes that on such subjects as improvisation, discipline, and tradition Murray (and, by extension, disciples of his like Stanley Crouch and Wynton Marsalis) sounds "like an echo." He maintains that the recently published volume of Ellison's collected essays "makes clear [that] Ellison was the wellspring for the ideals advanced by Murray, Crouch, and Marsalis."

It's a thorny subject. At one point, Murray tells me about V. S. Naipaul's visit with him in the late eighties—a visit that was recorded in Naipaul's "A Turn in the South." Naipaul wrote, "He was a man of enthusiasms, easy to be with, easy to listen to. His life seemed to have been a series of happy discoveries." At the same time, Naipaul identified Murray as a writer who "was, or had been, a protégé of Ralph Ellison's." Murray makes it clear that this gloss does not sit well with him. He counters by quoting something that Robert Bone, a pioneering scholar of African-American literature, told him: "I've been trying to figure out *who* is the protégé of *whom*."

Bone, an acquaintance of both principals, suggests beginning with a different set of premises. "On Murray's part, it must have been a terribly difficult thing for him to have been overshadowed by Ralph in terms of the timing of their two careers," he says. "In a way, they started out together at Tuskegee, and then they cemented that friendship in New York, but Murray got such a later start in his career as a writer. So when he came on the scene Ralph was, of course, a celebrity." What escapes us, Bone says, is that many of the positions with which Ellison was associated were ones the two had mulled over together and corresponded about—especially "the link between Afro-American writing and Afro-American music." Reverse all your assumptions, though, and one thing remains constant: "Murray, I think, naturally must have felt a good deal of envy and resentment." Where others see Darwin and Huxley, Bone sees Watson and Crick. Of Ellison and Murray he says, "There was a time when they were both young and aspiring writers, and they shared these ideas and they worked on them together, but Ralph got into print with them first, by a kind of accident." Speaking like a true literary historian, he adds, "I think these matters will be resolved when Murray leaves his papers—he has a box full of correspondence with Ellison. I think that that correspondence is going to bring out the mutuality of these explorations and discoveries."

IT'S CLEAR THAT, BENEATH ELLISON'S UNFAILINGLY COURTLY DEMEANOR, his own internal struggles may have taken their toll. The fire, in the fall of 1967, is often mentioned as a watershed moment for him, one whose symbolic freight would only increase over the years. He had been busy that summer in his Massachusetts farmhouse, making extensive revisions on his novel in progress—Murray recalls seeing a manuscript thick with interlinear emendations during a visit there. At times, Ellison had called Murray to read him some of the new material. The fire occurred on the very evening that the Ellisons had decided to return to New York. Murray says, "He packed up all his stuff and got everything together, put it all in the hallway leading out, with some of his cameras and some of his shooting equipment. Then they went out to dinner with Richard Wilbur. On the way home, when they got to a certain point, they saw this fire reflection on the skyline, and, the nearer they got, the more it seemed like it was their place. And as they turned in, they saw their house going up in flames." Ellison had a copy of the manuscript in New York, but the rewriting and rethinking that had occupied him for months were lost. "So he went into shock, really. He just closed off from everybody." Murray didn't hear from him until Christmas. In the months that followed, Ellison would sometimes call Murray up and read him passages—trying to jog Murray's memory so that he would jog Ellison's. "It took him years to recover," Murray says. Meanwhile, Murray's career was following an opposite trajectory. As if making up for lost time, he spent the first half of the seventies averaging a book a year; during the same period, Ellison's block as a novelist had grown to mythic proportions. Bellow says, "Ralph was suffering very deeply from his hangup, and it was very hard to have any connection with him. He got into a very strange state, I think."

Did Ellison feel betrayed? It seems clear that he did. ("Romie used to call it 'Oklahoma paranoia,'" Murray says, musing on the froideur that settled between them.) Did Ellison have reason to? That's harder to answer. The African-American poet Michael S. Harper, an Ellison stalwart, says, "The most important word I ever heard Ralph say was the word 'honor.' I happen to know some of the difficulties they went through when Albert was in a phase of making appearances in white literary salons, and reports came back from various people." Theories of the estrangement abound. One writer acquainted with the two men says that Ellison had learned that Murray was bad-mouthing him; another suggests that Ellison simply felt crowded, that Murray was presenting himself as Ellison's confidant—"As the man to see if you want to know"—in a way that Ellison found unseemly. The chill could make things awkward for acquaintances. One of them says, "I remember on one occasion Ralph and I were lunching at the Century Club, when Al saw me in the downstairs lobby. He came up immediately and we chatted briefly, and as we were talking to each other Ralph walked away and would have nothing to do with Al. Theirs had become a difficult relationship."

Murray, for his part, is inclined to see the matter in almost anthropological terms, as falling into the behavior patterns of out-group representatives amid an in-group: "Here's a guy who figures that he's got *his* white folks over here, and he got them all hoodwinked, so he don't want anybody coming in messing things up." In anthropological terms, the native informant never relishes competition. "Hell, it was probably inevitable," Willie Morris says of the estrangement.

FOR ALL THEIR SIMILARITIES IN BACKGROUND, EDUCATION, SENSIBILITY, even dress (they shared a tailor, Charlie Davidson, himself something of a legend in sartorial circles), the two men inclined toward rather contrasting styles of public presentation. A private man who in later years grew intensely aware of being a public figure, Ellison had contrived a persona designed to defeat white expectations of black brutishness. Hence the same words come up again and again when people try to write about him—words like "patrician," "formal," "aristocratic," "mandarin," "civilized," "dignified." James Baldwin once observed, shrewdly, that Ellison was "as angry as anybody can be and still *live*." It was this banked anger that kept his back so straight in public settings, his manners so impeccable; even his spoken sentences wore spats and suspenders. Murray, who enjoyed verbal sparring as much as anybody, lacked that gift of anger, and as a conversationalist he had always taken delight in the saltier idioms of the street. (Imagine Redd Foxx with a graduate degree in literature.) The writer Reynolds Price, a friend of both Ellison and Murray, says, "Ralph had a kind of saturnine, slightly bemused quality. I thought Al always seemed the more buoyant person."

Writing is at once a solitary and a sociable act, and literary relationships are similarly compounded of opposites. So it was with Ellison and Murray, two country cousins. Many people speak of Ellison's eightieth-birthday party—to which Murray had been invited and at which he delivered a moving tribute to his old schoolmate—as a significant moment of reconciliation. "I think it was Ellison's way of reaching out to Murray," a friend of Ellison's says.

Then, too, for all his companionability, Murray's literary inclinations ran strongly toward the paternal. He takes deep satisfaction in that role, and there are many who can attest to his capacity for nurturance. James Alan McPherson, one of the fiction writers who have most often been likened to Ellison, recalls a time in the late seventies when he was in Rhode Island with Michael Harper, the poet, and Ernest J. Gaines, whose novels include "The Autobiography of Miss Jane Pittman." In a moment of mad enthusiasm, they hit on the idea of going to New York and letting Ellison know how much they admired him. When they phoned him, he told them, to their unbounded joy, that they should come right down. And so, after an almost mythic trek, these young black writers arrived at Riverside Drive to pay a visit to their hero.

"Mr. Ellison can't see you," they were told at the door. "He's busy working."

They were crushed. They were also adrift: with the destination of their pilgrimage closed to them, they had no place to go. "So we called Al Murray, and he picked up the slack," McPherson recounts. "He brought us to his apartment, where he had some apples and some bourbon and some fancy French cheese. And he said, 'Have you ever met Duke Ellington's sister?' We said no, so he took us over to meet Duke Ellington's sister. And he said, 'Do you want to see the Bearden retrospective?'" He took them to the Brooklyn Museum and on to the Cordier and Ekstrom gallery, where Bearden was then showing his work. "And I'll always remember Al for that," McPherson says. (Murray tells me, "Most guys forget that I'm just two years younger than Ralph, but they feel closer to me because I'm more accessible. They kid with me all the time.") Perhaps, in the end, Ellison was the better student of Lord Raglan: he knew that patricide, or some variant of it, was a staple of heroic literature. McPherson says, quietly, "Ellison didn't want any sons."

For McPherson, what crystallized things was a ceremony that City College held in 1984 to honor Ellison. McPherson and Harper were both there to give tributes. At the luncheon, Harper tapped on his glass and handed Ellison a wrapped box, saying, "Ralph, here's a gift from your sons."

"Then you'd better open it yourself," Ellison replied dryly. "I'm afraid it might explode."

ALBERT MURRAY HAS NOW REACHED THE AGE WHERE HIS PROGENY have progeny, two of the most prominent in his line being, of course, Stanley Crouch and Wynton Marsalis. Both are frequent guests at Lenox Terrace, and Marsalis tells me of dinner-table conversations that roam from Homer to Galileo, from the commedia dell'arte to Faulkner and Neruda. "Murray has given me a first-class education," he says. And he speaks eloquently about the impact that "Stomping the Blues," and Murray's very notion of jazz as an art form, had on him; he speaks about tradition, blues idioms, a poetics of inclusion. As he puts it, "I'm a Murrayite." Crouch, whose writing has brilliantly championed Murray's difficult aesthetic and emulated his pugnacious style of critique, says, "I think he's one of the foremost thinkers to appear in American letters over the last twenty-five years." (He also suggests that Murray would have been a far worthier candidate for a Nobel Prize than Toni Morrison.) "The last of the giants," McPherson calls him.

There is much to be said for having descendants. They spread the insights you have given them. They worry about why you are not better known. (Crouch has a simple explanation for Murray's relative obscurity: "It's because he spent all that time on the Basie book—there was that very long silence. I think what happened was that his career lost momentum.") They remind you, fetchingly, of your own callow youth. And they take inspiration from your fearless style of analysis and critique, and apply it to your own work—though this can be a mixed blessing.

No doubt it's the ultimate tribute to Murray's legacy of combative candor that his most fervid admirers are quite free in expressing their critical reservations—notably with regard to the new novel. "The Seven League Boots" has the distinction of being the least autobiographical of Murray's three novels: its protagonist leaves Alabama with his bass and joins up with a legendary jazz band— one not unlike Ellington's. The band is blissfully free of quarrels and petty jealousies, and Murray's alter ego, Scooter, inspires only affection in those he encounters. Indeed, this is, in no small part, a novel about friendships, about literary and intellectual conversations and correspondences, including those between Scooter and his old college roommate. On a trip across the Mississippi River Bridge, Scooter finds himself thinking about

> my old roommate again. But this time the writer he
> brought to mind was not Rilke but Walt Whitman, about
> whom he had said in response to my letter about joining
> the band for a while. . . . *According to my old roommate,*
> *old Walt Whitman, barnstorming troubadour par excellence*
> *that he was, could only have been completely delighted with*
> *the interplay of aesthetic and pragmatic considerations*
> *evidenced in the maps and mileage charts and always tentative*
> *itineraries.* . . . It was Ralph Waldo Emerson who spoke of
> "melodies that ascend and leap and pierce into the deeps
> of infinite time," my roommate also wrote, which, by the
> way, would make a very fine blurb for a Louis Armstrong
> solo such as the one on "Potato Head Blues."

In the next few pages, there are allusions to, among others, Melville, James Joyce, Van Wyck Brooks, Lewis Mumford, Constance Rourke, Frederick Douglass, Paul Laurence Dunbar, and Antonin Dvorak. Perhaps the critic's library overstocks his novelistic imagination. In the *Times Book Review*, the novelist and critic Charles Johnson—who must be counted among Murray's heirs, and is certainly among his most heartfelt admirers—described it as "a novel without tension." It may well be that the pleasures this novel affords are more discursive than dramatic, more essayistic than narrative. Murray tells me, "I write hoping that the most sophisticated readers of my time will think that I'm worth reading." They do, and he is.

T HE poet Elizabeth Alexander writes:

> Albert Murray do they call you Al
> or Bert or Murray or "Tuskegee Boy"?
> Who are the Omni-Ones who help me feel?
> I'm born after so much. Nostalgia hurts.

You could say of him what he said of Gordon Parks: "Sometimes it is as if he himself doesn't quite know what to make of what he has in fact *already* made of himself." Sometimes I don't quite, either. On the one hand, I cherish the vernacular; on the other, I've always distrusted the notion of "myth" as something deliberately added to literature, like the prize in a box of Cracker Jack. And though my first two books can be read as footnotes to "The Omni-Americans," I, like most in the demoralized profession of literary studies, have less faith in the cultural power of criticism than he has. All the same, I find his company immensely cheering.

We live in an age of irony—an age when passionate intensity is hard to find outside a freshman dining hall, and when even the mediocre lack all conviction. But Murray was produced by another age, in which intelligence expressed itself in ardor. He has spent a career *believing* in things, like the gospel according to Ma Rainey and Jimmy Rushing and Duke Ellington. More broadly, he believes in the sublimity of art, and he has never been afraid of risking bathos to get to it. (I think the reason he took so long to write

Basie's life story is that he wanted to step *inside* a great black artist, to see for himself how improvisation and formal complexity could produce high art.)

The last time I visited him at his apartment, I sat in the chair next to his writing desk as he talked me through the years of his life and his formation, and made clear much that had been unclear to me about cultural modernity. "Let me begin by saying that Romie frequently got me into trouble," Ralph Ellison told mourners at a 1988 memorial service for Bearden. "Nothing physical, mind you, but difficulties arising out of our attempts to make some practical sense of the relationship between art and living, between ideas and the complex details of consciousness and experience." In this sense, Murray, too, has always spelled trouble—for critics and artists of every description, for icon-breakers and icon-makers, for friends and foes. You learn a great many things when you sit with him in his apartment, but, summed up, they amount to a larger vision: this is Albert Murray's century; we just live in it.

GHOSTS IN THE HOUSE

HILTON ALS

October 27, 2003

No. 2245 Elyria Avenue in Lorain, Ohio, is a two-story frame house surrounded by look-alikes. Its small front porch is littered with the discards of former tenants: a banged-up bicycle wheel, a plastic patio chair, a garden hose. Most of its windows are boarded up. Behind the house, which is painted lettuce green, there's a patch of weedy earth and a heap of rusting car parts. Seventy-two years ago, the novelist Toni Morrison was born here, in this small industrial town twenty-five miles west of Cleveland, which most city-dwellers would consider "out there." The air is redolent of nearby Lake Erie and new-mown grass.

From Morrison's birthplace it's a couple of miles to Broadway, where there's a pizzeria, a bar with sagging seats, and a brown building that sells dingy and dilapidated secondhand furniture. This is the building Morrison imagined when she described the house of the doomed Breedlove family in her first novel, "The Bluest Eye": "There is an abandoned store on the southeast corner of Broadway and Thirty-fifth Street in Lorain, Ohio," she wrote. "It does not recede into its background of leaden sky, nor harmonize with the gray frame houses and black telephone poles around it. Rather, it foists itself on the eye of the passerby in a manner that is both irritating and melancholy. Visitors who drive to this tiny town wonder why it has not been torn down, while pedestrians, who are residents of the neighborhood, simply look away when they pass it."

Love and disaster and all the other forms of human incident accumulate in Morrison's fictional houses. In the boarding house where the heroine of Morrison's second novel, "Sula," lives, "there were rooms that had three doors, others that opened on the porch only and were inaccessible from any other part of the house; others that you could get to only by going through somebody's bedroom." This is the gothic, dreamlike structure in whose front yard Sula's mother burns to death, "gesturing and bobbing like a sprung jack-in-the-box," while Sula stands by watching, "not because she was paralyzed, but because she was interested."

Morrison's houses don't just shelter human dramas; they have dramas of their own. "124 was spiteful," she writes in the opening lines of "Beloved" (1987). "Full of a baby's venom. The women in the house knew it and so did the children. For years each put up with the spite in his own way." Living and dead ghosts ramble through No. 124, chained to a history that claims its inhabitants. At the center of Morrison's new novel, "Love," is a deserted seaside hotel—a resort where, in happier times, blacks danced and socialized and swam without any white people complaining that they would contaminate the water—built by Bill Cosey, a legendary black entrepreneur, and haunted by his memory.

MORRISON SPENDS ABOUT HALF HER TIME IN A CONVERTED BOAT-house that overlooks the Hudson in Rockland County. The boathouse is a long, narrow, blue structure with white trim and large windows. A decade ago, when Morrison was in Princeton, where she teaches, it burned to the ground. Because it was a very cold winter, the water the firefighters used froze several important artifacts, including Morrison's manuscripts. "But what they can't save are little things that mean a lot, like your children's report cards," she told me, her eyes filling with tears. She shook her head and said, "Let's not go there."

We were in the third-floor parlor, furnished with overstuffed chairs covered in crisp gray linen, where we talked over the course of two days last summer. Sun streamed through the windows and a beautiful blue-toned abstract painting by the younger of her two sons, Slade, hung on the wall. As we chatted, Morrison wasn't in the least distracted by the telephone ringing or the activities of her housekeeper or her secretary. She is known for her powers of concentration. When she is not writing or teaching, she likes to watch "Law & Order" and "Waking the Dead"—crime shows that offer what she described as "mild engagement with a satisfying structure of redemption." She reads and rereads novels by Ruth Rendell and Martha Grimes.

Morrison had on a white shirt over a black leotard, black trousers, and a pair of high-heeled alligator sandals. Her long silver dreadlocks cascaded down her back and were gathered at the end by a silver clip. When she was mock-amazed by an insight, she flushed. Her light-brown eyes, with their perpetually listening or amused expression, are the eyes of a watcher—and of someone who is used to being watched. But if she is asked a question she doesn't appreciate, a veil descends over her eyes, discontinuing the conversation. (When I tried to elicit her opinion about the novels of one of her contemporaries, she said, "I hear the movie is fab," and turned away.) Morrison's conversation, like her fiction, is conducted in high style. She underlines important points by making showy arabesques with her fingers in the air, and when she is amused she lets out a cry that's followed by a fusillade of laughter.

"You know, my sister Lois was just here taking care of me," she said. "I had a cataract removed in one eye. Suddenly, the world was so bright. And I looked at myself in the mirror and wondered, Who is that woman? When did she get to be that age? My doctor said, 'You have been looking at yourself through the lens that they shoot Elizabeth Taylor through.' I couldn't stop wondering how I got to be this age."

When "The Bluest Eye" was published, in 1970, Morrison was unknown and thirty-nine years old. The initial print run was modest: two thousand copies in hardcover. Now a first edition can fetch upward of six thousand dollars. In 2000, when "The Bluest Eye" became a selection for Oprah's Book Club, Plume sold more than eight hundred thousand paperback copies. By then, Toni Morrison had become Toni Morrison—the first African-American to win the Nobel Prize in Literature, in 1993. Following "The Bluest Eye," Morrison published seven more novels: "Sula" (1973), "Song of Solomon" (1977), "Tar Baby" (1981), "Beloved" (1987), "Jazz" (1992), "Paradise" (1998), and now "Love." Morrison also wrote a critical study, "Playing in the Dark: Whiteness and the Literary Imagination" (1992), which, like all her novels since "Song of Solomon," became a best-seller. She has edited several anthologies—about O.J., about the Clarence Thomas hearings—as well as collections of the writings of Huey P. Newton and James Baldwin. With her son Slade, she has co-authored a number of books for children. She wrote the book for a musical, "New Orleans" (1983); a play, "Dreaming Emmett" (1986), which reimagined the life and death of Emmett Till, the fourteen-year-old black boy who was murdered in Mississippi in 1955; a song cycle with the composer André Previn; and, most recently, an opera based on the life of Margaret Garner, the slave whose story inspired "Beloved." She was an editor at Random House for nineteen years—she still reads the *Times* with pencil in hand, copy-editing as she goes—and has been the Robert F. Goheen Professor in the Council of the Humanities at Princeton since 1989.

"I know it seems like a lot," Morrison said. "But I really only do one thing. I read books. I teach books. I write books. I think about books. It's one job." What Morrison has managed to do with that job—and the criticism, pro and con, she has received for doing it—has made her one of the most widely written-about American authors of the past fifty years. (The latest study of her work, she told me, is a comparison of the vernacular in her novels and William Faulkner's. "I don't believe it," I said. "*Believe* it," she said, emphatically.) Morrison—required reading in high schools across the country—is almost always treated as a spokeswoman for her gender and her race. In a review of "Paradise," Patricia Storace wrote, "Toni Morrison is relighting the angles from which we view American history, changing the very color of its shadows, showing whites what they look like in black mirrors. To read her work is to witness something unprecedented, an invitation to a literature to become what it has claimed to be, a truly American literature." It's a claim that her detractors would also make, to opposite effect.

"I'm already discredited, I'm already politicized, before I get out of the gate," Morrison said. "I can accept the labels"—the adjectives like "black" and "female" that are often attached to her work—"because being a black woman writer is not a shallow place but a rich place to write from. It doesn't limit my imagination; it expands it. It's richer than being a white male writer because I know more and I've experienced more."

Morrison also owns a home in Princeton, where nine years ago she founded the Princeton Atelier, a program that invites writers and performing artists to workshop student plays, stories, and music. (Last year, she brought in the poet Paul Muldoon as a co-director.) "I don't write when I'm teaching," she said. "Teaching is about taking things apart; writing is about putting things together." She and her sons own an apartment building farther up the Hudson, which houses artists, and another building across the street from it, which her elder son Ford, an architect, is helping her remodel into a study and performance center. "My sister Lois said that the reason I buy all these houses is because we had to move so often as children," Morrison said, laughing.

Morrison's family—the Woffords—lived in at least six different apartments over the course of her childhood. One of them was set on fire by the landlord when the Woffords couldn't pay the rent—four dollars a month. In those days, Toni, the second of four children (she had two brothers, now dead), was called Chloe Ardelia. Her parents, George and Ramah, like the Breedloves, were originally from the South (Ramah was born in Greenville, Alabama; George in Cartersville, Georgia). Like many transplanted Southerners, George worked at U.S. Steel, which was particularly active during the Second World War and attracted not only American blacks but also displaced Europeans: Poles, Greeks, and Italians.

Morrison describes her father as a perfectionist, someone who was proud of his work. "I remember my daddy taking me aside—this was when he worked as a welder—and telling me that he welded a perfect seam that day, and that after welding the perfect seam he put his initials on it," she recalled. "I said, 'Daddy, no one will ever see that.' Sheets and sheets of siding would go over that, you know? And he said, 'Yes, but I'll know it's there.'" George also worked odd jobs, washing cars and the like, after hours at U.S. Steel. Morrison remembers that he always had at least two other jobs.

Ramah, a devout member of the African Methodist Episcopal Church, was a homemaker. From the first, it was clear that Morrison was not made to follow in her footsteps. "I remember going outside to hang some clothes on the line," she said. "And I held the pants up, I hooked them by the inside pockets. And whatever else I was doing, it was completely wrong. Then my mother or my grandmother came out and they just started to laugh, because I didn't know how to hang up clothes." Her parents seemed to have different expectations for her, anyway. "I developed a kind of individualism—apart from the family—that was very much involved in my own daydreaming, my own creativity, and my own reading. But primarily—and this has been true all my life—not really minding what other people said, just not minding."

The Woffords told their children stories and sang songs. After dinner, their grandfather would sometimes take out his violin and everyone would dance. And no matter how many times Ramah told the ghost stories she had learned from her mother and her Auntie Bell in Alabama, Chloe always wanted to hear more. She used to say, "Mama, please tell the story about this or that," her mother recalled in a 1982 interview with the Lorain *Journal*. "Finally I'd get tired of telling the stories over and over again. So I made up a new story." Ramah's stories sparked Morrison's imagination. She fell in love with spoken language.

Morrison always lived, she said, "below or next to white people," and the schools were integrated—stratification in Lorain was more economic than racial—but in the Wofford house there was an intense suspicion of white people. In a 1976 essay, Morrison recalled watching her father attack a white man he'd discovered lurking in their apartment building. "My father, distrusting every word and every gesture of every white man on earth, assumed that the white man who crept up the stairs one afternoon had come to molest his daughters and threw him down the stairs and then our tricycle after him. (I think my father was wrong, but considering what I have seen since, it may have been very healthy for me to have witnessed that as my first black-white encounter.)" I asked her about the story. "The man was a threat to us, we thought," Morrison replied. "He scared us. I'm sure that man was drunk, you know, but the important thing was the notion that my father was a protector, and particularly against the white man. Seeing that physical confrontation with a white man and knowing that my father could win thrilled, excited, and pleased me. It made me know that it was possible to win."

Morrison's family was spread along a color spectrum. "My great-grandmother was very black, and because we were light-skinned blacks, she thought that we had been 'tampered with,'" she said. "She found lighter-skinned blacks to be impure—which was the opposite of what the world was saying about skin color and the hierarchy of skin color. My father, who was light-skinned, also preferred darker-skinned blacks." Morrison, who didn't absorb her father's racism, continues to grapple with these ideas and argue against their implications. In a television interview some years ago, she said that in art "there should be everything from Hasidic Jews to Walter Lippmann. Or, as I was telling a friend, there should be everything from reggae hair to Ralph Bunche. There should be an effort to strengthen the differences and keep them, so long as no one is punished for them." Morrison addressed her great-grandmother's notion of racial purity in "Paradise," where it is the oppressive basis for a Utopian community formed by a group of dark blacks from the South.

As a child, Morrison read virtually everything, from drawing-room comedies to Theodore Dreiser, from Jane Austen to Richard Wright. She was compiling, in her head, a reading list to mine for inspiration. At Hawthorne Junior High School, she read "Huckleberry Finn" for the second time. "Fear and alarm are what I remember most about my first encounter" with it, she wrote several years ago. "My second reading of it, under the supervision of an English teacher in junior high school, was no less uncomfortable—rather more. It provoked a feeling I can only describe now as muffled rage, as though appreciation of the work required my complicity in and sanction of something shaming. Yet the satisfactions were great: riveting episodes of flight, of cunning; the convincing commentary on adult behavior, watchful and insouciant; the authority of a child's voice in language cut for its renegade tongue and sharp intelligence. Nevertheless, for the second time, curling through the pleasure, clouding the narrative reward, was my original alarm, coupled now with a profoundly distasteful complicity."

When she was twelve years old, Morrison converted to Catholicism, taking Anthony as her baptismal name, after St. Anthony. Her friends shortened it to Toni. In junior high, one of her teachers sent a note home to her mother: "You and your husband would be remiss in your duties if you do not see to it that this child goes to college." Shortly before graduating from Lorain High School— where she was on the debating team, on the yearbook staff, and in the drama club ("I wanted to be a dancer, like Maria Tallchief")— Morrison told her parents that she'd like to go to college. "I want

to be surrounded by black intellectuals," she said, and chose Howard University, in Washington, D.C. In support of her decision,
George Wofford took a second union job, which was against the
rules of U.S. Steel. In the Lorain *Journal* article, Ramah Wofford
remembered that his supervisors found out and called him on it.
"'Well, you folks got me,'" Ramah recalled George's telling them.
"'I am doing another job, but I'm doing it to send my daughter to
college. I'm determined to send her and if I lose my job here, I'll
get another job and do the same.' It was so quiet after George was
done talking, you could have heard a pin drop. . . . And they let him
stay and let him do both jobs." To give her daughter pocket money,
Ramah Wofford worked in the rest room of an amusement park,
handing out towels. She sent the tips to her daughter with care pack-
ages of canned tuna, crackers, and sardines.

Morrison loved her classes at Howard, but she found the social
climate stifling. In Washington in the late forties, the buses were
still segregated and the black high schools were divided by skin
tone, as in the Deep South. The system was replicated at Howard.
"On campus itself, the students were very much involved in that
ranking, and your skin gave you access to certain things," Morrison said. "There was something called 'the paper-bag test'—darker
than the paper bag put you in one category, similar to the bag put
you in another, and lighter was yet another and the most privileged
category. I thought them to be idiotic preferences." She was drawn
to the drama department, which she felt was more interested in
talent than in skin color, and toured the South with the Howard
University Players. The itineraries were planned very carefully, but
once in a while, because of inclement weather or a flat tire, the
troupe would arrive in a town too late to check in to the "colored"
motel. Then one of the professors would open the Yellow Pages
and call the minister of the local Zion or Baptist church, and the
players would be put up by members of the congregation. "There
was something not just endearing but welcoming and restorative in

the lives of those people," she said. "I think the exchange between Irving Howe and Ralph Ellison is along those lines: Ralph Ellison said something nice about living in the South, and Irving Howe said, 'Why would you want to live in such an evil place?' Because all he was thinking about was rednecks. And Ralph Ellison said, 'Black people live there.'"

After graduating from Howard, in 1953, she went on to Cornell, where she earned a master's degree in American literature, writing a thesis titled "Virginia Woolf's and William Faulkner's Treatment of the Alienated." What she saw in their work—"An effort to discover what pattern of existence is most conducive to honesty and self-knowledge, the prime requisites for living a significant life"—she emulated in her own life. She went back to Howard to teach, and Stokely Carmichael was one of her students. Around this time, she met and married Harold Morrison, a Jamaican-born architect. She joined a writing group, where the one rule was that you had to bring something to read every week. Among the writers in that group were the playwright and director Owen Dodson and his companion the painter Charles Sebree. At first, Morrison said, she brought in "all that old junk from high school." Then she began writing a story about a little black girl, Pecola Breedlove, who wanted blue eyes.

"I wanted to take the name of Peola"—the "tragic mulatto" character from the 1934 movie "Imitation of Life"—"and play with it, turn it around," Morrison said. When she was young, she said, "another little black girl and I were discussing whether there was a real God or not. I said there was, and she said there wasn't and she had proof: she had prayed for, and not been given, blue eyes. I just remember listening to her and imagining her with blue eyes, and it was a grotesque thing. She had these high cheekbones and these great big slanted dark eyes, and all I remember thinking was that if she had blue eyes she would be horrible."

When Morrison read the story to the writing group, Sebree turned to her and said, "*You* are a writer."

IN 1964, MORRISON RETURNED TO LORAIN. HER MARRIAGE HAD FALLEN apart and she had to determine how she was going to take care of her family—her son Ford was three years old and Slade was on the way. An ad in *The New York Review of Books* listed a position with L. W. Singer, a textbook division of Random House that was based in Syracuse. Morrison applied for and got the job. She took her babies (Slade was born in 1965) and moved East. She was thirty-four years old. In Syracuse, she didn't care to socialize; instead, she returned to the story about the girl who wanted blue eyes and began to expand it. She wrote when she could—usually after the children went to sleep. And since she was the sole support for her children, she couldn't sacrifice the real world for her art. "I *stole* time to write," she said. "Writing was my other job—I always kept it over there, away from my 'real' work as an editor or teacher." It took her five years to complete the book, because she enjoyed the process so much.

Holt, Rinehart & Winston published "The Bluest Eye" in 1970, with a picture of Morrison lying on her side against a white backdrop, her hair cut in an Afro. Taken at the moment when fashion met the counterculture—when Black was coöpted as Beautiful and soul-food recipes ran in fashion magazines next to images of Black Panther wives tying their heads up in bright fabric—the picture was the visual equivalent of the book: black, female, individualistic.

Set in Lorain at the end of the Depression, "The Bluest Eye" remains the most autobiographical of Morrison's novels. In it, she focusses on the lives of little black girls—perhaps the least likely, least commercially viable story one could tell at the time. Morrison positioned the white world at the periphery; black life was at the center, and black females were at the center of that. Morrison wasn't sentimental about the black community. Cholly Breedlove rapes his daughter Pecola because it is one of the few forms of power he has ("How dare she love him?" he thinks. "Hadn't she any sense at all? What was he supposed to do about that? Return it? How? What could his calloused hands produce to make her smile?"); a group of children scapegoat her as her misfortune worsens ("All of us—all who knew her—felt so wholesome after we cleaned ourselves on her. We were so beautiful when we stood astride her ugliness"); and three whores are her only source of tenderness ("Pecola loved them, visited them, and ran their errands. They, in turn, did not despise her").

The writing, on the other hand, was lush, sensible-minded, and often hilarious. If Morrison had a distinctive style, it was in her rhythms: the leisurely pace of her storytelling. Clearly her writing had grown out of an oral tradition. Rather than confirm the reader's sense of alienation by employing distancing techniques, Morrison coaxed the reader into believing the tale. She rooted her characters' lives in something real—certainly in the minds of black readers.

This came at a time when the prevailing sensibility in most American novels was urban and male, an outgrowth of the political and personal concerns that Ellison and Bellow, Baldwin and Roth had developed living in predominantly black or Jewish neighborhoods. Morrison was different. She grew up in an integrated town in the heart of America. "The point was to really open a book that's about black people, or by a black person, me or anybody," she said. "In the sixties, most of the literature was understood by the critics as something sociological, a kind of revelation of the lives of these people. So there was a little apprehension, you know—Is it going to make me feel bad, is it going to make me feel good? I said, I'm going to make it as readable as I can, but I'm not going to pull any punches. I don't have an agenda here."

One of the few critics to embrace Morrison's work was John Leonard, who wrote in the *Times*, "Miss Morrison exposes the negative of the Dick-and-Jane-and-Mother-and-Father-and-Dog-and-Cat photograph that appears in our reading primers and she does it with a prose so precise, so faithful to speech and so charged with pain and wonder that the novel becomes poetry. . . . 'The Bluest Eye' is also history, sociology, folklore, nightmare and music."

The poet Sonia Sanchez, who taught "The Bluest Eye" in her classroom at Temple University, saw the book as an indictment of American culture. For Pecola, the descendant of slaves, to want the master's blue eyes represents the "second generation of damage in America," Sanchez told me. "For this woman, Toni Morrison, to write this, to show this to us—it was the possible death of a people right there, the death of a younger generation that had been so abused that there was really no hope. What Toni has done with her literature is that she has made us look up and see ourselves. She has authenticated us, and she has also said to America, in a sense, 'Do you know what you did? But, in spite of what you did, here we is. We exist. Look at us.'"

"What was driving me to write was the silence—so many stories untold and unexamined. There was a wide vacuum in the literature," Morrison said. "I was inspired by the silence and absences in the literature." The story she told was a distinctly American one: complicated, crowded, eventful, told from the perspective of innocents. "I think of the voice of the novel as a kind of Greek chorus, one that comments on the action," she once said. She was a social realist, like Dreiser, with the lyricism and storytelling genius of someone like Isak Dinesen.

IN 1968, MORRISON WAS TRANSFERRED TO NEW YORK TO WORK IN Random House's scholastic division. She moved to Queens. ("I never lived in Manhattan," she said. "I always wanted a garden.") A couple of years later, Robert Bernstein, who was then the president of Random House, came across "The Bluest Eye" in a bookstore. "Is this the same woman who works in the scholastic division?" he asked Jason Epstein, then the editorial director of Random House. Morrison had been wanting to move into trade publishing, and went to see Robert Gottlieb, the editor-in-chief of Knopf, an imprint of Random House. Gottlieb recalled the interview: "I said, 'I like you too much to hire you, because in order to hire you I have to feel free to fire you. But I'd love to publish your books.'" He became her editor, and Morrison got a job under Epstein as a trade editor at Random House.

At Random House, Morrison published Gayl Jones, Toni Cade Bambara, and Angela Davis, among others. She was responsible for "The Myth of Lesbianism," one of the first studies of the subject from a major publisher, and "Giant Talk," Quincy Troupe and Rainer Schulte's anthology of Third World writing. Morrison gave me a copy of one of the first books she worked on, "Contemporary African Literature," published in 1972, a groundbreaking collection that included work by Wole Soyinka, Chinua Achebe, Léopold-Sédar Senghor, and Athol Fugard. (For some of them, it was their first publication in America.) The book is lavishly illustrated, with many color photographs of African tribesmen and African landscapes. Showing me the table of contents, Morrison said, "What was I thinking? I thought if it was beautiful, people would buy it." (Not many did.)

The women she worked with, in particular, became some of her closest friends. "Single women with children," she said, when I asked her about that era. "If you had to finish writing something, they'd take your kids, or you'd sit with theirs. This was a network of women. They lived in Queens, in Harlem and Brooklyn, and you could rely on one another. If I made a little extra money on something—writing freelance—I'd send a check to Toni Cade with a note that said, 'You have won the so-and-so grant,' and so on. I remember Toni Cade coming to my house with groceries and cooking dinner. I hadn't asked her." The support was intellectual as well as practical. Sonia Sanchez told me, "I think we all looked up and saw that we were writing in different genres, but we were experiencing the same kinds of things, and saying similar kinds of things." Their books formed a critical core that people began to see as the rebirth of black women's fiction.

Before the late sixties, there was no real Black Studies curriculum in the academy—let alone a post-colonial-studies program or a feminist one. As an editor and author, Morrison, backed by the institutional power of Random House, provided the material for those discussions to begin. The advent of Black Studies undoubtedly helped Morrison, too: "It was the academic community that gave 'The Bluest Eye' its life," she said. "People assigned it in class. Students bought the paperback."

In order to get attention for her authors—publishers still thought that the ideal book buyer was a thirty-year-old Long Island woman, and reviewers would lump together books by Ishmael Reed and Angela Davis, along with children's books, in a single article—Morrison decided to concentrate on one African-American text each season. She worked diligently. "I wanted to give back something," she said. "I wasn't marching. I didn't go to anything. I didn't join anything. But I could make sure there was a published record of those who did march and did put themselves on the line. And I didn't want to fail my grandmother. I didn't want to hear her say, 'You went to college and this is all you thought up?'" She laughed. "Compared to what my family had gone through and what I felt was my responsibility, the corporation's interest was way down on the list. I was not going to do anything that I thought was nutty or disrupt anything. I thought it was beneficial generally, just like I thought that the books were going to make them a lot of money!"

Morrison's view of contemporary black literature transcended the limitations of the "down with honky" school of black nationalism popularized by writers like Eldridge Cleaver and George Jackson. She preferred to publish writers who had something to say about black American life that reflected its rich experience. In

1974, she put together "The Black Book," a compendium of photographs, drawings, songs, letters, and other documents that charts black American history from slavery through Reconstruction to modern times. The book exercised a great influence over the way black anthropology was viewed.

At first, Random House resisted the idea of "The Black Book." "It just looked to them like a disaster," Morrison said. "Not so much in the way it was being put together, but because they didn't know how to sell it. 'Who is going to buy something called "The Black Book"?' I had my mother on the cover—what were they talking about?" She wrote about the project in the February 2, 1974, issue of *Black World:* "So what was Black life like before it went on TV? . . . I spent the last 18 months trying to do a book that would show some of that. A genuine Black history book—one that simply recollected Black Life as lived. It has no 'order,' no chapters, no major themes. But it does have coherence and sinew. . . . I don't know if it's beautiful or not (it is elegant, however), but it is intelligent, it is profound, it is alive, it is visual, it is creative, it is complex, and it is ours."

Despite all misgivings, the book garnered extraordinary reviews. Writing in the Cleveland *Plain Dealer*, Alvin Beam said, "Editors, like novelists, have brain children—books they think up and bring to life without putting their own names on the title page. Mrs. Morrison has one of these in the stores now, and magazines and newsletters in the publishing trade are ecstatic, saying it will go like hotcakes."

Morrison got a letter from a man in prison who had read the book. "Somebody had given him a copy, and he wrote to say thank you," Morrison told me. "And then he said, 'I need two more copies, because I need one to pass out to other people, and I need another one to throw up against the wall. And I need the one I have to hold close.' So there were readers on, quote, 'both sides of the street,' which is the way they put it." I recall buying "The Black

Book" as a teen-ager and feeling as if I had been given a road map of the Brooklyn community where I lived at the time.

"Toni became not a black editor but *the* black editor," a friend of hers told me. In 1975, D. Keith Mano, the "Book Watch" columnist for *Esquire*, devoted an entire article to Gayl Jones and her new book, "Corregidora," but the piece was as much about Morrison as about Jones. "Toni Morrison is Gayl's Svengali editor at Random House," Mano wrote. "Toni is dynamic, witty, even boisterous in a good-humored way. And sharp. Very sharp. She often uses the pronoun I. She'll say, '*I* published "Corregidora." '. . . I suspect the title page of 'Corregidora' should read, 'by Gayl Jones, as told to Toni Morrison.'" If Morrison had been a man or white, it seems unlikely that Mano would have noticed her championing of an author. Jones was uncommunicative and Morrison had books to sell. If a writer needed fussing, she fussed, and if not, not.

Morrison was a canny and tireless editor. "You can't be a slouch in Toni's presence," the scholar Eugene Redmond told me. "Her favorite word is 'wakeful.'" (She still gets up at 4 A.M. to work.) When she published the books of Henry Dumas—a little-known novelist and poet whose work was left fragmentary when he was murdered by a transit officer in the New York City subway in 1968, in a case of mistaken identity—she sent copies to Bill Cosby, Ossie Davis, Ruby Dee, and all the major movie executives and television hosts. In a letter inviting people to read at a tribute to Dumas, she wrote, "He was brilliant. He was magnetic and he was an incredible artist. . . . We are determined to bring to the large community of Black artists and Black people in general this man's work."

The racial climate in the mid-seventies made it especially hard for Morrison to promote certain books—books that might be taken as too radical. Morrison remembered that the marketing department balked when she wanted to have a publication party in a club on 125th Street. No one from Random House came—it was rumored that someone in management had cautioned the staff about the danger—except the publicist and her assistant, who said it was the best party they'd ever been to. A couple of news crews showed up, however, and the party was on the evening news, giving the book hundreds of thousands of dollars' worth of free publicity, by Morrison's reckoning. Similarly, Morrison said, when she brought out Muhammad Ali's autobiography, "The Greatest," in 1976, all the department stores that were approached about hosting the book signing backed out, fearing riots and looting. When E. J. Korvette's, the now defunct department store, agreed to host the signing, Morrison brought in members of the Nation of Islam, who came with their families, as peacekeepers. She also installed a white friend, a woman who worked in the sales department, to guard Ali. "You stand right next to Ali," she said. "And when people come up and punch him—'Hey, Champ!'—you stop them. Because he's not going to say it ever, that it hurts when you get a thousand little taps. And when you think Ali is tired give him a baby to play with. He likes babies." Two thousand people came to E. J. Korvette's, on a rainy night, and, with the Brothers of the Nation of Islam milling around in the crowd, everything was serene and orderly.

Throughout the seventies, Morrison worked as a teacher at Yale, SUNY Purchase, Bard, Rutgers, and SUNY Albany. "Random paid about ten cents, so Toni took on teaching jobs," Jason Epstein recalled. In a 1998 interview, she said, "When I wanted a raise, in my employment world, they would give me a little woman's raise and I would say, 'No. This is really low.' And they would say, 'But,' and I would say, 'No, you don't understand. You're the head of the household. You know what you want. That's what I want. I want that. I am on serious business now. This is not girl playing. This is not wife playing. This is serious business. I am the head of a household, and I must work to pay for my children.'"

"THE BLUEST EYE" HAD MADE THE LITERARY ESTABLISHMENT TAKE NO-tice. In "Sula," which was published three years later, Morrison's little colored girls grew up and occupied a more completely rendered world. "The Bluest Eye" was divided by seasons; "Sula" was divided into years, stretching from 1919 to 1965. Again, the story is set in a small Ohio town, in a neighborhood called the Bottom. ("A joke. A nigger joke. That's the way it got started.") Sula Mae Peace, Morrison's heroine, is the progeny of an eccentric household run by formidable women. She leaves the Bottom in order to reinvent herself. Morrison does not relay what Sula does when she ventures into the world, but her return is catastrophic. (The first sign of impending disaster is a plague of robins.) Her return also brings about a confrontation with her grandmother Eva—a parable of the New Negro Woman confronting the Old World.

> At Eva's house there were four dead robins on the
> walk. Sula stopped and with her toe pushed them into the
> bordering grass. . . . When Sula opened the door [Eva]
> raised her eyes and said, "I might have knowed them birds
> meant something. Where's your coat?"
>   Sula threw herself on Eva's bed. "The rest of my stuff
> will be on later."
>   "I should hope so. Them little old furry tails ain't going
> to do you no more good than they did the fox that was
> wearing them."
>   "Don't you say hello to nobody when you ain't seen
> them for ten years?"
>   "If folks let somebody know where they is and when
> they coming, then other folks can get ready for them.
> If they don't—if they just pop in all sudden like—then
> they got to take whatever mood they find."
>   "How you been doing, Big Mamma?"
>   "Gettin' by. Sweet of you to ask. You was quick enough
> when you wanted something. When you needed a little
> change or . . ."

"Don't talk to me about how much you gave me, Big Mamma, and how much I owe you or none of that."

"Oh? I ain't supposed to mention it?"

"OK. Mention it." Sula shrugged and turned over on her stomach, her buttocks toward Eva.

"You ain't been in this house ten seconds and already you starting something."

"Takes two, Big Mamma."

"Well, don't let your mouth start nothing that your ass can't stand. When you gone to get married? You need to have some babies. It'll settle you."

"I don't want to make somebody else. I want to make myself." . . .

"Pus mouth! God's going to strike you!"

"Which God? The one watched you burn Plum [Eva's son]?"

"Don't talk to me about no burning. You watched your own mamma. You crazy roach! You the one should have been burnt!"

"But I ain't. Got that? I ain't. Any more fires in this house, I'm lighting them!"

Where I come from, this dialogue doesn't sound so much fictional as documentary; it could be about the women—sisters and cousins—who passed Morrison's books on to me when I was growing up, women who didn't know they were "marginal."

Morrison's interest was in spoken language, heightened and dramatized. (Bob Gottlieb told me that he was always inserting commas into Morrison's sentences and she was always taking them out.) In describing her style, Morrison said, "I thought, Well, I'm going to drop 'g's where the black people dropped 'g's, and the white people on the same street in the same part of the state don't. But there was a distinction in the language and it wasn't in the spelling. It was someplace else." Morrison went on, "Maybe it's because African languages are so tonal, so that with the little shifts in pronunciation, the little shifts in placement, something else happens.

"I was just determined to take the language that for me was so powerfully metaphoric, economical, lunatic, and intelligent at the same time—just these short sentences or these developments of ideas that was the language of my family and neighbors and so on—and not make it exotic or comic or slumming." Zora Neale Hurston, the nineteen-thirties novelist and folklorist, was an example, Morrison said, of a black writer who treated dialogue as a transcript to show white people how it really was in the Florida swamps. Morrison's aim was different. "Street language is lyrical, plus it has this blend of the standard English and the sermonic, as well as the colloquial, you know—that is what I wanted to polish and show, and make it a literary vehicle," Morrison said. (She has succeeded in this to the point of irritating some readers. James Wood, in a review of "Paradise" titled "The Color Purple," wrote, "Morrison is so besotted with making poetry, with the lyrical dyeing of every moment, that she cannot grant characters their own words. . . . She seems to view her people as mere spokes of style, who exist to keep her lyricism in motion.")

Situating herself inside the black world, Morrison undermined the myth of black cohesiveness. With whiteness offstage, or certainly right of center, she showed black people fighting with each other—murdering, raping, breaking up marriages, burning down houses. She also showed nurturing fathers who abide and the matriarchs who love them. Morrison revelled in the complications. "I didn't want it to be a teaching tool for white people. I wanted it to be true—not from outside the culture, as a writer looking back at it," she said. "I wanted it to come from inside the culture, and speak to people inside the culture. It was about a refusal to pander or distort or gain political points. I wanted to reveal and raise questions." She is still raising questions: Bill Cosey, the deceased patriarch in "Love," is both beneficent and evil, a guardian and a predator.

Doing so, Morrison broke ranks—particularly with black male writers such as Larry Neal and Amiri Baraka, who were taking an increasingly militant stance against racism. Their attitude descended from the realistic portraits of black resistance in the novels of Wright, Baldwin, and Ellison—who, Morrison believed, were writing for a white audience. "The title of Ralph Ellison's book was 'Invisible Man,'" Morrison said. "And the question for me was 'Invisible to whom?' Not to me." Morrison refused to present an ideal or speak in unison, even if it meant she was perceived as a traitor. "There is that sense of firm loyalty for black people," she said. "The question is always, Is this going to be useful for the race?"

"I really liked that book," one black woman told Morrison after reading "The Bluest Eye." "But I was frustrated and angry, because I didn't want you to expose us in our lives." Morrison replied, "Well, how can I reach you if I don't expose it to the world?" Others, myself included, accused her of perpetuating rather than dismantling the myth of the indomitable black woman, long-suffering and oversexed. In a book about real and fictional black women, I wrote that the obsessive "man love" of Hannah, Sula's mother, was a stereotype. (At the time, I didn't see that Morrison's decision to burn her to death was a moral condemnation, not a melodrama.) Morrison is used to being challenged and isn't afraid to confront her critics. "I didn't like what you wrote," she said to me a few years ago. I was caught off guard, but she steered the conversation to another topic.

The reviews of "Sula"—like those of "The Bluest Eye"—were mixed. Writing in *The Nation*, the critic Jerry H. Bryant came closest to identifying the confusion: "Most of us have been conditioned to expect something else in black characters, especially black female characters—guiltless victims of brutal white men, yearning for a respectable life of middle-class security; whores driven to their profession by impossible conditions; housekeepers exhausted by their work for lazy white women. We do not expect to see a fierceness bordering on the demonic."

After "Sula," Bob Gottlieb advised Morrison to move on. "'O.K.,' I told her, 'that's perfect. As perfect as a sonnet,'" he recalled. "'You've done that, you don't have to do it again. Now you're free to open up more.'" She followed his advice with "Song of Solomon," a sprawling epic about a prosperous but tortured black family that drew comparisons to Gabriel García Márquez's "One Hundred Years of Solitude." As she turned her attention to history—taking on, in years to come, slavery, Reconstruction, the great migration, the Harlem Renaissance—writing began to occupy more of her time. "I went to Bob Bernstein twice," she told me. "Once, when I saw a house I wanted to buy. I didn't want to go through the whole black-woman thing—no man, no credit—and so I asked the company to get the mortgage for me. The second time was after 'Tar Baby' was published. I knew it was unorthodox, but I wanted to come into the office less. I was doing what the editors did—line editing—at home. It was such a waste of time to come in and drink coffee and gossip. So I started working one day a week. I'd get eighty letters done, stay until eight o'clock, but get my work done."

Eventually, she resigned. "The job at Random House was a life raft for her," Gottlieb recalled. "She had two sons and she was worried about losing that life preserver. After she published 'Tar Baby,' I said, 'Toni, you can depend on your writing to support you.'"

Morrison remembered Gottlieb's telling her, "O.K. You can write 'writer' on your tax returns."

MORRISON PROVOKES COMPLICATED RESPONSES FROM HER LITERARY progeny. She is routinely placed on a pedestal and just as frequently knocked off it. Black writers alternately praise her and castigate her for not being everything at once. With the deaths of Wright and Baldwin, Morrison became both mother and father to black writers of my generation—a delicate situation. (It's similar to the phenomenon James Baldwin noted in his essay on Richard Wright: "His work was an immense liberation and revelation for me. He became my ally and my witness, and alas! my father.") She spoke through her characters when we wanted her to speak to us. With every book, she loomed larger, and gave us more opportunities to define ourselves against her. In 1978, "Song of Solomon" won the National Book Critics Circle Award, beating out Joan Didion's "A Book of Common Prayer" and John Cheever's "Falconer." It was chosen as a main selection by the Book-of-the-Month Club—the first by a black since Wright's "Native Son." When "Tar Baby" came out, four years later, Morrison was on the cover of *Newsweek*, the first black woman to appear on the cover of a national magazine since Zora Neale Hurston in 1943.

"Beloved," too, was an instant sensation in 1987. It told the story of Margaret Garner, a runaway slave who murders her child rather than allow it to be captured. When "Beloved" failed to be nominated for a National Book Award (Pete Dexter's "Paris Trout" won that year), forty-eight prominent black intellectuals and writers, including Maya Angelou, Lucille Clifton, Henry Louis Gates, Jr., Alice Walker, and Quincy Troupe, protested "against such oversight and harmful whimsy" in a statement that was printed in the *Times Book Review*. "Alive, we write this testament of thanks to you, dear Toni: alive, beloved and persevering, magical. . . . For all America, for all of American letters, you have advanced the moral and artistic standards by which we must measure the daring and the love of our national imagination and our collective intelligence as a people." They contested the fact that Morrison had yet to be considered for a Pulitzer Prize. Later that year, "Beloved" did win a Pulitzer. Ralph Ellison, for one, disapproved of the special pleading. "Toni doesn't need that kind of support, even though it was well intentioned," he said.

"Beloved"'s profile only got higher as time went by. The contrarian critic Stanley Crouch called it "protest pulp fiction" and complained that it idealized black behavior "to placate sentimental feminist ideology, and to make sure that the vision of black woman as the most scorned and rebuked of the victims doesn't weaken." He objected to its commerciality. "Were 'Beloved' adapted for television (which would suit the crass obviousness that wins out over Morrison's literary gift at every significant turn) the trailer might go like this: 'Meet Sethe, an ex-slave woman who harbors a deep and terrible secret that has brought terror into her home.'" (As it happened, it was adapted for film, with Oprah in the role of Sethe.)

Best-selling books, film adaptations, television talk-show appearances all increased Morrison's celebrity and drew other famous people into her life. The actor Marlon Brando would phone to read her passages from her novels that he found particularly humorous. Oprah had her to dinner—on TV. By the time the film of "Beloved" was released, Morrison's fame was inescapable. I recall walking along the West Side piers in Manhattan and hearing a Puerto Rican queen, defending one of her "children," say to an opponent, "You want me to go 'Beloved' on your ass?"

Morrison's critics reached their loudest pitch when she was awarded the Nobel Prize, in 1993, a year that Thomas Pynchon and Joyce Carol Oates had been favored to win. "I hope this prize inspires her to write better books," Crouch said. Charles Johnson, a black novelist, called her writing "often offensive, harsh. Whites are portrayed badly. Men are. Black men are." He said that she had been "the beneficiary of good will" and that her award was "a triumph of political correctness." A piece in the Washington *Post* asked well-known American writers whom they would like to see receive the award. Erica Jong (whose choice, Doris Lessing, Jong described as "the wrong kind of African: white") wrote, "I wish that Toni Morrison, a bedazzling writer and a great human being, had won her prize only for her excellence at stringing words together. But I am nevertheless delighted at her choice. . . . I suspect, however, that her prize was not motivated solely by artistic considerations. Why can't art in itself be enough? Must we also use the artist as a token of progressivism?" The Nobel Committee said that Morrison "delves into the language itself, a language she wants to liberate from the fetters of race." To this, one critic retorted that she has "erected an insistent awareness of race (and gender and whatever else may be the 'identity'-defining trait du jour) as the defining feature of the self."

"I have never competed with other people," Morrison told me. "It just never occurred to me. I have to sort of work it up to understand what people are talking about when they complain about what this person did or that person shouldn't do. There were several contenders from the U.S. that year, and my wish was that they would've all gotten it, so that I could be left alone. I only compete with myself, with my standards. How to do better the next time, how to work well."

NEAR THE END OF ONE OF OUR INTERVIEWS LAST SUMMER, MORRISON took me on a tour of the house. Descending the staircase off the sitting room, we had a look at her office, with its two big desks stacked with paper and correspondence. Behind one desk was her assistant, John Hoppenthaler, a poet. Windows surrounded the room. "I don't really write that much in here," Morrison said. "Don't look at it—it's a mess." She decided that she would pick some tomatoes for lunch. She is what she calls a "pot" gardener—she enjoys gardening on a small scale. The room below the office is where Morrison does her writing. It has a slate floor, a big wooden table—"It's from Norway, not that I got it in Norway, and I'm sure the man who imported it overcharged for it, but I love all the grooves and cracks in it"—and a fully equipped kitchen. Sometimes she cooks Thanksgiving dinner for her family there (both sons are married, with children), but it's a room meant for work. French doors lead out to a stretch of grass and the river beyond. Morrison got to work picking tomatoes off a small vine trained against a stone wall. Two tomatoes that did not meet her standards she chucked into the river. Then she led me inside to get back to work.

SECRET HISTORIES

ALEXIS OKEOWO

October 26, 2020

On a clear night earlier this year, the writer and scholar Saidiya Hartman was fidgeting in a cab on the way to MOMA PS1, the contemporary-art center in Queens. The museum was holding an event to celebrate Hartman's latest book, "Wayward Lives, Beautiful Experiments," an account, set in New York and Philadelphia at the turn of the twentieth century, that blends history and fiction to chronicle the sexual and gender rebellions of young Black women. Several artists planned to present work that illustrated Hartman's influence on them. She was nervous just thinking about it. "I'm crying on the inside," she said. "I'm this shy person, and this feels so weird."

Hartman, who is fifty-nine, wore a blue batik tunic over slim black pants and plum-shaded ankle boots. A professor of English and comparative literature at Columbia, she occupies a singular position in contemporary culture: she is an academic, influenced by Michel Foucault, who has both received a MacArthur "genius" grant and appeared in a Jay-Z video. Hartman has a serene, patient demeanor, which the cultural theorist Judith Butler described as "withheld and shy, self-protective." She speaks at what seems like precisely three-quarters speed, to allow her to inspect her thoughts before releasing them. "She definitely has a bit of that holding-your-tongue thing as a power mode," the artist Arthur Jafa, a friend and collaborator of hers, told me. "She carries the universe in her head, and you can feel it in her presence." But her best friend, Tina Campt, a professor of visual culture at Brown, called her endearingly "goofy and awkward." On a recent trip to London, Campt told me, Hartman got lost returning to her hotel from a restaurant. The hotel was a block away.

At the museum, a tent had been set up in a courtyard, and a line of attendees snaked around it: artists, fashion people, writers, students, cool kids with their hair in topknots. Thelma Golden, the director of the Studio Museum in Harlem, greeted Hartman with a hug and warned, "Prepare for fan-girling."

The event's curator, Thomas Lax, was waiting inside the tent to show Hartman around. (Hartman's partner, Samuel Miller, a civil-rights attorney, had stayed home in Manhattan to help their teen-age daughter study for finals.) Lax had been a graduate student of Hartman's at Columbia, and they remain in touch. "Once you're in the circle, you don't want to leave," Lax said. Jafa, wearing a brocaded coat and gold-heeled boots, surveyed the crowd, which included the artists Glenn Ligon and Lorraine O'Grady. *"Every-body's* here," he said.

In three books and a series of essays, Hartman has explored the interior lives of enslaved people and their descendants, employing a method that she says "troubles the line between history and imagination." Her iconoclastic thinking on the legacy of slavery in American life has prefigured the current cultural moment. In 2008, five years before Black Lives Matter was founded, she wrote of "a past that has yet to be done, and the ongoing state of emergency in which black life remains in peril." Her writing has become a lodestar for a generation of students and, increasingly, for politically engaged people outside the academy.

At the museum, Jafa screened footage that showed how Hartman's ideas had "infiltrated" his art-making. The choreographer and performer Okwui Okpokwasili sang a piece inspired by characters in her book: domestic workers, chorus girls, juvenile delinquents, and wanderers. The artist Cameron Rowland read from a letter written by a South Carolina planter, detailing disobedience on his plantation—a litany of impudent acts that the planter seemed not to realize constituted a campaign of sly subversion. Rowland said that the letter evoked the "legacies of Black antagonism that are part of what Saidiya calls 'acts of everyday resistance.'" As Rowland read, the crowd erupted into laughter and cheers.

When the presentations were over, Hartman sat at a table at the back of the tent, where a line of people held copies of her book for her to sign. One woman said that she was having a "small crisis" and was about to change her name.

Hartman, whose given name is Valarie, responded soothingly. "That's O.K.," she said. "Which name do you want it signed to?" Another asked for advice on graduate programs; Hartman invited the woman to come see her at Columbia.

After the signing, a group of celebrants headed out to an Italian restaurant nearby. Hartman sat in the middle of a long table, the reluctant center of gravity. "She's royalty for us," Jafa said. "We're celebrating her, but we're also celebrating ourselves. It's a victory dance for the marginal, edgy, weirdo Black nerds."

HARTMAN GREW UP IN BROOKLYN, BUT HER PEOPLE ON HER MOTHER'S side are from Alabama. According to family lore, their forebears were enslaved first in Mississippi, but a slaveowner sold one of them to an Alabama plantation, to pay a debt. As a girl, Hartman occasionally visited Alabama during the summer, and remembers long Baptist services and cold bottles of Coca-Cola; her great-grandfather took her on country drives, pointing out farms that had once been owned by Black folks. The drives "deeply marked me," Hartman told me. But she also felt out of place in the conservative circles that her family occupied. "That Black social world was defined by a class and color hierarchy that was so extreme," she said.

Her mother, Beryle, grew up in Montgomery, among church-going activists; she and her parents took part in the bus boycott of the nineteen-fifties. During segregation, the family was proudly middle-class: one relative was among the first Black doctors in Selma, and another was a Tuskegee Airman. Beryle went to Tuskegee University and then to Tennessee State, where she studied social work. She was also schooled in propriety, encouraged to wear white gloves and forbidden to have male visitors in her dorm.

During college, Beryle met Virgilio Hartman, a private stationed at Maxwell Air Force Base. Her parents did not approve; Virgilio hadn't attended college, and he didn't come from the right kind of people. His family, immigrants to New York from Curaçao, were hardworking strivers, but, Hartman recalled, "there was less keeping up with the Joneses."

In Brooklyn, Hartman's parents' closest friends were a Jewish lesbian couple; her own friends were the children of immigrants from Panama and Haiti. Her mother took her and the neighborhood kids to the Guggenheim and the Museum of Modern Art, and to see shows like "For Colored Girls. . . ." Her father, a policeman, encouraged her to attend the highly competitive Stuyvesant High School.

Hartman, surrounded by people of varied ethnicities, considered herself a New Yorker first. Audre Lorde's daughter was a schoolmate; she also hung out with "privileged, disaffected white kids." She wrote poetry, played classical guitar, joined a physics club for a month. She wore overalls, flannel shirts, and a "wild Afro," to fit in with her leftist crew and also to reject the "Black American princess" image that her mother wanted her to present.

Hartman's early experience of politics was "simple and direct and radical," she said. She joined socialist organizations and reproductive-rights groups. While in high school, she interviewed the radical writer Amiri Baraka, and asked if there was a more effective way than poetry to bring about societal change. "Yes," he told her. "The gun." But her own inclinations were less combative. A few years before, her parents had sent her to a Black-nationalist summer camp in Crown Heights. On a camp trip to Pennsylvania, she accidentally stepped on the foot of a white boy and apologized. A counsellor told her that she should never apologize to a white person, and to go step on his foot again. Hartman made her way back to the boy and brushed his foot with hers. She vowed never to return to the camp.

HARTMAN WAS "QUESTING," SHE SAID. AFTER HIGH SCHOOL, SHE spent a year at Wesleyan, and then a year in a film program at New York University—an unhappy experience at what she describes as "vocational school for white guys from Long Island." Returning to Wesleyan, she sat in on a course on feminism, taught by Judith Butler. "She was so smart that I thought the windows were gonna blow out," Butler, who now teaches Hartman's books, said. "The quickness of her mind and the sharpness of her critique were breathtaking."

Hartman's mentors were working to erode the dominance of European perspectives. Hazel Carby gave Hartman a Marxist view of African-American, Caribbean, and African histories; Gayatri Spivak introduced her to post-structuralism, which holds that the truth of events is inextricably tied to the language used to describe them. Hartman began thinking about the invisible framework that governed her (relatively charmed) life as a young Black woman. "I wanted to understand the inequality that was structuring the world—even as I was feeling that it had not made anything impossible for me," she said. She changed her name from Valarie to Saidiya, which is derived from the Swahili word for "to help." The change, she wrote later, "extirpated all evidence of upstanding Negroes and their striving bastard heirs, and confirmed my place in the company of poor Black girls—Tamikas, Roqueshas, and Shanequas." (Her family called her by the new name reluctantly.)

Hartman was still marked by the experiences of her youth: following the rules down South, roaming free in New York. "I'm both a pessimist and a wild dreamer," she told me. She imagined getting involved in radical politics, going to Grenada to join Maurice Bishop's Black-liberation movement. Instead, she went to graduate school at Yale, and studied voraciously. The playwright Lynn Nottage, who met her there, recalled, "At parties, I'd be rocking to the music, and she'd be standing back trying to interrogate what was happening. I'd say, 'Just come into the party,' and she would be analyzing the lyrics to the song, how people are dancing, the gender and racial dynamics."

For her doctoral thesis, Hartman planned to write about the blues. But when she read Foucault's work on the ways that people are subjected to power, she saw a chance to do something new. Foucault, she realized, was "not thinking about Black people or slavery in the Americas." Her thesis would examine how totalizing, violent domination had shaped the status and agency of enslaved people.

The result was "Scenes of Subjection: Terror, Slavery, and Self-Making in Nineteenth-Century America," which argued, in dense and provocative detail, that Emancipation constituted another phase of enslavement for Black Americans, as they moved from the plantations to the punitive controls of the Black Codes and Jim Crow. Hartman was illuminating what she calls the "afterlife of slavery": limited access to health care and education, premature death, incarceration, and impoverishment—the "skewed life chances" that Black people still face, and the furious desire for freedom that comes with them. As Butler put it, "The question she returns to again and again is: 'Did slavery ever really end?'"

That question had been the subject of earlier scholarship; Hartman's book, with its compelling portrayal of lives caught between cruelty and resistance, helped move it toward the mainstream. Frank B. Wilderson III, a former student of Hartman's who now chairs the department of African-American studies at the University of California, Irvine, described her as quietly persuasive. "She's not an 'angry Black woman,'" he told me. "She's not Assata Shakur.

But what they don't know is that, where Assata Shakur will blow your head off, Saidiya has just put a stiletto between your ribs."

Wilderson interviewed Hartman in 2002 for an article called "The Position of the Unthought." In it, he criticized scholars of African-American history for underplaying the "terror of their evidence in order to propose some kind of coherent, hopeful solution"; he praised "Scenes of Subjection" for exposing the unrelenting violence of slavery. Hartman agreed that turning that legacy into a narrative of uplift was "obscene." But she has always been interested in portraying the agency of Black people. In "Scenes of Subjection," her subjects endure vicious circumstances through acts of imagination, making a way out of no way; they evaded work on plantations and, after Emancipation, refused to enter into contracts with their former masters. Hartman told me that her goal was to shift Black lives from the "object of scholarly analysis" to the basis for an "argument that challenged the assumptions of history." Once, while she was discussing "Scenes of Subjection" with her class at Columbia, a student expressed surprise that she gave the words of a slave the same weight as those of Foucault. "Yeah," she responded. "Exactly."

ONE RAINY EVENING, I VISITED HARTMAN AT THE APARTMENT THAT she shares with her family, in a stately building on the Upper West Side. Her labradoodle was barking excitedly, and Miller pulled him into the kitchen so that Hartman and I could talk in the living room. Behind her was a book-crammed study, with two handsome desks. Academic work has given Hartman a comfortable life—the apartment, provided by Columbia, is spacious, with hardwood floors, West African–cloth table runners, and a view of Riverside Park. But it has also, at times, been at odds with her creative instincts. She told me that she went to graduate school with no intention of becoming a professor: "I didn't have a trust fund, and I wanted to continue to study." That initial ambivalence has never really gone away.

Hartman's first teaching job was at the University of California, Berkeley, where she received early tenure on the strength of her draft of "Scenes of Subjection." The chair of the English department told her that, since she now had tenure, there was no need to finish the book. Hartman was taken aback, but ultimately she found freedom in her colleagues' low expectations. "As a Black woman intellectual, I am at the bottom of the food chain," she said during a talk at the Hammer Museum, in Los Angeles. But "within that space of no one taking me seriously, there was also all this space to work."

At Berkeley, Hartman wanted to reckon with the ways in which violence had been used to enforce social order. She also wanted to write with a resonance that was uncommon in scholarly literature. "I wanted to be a Wailer," she said—a member of Bob Marley's band. "What does it mean to describe Trench Town, in Jamaica, but be describing the world? What does it mean to have that kind of power articulating a condition, with poetry and beauty?"

Hartman is well versed in academic discourse; she sometimes describes her work as an effort to "topple the hierarchy of discourse" and to "jeopardize the status of the event." But she can also write with striking intimacy, evoking the feelings and the conditions of Black life. In her second book, a kind of anti-memoir called "Lose Your Mother: A Journey Along the Atlantic Slave Route," she described a pervasive sense of dispossession:

> Two people meeting on the avenue will ask, 'Is this where you stay?' Not, 'Is this your house?' 'I stayed here all my life' is the reply. Staying is living in a country without exercising any claims on its resources. It is the perilous condition of existing in a world in which you have no investments. It is having never resided in a place that you can say is yours.

The book grew out of a trip that Hartman took to Ghana, inspired by her great-great-grandmother Polly, who had been a slave in Alabama. As a girl, Hartman had been frustrated with the gaps in Polly's story: what she looked like, how her life had been. She wanted to investigate the rupture between Africa and the United States—the oceanic graveyard that transformed free people into slaves and, she believes, shaped the identity of the Black diaspora. "The routes traveled by strangers were as close to a mother country as I would come," she writes. In Ghana, she retraced the paths of captives, from ancestral villages to holding cells. But, instead of the words of enslaved Africans, she found only silence. Hartman wandered Accra and the Gold Coast for a year, disappointed that the Ghanaians she met saw her as an outsider, and upset that they refused to talk about African culpability in the slave trade.

The historical archive was little help. Hartman pored over records that often amounted to commercial transactions of enslaved bodies: slaver manifests, trade ledgers, food inventories, captains' logs, bills of sale. "In every line item, I saw a grave," she writes. "To read the archive is to enter a mortuary; it permits one final viewing and allows for a last glimpse of persons about to disappear into the slave hold."

The detailed narratives that did exist had been left by people like Thomas Thistlewood, a British plantation overseer in Jamaica. In his diaries, he described punishing a slave: "Gave him a moderate whipping, pickled him well, made Hector shit in his mouth, immediately put a gag in it whilst his mouth was full & made him wear it 4 or 5 hours." How could Hartman describe an enslaved life using such a passage, whose "annihilating force" revealed a great deal about Thistlewood but nothing about the slave?

Through those years, Hartman told me, "I was wrestling with what it means to have the colonial archive, the archive of the Western bourgeoisie, dictate what it is we can know about these lives."

Even later, more earnest attempts at historical memory were misleading; the Works Progress Administration's slave narratives, which often had white Southerners ask formerly enslaved people about their lives, made honest responses unthinkable. Hartman had been trying to overcome the silences about Black life, but she found herself reproducing them. As she once wrote, "The loss of stories sharpens the hunger for them."

FOR HARTMAN, RECKONING WITH HISTORY MEANS RETURNING AGAIN and again to old events and ideas. The writer Maggie Nelson told me that "Scenes of Subjection" is one of her favorite books, because it "uses historical record and trenchant argument to upend truisms." Nelson praised Hartman's ability to reframe events: "As a writer, she's continuing to shift the kaleidoscope and keep offering something different, like 'Now how about this? How about this?'"

In "Lose Your Mother," she wrote of a girl who was tortured to death on a British slave ship, possibly because she had refused to dance naked for the captain. The girl's death intensified a debate in England over the abolition of the slave trade. Hartman's account, re-creating the brutal killing and the trials that followed, briefly mentions another captive on the ship, a young girl who is referred to in legal documents only as Venus. After the book came out, Hartman said, "I was really haunted by that second girl."

A year later, in the essay "Venus in Two Acts," Hartman returns to the girl, criticizing herself for abandoning her. She admits to being tired of trying to tell stories based on "empty rooms, and silence, and lives reduced to waste," and wonders how to wring more from the archive. "What else is there to know?" she writes. "Hers is the same fate as every other Black Venus: no one remembered her name or recorded the things she said, or observed that she refused to say anything at all."

Hartman began exploring "what might have been," starting with a single invented detail, of a sailor testifying that the two

girls seemed like friends. In a process that she calls "critical fabula-
tion," she imagined a narrative: two doomed children passing days
together, finding solace and joy in each other's company; Venus
holding her friend as she died, whispering that everything would
be all right.

Hartman knew that such a counter-history would be seen as
less legitimate. "History pledges to be faithful to the limits of fact,
evidence, and archive," she wrote. "I wanted to write a romance
that exceeded the fictions of history." But a conventional history of
the girls' experience was impossible. As she noted, "There is not one
extant autobiographical narrative of a female captive who survived
the Middle Passage."

Still, she spends much of the essay describing her own uncertainty about what she's doing. Can stories fill in the archive? They
might provide comfort, but to whom? For the dead, it is too late.
In the end, Hartman decides that the goal is not to "recover" or
"redeem" the dead girls but to create a fuller picture of their lives.
Campt, her friend and colleague, said, "She gave us a way of seeing
them, not on the terms that society wanted to see them but on their
own terms."

IN 2017, ARTHUR JAFA DIRECTED A VIDEO FOR THE JAY-Z SINGLE "4:44,"
an apology for the rapper's romantic failings. Two and a half minutes in, a woman walks down a New York street, wearing a pensive,
purposeful expression: Hartman. "I was totally awkward and stiff,"
she said, laughing as she recalled the filming. "She had a certain
primness, properness," Jafa acknowledged. "But it's an image of a
person thinking in motion." When Jay-Z saw a cut of the video,
he asked who Hartman was. Jafa explained that she is "the arch-
angel of Black precarity." Her presence, he said, "may not register
to ninety-five per cent of his audience now, but five years down the
line, ten years down the line, twenty years down the line, that's going to be one of the most powerful moments of the video."

These days, Hartman is regularly referred to by activists, social-media influencers, and woke celebrities like Jeremy O. Harris, the author of "Slave Play." Her latest book, "Wayward Lives, Beautiful Experiments," might be her most daring; it is certainly her most popular. "After 'Scenes of Subjection' and 'Lose Your Mother,' I thought, I just can't write another book about slavery," Hartman told an interviewer at the London Review Bookshop last October. But Hartman, who describes her work as "a lot of sitting at my desk and staring off into space," has spent much of her writing life thinking about how Black people have resisted subjugation by means of "productive, creative, life-saving deviations from the norm." As she worked on the book, she began reimagining a scene from the life of W. E. B. Du Bois.

On an August day toward the end of the nineteenth century, Du Bois was on South Street in Philadelphia, amid day laborers and new migrants, pretty boys and brazen girls. Twenty-eight years old, Harvard-educated, and dressed in a gray three-piece suit, Du Bois was then a novice sociologist, hired to conduct a study of the Seventh Ward, the city's oldest Black neighborhood. Du Bois was scandalized by the slum's naked display of brawling, pleasure-seeking, and hustling; he blamed slavery's destruction of the Black family, but also the loose morals of the recent arrivals from the South. On South Street, he saw two young Black women window-shopping at a shoe store, and heard one tell the other, "That's the kind of shoes I'd buy my fellow." In Du Bois's view, "the remark fixed their life history." They must have been prostitutes, from one of the slums "where each woman supports some man from the results of her gains."

Hartman admires Du Bois, whom she sees as a model for innovative readings of the archive. In "Black Reconstruction," he narrates the lives of slaves who refused to work and who fled plantations; by describing these activities not as criminality but as a "general strike," he changed the way historians treated enslaved people.

But his telling of the encounter with the two young women felt incomplete to Hartman. "There was drama in that moment," she told me. "There's Du Bois's framing of it—but how did he look in *their* eyes? Why was female desire so scandalous that they could only be prostitutes?"

In "Wayward Lives," Hartman retells the scene from the women's point of view, as if she were a filmmaker, pulling back the lens to reveal characters at the margins of the frame. "They looked long and hard at all the objects on display in the shop window, expectant and dreaming of a way out," she writes. Stopping to admire a pair of boots, the color of oxblood and ivory, they imagine them worn by a "beautiful, dangerous" man, and fantasize about the adventures they might have with him. They pay no mind to Du Bois; he is just part of the hectic cityscape, an afterthought.

The young Black women in "Wayward Lives" arrived in New York and Philadelphia in the early days of the Great Migration, a generation or two removed from slavery. They were hoping for something more than what they'd left behind. What they found was decrepit slums, domestic work that felt akin to slavery, and social reformers and policemen who patrolled their most intimate activities. Laws to discourage "wayward minors" criminalized dancing, dating, and even walking in some streets. Under the guise of housing reform, young Black women were routinely arrested on "suspicion of prostitution," and sent to reformatories and workhouses. Hartman writes that they were arrested "on the threshold of their homes and inside their apartments, while exiting taxicabs, flirting at dance halls, waiting for their husbands, walking home from the cabaret with friends, enjoying an intimate act with a lover, being in the wrong place at the wrong time."

Many of the city's young Black women lived in a kind of "everyday anarchy," anyway; they took lovers, had lesbian relationships, dressed and behaved as they pleased. (Black women, Hartman notes, were flappers before the term existed.) She writes of Harriet

Powell, a seventeen-year-old who, despite being arrested for her "nocturnal wanderings," danced past midnight in Harlem clubs, went to movies, and rented a room where she met her lover. Powell and other Black girls in the city's sexual revolution had a freedom that their grandmothers could only dream of.

The archival material that Hartman draws on was mostly left by people who saw Black women as a "problem": journals of rent collectors, surveys of sociologists, trial transcripts and slum photographs, prison case files, interviews with psychiatrists and psychologists. To balance the portrait, Hartman does her most speculative work, exploring her subjects' shared horizon of desire and yearning. In one exchange, she writes about a white reform worker, Helen Parrish, fretting over her tenant Mamie Sharp, who saw other men besides her partner:

> There was no easy way to lead into the matter of adultery, so Helen broached the issue directly. "Mamie, have you been going around town with other men? Have you?" The question was as much an accusation as inquiry. Mamie's reply was no less direct: "Yes, I like to go about as I please." Mamie didn't apologize or offer any excuses for not being able to hold steady; she did not try to temper Helen's judgment by admitting that she had been lonely.

As Hartman worked on the book, she thought of her maternal grandmother, Berdie. She had gone to college to be a teacher, but became pregnant with Beryle, and her parents threw her out of the house, raising the child themselves.

Families like Beryle's, striving for respectability in a racist world, would have been embarrassed to acknowledge women who had children out of wedlock—let alone those who did sex work or had female lovers. "There is a certain kind of uplift and progress narrative that was saying, 'Oh, no, no, don't waste any time think-

ing about the past. Move on. Pull yourself up by your bootstraps,'"
Hartman said. In "Wayward Lives," though, women like these are
"sexual modernists, free lovers, radicals, and anarchists." They are
visionaries, imagining a different way of life.

Hartman's rethinking of the archive has enormous appeal
for readers hungry to see their identity—feminist, queer, gender-
nonconforming—mirrored in the past. Part of the book's argument
is that Black women originated a set of social arrangements that
were once considered deviant and are now commonplace: expansive
notions of family, generous intimacy and sociality, fluid romantic
relationships. Black women, Hartman says, have often operated
outside of gender norms, whether they wanted to or not. During
slavery, they had little control over their children or their repro-
duction. Afterward, poverty and discrimination forced them to do
things that few white women did: work for wages, lead households,
and enter and leave marriages freely. If they could not meet expectations set by white men, that allowed them to conduct experiments
in living. The poet and theorist Fred Moten told me, "Saidiya does
the very crucial work of expanding our understanding of the Black
radical tradition," revealing that it is "fundamentally the work of
working-class Black women and young Black girls."

But the historian Annette Gordon-Reed, writing recently in
the *New York Review of Books*, wondered if Hartman was project-
ing political aims onto people driven by necessity. She considered
the case of Mattie Nelson, who, on the way to a sexual awakening,
lost a baby in a teen-age pregnancy and was painfully abandoned
by several male lovers. "If Nelson were given the choice between
living a precarious life, depending upon men whom society prevented from realizing their potential, and being a wife and mother
under circumstances available to white middle- and upper-class
women, there is no reason to assume she would not have opted for
the latter," Gordon-Reed wrote. "We live after a sustained critique
of bourgeois values and lifestyles, decades in the making. Nelson

did not." For Hartman, though, rebels don't need to be motivated by ideology, or even to consider themselves revolutionaries. "Many of the people who have produced radical thought have not been imagined to be involved in the task of thinking at all," she said.

IN MARCH, "WAYWARD LIVES" WON THE NATIONAL BOOK CRITICS Circle Award—for criticism, rather than for nonfiction or fiction. No one seemed sure how to categorize it. "The book has had a very complex reception," Hartman told me. "I've been exploring the same set of critical questions since the beginning. But some people in the university world are, like, '"Scenes of Subjection" is the real thing. What are these other two books?'" Her publisher, W. W. Norton, had hoped for higher sales, and Hartman wondered if the book's marketing was partly to blame. The U.S. edition was published with extensive endnotes, and the interplay of factual and speculative sections may have confused readers new to her work. Her British publisher, Profile Books, classified "Wayward Lives" as both literature and history; it cut the endnotes and put them online, allowing the book to be read as creative nonfiction rather than as scholarship. "Some people told me, 'Oh, I like that novel,'" Hartman said, laughing. "I'm so unfaithful to genre, so it was fine."

But Hartman rejects the idea that her books should be understood as historical fiction. Instead, she calls her work a "history of the present"—writing that examines the past to show how it haunts our time. Many of her peers were engaged in the same project, she said; she points to the Canadian writer M. NourbeSe Philip's "Zong," a book of poems, extrapolated from legal documents, about a hundred and fifty Africans who were drowned on a British slave ship, so that the owners could collect an insurance payment.

For several decades, Black female scholars like Hortense Spillers, Sarah Haley, Erica Armstrong Dunbar, Tera Hunter, Farah Griffin, and Deborah Gray White have been creatively reading the archive, reconstructing the experiences of Black women using such alternative sources as cleaning manuals, Black newspapers, musical productions, and buried correspondence. Hartman sees her work as "enabled" by these women. But, she says, "the people who I really felt provoked and solicited by have been creative writers, the novelists and poets who are making other kinds of stories." Her inspirations include Caryl Phillips, Jamaica Kincaid, and, especially, Toni Morrison, whose novel "Beloved," inspired by a single newspaper clipping, was a painstaking effort to deepen the archive.

In 1987, the year that "Beloved" was published, Morrison wrote of a process of "emotional memory" that aimed to find truth in the gaps of verifiable fact. "They straightened out the Mississippi River in places, to make room for houses and livable acreage. Occasionally the river floods these places," she wrote. "It is remembering. Remembering where it used to be. All water has a perfect memory and is forever trying to get back to where it was. Writers are like that."

IN "WAYWARD LIVES," A CHORUS GIRL AT A HARLEM NIGHT CLUB FINDS herself in the luxurious apartment of A'Lelia Walker, the daughter of the Black hair-care entrepreneur Madam C. J. Walker. The girl, Mabel Hampton, sees men and women—"Voyeurs, exhibitionists, the merely curious, queers, the polyamorous, and the catholic"— stretched out on silk pillows. They are drinking champagne, eating caviar, and smoking marijuana; to Hampton's surprise, they are also having sex out in the open.

Walker—who, Hartman writes, "drank excessively, played cards with her intimates, gorged on rich food"—arrives late but makes an impression:

> She conversed with her guests, wearing a little silk short set, but it might as well have been an ermine coat; she had the bearing of a queen, and wore the flimsy little outfit with a stately air. Even without her infamous riding crop, there remained something forbidding and dangerous about her.

The scene is rooted in archival fact; historians agree that Walker had queer friends, threw decadent parties, and hosted salons during the Harlem Renaissance. In an interview in 1983, Hampton recalled attending a sex party in the early twenties. "There was men and women, women and women, and men and men," she said. "And everyone did whatever they wanted to do." But the vivid specificity of Hartman's portrayal drew criticism.

"I'm uncomfortable with people making claims and drawing conclusions," A'Lelia Bundles, a journalist who is Walker's great-granddaughter, told me, "just because they want to project something onto her." Bundles, who has published several books about Walker and is working on a new biography, said that Hartman had not consulted her or examined Walker's letters. She disputed the detail of the riding crop, which suggested that Walker was interested in S & M; in Bundles's photographic archive of Walker, she never carried a crop. A private sex party "would have not been impossible," Bundles said. But her research made it seem unlikely that Walker would have led such a visibly queer life.

Hartman said that she never interviews her subjects' relatives, and pointed out that the crop appeared in earlier historians' work. She believes that the pushback revealed "an anxiety around queerness." Her goal, she said, is "not about trying to pin down an identity, but thinking about the queer networks of love and friendship, and depending on the ephemera and rumors when the archive refuses to document these lives. So much of queer life could only survive without being detected."

The historian and artist Nell Painter saw value in Hartman's interrogation of the archive: "She can raise questions for historians to do historical work that they might not have thought of." But, she told me, "her work is not history—it's literature. She has a lot to say to history, but historians do something that's somewhat different. We can't make up an archive that doesn't exist or read into the archive what we want to find." Painter believes that there is still more evidence to be found about the history of Black life. "The past changes according to what questions we ask," she said. "The archive is a living, moving thing. The sources we can put our eyes on are changing as we speak."

All historians make imaginative leaps, but filling in blanks with precise details makes some uneasy. A fellow-academic and admirer of Hartman told me, "When it comes to specific people who lived real lives, I think fiction is the only place where we should speculate."

Hartman tends to be less interested in honoring the archive than in considering "the way in which language and narrative and plot are entangled in the mechanisms of power." She argues that much of what the archive contains about enslaved people was left by people whose views were so compromised as to be effectively made-up. "Fact is simply fiction endorsed with state power . . . to maintain a fidelity to a certain set of archival limits," she said, at the Hammer Museum. "Are we going to be consigned forever to tell the same kinds of stories? Given the violence and power that has engendered this limit, why should I be faithful to that limit? Why should I respect that?"

AS THE CORONAVIRUS FORCED NEW YORK INTO LOCKDOWN, I VISITED Hartman's corner office at Columbia, where she had begun teaching a seminar remotely. A framed print of Lorna Simpson's photograph "Two Sisters and Two Tongues" leaned against a bookcase; outside, students in graduation gowns posed for distanced photos on the steps.

The university sprawls along the southern edge of Harlem, where Hartman once lived, in a housing project with her film-school boyfriend. ("My family was mortified," she recalled.) I asked if she ever felt nostalgic when she went uptown. Looking out the window, she said, "It feels like a museum. All I see on the streets is private capital and rapaciousness, moving people of color out of New York."

A few days later, Hartman and her family left for Massachusetts, where they have a home. When I spoke to her recently, she had been at her desk, working on a project that she prefers to keep secret. "I'm very superstitious about that," she said, laughing. She would say only that it has to do with chronicling the history of the world from the perspective of Black women. She had also been gardening, rereading Morrison and Claudia Rankine, and watching "Greenleaf," a TV melodrama about a Southern Black church, with her daughter.

The news from the city had been on her mind. "Witnessing so many Black and brown people die, it was really emotionally devastating," Hartman said. As the lockdown intensified, New York assigned police to enforce social-distancing and mask-wearing rules. In six weeks, Brooklyn officers arrested forty people for violations; thirty-five were Black. Reports emerged of officers breaking up an evening cookout, swinging batons and knocking out someone's tooth.

In "Wayward Lives," Hartman lingers on the incongruous beauty of dark hallways where lovers could meet. For residents of Black neighborhoods, the halls, staircases, fire escapes, stoops, and courtyards became an extension of living spaces; if your apartment was too small or too uncomfortable, you could go a few feet outside and still feel at home. But that practice of escape has become fraught and, during the lockdown, criminalized. "You're not permitted to take up space in the public sphere," Hartman said. "We see this in gentrifying neighborhoods in New York. The new homeowners will try to pass ordinances like 'No barbecues in the front yard.'"

During the pandemic, the tense relationship between Black residents and the police worsened. Mass protests against the police killing of George Floyd, in Minneapolis, swept through the city, and video footage captured incidents of violence from officers. Black New Yorkers were not only dying from the coronavirus at twice the rate of their white neighbors; they remained disproportionately vulnerable to police brutality. But Hartman saw reason for hope. "Millions of people are involved in the critique of anti-Black racism and state violence," she said. "They're not settling for a tinkering with this order, but saying that the foundation of this order is slavery and settler colonialism, and that we have to build something new." They were imagining a different way of life.

PART V

ONWARD AND UPWARD WITH THE ARTS

VOICE OF THE CENTURY

ALEX ROSS

April 13, 2009

On Easter Sunday, 1939, the contralto Marian Anderson sang on the steps of the Lincoln Memorial. The Daughters of the American Revolution had refused to let her appear at Constitution Hall, Washington's largest concert venue, because of the color of her skin. In response, Eleanor Roosevelt resigned from the D.A.R., and President Roosevelt gave permission for a concert on the Mall. Seventy-five thousand people gathered to watch Anderson perform. Harold Ickes, the Secretary of the Interior, introduced her with the words "In this great auditorium under the sky, all of us are free."

The impact was immediate and immense; one newsreel carried the legend "Nation's Capital Gets Lesson in Tolerance." But Anderson herself made no obvious statement. She presented, as she had done countless times before, a mixture of classical selections—"O mio Fernando," from Donizetti's "La Favorita," and Schubert's "Ave Maria"—and African-American spirituals. Perhaps there was a hint of defiance in her rendition of "My Country, 'Tis of Thee"; perhaps a message of solidarity when she changed the line "Of thee I sing" to "Of thee we sing." Principally, though, her protest came in the unfurling of her voice—that gently majestic instrument, vast in range and warm in tone. In her early years, Anderson was known as "the colored contralto," but, by the late thirties, she was *the* contralto, the supreme representative of her voice category. Arturo Toscanini said that she was the kind of singer who comes along once every hundred years; Jean Sibelius welcomed her to his home saying, "My roof is too low for you." There was no rational reason for a serious venue to refuse entry to such a phenomenon. No clearer demonstration of prejudice could be found.

One person who appreciated the significance of the occasion was the ten-year-old Martin Luther King, Jr. Five years later, King entered a speaking contest on the topic "The Negro and the Constitution," and he mentioned Anderson's performance in his oration: "She sang as never before, with tears in her eyes. When the words of 'America' and 'Nobody Knows de Trouble I Seen' rang out over that great gathering, there was a hush on the sea of uplifted faces, black and white, and a new baptism of liberty, equality, and fraternity. That was a touching tribute, but Miss Anderson may not as yet spend the night in any good hotel in America." When, two decades later, King stood on the Lincoln Memorial steps to deliver his "I Have a Dream" speech, he surely had Anderson in mind. In his improvised peroration, he recited the first verse of "My Country, 'Tis of Thee," then imagined freedom ringing from every mountainside in the land.

Ickes, in 1939, bestowed on Anderson a word that put her in the company of Bach and Beethoven: "Genius, like justice, is blind. . . . Genius draws no color line." With the massive stone image of Lincoln gazing out over her, with a host of powerful white men seated at her feet—senators, Cabinet members, Supreme Court Justices— and with a bank of microphones arrayed in front of her, Anderson attained something greater than fame: for an instant, she became a figure of quasi-political power. In Richard Powers's novel "The Time of Our Singing" (2003), a magisterial fantasia on race and music, the concert becomes nothing less than the evocation of a new America—"A nation that, for a few measures, in song at least, is everything it claims to be." Fittingly, when Barack Obama became President, "My Country, 'Tis of Thee" floated out over the Mall once more, from the mouth of Aretha Franklin to a crowd of two million.

THE SEVENTIETH ANNIVERSARY OF THE EASTER SUNDAY CONCERT AR-
rives on April 9th, and various commemorations are under way.
The mezzo-soprano Denyce Graves will lead a tribute concert at
the Lincoln Memorial on the twelfth, and the historian Raymond
Arsenault has published a book entitled "The Sound of Freedom:
Marian Anderson, the Lincoln Memorial, and the Concert That
Awakened America" (Bloomsbury; $25). Last month, at Carnegie
Hall and other venues, the soprano Jessye Norman curated a festival of African-American cultural achievement, entitled "Honor!,"
during which Anderson was often invoked. (In 1965, Norman saw
Anderson sing at Constitution Hall, which had by then dropped its
exclusionary policies.) Yet Anderson's legacy seems in some way incomplete. The Lincoln Memorial concert has lost much of its iconic
status; many younger people don't know the singer's name. Within
classical music, meanwhile, black faces remain scarce. No African-
American singers were featured at the Metropolitan Opera's recent
hundred-and-twenty-fifth-anniversary gala. A color line persists,
more often politely ignored than confronted directly.

Anderson was born in 1897, in a poor section of Philadelphia.
Her father died when she was young; her mother worked in a tobacco factory, did laundry, and, for some years, scrubbed floors at
Wanamaker's department store. Her musical gifts were evident
early, and new possibilities seemed open to her. Four years before
she was born, the Czech composer Antonín Dvorák, the director of
the National Conservatory, in New York, had declared that spirituals and Amerindian themes would form the basis of American
music, and African-Americans were admitted to the school free of
charge. Because of those encouraging signals, many black families
saw classical music as a realm of opportunity. Yet, of thousands who
pursued a hopeful regimen of piano lessons and vocal coaching,
Anderson was one of very few who graduated into a real classical
career. A core of self-confidence, rarely visible behind her reserved

façade, allowed her to endure a series of potentially crushing disappointments. The sharpest setback is described in her autobiography, "My Lord, What a Morning": when she applied to a Philadelphia music school, in 1914, a young woman at the reception desk made her wait while everyone behind her in line was served. Finally, the woman said, "We don't take colored."

Anderson received enthusiastic notices throughout the nineteen-twenties—her first *Times* review, in 1925, described "a voice of unusual compass, color, and dramatic capacity"—but she needed time to master the finer points of style and diction in foreign-language songs. A notable aspect of her story, related in Arsenault's new book and at greater length in Allan Keiler's "Marian Anderson: A Singer's Journey," is that she found real recognition only when she began an extended European residency, in 1930, giving numerous recitals with piano accompaniment. German critics received her respectfully, and with little condescension. In Finland and the Soviet Union, there were near-riots of enthusiasm. In 1935, she sang in Salzburg, eliciting from Toscanini his voice-of-the-century plaudit, which the impresario Sol Hurok promptly spread through the press. During a series of American tours in the late thirties, she performed in sold-out halls night after night and found herself one of the better-paid entertainers of her time. (In 1938, she earned nearly a quarter of a million dollars, which, adjusted for inflation, comes to $3.7 million.) The American critics capitulated. Howard Taubman, of the *Times*, who later ghostwrote her memoir, called her the "mistress of all she surveyed."

What did she sound like in her prime? A slew of recordings made between 1936 and 1939 give an indication, although her voice plainly possessed the kind of incandescent glow that no machine can capture fully. The disks certainly demonstrate her legendary ability to produce a fine-grained, rich-hued timbre in all parts of her range, from the lowest tones of the female voice well up into the soprano zone. When she sings Schubert's "Erlkönig"—in which a child, his father, and the headless horseman speak in turn—you seem to be hearing three singers, yet there are no obvious vocal breaks between them. She is fastidious but seldom stiff; caressing little slides from note to note and a delicately trembling tone warm up what might have been an excessively studious approach. The incalculable element is the air of spiritual elevation that dwells behind the technique. Perhaps Anderson's most famous performance was of Brahms's "Alto Rhapsody," which she first recorded in 1939, with Eugene Ormandy conducting the Philadelphia Orchestra. (It can be heard on a Pearl CD that collects some of her finest early recordings.) In the Goethe poem on which Brahms's work is based, an embittered soul wanders the desert, eliciting a prayer for his redemption: "If there is on your psaltery, O father of Love, one sound acceptable to his ear, refresh his heart with it." Anderson effortlessly embodies the healing tone, but, before that, she mobilizes the lowest register of her voice to evoke the dark night of the soul.

Anderson was a musician of a pure, inward kind, to whom grand gestures did not come naturally. The historical drama at the Lincoln Memorial was not something she sought, and, in fact, she contemplated cancelling the concert at the last minute. Throughout her life, she preferred not to make a scene. As Arsenault writes, her negotiation of Jim Crow America displayed a "spirit of pragmatism" that could also be interpreted as "quiescence." Although she refused to sing in halls that employed "horizontal segregation"—that is, with whites in the orchestra and blacks in the galleries—for many years she did accept vertical segregation, with whites on one side of the aisle and blacks on the other. She usually took her meals in her hotel room, in order not to cause complications in restaurants. "I always bear in mind that my mission is to leave behind me the kind of impression that will make it easier for those who follow," she explained in her memoir. Sometimes she extracted a certain dignity from the ugliness of segregation: when the Nassau Inn, in Princeton, New Jersey, refused to give her a room, she spent the night at the home of Albert Einstein. But at other times the humiliation must have been intense. In Birmingham, Alabama, during the Second World War, she had to stand outside a train-station waiting room while her accompanist, the German pianist Franz Rupp, went to fetch a sandwich for her. Sitting inside was a group of German prisoners of war.

By the time Anderson's career entered its final phase, in the fifties and sixties, such obstacles had begun to disappear. Segregated halls were no longer on her schedule. She broke a momentous barrier in 1955, when she became the first black soloist to appear at the Metropolitan Opera, as Ulrica, in Verdi's "Un Ballo in Maschera." By then, her voice was past its prime, the pitch unstable and the vibrato distracting. She went on singing for ten more years, less because she couldn't leave the spotlight than because audiences wouldn't let her go. They cherished not only what she was but also what she had been. And she might have achieved even more if the world of opera had been open to her earlier. To hear her assume soprano arias such as "Casta diva" or "Pace, pace, mio Dio" (transposed down a step) is to realize that she was capable of singing almost anything. If, as Toscanini said, such a voice arrives once a century, no successor is in sight.

WHAT HAS CHANGED SINCE ANDERSON MADE HER LONELY ASCENT, basking in ecstatic applause and then eating alone in second-class hotels? Certainly, she made it easier for the black singers who came after her, especially the women. Leontyne Price attained the operatic triumphs that were denied to Anderson, and after Price came such female stars as Shirley Verrett, Grace Bumbry, Jessye Norman, and Kathleen Battle—although the rapid flameout of Battle's career might indicate the difficulties that await a black diva who doesn't go out of her way to avoid making a scene. Opportunities for black males have been markedly more limited, despite the pioneering work of Roland Hayes, Paul Robeson, Todd Duncan, and

George Shirley, among others. African-American conductors are hard to find; the most prominent is James DePreist, who happens to be Marian Anderson's nephew. According to statistics compiled by the League of American Orchestras, only two per cent of orchestral players are black. African-American composers are scattered across college faculties, but they seldom receive high-profile premières. The black contingent of the classical audience is, in most places, minuscule.

As part of Norman's "Honor!" festival at Carnegie, Charles Dutoit led the Philadelphia Orchestra in an impressive concert dedicated to Anderson's memory. The program consisted of Darius Milhaud's "La Création du Monde," the first great classical takeoff on jazz; "Lilacs," a tersely eloquent Whitman song cycle by the African-American composer George Walker; Mahler's "Lieder Eines Fahrenden Gesellen," which Anderson sang at Carnegie in 1946; and Dvořák's "New World" Symphony, in which intimations of spirituals can be heard. Two gifted black singers, Russell Thomas and Eric Owens, performed the Walker and Mahler songs. There weren't many other African-Americans in the building that night. A far more diverse crowd turned up when Norman headlined a performance of excerpts from Duke Ellington's "Sacred Concerts," at the Cathedral of St. John the Divine. For many black listeners, "classical music" means Ellington, Armstrong, and Sarah Vaughan; the European kind doesn't enter the picture.

To a great extent, this racial divide stems directly from racial prejudice. Racism hardly disappeared from classical institutions after Anderson reached the zenith of her fame. Nina Simone, for one, aspired to become a concert pianist, but when she failed to win a place at the Curtis Institute of Music—for what she surmised were racial reasons—she turned instead to playing and singing in clubs. In her autobiography, "I Put a Spell on You," she wrote, "My music was dedicated to a purpose more important than classical music's pursuit of excellence; it was dedicated to the fight for freedom and the historical destiny of my people." Miles Davis used harsher language when he explained why he gave up studying trumpet at Juilliard: "No white symphony orchestra was going to hire a little black motherfucker like me." He went on to mock a teacher who stated that "the reason black people played the blues was because they were poor and had to pick cotton." Davis, the son of a successful dentist, lost confidence in the school soon afterward.

Yet there is another, less baleful explanation for the absence of African-Americans from classical music: beginning with jazz, black musicians invented their own forms of high art. The talent that might have dominated instrumental music and contemporary composition migrated elsewhere. Perhaps Simone would have made a fine concert pianist, and Davis surely would have been a sensational first trumpeter in a major orchestra, but it's difficult to imagine that they would have found as much creative fulfillment along those paths. Instead, they used their classical training to add new dimensions to jazz and pop. Davis, an admirer of Stockhausen, made a point of criticizing the "ghetto mentality" that prevented some black musicians from investigating classical music. Several of Simone's songs are shot through with Bachian figuration, and her terrifying version of "Strange Fruit" rests on Baroque harmonies of lament.

Sadly, African-American classical musicians today seem almost as lonely as ever. They are accustomed to being viewed as walking paradoxes. The irony is that classical music has become a far more heterogeneous culture than it was when Anderson sang on the Mall. The most talked-about conductor of the moment is Gustavo Dudamel; the superstar pianist is Lang Lang; the most famous of all classical musicians is Yo-Yo Ma. (When people talk about the "whiteness" of this world, they tend to count Asians as white.) No longer a European patrimony, classical music is a polyglot business with a global audience. Why does it still somehow seem inherently unlikely that a black person should compose an opera for the

Met, or become the music director of the Philadelphia Orchestra? Unlikelier things have happened, such as the election of a half-Kansan, half-Kenyan as President of the United States.

Anderson died in 1993, at the age of ninety-six. The obituaries singled out the Lincoln Memorial concert as the supreme moment of her career, but her autobiography gives the impression that other experiences gave her a deeper satisfaction. For Anderson, Easter Sunday, 1939, may have been an ambiguous triumph—marking a great moment in civil-rights history but, on a private level, intruding on her dream of a purely musical life. An artist became a symbol. Her happiest memories, one gathers, were of those international tours in the thirties, when the European critics declared her a singer to watch, and the Finns went wild, and Toscanini blubbered his praise, and she became nothing less—and nothing more—than one of the great voices of her time.

THE COLOSSUS

STANLEY CROUCH

May 9, 2005

Not long ago, the jazz drummer Victor Lewis was hanging out at the Village Vanguard, and declared that he had finally decided what he wanted to be when he became an old man: Sonny Rollins. Lewis had recently performed with Rollins in Antibes. "Do you know that man stood up there and gave a three-and-a-half-hour concert and did most of the playing?" Lewis said. "He wasn't coasting or floating, either. He was deep in it, playing his ass off. That's surreal. Seventy-three years old, out in the hot sun, blowing a saxophone for that long—who can believe that?"

Rollins works at extremes. He is either astounding or barely all right. He hates clichés and signature phrases—"licks"—and refuses to play them. Consequently, for him there are no highly polished professional performances. When he's on, which is seven or eight times out of ten, Rollins—known as "the saxophone colossus"—seems immense, summoning the entire history of jazz, capable of blowing a hole through a wall. On his off nights, though, he can seem no more than another guy with a saxophone and a band, creeping through a gig. Those who hear him on such nights come away convinced that the Sonny Rollins of legend is long gone.

I've heard Rollins play many times during the past several years, and I've seen many versions of him. In an amphitheatre in Washington, D.C., a few summers ago, he was in good form, teasing the audience by embellishing familiar songs with new, invented melodies and fast themes. For an encore, he played "I'll Be Seeing You," a ballad turned swinger, and sent the notes soaring out over the crowd. Later, at the New Jersey Performing Arts Center, in Newark, he pulled out a song that very few in the audience would know, "Let's Start the New Year Right," which was played by Louis Armstrong, one of Rollins's musical heroes. ("He found the Rosetta stone. He could translate everything," Rollins has said of Armstrong. "He could find the good in the worst material.") Rollins's calypso "Global Warming" was shrieking and rhythmic; the low notes hit with a thud. He played his horn almost to the point of hyperventilating. On the song "Why Was I Born?," he came up with a distinct motive for each eight-bar section—a remarkable expression of the power of his idiom. Rollins was heard over the hill that night.

But when Rollins is faced with a young crowd he often resorts to banal calypso tunes, playing one after another. This was the case at the House of Blues in New Orleans one night a few years ago, when I went to hear him with a writer and pianist friend. My friend was so disgusted that he vowed never to take another chance on seeing Rollins live. "Sonny gets insecure in front of young people and doesn't have the confidence to depend on his swing," a musician who used to play regularly with Rollins told me. "He knows the kids can hear that calypso beat, and he gives it to them."

Since 1980, Rollins has made more than a dozen records in the studio, but unlike many of his fellow-titans on the tenor saxophone—Coleman Hawkins, Lester Young, John Coltrane—he has realized his talent almost exclusively on the bandstand. His finest recordings in the past twenty-five years have been live ones, legal and bootlegged. Running through a repertoire of Tin Pan Alley songs, jazz standards, originals, and festive calypsos—something old, something new—Rollins seems to have an endless catalogue on which to draw. If jazz improvisation is a kind of democratic expression, then Rollins may well be our greatest purveyor of utopian feeling.

FOR MORE THAN THIRTY YEARS, ROLLINS HAS LIVED IN A MODEST two-story house in Germantown, New York, a couple of hours north of Manhattan. (He kept an apartment in Tribeca, near the World Trade Center, but gave it up after September 11th. Television audiences saw Rollins board the evacuation bus wearing a surgical mask and carrying his saxophone.) The Germantown property includes a large converted stable that is used as a garage. There is a swimming pool in the back and, beyond it, a small house where Rollins writes and practices music for many hours a day. In the studio, there are pictures of Rollins on bandstands around the world; a Japanese ceramic version of him wearing Oriental robes and blowing a horn; stacks of music; an electric keyboard; and various trophies and mementos.

Rollins lives alone; Lucille, his wife of nearly forty years, died in November. (They had no children.) The bucolic simplicity of the place and the soft tones in which Rollins tends to express himself are at odds with the muscularity of his music. "I like the quiet, and I prefer being left alone," Rollins said when I went to visit him last spring. "Up here, I can choose contact with the world when I want it. That kind of freedom is a blessing, and I don't take it lightly."

Unlike Armstrong or Dizzy Gillespie, Rollins has no talent for stagecraft or show. He doesn't tell jokes onstage; he barely even smiles. He conveys his sense of humor subtly, through his music, quoting Billy Strayhorn's "Rain Check" when caught performing in a drizzle, or arriving late and walking through an irritated audience playing "Will You Still Be Mine?" And yet he has a gift for unexpected display. He shaved his head in the sixties, when a hairless dome was cause for comment, and changed his style constantly, alternating beautiful suits with ethnic robes, T-shirts, floppy purple hats, and tennis shoes. In the eighties, he dyed his hair and beard shoe-polish black. Nowadays, he has come to himself: he wears a silver-white beard and mustache, and the effect is handsome and majestic.

The youngest child of hardworking Caribbean parents, Rollins was born in Harlem on September 7, 1930. His parents were from the Virgin Islands. His father, a Navy man, was often away at sea. He had an older brother, Valdemar, and an older sister named Gloria. Rollins's given name was Walter Theodore, but, he told me, "they started to call me Sonny because I was the baby, the youngest."

When Rollins was a boy, Harlem suffered—as parts of it still do—from terrible poverty. Yet there was an intellectual and artistic renaissance. Ralph Ellison described Harlem in the nineteen-thirties as "an outpost of American optimism" and "our own homegrown version of Paris." Rollins recalls the period as a happy time. "I remember us kids playing in the lobbies of the old theatres," he said. "I remember all that wonderful music that came out of Abyssinian Baptist Church and Mother Zion. There was a great feeling then. It was a very warm thing." In 1939, the Rollins family moved to 371 Edgecomb Avenue, between 150th and 155th Streets. This was Sugar Hill, an élite neighborhood. There, Rollins often saw three very striking men: W. E. B. DuBois; Thurgood Marshall; and Walter White, the executive secretary of the N.A.A.C.P., a Negro whose light skin allowed him to go on daring undercover missions among violent Southern white racists.

But it was Coleman Hawkins, the father of the jazz tenor saxophone, who most impressed him. Around the time the family moved to Sugar Hill, Hawkins's version of "Body and Soul" was on jukeboxes across the country. "When I was a kid, even though I didn't really know what it was, you could hear Coleman playing that song all over Harlem," Rollins said. "It was coming out of all these windows like it was sort of a theme song." To the consternation of his family, who were conservative and practical-minded, he fell in love with the saxophone and decided to become a musician. Only his mother supported his ambition, and it was she who bought him his first horn, an alto saxophone, when he was nine.

Living on the Hill gave Rollins a chance to get close to the musicians he revered. "I used to see all of these great musicians," Rollins said. "There was Coleman Hawkins, and his Cadillac and those wonderful suits he wore. Just standing on the corner, I could see Duke Ellington, Andy Kirk, Don Redman, Benny Carter, Sid Catlett, Jimmy Crawford, Charlie Shavers, Al Hall, Denzil Best, and all of these kinds of men. Those guys commanded respect in the way they carried themselves. You knew something was very true when you saw Coleman Hawkins or any of those people. They were not pretending. When they went up on the bandstand, they proved that they were just what you thought they were. You weren't dreaming. It was all real. You couldn't be more inspired."

Though the dictates of show business meant that Negro musicians had to tolerate minstrelsy and all the other commonplace denigrations, most jazz musicians of the era formed an avant-garde of suave, well-spoken men in lovely suits and ties, with their shoes shining and their pomaded hair glittering under the lights, artists ranging in color from bone and beige to brown and black. Their very sophistication was a form of rebellion: these musicians made a liar of every bigot who sought to limit what black people could and could not do, could and could not feel.

Having switched to tenor saxophone in the early forties, Rollins then led a band with some other young men from the Hill: the alto saxophonist Jackie McLean, the drummer Art Taylor, and the pianist Kenny Drew. They played "cocktail sips" in the early evening for working people and the numbers runners who moved through the crowd. "Those gigs could be something else, man," Rollins said. "Those weren't always peaceful people out to have a good time. They could get ugly. At the dances particularly, it could get very rough. You had to be vigilant every second, because fights could break out and you would have to protect yourself and your horn." What he observed in those situations—the frailty of peace and calm, as well as the ballroom ambience of slow, close dancing and whispered courtship—has never left his ballad playing.

Rollins intently studied the tenor players: Ben Webster, of Kansas City; Don Byas, of Muskogee, Oklahoma; and Lester Young, of Woodville, Mississippi, and New Orleans. "That was the best ear training," he told me. "Natural musicians have to be able to do that, to cop stuff quickly by ear. That's what I am, an intuitive player. I didn't go to school to learn what I do. I spent a lot of time just practicing my horn. So I think I was playing a lot of stuff before I knew what it was. I was in the middle of that golden period of popular songs and movie music, and I retained all of that stuff. I know most of those songs, and most of the lyrics. The story begins with the melody; you keep the story going by using the melody the way you hear it as something to improvise on. In reality, it should all be connected—the melody, the chords, the rhythm. It should all turn out to be one complete thing."

Rollins also spent a lot of time at the Apollo Theatre, in Harlem. "You could get it all at the Apollo, man, all of it," he said. "If you wanted to hear Frank Sinatra, you had to go downtown, but everything else—I'm talking about giants like Billy Eckstine, Billie Holiday, and Sarah Vaughan—was at the Apollo. There would be two movies, maybe a Western and a jungle movie, or a comedy and a detective or gangster picture. There would be comedians, jugglers, dancers, and Duke Ellington, Count Basie, and every kind of band. You would have experienced all of these styles and emotions by the end of the shows." Even then, Rollins's playing was imbued with a vast array of musical Americana.

Rollins didn't become aware of the alto saxophonist Charlie (Bird) Parker until he bought a recording in the mid-forties that featured Don Byas playing "How High the Moon" on one side and Parker sailing through "Koko" on the other. Soon, he was hearing Parker at the Apollo, too. Parker was considered the most important musician in the emerging school of bebop, which demanded a new level of velocity technique, melody, and harmony, and a mastery of slippery triplet rhythms. He also brought with him the troubles of heroin. Just as musicians a generation earlier had smoked reefers when they found out that Louis Armstrong liked the stuff, so, now, did the members of the bebop movement follow Parker's self-destructive path. The result was disastrous, with many musicians dying young. Rollins said that he and his musical buddies from Sugar Hill foolishly thought that taking heroin "would make us play better."

By the end of the nineteen-forties, Rollins had an addiction he couldn't shake. "Sonny was a real junkie," one musician recalls. "He was a bandit, and he even looked like one. His hair was gassed up and looked real greasy. He burned just about everybody he came in contact with. That heroin had him so desperate that if he got his hands on your instrument it would end up in the pawn shop." Rollins became, as he himself put it, "persona non grata among my family." He went on, "It made me mad then, but I can understand, because I did a lot of bad things. Always stealing, always lying, always trying to get the money for those drugs. I was lost out there, like all of us were, and the only person who would forgive me and still believe in me was my mother. She never turned her back on me. I was her baby son, no matter what." For much of 1951, Rollins was in prison for attempted robbery. "When I was out there on Rikers Island, imprisoned among those criminals, I was disgusted with myself, when I wasn't thinking about the time I was losing not practicing my horn," he told me.

But even as Rollins struggled, he began to emerge as an artist. Jackie McLean told me, "I remember when Sonny came back from Rikers Island and he was standing in the door listening to one of the gigs I was holding down for him while he was gone. He asked if he could play my horn, the alto, and I handed it over. People missed that Sonny Rollins on *alto*. Sonny got up there and played 'There Will Never Be Another You.' He spat out so much music—so *much* music—that when he finished I didn't want to *touch* that horn. It was on *fire*."

In December of 1951, Rollins made a surprisingly mature recording, "Time on My Hands." His tone is big and sensual, as delicate as it is forceful. Already, at twenty-one, he had the ability to express as much tenderness as strength, melding the romantic ease of Lester Young, the robust power of Coleman Hawkins, and the lyricism of Charlie Parker. In pacing, tone, feeling, and melodic development, "Time on My Hands" is Rollins's first great piece. Loren Schoenberg, a jazz musician and scholar, says of the performance, "Compared to the other young saxophone players recording during that period—Stan Getz, Wardell Gray, Sonny Stitt, Zoot Sims, Gene Ammons—Rollins is accessing everything that had happened to the tenor saxophone. He was not just approaching the surface of the sound and the technique but the emotional depth and breadth. What is most shocking about it is that all of these other men were several years older. But Rollins sounds more mature than any of them sounded at that time."

Out of Rollins's attentiveness to his musical forebears had come a heightened sensitivity to melody, harmony, rhythm, and timbre, the shading that gives a note its emotional texture. "Those kinds of hearing are exactly the elements that make jazz so great," Gunther Schuller, the conductor and composer, says. "In the arena of art, they make the idea of schizophrenia—or multiphrenia, perhaps—not a problem but a profoundly positive thing. One is splitting up the brain to achieve all of these tasks in the interest of creative order, not any kind of fumbling disarray.

"These are the things that are beyond even most concert musicians, because, unlike Sonny Rollins and Ben Webster and those kinds of musicians, the classical musician—no matter how great—is, on the one hand, reading music or playing it from memory. On the other, he is too closely connected to what he was told about how to play by his most influential teachers. This makes it veritably impossible for him even to encounter, much less master, that kind of personal hearing knowledge from within his own being. Sonny

Rollins discovered those things for himself, as all jazz musicians must, and what he has done with those discoveries makes him one of the greatest musicians of any serious music, no matter what name we give it, and no matter what the era or century in which it was made."

In the mid-fifties, after recording classic numbers with a variety of musicians, including Miles Davis, Thelonious Monk, and the members of the Modern Jazz Quartet, Rollins checked into a rehab program in Lexington, Kentucky, where he kicked his heroin habit. From there, he went to Chicago, where he began playing with the trumpeter Clifford Brown and the drummer Max Roach. Rollins had a special affection for Brown. "Clifford was pure," he said. "He didn't do any of the things the others of us got messed up in. He was a witty guy, very quick. He could play a strong game of chess." Brown's music reflected his acuity. "His command of his horn was intimidating," Rollins said. "He had an angelic sound. Other musicians were free to ask him technical questions and he would tell them. He didn't try to mislead you and stunt your growth like some of the competitive guys out there. Being around him lifted me up completely. Near the end, we got that unified sound you almost never hear—there was no saxophone, there was no trumpet." In Chicago, Rollins met Lucille Pearson at one of his performances. Lucille was white, and when, in 1971, she took over Rollins's business affairs, he noticed that she got more respect than he ever did.

In 1956, Brown died, at the age of twenty-five, in an automobile accident on the Pennsylvania Turnpike. He and the band's pianist, Richie Powell, who also died, were on their way to Chicago for a gig. Roach and Rollins were waiting for them there in a hotel when they got the news. "When I told Sonny what had happened, he just turned around and went back to his room," Roach said. "You could hear that tenor saxophone playing all night."

Shortly thereafter, Rollins and Lucille moved back to New York, and he recorded "Saxophone Colossus." One of the great small-group recordings, it showcased Rollins's improvisational powers. In 1957, he made the equally extraordinary "Way Out West," his first recording using only bass and drums. On the album cover, Rollins wears the high-camp garb of a gunslinger: a ten-gallon hat and a holster. The following year, he recorded his most adventurous composition, "Freedom Suite," a twenty-minute trio piece for tenor, bass, and drums, and revealed his skill as an arranger, giving the piece four distinct themes. Part of its excitement stems from the interplay between Rollins and Roach, which clearly anticipates the avant-garde elasticity of the sixties.

Rollins, an activist before "protest music" became common fare in jazz, wrote a manifesto to accompany the album: "America is deeply rooted in Negro culture: its colloquialisms, its humor, its music. How ironic that the Negro, who more than any other people can claim America's culture as his own, is being persecuted and repressed; that the Negro, who has exemplified the humanities in his very existence, is being rewarded with inhumanity." It is hard to find the precise political meaning of the music itself, but it is clearly less playful than his earlier recordings. Gone are the witty quotations from other tunes and the unexpected shifts of color that Rollins had so often inserted into his playing. The music has a stoic quality, a heroic certitude, and a grand lyricism without being stiff or cold or pretentious. It is a timeless achievement.

JUST WHEN ROLLINS WAS BECOMING ONE OF THE LEADING FIGURES IN jazz, a new force emerged, in the form of John Coltrane, a tenor player from Philadelphia by way of North Carolina. Coltrane, who also struggled with drugs, was then in the process of leaving the Miles Davis Quintet. After playing with Monk at New York's Five Spot in 1957, Coltrane began to ascend very quickly, startling the jazz world with his innovative harmonic schemes and the complex originality of his phrasing. Before long, people were saying that Rollins had been left behind; he felt the slight profoundly.

"Sonny never found a way to discover how great he really was, and he never recovered from the disapproval of the jazz community when Coltrane was coming up," Branford Marsalis told me. "It's a shame that he never understood that they didn't have the capacity to understand how great he was."

In 1959, Rollins decided to stop performing for a few years, and Lucille helped support him with a secretarial job in the physics department at New York University. Rollins often practiced his horn on the Williamsburg Bridge, pushing himself to play loud enough to compete with the industrial noise of the city. Though he was working earnestly on his music, it was hard to avoid the impression that he had been eclipsed by Coltrane. "You know what happened to Sonny Rollins?" went a joke that circulated in the jazz world at the time. "A 'Trane ran over him."

Even now, Rollins resents that suggestion. "I left the scene to work on some things because I was getting all of this press and I was near the top in the polls, but I wasn't satisfying myself and I didn't feel like I was satisfying the public," he said. "I wanted to work on my horn, I wanted to study more harmony, I wanted to better myself, and I wanted to get out of the environment of all that smoke and alcohol and drugs. In order to avoid disturbing anyone, I went up on the Williamsburg Bridge and practiced."

"What he was playing at the time was so powerful you couldn't believe it," Freddie Hubbard, the great trumpeter, told me. "Other saxophone players were scared of him. He was feared. I played with him and I played with Coltrane, and Sonny was definitely the strongest. He could play so fast you couldn't pat your foot, and then he could double that. Plus, he could keep that big sound going at that tempo, which is impossible. And when he was going at those notes like a tornado, or something like that, each one was right. He wasn't hotfooting along and missing any of those damn chords.

"The difference between him and Coltrane was that Coltrane worked his harmony out very scientifically. He studied Nicolas

Slonimsky's 'Thesaurus of Scales and Melodic Patterns.' Sonny was different. Spontaneous. There was no fear in him—not of the saxophone, not of the music. He was like Bird, because he wasn't thinking about practicing intervals and scales and all that stuff, like Coltrane. All he needed was a song and he could hear the freedom of the music through his own personality."

Though Rollins and Coltrane were considered rivals by the music community, they admired each other. Hubbard said, "Oh, man, Coltrane loved Sonny. And Sonny loved Coltrane. They didn't talk too much about each other, but whatever they said was always complimentary. But, when I would practice with one of them and then go practice with the other one, they both wanted to know what the other was doing. Both of them were fired up about music, too, because they had both been drug addicts and were trying to make up for the time they lost out in the streets chasing that heroin."

Rollins and Coltrane also had an intellectual kinship, based on shared spiritual concerns. "During the time that I was on the bridge," Rollins recalled, "Coltrane and I were both reading a lot of books about spiritual things—Buddhism, Sufism, and I was into Rosicrucianism. And we talked about music reflecting those disciplines. We were optimistic about things. Coltrane and I would talk about changing the world through music. We thought we might get so good that our music would influence everything around us. I think he stuck to that path, but sometimes I became disconsolate about whether music could change the world. I thought about all the music that Louis Armstrong, Billie Holiday, and Art Tatum and all these people played, and how it hadn't had any effect. But now I know that you can uplift people with your music. They can feel bad, and, if you play something, they might feel better. I have to satisfy myself with that kind of contribution."

WHEN ROLLINS RETURNED TO THE STAGE, IN LATE 1961, FRONTING A band that featured the guitarist Jim Hall, the jazz scene had fractured. Some critics and musicians felt that they were in the midst of a new bebop revolution; others felt that jazz, rather than expanding, was being overthrown in favor of self-indulgence and chaos. Ornette Coleman, a composer and alto saxophonist from Fort Worth, Texas, was considered the most outrageous jazz innovator. Coleman played "free" jazz, which used neither chords nor set tempos. His music, with its floating melodies, idiosyncratic phrasing, and echoes of the blues, was exalted as being primitively profound; it was also dismissed as inept. Then, there was Coltrane's furnace-blast modality. He stacked scales and used few chords, and his music was driven by the dense triplet complexities of the drummer Elvin Jones. Coltrane performed forty-minute solos, and sometimes so exhausted himself that he fell to his knees on the bandstand, still playing.

In contrast to Coleman and Coltrane, Rollins—who now kept his hair close-cropped, and wore tailored suits and tuxedos—was seen as a standard-bearer of convention, and perhaps as the only one who could save jazz. He was hardly comfortable in this role. "I didn't feel like I was there to save anything—I was just ready to play," Rollins said. "The Bridge," his first recording after returning to professional life, documents a luminous moment when he used superior arrangements, including tempo and metric modulations, saxophone and guitar riffs, and group phrasing that resembled conversation. He hadn't lost his sense of adventure, but it seemed impossible for him to fake the shrieks and screams that characterized the tumultuous avant-garde. He obviously still believed in the many powers of the musical notes, which put him at odds with someone like the late Albert Ayler, a screeching saxophonist who influenced Coltrane. "It's not about notes anymore," Ayler once said. "It's about feelings."

But then Rollins began playing standard songs and his own originals from the nineteen-fifties in the style of Ornette Coleman. "I figured if that kind of playing was valid you could do it on any kind of material, just like every other style," he said. "You didn't need special material. If the conception was valid, the playing should be special enough." Rollins hired two of Coleman's former sidemen, the trumpeter Don Cherry and the drummer Billy Higgins. The music that resulted—the RCA Victor recordings (particularly "Our Man in Jazz"), a series of European bootlegs, and an especially stunning appearance on Italian television—seemed even more daring than what either Coltrane or Coleman was up to at the time. The music, based on split-second shifts in direction, mutated rapidly, sometimes turning a song into a suite, as with "Oleo." Rollins told a European interviewer at the time, "I think I sound like Ornette now." But the band was short-lived. Cherry and Higgins, both of whom were drug addicts, tended to arrive at gigs high. Rollins, who was trying to stay clean, fired them and hired the pianist Paul Bley, who had brought Coleman's approach to the keyboard.

Rollins, meanwhile, was becoming more and more eccentric. Still known as a sharp dresser, in 1963 he started wearing a Mohawk. "The Mohawk, to me, signified a form of social rebellion and it was a nod to the Native American," he said. "I was listening to some Native American music and reading some Native American cultural stuff, and I felt very close to the aboriginal feeling. It made me feel more powerful." Most people thought that the Mohawk made Rollins look both ridiculous and dangerous. A sizable man to begin with, he took up bodybuilding and yoga, grew a thick black mustache, and came to resemble an ominous bouncer. There was a new strangeness to his stage persona as well. At the Five Spot, in 1964, when he wasn't playing to the walls or walking among the tables as he performed, he might come onstage in a cowboy hat and a Lone Ranger mask, with cap pistols strapped on. "Maybe my memories of shows at the Apollo had gotten the best of me," Rollins said sheepishly.

While recording for RCA Victor, Rollins produced a number of successful pieces and masterly performances that influenced younger players, such as Pharoah Sanders and Archie Shepp. To some, this creative ingenuity seemed forced. One person who was involved with the RCA recordings has said, "It was almost a tragic period for him. Sonny was really at sea. He didn't know what to do, which way to go. Sonny was absolutely confused by the press, the music community, and everything else. He seemed afraid of being considered old-fashioned. I think the attention that Coltrane was getting and the many who were starting to imitate him made Sonny feel left out, not at the center of things. It was very sad, this tremendous talent turning in circles as he lost more and more confidence. He could do anything he wanted; it was just that he didn't know what to do."

Rollins now admits, "I don't think that Coltrane was thinking about competing with me or had any bad feeling toward me, but I did start to resent him at one point and I feel very embarrassed by that now. When I was up on the bridge and he used to come by my place and see me, we were together. In fact, if I was uptight for money I could get a loan from him, or from Monk, and know that it would never end up in the gossip of the jazz world about how bad off Sonny was. They were real friends. But when I came down from the bridge I think I let his success and the attention that he was receiving get to me. It should never be like that. Never."

By the summer of 1965, Rollins had recovered from his insecurities enough to make the excellent "On Impulse!" Ray Bryant, who played piano on the album, says that the title was perfect, because Rollins just came into the studio and began playing. "He might say a title and be gone!" Every track is strong. Rollins handles his instrument with the authority that James Joyce attributed to the superior artist, who works with the ease of a god paring his nails. Early in 1966, he recorded the score for the film "Alfie," another triumph. The trumpeter Nicholas Payton says of "Alfie," "Except for Monk, I don't know if anybody else could play with that architecture, except that Sonny was doing it all his own way, which made it an innovation. The title track is actually like a movie being made right in front of you, from start to end, with major characters and minor characters functioning inside a serious plot that takes them here and there, some disappearing and popping up later in a dramatic way. Harmonically, he knew how to play a phrase that never resolves, that hints at something that is never played, but he won't finish the phrase. He creates more and more suspense by playing a series of these phrases, then he'll drop that bomb that brings it all together, that resolves everything. Boom. If you could do something like that and not be noticed, I can understand why some people say Sonny was acting crazy during that period."

Like Louis Armstrong, who always claimed to be nostalgic for the way things were before he became famous, Rollins didn't particularly enjoy the responsibilities of leadership or notoriety. "Well, I'll tell you, I never really liked being a bandleader, because if things didn't sound good all the disappointment fell on me," he said. "At the same time, I couldn't be the real Sonny unless I was leading the band. So it was a riddle that I couldn't solve, and I don't think that I solved it for a long time. Now, even though I still don't really like it, they have my name up there and I have to show up and call the tunes and lead the musicians I've hired to play with me."

In 1969, Rollins retreated again and did not return to the studio or the bandstand until 1971. "I was looking for something spiritual, something that would make sense out of the mess I felt that I was in," he said. "I hated music at the time, because there didn't seem to be enough love between the musicians, not the kind I grew up with. I was sick of the whole thing. The clubs, the travelling—everything meant nothing to me at that time. I went to India, and had no idea whether I would ever play the saxophone professionally again."

By the time Rollins reappeared, things had begun to change once more. Imitating Miles Davis, certain major jazz musicians, such as Freddie Hubbard, Herbie Hancock, and Wayne Shorter, began to embrace rock, or submit to it, or sell out entirely. To the annoyance of many of his fans, Rollins began using electric bass and electric keyboards, while abruptly transforming himself into a rhythm-and-blues player. His recordings were dismal, and he seemed incapable of making a good one. To this day, he hasn't recorded anything that approaches "Saxophone Colossus," "Way Out West," "Freedom Suite," "The Bridge," "On Impulse!," or "Alfie." The late Joe Henderson, whose style was firmly based in the Rollins mode of the early sixties, made recordings in the eighties and nineties that were so much better than his mentor's that uninformed listeners might rank him above Rollins. The formidable jazz drummer Al Foster, who worked with both of them, told me, "Joe always sounded great, but when I was going back and forth between his band and Sonny's I realized that Joe, who could outplay almost everybody, wasn't even close to Sonny. There was no contest. Joe was a master; Sonny is *the* master. But you have to hear him in person to know that."

UNTIL RECENTLY, IT APPEARED THAT ROLLINS WAS DESTINED TO BECOME a legend whose best work in the last phase of his career would probably go undocumented. Thankfully, this is not to be. Not long ago, I went to Portland, Maine, to see Carl Smith, a collector in his sixties who already has more than three hundred bootleg performances of Rollins—seemingly every session, radio broadcast, night-club appearance, and concert recorded from 1949 to the present. He is trying to persuade Rollins's label, Milestone Records, to put out the best of them, at no profit to himself. He wants the world to enjoy what he has enjoyed, and he believes that those recordings, properly selected and edited, would not only create a major shift in Rollins's stature but also rejuvenate jazz by showing what a great living improviser can truly do. I agree. The first such album, "Without a Song (The 9/11 Concert)," recorded at a performance in Boston on September 15, 2001, is due out in August.

Sitting in Smith's neat apartment—it has a harbor view—and

listening to performance after performance, I came to realize that Rollins is like all truly great players: no matter how well you think they can play, they always exceed your expectations. Smith said that during the bewildering period of the mid-seventies, Rollins "never matched the classics of the fifties." He went on, "The records show that. He seemed to have lost it. Then, in performance at least, he rediscovered himself around 1978. He stood up again, and began to build back up to a kind of ecstatic playing that achieved miraculous heights in the eighties and has sustained itself to this very day."

Over and over, decade after decade, from the late seventies through the eighties and the nineties, there he is, Sonny Rollins, the saxophone colossus, playing somewhere in the world, some afternoon or some eight o'clock somewhere, pursuing the combination of emotion, memory, thought, and aesthetic design with a command that allows him to achieve spontaneous grandiloquence. With its brass body, its pearl-button keys, its mouthpiece, and its cane reed, that horn becomes the vessel for the epic of Rollins's talent and the undimmed power and lore of his jazz ancestors.

"We never really know too much, not really," Rollins told me. "We need to be humble about that. But we do get to know certain things, and we have to do the best with them. Right now, I know what I got from Coleman Hawkins, from Ben Webster, from Dexter Gordon, from Don Byas, from Charlie Parker, and all the other guys who gave their lives to this music. I know that without a doubt. From childhood, I've known this. All the way from back then, when it was coming out of the windows, when it was on the stage at the Apollo, when it was on the new records coming out. So now, after all these years, it's pretty clear to me, finally. All I want to do is stand up for them, and for the music, and for what they inspired in me. I'm going to play as long as I can. I want to do that as long as I can pick up that horn and represent this music with honor. That's all it's about, as far as I can see. I don't know anything else, but I know that."

AMERICAN UNTOUCHABLE

EMILY NUSSBAUM

December 7, 2015

Racial diversity on television is in a state of rapid acceleration. In 2012, when "Scandal" débuted, it was the first network drama to feature a black female lead in thirty-eight years—a shameful milestone. Just three years later, black and brown ensembles have begun proliferating, from "Black-ish" to "Jane the Virgin," "American Crime" to "Empire." There has been a remarkable migration of black actresses from movies to TV, a deluge of new talent on shows like Netflix's "Orange Is the New Black," and most strikingly, an emerging class of showrunners of color, on both cable and network: Aziz Ansari and Mindy Kaling, Shonda Rhimes and Kenya Barris, Lee Daniels and Larry Wilmore, Nahnatchka Khan and John Ridley, Dee Rees and Mara Brock Akil.

None of this means that white men don't still run Hollywood, of course: The recent season of "Project Greenlight," on HBO, made it clear how resistant to race talk Hollywood can be, a stifling culture of bros bonding with mirror versions of themselves. And yet there's something in the air, along with a new bluntness about the stakes. When Viola Davis won an Emmy for Best Actress, for ABC's "How to Get Away with Murder," she quoted Harriet Tubman and declared, "The only thing that separates women of color from anyone else is opportunity. You can't win an Emmy for roles that are simply not there."

This is an encouraging development—certainly, it's long overdue. And yet for observers inside the industry, there's also a built-in wariness, because this has all happened before, only to recede, each time: in the early fifties, when television seemed like it might offer an open door; in the seventies, the era of "Roots" and Norman Lear; and again in the early nineties, post-Cosby, when black sitcoms thrived. One person understood this maddening phenomenon more than most: P. Jay Sidney, an African-American actor who built a four-decade career in television, all the while protesting network racism, in what Donald Bogle's book "Primetime Blues" recounts as a "one-man crusade to get African-Americans fair representation in television programs *and* commercials."

Sidney is a footnote in history books, while other activists of his era are heroes. But he was there when the medium began, appearing on TV more than any other black dramatic actor of the time. Even as his résumé grew, Sidney picketed, he wrote letters, he advocated boycotts, he taped interactions with executives, lobbying tirelessly against TV's de-facto segregation. In 1962, he testified before the House of Representatives. Nothing made much headway; he grew disgusted and disaffected. By the time Sidney died, in Brooklyn, in 1996, he had largely been forgotten, a proud loner who never got to see his vision become reality. "People today benefit from things that were sacrificed years ago," his ex-wife Carol Foster Sidney, who is now eighty-seven, told me. "And they haven't a clue."

Sidney was born Sidney Parhm, Jr., in 1915 in Norfolk, Virginia, and grew up in poverty, in an era of public lynchings and Jim Crow. His mother died when he was a child; his father moved the family to New York, then died when his son was fifteen. According to a 1955 profile, titled "Get P. Jay Sidney for the Part," he was a "difficult" child who landed in foster care but excelled academically—he graduated from high school at fifteen, then went to City College for two years, dropping out to enter the theatre. A lifelong autodidact, he is described by those who knew him as a guarded, sardonic figure, eternally testing those around him against an intellectual ideal. But even during the Depression he got jobs: he was in Lena Horne's first stage play, in 1934; in the forties, he appeared in "Carmen Jones" and "Othello." In a photograph taken at a campaign event for Franklin D. Roosevelt, Sidney is a dapper bohemian with a clipped beard. He also built a radio career, producing a series called "Experimental Theatre of the Air," which, in a radical move, cast voices without regard to racial categories. Sidney collected his press clippings in a binder, which is saved at the New York Public Library's Schomburg Center.

As the country came out of the Depression, and the civil-rights movement began, progress for black actors finally seemed to be on the horizon. Television, in the forties, was a low-status but experimental medium, with an anything-goes openness, suggesting tantalizing opportunities for innovators. That possibility blinked out. In a newspaper article from the mid-fifties, headlined "TV'S NEW POLICY FOR NEGROES," Sidney is depicted as the "single exception" to the exclusion of black dramatic actors. In TV's infancy, the article laments, "The video floodgates were expected to be thrown open to experienced Negro actors. It never happened."

"We took it for granted that we would be the last hired if hired at all and the first fired," Ossie Davis recalled, in "The Box," Jeff Kisseloff's oral history of television. "And that we would wind up doing the same stereotypical crap that we did on Broadway." "Amos and Andy" was typical fare. There was some pushback from the black community: In the late fifties, Davis participated in a TV boycott in Harlem, in which black viewers turned off their sets one Saturday night. Sidney went farther than that, and while his rabble-rousing didn't especially improve his own career prospects, it had a knock-on effect on Davis's: "He used to walk around with a sign, accusing the broadcast industry of discriminating against black folks. As a response to P. Jay's accusations, CBS didn't give him a job, but they gave me one."

From 1951 on, Sidney made a living on TV, getting a few notable roles, including Cato, Hercules Mulligan's slave and fellow-spy, in "The Plot to Kidnap General Washington," in 1952. For two years, he appeared as one of two African-American soldiers on "The Phil Silvers Show"—a casting move protested by Southern stations. (The writers ignored them.) Over time, he amassed roles on more than a hundred and seventy shows, as well as a lucrative sideline in voice-over work and advertisements, playing the role of Waxin Jackson for Ajax. But the majority of his parts were walk-ons: doormen, porters, waiters. "I had a whole goddamned career of 'Yassuh, can I git ya another drink, sir?,'" he told Kisseloff. "But I did what was available. I did not mix feelings with the fact that I needed money to live."

With each setback, Sidney grew more frustrated, according to Foster Sidney, who married Sidney in 1954. Foster Sidney was the daughter of a dentist, educated at Howard University, a member of the Washington, D.C., African-American élite. She had persuaded her family to let her move to New York to be a French translator but dreamed of being an actress. Foster Sidney recalls, "He knew I had these aspirations, but he said, 'One actor in the family.' I, timid little thing, said, 'Yes, dear.'" Their marriage was contentious, with Sidney resenting Foster Sidney's "bourgeois" background; they separated, and had no children, but did not divorce until 1977. (In later years, Foster Sidney returned to acting, a period she calls "ten years in Heaven.")

Nonetheless, Foster Sidney supported her husband's activism, marching with him, as did a few other friends, including Sidney's lawyer and close friend Bruce M. Wright—who later became a flamboyant activist judge, derided as Turn 'Em Loose Bruce for his opposition to racist bail policies. Even in freezing January, Sidney picketed CBS, the advertising agency BBDO, and other places, passing out flyers. He bought ads in the *Times* advocating a boycott against the sponsor Lever Brothers, which used black talent only in ads aimed at blacks. "It was his *life*," Foster Sidney said. "There was nothing else he wanted."

Sidney was particularly impatient with actors who hesitated to join his protests for fear of alienating their employers. "I didn't give a shit about jobs for blacks," he told Kisseloff. "I was concerned about the image of black people in television." As early as 1954, he was writing to the Footlights and Sidelights column in the *Amsterdam News*, encouraging a write-in campaign, noting that "by not including Negroes in at least approximately the numbers and the roles in which they occur in American life, television and radio programs that purport to give a true picture of American life malign and misrepresent Negro citizens as a whole."

In 1962, he testified before the House, arguing against "discrimination that is almost all-pervading, that is calculated and continuing." He described two-faced producers, who used a nepotistic, friend-of-a-friend hiring approach, saying, "for most white people, Negroes are not actors, or doctors, or lawyers—not really—but are rather, all members of a secret lodge, domiciled in Harlem or some other Colored Town—all knowing each other and all experts on one another." In 1967, *Variety* reported that Sidney had quit a job on "As the World Turns," protesting the soap opera's policy of not offering black actors contracts, as it did white actors. In 1968, he was quoted in the *Times* on whether the representation of black people in ads had improved. "It was like a man who's been gravely ill with a temperature of 104 if it drops to 102 it's better," he said. "But, if the question is, 'Has the progress been commensurate with the need?' The answer is 'No.'"

Sidney was a particular thorn in the side of David Susskind, the powerful producer and talk-show host, whose "The David Susskind Show" offered a free-wheeling space for debates about social issues. Susskind was the model of the white-liberal media elite, as well as a supporter of civil-rights causes, but when he produced a show about American history that omitted blacks Sidney promptly targeted his office. After Susskind died, Claude Lewis recounted Sidney's confrontation with Susskind in the Philadelphia *Inquirer*. "You're killing me," Susskind said. "I mean to," Sidney replied. "You talk that good stuff on TV, but you don't practice what you preach. We're here to say you're a phony. If you really want to be the decent guy you pretend to be, you'll offer opportunities to talented Negro performers, just as you do to whites." When Susskind told Sidney that he would "earn an ulcer," Sidney replied, "Mr. Susskind, I don't get ulcers. I give ulcers. I'm on this line, not to win parts for me, but for others who deserve them." A few years later, Sidney was hired to act in a Susskind production, the gritty and iconoclastic social-justice procedural "East Side/West Side," along with James Earl Jones and Cicely Tyson. The series was cancelled after one season.

Tom Scott, a younger actor and a model—he was one of the first African-Americans to be hired by Ford—picketed with Sidney. The two men talked nightly, strategizing; Scott was inspired by his friend's savvy, as well as his willingness to take extreme measures to attract attention to the cause. When he couldn't get press coverage, Scott recalls, Sidney had a female friend call the police and tell them, "There's a nigger out there with a knife!" The cops showed up—and, with them, the media.

Yet, as the years passed, the door stayed locked. TV was still run by white people, emphasizing white stories. And somewhere along the line, Sidney stopped picketing and handing out leaflets. He'd bought a brick house in the Prospect Lefferts Gardens neighborhood of Brooklyn, where he retreated. In 1988, the *Amsterdam News* lamented the minuscule presence of black TV producers and writers, adding that Sidney's activism had had as much effect as "ice cubes at the South Pole." Sidney made one last significant TV appearance, in the TV movie "A Gathering of Old Men." But in some ways little had changed: in his final movie, "A Kiss Before Dying," in 1991, he played a bellman.

Foster Sidney lost touch with her ex-husband after their divorce; so did Scott and Lewis. But someone must have known him—the person who saved a document, labelled "ephemera," that showed up at the Schomburg Center. On the envelope is scrawled "P. Jay

Sidney memoir." Inside is a fifteen-page handwritten account of Sidney's life, on lined yellow paper, ending with a description of his death, from prostate cancer. It's unclear who the author is, but the narrative is a raw and intimate confession, seemingly notes for a book. It's possible that this is the project Sidney mentioned in a 1946 playbill, in a bio that describes him writing a book whose title is underlined at the top of these pages, "Memoirs of an American Untouchable."

Written in the third person, the document swings wildly in tone; it's laceratingly self-critical at some points, grandiose at others. It recounts Sidney's father's warnings: never to trust women or white people, never to be dependent. It ruminates on the cruel tumult of Sidney's romantic life, including his affairs with married women, but also on his longing, never-fulfilled, for an intellectual soul mate. He rails against institutions: the Catholic Church, Hollywood, even the civil-rights movement, which he felt made black people complacent. To the end, the document says, Sidney was rankled by a world that thought small. He had picketed for "black actors to be portrayed as respected people," but an award he won honored only "his fighting to get black actors work on TV—just work, any old part. (This was not his aim at all! No one understood. He became very discouraged.)"

By all accounts, Sidney grew irascible with age: Lewis describes him as having become so sensitive that he saw slights everywhere. But there was a moment when Sidney believed that TV might someday reflect African-Americans in their full humanity. In a speech Sidney gave at a National Freedom Day dinner, in Philadelphia in 1968, he laid out this vision, with wit and elegance. The "bad image" of blackness, he said, was "like the air we breathe, and that makes it harder to recognize." While African-Americans were accepted as "entertainers" for whites, only on dramatic shows might they be seen as "real people with real problems and real feelings." White-centered programs "imply, insinuate, suggest—and I will use this word in the special way that possibly only Negroes will understand—they signify" that African-Americans were not truly citizens. Black audiences absorbed this message, too, learning to discount their own power—their economic leverage, especially. Sidney's speech urged viewers to demand their place onscreen, to refuse to settle for anything less than a full portrait of their own lives, the source of true artistic liberation. Read today, it feels like a map to a world always just beyond the horizon.

BROTHER FROM ANOTHER MOTHER

ZADIE SMITH

February 23, 2015

The wigs on "Key and Peele" are the hardest-working hairpieces in show business. Individually made, using pots of hair clearly labelled—"Short Black/Brown, Human," "Long Black, Human"—they are destined for the heads of a dazzling array of characters: old white sportscasters and young Arab gym posers; rival Albanian/Macedonian restaurateurs; a couple of trash-talking, churchgoing, African-American ladies; and the President of the United States, to name a few. Between them, Keegan-Michael Key and Jordan Peele play all of these people, and more, on their hit Comedy Central sketch show, now in its fourth season. (They are also the show's main writers and executive producers.) They eschew the haphazard whatever's-in-the-costume-box approach—enshrined by Monty Python and still operating on "Saturday Night Live"—in favor of a sleek, cinematic style. There are no fudged lines, crimes against drag, wobbling sets, or corpsing. False mustaches do not hang limply: a strain of yak hair lends them body and shape. Editing is a three-month process, if not longer. Subjects are satirized by way of precise imitation—you laugh harder because it looks like the real thing. On one occasion, a black actress, a guest star on the show, followed Key into his trailer, convinced that his wig was his actual hair. (Key—to steal a phrase from Nabokov—is "ideally bald.") "And she wouldn't leave until she saw me take my hair off, because she thought that I and all the other guest stars were fucking with her," he recalled. "She's, like, 'Man, that *is* your hair. That's your hair. You got it done in the back like your mama would do.' I said, 'I promise you this is glued to my head.' And she was squealing with delight. She was going, 'Oh! This is crazy! This is crazy!' She just couldn't believe it." Call it method comedy.

The two men are physically incongruous. Key is tall, light brown, dashingly high-cheek-boned, and L.A. fit; Peele is shorter, darker, more rounded, cute like a Teddy bear. Peele, who is thirty-five, wears a nineties slacker uniform of sneakers, hoodie, and hipster specs. Key is fond of sharply cut jackets and shiny shirts—like an ad exec on casual Friday—and looks forty-three the way Will Smith looked forty-three, which is not much. Before he even gets near hair and makeup, Key can play black, Latino, South Asian, Native American, Arab, even Italian. He is biracial, the son of a white mother and a black father, as is Peele. But though Peele's phenotype is less obviously malleable—you might not guess that he's biracial at all—he is so convincing in voice and gesture that he makes you see what isn't really there. His Obama impersonation is uncanny, and it's the voice and hands, rather than the makeup lightening his skin, that allow you to forget that he looks nothing like the President. One of his most successful creations—a nightmarish, overly entitled young woman called Meegan—is an especially startling transformation: played in his own dark-brown skin, she somehow still reads as a white girl from the Jersey Shore.

Between chameleonic turns, the two men appear as themselves, casually introducing their sketches or riffing on them with a cozy intimacy, as if recommending a video on YouTube, where they are wildly popular. A sketch show may seem a somewhat antique format, but it turns out that its traditional pleasures—three-minute scenes, meme-like catchphrases—dovetail neatly with online tastes. Averaging two million on-air viewers, Key and Peele have a huge second life online, where their visually polished, byte-size, self-contained skits—easily extracted from each twenty-two-minute episode—rack up views in the many millions. Given these numbers, it's striking how little online animus they inspire, despite their aim to make fun of everyone—men and women, all sexualities, any subculture, race, or nation—in repeated acts of equal-opportunity offending. They don't attract anything approaching the kind of critique a sitcom like "Girls" seems to generate just by existing. What they get, Peele conceded, as if it were a little embarrassing, is "a lot of love." Partly, this is the license we tend to lend to (male) clowns, but it may also be a consequence of the antic freedom inherent in sketch, which, unlike sitcom, can present many different worlds simultaneously.

This creative liberty took on a physical aspect one warm L.A. morning in mid-November, as "Key and Peele" requisitioned half of a suburban street in order to film two sketches in neighboring ranch houses: a domestic scene between Meegan and her lunkhead boyfriend, Andre (played by Key), and a genre spoof of the old Sidney Poitier classic "Guess Who's Coming to Dinner." "One of our bits makes you laugh? We have you, and you will back us up," Peele suggested, during a break in filming. "And, if something offends you, you will excuse it." Sitting at a trestle table in the overgrown back garden of "Meegan's Home," he was in drag, scarfing down lunch with the cast and crew, and yet—for a man wearing a full face of makeup and false eyelashes—he seemed almost anonymous among them, speaking in a whisper and gesturing not at all. On set, Peele is notably introverted, as mild and reasonable in person as he tends toward extremity when in character. Looking down at his cleavage, he murmured, "You often hear comments, as a black man, that there's something emasculating about putting on a dress. It may be technically true, but I've found it so fun. It's not a downgrade in any way."

When Key sat down beside Peele, he, too, seemed an unlikely shock merchant, although for the opposite reason. Outgoing, exhaustingly personable, he engages frenetically with everyone: discussing fantasy football with a cameraman, rhapsodizing about the play "Octoroon" with his P.R. person, and ardently agreeing with his comedy partner about the curious demise of the short-lived TV show "Freaks and Geeks" ("Ahead of its time"), the present sociohistorical triumph of nerd culture, and a core comic principle underpinning many of their sketches. ("It's what we call 'peas in a pod': two characters who feel just as passionate about the same thing.")

Peele loves "a comedy scene that makes you cry"—like the last episode of Britain's "The Office"—and cites Ricky Gervais's creation, Regional Manager David Brent, as a personal touchstone. Key loves Gervais, too, though his "favorite performer of all time ever" is another Brit, Peter Sellers. "Because it's all pathos, pathos, pathos." When considering these matters, the two men laugh at each other's jokes and finish each other's sentences, apparently free of the double-act psychodrama made infamous by such toxic pairings as Martin and Lewis, Crosby and Hope, and Abbott and Costello. Like their Comedy Central stablemates Abbi Jacobson and Ilana Glazer, from the sitcom "Broad City," they pull off the unusual trick of wringing laughs out of amity. One of the network's original concepts for the show was "Key Versus Peele," which was soon abandoned when the two stars couldn't find enough topics on which to disagree, even comically.

Both men have an improv background, and improv's culture of mutual support suffuses their material. (Faced with an empty stage, Key explained, "If I bump into a 'desk,' then he walks into the room five minutes later and walks around that 'desk.' You don't act, you react.") From their enthusiastic L.A. valets, avid fans of the actor they call "Liam Neesons" (catchphrase: "Liam Neesons is my shit!"), to the two homoerotic Arabic gentlemen who frot each other while supposedly admiring passing hotties in full burkas ("You saw ankle bone?"), a natural chemistry—the product of a genuine relationship—is being turned up to eleven. "We're brothers," Peele said. "It's not even best friends. It's a total brother understanding."

TWENTY MINUTES LATER, KEY AND PEELE HAD A NINE-ALARM FIGHT—as Andre and Meegan. Andre was attempting to break up with Meegan, and Meegan was refusing to let him. She sat on a plush white sofa, surrounded by reality-TV-show-inspired furnishings, filing her nails and becoming, despite a veil of self-help language, increasingly incensed. ("Can I ask why? Because I'm doing a lot of, like, growth work on myself.") Peele played it perfectly, but the camera angle was awkward, and his wrist hair kept escaping the cuffs of Meegan's pink velour tracksuit. As they reset, Peele subtly extemporized. The moment in which Meegan demands an explanation—"Grown adults give reasons!"—morphed into "Grown individuals present examples!"—a lift in register that proved unaccountably funnier. In response, a hapless Andre could only bellow and writhe in frustration.

"Meegan and Andre" is one of Key and Peele's most popular recurring sketches, and plays to their strengths: Peele's pitch-perfect ear for verbal tics and Key's long-limbed physical comedy. As the sophistic, motormouthed Meegan, Peele gets to the core of what contemporary entitlement looks like—concern with one's personal rights combined with non-interest in one's duties—managing to place Meegan in that comedy sweet spot where girl power meets good old-fashioned narcissism. Key, meanwhile, uses all his native brio to embody an amiable jock, utterly dominated and forever perplexed as to why. "I was almost out the door," Andre said twice to himself, as Meegan, satisfied that the breakup had been averted, grew bored and wandered off into the kitchen. Key put his head in his hands and arranged his body in the manner of a man drained of hope. This improvised gesture solved the problem of an explosive scene that seemed to dribble away, and Key carried if off with a sincerity that tipped the scale gently from comic toward tragic.

A little later, on a raised wooden deck at the back of the house, Key and Joel Zadak—who manages both Key and Peele—sat on high stools watching the footage. It was clear that Key had expanded

Andre from the confused putz of previous seasons to something close to an emotionally abused person. If the depth Key brings to comic moments is unexpected, the bigger surprise is that he's doing comedy at all: he intended to be a classical actor. After attending the University of Detroit Mercy, he got an M.F.A. from the Pennsylvania State University School of Theatre, and claims to have been a tad put out when, in 1997, he was invited to become a member of the Second City Detroit: "I've got an M.F.A.! A Mother-Fucking-A.! I took total umbrage!" (He still has dreams of playing the Dane, although, given his age and his schedule, he may have to wait for Lear. "'Remember that night you said you'd do 'Hamlet?'" he said wistfully, quoting a Chicago actor friend's recent query. "I was, like, 'Call me in 2017.'") But it is the mixture of the classical and the contemporary in him—the voice that sounds as natural saying "umbrage" as saying "motherfucking"—that provides much of his comic charm.

Perhaps because of this background in dramatic theatre, Key is the showman, the all-rounder, while there is a detail and a level of delicacy to Peele's craft that require just the right frame to set it off. Beyond "Key and Peele," it's hard to imagine Peele in any vehicle not constructed around a comic character of his own devising, just as the "Pink Panther" series was essentially an elaborate showcase for the marvel that was Peter Sellers's Inspector Clouseau. By contrast, you can envision Key in a variety of projects: Off Broadway as Hamlet, but also presenting the Oscars, floating in space next to Sandra Bullock, or putting his hand on Tom Hanks's shoulder, delivering some bad news. Whatever scene you set, Key will give you everything he's got. But the same qualities that make Key such an easy and pleasant presence on set—amiability, flexibility, absence of dogma—also make him hard to pin down as a personality. He's so good at reacting, so attuned to other people's feelings, that it's not always easy to assess what he feels. "I very often don't know what's fuelling my passion," he confessed, while someone fussed with Andre's ludicrous ducktail. "I'm just being practical with the skill set that I have."

THAT AFTERNOON, DURING THE POITIER SKETCH, WHICH FEATURED only Key, Peele unburdened himself of Meegan, re-dressed as himself, and sat down beneath the dappled light of an orange tree, where he considered his career: "Fifteen, twenty years ago, I decided I wanted to be a sketch performer." Not an unusual dream, perhaps, for a funny kid raised on the Upper West Side, a mile and a half from the "Saturday Night Live" studios, although few would have pursued it with Peele's single-minded persistence. While at P.S. 87, the Metropolitan Opera did a workshop with his fifth-grade class; Peele was given the shy kid's job of assistant stage manager, the duties of which included being understudy to one of the leads. When that actor called in sick, Peele filled in for several performances, playing the part of a "cool guy" (black leather jacket, sunglasses, chain), and discovering, in the process, how much he liked having an audience. Later, as a student at Sarah Lawrence—where he had intended to study puppeteering—he joined an improv troupe, which soon became his main concern; two years in, he dropped out of college entirely to form a comedy partnership with his college roommate and fellow troupe member, Rebecca Drysdale, who's now a writer on "Key and Peele." (He realized, he has said, that he had no need of puppets. He would use himself: "the most intricate puppet of all.") Drysdale and Peele called themselves "Two White Guys," although they were—as the publicity made explicit—"A black guy and a white Jewish lesbian," and went on to perform two well-received sketch shows at Chicago's Improv-Olympic theatre before the rest of Peele's Sarah Lawrence class had even graduated. Soon afterward, Peele joined Boom Chicago, an improv troupe based in Amsterdam, which has a remit to create comedy that "addresses Dutch, American and world social and political issues," although Peele made his mark playing Ute, a vapid

Danish supermodel and an occasional presenter of the Eurovision song contest. (She had a Euro-trash accent and said things like "Yes, because, like, if you have English as a second language it's hard to make your head talk!")

Becoming other people: this is Peele's gift. The small scraps online of his forays into standup reveal a man who doesn't quite know who to be onstage—there's no persona he's happy to be stuck in—and Peele, recognizing this, abandoned the form early. "The one thing that you don't figure out as an improviser or a sketch performer is 'What am I?'" he observed. The essence of his talent is multivocal, and he has, in the past, attributed this to his childhood anxiety at having the wrong voice, which, in his case, meant speaking like his mother—that is, speaking "white." ("It cannot be a coincidence that I decided to go into a career where my whole purpose is altering the way I speak and experiencing these different characters and maybe proving in my soul that the way someone speaks has nothing to do with who they are," he told Terry Gross, on "Fresh Air.") In improv, the question of authenticity becomes irrelevant: the whole point is to fake it.

To watch the afternoon's filming, I walked next door, into a modern living room disguised as a late-fifties interior, complete with sideboard and drinks cabinet and cut-glass tumblers half filled with fake whiskey. Key was struggling through an awkward meal with his white girlfriend and her parents, who he believes dislike him because he's black. It's only when he stands up, affronted, and prepares to walk out—"There's no point in trying to reason with people who can't appreciate the differences in others"—that we see that he has a great big tail (to be added in postproduction). The mother says, "I cannot *believe* you brought a black man into our house!" A moment later, the camera pulls back for the punch line: everybody has a tail. During a pause in filming—as the crew discussed the timing of the tail reveal—Bonnie Bartlett, the actress playing the mother, who is in her mid-eighties, turned to Key and

murmured, "It must have been interesting to be *your* mother, because you're so . . ." She touched her own, pink, face. A moment
later, perhaps worried that she'd given offense, Bartlett looked
stricken, but Key smiled kindly. "I think that's a fair statement of
the case," he said. "Now, where are you from, Bonnie?" "Illinois."
"You're kidding me!" The actress, encouraged, began to tell her story:
"My hometown was settled by men taken there to work . . . these
Swedish men. . . ." She faded. "*Really*," Key persisted, with great
warmth. "That's such an interesting story." The crew reset the cameras. This time, when Bartlett's line came around, she said, "I can't
believe you would bring a dark man into this house." Cut. Bartlett
looked stricken once more: "I can't believe I said 'dark'! But we
didn't say 'black' in those days. . . ." Key turned anthropological, objectively curious: "What did you say? Did you say 'Negro?'"
Bartlett, relieved, considered the question: "'Colored,' I think . . ."
Key thanked her for the smart correction: they went with "colored."

KEY AND PEELE MET—AS KEY RECENTLY TOLD JIMMY KIMMEL—IN 2003,
when they "fell in comedy love" while performing on consecutive
nights in Chicago, at the Second City Theatre. Peele was visiting
with Boom Chicago, doing his Ute bit; Key was playing a socio-
pathic high-school gym instructor called Coach Hines, who "inspires" his teen-age students by regularly enumerating all the ways
in which he will violently murder them if they do anything wrong.
Improv is not a world overburdened with people of color, but neither man felt territorial when, soon after, they each auditioned for
Fox's raucous, satirical sketch show "Mad TV." In the end, they
were both hired, and quickly put to work, mainly impersonating
black celebrities—Ludacris, Bill Cosby, Snoop Dogg—but also doing some of the kind of detailed fictional work they would later
develop on "Key and Peele." Coach Hines became a recurring spot,
while Peele turned an impersonation of the rapper 50 Cent into a
character study, in which Key, as 50's manager, phones the rapper

to tell him of the chart dominance of his rival, Kanye West. 50, heartbroken, sings a maudlin song called "Sad 50 Cent." (Sample lyric: "I walk around my prostitute garden, and my carousel. Nothing seems to make me smile today." The song was nominated for an Emmy in 2008.) The humor on "Mad TV" was broad—and too reliant on celebrity subjects—but it was a great place to hone your sketch-writing skills, and made both men, especially Peele, usefully hunger for a time when a joke wouldn't have to pass through a dozen producers to get on the air.

Toward the end of their five-season stint, a big-eared, biracial senator began to make headlines and, a short while later, became President. "S.N.L." needed an impersonator. This was, for Peele, "the dream. That was what I set out to do." But when the call came he was under contract with "Mad TV." He was devastated that a legal matter was screwing him up, especially when he had, he felt, "strategized everything perfectly." Watching the other Obamas on "S.N.L." was a "strange, strange little period" in his life, but also motivating: "I think the strategist in me went, 'All right, well what does this mean? This means there's gotta be something that I can put these skills into; there's gotta be a reason I'm not doing this, ultimately.'" When Peele was freed from his "Mad TV" contract, in 2009—and after a pilot for Fox went nowhere—he and Key began discussing a sketch show, and a young director named Peter Atencio immediately came to mind.

Key had met Atencio when they made a Web series on a green screen in the "crappy one-bedroom apartment in Hollywood" that Atencio describes himself as living in at the time ("It was for MySpace, which dates how long ago that was"), having moved from Boulder, Colorado, at nineteen, in the hope of making movies. They liked each other and kept in touch; Key introduced Peele to Atencio. Only thirty-one now, he was twenty-seven when Key and Peele managed to persuade Comedy Central to accept him after the studio's first choice for director dropped out. With a small team of eight writers and four producers, the first season was written over thirteen weeks, creating two hundred and sixty sketches that were later pared down to fifty-four. Atencio has directed every episode of "Key and Peele," until this current season. After the network put in for a double order of episodes, postproduction on the first half began overlapping with the filming of the second; unwilling to relinquish control of color and sound mixing, Atencio conceded a third of the season to a trio of directors. But, even when he's not directing himself, he's a frequent visitor wherever "Key and Peele" is filming, which, on the day we spoke, happened to be a standard-issue black box of a set, deep within the Universal Studios complex.

Extras were filing through the sun-baked parking lot to play the crowd at a basketball game, and Atencio stood in the studio's doorway like a benign house spirit, watching them pass, nodding at producers, and then walking across the room to greet Key and Peele, where they sat "courtside," having their wigs tweaked. Tall and lumbering, with a soft, pale, pouchy face, partly obscured by thick geek glasses and a baseball cap, he was dressed in baggy streetwear, all of it a little lopsided on his large frame, and looked more like a visiting weed dealer than like the man who usually runs the show. Back outside, he blinked moleishly in the sun. "I live within it," he said, speaking of the series. "It is my life. It's definitely the only way I know how to do it. It's probably the only way it could be done."

From the outset, Atencio wanted "Key and Peele" to have a distinct look. He recalled that his pitch was to "make every sketch the funniest set piece in a movie." Rather than resorting to the kind of verbal exposition on which so much sketch comedy relies, he suggested using "visual information, editing cues, things that kind of set the tone and the mood so that you don't have to do it in the writing." A goofy scene concerning the frustration of holding a "Group 1" boarding card as various groups file onto the plane right in front you—"Uniformed military personnel . . . People in wheelchairs. Any priests, nuns, rabbis, imams. Any old people in wheelchairs. Any old people in wheelchairs with babies. Any old religious people with military babies. Jason Schwartzman. Anyone with a blue suitcase"—culminates with Key, still clutching his ticket, sitting amid the movie-grade wreckage of a commercial airliner. It looks so epic and expensive, it draws gasps as well as laughs, but was shot relatively cheaply by Atencio on the "War of the Worlds" set at Universal Studios.

COMEDY CENTRAL PROMOTED THE FIRST *SEASON* WITH THE TAGLINE "If you don't watch this show, you're a racist," but "Key and Peele" rarely resorts to the kind of binary racial humor so appreciated by Homer Simpson—*black people do this, white people do that*—and the color line is far from being its sole concern. (Nor is it all pathos, pathos, pathos. One sketch ponders the eternal question "What if names were farts?") Where the comedy is racial, the familiar, singular "race card" is switched for something more like the whole pack fanned out, with the focus on what Peele has called "the absurdity of race." "I always look back at standardized tests," he said, as he sat in Hair and Makeup, making a small but significant wig transition from "sports announcer" to "sportscaster." "They make you say what race you are, where you check out, and I think that's ultimately an unhealthy tradition." His eyes, naturally rather narrow, widened dramatically. "It is *crazy* that as a kid we're taught, 'What is your identity?' We're *asked* that!" Key, who sat at the other end of the trailer, going from having hair to being bald to having hair again, is similarly struck by the irrational nature of racial categories. "The limbic system is alive and well," he said. "And it's going, '*I need to find a category. I need to find a category. If I don't find a category, I'm not safe.*'"

He seemed to be referring to a neurological theory according to which the limbic system is responsible for our primal reactions—such as recognizing membership within a certain tribe—because it looks for visual equivalences between things, whereas our prefrontal cortex, which developed later, is able to make complex cognitive decisions. "So the thing is: the limbic system is still kicking it, hard," he continued. "And people are going to fight it, but naturally try to categorize themselves. Because when all we had was a limbic system people were, like, 'Dude, there's us and those fucking sabre-toothed tigers, *so we all have to stick together.*'" This led to a discussion of how tiny differences in phenotype—the relative "flatness" of Peele's nose compared with the higher bridge of Key's—can create differences in people's lives, both in the way that we are comprehended by others and in the way, especially as children, that we comprehend ourselves.

Key: "Jordan and I are . . . we're biracial."

Peele: "Yes. Half black, half white."

Key: "And because of that we find ourselves particularly adept at lying, er, because on a daily basis we have to adjust our blackness."

This moment occurs onstage, in the first episode of "Key and Peele," while they are out of character, speaking to a live studio audience, and it has some of standup's confessional feel. Sometimes, they explain, this adjustment has to happen simply to "terrify white people." (Without it, "we sound whiter than the black dude in the college a-cappella group. We sound whiter than Mitt Romney in a snowstorm.") But it may also be a way of seeking approval from the other side of the line. "When we're around other brothers and sisters," Peele says, with a sly smile, "you gotta dial it up." This leads to a demonstration of blackness dialled up ("You know what I'm talking about, brother—and you know I know what you're talking about; and you know I know you know; no doubt no doubt no doubt. . . ."), complete with physical gestures, which aren't the familiar, supposedly "black" gestures of TV comedy (no gang signs or exaggerated side-to-side head bopping) but are still, of course, stereotypical. The heads move, but the movement is far more closely, accurately, observed, and then expanded upon: Peele's little shuffling dance of joy, the way Key closes his eyes to signify assent. I would describe it as a fond imitation.

The skit alerts us to a shared trait that we may not have noticed until presented with it. But this is not the mild Jerry Seinfeldesque communality of coffee-drinking and airplane etiquette. It concerns the communality of race, about which we are rarely allowed to laugh. To say that the two men become, in that moment, "more black" is to concede, in one sense, to a racial stereotype—and yet if there is not such a thing as "blackness," upon what does "being black" hinge? (To fondly identify a community, you have to think of its members collectively; you need to think the same way to hate them. The only thing a rabbi and an anti-Semite may share is their belief in the collective identity "Jewishness.") "You never want to be the whitest-sounding black guy in a room," Peele concludes. (In response to which Key muses, "You put five white-talking black guys in the same room. . . . You come back in an hour? It's gonna be like Ladysmith Black Mambazo up in here!")

A few months after this sketch aired, Obama—surely the whitest-sounding black man in most rooms he enters—went on "Jimmy Fallon," and gave an unexpected shout-out to Key and Peele. He was responding to the "Obama Loses His Shit" sketch, in which Peele, as Obama, sits in a wingback chair for his weekly Presidential address and calmly outlines the concerns of early 2012—Iraq, North Korea, Tea Party pushback, his own legitimacy—while Key, as his Anger Translator, Luther, paces up and down the room, saying the unsayable ("I have a birth certificate! I have a hot-diggity-doggity-mamase-mamasa-mamakusa birth certificate, you dumb-ass crackers!"). The sketch seemed to articulate an unspoken longing among many Obama supporters, and perhaps within the black community as a whole. I certainly hadn't realized how much I wanted Luther until I saw him. Later that year, Obama asked to meet with Key and Peele, and wryly acknowledged the same desire. "I need Luther," he told them. "We'll have to wait till second term."

The sketch employs a comic reversal (Key: "I think reversals end up being the real bread and butter of the show"), but the emotional recognition gets the belly laugh. It has a famous antecedent in a 1986 sketch from "S.N.L.," in which Phil Hartman, playing Ronald Reagan, bumbles around the Oval Office—photo-ops with Girl Scouts, speaking inanities to journalists—but as soon as the press corps leaves, he's all business: conversing in Arabic, understanding the Contras, quoting Montesquieu. "And that's informed a handful of scenes of ours," Peele explained. "It's a version of that." When they're writing, they're looking for the emotional root of the humor. "What's the mythology that is funny just because people know it's not true?" he continued. You need to be able to guess what many people really feel about something, even if they won't ever dare say it. It's this skill that is, in the end, every comic's bread and butter. How does one develop it? Key, who has given a lot of thought to the matter, feels that both his empathic and his imitative skills are essentially a form of hyper-responsiveness. "The theory is: There's no one in the world—there may be people as good as I am at this, but no one's better than me at adapting to a situation." If comic skill is a form of adaptation, Key and Peele had completed the necessary apprenticeship while still in short pants.

PEELE, REARED IN A ONE-BEDROOM WALKUP BY A WHITE "BOOKISH" mother (a fact one might have been able to glean solely from his middle name: Haworth), barely knew his black father. (He was mostly absent and died in 1999.) A sketch from the second season, written by Peele's old roommate Rebecca Drysdale, has Peele, playing himself, visiting a trailer park in search of his long-lost father (played by Key), who treats Peele with contempt until Peele lets slip that he has his own TV show. It's a brutally funny scene, painful to watch once you're aware of the personal history behind it. "I was in this ABC special called 'Kids Ask President Clinton Questions,'" Peele recalled. "It was the last question of the day. I ask him, 'What would you do: Is there any way for you to help kids who aren't getting child support?'" Yet Peele has, in common with Key, a tendency to interpret past pain as productive: "I was a kid that got to go to the White House and talk to the President. I was really in seventh heaven!" As well as appearing on television, Peele watched an epic amount of it—"Everything I do now, part of it is the fact that I had television as my second parent. Hours and hours"—and, for him, after the age of six, the most consistent black father figure in the home was on TV, refracted through the fun-house mirror of American pop culture. Many of the sketches on "Key and Peele" seem to play off black shows of the period, or reruns ("Roots," "Good Times," "Family Matters"), in scenes both loving and accusatory. In one, Steve Urkel turns up as a homicidal maniac.

But if Peele wasn't lonely, exactly—"There was a precedent for biracial latchkey kids"—and always, he says, felt loved, other people's reactions complicated things. "I went to school, and the first kid goes, 'Your mom's *white*?'" he said. He had to quickly adapt to "what other people were used to and what other people were taught, and we were asked to identify what I was or whose side I was on: was I one or the other?" Key and Peele's somewhat unusual insistence on their biracialism is motivated in part by a refusal to obscure white mothers to whom they were very close. For Peele's mother, Lucinda Williams, who still lives in that walkup on the Upper West Side, the situation was made easier by living in Manhattan. "Having parents with different ethnic identities was not a particularly unusual situation here, nor was being raised by a single parent," she told me. Peele, Williams says, was "obviously my joy," but she had her share of dealing with other people's incredulity, especially as a pale, blue-eyed blonde. Strangers, she said, tended to "assume he was adopted or I was watching someone else's child. When he was still in a stroller, I would see people's faces freeze and then look away upon leaning in to admire the baby. You could almost see a 'Does Not Compute' sign light up in their eyes."

As Peele grew, his increasing interest in performing surprised his mother. He had always seemed shy, "the quiet kid who likes to draw," who loved movies about aliens, monsters, and robots—all of whom tend to have no race at all. There were many literary books on the shelves, but Peele gravitated toward fantasy. ("'Labyrinth.' That's my world," Peele confirmed. "'NeverEnding Story.' 'Willow.'") Twenty years later, "Key and Peele" features many zombies and vampires, and annually delights in its Halloween episode. But Peele was part of that generation of nerds who, as Key pointed out, have conquered the earth—at least, the part that makes most popular entertainment. Wendell, whom Peele plays on the show—a three-hundred-pound recluse, fond of cheesy crusts and action figures, overly anxious to convince people that he's "seeing someone, sexually"—is only a kind of obscene, comic extrapolation of Peele-the-fantasy-fan. "I think that 'nerd' is kind of an elusive term," Peele said. "I guess technically it means someone who is obsessed with pop culture, and possibly without having the social graces themselves to deal with things. But the term 'nerd' that I relate to is more of the first part, where it's just to be an unabashed fan of something." Fandom remains the easiest way to draw Peele out. He is cautious on intimate subjects, happier discussing the classic nerd topics of his peers: Kubrick movies, nineties hip-hop, the inadvertent comic genius that is Kanye West.

Key, who thinks of himself as being from a slightly different era, has no interest in hip-hop ("I'm a sixties R. & B. man") and speaks of his personal life and history more readily, in a great flowing rush, though perhaps this is simply to save time, as the story comprises an unusual number of separate compartments. Born in Detroit, he is the child of an affair between a white woman and her married black co-worker, and was adopted at birth by another mixed-raced couple, two social workers, Patricia Walsh, who is white, and Michael Key, who hailed from Salt Lake City, "with the other twelve black people." The couple raised Key but divorced while he was an adolescent. Key's father then married his stepmother, Margaret McQuillan-Key, a white woman from Northern Ireland. Key's familial situation was often in flux: after his own adoption came a sibling; then his parents' divorce and his father's remarriage.

As a boy, he had ambitions in veterinary science, movie stardom, and football, but when childhood epilepsy ruled out football his interest in performing surged ahead of everything else, a passion in which he was encouraged by his mother. Later, his stepmother suggested that he go abroad to study drama, and when he was eighteen she and his father sent him on a reconnaissance trip: "That was my end-of-high-school gift: to go to England. My stepmother said, 'If you're going to do theatre for a living, you've got to do it right'"—here Key took a stab at a Belfast brogue—"*They don't fookin' do it right here.*" Key is, like Peele, a man of many voices. (His wife, Cynthia Blaise, is a dialect coach, though Key claims that her role is more supportive than instructive: "She doesn't usually help me. She's very sweet to say things like 'No, I think you've got that, honey.'") He picked up a few voices during his stay in London, where he had to adapt to yet another culture and another concept of "blackness." While visiting family in Northern Ireland, he watched some TV coverage of Brixton and had a minor racial epiphany: "Holy shit, those are black people!" He loved the Olympic sprinter Linford Christie, amazed to hear such an unfamiliar voice emerging from so familiar a face. "My brain started to make that adjustment almost immediately, at eighteen years of age. My brain said, 'Oh, I get it. It's all cultural. None of it's about melanin.'" Seven years later, he had a profoundly affecting reunion with his biological mother, Carrie Herr, which brought with it more siblings ("I literally went to bed one day with one sibling and woke up the next morning with seven"), and a sudden acceptance of Jesus Christ as his personal savior, an event that he has described as "pretty unexpected." But adapting to unexpected emotional contingencies is what Key does best. "I'm not the smartest person in the world," he offered. "But my E.Q., my 'emotional quotient'—off the charts."

On set, this serves him well. Key acknowledges that his flitting between personas can seem a spooky art to those of us who are stuck with our singular selves: "Very often, humans latch on to the first thing they can get hold of and go, 'This is working. I'm gonna do this,'" he told me. "And what Jordan and I have latched on to is: '*All* of this is working.'" To Key, "the varied thing is the normative thing." This brought to mind Alice Miller, the author of "The Drama of the Gifted Child," who argued that the empathic skills one often finds in gifted children represent a symptom as much as a gift, a child's reactive response to the inconsistencies and unexpectedness around him. Key has read the Miller—he calls it "an amazing book"—but considers himself removed now from the traumas that may have shaped his skills: "It was a tool you were using to survive when you were younger, and now you can use for other ends." The way he rattles off his complex past, as if it had all happened to another man, seems related to this; able to see himself from a distance, he speaks like a writer describing a character. He notes, too, that he seldom feels "strongly about things," and when observing other people he has an almost anthropological reaction: what would it be like to feel so deeply attached to one point of view?

WHILE RACE CAN APPEAR ABSTRACT TO KEY AND PEELE, ESPECIALLY when seen through the lens of their own unconventional backgrounds, for many of their viewers race is neither an especially fluid nor a changeable category; it is the determining fact of their lives. Within the rigid categories of media representation, for example, Key and Peele are two black men who star in a TV show that has unusual crossover appeal, and matters that might seem neutral on other shows—like the casting of "love interests"—must be more carefully considered. Key, whose wife is white (Peele's partner, the standup and comic actress Chelsea Peretti, is also white), pronounced himself "hyperaware" of the issue: "It's one thing that you can control." For a recent sketch, in which Key finds a woman collapsed on the ground, and during his subsequent 911 call falls in love with her, the script required that the woman be "staggeringly gorgeous." When casting her, Key said, "it was very important to me not to have a light-skinned woman." In telling this story, he assumed, for the moment, the voice of a disgruntled viewer: "*These two niggas ain't got nothing but white women on this show!*"

Once, backstage on a "Key and Peele" college tour, taking pictures with the student volunteers, hugging and chatting with them, Key mentioned to Peele that he sometimes had a bad feeling about the way he conducted these interactions. "And then Jordan said, 'Why?'" he recalled. "And I said, 'Because when I'm around the black girls I hug them and give them more attention.' Because ain't *nobody* been shit on more than black women. They just deserved more because of the fucking shit. It's one thing to get whipped. It's another thing to get whipped *and* raped. Do you know what I mean? It's just horrible. And not that white women don't have problems." The painful history of black women in America, Key stressed, "won't leave me. I think of my grandmother and my aunts. It reverberates. And so it's, like, a woman with dark-chocolate skin should be an image of beauty for anybody just as much as a woman with milk-white skin." Although, he added, "none of it actually should matter." But it does, of course. A scene in which Key and Peele play two husbands mortally afraid of their wives could be read as a satire on middle-class marital mores, regardless of race, but when Key appeared on "Conan" and claimed, in reference to the sketch, that "there is nothing more dangerous on planet Earth than a black wife," he resurrected a familiar insult, too often directed at black women, some of whom pointed out, online, that Key

has no personal experience on which to draw his conclusion. They felt hurt precisely *because* they were black women, speaking from a singular place and with a singular experience.

Peele, when asked about how race is dealt with on the show, said, "Really, there's no actual strategy, and there's no perspective that would be easy to . . . to state. Much like race in this country. It's so nuanced. It's so complicated. It's so deep-seated, and, at the same time, it's evolving, and then it feels like it devolves. And it's this nebulous thing." I thought of that William Gibson quote: "The future is already here—it's just not very evenly distributed." It can't be easy making race comedy in such a mixed reality: a black President on the one hand, black boys dying in the streets on the other. It's a difficult omelette, and you're going to break some eggs trying to make it. But getting it right means penetrating the heart of a long and painful national conversation.

In one sketch, Peele appears as a young black man walking through a white suburb. A mother shoos her children indoors; a man mowing his lawn gives Peele a warning glare; a cop slowly tracks him in his squad car, his eyes filled with preëmptory violence. Then Peele puts up his hoodie: the face of a young white man is painted in profile on the side, obscuring Peele's. The cop smiles and waves. A minute long and wordless, it's a wonderfully pure comic provocation. "We just kind of put ourselves in the center of it, moment to moment," Peele said, referring to America's race issue. Ultimately, he said, they hope that their show will be "a mirror. I think there's even an element of the Rorschach test." He meant a mirror held up to the audience, but it is, of course, also a mirror of Key's and Peele's own attitudes, which, like everybody's, aren't always completely within their control.

ON MY LAST DAY ON SET, I SAT BEHIND THE CAMERAS, NEXT TO JO' Zadak. We had some dead time on our hands; Key's and Pee stand-ins, Shomari (tall, light brown) and Brian (shorter,

brown), were texting while the crew tested the lights against their complexions. Zadak is a youthful forty-three, with a sharp quiff and an unlined face, and was a comedy nerd before he became a comedy manager: hanging around the Second City Chicago, moving to L.A. to study screenwriting, hoping to be an improv guy himself. Now, as one of the executive producers on the show, he is content to be behind the scenes, and has the aura of a laid-back dude, despite his typical L.A. TV schedule. ("You know, I wake up in the morning at five o'clock. I read for an hour. I go to the gym for an hour. I take one of the kids to school, come to work. . . .") Describing the pair, he reached for a Beatles analogy "where Keegan is Paul, and Jordan is John. Where Keegan can write and perform a hit song all day long, and people will love him, and Jordan can do the same, but I think people look a little bit more deeper into what Jordan's doing. He's a little bit more of a deep thinker." (The previous day, Atencio had made the same analogy.) What most impresses Zadak about his clients, though, is their openness. They never "dismiss anything out of hand. They listen to everything."

Beyond the introvert-extrovert paradigm, it is perhaps this openness that strikes people as Beatle-like, for, to keep moving forward, as the Beatles did, you have to be constantly listening, second-guessing reactions, preëmpting tastes, adapting. If this is hard enough to do in music, it is even more difficult in comedy. The world is full of calcified comedians who stop—sometimes very suddenly—being funny, too attached to a joke's familiar neural pathway, perhaps, or too dogmatic, unable to change. How do you stay funny? It's a question that "haunts" Peele: "My biggest fear is someday reaching that point at which I see a lot of artists and comedians, where they stop growing. They had that success at a certain point, and it worked. And they cash in and they forget to continue to evolve."

The stand-ins left; Key and Peele arrived, having been transformed into basketball commentators who seem to have taken a

truth serum ("Welcome back to another few hours and several million dollars spent on watching adult men play a simple child's game, all while being paid more than the President!"). On form, as funny as I'd ever seen them, their faces were barely dusted with a few whitish wrinkles, yet they appeared as unmistakably Caucasian as Mitt Romney. Every now and then, Jay Martel, one of the show's executive producers—and an occasional writer for this magazine—walked over to their desk to discuss some verbal tweaking. Tall, thin, tonsured, he looked like a mild-mannered Quaker, and turned out to be a descendant of ministers and missionaries. ("I'm deciding whether a donkey dick is funnier than a dog dick. My ancestors would have been horrified.") At one point, Martel went over to discuss a line Key didn't like: "The alleged rapist passes the big orange ball to the sweaty legal giant; the sweaty legal giant passes it to the pituitary case." The term "pituitary case," Key argued, had "too much math in it," which meant, Martel explained, that too many mental steps were required to get to the laugh. On set and in the writing room, a series of terms are deployed as useful shorthand. "A clam": an old joke. "Lateral": an absence of escalation. "Map over": to take the beats of a genre piece and "map" a joke over them, as in the Poitier sketch. "Dookie": a joke that isn't yet fully formed. In place of "pituitary case," Martel offered "huge child-man." Dookie completed. Key and Peele moved on to trying to amuse each other with improvised catchphrases:

"Shploifus!"

"Hamhocks!"

"Biscuit time!"

"Gudeek!"

"Ebola!"

The last was Peele's, and Key looked at him despondently: "But they'll probably have Ebola all figured about by 2015." (When the scene will air.) "Cut to: urban wasteland," Peele said, and Key picked up the joke: "Resident Evil: Whole of the Western World." Even their off-the-cuff commentary on their genre sketches is framed as genre sketch.

SO FAR, KEY AND PEELE HAVE EVOLVED TOGETHER WITHIN THEIR happy comedy marriage, but it is still subject to all the normal pressures of a marriage (pulling in different directions, wanting different things), and many people close to them, including Zadak, have suggested that it is nearing its natural end. They have other projects under way, some together (including an as yet unnamed Judd Apatow feature) but several apart, though here the Paul-and-John analogy falls short. If and when Key and Peele separate, it will surely be more conscious uncoupling than brutal divorce. Still, there were moments on set when it felt as if they wanted something new thrown at them. Sitting behind a desk at the end of a long day, they tried to nail a short skit with the following mapped-over premise: What if public-school teachers were traded—and paid—like football players? ("Apparently, P.S. 431 made Ruby an offer she couldn't refuse: eighty million dollars guaranteed over six years, with another forty million dollars in incentives based on test scores. This salary puts her right up there with Rockridge Elementary's Katie Hope.") There wasn't much math to do, and hardly any physical business, and they seemed a little bored, making a few uncharacteristic errors. Key, waiting for the cameras to reset, turned to Peele and noted the cushy situation of sports announcers: "Some people do this shit for a living, *and that's all they do.* This shit is *easy.* Why don't we do this shit?" Peele agreed, but then started laughing, replying in his sports-announcer voice, "Haven't done it right so far—but still!" The cameras ready, they tried again, messed up again. I got the sense that the problem was that there weren't enough problems.

Some people are simply best suited to a challenge, as Jay Martel reminded me, when he e-mailed, a few days later, with a favorite anecdote from the show: "In our sketch about competing actors playing Malcolm X and Martin Luther King, we stacked up heightening physical bits, without really stopping to consider if they were physically possible—including asking Keegan (playing Malcolm X) to do the Worm across the stage. When we shot it, Keegan executed a perfect Worm. After the take, he stood up and said, 'Apparently, I can do the Worm.' He'd never even attempted it before."

RADICAL ALIENATION

CALVIN TOMKINS

December 21, 2020

The most spellbinding art work of the past decade is a seven-and-a-half-minute film called "Love Is the Message, the Message Is Death," by the artist and filmmaker Arthur Jafa. Word spread quickly after its New York première, in November, 2016, at Gavin Brown's gallery. People crowded the gallery to see it, but nothing they had heard prepared them for the rapid-fire sequence of a hundred and fifty film clips of Black people in the maelstrom of American life: a teen-age girl being thrown to the ground by a white police officer, burning cars and hip-hop dancers, Martin Luther King, Jr., in an open car, a man being beaten by several uniformed policemen, LeBron James soaring in for a gorgeous dunk, Barack Obama singing "Amazing Grace" at a memorial service in Charleston, a woman saying, "What would America be like if we loved Black people as much as we love Black culture?" Most of the images are found footage, taken from YouTube. Their emotional impact comes from the way Jafa has put them together, shifting and editing and choreographing to create a flow of deeply resonant juxtapositions, over a soundtrack of Kanye West's ecstatic "Ultralight Beam."

For Jafa (pronounced Jay-fa), who turned sixty in November, the film's reception was startling. A dozen major museums in this country and in Europe acquired copies of "Love Is the Message," and many more borrowed it for special screenings. As Jafa's friend John Akomfrah, the British artist and filmmaker, said to me, it was ironic that "this figure who was heralded for a long time as a kind of prophet in the world of cinema would turn out to be the savior of the art world." Jafa had a lively interest in contemporary art, and from 1999 to 2005 he had shown sculptures and other works in art galleries here and abroad, but cinema had been his primary focus since the seventies, when he was an undergraduate at Howard University, in Washington, D.C. Howard had an excellent film department, and in Jafa's third year there his interest had shifted from architecture to film studies. Incorrigibly curious and hugely ambitious, A.J., as everyone called him, identified his goal very early: "To make Black cinema with the power, beauty, and alienation of Black music." Jafa was not the first to stake this claim, but, as Akomfrah said, "somebody needed to articulate it for our generation, and A.J. was that figure."

Jafa's thinking was based on a concept that he calls "Black visual intonation." "Something I've pointed out a million times is that, if you look at Black folk and our visual expressivity, it's very, very undeveloped in comparison to what we've been able to achieve in music," he told me, one day this summer. "It's undeveloped despite the fact that we come from a visual tradition that's just as rich as the musical one. There is no contemporary art without African descent. Cubism is Picasso trying to understand African artifacts." Africans brought music with them on the slave ships, he said, and the music changed and developed in response to the new context, and this led to "everything from Billie Holiday to Jimi Hendrix to Motown, Charlie Parker, Thelonious Monk—you can go on and on." But nothing comparable had happened in African-American visual expression, and when Jafa's teachers in the film department at Howard introduced him to the idea of cinema devoted to Black lives, he said, "I was very excited. It sort of fired my imagination."

"Love Is the Message" is the closest he has come to realizing the goal he set for himself forty years ago. "I think what the film captures is the Black struggle to live," the writer and scholar Saidiya Hartman, who has known Jafa for many years, said to me. "It's a series of iconic images that show the brilliant virtuosity of the Black thinkers, artists, and athletes that ordinary Black folk have given to the world, alongside some of the forces that have negated Black life. You don't have to know the exact reference for each image to feel the work's density and power." The poet Fred Moten, another friend of Jafa's, talked to me about the "entanglement of absolute joy and absolute pain" that is fundamental to Black art and Black music. "'Love Is the Message' has all of that, and you know it immediately," he said. "It's in every moment. There is no break, and this is why it's good that it lasts only seven minutes, because that's as much as anyone can take."

TWO OF JAFA'S TEACHERS AT HOWARD, HAILE GERIMA AND BEN Caldwell, were recognized independent filmmakers. Gerima, who was born in Ethiopia, had been a leader of the L.A. Rebellion, a group of cinema students at U.C.L.A. in the nineteen-sixties and seventies, whose rebellion, in Gerima's words, was against "the white supremacist vocabulary" of mainstream Hollywood. Gerima was Jafa's mentor and role model. His films ("Bush Mama," "Ashes and Embers," "Sankofa"), along with those of Caldwell, Charles Burnett, Larry Clark, and other pioneers of L.A.'s Black film movement, opened Jafa's eyes to the boundless possibilities of cinema, but he gradually came to feel that something was missing in their approach. "It seemed to me early on that it wasn't enough to say a Black person made the film," he said. "It had to be something more. And, in trying to think about what I consider fundamental Black aesthetic values, one of the things that came up was rhythm. Most people will say Black people have rhythm—they seem able to do things with time. So I became interested in how cinema could be inscribed with a more idiomatic sense of timing."

Jafa had been an omnivorous reader since he was seven or eight. In the Howard library, where he spent much of his free time, he discovered a citation, in a musicology book, about a missionary who

had listened to the music in African villages and had tried to transcribe it. "One of the things I remember is the missionary saying
that the difficulty in studying the music of the Negroes is their
tendency to worry the note." He paused, and rubbed the graying
thatch of beard on his chin. "Worry the note," he repeated. "Basically, what he means is that, in most African music, and in fact
many musics of the non-Western world, the thing you call a note,
which in Western music is a pure sound that vibrates in a measurable fashion, is neither pure nor measurable. A B-flat has a very
specific tonal vibration. But what you hear in a lot of African and
non-Western music—certainly in Black music—is a vibrational fre-
quency that fluctuates. So when this guy tried to notate their music,
he'd say, 'That sounds like a B-flat to me,' but in fact it was never
only a B-flat. There is a certain quiver in a Black person's playing.
Even M.L.K.'s 'I Have a Dream' speech is a combination of the
words and the thing he's doing with his voice." Jazz historians and
other musicologists may well dispute aspects of Jafa's analysis, but
it gave him the insight he needed. "What I realized," he concluded,
"is that there must be techniques, ways to get visual movement in
cinema that has something of what Black vocal intonation does in
Black music."

Gerima remembers Jafa as a "very noticeable" student, "brilliant, energetic, and full of imagination." Jafa says he gave Gerima
and his other teachers a lot of trouble. "I argued a lot," he told me.
"It bothered Haile that I was swinging my Super 8 camera around
and just burning film—I was being Jackson Pollock." His talent
was unmistakable, though, and in the summer of 1980 Gerima sent
him to Los Angeles to work with Charles Burnett on his new film,
"My Brother's Wedding." Jafa thought Burnett's previous film,
"Killer of Sheep," a deeply evocative study of working-class people
in Los Angeles, was the best movie yet made by a Black director.
"My Brother's Wedding," about a quiet young man and his reckless best friend, received a poor review in the *Times*, because the

producer had shown the film before Burnett had finished editing it. But Jafa learned a great deal about cinematography from Burnett, who shot his own films, and he fell in love with the film's assistant director, a dazzlingly gifted woman named Julie Dash.

Eight years older than Jafa and a graduate student at the U.C.L.A. film school, Dash had already made three films of her own, and she was working on a series of shorts about Black women in America at the turn of the century. When their time on the Burnett film came to an end, Jafa moved in with Dash. (Although he went back to Howard a few times after that and took classes, he never graduated.) "A.J. admired my independent spirit," Dash told me. "When we first met, he thought I was gay. Why? I don't know. We'd have conversations that went long into the night, so long I'd sometimes go to sleep. We wore each other's clothes. Everybody we knew wore surplus Army khakis, and we were actually the same size." Jafa urged her to put aside the series of short films so that they could concentrate on one of them, about Black people in an isolated Gullah community on an island off the coast of South Carolina. Dash was persuaded—her father's people had come from this region. The result, eleven years later, was "Daughters of the Dust," one of the enduring classics of independent cinema.

The script for "Daughters" called for a large cast—three or four generations—and required serious funding. Dash had managed to raise about thirty thousand dollars, enough to start putting together a production team. Jafa was the cinematographer, and he brought in Kerry James Marshall, a young artist he had never met, to be their production designer.

"I'd just had a show in Los Angeles, and A.J. read an interview with me in the paper and called out of the blue," Marshall recalled. "We were on the phone for a couple of hours. I said, 'Why don't you come by?,' and a few days later he came and we stood near the door talking for another two hours before we sat down. He is a talker. One of the things that really got us together was my deep interest in Mississippi Delta blues. I was always trying to paint a visual equivalent to things like the Robert Johnson songs 'Cross Road Blues' or 'Devil Got My Woman,' and when I read Julie's script that's what it sounded like to me. I hadn't had any experience at all in making a film, but, as it turned out, I had the combination of skills they needed to help that happen." Marshall became an essential third figure in the collaboration, and his wife, the actress Cheryl Lynn Bruce, played the role of Viola Peazant.

Dash and Jafa married in 1983, and their daughter, N'Zinga (named for an Angolan queen), was born a year later. They moved from Los Angeles to Atlanta in 1986, to be closer to where "Daughters of the Dust" would be filmed. Jafa's parents, who had recently moved there, were delighted to look after N'Zinga—they called her Zing—while Jafa and Dash scouted locations. They were still far short of their funding goal, which was eight hundred thousand dollars, but in the fall of 1987 they assembled a small team and went to the island of St. Helena, South Carolina. They managed to shoot a trailer and some of the film that fall. Soon afterward, Lindsay Law, the executive producer of PBS's "American Playhouse," saw the trailer and loved it. He arranged for "American Playhouse" to give Dash and Jafa eight hundred thousand dollars, which allowed them to go back to St. Helena in 1989 and reshoot the film from scratch, with new costumes and equipment.

Jafa rented two 35-mm. movie cameras, and a computer that allowed him to weave together normal-motion and slow-motion footage. "He wanted the camera to move through space like Michael Jordan driving through the lane," Marshall said. Jafa also had specific ideas about lighting that would bring out the subtle variations in Black skin. He made his own reflectors—instead of using the usual large aluminum sheets, he cut out small, hand-held ones that threw light on the actor's face. When they finished shooting, though, the money was gone, and there was nothing left for the editing. "We went back to 'American Playhouse,'" Jafa said. "They gave us the money to edit, but in return we had to give up most of our financial interests in the film."

"Daughters of the Dust" premièred in 1991 at the Sundance Film Festival, where it was nominated for the Grand Jury Prize, and Arthur Jafa won the award for Excellence in Cinematography. But the film's nonlinear narrative structure and the fact that some of its dialogue was in the Gullah language made distributors nervous, and none of them would go near it. Jafa eventually negotiated an agreement with Film Forum, the art-house theatre in Greenwich Village, which showed "Daughters" in 1992. Dash went on the "Today" show, and when the film started drawing sellout crowds the run was extended. "Daughters of the Dust" was the first film by an African-American woman to get a theatrical release.

"That was a weird time," Jafa said. "'Daughters' was the toast of the New York film community, but we'd given away a large part of our financial interests, and knew we weren't going to make any money on it. Plus, Julie's and my relationship at that point was not in the best place." By 1991, they had separated. "I was struggling with some personal stuff, psychological stuff, and Julie, what with the child and the movie, couldn't help me," he said. "I was just very immature." He also said, "I didn't want to become Mr. Dash."

TALKING ON SKYPE, AS JAFA AND I WERE OBLIGED TO DO BECAUSE OF the pandemic, has unexpected limitations. I was on the East Coast, and Jafa was in Los Angeles, and it took me three sessions to realize that Jafa's brother Boston was sitting across the desk from him, working quietly while we talked. I finally "met" him when he got up and walked into view and waved. The brothers don't look alike, but they sound very much like brothers, with Deep South accents. A.J., who is interested in clothes and gets invited to openings at Gucci, wears a small diamond stud on his right eyebrow, and another one just under his lower lip. "I've had the studs for more than twenty years," he told me. "People used to think the one below my lip was a crumb—before COVID, they'd try to brush it off."

Jafa usually sat with his back to a window, so on bright days he was in shadow, and only gradually did I become aware of his tattoos. They were more or less everywhere: a black panther on his neck; a drawing of an early work by Zaha Hadid, "The Peak," which was never built, on his left arm; "FRODO," from "The Lord of the Rings," in capital letters and also on his left arm; Krazy Kat on the back of one hand. There were a lot more of them, he said, and a story to go with each. So, Krazy Kat? "People have pointed out to me that it's ironic, because I don't like cats," Jafa said. "They don't respect your personal space. But Krazy Kat at one point was the biggest thing in American popular culture, and the artist who drew him, George Herriman, is such an interesting figure to me— his own kids never knew their father was Black."

When Jafa tells stories, the words come slowly at first, in a baritone drawl, but as he gets going the pitch rises and the tempo accelerates. "The cat loves the mouse, the mouse hates the cat," he said. "The dog, Officer Pupp, loves the cat, but the cat can't see him because the cat loves the mouse. And what makes it worse is that the mouse keeps throwing a brick at Krazy Kat's head, which is an act of violence, but the cat sees the violence as an act of love, and so the circle continues. The absurdity of it strikes me as being as good a model of Black love and hate in white society as we've ever seen, a profound and absurd meditation on the thin line between love and hate."

JAFA WAS BORN IN 1960 IN TUPELO, MISSISSIPPI, THE BIRTHPLACE OF Elvis Presley. "My mom was born in Tupelo, and so were my aunt and uncle, and my grandparents grew up there," Jafa told me. His aunt Nettie has served on the Tupelo City Council since 2001. Jafa's full name is Arthur Jafa Fielder; he dropped Fielder (as his grandfather, another Arthur Jafa, had done) when he was in his early twenties, but his family ties have never weakened. Arthur and Rowena, his parents, were teachers, and his siblings—three younger brothers—have all found arts-related careers: Boston, the second oldest, is a musician and a filmmaker. (Named for their father's cousin, Ralph Boston, he was called Ralph until he got to high school, where everyone started calling him Boston.) Jim teaches film production in New York City high schools, and his twin brother, Tim, writes graphic novels.

Jafa's school integrated the year he entered first grade, and he was one of a handful of African-Americans in his class. Two years earlier, the family had moved to Russellville, Alabama, but Jafa was sent back to Tupelo to live with his grandparents so that he could go to school there. When the Ku Klux Klan burned down their house in Russellville (Arthur had been named football coach of the recently combined white and Black high schools), they returned to Tupelo. The whole family moved again, less than a year later, to Clarksdale, Mississippi, where Arthur and Rowena had been offered positions at Coahoma Junior College, an innovative school for Black students. Arthur taught physical education and coached football and basketball; Rowena, who taught business administration, became the school's financial director.

Clarksdale is in the Mississippi Delta, which Jafa describes as a Black Jurassic Park. "I grew up in a region where some of the more horrific acts in the century occurred," Jafa said. "Emmett Till was killed, the three civil-rights workers were killed, people were tortured and murdered and nobody was brought to trial." Unlike Tupelo, Clarksdale had held on to hard-core segregation long after it became illegal. And yet, growing up in a supportive family and on a college campus, the Fielder children felt protected and encouraged. For the first few years, the family lived on the campus in a blue-and-white trailer with three bedrooms. "Art and I shared a room," Boston recalled. "It was filled with Marvel and

DC comic books, and boxes of the magazines that Art cut pictures out of and pasted in notebooks. He slept in the top bunk, and I was on the bottom. We'd tell each other stories and make drawings— he'd draw something and hand it down to me, and I'd hand one up to him."

"The move from Tupelo to Clarksdale was mainly a change in soundtrack," Jafa said. "In Tupelo, the radio was dominated by Elvis Presley. I remember my grandmother telling stories about Elvis. They knew him in the Black part of town—that's how poor he was. When Elvis was a kid, he would sit on the porch of a nearby house and play guitar." Jafa was never a Presley fan. In Clarksdale, where the soundtrack was Memphis soul, all four Fielder boys went to Catholic school, because their non-Catholic parents thought they would get a better education that way. (Their father eventually converted to Catholicism.) Jafa was an altar boy and a straight-A student, and in high school he became a National Merit Scholar. "I was just elated to know that I had one student, just one, who could have gotten into M.I.T.," Olenza McBride, his social-studies teacher, recalled.

Jafa read all the time—first comics, then science fiction, the World Book (his parents bought the series, and later they added the Encyclopædia Britannica), history, sociology, and world literature. "Our neighbor was head librarian at the college," he said. "She would let me stay there after hours—I'd fall asleep in the stacks, and my dad would come to pick me up at two in the morning." Jafa and Boston saw every movie they could get to. One Saturday afternoon, when Jafa was ten, their parents dropped them off at the white people's theatre on the other side of town to see Stanley Kubrick's "2001: A Space Odyssey." The theatre was empty except for a few white couples, who left before the intermission. "The lights go down, the movie begins, and it's like being buried alive," Jafa wrote, in a 2015 essay called "My Black Death." "Even now, I'm still searching for an art experience capable of matching the effect this film had on me." When it ended, he and Boston walked out in a daze to the empty lobby, where the white theatre manager sat in the ticket booth reading a newspaper. "At this point in my life I didn't have un-chaperoned interactions with white people, young or old," Jafa wrote. "He was sitting in the ticket booth with the door open, so I walked over to him and said, 'Excuse me, sir, I've just come out of the movie, could you tell me what it was about?' He looked at me over his paper, paused a moment, and said, 'Son, I've been looking at it all week and I haven't got a clue.'"

There was a coda to the experience. In the mid-nineties, when Jafa was working as a cinematographer, Kubrick hired him to be a second-unit cameraman for "Eyes Wide Shut." Kubrick shot most of the film in England, but it was set in New York, and Jafa spent a lot of time filming locations there. "We were constantly shooting things over and over, because Kubrick kept sending notes saying would we try it again three degrees to the left, or three degrees to the right," Jafa recalled. "He called many times a day, and occasionally the assistant director would say, 'Stanley's on the phone, he wants to say hi,' and I would say, 'Not now, I'm shooting.'" In 1999, returning from Europe to attend the film's New York première, Jafa saw a newspaper headline: "STANLEY KUBRICK DIES AT 70." "Stanley Kubrick was one of my heroes," he said. "There was so much I wanted to say to him, and I'd had this fantasy that when we finished shooting we'd be able to have a proper conversation. I went to the première and got very depressed, trying to figure out why I had never spoken to him."

SHOOTING OTHER PEOPLE'S FILMS WAS ALWAYS, FOR JAFA, A STEPPING stone to shooting his own. "I love cinematography, but once I'd mastered the craft it was never fulfilling on its own," he told me. "Daughters of the Dust" had brought no directing offers, though, and until recently neither Dash nor Jafa could get funding for a second feature. Hollywood producers had financed and profited from nineteen-seventies blaxploitation films, some of which had Black directors, but the first Black filmmaker of Jafa's generation to break into the Hollywood system and establish a career on his own terms was Spike Lee. Lee went to a screening of "Daughters" and as he was leaving the theatre he introduced himself and asked if Jafa would like to work on a film about Malcolm X. Jafa said yes, and his skill as a cameraman on the movie led to his becoming the cinematographer for Lee's next feature, "Crooklyn." "Spike changed my life," Jafa said. "He put me on the path to being a legitimate entity in the film universe." The two of them didn't get along, though, and they haven't worked together since. Lee had no interest in Jafa's urge to experiment on "Crooklyn" with lenses and film speeds, cinematic rhythms, and nonlinear storytelling. "We had a rocky collaboration, but we've finally reached a rapprochement, and I want to keep it that way," Jafa told me.

I asked him to name the filmmakers he most admired. "I like films more than filmmakers," he said. "But, anything Andrei Tarkovsky ever did, especially 'The Mirror' and 'The Sacrifice,' his last. Tarkovsky's films are philosophical meditations on life, time, aging, things like that." Yasujirō Ozu, he said, was "right up there, not quite as high as Tarkovsky. Ozu will sit with things." The Italians? "I love Fellini, Pasolini, Antonioni. Antonioni is a great filmmaker, but to me that really does come down to 'L'Avventura,' the film where he plays with dimensions of dramatic time and space. There's a scene with Monica Vitti in a hotel corridor. She walks into the frame, and then out of the frame, and in a Hollywood film you would cut, but the camera just stays on that long, empty hallway."

Jafa respects Ingmar Bergman, but, he said, "I don't know if his films have aged so well, even 'Persona,' which is clearly a great film." He likes Godard more than Truffaut, and, he said, "Bresson is above anybody we've mentioned, except Tarkovsky—Bresson is the Beethoven and Bach of cinema." He also paid homage to Oscar Micheaux, whom he called "the godfather of Black American cinema." I asked him about Andy Warhol. "Neck and neck with Bresson," he said, to my surprise. "Every moment in a Warhol film is an extended moment. You think of Miles Davis, the speed at which he improvises. His notes sit in the air like they're unfurling in slow motion. They always feel introspective, considered, not in the moment." Jafa puts "The Godfather: Part II" in his top ten films, "but Coppola is not in my top ten directors."

FROM THE EARLY NINETIES TO 2000, LIVING IN NEW YORK, JAFA SHOT documentaries (on Audre Lorde and W. E. B. Du Bois, among others), music videos, and television commercials. "The early nineties was when you started to see more Blacks in Hollywood movies," he said. "I wanted to direct music videos, and I was very unsuccessful. I could never crack it. I guess I could have moved to Hollywood and done what everybody else does, but I didn't see that." Ideas for films proliferated in his head. The schoolboy notebooks in which he'd pasted images from comic books and magazines when he was ten had been succeeded by three-ring binders filled with movie stills, advertisements, news photographs, and reproductions from art books and countless other sources—images that he liked to show to people. He often had binders with him. "A.J. was always a great storyteller of his own film ideas," the writer and critic Greg Tate recalled. "He would act out all the parts." Tate and Jafa connected when they were both returning books to the Founders Library at Howard. They talked for six hours on the library steps, and the conversation has been going on ever since.

Jafa also spent time in art galleries and museums, and immersed himself in art history and theory. His fascination with Marcel Duchamp kept surfacing in our conversations. "My whole understanding of Duchamp has to do with African artifacts, aesthetic artifacts, and their profound effect on Western art," Jafa said. Picasso, Matisse, Derain, and other artists in Paris during the early years of the twentieth century had discovered African sculpture at the Musée d'Ethnographie du Trocadéro, and it had changed the way they saw the world. "All those people used African artifacts to make paintings, because they had certain spatial and formal implications, and the massing of those implications produced Cubism," Jafa said. "Duchamp made paintings in that modality—'Nude Descending a Staircase,' where you see the figure multiple times at the same moment and from different vantage points. But Duchamp was smarter than anybody around. I think he realized that a lot of the energy produced by African objects came not from their formal and spatial qualities but from their being what I would call radically alienated. It was contextual. An African artifact in a white museum space, with all this baggage of ideas about painting and contemplation, was deeply alien."

Jafa believes that Duchamp's 1917 "Fountain," a porcelain urinal from a plumbing-supply store, turned upside down and signed "R. Mutt," was directly influenced by African sculpture and drew its undeniable power from the same sort of radical alienation. "What Duchamp did better than any other artist was to take something that existed and turn it into another thing," Jafa said. "He didn't make it—he turned it into something else. It's like what I say about Black people and basketball. We didn't invent basketball, but we created it. One of the more telling things about Black people is that we do things that don't make our job easier. Why do a three-sixty before you land a basketball? You don't get more points—it just raises your level of difficulty. What is that about?" (His voice went up about an octave.) "Folks argue that it's entertainment, but it's central to who we are. It's refusing the structures that want to turn the game into a business. We know it's a business—winning—but we refuse to acquiesce in the elimination of play. And I don't think it's a big leap to say that's central to Duchamp's entire practice. For all the intellectualism around Duchamp, what did he always insist on? That it was playful. His tongue was definitely in his cheek."

So was Jafa's when he revealed his "secret theory" that Jeff Koons is "a very light-skinned Black guy passing for white." He argued, "Look at the works that made his reputation. The vacuum cleaners refer to Black women, domestic workers. The two basketballs floating in vitrines, I insist, are testicles, connoting everything from castration to Black sexual prowess. The bunny rabbit, which most people say is his masterpiece, is clearly Brer Rabbit." Jafa went on in this vein for quite a while before returning to Duchamp.

"He is one of the non-musicians I would put in the company of John Coltrane and Miles Davis," he said. "There were occasionally white people at our family reunions, in-laws and white friends of my parents. Duchamp is one of the people we will always reserve a seat for."

IN 1999, JAFA DECIDED TO QUIT THE FILM WORLD. HE WASN'T GETTING any closer to directing his own films, and it seemed to him that the art world offered more opportunities to realize the ideas swarming in his head. He'd been interested in art since his second year at Howard, when one of his architecture teachers sent the class to see I. M. Pei's new East Building, at the National Gallery of Art. "There was an exhibition of Mark Rothko, eight brownish paintings that all looked the same to my untrained eye, and they infuriated me," Jafa recalled. "I told the instructor it was bullshit. I was irate. I went back to that show ten times, kept going back, couldn't get it out of my mind. I was obsessed. He's still my favorite painter."

Twenty years later, when Jafa decided to do "this art thing," success came almost immediately. A group of his short videos appeared in the 2000 Whitney Biennial—one of the curators, Valerie Cassel Oliver, described them in *ARTnews* as "very subtle, very poetic." Jafa's "Tree" was included in the Whitney's "BitStreams" exhibition a year later; it's an eight-minute video of a blurry, constantly moving tree that looks like it's escaped from a Monet painting and gone off on its own. Other art works by Jafa appeared in group shows in this country and abroad: a metal bench he had found on a visit to Bamako, Mali; a Pontiac Firebird Trans Am, resting on a frame that gave it the appearance of floating; a video of a man in a yellow jacket lying on a sidewalk with people walking past. By 2005, though, the overbearing whiteness of the art world had driven him back to filmmaking. "I was invited to parties where I was the only Black person," he recalled. "It just didn't feel right, so I walked away from the art world."

In 2002, at a New Year's Eve party in New York, he met Suné Woods, a young woman on her way to becoming an artist. "It was almost like a force turned me around, and I said to Greg Tate, 'Hey, man, who is that? I'm going to marry her.'" Woods and Jafa never married, but in 2004 they had a son, Ayler. "Then we just fell apart," Jafa said. "Suné said she was going to graduate school in San Francisco and taking Ayler with her, and that was terrifying to me, because I'd had the same experience when I split up with Julie." Jafa commuted between New York and San Francisco for two years, before moving to Los Angeles in 2010. He wanted to be closer to Ayler, and also to N'Zinga, who was living with her mother in L.A. Dash had built an impressive reputation as a director of film biographies (she's currently doing one on Angela Davis), and she and Jafa had never been out of touch. ("We're still best friends," Dash told me recently. Their first grandchild, Adrian Julian Arana, born to N'Zinga in 2017, brought them even closer.) When Jafa moved to Los Angeles, his self-confidence was at a low ebb. The film industry seemed less and less interested in hiring him. He was approaching fifty, and he felt as though he hadn't achieved any of his goals. His friends were worried. "He was like a falling star," John Akomfrah said. "He'd always been a figure of such promise. All of us expected something great to happen, and as the years went by some people were thinking maybe it wasn't going to come."

In 2011, he hit rock bottom. Depressed and suicidal, he went to stay with his parents, in Atlanta. ("You can always come home," they had told their children.) After the breakup with Dash, Jafa had dealt with his depression by going into therapy. This time, the film world intervened. Sitting in his parents' living room, wondering what to do with his broken life, he got a telephone call from Paul Garnes, a Hollywood producer who worked with the show-runner Salim Akil. "Paul said I was like a mythical beast, because everybody out there had heard of me but nobody knew me," Jafa told me. He had called to see if Jafa was available to shoot the pilot for a new TV series, a comedy-drama like "Entourage," about Black people, that Akil was directing. "Available? I was broke and out of work. The producers must have liked the pilot, because they asked me to shoot the series—for a shitful of money. I thought, Well, maybe just grow the fuck up and take the money."

Jafa used the forty-five thousand dollars he'd been paid for the pilot to buy a new Prius and to rent a small apartment in L.A. The series wasn't picked up, though, and he had to find something to do right away—he was determined not to sink back into despair. Kahlil Joseph, a filmmaker and a close friend, called to say that ZDF, a German public-television network, had commissioned him to make a documentary about the March on Washington, whose fiftieth anniversary was coming up in 2013. Joseph had scheduling conflicts. Would Jafa be interested in directing it? Jafa said he would—and he had ideas about how. "I wasn't interested in looking back," Jafa told me. "I was interested in where Black people are now. I wrote a really insane, crazy treatment that had very little to do with the March on Washington, and they gave me the money and I went off and did it. And that was the beginning of the work I'm doing now."

JAFA'S FILM, CALLED "DREAMS ARE COLDER THAN DEATH," IS A FIFTY-two-minute collage of brief and not so brief interviews with African-American artists, writers, filmmakers, academics, and friends, alternating or coinciding with images of houses and back yards, waves breaking over rocks, Civil War photographs, extreme closeups of eyes, mouths, and faces, photographs of Martin Luther King, Jr., and James Baldwin. The speakers pull no punches, and what comes through is an orchestrated assault of incendiary thinking about racism. There were financial disagreements with a producer, and "Dreams" wasn't televised in the U.S. But it was shown in 2014 at the BlackStar Film Festival, in Philadelphia, and at the New York Film Festival. By then, Jafa had started working on a project that he called "APEX."

Close to eight hundred separate images flash by in "APEX"'s eight minutes and twenty-two seconds, against a pounding techno beat: a man's deeply scarred back, Walt Disney and Mickey Mouse, the fiery surface of the sun, a cartoon shark, lynchings, Sojourner Truth, Aretha Franklin, a cross-legged monk on fire, movie stills of white actors in blackface, Black people being fire-hosed, a 1920 Harlem street parade beneath a sign that reads "The New Negro Has No Fear." Jafa worked on "APEX" for four years, off and on, without knowing what it was. "I didn't understand it as a film, or as art," he told me. "I assumed it was an internal document that I showed to my friends."

Early in 2016, working again as a cinematographer and staying in a New York hotel room between jobs, Jafa put together the basic elements of "Love Is the Message, the Message Is Death." There was no concept and no script. "It was a response to the influx of footage of Black people being assaulted, which I had just been throwing in a file." A week later, he heard Kanye West's "Ultralight Beam" performed on "Saturday Night Live" and decided to use it as the soundtrack—without notifying West or getting permission. (West's reaction, when he and Jafa met, in 2020, was to say that Jafa's film had brought him "back to life," and to hire him to direct a music video for the song "Wash Us in the Blood.") Jafa showed an early version of "Love Is the Message" to Greg Tate, Fred Moten, Saidiya Hartman, the cinematographer Bradford Young, and other friends. Tate said, "There's something about the construction of it, the flow and the velocity, that's very much the way young people experience the Internet. It resonates with this generation's hip-hop culture."

Jafa wanted to post the film on YouTube, but Kahlil Joseph urged him not to give it away. Joseph screened it several times on film nights at the Underground Museum, in Los Angeles, as an unannounced opener for the main feature. Soon afterward, in June, Joseph showed it to a small, private audience in Switzerland during Art Basel, the international art fair. Gavin Brown, a British-born artist who had become a New York art dealer, and who had a long history of finding and nurturing new talent, saw it there. "I remember being stuck to my chair, eyes wide, trying to keep up with it, and then as it ended I felt the air being expelled from my body," he said.

Brown had never heard of Jafa. When he got back to New York, he tracked down a number and called him. Jafa was in Los Angeles, driving Ayler to school. Brown started to introduce himself, but Jafa broke in and said, "I know who you are. I'm coming to New York next week—we should meet." They met at Brown's gallery in Harlem, and walked to Maison Harlem for a four-hour lunch. "It was like being in a storm," Brown recalled. "Toward the end, he said, 'What are we doing here? Why are we meeting?' I told him I would love to show his film. He said, 'Nah, I don't want that,' but then we talked some more, and he asked, 'When would you want to do this?' I said, 'In a couple of weeks.' He said that was crazy, and then he left, and the next day we talked and he said, 'Let's do it.'"

"Love Is the Message" opened at Gavin Brown's gallery on November 12th, four days after Donald Trump was elected President. "Everybody was stunned by what had happened to this country, or by what this country really is," Brown said. Projected onto a large wall in an empty, darkened gallery, the images of "Love Is the Message" were larger than life, and the sound was enveloping. Several viewers wept openly. Jafa hadn't expected this response, and, later, when he kept hearing about the film making people cry, he felt uneasy. "Why are tears the metric of having a critical or productive engagement with it?" he wondered. "I don't know if I completely understand." That his success had come in the art world, which he'd given up on more than a decade earlier, made it even more unexpected. The art world had changed since 2005, and many more Black artists were being shown—Jafa among them. The Hammer Museum, in Los Angeles, had exhibited sixty-three of Jafa's three-ring binders in its 2016 "Made in L.A." show.

Hans Ulrich Obrist, the director of London's Serpentine Galleries, saw the Hammer show and gave Jafa a large solo exhibition in 2017; it was a retrospective, although many of the works in it were new. In June, "APEX" made a sensational début at Art Basel. Jafa had his second show at Gavin Brown's gallery a year later. It occupied three floors, and included a sculpture of two eight-foot-high truck tires wrapped in heavy chains; a mural-size montage of the eight hundred images he had used to make "APEX"; and a new, two-hour-long film called "akingdoncomethas," which was devoted largely to footage of preachers and gospel singers. When asked by a young woman in a lecture audience whether he had now chosen the art world over the film world, Jafa laughed and said, "I didn't choose the art world, the art world chose me. I thought I was done with it."

Jafa's next film, "The White Album," won the Golden Lion, the top prize at the 2019 Venice Biennale. As a political document, it overpowers "Love Is the Message." A fat, middle-aged white man delivers an anguished mea culpa on white supremacy: "We're scared of Black vengeance. We're scared shitless, and we always have been. Since Day One, we've put our hands on Black people, grabbed 'em, snatched 'em up, put 'em on a boat, and made 'em our own friggin' personal slaves and assistants for no pay. We did all that. You're goddam right we're scared. . . . So we got a lot of fuckin' fear, man." A blond Valley Girl type, echoing Trump, tells us that she is "the farthest person from being racist," and complains that "white people have the hardest time nowadays because we try so hard. . . . Have some respect for white people, O.K.?" Nearly all the speakers are white. At one point, we're airborne, watching bombs explode on the ground and people flee machine-gun fire from a helicopter. In another sequence, a handcuffed white man sits on a curb yelling "Niggah, niggah, niggah" and "Fuck you" at an impassive Black policewoman. The film, to which Jafa keeps adding, also offers brief glimpses of Gavin Brown and other white people Jafa loves and respects. "Like many of my best ideas, 'The White Album' started as a joke," he said. "Echoing the Beatles' title was super-intentional. But a very thoughtful friend of mine said, 'Man, this is something huge. White folks are going to *love* it.'"

The horrifying death of George Floyd, in May, has had lasting repercussions. "I was tremendously moved the first time I saw images of the protest marches in Paris and London and other places," Jafa said recently. "I was moved, but I was also very reticent to unblock my heart. We've been living with this for so long." A week later, his thinking had shifted: "This is such a complex moment. I don't know if we've had a moment like this, where we have a pandemic and on top of that an insurrection. George Floyd's murder is as close to a straight-up lynching as anybody has seen. So many of my friends have parsed and dissected over and over why this particular instance of something that Black people have been complaining about from time immemorial—what is it about this instance that triggered people? One of the things I've heard, and that I think is true, is the unflinching nature of George Floyd and the cop looking at the camera. It's that rare instance of white America looking into a mirror and being frightened by what it sees staring back. Cornel West says there are certain things that Black people cannot not know in America. We know these things, even though they are fearsome, horrible things. And I've hardened my heart, because I don't want to be debilitated by the lack of empathy for Black people. But I think maybe people are starting to realize that the way we have been treated for the last couple of hundred years doesn't just diminish the collective lives of Black people—it diminishes the living force of everybody. I think they are starting to get that."

THERE IS NO LONGER A SEPARATION IN JAFA'S WORK BETWEEN FILM-making and art. A large Jafa retrospective is scheduled to open in January at the Louisiana Museum, in Denmark. Many of his recent films will be on view, and the show has given him the chance to fabricate new works that he's been thinking about for years. A film made with computer technology alone (no camera was used) conjures up what looks like black, turbulent water endlessly plunging and crashing in on itself. A series of long, wall-mounted sculptures that resemble railroad tracks, in varying lengths, relate to something Jafa talked about with David Bowie thirty years ago: "The idea of taking things that don't have any value, that are detritus, and making something magnificent of them. They feel like found objects, readymades, but they are imagined and generated."

Jafa also has several full-length films in development. In 2014, he and two friends, the cinematographer Malik Sayeed and the curator Elissa Blount Moorhead, joined forces in a film production company called TNEG, but it never quite got off the ground. "I couldn't decide whether I wanted to be Walt Disney or Mickey Mouse," Jafa joked. The attention paid to "Love Is the Message" wasn't lost on potential backers, though, and early in 2020 Jafa, Gavin Brown, the Hollywood producer Melinda Nugent, whom Jafa has known for twenty-five years, and the Swiss collector and entrepreneur Maja Hoffmann started a company called SunHaus to support Jafa's projects and also to develop film work by other artists. "Our funding is coming from the art world, and we're confident that we will be able to control the process," Nugent told me.

An investor has pledged enough money to keep them running for three years.

Jafa had planned to start work this past spring on "Cudhial," a narrative film, set in the Mississippi Delta, about a love affair between a seventeen-year-old high-school student and his teacher. (The pandemic intervened; he will try again next spring.) This is the kind of film that Haile Gerima has always wanted Jafa to make: personal, relational, and deeply felt. "Daughters of the Dust" had been a "promissory note" for both Jafa and Dash, according to Gerima—a preview of the storytelling talent they shared in such abundance. Jafa read the "Cudhial" script to Gerima thirty years ago, on the phone; it took hours. "The first script was lost," Jafa said. "I moved so many times over the years." He is rewriting it, with help from Boston. "A lot of my feelings about Julie Dash are bound up in 'Cudhial,'" he said. "She was the most beautiful, the most sophisticated . . ." His voice trailed off. "She taught me so many things."

"Cudhial" (pronounced "Cu-jul") is a word Jafa made up. He does this now and then, if the language seems to need it. "I used to have a tight grasp of what 'Cudhial' meant, but now it's just a feeling, a kind of nostalgia—not longing for a moment as much as am-bivalence about a moment," he said. "I think it's about my personal notion of Black being. It's like saying, 'That painful experience I went through made me who I am. I wouldn't want to relive it, but I constantly return to it, and I luxuriate in it in a certain way. But the parts that were amazing, the parts that were pleasurable, are strictly bound up with the parts that were painful.'"

In a remark that was widely misunderstood, Jafa once said that he wasn't addressing white people in his work. "I never said I don't care what white people think about it," he told me. "I'm super-pleased when white people like my work, or are interested in it, or provoked by it. But I'm talking to Black people, not to everybody. I'm certainly not trying to talk to white people, and I don't think it serves white people to be spoken to. It makes them feel like they're the center of the universe, in a way that is profoundly problematic. In Eric Clapton's 'Layla,' which I think is the greatest hard-rock love song ever, he's not singing to everybody. He's singing to Pattie Boyd. He fell in love with his best friend's wife, and he's singing to her. And everybody else is listening in."

THE *SHADOW* ACT

HILTON ALS

October 8, 2007

Octavia picked up her pen in the dimly lit Moroccan restaurant and leaned over her notebook. A bespectacled nine-year-old who aspires to a career in fashion, she thought for a moment and then set to work. It was June, 2007. Outside, Paris was thick with humidity in the twilight. Inside, the restaurant's pillows and rugs were redolent of tagines past. But Octavia's concentration was complete as she drew first a head, then a neck, then a pair of wide, staring eyes. Gradually, it became clear that the figure she was sketching was her mother, the thirty-seven-year-old black American artist Kara Walker, who was in Paris for the opening of her travelling retrospective, "My Complement, My Enemy, My Oppressor, My Love." The show, which had originated at Walker Art Center, in Minneapolis, in February, was due to open two days later at the ARC/Musée d'Art Moderne de la Ville de Paris. (Curated by Philippe Vergne, Walker Art Center's deputy director and chief curator, "My Complement" will open at the Whitney Museum of American Art, in New York, this month.) Intellectually and emotionally ambitious, Walker's retrospective showcases more than two hundred of the provocative—frequently incendiary—and racially charged images that she has produced in her thirteen-year career.

A kind of latter-day Daumier, Walker presents—in huge tableaux constructed from black-paper cutouts or silhouettes, as well as in watercolors, drawings, and films—a visual world that rivals the French master's. Instead of industrial Paris, Walker combs the mansions and swamps of the antebellum South to find her characters, whose surroundings are a visual corollary of their fetid imaginations and musty souls. Like Daumier, she pays attention to costume, which functions in her work as a signifier not only of race and class but of ethics. Her white characters are often creatures of fashion, morally bankrupt beneath their silken folds, while her black characters wear the uniform of the oppressed: head rags, aprons, or tattered britches. But Walker is much more than a caricaturist. Her work has a spiritual quality, a meditative thoroughness that recalls the canvases of the late Haitian master Hector Hyppolite. Where Hyppolite used Catholic and voodoo symbols, Walker's saint figure is a character she calls the Negress. Small, with braided hair and sometimes oversized boots, the Negress appears in a number of Walker's works, often shitting, vomiting, or farting her way through a beautiful composition on the subject of bestiality, lynching, or the Christian ethos of slavery. Still, Walker's belief in the Negress's trickster nature—in her wiles and her will to survive—makes *us* believe that the girl can beat the odds and make it through.

At the restaurant, Walker sat on her daughter's left. On Octavia's right were two other Walker women: Kara's sister, Dana, who runs the continuing-studies division of a design college, in Pasadena, California, and her mother, Gwendolyn, who is a former amateur dress designer and seamstress. (As a girl, Kara modelled Gwendolyn's designs in her home town, Stockton, California.) In a sense, visual culture is the family business. (Walker's father, Larry, is a painter.) But Walker—who as a child dreamed of becoming the next Charles Schulz—is, so far, the only family member to have achieved international visibility in the art world. In 1997, at the age of twenty-eight, she became one of the youngest people to be given a MacArthur "genius" fellowship. The award followed an outpouring of works like "The End of Uncle Tom and the Grand Allegorical Tableau of Eva in Heaven" (1995). In this large-scale cutout wall piece, Walker laid out, among other things, a trio of female slaves suckling one another while a plantation floats in the distance; a prepubescent slave girl—Walker's Negress—defecating and brandishing a tambourine; a white girl in a hoopskirt wielding an axe; and a potbellied gentleman with a wooden leg and an erect penis, which is shaped not like a male member but like a slave boy (in his hand is a sword impaling a slave baby). Walker's vision, here and elsewhere, is of history as trompe-l'oeil. Things are not what they seem, because America is, literally, incredible, fantastic—a freak show that is almost impossible to watch, let alone to understand. In Walker's work, slavery is a nightmare from which no American has yet awakened: bondage, ownership, the selling of bodies for power and cash have made twisted figures of blacks and whites alike, leaving us all scarred, hateful, hated, and diminished. "The End of Uncle Tom" not only takes on Harriet Beecher Stowe's 1852 masterwork—which James Baldwin called "a catalogue of violence"—but also explores the psychological legacy of the acts of brutality it described. Both historical and contemporary, the piece is a critique of slavery, as well as of the casual racism that modern blacks are exposed to on a daily basis in our post–politically correct times. Walker throws hatred back in our faces.

She uses the country's pre- and post-Reconstruction past to examine her personal history, too. "I am driven by myself . . . the capture of myself in the mirror, the auctioning off of myself . . . teeth and hair, tits and ass," she once wrote. And she is not unaware of the ambivalence—or anger—that the graphic and accusatory nature of her work inspires in some viewers. "Dear you insufferable cunt, you with your Black wailings, your Hungry ghosts, your vengeful heart," she wrote in the voice of an imaginary critic, on one of a series of index cards in a piece titled "Texts" (2001). "Why do you insist on tormenting yourself, as well as your loved ones, with Ingratitude? . . . You are given 'chances' 'opportunities' 'inches,' as well as Miles. And you take them all. And spit,

spit in those faces, bite those hands defecate on heads from your bare branch perch."

In 2000, Walker gave a talk at the Des Moines Art Center. Afterward, a white man in the audience asked her how long she intended to make the type of work she did. Walker responded, "Oh, probably as long as I'm black and a woman." (This exchange has been quoted as an example of Walker's "fearlessness," with Walker depicted in the press as the art community's very own Sojourner Truth, a paragon of black righteousness in a corrupt white world—an image that Walker, who has said that she occasionally feels like "somebody's pet project," is very much aware of.) But, of course, the subtext behind the Des Moines man's question remains: Why—or how—does a Kara Walker come to exist at all?

THE FOUR WALKER WOMEN COVERED THE SPECTRUM OF THE COLOR brown. Octavia was the lightest (her father—the German-born jewelry designer Klaus Bürgel, from whom Walker recently separated—is white), Walker the darkest. The adult Walkers were tall and thin, with a graceful bearing and prominent clavicles. Their speaking voices were almost indistinguishable. Before answering any question, no matter how trivial—Moroccan waiter: "The couscous is *super!* You try, yes?"—they murmured among themselves like doves.

The men of the family were absent. Walker's father had stayed home, in Lithonia, Georgia. Her brother, Larry, Jr., a tax consultant who lives in a suburb of Atlanta, was not on speaking terms with Dana at the time. The Paris trip was important to Walker for reasons beyond the exhibition. "Because my family is so disparate and weird in some ways, it wasn't until recently that I had the feeling of having a family," she'd told me in late May, at her apartment on New York's Upper West Side. Two years earlier, when Dana was ill, Walker and her mother had travelled to California to help her as she recovered. "And for about ten days we were all in her little apartment with her three cats, just helping one another out, and I was so taken by the whole thing," Walker said. She hoped to duplicate the experience in Paris. "It's still kind of an experiment," she said thoughtfully.

At the end of the meal, Walker's mother raised her eyes from Octavia's drawing and said, "You know, as a child Kara drew first from paintings and photographs. When I told her it was good, she'd say, 'Mom, anyone can do that.' And I said, 'No, they can't.'" She turned to her daughter. "After a while, you were drawing what was there, what was around."

"No, I wasn't," Walker insisted. "I was drawing what I *saw*."

"THE ARTIST IS LIKE AN ABUSER OF EVERYTHING—PICTURE-PLAYING, HIStory, other people," Walker told me. Her vision of her work as an antidote to politeness has its roots in a number of events. In 1983, when Walker was thirteen, her father moved the family from Stockton, where he had chaired the art department at the University of the Pacific, to Atlanta, where he took on similar responsibilities at Georgia State University. Larry, whom Walker describes as having a "big personality," like Bill Clinton's, had grown up partly in Georgia, and every time he came back to California from an interview there he'd say, "It's a changed place. The New South."

The family eventually settled in Stone Mountain, a suburb of Atlanta, which was known for a giant carving commemorating Confederate Army leaders and was a historical meeting place for the Ku Klux Klan. "There was some kind of welcoming reception for my dad," Walker said. "The chairman of the Fine Arts Department had this kind of patrician accent, and he made these boring pin-striped paintings. And there was my dad, all six foot four of him, Mr. Can-Do, much respected in California, and Mr. Patrician talking down to him in a way that I couldn't conceive of: 'Very good, young man.' My dad stood there with this sort of nervous posture." Walker bowed her head and hunched her shoulders, striking an attitude of little-boy defeat. "I've never asked him about that moment. It was sad, because we had just left a place where there was a celebration for my dad's contributions—to the university and the city and the schools. And then, at this place, there were these people just looking at him, like, Hmm."

For many black American children, the primal scene is not the sight of their parents having sex but the sight of their parents being diminished by white condescension. The question that the child asks himself, then, is this: If whites can reduce my father—my protector—to powerlessness, what can they do to me? Walker claims to have absorbed her father's generally optimistic perspective—"It's all possible, and good things will come if you work toward them"—as well as her mother's subtle undercutting of it: "The things I remember my mom sort of intuiting under the radar were, like, Well, life ain't fair. So as a child I opted for my father's world view, with a kind of freaked-out understanding of there being something darker at work."

When it comes to Walker's art, the black male figure—generally a slave, sometimes engaged in homosexual acts with a white slave owner—has special meaning for her. She told me that, in order to bring emotional validity to her black male figures, "I've consulted 'official' black men. I look to my father and my brother. And they're sort of opposites in interesting ways." Larry, Jr., was, she said, "a problem kid until recently. He's got sort of a violent personality. Also very smart. So he's a searingly brilliant person who takes all these super-interesting wrong turns. When I was a kid, I thought of my brother as the guy who was always disappearing. He was a little bit aimless. But he became very religious—that was his thing. Right-wing. Jimmy Swaggart. The TV was at full blast all day long. He would go off on tangents, and I was his disciple, because I was home and I didn't have a driver's license, and I'd think, That's my role. That's what I do. If I can't beat him, I just have to sit here and wait until this is over."

Walker found refuge in art. She believes that Larry, Jr.,'s powerful reactions to things—"Sometimes my brother would go off like fireworks"—are "part of my makeup now. I have a big fear of losing control, or losing control in ways that I can't control. A studio, or just a sketchbook, has always been the place where I could do that, but it was confined and finite." Art was also a way of connecting with her father, who, despite his reserve, celebrated her childhood ambitions by using her drawings as Christmas cards. (His restraint has held strong. Walker mentioned a show of her drawings that her parents had come to see: "My dad talked about all kinds of superficial things, like the push and pull in the use of graphite and the eraser. And I kind of sat there next to him, wanting to say, 'We're looking at a disintegrating Negro pussy!'")

As an adolescent, Walker sat in on her father's life-drawing classes. "Sometimes I would venture into his studio, which was the garage, bug him and hang around, wait for something," she said. What she was waiting for was her own voice, her particular vision. In 1987, she was accepted at the Atlanta College of Art. While there, she began to question not only her family's precepts but her identity as a painter. "There were definitely accepted artistic modes in the South in the eighties," she recalled. At the A.C.A., the work that was encouraged, she said, involved "this kind of crafty, gothic Southern sensibility." Conceptual art was not encouraged; "the mere use of the word 'conceptual' implied a violence to that universe," she said. Still, when Walker was nineteen, an instructor referred her to the work of the conceptual artist Adrian Piper. Since the nineteen-sixties, Piper, a light-skinned black woman who is sometimes mistaken for white, had been making photographs, word pieces, and sculptures that addressed race and gender and the ways in which we internalize the roles assigned to us. In response to the work, Walker wrote a paper that she titled "Black/White (grey) notes on Adrian Piper." The piece is a series of lyrical statements and questions that Walker asked herself: "I'm not an Other in some eyes / I think / and yet a black woman-artist-philosopher has a / calling card to announce when she has been stumbled upon / injured, ignored by the elite / over whom she strives to soar." Walker was not only announcing her ambitions; as she makes clear in the next line—"Am I ignorant of all strife?"—she was pushing herself toward identity politics, and beginning to question her own existence between two worlds, as a relatively privileged black woman. Walker now says of the paper, "I think it reveals something of my inhibitions at the time about making any kind of racialized gesture in my work." Back then, she said, her attitude toward race and art was "I'm not going to ghettoize. You have 'real' art, and then the art of the ethnic minority." But, as she examined the work of other contemporary black female conceptual artists, such as Lorna Simpson, things began to change. Life—and race—intruded on her "universalist" approach to her work. One pivotal episode for Walker was an event at the A.C.A. in which the school's relatively small contingent of black students arranged a study group to talk about race. "I was working in the slide library," Walker said, "and a black artist was invited to give a talk. All the black students went to this thing, and I was working in the library where it was happening, but I didn't attend. I was outside the door, doing the slides." Her habit of keeping herself, literally, apart from blackness was, she said, "the kind of thing I felt I needed to address." She was also doing work—a series of allegorical paintings involving birdlike creatures—that didn't please her. "It was just painting in general," she said. "It was just moving my hand, but to what purpose, you know?"

During her senior year, she added, "I started to recognize what sort of role I played, what place I occupied in the world of white students. I remember these students talking about 'In Living Color'"—the sketch-comedy television series with a primarily black cast. "It was sort of the heyday. And they were talking about the 'fly girls' on 'In Living Color,' and an older female student said, 'They have such big bottoms!' And another guy was trying to clarify, saying, 'I think that's something that black people are known for.' And I was sitting there alone, just sort of listening." The discomfort that Walker felt on overhearing the exchange fuelled her work as an artist. "At the time, I was mainly interested in sex and falling in love," she said. "And I had these romance magazines—*Bronze Thrills* was one of them, and *Jive*, I think. I was interested in the ads for clairvoyance and the romance photoplays in the back, and the advertisements for body enhancements. It was a devious little moment." At the A.C.A., she was given a wall on which to do a mural. "I wound up doing a mural of a booty implant. It was shortly after that conversation about butts."

Walker didn't fall in love during this period—she says now that there "wasn't really a real relationship before my husband"—but she had what she calls "experiments." "What I was getting out of the experiment is unclear," she said, "but something was received. And one of those things had to do with becoming a black woman— being objectified, being an object of white male desire. Without hitting a couple of dark milestones in my sense of self, I wouldn't have started making the silhouettes." One such dark milestone was Walker's on-again, off-again sexual relationship with a complicated white man. "I have for years been overcoming the vast mythology I constructed around him . . . certain that to acknowledge him publicly would mean my imminent death," she told me in an e-mail. "As I think I have alternately suggested he is a sadist, a racist, a misogynist . . . and, perhaps less credibly: Satan himself. At the time of my entanglement with him I suffered something my therapist later called a 'schizoid reaction' . . . where I became two very different people, kind of Jekyll and Hyde-ish, and behaved a bit like a trapped animal. It is true, I learned a lot during that time, but all of it couched in silence and a deep sense of terror. . . . I was to him 'an enigma' and there was no love lost."

Walker's self-scrutiny on this and other issues forced me, as it has other viewers of her work, to see my questioning in a different light. By treating her as a journalistic "subject" and pressing her for self-revelation, had I also inadvertently turned her into an object? Just as she does in her art, she exposed herself—left herself vulnerable—in order to set me right. Thelma Golden, the director of the Studio Museum in Harlem, who has worked with Walker on a number of occasions, told me that she admires the artist's compulsion to reveal herself. Still, she worries for her. "Sometimes, when we're having a dialogue that's meant for publication, I say to Kara, 'Do you *really* want to say that?,' and the answer is always yes."

When Walker enrolled in the M.F.A. program at the Rhode Island School of Design, in Providence, in 1992 (she received a degree in painting and printmaking, in 1994), she found herself "far from bad influences." In Providence, Walker said, she felt, for the first time, that "I could make it my mission to discover why did I see this put-upon, burdened black girl when I looked at myself? Why did a girl like me, who grew up in the suburbs, safe and declawed, have this feeling?" She added, "Maybe early on, if I'd had sort of a critical input from black women in my life or a less silent black family, I wouldn't have been so curious." History was merging with the personal, and the dialogue that Walker was having with herself was supplemented by reading. "I kept getting books that had 'sex' in the title," she recalled. "'Making Sex' was one—looking at how gender is described in nineteenth-century texts. Things like that." But there was one book that was especially significant, "Home Girls," an anthology of black feminist writing from the eighties. "It was kind of dated, but it was really useful," she said. "The book was so new for me, in a way." Hearing black feminist concerns articulated by other women and artists of color helped Walker to recognize how she was viewed in the eyes of her fellow-countrymen.

"One of the most interesting reversals of cultural prejudice . . . comes from the old notion that black women represented the lowest possible moral standard for any (white supremacist patriarchal) nation or state," Walker said, in an interview with Silke Boerma, before her 2002 show, "Kara Walker: For the Benefit of All the Races of Mankind An Exhibition of Artifacts, Remnants, and Effluvia EXCAVATED from the Black Heart of a Negress." She went on:

> Why? And what does that mean, or how has that viewpoint changed (or has it) in view of powerhouses like Oprah Winfrey or the hundreds of black entertainers and black female politicians and activists? Well, the myth comes about sometime in pre-Enlightenment Europe when whites confused Negroes with animals and then surmised that black women were fucking orangutans. I mean being fucked by them. Voltaire lampoons this myth in "Candide," William Blake made a print of helpless "primitive" girls being ravaged by apes. . . .
>
> So one of the motifs in my work is that as a Black Girl I am a thing which is violated by filthy beasts. The other is that Western progress and colonization, slavery, Modernism, etc., grew out of a white European need to not feel like the filthy beasts they feared they might be. . . .
>
> The other motif is that as a black woman seeking a position of power I must first dispel with (or at least reckon with) the assumption (not my own, but given to me like an inheritance) that I am amoral, beastly, wild. And that because of this I must be chained, domesticated, kept, traded, bred. And out of this subservient condition . . . I must escape, go wild, be free, after which I have to confront the questions: How free? How wild? How much further must I go to escape all I've internalized?

Not long before arriving in Providence, Walker told me, "I just sort of burst. And that's when I realized that everything I was doing, painting-wise, was just a lie and a cover. There was something in me that was never going to be relevant unless I sort of pulled back my skin and the skin of the painting that I was doing and looked at it for what it was." Walker's silhouette technique was the result of an intense period of looking. While she was immersing herself in the writings of black feminist critics and novelists, such as bell hooks, Michele Wallace, Toni Morrison, and Octavia Butler, she was also poring over reference books on early American art. One image captured her imagination: a nineteenth-century silhouette of a little black girl in profile. "I had a catharsis looking at early American varieties of silhouette cuttings," she wrote to me. "What I recognized, besides narrative and historicity and racism, was this very physical displacement: the paradox of removing a form from a blank surface that in turn creates a black hole. I was struck by the irony of so many of my concerns being addressed: blank/black, hole/whole, shadow/substance, etc. (There's also that great quote from Sojourner Truth: 'I sell the shadow to support the substance.')" Making silhouettes, Walker wrote to Gwendolyn Dubois Shaw for her book "Seeing the Unspeakable: The Art of Kara Walker," in 2004, "kind of saved me. Simplified the frenzy I was working myself into. Created the outward appearance of calm."

In using the silhouette, Walker was appropriating a sentimental form to build a narrative about power. First drawing on black paper, and then cutting her figures out freehand, she was engaging in a "reversal of the cultural prejudice" that she had experienced as a student in Atlanta. Now she was creating an art history of her own, one that not only took on the image of blacks in Western art—much as the black American Robert Colescott had done in the nineteen-seventies, when he replaced the Dutch figures in van Gogh's "The Potato Eaters," for instance, with slaves and retitled the painting "Eat Dem Taters"—but went a step further, both through sheer technical skill and by shifting the axis of the work away from satire and toward the realm of social realism, as well as social comedy. Walker's realism centered on her interpretation of the Negress, a figure that other artists had tackled before her. The black assemblage artist Betye Saar had made a name for herself in the seventies with pieces, such as "The Liberation of Aunt Jemima" (a depiction of Aunt Jemima holding a shotgun), that sought to "empower" the stereotypes of black women. Ellen Gallagher had rendered the Negress abstract, in perhaps too pretty works devoted to the notion of beauty in black female hair culture. But Walker incorporated a violence and an honesty that were unprecedented. It was as if she had ripped the slave woman out of Manet's "Olympia" and pasted her to a wall, forcing her to stand on her own and answer for herself as the heroine—or villain—of the narrative, instead of simply offsetting Olympia's white beauty.

The first silhouettes that Walker exhibited in New York were part of the "Selections 1994" show at the Drawing Center, in SoHo. Walker had come to New York from Rhode Island to interview at the College Art Association—a yearly forum where art historians and artists check out the academic job market. Walker was still a student, and she was intent on a career as a teacher. She had brought some slides of her first silhouettes. "I know there was a group of images on paper, and one was a Little Eva figure," she recalled, "and one was kind of a pickaninny melon, bursting in half, and the other one was a girl figure, with exaggerated black features in her face, while the rest of her body was like a mass, a kind of explosion of black paper." An artist friend encouraged her to leave her slides at the Drawing Center, which was run by an enthusiastic young curator named Annie Philbin. (She now heads the Hammer Museum, in Los Angeles, where "My Complement" is scheduled to open in March.) Philbin's associate James Elaine insisted that she take a look at Walker's work. "It was astonishing," Philbin recalled. She contacted Walker and asked if she could render her images in a larger scale and make a wall drawing.

The resulting piece, the thirteen-by-fifty-foot "Gone, An Historical Romance of a Civil War as It Occurred Between the Dusky

Thighs of One Young Negress and Her Heart," was the most blatantly romantic of Walker's early works. On the far left, two white lovers in the antebellum South stand on the banks of a river beneath a tree heavy with moss and lean into each other for a kiss. The gentleman's sword points to the backside of a small male slave, who holds a strangled bird, which may have just emerged from between the legs of the female slave sitting before him. In the center of the wall is a Plymouth Rock–like shape, from which a white man being fellated by a slave girl looks to the sky and sees a slave boy floating away, his phallus swollen into an enormous, almost human shape. (The viewer is reminded of the lovers, ghosts, and fabulist foliage in Toni Morrison's 1981 romance, "Tar Baby.") Clearly, Walker was still working somewhere between "pure" beauty—the elevation of shapes—and the search for a narrative that could capture both the eye and the heart. "There was this huge gesture that came out of me," she said. "And I felt like I got it back in waves." In a review of the resulting work that ran in the *Times*, the art critic Holland Carter wrote, "In a large figurative tableau . . . she fashions a surreal, raunchy, angry fantasia on the world of antebellum slavery. Looking like a cross between a children's book and a sexually explicit cartoon, this is skillful, imaginative work and will doubtless be showing up elsewhere soon."

"It was my proudest moment," Walker told me. "Honestly and truly. There's a little grainy picture of me, and I think that face is a proud face." But after the show, she says now, "I went, O.K., I don't know what happens after this. I didn't have a very good game plan." What Walker did have was a number of dealers who were eager to represent her. In the end, she signed on with Brent Sikkema, who is known for his political commitment to artists of color and women, and who has been her sole dealer ever since. "I think, maybe, one of the reasons Kara came to the gallery is that I went to Providence," Sikkema told me. "I had phoned Annie, who took care of the artists she showed at the Drawing Center. I thought, I love this, but there's no way I can go up against the other dealers who have money. I was struggling; my gallery was in my apartment." But one day, not long after the show opened, Sikkema found himself driving through Rhode Island with a friend. "I said, 'You know, I think Kara Walker lives around here.' And my friend said, 'Why don't you call her?' So I jumped out of the car and went to a phone booth. She was listed, and she asked us over and started showing us her work. It was like being in someone's laboratory. She was like a scientist who had been working away on all these gorgeous, strange, unforgettable experiments."

After Walker joined Sikkema, in 1994, the gallery blossomed. (It is now housed in a large, pristine space in Chelsea.) "I call the gallery the house that Kara built," Sikkema says. Walker's career and her personal life flourished, too. In 1993, she met Klaus Bürgel, who was then an instructor at the Rhode Island School of Design. They were married in Atlanta in 1996. Between 1994 and 1997, when she was awarded the MacArthur, Walker had eight solo exhibitions, and took part in more than fifteen group shows. The fellowship, however, resulted in an attack waged by what one observer called the "thought police": a group of artists who believed that visual art should be used to ennoble black Americans, not to expose their family secrets. In the summer of 1997, Betye Saar sent more than two hundred letters to prominent artists, writers, and politicians asking them to join her in a campaign to prevent Walker's art from being exhibited. "I am writing you, seeking your help to spread awareness about the negative images produced by the young African-American artist, Kara Walker," she wrote. "Are African-Americans being betrayed under the guise of art?" her accompanying statement began. Saar objected not only to the content of Walker's work—which she termed "revolting"—but to its lack of a relevant social consciousness, at least as she understood it. Saar's own satirical pieces about stereotypes in advertising were safely ensconced in a folk tradition and presented with a certain knowingness and warmth—with a wink at the audience. In Saar's predictable world, "whitey" was mostly to blame. Walker, on the other hand, explored not only the white world's fetishization of control and dominance but the black community's complicity in its own emotional enslavement.

Shortly afterward, Juliette Harris, the editor of the *International Review of African American Art*, wrote a long piece on the response of black artists and intellectuals to Walker's work and to that of another black artist, Michael Ray Charles. "I have nothing against Kara except that I think she is young and foolish," Saar told Harris. "Here we are at the end of the millennium seeing work that is very sexist and derogatory. . . . The trend today is to be as nasty as you want to be: TV, Rodman, rap. The goal is to be rich and famous. There is no personal integrity. . . . Kara is selling us down the river." With a flourish, Saar announced, "Aunt Jemima is back with a vengeance." (Of the article, Walker noted, "It's beautiful, because, to dismiss what I do, it basically does what I do: creates a stereotype where once there was a person. Uses all of the accoutrements of that person's humanity—their skin, their hair, their social life—to construct another character. The only thing that's missing is the signature, saying, 'This is my piece. This is *my* Kara Walker.'")

In October of the same year, the black American artist Howardena Pindell joined the fray when she said, in a talk at the Johannesburg Biennale, "What is troubling and complicates the matter is that Walker's words in published interviews mock African-Americans and Africans. . . . Walker consciously or unconsciously seems to be catering to the bestial fantasies about blacks created by white supremacy and racism." From Walker's perspective, she was exposing, not catering to, white male fantasies about black women. In 1998, in an interview with her cousin the writer James Hannaham, she addressed the prevalence of those attitudes today. "At some point in Atlanta," she recalled, "I was with my then boyfriend, John, in the park, thinking we were alone, but when we got back to the car there was a flyer from the Ku Klux Klan, spelling out for him all the evils of black women, describing what sort of peril he was in, and identifying stereotypes of disease and moral degradation. That was an awakening for naïve me. So I guess I needed a way to question how these types of issues have been represented in art previously."

In the *International Review* article, Henry Louis Gates, Jr., was one of several intellectuals and artists who came to Walker's defense. Walker, he argued, was "seeking to *liberate* both the tradition of the representation of the black in popular and high art forms and to liberate our people from residual, debilitating effects that the proliferation of those images undoubtedly has had upon the collective unconscious of the African-American people." He went on, "No one could mistake the images of Kara Walker . . . as *realistic* images! Only the visually illiterate could mistake their postmodern critiques for realistic portrayals, and that is the difference between the racist original and the post-modern, signifying, antiracist parody that characterizes this genre of artistic expression."

When I asked Kathy Halbreich, the director of Walker Art Center, about the uproar, she said, "I'm amazed that Kara continued to make stronger and stronger work. I think a lesser psyche would have collapsed." To Halbreich, Saar's and Pindell's criticisms seemed "largely generational. I understand that these women came of age when ambiguity was poison, but their efforts to silence Kara made me sad, even as I sort of understood the context out of which their speech arose. Here were women who'd worked so hard to get a voice, and they were trying to paralyze a younger set of vocal cords." Walker, who was pregnant at the time of the attacks, told me that she had been "pretty upset." "It was a triple whammy—the accolades, the dismissals, the hormones, all at the same time," she said. "You know, I had just started, *kaboom*, fireworks going on, and I felt, Well, I have to redouble my efforts if I'm going to keep all this going, and I've got to take this child and go charging through, like in football."

IN A SENSE, THE ARGUMENT OVER WHAT IS AND IS NOT RACIALLY "correct" in the art world originated in 1984, when Walker was still in high school and the late curators William Rubin and Kirk Varnedoe mounted a show called "'Primitivism' in 20th Century Art" at the Museum of Modern Art. The exhibition, which sought to find the "affinities" between European modernists, such as Gauguin and Picasso, and "tribal" art from Africa and elsewhere, caused a sensation. After it opened, the writer Thomas McEvilley published an essay titled "Doctor Lawyer Indian Chief," in *Artforum.* The show, McEvilley argued, "illustrates, without consciously intending to, the parochial limitations of our world view and the almost autistic reflexivity of Western civilization's modes of relating to the culturally Other." Janet Malcolm, commenting on McEvilley's essay, in this magazine, in 1986, noted, "There was something about the piece that was instantly recognized as more deeply threatening to the status quo than it is usual for a critique of a museum show to be. . . . McEvilley's article was like the knocking on the door dreaded by Ibsen's master builder—the sound of the younger generation coming to crush the older one."

What McEvilley set out to crush was the vision of "tribal art" as a tool to be used by more sophisticated Western artists. He decried "the museum's decision to give us virtually no information about the tribal objects on display, to wrench them out of context, calling them to heel in the defense of formalist modernism," adding, "No attempt is made to recover an emic, or inside, sense of what primitive esthetics really were or are. . . . The point of view of Picasso and others . . . is the only focus of MOMA's interest. . . . By their absolute repression of primitive context, meaning, content, and intention . . . [Rubin and Varnedoe] have treated the primitives as less than human, less than cultural—as shadows of a culture, their selfhood, their Otherness, wrung out of them." In other words, the message McEvilley drew from the MOMA show was that people of color don't exist unless whites say they do—and, even then, they exist only as they are seen by whites. What person wouldn't rebel in the face of declarations of his nonexistence?

The "'Primitivism'" show came at a time when the art world was redoubling its efforts to be inclusive, embracing first the feminist artist Sue Williams, then the performance artist Karen Finley, and the black artist Fred Wilson, among others. "Difference" had hit the mainstream, in both art and fashion. (The vogue for including artists of color and "queer" artists in major surveys reached its apotheosis in 1993, when Daniel Joseph Martinez created buttons for that year's Whitney Biennial that read, "I CAN'T IMAGINE EVER WANTING TO BE WHITE.") Nevertheless, more than twenty years later, Walker and others registered the same kind of blindness to the fate of black people that had incensed McEvilley, in the tardy response of the primarily white political élite to the devastation caused by Hurricane Katrina, which destroyed the lives and livelihoods of thousands of poor black Americans. Earlier that year, Walker had been invited by Gary Tinterow, the head of modern art at the Metropolitan Museum of Art, to do some work in the museum's twentieth-century wing. (Walker had moved to New York in 2002, to teach at Columbia University.) As Tinterow put it to her, she could curate a show of her own works, or one that also utilized the museum's holdings by other artists. Walker chose the second option. Then Katrina happened. Hence not only the title of the show, "After the Deluge," but the themes expressed in the works chosen: black people, poverty, water, disaster. Writing in the *Times*, the art critic Roberta Smith said of the show, "If, like Goya, Ms. Walker is a pitiless satirist who skewers the human condition with a grace and precision tantamount to tenderness, you could almost say that Katrina is Ms. Walker's version of Goya's Napoleonic Wars. But not quite: 'After the Deluge' includes no post-Katrina work by Ms. Walker. Instead, it reminds us that poverty and even water have also been longtime themes for Ms. Walker; if anything, her work warned of the pathologies that Katrina unleashed." (For the second anniversary of Hurricane Katrina, in August, Walker created a cover for this magazine, showing the continued plight of the hurricane victims, titled "Post Katrina—Adrift.")

A DAY BEFORE THE RETROSPECTIVE OPENED IN PARIS, I SAT IN FRONT OF the wall that separated the exhibition space from the lobby. On it, Vergne had installed Walker's "Endless Conundrum, an African Anonymous Adventuress" (2001). In the piece, which measures fifteen by thirty-five feet, were images on the subject of "modernism and primitivism." Witness the black American star Josephine Baker shaking loose her famous skirt made of artificial bananas, as another black woman, naked, crouches beneath her, expelling gas. Nearby, Walker had placed silhouettes of sculptures resembling works by Giacometti and Brancusi—what McEvilley would surely have seen as symbols of the European stealing from the African and then stamping out his source. Richard Flood, who is the chief curator of the New Museum of Contemporary Art, in New York, explained that Walker had originally created the piece for the Fondation Beyeler, a Swiss museum that exhibits African tribal sculptures next to modernist works: "'Primitivism'" redux. Still, Vergne hoped that, by confronting the French audience with "Endless Conundrum" first, he could show them something of Walker's message. "She uses pretty forms for content that hurts," he told me.

As I strolled through the galleries, I watched Walker at work. She had pressed Octavia into service for the installation of "Slavery! Slavery!" (1997). "Put the clouds there," she told her softly. Octavia complied, and then stepped back to have a look. Walker said, "I don't know if it's right, but it looks right." Farther down the hall, Walker's three short films were playing in separate rooms. The film I kept returning to—which played in a loop in my head, as it did at the museum—was called "8 Possible Beginnings. Or: the Creation of African-America" (2005). It is, for me, her most sophisticated and haunting work in the medium. The film shows a series of shadow puppets—Walker cutouts. Projections of blacks on a slave ship are intercut with daguerreotypes from the period, showing the journey across the Middle Passage. A great black head rears up and swallows some black stick figures: the motherland. A black male slave has sex with a puny white slave owner, but only after fellating himself, to the sound of cheerful antebellum ditties. The black male slave gives birth to a child, one of various smiling Topsy-like angels who hover throughout the movie. In one of the final tableaux, slaves hang from a tree. A slave girl, pursued by a white man, makes her way through the landscape as Walker and her daughter intone, among other things, "I wish I were white" and "Maybe all of this will dream away and I will disappear." (When I asked Walker how she felt about including Octavia in her work, she said that she'd considered asking one of Octavia's classmates, but felt that it would be too strange. "I didn't want to exploit her or put her in that weird spot," she added. "I just asked her if she would do it. She was hanging around the studio a fair amount when I was working on the film, anyway. Then I had to find a proper way to pay her!")

"Eight Possible Beginnings" brought to mind the white South African artist William Kentridge's shadow-puppet films, which were inspired by his experience of apartheid. Like Kentridge's works, Walker's are laden with powerful, profound treasures, as well as with the junk that clogs up our collective sensibility when it comes to race. I also heard in the film the plea for understanding put forth by Charlotte Forten, a "free" black woman, in her Civil War diaries, as well as references to Kate Chopin's 1894 story collection "Bayou Folk" and to various blaxploitation movies from the nineteen-seventies. (Oscar Micheaux, the father of "race" films, was an influence on Walker. "I love his complex, Ed Wood style of directing," she told me.) As the scenes played over and over, I tried to divorce the images from issues of race, and found them even more arresting. What became clearer was Walker's less provocative but equally poignant theme: our desire to be dominated by someone else, whom we will always call Other.

TOUT PARIS SHOWED UP FOR WALKER'S OPENING, OR AS *TOUT* AS Paris could be in late June. Most people walked through the exhibition silently, respectful if slightly baffled. The response to the show was somewhat different from what it had been at Walker Art Center. There, for instance, Halbreich and Vergne received a three-and-a-half-page, single-spaced letter about the show from a black museum employee named Marcus Harcus, in which he wrote, in part, "Obviously Kara Walker is a world-class talent. . . . I feel her artwork is impressive & important, but also potentially dangerous & corrupting. K.W.'s artwork forces everyone who experiences it to confront the realities of the daily atrocities suffered by 'New World' Africans over the course of 400 years. This could be highly valuable. When people view the silhouettes on cycloramas or film, we feel like eyewitnesses to the scenes. This could be damaging." By which Harcus meant that it was Walker's responsibility both to illustrate history and to protect us from it. This is the kind of dialogue that Walker welcomes. (A few days after the opening in Paris, she told me that she was most engaged by a couple of black museum workers there who asked her how black Americans had responded to the pieces.)

Walker attended the Paris opening in a white dress with a black bow that resembled an artist's smock. She swayed to the music, while well-wishers stopped by to greet her. As Octavia played with a friend, her grandmother asked her to keep the noise down. "I always try to teach my children not to annoy people," she said. There were no speeches after the show. Instead, Vergne and Halbreich took the Walkers, Sikkema, and others to dinner at a restaurant across the street. There, Halbreich toasted Walker. Then Walker toasted Vergne and the installers. Octavia sat to her left, drawing. Walker, her eyes cast down toward her place setting, recalled a story that she wanted to share with the assembled. With a smile, she said, "When Octavia was four, we were at an event like this." Octavia groaned, and worked more assiduously on her sketch. Walker continued, "And people were saying my name. And Octavia looked up and said, exasperated, 'Kara Walker, Kara Walker. When is it gonna be *my* turn?'"

GETTIN' PAID

KELEFA SANNEH

August 20, 2001

Earlier this year, VH1, the music-video channel, broadcast a television series called "Bands on the Run." Four rock groups were sent on tour, competing to see which one could sell the most merchandise; the winner would get a hundred thousand dollars' worth of new equipment, fifty thousand dollars in cash, a VH1-financed video, and a showcase concert with industry executives. The bands weren't very good, but the animosity of the competition was entertaining. In one episode, a group called Soulcracker started a grassroots smear campaign, telling fans that a victory for the rival group Flickerstick would be a victory for "corporate rock." It was an absurd claim—both bands were, after all, angling for a corporate contract, on a corporate television show—and the insult backfired: Flickerstick demanded an apology, and got one. The next week, Flickerstick won the competition.

What's funny about the insult is how old-fashioned it seems. The term "corporate rock" is a relic of the nineteen-seventies, popularized by critics who felt that the big record companies had coöpted a rebellious, authentic genre for mass consumption. In 1978, the rock journalist Lester Bangs wrote, "The music business today still must be recognized as *by definition* an enemy, if not the most crucial enemy, of music and the people who try to perform it honestly." Over the past ten years, though, "corporate rock" has been upstaged by "corporate rap," which has emerged as the country's new music. Rappers are responsible for three of the country's ten most popular albums, and the Recording Industry Association of America estimates that last year rap music generated more than $1.8 billion in sales, accounting for 12.9 per cent of all music purchases; it has surpassed country music as the nation's second most popular genre, after rock and roll. The obscure rap record labels Fo' Reel and Hypnotize Minds have teamed up with the media conglomerates Vivendi Universal and Sony, respectively, and have found millions of customers. Rappers, with a few notable exceptions, are black men, but their listeners are not: about seventy per cent of the people who buy rap albums are white, and an increasingly large percentage are female. "Hip-hop," once a noun, has become an adjective, constantly invoked, if rarely defined; people talk about hip-hop fashion and hip-hop novels, hip-hop movies and hip-hop basketball. Like rock and roll in the nineteen-sixties, hip-hop is both a movement and a marketing ploy, and the word is used to describe almost anything that's supposed to appeal to young people.

What's most unexpected about this boom is the reaction of the rappers themselves, who rose to prominence as icons of rebellion and authenticity. They have not only accepted corporate rap but embraced it. Like Frank Sinatra before them, they are chairmen of the board: *Fortune* put the rapper Master P on its cover in 1999, after he branched out into film production, sports management, and fashion, and today's biggest rap acts, from OutKast to Snoop Dogg, are diversifying, leveraging their popularity to create their own companies. Eminem may deliver antisocial lyrics, but as a businessman he's a model citizen, an entrepreneur who recently put his solo career on hold so he could build up his new imprint, Shady Records.

The greatest of the corporate rappers is Jay-Z, a thirty-one-year-old tycoon from the Bedford-Stuyvesant section of Brooklyn. He has all the necessary credentials: a record label (Roc-A-Fella Records), a clothing company (Rocawear), a production house (Roc-A-Fella Films). What's more, he has the right sensibility: nonchalant, devious, witty. He has put out five successful albums in five years—the only rapper to have done so—starting with "Reasonable Doubt," his début, in 1996, and he's sold more than eleven million records. Many rappers have made money, and lots of it, but none have rapped so eloquently about making money, or about the lure of wealth and ambition. Jay-Z has succeeded by treating hip-hop above all as a corporate enterprise, by embracing ruthless professionalism as his guiding aesthetic. As he once put it, "What y'all about to witness is big business, kid."

I MET JAY-Z FOR THE FIRST TIME THIS SPRING, IN LOS ANGELES. HE WAS in town for the Soul Train Music Awards (he'd been named male entertainer of the year), and I spent a day watching him rehearse and shop for sneakers at a nearby mall. There was a constant procession of well-wishers and autograph-seekers, and he greeted most of them wordlessly, with faint smiles and loose handclasps. Jay-Z is not flamboyant in the way that rappers are expected to be flamboyant. He doesn't have a gimmick, or an outlandish persona, or an especially fancy wardrobe. He usually wears a T-shirt and jeans, invariably made by Rocawear. He's tall and lanky. His hair is shaved barbershop-close, and there is the hint of a goatee on his chin. Diamond earrings and a diamond pendant are the only indications of his fortune and, indirectly, his fame.

Jay-Z was born Shawn Corey Carter in 1969. He grew up in the Marcy City Housing Projects, a forbidding bastion in Bedford-Stuyvesant; he has turned the project name into a hip-hop brand name. (At a recent concert in Washington, D.C., he was introduced with the words "Marcy projects, y'all!") He was the youngest of four children, two boys and two girls, and was brought up by his mother, Gloria; his father left the family when Jay-Z was eleven. Jay-Z is among the few rappers who memorize rhymes without committing them to paper, but he says that as a kid he always kept a green notebook with him. "I used to write in it every day, at my mom's house, banging on the table and saying my raps," he says.

When an older neighbor called Big Jaz got a record deal, Jay-Z left George Westinghouse Technical High School to become his side-kick. "He took me to London, and I was, like, 'People pay you? To make raps? Oh, shit!'" After a few years, when it was clear that Big Jaz would never become a major rap star, Jay-Z left him to tour with Big Daddy Kane, a popular rapper whose career was beginning to decline.

Jay-Z returned to Brooklyn, where, he says, he spent his early twenties selling crack cocaine. He is vague about the specifics. "I was running the streets," he told me, and that's about as far as he would go. In song, he's more forthcoming:

I took trips with so much shit in the whip that if the
cops pulled us over, the dog would get sick.

In 1995, after Jay-Z was shot at from six feet away, he decided to give rapping another try. A producer named Clark Kent introduced him to Damon Dash, a Harlem entrepreneur who had contacts in the rap industry, but no one was interested in signing Jay-Z. His old songs were considered too "sophisticated," he told me. "You had to really like rap to be, like, 'This dude's clever: the way he's using his words, the way he tackles his subjects—that's different.'" So Jay-Z and Dash, along with a silent partner, Kareem (Biggs) Burke, formed Roc-A-Fella Records, to put out Jay-Z's music themselves. Roc-A-Fella eventually struck a distribution deal with Priority Records (which it later left for Island/Def Jam), and issued Jay-Z's first album, "Reasonable Doubt," in 1996. A cheerful, filthy love song called "Ain't No Nigga" became his first hit; it also launched the career of Foxy Brown, who rapped as Jay-Z's girlfriend.

"Reasonable Doubt" is filled with rhymes as smooth as the hustlers Jay-Z sings about, and even the grittiest (or most exuberant) song suggests the poise and strength of a shrewd businessman. The first thing you notice listening to the album is the high, nasal voice, steely and precise; the enunciation is clear, and Jay-Z moves over each syllable lightly. The words pour out so effortlessly that rhyme and rhythm seem almost like an afterthought. His style is suggestive rather than declamatory; instead of shouting threats of murder, he sighs, "Believe you me, son, I hate to do it just as bad as you hate to see it done."

"Reasonable Doubt" sold more than half a million copies, but in order to cross over to the pop audience Jay-Z needed catchier tunes. Rap songs are a combination of rhyming and "beats"—heavily rhythmic tracks built from synthetic sounds, live instrumental music, and samples of other songs. In 1997, Jay-Z tried to find a more beat-driven sound; the result was a disappointing album called "In My Lifetime, Vol. 1" ("I wish I could have nailed that one," he says now) that sampled eighties rock songs such as "You Belong to the City" and "I Know What Boys Like." Then, in 1998, he bought an unlikely beat from a veteran producer named Mark 45 King, which added a heavy bass line to "It's the Hard-Knock Life," from the musical "Annie." Jay-Z slowed down his delivery to match the tempo, and the result was the crossover hit "Hard Knock Life (Ghetto Anthem)":

> I'm a be on top, whether I perform or not. I went from
> lukewarm to hot, sleeping on futons and cots to king-size
> dream machines.

An accompanying album, "Vol. 2 . . . Hard Knock Life," sold more than five million copies, and made Jay-Z rap's biggest star.

Jay-Z has made two albums since. "Vol. 3 . . . Life and Times of S. Carter," was released in 1999, and "The Dynasty: Roc La Familia (2000–)," a showcase for other artists on Jay-Z's record label, was released last October. Since his first album, Jay-Z has simplified his intricate rhyme style: his lyrics have become less tightly constructed, and less descriptive—an approach that appeals to mainstream fans, who buy hip-hop for the beats, not the words. He explains by affecting the pinched voice of a casual, presumably white listener: "I'm from West Motherfuck. I don't know what they're talking about. But the music is good." When I asked him if he thought the transformation was an improvement, he responded with an unsentimental comparison to Michael Jordan. "In his early days, Jordan was rocking a cradle, cranking it, all crazy, but he wasn't winning championships," Jay-Z said. "And then, later in his career, he just had a fadeaway jump shot, and they won six titles. Which was the better Jordan? I don't know."

In an earlier era, a rapper might have been tempted to ignore mainstream listeners, or to pretend to, but for Jay-Z sound business practice trumps artistic ambition. Still, no one wants to watch a man make jump shots forever—not even perfectly executed fadeaway jump shots—and so Jay-Z has to find a way to keep people interested, including aficionados. On "The Dynasty," he rapped about a girlfriend's miscarriage, and he and one of his protégés, Beanie Sigel, have written a pair of songs that berate their deadbeat dads. Songs such as these convincingly convey personal desperation, but they suggest a professional desperation as well.

IN THE BEGINNING, HIP-HOP WASN'T "ABOUT" ANYTHING AT ALL: IT was invented not by rappers but by disk jockeys. In 1973, a Jamaican immigrant in the Bronx who called himself DJ Kool Herc popularized the art of manipulating two turntables at once, so he could repeat his favorite drum patterns over and over. The jumpy music that resulted was given the name hip-hop. D.j.s who performed regularly in parks or clubs or roller rinks began hiring m.c.s to extoll their skills to the crowd, drawing on the African-American tradition of street-corner rhyming. In the studios, when the first hip-hop records were made, d.j.s were sometimes replaced by live bands, and the m.c., or rapper, became central to the music. In 1979, a group of dilettantes called the Sugarhill Gang released a song called "Rapper's Delight," and it became a hit. "Hip-hop" had become "rap music."

The first generation of stars were cartoonish figures from New York City—Kurtis Blow, Whodini, Run DMC, the Fat Boys, the Beastie Boys, and LL Cool J. They had whimsical names and wore whimsical clothes, and their records were filled with whimsical boasts. Run DMC proclaimed itself "the big, bad wolf in your neighborhood—not bad meaning bad, but bad meaning good." Then, in 1988, Public Enemy, a Long Island collective, released an album entitled, "It Takes a Nation of Millions to Hold Us Back." The group presented itself as a paramilitary outfit agitating for black power, and, just as the Beatles established the idea that pop songs could be art, Public Enemy established the idea that hip-hop could be politics.

Hip-hop has an insatiable appetite for new characters and new stories, and Public Enemy was soon overshadowed by a West Coast counterpart, NWA (or Niggaz with Attitude). NWA had a different arsenal of slogans—"Fuck tha Police" instead of Public Enemy's "Fight the Power"—which were delivered in first-person tales of crime and sex influenced by nineteen-eighties storytellers like Too $hort, Slick Rick, Kool G Rap, and Ice-T (who named himself after the pulp novelist and ex-pimp Iceberg Slim). A new term was coined to describe this foulmouthed genre: gangsta rap. And yet, for anyone who follows hip-hop closely, "gangsta rap" isn't a very useful term; over the past ten years, it has come to denote any rapper who talks about gunplay in the first person—and this includes almost every one.

Rappers may emulate businessmen these days, but they are still linked to crime and violence. The story of corporate rap starts with the murder of two of the most popular rappers of the nineteen-nineties: in September of 1996, in Las Vegas, Tupac Shakur (who recorded as 2pac) was shot and killed, and six months later, in Los Angeles, Christopher Wallace, better known as the Notorious B.I.G.

(or Biggie Smalls) was shot and killed; neither case has been solved. Shakur and the Notorious B.I.G. followed NWA, putting NWA's thuggish imagery to more personal use. On albums such as "Me Against the World" and "All Eyez on Me," Shakur turned his life into an epic tale of self-sacrifice. Biggie was a superior stylist and a great narrator; he told his life story in a series of morbid jokes and pointed anecdotes. Both Biggie and Shakur celebrated money, but mainly they celebrated themselves, and you got the sense that they might have rapped for nothing, if they'd had to. The two had once been friends, but they had become embroiled in a seemingly baseless feud—it involved a mugging and, of course, a woman—when Shakur was killed.

The Notorious B.I.G. was a protégé of Sean (Puffy) Combs, a music executive who moonlighted as a rapper under the name Puff Daddy. In the summer of 1997, Combs initiated hip-hop's big-money boom with a eulogy for Biggie called "I'll Be Missing You," in which he rapped over "Every Breath You Take," the eighties chestnut by the Police. "I'll Be Missing You," which became the most popular song of the summer, seemed to be the paradigmatic story of hip-hop: a flashy businessman mourning a slain thug.

Most people thought of Puffy and Biggie as opposites—the executive and the thug, the businessman and the artist, the pop star and the rapper—but Jay-Z's insight was to seize upon the avarice that united them. Rappers had long suggested that the music industry wasn't much different from the drug world (as Biggie put it, "If I wasn't in the rap game / I'd probably have a ki, knee-deep in the crack game"); now Jay-Z conflated Biggie's eloquent thug and Puffy's smooth executive to create the image of an utterly mercenary man who just happens to rap. In an industry characterized by pumped-up personae, it reminded the listener that rapping is nothing more or less than a job. And in the wake of two murders, that seemed like good news—and good business.

Still, it is tempting to believe that rappers are the deadliest rich people in the country, forever guzzling champagne and spilling blood, and the arrests that have accompanied hip-hop's mainstream success have only reinforced this perception. In 1999, Combs was charged with beating a record executive with a chair, a telephone, and a champagne bottle (hip-hop has a weakness for leaden symbolism). The charges were later dropped. Recently, Combs stood trial for weapons and bribery charges in connection with a 1999 night-club shooting. (He was acquitted, but his protégé Shyne was convicted of assault, reckless endangerment, and gun possession, and was sentenced to ten years in prison.) Three weeks before the Combs shooting, Jay-Z was arrested for the stabbing of Lance (Un) Rivera, a record executive (and former friend) whom the rapper reportedly suspected of pirating his new album before its official release date. (The trial is scheduled to start next month.) In April, Jay-Z was arrested again; police said that his bodyguard had been found outside a night club with an unlicensed Glock 9-mm. semiautomatic.

Earlier this year, it was reported that New York police were "profiling" rappers, and last month the Senate held hearings on "media violence," focussing on the world of hip-hop. Hip-hop is a particularly easy target for cops and senators, because rappers make their living by telling stories that sound like autobiography, and they do so in lyrics that are spoken, not sung. Six months before his most recent arrest, Jay-Z seems to have predicted it in rhyme, right down to the kind of gun:

> See me with a bodyguard? That means police is watching. And I
> only use his waist just to keep my Glock in. But
> when shit goes down, you know who's doing the popping.

Life rarely imitates art that faithfully, but the convergence of rap and rap sheet is so common in hip-hop that it was barely noted even by Jay-Z's most vigilant fans.

To a casual listener, it may not be immediately obvious what makes one rapper better than another. But, like the generation of fans who dissected Bob Dylan's lyrics and debated the merits of various bootleg recordings, rap fans pore over arcana in magazines and squabble about literary prowess online. On one hip-hop Web site, visitors recently debated "What is the hottest metaphor or simile ever written?" From the beginning, Jay-Z was admired for the quality of his verse. He compared his rhymes to luxury goods, as a way of flattering his listeners' powers of discernment:

Time to separate
   the pros from the cons, the platinum
   from the bronze,
that butter soft shit from that leather on the Fonz.

Much attention has been paid to rap's content—the prevalence of words like "nigga" and "bitch," the forthright treatment of sex and violence—but surprisingly little to the construction of the lyrics. And yet success in hip-hop has as much to do with style as with content. For much of the nineteen-eighties, rap was bound by strict metric conventions: each line had four beats, with the stress on the second and the fourth, and each verse was a series of couplets. Run DMC perfected doggerel in 1984 ("Cool chief rocker, I don't drink vodka/But keep a microphone inside my locker"), and by 1988 the rhyme virtuoso Rakim had stretched the rules with tricky alliteration and run-on lines ("Music mixed mellow maintains to make / melodies for m.c.s, motivates the breaks").

Jay-Z's lyrics, on the other hand, sound like everyday speech. He throws in conversational tics—a little laugh in the middle of a line, or a pause, as if he were thinking something through—to heighten the effect. This style creates a sense of intimacy, which is undermined by a chilly sensibility, a frankly avaricious way of looking at the world, and an aversion to sentiment. In his best songs,

Jay-Z exploits this contradiction by telling stories that balance a C.E.O.'s suave self-confidence with a memoirist's introspection, using unpredictable rhyme schemes to keep the listener off balance. "D'evils," from "Reasonable Doubt," begins with a criminal's monologue:

> The shit is wicked on these mean streets—none of my
> friends speak, we all tryna win. But then again,
> maybe it's for the best, though, 'cause when they seeing too
> much, you know they tryna get you touched. Whoever said
> illegal was the easy way out couldn't understand the
> mechanics and the workings of the underworld. Granted,
> nine to five is how you survive—I ain't tryna survive,
> I'm tryna live it to the limit and love it a lot.
> Life ills poison my body, and used to say, "Fuck
> mic skills!" I never prayed to God, I prayed to Gotti. . . .
> It gets dangerous, money and power is changing us,
> and now we're lethal, infected with d'evils.

"D'evils" (the title is pronounced "da evils") is a song about money and power, and it describes a world in which ambition is the root of all evil (and all success), a world where the criminal ethic— "We all tryna win"—sounds a lot like a capitalist code. In the second verse, we find a young hustler kidnapping a young mother, desperate to locate her lover, who has, it seems, betrayed him in a business deal. The hustler pays her to squeal, and there's an implication of violence—"My hand around her collar"—suggesting that he might be literally stuffing her mouth full of bills: "About his whereabouts I wasn't convinced. / I kept feeding her money till her shit started to make sense." It's a sardonic joke about the rap industry, which feeds its stars money and power in exchange for a convincing story. Jay-Z aspires to the hustler's merciless attitude, but, as a rapper, he also resembles the kidnapped girlfriend, squealing for cash.

Part of what makes "D'evils" compelling is this sense that Jay-Z's persona—his professionalism—might be at odds with his profession. The first verse described d'evils as a criminal compunction; now it seems more like a narrative compunction—a disease that makes you talk too much.

If Jay-Z's skill accounts for his reputation, and his practical approach to marketing his skill accounts for his success, then his ability to sense what his audience wants to hear before his audience senses it—to tell stories that don't just demand belief but inspire it—accounts for his longevity. A few times a year, there's a meeting in the Def Jam offices to decide what the next Jay-Z single and music video will be. Last year, after the release of "Vol. 3 . . . Life and Times of S. Carter," none of the executives could decide what single to release. The obvious choice was "Things That You Do," because it featured the pop singer Mariah Carey, but Kevin Liles, the president of Def Jam, thought it was "too mainstream." Then support started building for "Big Pimpin'," an unlikely candidate— its beat sounded North African, and it lacked a sung hook, which is generally considered essential for a hip-hop single. Liles, a convivial, round-faced man, and an energetic storyteller, recalled the conversation: "Jay said, 'It's a movement: This is how you big pimp.' I said, 'I don't know, Jay.' He said, 'Nah, we gotta do a video. We gotta show people what big pimping is all about. Let's make the movement.' So I said, 'Let's go, let's do it.' And the rest is history." The "movement" they created was this: Jay-Z on an enormous yacht somewhere warm, drinking champagne with women in swimsuits, and rapping about a life of sex and cash. As he put it:

On a canopy my stamina be
enough for Pamela Anderson Lee.
MTV, "Jam of the Week."
Made my money quick then back to the streets.

The video cemented Jay-Z's reputation as hip-hop's smoothest hustler, and "big pimpin'" became slang for living large; Jay-Z even made a follow-up song, "Parking Lot Pimpin'."

Expensive cars, yachts, champagne, and jewelry are everywhere in contemporary rap songs and videos. While hip-hop was once attacked for what was perceived as political rage, it has now given critics a different sin to excoriate: greed, or "bling bling" (after a song that asked, "What kinda nigga got diamonds that'll—bling!—blind ya?"). Last year, *Newsweek* ran a cover story that announced, "Welcome to the bling-bling generation." Hip-hop, the article claimed, had become "a Frankenstein's monster—with fifty thousand dollars worth of white gold draped over its neck pegs." (In fact, this characterization is inaccurate: most major rappers disdain white gold, considering it inferior to platinum.) Ever since the Sugarhill Gang rhymed about having "more money than a sucker could ever spend," it's been clear that hip-hop isn't an ascetic culture, and in the late nineteen-nineties it became more infatuated than ever with earning power and spending habits.

"When everybody else was doing gold," Jay-Z says, "I was, like, 'I want something platinum.' And then seeing the whole world switch—the whole world, you know what I'm saying? For a kid from Marcy? No one can take that away from me." In hip-hop, achievement comes down to style: life style, musical style, rhyme style. Jay-Z has moved out of the Marcy projects and into a penthouse apartment in Fort Lee, New Jersey (rich rappers inevitably move to the suburbs, for safety and privacy), which has a view of the Manhattan skyline and a private screening room. Roc-A-Fella Films has made a distribution deal with Miramax, and Rocawear, available at Macy's, among other places, has replaced Phat Farm and Fubu as New York's most visible brand. Jay-Z's latest hit, "I Just Wanna Love U (Give It 2 Me)," was a champagne-fuelled celebration song inspired by a birthday party for Kimora Simmons, the wife of Def Jam's co-founder Russell Simmons. But, despite all his big-money rhymes and real-life wealth, Jay-Z has never once described what champagne tastes like. His is the pleasure of a man obsessed with status (he recently called himself a "status-tician"), rather than the simpler pleasure of a hedonist.

Hippies and punk rockers used to talk about artists "selling out," chasing money at the expense of art. As the years passed, rockers got not only older but richer, and their newfound wealth was, inevitably, a bit of an embarrassment, or, at any rate, an absurdity: a rich society guy in late middle age singing about being a "Street Fighting Man." Rappers, on the other hand, don't sell out; they "fall off"—that is, they lose their artistic credibility and their financial viability at the same time. Punks (and their descendants in the world of underground rock) were afraid that big audiences and big money would ruin their subculture of authenticity, but in hip-hop success is a form of validation—a rapper's riches are proof that he's good at what he does. Platinum jewelry and platinum plaques are metaphors for artistic achievement, not just commercial success. It's hard to imagine a major rapper refusing to make a video at the height of his career, the way Pearl Jam did. In hip-hop, stories are either convincing or they're not; when a rapper loses his power to convince, it's usually a failure not of authenticity but of rhetoric. Jay-Z will be a master criminal and a brilliant business mind and a great rapper until people stop believing him.

JAY-Z'S RECENT ARRESTS HAVE GIVEN HIM NEW MATERIAL. HE HAS even made a music video, for a song called "Guilty Until Proven Innocent," loosely based on the stabbing of Lance (Un) Rivera, in which he takes the witness stand, delivers a defiant defense, and celebrates his acquittal. But on a spring morning in a Manhattan courthouse, where Jay-Z was attending a scheduling hearing in the Rivera case, the discrepancy between Jay-Z the rapper and Shawn Carter the defendant couldn't have been clearer: being on trial mainly means keeping your mouth shut, in the courtroom and outside it, and that's exactly what Jay-Z did.

I arrived just in time to see Jay-Z sprinting up the steps to meet one of his lawyers, Murray Richman. It was the first time I'd seen him without a flock of handlers and bodyguards and managers and friends trailing him. I passed through the metal detector with Jay-Z and Richman, and as we got to the elevators Jay-Z turned around and looked at me, not quite smiling. "What's going on?" he said.

It was not a day of high legal drama. The court date was a mere formality—a request for a postponement. There were only half a dozen other people in the courtroom; no reporters, no fans.

Jay-Z sat alone at a small desk before the bench, dressed in a Rocawear T-shirt and Rocawear jeans. The hearing took almost no time: the lawyers stepped forward and murmured to the judge. The judge murmured back, one hand over the microphone. Richman smiled broadly and said, "Thank you so much." The postponement had been granted, and Jay-Z strode out of the courtroom. A few weeks later, a publicist from Def Jam called me. She told me that for "legal reasons" Jay-Z wouldn't talk to me anymore.

AS JAY-Z'S LAWYERS WOULD BE THE FIRST TO TELL YOU, RAPPING about crime doesn't make you a great criminal. By the same token, rapping about money doesn't make you a great businessman. Jay-Z is a part owner of Rocawear and Roc-A-Fella Films, but Damon Dash takes most of the meetings himself. "If I gotta bring Jay, that mean we got a problem," he says. Jay-Z is more actively involved in Roc-A-Fella Records, which he intends to establish as hip-hop's ruling family. In recent years, realizing, perhaps, that his own career won't last forever, he has been shilling for Roc-A-Fella at every turn. "Y'all niggas truly ain't ready for this dynasty thing / Y'all thinking Blake Carrington, I'm thinking more like Ming," he rapped in a recent song. And yet he has had a rough time with his protégés: Amil, a young female rapper, left the Roc-A-Fella stable shortly after releasing a poorly received début album last year, and Memphis Bleek, a Marcy-projects alumnus, hasn't quite found his own style or marketing niche. Jay-Z's most promising protégé is Beanie Sigel, a hard-bitten twenty-seven-year-old, who is as forthcoming as Jay-Z is guarded. "My style is crack houses in South Philly," Beanie says. "That's where most of my life was written."

The first time I heard "The Reason," Beanie Sigel's new album, I was sitting in an S.U.V. that was hazy with marijuana smoke. Half a dozen of Beanie's friends and handlers were nodding their heads in unison, and Beanie himself was rapping along, offering running commentary: "Yo, we in church right now—this one make you get the Holy Ghost." His first album had been uneven, but "The Reason" is one of the year's best, full of verses knotted with syllables:

> Crack topic: back block it, thirty-one long
> blacktop it, you can't stop it, Gat top it
> black Mack, black Glock it, blast rocket
> sit your faggot-ass on your back pocket.

Sitting in a deserted pool hall in Chelsea later that night, Beanie recalled the day that a friend of a friend got him an audition with Jay-Z. "Meeting Jay was like meeting the perfect hustler," he said. "It was like being a young kid on the block, when a dude drive up in a big Caddy and throw you the keys, like, 'Park the car, shorty.' It was like meeting that guy."

Along with most of his hip-hop contemporaries, Beanie Sigel has internalized the rules of corporate rap—he explained to me that you have to have a "good marketing plan" when you're "selling your product," whether it's music or crack. And yet he doesn't come across like a C.E.O. If Jay-Z is a salesman, then Beanie Sigel is a product, a charismatic hustler who senses that part of his appeal is his roughness (he described himself as "all edges, all the way around, three-sixty"), a slick talker whose style emphasizes word-play over plain speech. (He even answered some of my questions in rhyme.)

The new corporate rapper is intensely self-aware. Eminem has rhymed, with seeming amusement, about being a "commodity." One of rap's new stars calls himself Ludacris. Even Master P has recognized this changing atmosphere: his own career has slowed down, and his empire has fallen apart, but he's found new success through his son, an eleven-year-old rap star named Lil' Romeo. Maybe, after four years of corporate rap, the obsession with businessmen is turning into an obsession with products.

Fifteen years ago, a rapper might have called himself a "microphone controller" or a "rhyme animal"—epithets that called attention to lyrical skill. Today, rappers distract listeners from the fact that there's any rapping going on at all, claiming to be pimps and thugs and cocaine dealers and businessmen and leaders and commodities. "Where I'm from, it wasn't cool to be a rapper," Beanie Sigel told me. "If you was a rapper, you was a sucker, straight up. So I kept it under my hat. I'd say, 'Nah, man, I ain't no rapper.'"

Beanie Sigel's disavowal of rapping reminded me of something I'd heard before. Later that night, I pulled out his first album and confirmed a hunch: there's a moment early on when Beanie tries to get rid of a fan by sneering, "I ain't no fucking rapper," as if he wished it were true. You can hear the same ambivalence in Jay-Z's willingness to sacrifice complex rhymes for a good beat, in his insistence that "without rap I was crazy straight," and in his half-serious threats of retirement: "Back to Shawn Carter the hustler, Jay-Z is dead." The success of corporate rap has inspired a kind of self-loathing among rappers, who have begun to suspect that rapping itself is beneath them; if the hip-hop boom is drawing to a close, it can't be said that the rappers didn't see it coming.

It would be somehow fitting if rappers, who made d.j.s obsolete, ended by talking themselves into obsolescence, unable to compete with their own tall tales. You get the feeling that some rappers envy

Shakur and the Notorious B.I.G., who were killed mid-act, im-
mortalized in character. Jay-Z has been talking about retirement
ever since he released his first album, which he also claimed would
be his last. He wasn't planning to be a rapper all his life, and he
certainly wasn't planning to stay in the game long enough to fall
off. He said that, having established himself as the consummate
smooth criminal, he would move on—back, perhaps, to the streets.
Like a gangster looking for one last big score, or a corporate boss
angling for a lucrative buyout, he dreamed of quitting while he was
ahead, of getting out before he was pushed out. That's what the
sound of "Big Pimpin'" is—a celebration before the falloff.

Rapping as a means to a financial end: this is the narrative of
the era of corporate hip-hop. Strangely, it's kept hip-hop interesting and exciting, because it has forced rappers to find new ways to
talk about themselves, new ways to tell their stories. But for Jay-Z
it poses a question: If you're so good, why are you still rapping? As
he prepares to release his sixth album in six years, he sounds apologetic. "Can't leave rap alone, the game needs me," he explains in his
new single, and it's true, for now. It won't be true forever.

THE MASK OF METAL-FACE DOOM

TA-NEHISI COATES

September 21, 2009

I first heard the rapper Daniel Dumile (pronounced DOOM-ee-lay) when I was fourteen and hip-hop was just beginning to bloom. The music was not so much "CNN for black people," as Chuck D would later dub it, as a lingua franca. I came up awkward in West Baltimore—a tall black boy with no jumper, no gear, and no game. But my mastery of the arcane verses of X-Clan, my sense that the decoupling of EPMD was an irreparable tragedy, and my abiding hatred of Vanilla Ice ushered me into the scowling ranks of my generation.

In those days, you could tune in to "Yo! MTV Raps" and see everything from the gangsta stylings of N.W.A. to the mysticism of Rakim and the goofy musings of the Afros. This was the heyday of sampling—most rap was too small for lawsuits—and a hard-ass beat could come from anything: the opening piano riff from Otis Redding's "Hard to Handle," the horns from Inspector Gadget's theme song, a hook from "Schoolhouse Rock."

Dumile was typical of that motley generation. Performing under the name Zevlove X, he made his début in 1989 with a verse on a song called "The Gas Face," the second single by the group 3rd Bass. In the video, an assortment of hip-hop royalty gives "the gas face" (a maneuver that involves shaking your face in a slack-jawed manner, while moaning) to Adolf Hitler, the South African President P. W. Botha, and the mainstream rapper MC Hammer.

Dumile, who was eighteen years old when the video was made, wears a gas-station attendant's uniform and a baseball cap cocked to the side. His babyish face seems to shrink behind a pair of over-sized glasses.

Two years later, as a member of the group KMD, Dumile re-leased the album "Mr. Hood." It was uneven, notable mostly for the cult hit "Peach Fuzz" ("By the hairs of my chinny chin chin, gots many plus plenty / String by string, I think I counts like twenty"). Dumile's style is vibrant and freewheeling; he skates over the beat, undisturbed by guitar and piano riffs, sliding words into the empty spaces between the snare and the kick drums. "At the time, it was people coming out everywhere," he told me recently. "It was 'Such-and-such over there is live. Such-and-such over here is live.' And we were all going hard. It was slightly competitive, and everyone was blowing before us. We were kind of the fringe group. It was like, 'You know about KMD, yo?'"

KMD never got the chance to blow up. In 1993, Dumile's brother Dingilizwe, also a member of KMD and known as Subroc, was hit by a car and killed. Later that year, KMD's label, Elek-tra, refused to release the group's second album, "Black Bastards," fearing a controversy over the cover art (a Sambo figure being sent to the gallows). The group left the label, just as rap's commercial appeal was becoming undeniable. Artists like Snoop, Tupac, and Dr. Dre were going multiplatinum, and by the end of the decade rap had gone from American cult music to American pop music.

Meanwhile, I kept the assembled works of Wu-Tang Clan on repeat and stewed, convinced that somewhere around 1998 hip-hop had run out of things to say. I was not alone. Disaffected music fans began to refer to the halcyon days of the eighties and nineties—when every rapper had a d.j., and label owners didn't vamp in vid-eos, confusing themselves with artists—as "the Golden Era."

We were the kind of fundamentalists that haunt every genre of popular music. By the end of the nineties, we had started seeking a sound that offered something other than guns, girls, and drugs. Some of us found neo-soul. Others got lost in our parents' jazz records. And still others were radicalized and turned to U2 and Björk.

Dumile vanished from the national scene and began living as a civilian in New York City. He had a child. "I was just doing regular stuff, just raising my son," he told me.

Then, in 1999, Dumile released a solo record, "Operation: Doomsday," under the moniker Metal Face Doom. His verbal agility was intact, and his lyrics had grown more sinister. There was a mean streak to his humor, and he made references to the death of his brother ("On Doomsday—ever since the womb, till I'm back where my brother went / That's what my tomb will say"). And something else—Dumile, in the guise of MF Doom, did literally what most rappers only do metaphorically: he wore a mask.

A RAP ALBUM IS AN AUTOBIOGRAPHICAL COMIC BOOK, WHOSE author styles himself as a twisted, oft put-upon antihero. Carlton Ridenhour, a Long Island native who studied graphic design in college, picked up a mike and became Chuck D, an enemy of the state, a revealer of racist conspiracies, a militant watched by the F.B.I. Christopher Wallace was morbidly obese and, by his own assessment, "black and ugly as ever," but when he became Biggie Smalls he transformed himself into a Lothario whose hits, like "One More Chance," portrayed him as a prolific cuckold artist—"Where you at flipping jobs, playing car-notes? / While I'm swimming in your women like the breaststroke." At various moments, the rapper Nas billed himself as Nasty Nas (corner seer), Nas Escobar (gangsta drug kingpin), and Nastradamus (sanctimonious, persecuted celebrity).

When Dumile began performing as MF Doom, he extended hip-hop's obsession with façades. While other m.c.s fashioned themselves after outlaws, thugs, or drug dealers, Dumile, whose handle is inspired by the Fantastic Four villain Dr. Doom, called himself "the Supervillain." When he raps, he often refers to Doom in the third person. Other m.c.s are obsessed with machismo; Dumile is obsessed with "Star Trek" and "Logan's Run."

When I rediscovered Dumile, in his new guise, I was on the cusp of fatherhood and life-partnership, and considering divorce from the music of my youth. My outlook was that of any Golden Age proponent—I was worn down by the petty beefs between rappers, by the murders of Tupac and Biggie, and by the music's assumption of all the trappings of the celebrity culture in which it now existed.

Doom's music was revanche, and the Doom persona felt as though it had emerged from the graveyard of rappers murdered by glam-hop. Onstage, Doom looked the part. He cultivated a dishevelled aspect—ill-fitting white tees or throwback Patrick Ewing jerseys. His paunch gently rebelled against the borders of his shirt. He was visibly balding. His manner suggested a retired B-boy tossing off the trappings of domesticity for one last boisterous romp.

THE MASK "CAME OUT OF NECESSITY," DUMILE EXPLAINED. IT WAS A warm afternoon in Atlanta, where he lives now, and we were sitting in black vinyl chairs in an alley in midtown. Dumile wore a green polo shirt, matching green shorts, a pair of black Air Jordans without socks, and a New York Mets cap. His glasses were missing a lens and sat crooked on his face. He removed the Mets cap and placed it on his knee.

Dumile, who is now thirty-eight, was raised on Long Island, home of several prominent rap groups of the Golden Era—De La Soul, Public Enemy, EPMD, and Leaders of the New School. He started performing during the infancy of hip-hop, when no one had yet realized the potential for big money in a guy talking into a microphone.

"Rhyming wasn't that popular back then, but it was fun," Dumile told me. "And people would say, 'Oh, you rhyme? Oh, snap, say a rhyme for me! Say another one! Say the one about the girl!' Everybody had a cousin who came out for the summer and could rhyme. And you'd be like, 'Oh, he rhymes? Oh, he rhymes? I gotta meet him.'

"Ever since third grade, I had a notebook and was putting together words just for fun," Dumile went on. "I liked different etymologies, different slang that came out in different eras. Different languages. Different dialects. I liked being able to speak to somebody and throw it back and forth, and they can't predict what you're going to say next. But once you say it they're always like, 'Oh, shit!'"

For MF Doom, Dumile wanted to create a character with a complete backstory, which he would reference through a series of albums. "The story was coming together, and it worked and became popular. And now people wanted to see shows, and I'm like, how do I do that?

"I wanted to get onstage and orate, without people thinking about the normal things people think about. Like girls being like, 'Oh, he's sexy,' or 'I don't want him, he's ugly,' and then other dudes sizing you up. A visual always brings a first impression. But if there's going to be a first impression I might as well use it to control the story. So why not do something like throw a mask on?"

Or throw the mask on someone else—Dumile routinely sends out one of his comrades in the Doom costume and has him lip-sync the entire show. He sees this as a logical extension of the Doom idea. Fans who have paid for tickets tend to disagree. Across the Internet there are videos of imposters—"Doomposters"—being booed off the stage, with comments posted like "I waited an hour for this bullshit," or "This shit is tenfold worse than Ashlee Simpson or Milli Vanilli."

If Dumile had his way, he would take it further. He jokes that he'd like to dart backstage after a performance, take off the mask, and then wade into the crowd—beer in hand—and applaud his own work. In conversations with strangers, if the subject of Doom comes up, Dumile will simply play along, like Peter Parker or Bruce Wayne.

"I'm the writer, I'm the director," Dumile said. "If I was to go out there without the mask on, they'd be like, 'Who the fuck is this?'" He went on, "I might send a white dude next. Whoever plays the character plays the character . . . I'll send a Chinese nigger. I'll send ten Chinese niggers. I might send the Blue Man Group."

Dumile has released seven albums since "Operation: Doomsday." Most of them have been under the name MF Doom, but he has also used semi-related personas like Viktor Vaughn (inspired by Dr. Doom's real name in Marvel comics) and King Geedorah (the three-headed monster in Godzilla movies). The most highly regarded of his recent albums is "Madvillainy" (2004), a collaborative effort between Dumile and the Los Angeles–based underground producer Madlib. (The duo dubbed themselves "Madvillain.") The album's production was minimalist, like much of Doom's solo work. A great hip-hop producer can hear music that spans many genres and assemble it, in bits, into a coherent aesthetic—and Madlib has an ear for samples ready-made to be looped. But the album's singular sound came mostly from Doom's raspy baritone rendering a sort of nerdcore poetry: "Off pride, tykes, talk wide through scar-meat / Off sides, like how Worf ride with Star-Fleet."

ONE FRIDAY IN APRIL, I FLEW OUT TO MEET DUMILE IN LOS ANGELES, where he was working on his next project, a second collaboration with Madlib. He planned to work the first night, and offered to let me watch the session. But he was running late, and we settled on simply having dinner and starting up on Saturday.

From that point, the weekend took on the feel of juvenile fantasy. My hotel, in West Hollywood, looked like a set from "Entourage." On Friday evening it became a night club, and in order to get back to my room I had to present my key to two people manning a velvet rope. Behind the reception desk, a woman lounged on a bed perched in an elevated alcove.

When I called Dumile the next morning, he offered to send his driver and cohort, Five (named for Johnny Five, the robot from "Short Circuit"), to pick me up at the hotel at one o'clock. By two, I hadn't heard anything, so I picked up a book and headed downstairs.

The party had started early. There was a d.j. playing MP3s from his laptop a few yards from the pool. Women in bikinis wandered out from the deck into the lobby. Anxious young men in shorts filed in from the entrance. It was exactly what I would have wanted all my Saturdays to be like when I was sixteen. Except that almost everyone was white.

I spotted Five at a table drinking a Bloody Mary. Short and bespectacled, with a long ponytail, he waved happily as I approached. "Doom didn't give me your number," he explained. He did not look as though he'd been trying hard to rectify the problem.

We got into his black Chevy Avalanche and drove down Sunset, presumably to see Dumile at work. But there was much to be done before that. We stopped at Amoeba Records to pick up Doom's new album, "Born Like This," since Dumile had not yet heard the finished product. We had to pick up beer, too, a necessity for the transition from Dumile to Doom. We had to wait for forty-five minutes in front of the house north of downtown where Dumile was staying. When he emerged, he was carrying some audio equipment, and was accompanied by a woman clutching a large bottle of Grey Goose vodka. Dumile packed the equipment in the trunk. The woman handed him the bottle, and he hopped in the back. He picked up the new record and groused about the cover art.

"Five, ride around," he said. "I want to hear how it sounds."

A great m.c. is, on one level, a drummer performing a solo. But, more than that, he is a poet, assembling words according to the rules of a particular meter. Dumile offers a darkly humorous take on the life of the Doom character. There is no single narrative, as much as there are variations on a theme, the most constant being his mask. From the song "Beef Rap" off of his album "MM . . . Food": "He wears a mask just to cover the raw flesh / A rather ugly brother with flows that's gorgeous."

Hip-hop feeds on the aggression of post-pubescent males. And Dumile draws on the aggression of a particular type of male who came of age in a particular era. When he claims to "eat rappers like part of a complete breakfast," when he challenges other m.c.s to battle for Atari cartridges, when he yells "Zoinks!" mid-rhyme, he's signalling those who grew up with Saturday-morning cartoons and "The Dukes of Hazzard." For his listeners, his references—"Good Times," popping wheelies, karate classes—evoke lost innocence, even when the topic is grim. On "Hey!," Doom delivers a couplet about some old neighborhood friends, now incarcerated, over a sample from the theme song to "Scooby-Doo":

To all my brothers who is doing unsettling bids
You could have got away if it was not for them meddling kids.

"When I do it, I feel like I'm thirteen again," Dumile told me. "I remember, when we were that age, everybody was nice, and everybody was getting nicer. That same well of energy we were drawing from then, I go to there. . . . To me it feels like that time was richer, every second was really five minutes. Being older now, grown, I'm like, what do we really do that's fun? I'm kind of corny when you think about it. What could I rhyme about? Let me see, um, I gotta pay the rent today."

The rest of our day bore this out. We spent the hours in the manner of teenagers with nowhere to be, and I saw that Dumile's music sends me back to adolescence because he lives—at least while he's creating—as though he were back there, too.

We wound through the hills of Los Angeles with "Born Like

This" blasting at full volume. Hip-hop is music for warriors—or, at least, for those who imagine themselves as such. I'd listened to "Born Like This" on my iPod during the flight out and come away unmoved. But hearing a song like "Cellz"—with its lengthy jacking of a poem by Charles Bukowski, pounding drums, and high slicing whistles—at high volume changed my mind.

Dumile had said he'd be working by noon; it was now four o'clock. We came off a sharp curve, and he pointed out a large house on a cliff, which the producer Danger Mouse had recently bought. We stopped at a broad opening, high up. You could see the neighborhoods of Mount Washington and Cypress Park, a commuter-train line, the skyscrapers of downtown Los Angeles. With the music still pumping, he walked around for a bit, nodding and making small talk with Five.

Then they hopped back in the car, and Five drove to the studio, a cottage behind a friend's house. Dumile opened the trunk and pulled out a heavy bag filled with rhyme books, which he'd Fed-Exed out the night before, and passed it to me. "If I'm gonna let you see my rhyme books, you could at least carry the bag," he said.

Dumile took some audio equipment inside. Then he reiterated instructions that he'd given me the night before: there was to be no talking while he was working, not from me, from Five, or from him. He fiddled with a two-hundred-and-fifty-gig hard drive until Madlib's instrumentals pounded out from the speakers, filling the room.

He paused to explain his approach. "When I'm doing a Doom record, I'm arranging it, I'm finding the voices. . . . All I have to do is listen to it and think, Oh shit, that will be funny. I write down whatever would be funny, and get as many 'whatever would' funnies in a row and find a way to make them all fit. There's a certain science to it. In a relatively small period of time, you want it to be, That's funny, that's funny, that's funny, that's funny. I liken it to comedy standup."

So do his fans. Online threads about Dumile's work tend to feature nothing but a series of favorite lines: "Oh my aching hands, from raking in grands / And breaking in mike stands," or "What? These old things? About to throw 'em away / With the gold rings that make 'em don't fit like O.J."

I opened the bag and began paging through the rhyme books. It was a great honor—an m.c. sharing his rhyme books is like a magician sharing notes for his tricks. I half expected a column of light to bloom from the pages. But Dumile's books were like his songs— scatterbrained and disorganized, a series of potentially humorous couplets. The best ones were written over in black ink two or three times. Few were arranged into verses.

Despite his edict of silence, he spent most of the evening trading jokes with Five, yelling nonsensical phrases ("Flurk! Flurk! Flurk!") into my tape recorder, making bets centered on Five's bad Spanish, and drinking beer. By 11 P.M., it was apparent that very little would get done. We walked out around midnight. "Give it a day," he said, "and see how things sound in the morning."

WHEN I WAS TWELVE, I TOOK A SHORT WALK FROM MY PARENTS' West Baltimore row house to Mondawmin Mall. I rode the escalator up, walked into the music store, flipped through the bound platters, and with my own money purchased my first record, Stetsasonic's "Talkin All That Jazz."

That was 1988. R. & B. had devolved into synth-pop, and seemingly every respectable radio station was advertising itself with the tagline "No Rap." Stetsasonic's "All That Jazz" was a new generation's effort to reach back and pull black music out of the mire of disco:

Tell the truth James Brown was old
Until Eric and Ra came with I Got Soul.

I played that record for most of the year. When no one was look-ing, I'd place my fingertips on the wax and scratch, trying to make the record tweet like a bird. That was how I inaugurated the Golden Era—in my small bedroom, doing my best rendition of Jazzy Jeff.

One afternoon last May, I met Stetsasonic's d.j., Prince Paul, in front of the VH1 building in SoHo. Paul is best known for pro-ducing De La Soul's first three albums, all of them classics of the Golden Era. He also produced the track "The Gas Face." New York had just started to warm up. At all the cafés, people were seated at outdoor tables, laughing. But Paul was dressed as though he dis-trusted the recent change in the weather—pants and a short-sleeved brown shirt over white long johns. He had a baseball cap pulled low over his face.

I had talked to him once on the phone, but still I was off bal-ance. He was all of five-nine, yet it was hard not to see him as monumental, as a part of my history. We walked uptown, stopped at a diner, ordered turkey burgers, and talked about his days with Stetsasonic and De La Soul and what had changed.

"Now every m.c. wants a beat tape, like 'Yo! Gimme a beat,'" he said, noting that m.c.s have become more like singer-songwriters, with the egos to match. "But back then it was like '3rd Bass? Hmm . . . This and this! These are two songs I hear y'all on.'" Paul recalled working with Dumile for the first time. "He came in rhyme-ready when it was time to record. I met him and his brother Subroc. They were just really nice dudes. . . . I remember shortly after hear-ing about his brother passing, and then hearing about him going through a struggle with Elektra and that record getting dropped. And then after that I didn't hear from him."

Paul reconnected with Doom after hearing a single off "Opera-tion: Doomsday," and the two have worked together intermittently for the past ten years. Dumile appeared on Paul's "Politics of the Business." Paul did some comic voice-overs for "Born Like This."

Their creative bond extends from a similar outlook toward the past, a sense that rap isn't what it was. "If you go to a rapper today and say, 'Yo, I got better rhymes than you,' he'll go, 'Yeah, you probably do, but I sold more records,'" Paul said. "The pride isn't in the lyrical content."

Two years ago, the rapper 50 Cent challenged Kanye West, not by claiming to be a more creative artist or having superior mike skills but by daring him to sell more records. (50 Cent lost.) The ethos consecrated by Sean (Diddy) Combs—that what sells is what's classic—has essentially carried the day. For the fan who is no longer obsessed with the pose of rebellion, with fending off other young men, or with sexual frustration, beholding hip-hop in the aughts is like stumbling across an old journal and then seeing its most inflammatory and narcissistic elements turned into a marketing plan. All the moments of tenderness (De La Soul's "Eye Know"), idleness (the Roots' "Lazy Afternoon"), and black comedy (Ice Cube's "It Was a Good Day") have been drained away.

ON MY LAST DAY IN L.A., I FOLLOWED FIVE FROM MY HOTEL TO Dumile's studio. Today, Five explained, the ground rules were to be strictly followed. There was to be absolutely no talking and no joking. When I arrived, Dumile was sitting behind his computer cycling through the Madlib beats and taking notes. He was replaying video news reports about the chimp who had attacked a woman in Connecticut that February. The beat on loop was the same one he'd played the night before—jangling piano and a man muttering.

He clicked a button, and the news reports played over the beat. I struggled to find some connection between the two but said nothing. Dumile explained that he was working on retelling the story from the chimp's perspective.

"I'm digging through these to get pictures for the actual facts of the piece," he said. "It's still the fact of shooting a monkey. What is this disrespect for life?"

He took his pad and walked outside, sat at picnic table, and started to write. I drove off to make a Starbucks run for the group. I plugged in my iPod and cranked up the Yeah Yeah Yeahs.

Dumile's success, by hip-hop standards, has been modest. He has no platinum or gold records, or anything that could be called a hit. He is uninterested in hooks, displays a flagrant disregard for linear storytelling, and insists on cutting songs that time out before the three-minute mark. "The Gas Face" made him a local celebrity in 1989. He says that he got into a fight with some jealous rivals just before he was scheduled to perform the track on "The Arsenio Hall Show," and he had to do the show with his arm in a cast. "Fame never helped the situation," he told me. "Fame, in the streets, is something you don't want." As a member of KMD, alongside his brother, Dumile seemed to enjoy the spotlight, but he has never reconciled himself to performing as a solo act—hence his use of Doomposters. He'd rather be alone in a studio writing about a pet chimp gone berserk.

When I returned, Dumile had finished writing and come back inside to record. He had asked that I not watch him do this, but I could hear him reciting muffled lyrics. When the music paused, he peeked out and Five handed him a Frappuccino. I could see his mask hanging from a mike stand. He nodded and closed the door, and that was the last I saw of the villain.

THE AUTOFICTIONS OF KENDRICK LAMAR

DOREEN ST. FÉLIX

July 26, 2017

At the start of his popular ascendance, Kendrick Lamar made a point of hiding. In the 2012 video for "Money Trees," he was shot askance, frequently blocking the camera's view with his hand in a gesture of cool self-protection. The "spectacle" of Lamar was instead his own handle on his voice—or voices. Lamar is a rapper who engages modulations like singers do; his voice is an instrument of feeling. With it, he darts easily across the range of masculine consciousness; he can sound wry, and then, all of a sudden, grave, suspicious, excitable, crass, sombre, and full of awe—often all on the same song. The first time I saw him perform, at an open-air college concert, in 2014, two years after the release of his melancholic masterpiece "good kid, m.A.A.d city," he was wearing a baggy white hoodie, which, when he crouched, veiled his entire profile. At one point, Lamar spotted a reveller in the crowd wearing headphones, and commanded him to remove them. How could he? The point of a Lamar performance, back then, was to marvel at the artist's aural athleticism. One could see him without seeing his face.

The first blushes of Lamar's aesthetic expansion came with the video for "Bitch, Don't Kill My Vibe," in 2013. Clad in crisp white churchwear, Lamar frolicked with a congregation, first in a hearse and then in a wheat field, as he led a casket to a sun-drenched resting place. In 2014, the videos for "To Pimp a Butterfly," a difficult, pluralistic blues album, were darkly resplendent: "i" depicted Lamar leaning out of the window of a moving car, his eyes closed in the moonlight, his torso a whir of urban recklessness; in "Alright," he hung upside down, lifted by a mass of grinning black men. American terror, through the eyes of Lamar, is appropriated into fugitive visions of ecstasy; as Jason Parham wrote recently, in *Wired*, Lamar's videos have captured "black existence viewed from the inside, a way of being that sits at the nexus of reality, fantasy, and abstraction."

"DAMN.," Lamar's fourth album, which scored double-platinum sales this week, pushes the artist further toward flamboyance. (Lamar still honors his foundational interest: uncovering black people in poses of grandeur and of precariousness. The video for "ELEMENT." brings to life photographs of the legendary Harlem photographer Gordon Parks.) The creation of evolving personae has generally been considered the province of pop artists. Rappers, uniquely burdened by vague standards of authenticity, have cultivated complex, performative autofictions. Tupac, Lamar's technical model, fashioned himself the sagacious Californian Makaveli; Flying Lotus, Lamar's associate, metamorphosed into an animated strongman named Captain Murphy. For the past month, Jay-Z has been serializing the videos attendant to "4:44," packaging the load of a much-appraised biography in the glamour of myth. On "DAMN.," Lamar has developed a curious id called Kung Fu Kenny—"A savage, an asshole, a king," to quote the slinky boast track "LOYALTY.," which features Rihanna.

On Sunday night, thousands flocked to see this latest incarnation of the rapper at Brooklyn's Barclays Center. It was Lamar's second New York stop on the "DAMN." tour. On Instagram, snippets of the first New York City performance, also at Barclays, three days earlier, teased orange pyrotechny and billows of white smoke. I wondered if such stadium-sized antics might make Lamar's set feel shallow—a fear that was not abetted when, on Sunday, the rapper Travis Scott opened with wily frenzy, at one point straddling a massive, phoenix-like structure (a reference to his lavishly titled second album, "Birds in the Trap Sing McKnight") suspended in midair above the crowd.

Lamar, when he emerged, finally, out of a cloud of silver froth, stayed grounded. He crouched, in a position of attack, or perhaps of prayer, for most of his first song, the anthemic "DNA" ("I got, I got, I got, I got loyalty, got royalty inside my DNA"). He was dressed in a bright yellow tracksuit; his hair was braided and gathered into a warrior's knot. Behind him, on a massive screen, a film—"The Damn Legend of Kung Fu Kenny"—flickered in and out over the course of the ninety-minute-long performance, during which Kung Fu Kenny encountered and defeated numerous adversaries, sometimes real people, sometimes shadows, sometimes with a smirk on his face. Lyrics flashed in Mandarin. It was a sleek appropriation of an appropriation—a flashback to the enthusiasms of Wu-Tang and Missy Elliott. In our era of political sanctimony, where the biggest stars in pop have abandoned concept for virtue-signalling, Lamar's was an elegant escapism.

In contrast to Kung Fu Kenny, the Lamar onstage was serious and solitary. He did not perform with a band or with hype men, and—apart from a guest appearance from the rapper 2 Chainz and Scott—managed the massive Barclays stage on his own. He seemed to have forgotten about the film behind him, about his costume. The visual busyness of the stage only emphasized how Lamar's fiercely concentrated stage presence can overwhelm all activity around him. His delivery is a testament to the enduring power of an unvarnished rap performance. "This will be the livest experience of your motherfucking life," he said at one point, in a very low voice. "Before we do that, we have to prove where we came from," he added, launching into a moment of mournfulness, which was twisted, by his crowd, into exhilaration. "Now, I done grew up 'round some people living their life in bottles," he intoned. A projection of a rippling body of water vibrated behind him. People screamed. Lamar glowered. "Swimming Pools" is an exercise in misdirection: Lamar maneuvers the darkness of his subject—the song is about the effects of alcoholism—with lithe, jumpy delivery.

Lamar is a master of storytelling—he has a feel for cadence. That night, for longer than most of his few peers tend to do onstage, Lamar was a modern griot. His velocity on the grinding "HUMBLE." was stunning; the menacing calm of "ELEMENT." made the air constrict. Sweat gathered under his neck as he scaled the syncopated peaks and valleys of "King Kunta." During "PRIDE.," Lamar seemed to genuflect before asking, up from his knees, "Happiness or flashiness? How do you serve the question?" The crowd had, impressively, quieted. Lamar seemed to have found his answer.

PART VI
ANNALS OF THE LAW

OPERA IN GREENVILLE

REBECCA WEST

June 14, 1947

On February 15, 1947, an incident occurred that drew the taxi-drivers of Greenville very close together. A driver named Brown picked up a Negro fare, a boy of twenty-four called Willie Earle, who asked him to drive to his mother's home in Pickens County, about eighteen miles from Greenville.

Willie Earle reached his home that night on foot. Brown was found bleeding from deep knife wounds beside his taxi a mile or two away and was taken to a hospital, where he sank rapidly. Willie was arrested, and put in Pickens County Jail. Late on the night of February 16th, the melancholy and passionate Mr. Roosevelt Carlos Hurd was, it was said, about certain business. Later, the jailer of the Pickens County Jail telephoned to the sheriff's office in Greenville to say that a mob of about fifty men had come to the jail in taxicabs and forced him to give Willie Earle over to them. A little later still, somebody telephoned to the Negro undertaker in the town of Pickens to tell him that there was a dead nigger in need of his offices by the slaughter-pen in a byroad off the main road from Greenville to Pickens.

THE MEN WHO TOOK WILLIE EARLE AWAY WERE IN A STATE OF MIND not accurately to be defined as blood lust. They were moved by an emotion that is held high in repute everywhere and especially high in this community. All over the world friendship is regarded a sacred bond, and in South Carolina it is held that it should override nearly all other considerations. It is not to be wondered at, therefore, if in Greenville a group of very simple people, grieving over the cruel slaughter of a beloved friend, felt that they had the right to take vengeance into their own hands. They would feel it more strongly if there was one among them who believed that all is known, that final judgment is possible, that if Brown was a good man and Willie Earle was a bad man, the will of God regarding these two men was quite plain. It would, of course, be sheer nonsense to pretend that the men, whoever they were, who killed Willie Earl were not affected in their actions by the color of Willie Earle's skin. They certainly did not believe that the law would pursue them—at least, not very far or very fast—for killing a Negro. But it is more than possible that they would have killed Willie Earle even if he had been white, provided they had been sure he had murdered Brown. The romances in statement form throw a light on the state of mind of those who later told of getting Willie Earle into a taxi and driving him to a quiet place where he was to be killed. One says that a taxi-driver sat beside him and "talked nice to him." He does not mean that he talked in a way that Willie Earle enjoyed but that the taxi-drivers thought that what he was saying was elevating. Mr. Hurd described how Willie Earle sat in the back seat of a Yellow Cab and a taxi-driver knelt on the front seat and exhorted him, "Now you have confessed to cutting Mr. Brown, now we want to know who was the other Negro with you." Willie Earle answered that he did not know; and it appears to be doubtful that there was another Negro with him. The taxi-driver continued, in the accents of complacent pietism, "You know we brought you out here to kill you. You don't want to die with a lie in your heart and on your tongue."

Brown's friends were in the state of bereavement that is the worst to bear. Brown was not dead. He was dying, and they could do nothing to save him. They were in that state of frustration that makes atheists at the deathbed of their loved ones curse God. "They then drug the Negro out of the car," said Mr. Hurd in his statement. ("Drug" is certainly a better word than "dragged.") Nobody speaks of doing anything there beside the slaughter-pen; they all speak of hearing things. One heard "the tearing of cloth and flesh," another heard "some licks like they were pounding him with the butt end of a gun." Some heard the Negro say, "Lord, you done killed me." Some saw as well as heard. "I saw," stated one, "Hurd aim the single shotgun towards the ground in the direction of where I judged the Negro was laying and pulled the trigger; I then heard the shot fired. I then heard Hurd ask someone to give him another shell." But Mr. Hurd also is among those who heard but did not do. He did not even see. "When I seen they were going to kill the Negro," he stated, "I just turned around, because I did not want to see it."

NO MORE NEGROES WENT INTO THE GALLERY. THERE WERE STILL ONLY thirteen when the verdict was given. But the courtroom slowly filled up during the hour and a half that elapsed before the Judge's return. The bondsman who had organized the defense fund came in and sat with a friend, who also resembled a giant baby; they whispered secrets in each other's ears, each screening his mouth with a huge hand while the other hand held, at arm's length, a tiny cigarette, as if a wreath of smoke could trouble their massiveness. The widow Brown ranged the aisles hungrily, evidently believing that an acquittal would ease her much more than it possibly could. The attorneys came in one by one and sat at their tables. Mr. Wofford was, as they say down there, happy as a skunk, flushed and gay and anecdotal. He and his group made a cheerful foreground to the benches where the wives of the defendants, fortified by their returning friends, wept less than before but still were weeping. As one of the Southern newspapermen looked about him at the scene, his face began to throb with a nervous twitch. At length, the Judge was seen standing at the open door of his chambers, and the defendants were brought into court. They were all very frightened.

They bore themselves creditably, but their faces were pinched with fear. Mr. Hurd, though he was still confused, seemed to be asking himself if he had not been greatly deceived. Fat Joy was shifting along, wearing sadness as incongruously as fat men do. As they sat down, their wives clasped them in their arms, and they clung together, melting in the weakness of their common fear. The Judge came onto the bench and took some measures for the preservation of order in the court. He directed that all people should be cleared from the seats within the bar of the court unless they had a direct interest in the case or were of the press. The bondsman who had organized the defense committee was in such a seat and did not at first rise to go, but the court officials made him go. The people thus ejected stood around the walls of the room. Those by the windows turned to look at the downpour of the rain, which was now torrential. The Judge ordered all the officers of the court to take up positions in the aisles and to be ready for anyone who started a demonstration. They stood there stiffly, and the defendants' wives, as if this were the first sign of a triumph for severity, trembled and hid their faces. The jury entered. One juror was smiling; one was looking desperately ashamed; the others looked stolid and secretive, as they had done all through the trial. They handed the slips on which they had recorded their verdicts to the clerk of the court, who handed them to the Judge. He read them through to himself, and a flush spread over his face.

As soon as the clerk had read the verdicts aloud and the Judge had left the bench and the courtroom, which he did without thanking the jury, the courtroom became, in a flash, something else. It might have been a honky-tonk, a tourist camp where they sold beer, to use Mr. Culbertson's comminatory phrase. The Greenville citizens who had come as spectators were filing out quietly and thoughtfully. Whatever their opinions were, they were not to recover their usual spirits for some days. As they went, they looked over their shoulders at the knot of orgiastic joy that had instantly been formed by the defendants and their supporters. Mr. Hurd and his father did not give such spectacular signs of relief as the others. They gripped each other tightly for a moment, then shook hands stiffly, but in wide, benedictory movements, with the friends who gathered around them with the ardent feeling that among the defendants Mr. Hurd especially was to be congratulated. The father and son were grinning shyly, but in their eyes was a terrible light. They knew again that they were the chosen vessels of the Lord. Later, Mr. Hurd, asked for a statement, was to say, "Justice has been done . . . both ways." Meanwhile, the other defendants were kissing and clasping their wives, their wives were laying their heads on their husbands' chests and nuzzling in an ecstasy of animal affection, while the laughing men stretched out their hands to their friends, who sawed them up and down. They shouted, they whistled, they laughed, they cried; above all, they shone with self-satisfaction. In fact, make no mistake, these people interpreted the verdict as a vote of confidence passed by the community. They interpreted it as a kind of election to authority.

They must have been enormously strengthened in this persuasion by the approval of Mr. Culbertson, who, as soon as the Judge had left court, had leapt like a goat from chair to table and from table to chair, the sooner to wring the hands of his clients. Oddly, Mr. Ashmore, the prosecuting attorney, was also busy telling the defendants how glad he was that they had been acquitted, with the rallying smile of a schoolmaster who is telling his pupils that he had to keep them in for a little because they really were too boisterous, but that he knew all the time what fine, manly fellows they were. Clark had now produced his camera and flashlight and was standing on a chair, taking photographs of the celebrations. The defendants were delighted and jumped up on chairs to pose for him, their friends standing below them and waving and smiling toward the camera, so that they could share in the glory. In these pictorial revels, Mr. Culbertson was well to the fore. First he posed with the Hurds. Then he formed part of a group that neither Greenville nor the C.I.O. could greatly enjoy if they should see it in *Life*. On a chair stood Fat Joy, bulging and swelling with pleasure, and on his right stood the bondsman and on his left Mr. Culbertson, baring their teeth in ice-cold geniality, and each laying one hard hand on the boy's soft bulk and raising the other as if to lead a cheer. It is unlikely that Mr. Culbertson was unaware of the cynical expression on Clark's face, and he knew perfectly well what other members of the press were thinking of him. But he did not care. *Life* is a national weekly. Mr. Culbertson does not want to be a national figure. He means to be a highly successful local figure. My future, he was plainly saying to himself, is in Greenville and this is good enough for Greenville, so let's go. It will be astonishing if he is right. At that, he was a more admirable figure than Mr. Wofford, however, because at least his credo had brought him out into the open standing alongside the people whose fees he had taken and whose cause he had defended. But on hearing the verdict, Mr. Wofford, who possibly has an intention of becoming a national figure, had vanished with the speed of light and was doubtless by this time at some convenient distance, wiping his mouth and saying, "Lord, I did not eat."

There could be no more pathetic scene than these taxi-drivers and their wives, the deprived children of difficult history, who were rejoicing at a salvation that was actually a deliverance to danger. For an hour or two, the trial had built up in them that sense of law which is as necessary to man as bread and water and a roof. They had known killing for what it is: a hideousness that begets hideousness. They had seen that the most generous impulse, not subjected to the law, may engender a shameful deed. For indeed they were sick at heart when what had happened at the slaughter-pen was described in open court. But they had been saved from the electric chair and from prison by men who had conducted their defense without taking a minute off to state or imply that even if a man is a murderer one must not murder him and that murder is foul. These people had been plunged back into chaos. They had been given by men whom they naïvely trusted the most wildly false ideas of what conduct the community will tolerate. It is to be remembered that in their statements these men fully inculpated each other. At present they are unified by the trial, but when the tension is over, there will come into their minds that they were not so well treated as they might have been by their friends. Then the propaganda for murder which was so freely dished out to them during their trial may bear its fruit. Not only have they, along with everyone else, been encouraged to use the knife and the gun in ways that may get them into trouble—for it is absurd to think of Greenville as a place whose tolerance of disorder is unlimited—but they have been exposed to a greater danger of having the knife and the gun used on them. The kind of assault by which Mr. Brown died is likely to be encouraged by the atmosphere that now hangs over Greenville. These wretched people have been utterly betrayed.

It was impossible to watch this scene of delirium, which had been conjured up by a mixture of clownishness, ambition, and sullen malice, without feeling a desire for action. Supposing that one lived in a town, decent but tragic, which had been trodden into the dust and had risen again, and that there were men in that town who threatened every force in that town which raised it up and encouraged every force which dragged it back into the dust; then lynching would be a joy. It would be, indeed, a very great delight to go through the night to the home of such a man, with a few loyal friends, and walk in so softly that he was surprised and say to him, "You meant to have your secret bands to steal in on your friends and take them out into the darkness, but it is not right that you should murder what we love without paying the price, and the law is not punishing you as it should." And when we had driven him to some place where we would not be disturbed, we would make him confess his treacheries and the ruses by which he had turned the people's misfortunes to his profit. It would be only right that he should purge himself of his sins. Then we would kill him, but not quickly, for there would be no reason that a man who had caused such pain should himself be allowed to flee quickly to the shelter of death. The program would have seemed superb had it not been for two decent Greenville people, a man and a woman, who stopped as they went out of the courtroom and spoke to me, because they were so miserable that they had to speak to someone. "This is only the beginning," the man said. He was right. It was the beginning of a number of odd things. Irrational events breed irrational events. The next day I was to see a Negro porter at the parking place of a resort hotel near Greenville insult white guests as I have never seen a white hotel employee insult guests; there were to be minor assaults all over the state; there was to be the lynching party in North Carolina. "It is like a fever," said the woman, tears standing in her eyes behind her glasses. "It spreads, it's an infection, it's just like a fever." I was prepared to admit that she, too, was right.

BLACK BODIES IN MOTION AND IN PAIN

EDWIDGE DANTICAT

June 22, 2015

This past weekend, between not sleeping and constantly checking the news, I walked the long rectangular room at New
York's Museum of Modern Art, where Jacob Lawrence's "Migration Series" is currently on display. I had seen many of the paintings
before, in books and magazines, but never "in person." I'd somehow
expected them to be as colossal as their subject, the fifty-five-year-
plus mass migration of more than six million African-Americans
from the rural south to urban centers in the northern United States.
The sixty spare and, at times, appropriately stark tempera paintings in the series each measure twelve-by-eighteen inches and are
underscored by descriptive captions written by the artist, whose
parents moved from Virginia and South Carolina to New Jersey,
where he was born. The size of the paintings quickly became inconsequential as I moved from panel to panel, the first one showing
a crowd of people crammed into a train station and filing toward
ticket windows marked Chicago, New York, Saint Louis, and the
last panel returning us to yet another railroad station, showing that
in spite of dangerous and unhealthy working conditions and race
riots in the North, the migrants "kept coming."

At the end of a week when nine men and women were brutally
assassinated by a racist young man in Charleston, South Carolina,
and the possibility of two hundred thousand Haitians and Dominicans of Haitian descent being expelled from the Dominican

Republic suddenly became very real, I longed to be in the presence of Lawrence's migrants and survivors. I was yearning for their witness and fellowship, to borrow language from some of the churches that ended up being lifelines for the Great Migration's new arrivals. But what kept me glued to these dark silhouettes is how beautifully and heartbreakingly Lawrence captured black bodies in motion, in transit, in danger, and in pain. The bowed heads of the hungry and the curved backs of mourners helped the Great Migration to gain and keep its momentum, along with the promise of less abject poverty in the North, better educational opportunities, and the right to vote.

Human beings have been migrating since the beginning of time. We have always travelled from place to place looking for better opportunities, where they exist. We are not always welcomed, especially if we are viewed as different and dangerous, or if we end up, as the novelist Toni Morrison described in her Nobel lecture, on the edges of towns that cannot bear our company. Will we ever have a home in this place, or will we always be set adrift from the home we knew? Or the home we have never known.

The nine men and women who were senselessly murdered at Emanuel African Methodist Episcopal Church last Wednesday were home. They were in their own country, among family and friends, and they believed themselves to be in the presence of God. And yet before they were massacred they were subjected to a variation of the same detestable vitriol that unwanted immigrants everywhere face: "You're taking over our country, and you have to go."

In the hateful manifesto posted on his Web site, the killer, Dylann Roof, also writes, "As an American we are taught to accept living in the melting pot, and black and other minorities have just as much right to be here as we do, since we are all immigrants. But Europe is the homeland of White people, and in many ways the situation is even worse there." I wonder if he had in mind Europe's most recent migrants, especially those who have been drowning by the hundreds in the waters of the Mediterranean Sea, brown and black bodies fleeing oppression and wars in sub-Saharan and northern Africa and the Middle East. Or maybe he was thinking of all those non-white people who are European citizens, though not by his standards. This bigoted young man charged himself with deciding who can stay and who can go, and the only uncontestable way he knew to carry out his venomous decree was to kill.

In "The Warmth of Other Suns," the Pulitzer Prize–winning journalist Isabel Wilkerson writes that, during the Great Migration, "The people did not cross the turnstiles of customs at Ellis Island. They were already citizens. But where they came from, they were not treated as such." Nearly every migrant Wilkerson interviewed justifiably resisted being called an immigrant. "The idea conjured up the deepest pains of centuries of rejection by their own country," she writes.

Tragically, we do not always get the final say on how our black bodies are labelled. Those fleeing the South during the Great Migration were sometimes referred to not only as immigrants but as refugees, just as the U.S. citizens who were internally displaced by Hurricane Katrina were given that label ten years ago.

Dominicans of Haitian descent also thought themselves to be at home in the Dominican Republic. The Dominican constitution, dating back to 1929, grants citizenship to all those who are born in the country, unless they are the children of people "in transit." Dominicans of Haitian descent who were born during the past eighty-six years are still considered to be in transit. Black bodies, living with "certain uncertainty," to use Frantz Fanon's words, can be in transit, it seems, for several generations.

White supremacists such as Dylann Roof like to speak of black bodies as though they are dangerous weapons. Xenophobes often speak of migrants and immigrants as though they are an invasion force or something akin to biological warfare. In an essay called "The Fear of Black Bodies in Motion," Wallace Best, a religion and Great Migration scholar, writes that "a black body in motion is never without consequence. It is always a signifier of something, scripted and coded. And for the most part, throughout our history black bodies in motion have been deemed a threat."

These days, it seems that black bodies are more threatened than they have ever been so far in this century. Or maybe we just have more ways to document the beatings, shootings, and other abuses that have been suffered in the recent past. As means of transportation have become more accessible, it also seems that we have more migration than ever. Even children are migrating by the thousands in our hemisphere, crossing several borders to flee gang violence in Central America, while hoping to be reunited with their U.S.-based parents. Still, we live in a world where, as the late Uruguayan writer Eduardo Galeano said, money can move freely, but people cannot.

Black bodies are increasingly becoming battlefields upon which horrors are routinely executed, each one so close to the last that we barely have the time to fully grieve and mourn. The massacre at Emanuel African Methodist Episcopal Church and the racist rant that preceded it highlight the hyper-vigilance required to live and love, work and play, travel and pray in a black body. These killings, and the potential mass expulsions from the Dominican Republic, remind us, as Baby Suggs reminds her out-of-doors congregation in Toni Morrison's "Beloved," that, both yonder and here, some do not love our flesh and are unwilling to acknowledge our humanity, much less our nationality or citizenship.

As many Haitian migrants and immigrants and Dominicans of Haitian descent now either go into hiding or leave the Dominican Republic out of fear, we are witnessing, once again, a sea of black bodies in motion, in transit, and in danger. And as Emanuel African Methodist Episcopal Church and the larger community of

Charleston, South Carolina, prepare to bury their dead, we will once again be seeing black bodies in pain. And we will be expected to be exceptionally graceful mourners. We will be expected to stifle our rage. And we will keep asking ourselves, When will this end? When will it stop?

A DARKER PRESENCE

VINSON CUNNINGHAM

August 29, 2016

A few years ago, Rex Ellis, the associate director of curatorial affairs for the National Museum of African American History and Culture, which will open in September on the Mall in Washington, D.C., made a phone call. Ellis is a natural storyteller, with a voice that mixes congestion and control in a manner reminiscent of Jesse Jackson's. He'd clearly told the story of the call before, but when I spoke with him this past spring, in his office on an upper floor of the glassy Capital Gallery Building, on Maryland Avenue, he repeated it for me with all the shock and wonder that it warranted.

"A phone call," he began. "To a young lady by the name of Wendy Porter." She had e-mailed him, saying that she had Nat Turner's Bible. Ellis smirked slightly and rolled his eyes. "Well, there are a lot of folk who call and make all kinds of claims. So I said, 'Mmm-hmm.' But then she told a little bit about her history, and she mentioned Nathaniel Francis. And I said"—deeper this time, slower—"'Mmm-hmmmm.'"

Nathaniel Francis owned the property on which Nat Turner was captured, in October, 1831. There, on Francis's land, the slave preacher hid, having led a revolt of fellow-slaves that drew its inspiration from the Bible in question and ended in the deaths of at least fifty-five white residents of Southampton County, Virginia. Turner was tried and hanged in the nearby town of Jerusalem. It is not clear to Ellis or to his staff just how Francis came to have Turner's Bible; later, by searching through library documents and photographs, they learned that his family had held on to it until at least 1900. As if to complete the circle of haunted serendipity, Wendy Porter's stepfather was related to one of Nathaniel's descendants, Rick Francis, a prominent member of the Southampton County Historical Society, which owns the sword that Nat Turner had with him when he was captured.

"So," Ellis said, tracing ecstatic connections on his desk with his fingers, "everything just started to fit together." He travelled to Virginia Beach to see the Bible. Porter, who was seven or eight months pregnant, greeted him at the door of her home and introduced him to her mother, who took him to the dining room. Porter's mother went into a closet and pulled down an object wrapped in a thinning dishtowel. She placed it on a table in front of Ellis. Sitting in Washington, Ellis pantomimed the gesture, sliding an invisible book across his desk, to me.

When Ellis unwrapped the Bible at the Porters', the binding was long gone. What he saw was its first yellowed page, the edges rounded by much use. He turned a few pages, gingerly, then stopped. He looked at the mother. "We only bring it out during family reunions," she said. "And only when someone asks do we bring it out so that they can see it. Then we wrap it up and put it back in the closet."

She looked at the Bible. "We thought that this was something—we knew it was important," she said. "Yes, Ma'am," Ellis replied. Then she spoke again, as if urged, Ellis said, by some outside force. "It was time for it to leave here," she told him. Ellis looked me in the eyes when he repeated what she said next: "Because there's so much blood on it."

IN THE INTRODUCTION TO "AMERICA'S BLACK PAST," AN ANTHOLOGY published in 1970, the historian Eric Foner wrote that, among this country's "myths and misconceptions, one of the most pervasive and pernicious . . . is the picture of blacks as inactive agents in history." An active history, like the one that lay behind Nat Turner's bloody Bible—full of inscrutable decisions and odd happenings, shaped but not determined by suffering—often stays hidden. The Bible will soon go on display at the new museum on the Mall, our latest opportunity to bring such a history into the light.

The museum's mouthful of a name—and its inelegant initialism, N.M.A.A.H.C.—testifies to a bureaucratic slog that began in 1915, when black veterans of the Union Army, together in Washington to celebrate the fiftieth anniversary of the war's end, and fed up with the discrimination they found in the capital city, organized a "colored citizens' committee" to build a monument to the civic contributions of their recently emancipated people. In 1929, Herbert Hoover appointed a commission, which included the civil-rights leader and educator Mary McLeod Bethune and the N.A.A.C.P. co-founder Mary Church Terrell, to come up with a plan. Unfunded and largely ignored, the commission languished, and was eventually dissolved by Franklin D. Roosevelt. The effort began again in the nineteen-seventies, with several abortive attempts at legislation and much controversy within the Smithsonian Institution, under whose aegis each national museum is administered. Finally, in 2003, George W. Bush signed the National Museum of African American History and Culture Act, which had been sponsored in the Senate by Sam Brownback and in the House by John Lewis, the project's most consistent contemporary champion.

In 2005, Lonnie Bunch was hired to be the museum's founding director. Bunch, now sixty-three, previously served as the associate director for curatorial affairs at the National Museum of American History, and then spent five years as the president of the Chicago Historical Society. We spoke this past April, on a muggy day in Washington, in his office at the Capital Gallery Building. He told me the story of how, after being hired by the N.M.A.A.H.C., which had "no collection, no money, no staff, no site," he was greeted at an earlier set of offices, at L'Enfant Plaza.

"I go over there—door's locked," he said. "So I go to security and say to the guard, you know, 'I'm the director of this new museum.' He says, 'We don't know who you are—you can't get in.' So I go to the manager's office: *he* won't let me in. I call back to the Smithsonian and say, 'What's going on here?' They say, 'We don't know.' So I'm standing in front of the door, really ticked off, thinking, Why'd I take this job? But then this maintenance guy walks by, and in his cart he's got a crowbar. So I take the crowbar and break into the offices."

I may have looked skeptical. "Nobody was ready for us," he insisted. "I had to break in."

The difficulty of the past decade's work is a theme with Bunch—he says he plans to publish a book about the experience, called "A Fool's Errand"—and this story was perhaps offered as an allegory, both for the tortuous process of opening a national museum and for the history of black people in America. Or, at least, one version of that history: first a promise; then a series of closed doors; then despair; then, at last, access by way of force instead of grace. "I'm a kid born in Newark," Bunch said, arching an eyebrow, "so I know how to fight."

That pugilist's impulse, along with an intimate understanding of the politics and the pace of the Smithsonian, has, from the beginning, informed Bunch's approach to the technical and diplomatic aspects of his directorship. When he was deciding whether to leave his job in Chicago, he spoke with Richard M. Daley, the city's former mayor. Daley, characteristically blunt, asked, "Why would you leave to run a *project*?" The question stayed with Bunch, and led him to conclude that, even without a physical space of its own, the museum must exist, not aspirationally but in fact, starting soon after his appointment.

Rather than focussing solely on fund-raising and acquisitions, Bunch pulled Robert Moses's old trick: quickly driving stakes into the ground. He commissioned a series of books, online displays, and travelling exhibitions, including one that opened last year, in a gallery on the second floor of the National Museum of American History, called "Through the African American Lens." The eclectic show serves as a preview of the museum to come; among the objects on display are a sword and a canvas tent used by the Union soldier George Thompson Garrison; a desk from the Hope Rosenwald School for rural black children, dating from the beginning of the twentieth century; and a set of colorful costumes from the original Broadway production of "The Wiz."

The museum did not own a single artifact when Bunch began, so he instituted a program called Saving African American Treasures, a take on the PBS favorite "Antiques Roadshow." Professional conservationists specializing in paper, textiles, and other delicate materials travelled around the country, helping interested amateurs to, as he put it, "preserve Grandma's old shawl, or that wonderful photograph." Bunch's hope was that the tour would inspire a certain generosity of spirit, as well as some "buzz" about the museum's ambitions. It did. Bunch's curators have now collected more than thirty-five thousand objects, most of them donations. They range from a chillingly anonymous pair of rusted slave shackles to a frilled shawl of lace and linen given to Harriet Tubman by Queen Victoria; from an advertisement for a Memphis slave market that featured a "general assortment of Negroes" to a pocket watch owned by the abolitionist William Lloyd Garrison; from Muhammad Ali's headgear to James Baldwin's passport, crowded with stamps. One room in the museum will contain the coffin of Emmett Till.

The collection's dependence on viscerally affecting items reflects the Smithsonian's tendency toward a broad, largely artifact-based history—Here's somebody's Buick! Here's something Walt Whitman once touched!—meant to induce gooseflesh, or thoughtful moans. Its curators know how impatient tourists and students can be. Eleven of the Smithsonian's twenty enormously popular museums are situated on the Mall, and the lawn is perpetually bright with camera flashes and school-group T-shirts. "People are gonna give you two hours per museum," Bunch told me with a shrug.

But artifacts cannot speak for themselves; the meaning of a museum is determined by acts of interpretation. It's natural to see the museum's opening as part of a continuum that began in the nineteen-sixties and seventies, with the advent of black-studies programs, or even earlier, with the work of Carter G. Woodson, an author and scholar who was the son of slaves—in other words, as part of the history of black history. Bunch, however, rejects this idea. "What I argue is: This is not a *black* museum. This is a museum that uses one culture to understand what it means to be an American. That, to my mind, is the cutting edge."

He spoke in terms like this throughout our conversation, with an unrelenting deliberateness, as if from a page of talking points. "This is a story that is too big to be in the hands of one community," he said at one point, describing the story that is America. And then, speaking of the sojourn of black people in this country: "This is, in some ways, the quintessential American story." And, later, contrasting the efforts of his staff with other, more possessive ethnic histories: "Instead of simply saying, 'This is *our* story, period,' we want to say, 'This is everybody's story.'"

Bunch's framing of black experience, as a lens through which one may better see some static American text, sidesteps more than a century of scuffles over the nature, and the meaning, of that experience. Between the accommodationism of Booker T. Washington and the activism of W. E. B. Du Bois, the romance of Zora Neale Hurston and the social realism of Richard Wright, the defiance of the Black Lives Matter movement and the caution of "respectability politics," there has always been something along these lines: go along or fight back, persuade or condemn, love or leave, use a common language or create one of your own.

Bunch may be a fighter, but he seems eager to avoid such

a clash—the cost, perhaps, of doing business with Congress, on whom so much concerning the museum depends. (More than half of the funds for the building have come from the federal government; the balance has been provided by a star-studded group of private donors, including Michael Jordan, the television producer Shonda Rhimes, and Oprah Winfrey, whose contribution of more than twenty million dollars is commemorated by the museum's Oprah Winfrey Theatre.) Bunch told me about a meeting he had with Jim Moran, a former U.S. congressman from Virginia, who initially opposed the museum: "He says, 'O.K., Lonnie, I don't wanna be rude, but I don't think there should be a black museum just for black people.' And I said, 'Neither do I.' Blew him out of the water."

With benefactors like these, there may have been little incentive to engage more directly with the most heated debates about black identity and culture, or to empower the scholars best known for leading, and reflecting upon, those exchanges. Seven years ago, one such scholar, Henry Louis Gates, Jr., was arrested by a white police officer while trying to gain entrance to his own home, in Cambridge, Massachusetts. This led to the now infamous "Beer Summit" with Gates, President Obama, and the arresting officer. Gates later offered the museum the handcuffs used to detain him. Bunch initially declined the gift, before reversing himself.

"We *listened* to all the best scholars, even if we didn't always end up doing what they thought we should," Bunch told me. Eric Foner has offered his expertise to Bunch and his team throughout the planning process. "They've made a very big effort to engage scholars, at all points of planning," Foner said. "This museum cannot satisfy everybody—I don't suppose any museum can—and I think the more Lonnie can point to input by current scholars, well-known scholars, this will help to deflect whatever criticism might be coming their way."

Perhaps Bunch hopes that the mere location of the museum

will, in its way, speak more freely. The symbolic axis of the Mall has always been a source of silent but tangible power, particularly with respect to the history of black Americans, beginning with the slave pens that once dotted the land and culminating, perhaps, in the subtle stage design of the March on Washington. "The Mall is America's front yard," Bunch said, when I asked him about the importance of the real estate, "but it is also, in some ways, the place where more people come to understand what it means to be an American than anyplace else in the country." His familiarity with the Mall, and its conventions, led to one of the museum's most striking features. "I wanted a darker building," he said. "I didn't want the white marble building that traditionally was the Mall. What I wanted to say was, there's always been a dark presence in America that people undervalue, neglect, overlook. I wanted this *building* to say that." Then, as if to balance out this quick foray into confrontational talk, he added, "I also wanted a building that spoke of resiliency and uplift."

THE MUSEUM STANDS ON THE LAST AVAILABLE PLOT ON THE MALL, just east of the Washington Monument, finished but not yet full. Designed by the Ghanaian-British architect David Adjaye, the building is a glass cube, sheathed in three broad, overlapping aluminum bands coated with bronze. Adjaye and his partner, Philip Freelon, call this outer cladding a "corona," a reference to the beaded crowns characteristic of Yoruba art, from West Africa. The corona is decorated with a kind of lattice, a stylized version of the filigree ironwork made by slaves in New Orleans and South Carolina, giving the museum the look of a temple devoted to a vaguely benevolent god. The aluminum bands open as they ascend; trace their angles upward, and they might be arms raised in joy. Follow them downward, and you see the tips of arrows, pointing toward a burial ground, or to a thick knot of invisible roots. The Mall is one of the most tightly regulated spaces in the country, and Adjaye was barred from building any higher; an extra story would have obstructed the sweeping east-west sight line from the Capitol to the Lincoln Memorial. More than half the building is underground.

For pedestrians on the Mall, the museum is hard to see from more than a few dozen yards away, especially during the spring and summer—the Mall's famous row of American elms is particularly thick on the plot where the building stands. It is set back from the street, on the other side of a neat, rectangular lawn; up from the grass pokes the top of a glass-enclosed circular fountain, called the Oculus, which allows sunlight into the museum's Contemplative Court, belowground, where visitors can pause to consider the treasures— and, if necessary, recover from the traumas—experienced so far. Over the building's shoulder looms the Washington Monument, its red eye blinking down as if from the height of the nation's founding.

Adjaye's structure is the latest installment in the Mall's meandering passage through trends in public art. The original design for the area, by Pierre L'Enfant, D.C.'s great planner-auteur, called for a shaggy informality. In his 1791 report to George Washington, L'Enfant imagined a lively promenade flanked not by museums and bureaucratic offices but by sites offering "diversion to the idle"— theatres, assembly halls, and public academies. This vision was never realized: financial strain and political gridlock stalled construction almost completely during the nineteenth century.

In 1902, the Senate Park Commission, in a report titled "The Improvement of the Park System of the District of Columbia," reimagined the Mall. The architects and artists on the commission, stirred by America's emergence as an imperial power, designed the space according to the neoclassical principles of the so-called American Renaissance. That visual style defines the Mall's most iconic structures: the Washington Monument and the Lincoln and Jefferson Memorials. Soon, however, a younger generation, influenced by the blossoming of modernism and by the shattered idealism brought on by two world wars, crashed awkwardly into the frame. Their work reached a nadir in the nineteen-seventies, with the brutalism of the Hirshhorn Museum and Sculpture Garden and the chunky Air and Space Museum. If the grand planners of the Mall were slightly grandiose, the late-century modernists zagged too far toward a tacky, post-human future.

Adjaye's building might be the most successful modernist design on the Mall so far. This is partly because of its unashamed approach to symbolism. Touches like the corona's outer lattice serve as a reminder of the human work that has gone into the making of America.

THREE STORIES BENEATH THE BUILDING'S AIRY UPPER VIEWS, ON THE museum's bottom level, is an exhibit called "Slavery and Freedom." Quotations from famous freedom-oriented national texts, presented chronologically—the Declaration of Independence, Absalom Jones's Thanksgiving sermon of 1808, a stanza from the spiritual "Steal Away to Jesus"—are carved into a vast, unbroken, slate-gray wall. The objects in the exhibit include a tin wallet containing neatly folded freedom papers, a slave identification button stamped "POR-TER," and a Union Army recruitment poster from 1863, featuring Frederick Douglass's rallying cry, "Men of Color, to Arms!" The chronological presentation and the tension between the relics and the promissory texts leave an impression of inevitability: the terrors of the slave trade giving way, gradually, to emancipation, hidden, from the beginning, somewhere deep within the national heart.

Slavery and freedom have, in America, always been intertwined, spinning toward and away from each other in a kind of ontological dance. But the museum's hand-in-hand treatment of the concepts conveys an implicit promise to museumgoers of the uplift to come. This assurance is reiterated by the design of the "history galleries," which, under one high ceiling, occupy the entire lower section of the museum. A series of wide, gently sloped ramps lift a visitor ever farther, in time and in elevation, from slavery—the title of Booker T. Washington's autobiography, "Up from Slavery," made literal, and almost eschatological. Above, like a promise flown in from the future, hangs a yellow-and-blue training plane operated during the Second World War by the Tuskegee Airmen, the first black American military pilots.

Slavery might be better presented without the escape hatch of freer air above. After all, this is how it was experienced: not as a step on the path to somewhere else but as a cruel normalcy, a permanent condition, the life that one's ancestors had lived, and that one's children would surely live, too. The Holocaust Memorial Museum, across the Mall, offers a sober acknowledgment: for millions, this was a lifetime—an entire edifice, not simply a floor. "In Washington, D.C., there is no museum of American slavery," Foner noted, when we spoke. He added, "We have a museum of the Holocaust in Washington, which is a great museum, but, you know, what would we think if the Germans put up a big museum of American slavery in Berlin and didn't have anything about the Holocaust?"

At the point on the wall's time line that marks emancipation, there stands a one-room slave cabin, made of whitewashed yellow pine in tidy slats. The cabin was dismantled where it stood originally, on the Point of Pines plantation, on Edisto Island, South Carolina, and reconstructed here. The roof looks flimsy; the simple brick fireplace reaches almost to the ceiling. The floor is clean and smooth. Something happens there, standing where others lived and likely died: the years ahead disappear. The quotidian catalogue that springs to mind—cooking, cleaning, sex, song—gives way to an awareness that such normalcy could exist, was *made* to exist, amid such evil. You look askance at that word, "home."

Outside the cabin, the time line reasserts itself, and the ramps speed history up, leading visitors to an exhibition called "Defending Freedom, Defining Freedom," which presents the era of de-jure and de-facto segregation and is anchored by a gleaming green Jim

Crow-era railway car. Soon, close to ground level, "A Changing America" takes us from the chaos of 1968 to the election of Barack Obama and the blood-fuelled rise of Black Lives Matter. Here you are surrounded by panels designed to look like picket signs, bedecked with quick-hit blurbs on "The Aftermath of King's Assassination" and "Feminist Writing," the Black Panthers and Black Power.

There is an irony in this approach: the leaders of these movements did not merely assemble a mountain of facts about life in America; they drew from those facts a world view. They offered interpretations of those facts, thus risking, even inviting, controversy and dissent. The new museum's one heavy-handed assertion—the fact of black advancement—is indisputable. But it makes no comment on which means, and which strategies, have secured this progress, or how it might be sustained and enlarged. The exhibits make a thorough sweep through the centuries; no one will leave without scores of wide-eyed did-you-know's to share. But by refusing to submit its wares to the refiner's fire of exegesis, or to make of the many ideas represented within its walls some new idea, useful for the future, the museum reduces history to a scattering of bright but unconstellated stars.

THERE IS A FEELING OF RELIEF WHEN YOU REACH THE UPPER FLOORS, where the "culture galleries" are housed, and where even Smithsonian-friendly artifacts begin to gather coherence. These items speak not with the wrenching power of the Point of Pines cabin but with a kind of roving intelligence, enabled by the symbolic wit of art. Take, for example, the MIDI Production Center, or MPC, owned by the late producer J. Dilla. The MPC, a tool for recording, mixing, and creating something new from found materials, evokes the process by which art can confound the course of events, not simply reflect or react to it.

The triumph of the building's interior is the gallery for fine art, which occupies the museum's fourth and most impressive floor. From a wide window, facing west, you can see from the White House, in the north, to the Ellipse, to the Washington Monument and the Jefferson Memorial, with the Lincoln Memorial just visible in the distance. When I visited, the art was not yet placed, but the collection, which the chief curator, Jacqueline Serwer, along with the curator Tuliza Fleming and the museum's deputy director, Kinshasha Holman Conwill, acquired mostly from private donors, is a genuine treasure—and a reminder of art's power to illuminate history's murkier passages. "There wasn't a place in the Smithsonian where you could go from Robert Duncanson to Carrie Mae Weems," Bunch told me, describing the museum's goal in bringing together black artists from America's past and its present. "I wanted us to be that place." Duncanson's stately "The Garden of Eden," painted thirteen years before emancipation, depicts a paradise, leafy and mountainous but also unsettlingly dark. The figures of Adam and Eve are distant and barely distinguishable from the wilderness beyond them. The painting conveys a post-Fall America, tinged with menace, in which sin and grace manage a dissonant coexistence. David Driskell's brown-toned canvas "Behold Thy Son," a work of anguished expressionism, was painted in 1956, a year after the lynching of Emmett Till. It depicts a body with a mangled face and outstretched arms, which could be Christ drooping from the Cross or Till at his funeral, where his mother, Mamie Till-Mobley, insisted on an open casket.

The museum's greatest example of the synthesis of art and history, beauty and tragedy, might be "April 4," a work from 1969, by the abstractionist painter Sam Gilliam, in which the artist memorialized Martin Luther King, Jr.,'s assassination. The canvas, smudged with purple, conveys an uneasy mood, but its key feature is a wild splattering of red. The suggestion of blood says much of what can be said about King's killing, or, for that matter, anyone's: that it is senseless, that it is blank fact, that no word could ever rise to its finality.

The museum's history galleries may, over time, find a way to communicate the power of events with a similar force—to achieve a kind of lift, away from the time line and into deeper places. Of course, as a public institution, it belongs to a nation still nervous about its meaning, and it depends, financially, on a Congress hardly interested in original thought along racial lines. It exists, massively, in three-dimensional space, not on the page or on canvas.

And the contemporary Mall, despite the loftiness of its monuments, is one of the country's great populist locales. The scene on a warm day—Frisbees floating, sunbathers dozing, those endless busloads of schoolkids—is a vindication of L'Enfant's original, bustling idea, a happy echo of America's largeness and its stubborn eccentricity. Seen this way, the appearance of the N.M.A.A.H.C. as a site of pilgrimage—and, more mutely, as a dark presence at a distinguished address—will not fail to do some good. Better that the children go home rattling off facts, however loosely grasped, about Jim Crow and James Brown than not. Still, for the new museum to become worthy of its expressive building, and to join the ranks of institutions that have helped us to better understand ourselves, it will need to borrow the tactics of art: a long and steady gaze, a bravery uncommon in bureaucracy, and a conception of experience not as a lens but as something that we must continue, indefinitely, to excavate—interpreting as we dig.

BEFORE THE LAW

JENNIFER GONNERMAN

October 6, 2014

In the early hours of Saturday, May 15, 2010, ten days before his seventeenth birthday, Kalief Browder and a friend were returning home from a party in the Belmont section of the Bronx. They walked along Arthur Avenue, the main street of Little Italy, past bakeries and cafés with their metal shutters pulled down for the night. As they passed East 186th Street, Browder saw a police car driving toward them. More squad cars arrived, and soon Browder and his friend found themselves squinting in the glare of a police spotlight. An officer said that a man had just reported that they had robbed him. "I didn't rob anybody," Browder replied. "You can check my pockets."

The officers searched him and his friend but found nothing. As Browder recalls, one of the officers walked back to his car, where the alleged victim was, and returned with a new story: the man said that they had robbed him not that night but two weeks earlier. The police handcuffed the teens and pressed them into the back of a squad car. "What am I being charged for?" Browder asked. "I didn't do anything!" He remembers an officer telling them, "We're just going to take you to the precinct. Most likely you can go home." Browder whispered to his friend, "Are you sure *you* didn't do anything?" His friend insisted that he hadn't.

At the Forty-eighth Precinct, the pair were fingerprinted and locked in a holding cell. A few hours later, when an officer opened the door, Browder jumped up: "I can leave now?" Instead, the teens were taken to Central Booking at the Bronx County Criminal Court.

Browder had already had a few run-ins with the police, including an incident eight months earlier, when an officer reported seeing him take a delivery truck for a joyride and crash into a parked car. Browder was charged with grand larceny. He told me that his friends drove the truck and that he had only watched, but he figured that he had no defense, and so he pleaded guilty. The judge gave him probation and "youthful offender" status, which insured that he wouldn't have a criminal record.

Late on Saturday, seventeen hours after the police picked Browder up, an officer and a prosecutor interrogated him, and he again maintained his innocence. The next day, he was led into a courtroom, where he learned that he had been charged with robbery, grand larceny, and assault. The judge released his friend, permitting him to remain free while the case moved through the courts. But, because Browder was still on probation, the judge ordered him to be held and set bail at three thousand dollars. The amount was out of reach for his family, and soon Browder found himself aboard a Department of Correction bus. He fought back panic, he told me later. Staring through the grating on the bus window, he watched the Bronx disappear. Soon, there was water on either side as the bus made its way across a long, narrow bridge to Rikers Island.

Of the eight million people living in New York City, some eleven thousand are confined in the city's jails on any given day, most of them on Rikers, a four-hundred-acre island in the East River, between Queens and the Bronx. New Yorkers who have never visited often think of Rikers as a single, terrifying building, but the island has ten jails—eight for men, one for women, and one so decrepit that it hasn't housed anyone since 2000.

Male adolescents are confined in the Robert N. Davoren Center—known as R.N.D.C. When Browder arrived, the jail held some six hundred boys, aged sixteen to eighteen. Conditions there are notoriously grim. In August of this year, a report by the U.S. Attorney for the Southern District of New York described R.N.D.C. as a place with a "deep-seated culture of violence," where attacks by officers and among inmates are rampant. The report featured a list of inmate injuries: "broken jaws, broken orbital bones, broken noses, long bone fractures, and lacerations requiring stitches."

Browder's family could not afford to hire an attorney, so the judge appointed a lawyer named Brendan O'Meara to represent him. Browder told O'Meara that he was innocent and assumed that his case would conclude quickly. Even the assistant district attorney handling the prosecution later acknowledged in court papers that it was a "relatively straightforward case." There weren't hours of wiretaps or piles of complicated evidence to sift through; there was just the memory of one alleged victim. But Browder had entered the legal system through the Bronx criminal courts, which are chronically overwhelmed. Last year, the *Times*, in an extended exposé, described them as "crippled" and among the most backlogged in the country. One reason is budgetary. There are not nearly enough judges and court staff to handle the workload; in 2010, Browder's case was one of five thousand six hundred and ninety-five felonies that the Bronx District Attorney's office prosecuted. The problem is compounded by defense attorneys who drag out cases to improve their odds of winning, judges who permit endless adjournments, prosecutors who are perpetually unprepared. Although the Sixth Amendment guarantees "the right to a speedy and public trial," in the Bronx the concept of speedy justice barely exists.

FOR AS LONG AS BROWDER COULD REMEMBER, HE HAD LIVED IN THE same place, a two-story brick house near the Bronx Zoo. He was the youngest of seven siblings; except for the oldest two, all the children were adopted, and the mother fostered other children as well. "Kalief was the last brought into the family," an older brother told me. "By the time it came to Kalief, my mom had already raised—in foster care or adoption—a total of thirty-four kids." Kalief was the smallest, he recalled, "so my mom called him Peanut."

As a child, Browder loved Pokemon, the W.W.E., free Wednesdays at the Bronx Zoo, and mimicking his brother's workout routine. "At six years old, he had an eight-pack," his brother said. When Browder was ten, their father, who worked as a subway cleaner, moved out, though he continued to help support the family.

For high school, Browder went to the small, progressive New Day Academy. A former staff member remembered him as a "fun guy," the type of kid others wanted to be around. Occasionally, he would grab a hall pass, sneak into a friend's classroom, and stay until the teacher caught on. He told me that his report cards were full of C's, but the staff member I spoke to said, "I thought he was very smart."

Inside R.N.D.C., Browder soon realized that he was not going to make many friends. He was assigned to a dorm where about fifty teen-age boys slept in an open room, each with a plastic bucket to store his possessions in. "Their conversations bored me," he told me. As far as he could tell, the other inmates were interested only in "crimes they committed and girls that they did." When Browder asked a guard how inmates were supposed to get their clothes cleaned, he was told that they had to wash them themselves. He thought this was a joke until he noticed other inmates scrubbing their clothes by hand, using their bucket and jailhouse soap. After he did the same and hung his wet clothes on the rail of his bed, he wound up with brown rust stains on his white T-shirt, his socks, and his boxers. That day, he told himself, "I don't know how I'm going to live in this place."

Browder's mother visited every weekend. In the visiting room, he would hand her his dirty clothes and get a stack of freshly laundered clothes in return. She also put money in a jail commissary account for him, so he could buy snacks. He knew that such privileges made him a target for his fellow-prisoners, who would take any opportunity to empty someone else's bucket of snacks and clothes, so he slept with his head off the side of his bed, atop his bucket. To survive inside R.N.D.C., he decided that the best strategy was to keep to himself and to work out. Before Rikers, he told me, "every here and there I did a couple pullups or pushups. When I went in there, that's when I decided I wanted to get big."

The dayroom was ruled over by a gang leader and his friends, who controlled inmates' access to the prison phones and dictated who could sit on a bench to watch TV and who had to sit on the floor. "A lot of times, I'd say, 'I'm not sitting on the floor,'" Browder said. "And then they'll come with five or six dudes. They'd swing on me. I'd have to fight back." There was no escape, no protection, and a suspicion that some of the guards had an agreement with the gang members.

Browder told me that, one night soon after he arrived, a group of guards lined him and several other inmates up against a wall, trying to figure out who had been responsible for an earlier fight. "They're talking to us about why did we jump these guys," he said. "And as they're talking they're punching us one by one." Browder said that he had nothing to do with the fight, but still the officers beat him; the other inmates endured much worse. "Their noses were leaking, their faces were bloody, their eyes were swollen," he said. Afterward, the officers gave the teens a choice: go to the medical clinic or go back to bed. But they made it clear that, if the inmates went to the clinic and told the medical staff what had happened, they would write up charges against them, and get them sent to solitary confinement. "I just told them I'll act like nothing happened," Browder said. "So they didn't send us to the clinic; they didn't write anything up; they just sent us back." The Department of Correction refused to respond to these allegations, or to answer any questions about Browder's stay on Rikers. But the recent U.S. Attorney's report about R.N.D.C. recounts many instances in which officers pressured inmates not to report beatings—to "hold it down," in Rikers parlance.

ON THE MORNING OF JULY 28, 2010, BROWDER WAS AWAKENED AT around half past four. He was handcuffed to another inmate and herded onto a bus with a group of other prisoners. At the Bronx County Hall of Justice, they spent the day in a basement holding pen, each waiting for his chance to see a judge. When Browder's turn came, an officer led him into a courtroom and he caught a glimpse of his mother in the spectator area. Seventy-four days had passed since his arrest. Already he had missed his seventeenth birthday, the end of his sophomore year, and half the summer.

A grand jury had voted to indict Browder. The criminal complaint alleged that he and his friend had robbed a Mexican immigrant named Roberto Bautista—pursuing him, pushing him against a fence, and taking his backpack. Bautista told the police that his backpack contained a credit card, a debit card, a digital camera, an iPod Touch, and seven hundred dollars. Browder was also accused of punching Bautista in the face.

A clerk read out the charges—"Robbery in the second degree and other crimes"—and asked Browder, "How do you plead, sir, guilty or not guilty?"

"Not guilty," Browder said.

An officer escorted him out of the courtroom and back downstairs to return to Rikers. It no longer mattered whether his mother could find the money to bail him out. The Department of Probation had filed a "violation of probation" against him—standard procedure when someone on probation is indicted on a new violent felony—and the judge had remanded him without bail.

Browder repeatedly told O'Meara, his court-appointed lawyer, that he would never plead guilty and that he wanted to go to trial. O'Meara assumed that his courtroom defense would be "Listen, they got the wrong kid." After all, the accusation had been made a week or two after the alleged robbery, and the victim had later changed his mind about when it occurred. (The original police report said "on or about May 2," but Bautista later told a detective that it happened on May 8th.)

With each day he spent in jail, Browder imagined that he was getting closer to trial. Many states have so-called speedy-trial laws, which require trials to start within a certain time frame. New York State's version is slightly different, and is known as the "ready rule." This rule stipulates that all felony cases (except homicides) must be ready for trial within six months of arraignment, or else the charges can be dismissed. In practice, however, this time limit is subject to technicalities. The clock stops for many reasons—for example, when defense attorneys submit motions before trial—so that the amount of time that is officially held to have elapsed can be wildly different from the amount of time that really has. In 2011, seventy-four per cent of felony cases in the Bronx were older than six months.

In order for a trial to start, both the defense attorney and the prosecutor have to declare that they are ready; the court clerk then searches for a trial judge who is free and transfers the case, and jury selection can begin. Not long after Browder was indicted, an assistant district attorney sent the court a "Notice of Readiness," stating that "the People are ready for trial." The case was put on the calendar for possible trial on December 10th, but it did not start that day. On January 28, 2011, Browder's two-hundred-and-fifty-eighth day in jail, he was brought back to the courthouse once again. This time, the prosecutor said, "The People are not ready. We are requesting one week." The next court date set by the judge—March 9th—was not one week away but six. As it happened, Browder didn't go to trial anytime that year. An index card in the court file explains:

June 23, 2011: People not ready, request 1 week.

August 24, 2011: People not ready, request 1 day.

November 4, 2011: People not ready, prosecutor on trial, request 2 weeks.

December 2, 2011: Prosecutor on trial, request January 3rd.

The Bronx courts are so clogged that when a lawyer asks for a one-week adjournment the next court date usually doesn't happen for six weeks or more. As long as a prosecutor has filed a Notice of Readiness, however, delays caused by court congestion don't count toward the number of days that are officially held to have elapsed. Every time a prosecutor stood before a judge in Browder's case, requested a one-week adjournment, and got six weeks instead, this counted as only one week against the six-month deadline. Meanwhile, Browder remained on Rikers, where six weeks still felt like six weeks—and often much longer.

Like many defendants with court-appointed lawyers, Browder thought his attorney was not doing enough to help him. O'Meara, who works mostly in the Bronx and in Westchester County, never made the trip out to Rikers to see him, since a visit there can devour at least half a day. To avoid this trek, some lawyers set up video conferences at the Bronx courthouse with their clients who are in jail. O'Meara says he's "pretty sure" he did this with Browder, but Browder says he never did. Court papers suggest a lawyer in a hurry: in the fall of 2010, O'Meara filed a notice with the court in which he mistakenly wrote that he would soon be making a motion on Browder's case in "Westchester County Court," instead of in the Bronx.

New York City pays lawyers like O'Meara (known locally as "18-B attorneys") seventy-five dollars an hour for a felony case, sixty dollars for a misdemeanor. O'Meara handles all types of cases, from misdemeanors to homicides. When I met him, earlier this year, he was eating a hamburger and drinking coffee at a diner in Brooklyn after an appearance at a courthouse there. He was about to take the subway back to the Bronx, and his briefcase was bulging with papers. He told me that Browder, compared with some of his other clients, "was quiet, respectful—he wasn't rude." He also noted that, as the months passed, his client looked "tougher and bigger."

Most of the time, however, Browder had no direct contact with

O'Meara; the few times he tried to phone him, he couldn't get through, so he was dependent on his mother to talk to O'Meara on his behalf. Every time Browder got the chance, he asked O'Meara the same question: "Can you get me out?" O'Meara says that he made multiple bail applications on his client's behalf, but was unsuccessful because of the violation of probation. Meanwhile, other inmates advised Browder to tell his lawyer to file a speedy-trial motion—a motion to dismiss the case, because it hadn't been brought to trial within six months. But, with so many one-week requests that had turned into six-week delays, Browder had yet to reach the six-month mark.

For a defendant who is in jail, the more a case drags on the greater the pressure to give up and plead guilty. By early 2012, prosecutors had offered Browder a deal—three and a half years in prison in exchange for a guilty plea. He refused. "I want to go to trial," he told O'Meara, even though he knew that if he lost he could get up to fifteen years in state prison. Stories circulate on Rikers about inmates who plead guilty to crimes they didn't commit just to put an end to their ordeal, but Browder was determined to get his day in court. He had no idea how rare trials actually are. In 2011, in the Bronx, only a hundred and sixty-five felony cases went to trial; in three thousand nine hundred and ninety-one cases, the defendant pleaded guilty.

NOT LONG AFTER ARRIVING ON RIKERS, BROWDER MADE HIS FIRST TRIP to solitary confinement. It lasted about two weeks, he recalls, and followed a scuffle with another inmate. "He was throwing shoes at people—I told him to stop," Browder said. "I actually took his sneaker and I threw it, and he got mad. He swung on me, and we started fighting." Browder was placed in shackles and transferred by bus to the Central Punitive Segregation Unit, which everyone on Rikers calls the Bing. Housed in one of the island's newer jails, the Bing has four hundred cells, each about twelve feet by seven.

In recent years, the use of solitary confinement has spread in New York's jails. Between 2007 and mid-2013, the total number of solitary-confinement beds on Rikers increased by more than sixty per cent, and a report last fall found that nearly twenty-seven per cent of the adolescent inmates were in solitary. "I think the department became severely addicted to solitary confinement," Daniel Selling, who served as the executive director of mental health for New York City's jails, told me in April; he had quit his job two weeks earlier. "It's a way to control an environment that feels out of control—lock people in their cell," he said. "Adolescents can't handle it. Nobody could handle that." (In March, Mayor Bill de Blasio appointed a new jails commissioner, Joseph Ponte, who promised to "end the culture of excessive solitary confinement.")

For Browder, this was the first of several trips to the Bing. As he soon discovered, a prisoner there doesn't leave his cell except to go to rec, the shower, the visit room, the medical clinic, or court; whenever he does leave, he is handcuffed and strip-searched. To pass the time, Browder read magazines—*XXL*, *Sports Illustrated*, *Hip Hop Weekly*—and street novels handed on by other inmates; one was Sister Souljah's "Midnight." He'd always preferred video games, but he told me, "I feel like I broke myself into books through street novels." He moved on to more demanding reading and said that his favorite book was Craig Unger's "House of Bush, House of Saud."

Summer is the worst time of year to be stuck in the Bing, since the cells lack air-conditioning. In the hope of feeling a breeze, Browder would sleep with the window open, only to be awakened at 5 A.M., when the cell filled with the roar of planes taking off from LaGuardia, one of whose runways is less than three hundred feet from Rikers. He would spend all day smelling his own sweat and counting the hours until his next shower. He thought about the places he would have been visiting if he were not spending the summer in jail: Mapes Pool, Coney Island, Six Flags. One day, when he called home to talk to his mother—he was allowed one six-minute call a day while in solitary—he could make out the familiar jingle of an ice-cream truck in the background.

There hadn't been much to do at R.N.D.C., but at least there was school—classrooms where the inmates were supposed to be taken every day, to study for a G.E.D. or a high-school diploma. The Bing had only "cell study": a correction officer slid work sheets under the door in the morning, collected them a few days later, and, eventually, returned them with a teacher's marks. Some inmates never bothered to fill in the work sheets, but Browder told himself, "I'm already in jail—I might as well keep trying to do something." There were times, however, when nobody came by to collect the work sheets on the day he'd been told they were due. If Browder saw a captain walk by through the small window in his door, he would shout, "Where is the school correction officer to pick up the work?"

Near the end of 2010, Browder returned to the Bing; he was there for about ten months, through the summer of 2011. He recalls that he got sent there initially after another fight. (Once an inmate is in solitary, further minor infractions can extend his stay.) When Browder first went to Rikers, his brother had advised him to get himself sent to solitary whenever he felt at risk from other inmates. "I told him, 'When you get into a house and you don't feel safe, do whatever you have to to get out,'" the brother said. "'It's better than coming home with a slice on your face.'"

Even in solitary, however, violence was a threat. Verbal spats with officers could escalate. At one point, Browder said, "I had words with a correction officer, and he told me he wanted to fight. That was his way of handling it." He'd already seen the officer challenge other inmates to fights in the shower, where there are no surveillance cameras. "So I agreed to it; I said, 'I'll fight you.'" The next day, the officer came to escort him to the shower, but before they even got there, he said, the officer knocked him down: "He put his forearm on my face, and my face was on the floor, and he just started punching me in the leg." Browder isn't the first inmate to make such an allegation; the U.S. Attorney's report described similar incidents.

Browder's brother reconsidered his advice when he saw him in the Bing visiting area. For one thing, he says, Browder was losing weight. "Several times when I visited him, he said, 'They're not feeding me,'" the brother told me. "He definitely looked really skinny." In solitary, food arrived through a slot in the cell door three times a day. For a growing teen-ager, the portions were never big enough, and in solitary Browder couldn't supplement the rations with snacks bought at the commissary. He took to begging the officers for leftovers: "Can I get that bread?" Sometimes they would slip him an extra slice or two; often, they refused.

Browder's brother also noticed a growing tendency toward despair. When Browder talked about his case, he was "strong, adamant: 'No, they can't do this to me!'" But, when the conversation turned to life in jail, "it's a totally different personality, which is depressed. He's, like, 'I don't know how long I can take this.'"

Browder got out of the Bing in the fall of 2011, but by the end of the year he was back—after yet another fight, he says. On the night of February 8, 2012—his six-hundred-and-thirty-fourth day on Rikers—he said to himself, "I can't take it anymore. I give up." That night, he tore his bedsheet into strips, tied them together to make a noose, attached it to the light fixture, and tried to hang himself. He was taken to the clinic, then returned to solitary. Browder told me that his sheets, magazines, and clothes were removed—everything except his white plastic bucket.

On February 17th, he was shuttled to the courthouse once again, but this time he was not brought up from the court pen in time to hear his case called. ("I'll waive his appearance for today's purposes," his lawyer told the judge.) For more than a year, he had heard various excuses about why his trial had to be delayed, among them that the prosecutor assigned to the case was on trial elsewhere, was on jury duty, or, as he once told the judge, had "conflicts in my schedule." If Browder had been in the courtroom on this day, he would have heard a prosecutor offer a new excuse: "Your Honor, the assigned assistant is currently on vacation." The prosecutor asked for a five-day adjournment; Browder's lawyer requested March 16th, and the judge scheduled the next court date for then.

The following night, in his solitary cell on Rikers, Browder shattered his plastic bucket by stomping on it, then picked up a piece, sharpened it, and began sawing his wrist. He was stopped after an officer saw him through the cell window and intervened.

BROWDER WAS STILL ON RIKERS ISLAND IN JUNE OF 2012, WHEN HIS high-school classmates collected their diplomas, and in September, when some of them enrolled in college. In the fall, prosecutors offered him a new deal: if he pleaded guilty, he'd get two and a half years in prison, which meant that, with time served, he could go home soon. "Ninety-nine out of a hundred would take the offer that gets you out of jail," O'Meara told me. "He just said, 'Nah, I'm not taking it.' He didn't flinch. Never talked about it. He was not taking a plea."

Meanwhile, Browder kept travelling from Rikers to the Bronx courthouse and back again, shuttling between two of New York City's most dysfunctional bureaucracies, each system exacerbating the flaws of the other. With every trip Browder made to the courthouse, another line was added to a growing stack of index cards kept in the court file:

June 29, 2012: People not ready, request one week.
September 28, 2012: People not ready, request two weeks.
November 2, 2012: People not ready, request one week.
December 14, 2012: People not ready, request one week.

By the end of 2012, Browder had been in jail for nine hundred and sixty-one days and had stood before eight different judges. He always maintained his composure, never berating his attorney or yelling protests in court. O'Meara was impressed by his control. "I can't imagine most people sitting in there for three years and not becoming very upset with their attorney," he says. "He just never complained to me." Privately, though, Browder was angry. About the prosecutors, he would tell himself, "These guys are just playing with my case."

On March 13, 2013, Browder appeared before a new judge, Patricia M. DiMango, who had been transferred from Brooklyn as part of a larger effort to tackle the Bronx's backlog. She was known for her no-nonsense style when dealing with defendants; at the Brooklyn courthouse, she was referred to as Judge Judy. (As it happens, this year she became a judge on "Hot Bench," a new courtroom TV show created by Judge Judy.) In the Bronx, Di-Mango's job was to review cases and clear them: by getting weak cases dismissed, extracting guilty pleas from defendants, or referring cases to trial in another courtroom. At the start of 2013, there were nine hundred and fifty-two felony cases in the Bronx, including Browder's, that were more than two years old. In the next twelve months, DiMango disposed of a thousand cases, some as old as five years.

Judge DiMango explained to Browder, "If you go to trial and lose, you could get up to fifteen." Then she offered him an even more tempting deal: plead guilty to two misdemeanors—the equivalent of sixteen months in jail—and go home now, on the time already served. "If you want that, I will do that today," DiMango said. "I could sentence you today. . . . It's up to you."

"I'm all right," Browder said. "I did not do it. I'm all right."

"You are all right?" DiMango said.

"Yes," he said. "I want to go to trial."

Back at Rikers, other prisoners were stunned. "You're bugging," they told him. "You're stupid. If that was me, I would've said I did it and went home." Browder knew that it was a gamble; even though he was innocent, he could lose at trial. "I used to go to my cell and lie down and think, like, Maybe I am crazy; maybe I am going too far," he recalled. "But I just did what I thought was right."

On May 29th, the thirty-first court date on Browder's case, there was another development. DiMango peered down from the bench. "The District Attorney is really in a position right now where they cannot proceed," she said. "It is their intention to dismiss the case." She explained that this could not officially happen until the next court date, which ended up being a week later. "I will release you today, but you have to come back here on time without any new cases," she said. "Do you think you can do that, Mr. Browder?"

"Yes," he said.

Browder could not believe what was happening. His battle to prove his innocence had ended. No trial, no jury, no verdict. An assistant district attorney filed a memo with the court explaining that Bautista, the man who had accused Browder, had gone back to Mexico. The District Attorney's office had reached his brother in the Bronx and tried to arrange for him to return and testify, but then the office lost contact with the brother, too. "Without the Complainant, we are unable to meet our burden of proof at trial," the prosecutor wrote.

Browder had to spend one more night on Rikers. By now, he had missed his junior year of high school, his senior year, graduation, the prom. He was no longer a teen-ager; four days earlier, he had turned twenty.

He didn't know what time he would be released, so he told his mother not to bother picking him up. The next afternoon, he walked out of jail, a single thought in his mind: "I'm going home!" He took the bus to Queens Plaza, then two subways to the Bronx, and his euphoria began to dissipate. Being around so many people felt strange. Except for a few weeks, he had been in solitary confinement for the previous seventeen months.

AFTER LEAVING RIKERS, BROWDER MOVED BACK HOME, WHERE HIS mother and two of his brothers were living. Everybody could see that he had changed. Most of the clothes in his bedroom no longer fit; he had grown an inch or two while he was away and had become brawnier. Many of his former pastimes—playing video games, watching movies, shooting hoops in the park—no longer engaged him. He preferred to spend time by himself, alone in his bedroom, with the door closed. Sometimes he found himself pacing, as he had done in solitary. When he saw old friends, he was reminded of their accomplishments and what he had not achieved: no high-school diploma, no job, no money, no apartment of his own.

Before he went to jail, he used to like sitting on his front steps with his friends, and when a group of attractive girls walked by he'd call out, "Hi. What are you doing? Where's the party at? Can I go with you?" Now, if he managed to get a girl's number, the first real conversation would always go the same way: she would ask him if he was in school or working, and he would feel his anxiety rise. Once he revealed that he was still living at home, without a job or a diploma, "they look at me like I ain't worth nothing. Like I ain't shit. It hurts to have people look at you like that." He could explain that he'd been wrongfully arrested, but the truth felt too complicated, too raw and personal. "If I tell them the story, then I gotta hear a hundred questions," he said. "It gets emotional for me. And those emotions I don't feel comfortable with."

Not long after Browder returned home, one of his relatives called an attorney named Paul V. Prestia and told him that Browder had spent three years on Rikers only to have his case dismissed. "Send him down," Prestia said. A former prosecutor in Brooklyn, Prestia now has his own firm. On his office wall hangs a 2011 *Post* story about a Haitian chef from the Bronx who was mistakenly arrested for rape and spent eight days on Rikers; Prestia got the case dismissed.

When Prestia first heard Browder's story, he thought there must be a catch; even by the sorry standards of justice in the Bronx, the case was extreme. "It's something that could've been tried in a court in a matter of days," he told me. "I don't know how each and every prosecutor who looked at this case continued to let this happen. It's like Kalief Browder didn't even exist." Earlier this year, Prestia filed a suit on Browder's behalf against the city, the N.Y.P.D., the Bronx District Attorney, and the Department of Correction.

Robert T. Johnson, the Bronx District Attorney, will not answer questions about Browder's case, because, once the charges were dismissed, the court records were sealed. But recently when I asked him a general question about cases that drag on and on, he was quick to deflect blame. "These long delays—two, three years— they're horrendous, but the D.A. is not really accountable for that kind of delay," he said. His explanation was that either the case did not actually exceed the six-month speedy-trial deadline or the defense attorney failed to bring a speedy-trial motion.

Prestia, in his lawsuit, alleges "malicious prosecution," charging that Johnson's prosecutors were "representing to the court that they would be 'ready' for trial, when in fact, they never were." Prestia said, "The million-dollar question is: When did they really know they didn't have a witness? Did they really not know until 2013?" He suspects that, as he wrote in his complaint, they were "seeking long, undue adjournments of these cases to procure a guilty plea from plaintiff." The city has denied all allegations of wrongdoing, and Johnson, when I asked about these accusations, said, "Certainly if there is something uncovered that we did wrong, I will deal with that here. But I don't expect that to be the case."

Prestia has represented many clients who were wrongfully arrested, but Browder's story troubles him most deeply. "Kalief was deprived of his right to a fair and speedy trial, his education, and, I would even argue, his entire adolescence," he says. "If you took a sixteen-year-old kid and locked him in a room for twenty-three hours, your son or daughter, you'd be arrested for endangering the welfare of a child." Browder doesn't know exactly how many days he was in solitary—and Rikers officials, citing pending litigation, won't divulge any details about his stay—but he remembers that it was "about seven hundred, eight hundred."

One day last November, six months after his release, Browder retreated to his bedroom with a steak knife, intending to slit his wrists. A friend happened to stop by, saw the knife, and grabbed it. When he left the house to find Browder's mother, Browder tried to hang himself from a bannister. An ambulance rushed him to St. Barnabas Hospital, where he was admitted to the psychiatric ward. In his medical record, a social worker describes the suicide attempt as "serious."

ONE AFTERNOON THIS PAST SPRING, I SAT WITH BROWDER IN A QUIET restaurant in lower Manhattan. He is five feet seven, with a high forehead, tired eyes, and a few wisps of hair above his upper lip. "Being home is way better than being in jail," he told me. "But in my mind right now I feel like I'm still in jail, because I'm still feeling the side effects from what happened in there."

When I first asked if I could interview him, he was reluctant, but eventually he agreed, and we met many times. We always met in downtown Manhattan, near Prestia's office. He didn't want to meet in the Bronx, and seemed to feel more comfortable speaking where nobody knew him. He almost always wore the same uniform: a hoodie with the hood pulled down; a pair of earbuds, one stuck in an ear and the other swinging free; rosary beads dangling from his neck—not because he is Catholic (his family are Jehovah's Witnesses) but "for fashion," he said. When I asked him about Rikers, he surprised me with his willingness to speak. At times, he seemed almost unable to stop, as if he had long been craving the chance to tell somebody about what he endured. Other times, though, the act of remembering seemed almost physically painful: he would fall silent, drop his gaze, and shake his head.

Ever since Browder left Rikers, he has tried to stay busy. He sat through G.E.D. prep classes, signed up for a computer course, searched for a job, and attended weekly counselling sessions. This past March, he learned that he had passed the G.E.D. on the first try. "I gained some of my pride back," he told me. He landed a job as a security guard—not his dream position, but it would serve while he looked for something better. By coincidence, one of the places he was sent was St. Barnabas. On his second day there, he overheard some employees talking about him; somebody seemed to have figured out that he had been in the psychiatric ward. Soon afterward, with a vague explanation, he was fired.

Prestia helped him find a part-time job, working for a friend who runs a jewelry business in the same building as Prestia's office, near Wall Street. On May 29th—four days after his twenty-first birthday, and a year to the day after DiMango told him that he would be set free—Browder stood on a sidewalk in front of a Chase bank, handing out flyers advertising the jewelry business. He told me that he liked Wall Street—being surrounded by people with briefcases and suits, everyone walking with a sense of purpose. "When I see professional people, I see myself," he said. "I say, 'I want to be like them.'"

Exactly how he would manage this he was not sure. Most days, the progress he had made since coming home did not feel like progress to him. "It's been a year now, and I got a part-time job, and I got my G.E.D.," he said. "But, when you think about it, that's nothing. People tell me because I have this case against the city I'm all right. But I'm not all right. I'm messed up. I know that I might see some money from this case, but that's not going to help me mentally. I'm mentally scarred right now. That's how I feel. Because there are certain things that changed about me and they might not go back."

This month, Browder started classes at Bronx Community College. But, even now, he thinks about Rikers every day. He says that his flashbacks to that time are becoming more frequent. Almost anything can trigger them. It might be the sight of a police cruiser or something more innocuous. When his mother cooks rice and chili, he says, he can't help remembering the rice and chili he was fed on Rikers, and suddenly, in his mind, he is back in the Bing, recalling how hungry he was all the time, especially at night, when he'd have to wait twelve hours for his next meal.

Even with his friends, things aren't the same. "I'm trying to break out of my shell, but I guess there is no shell. I guess this is just how I am—I'm just quiet and distant," he says. "I don't like being this way, but it's just natural to me now." Every night before he goes to sleep, he checks that every window in the house is locked. When he rides the subway, he often feels terrified. "I might be attacked; I might be robbed," he says. "Because, believe me, in jail you know there's all type of criminal stuff that goes on." No matter how hard he tries, he cannot forget what he saw: inmates stealing from each other, officers attacking teens, blood on the dayroom floor. "Before I went to jail, I didn't know about a lot of stuff, and, now that I'm aware, I'm paranoid," he says. "I feel like I was robbed of my happiness."

THE FORGOTTEN ONES

RACHEL AVIV

October 1, 2018

Seth Murrell, a four-year-old boy with dreadlocks to his chin, moved with his family to Atlanta in the fall of 2015. On his first day at his new preschool, he cried the whole morning. He wouldn't sit still in his chair. He'd pop up and snatch the glasses off a classmate's face, or spit at the teacher. When he was tired, he waved his arms in the air, begging his teacher to hold him. On the rare occasions that his teacher complimented him, he shouted "Yay!" too loudly.

His mother, Latoya Martin, a hair stylist, had moved with her husband and three children from Donalsonville, a rural town in Seminole County, in the southwest corner of Georgia, to be closer to psychiatrists and neurologists who would understand why her son was developmentally delayed. He couldn't string words together into a sentence. His teachers called Latoya nearly every day and told her to pick him up early, because he was disrupting the class. When Latoya resisted—she was busy looking for a new job—her friends warned her that the school might call child-protective services if she couldn't pick up Seth promptly. Latoya sensed that the teachers were accusing her of being a bad parent, so she informed the school's principal that she had never done drugs and that in high school her G.P.A. had been 4.0. Latoya's sister Anita said, "They kept saying we needed to work with him more at home. I'm, like, we work with him—that's not the problem. This is part of his disability!"

After a month, Latoya was told that Seth would be sent to a

school twenty minutes away, in the Georgia Network for Educational and Therapeutic Support, a constellation of schools, known as GNETS, attended by four thousand students with emotional and behavioral disabilities. Anita, a public-school teacher in Atlanta for nearly two decades, said, "I was just trying to figure it out in my head—we already have special-ed classes in the schools, so why is there this second system?" GNETS has a ten-per-cent graduation rate, compared with seventy-eight per cent for other public schools in Georgia.

Seth, who at twenty-one months had been given a diagnosis of pervasive developmental disorder—a loosely defined diagnosis often given to toddlers when their condition is not understood—was assigned to the Ash Street Center, one of a hundred and seventy-nine sites in the GNETS network. The school is surrounded by a gated fence. Latoya said that the next-youngest student in Seth's class was nine. The year before, a teaching assistant at Ash Street had been arrested after knocking a fourteen-year-old boy to the floor, choking him, and shouting, "I will kill that little motherfucker!"

Latoya said that, when she walked into her son's class, "I did not see one white child. All I saw was black boys." Seth's "target behavior," according to the center's intervention plan, was to "comply with adult directives." Latoya demanded that Seth be returned to his neighborhood school, but she was told that first he had to meet his performance goals, which included following instructions seventy per cent of the day. "You all know this is against the law, right?" she said to Seth's teacher. The federal Individuals with Disabilities Education Act, passed in 1975, states that children with disabilities must be educated with their nondisabled peers to the "maximum appropriate extent." They can be removed from their classrooms only if their disabilities are so severe that they can't learn in a less restrictive setting.

After Seth had gone to Ash Street for ten days, Latoya and

her husband, Tercel, who was working at a Toys R Us, returned with their children to Donalsonville, where Latoya's family has lived for as many generations as they can trace back. Latoya's sister Yvette, a high-school teacher, said, "She was just praying that a small town with teachers who had grown up around them would know how to take care of her baby." Latoya tried to enroll all three children in their former school, where she and her twelve siblings had gone. Though black and white students at the school had held separate proms as recently as the nineteen-eighties, Latoya trusted the teachers, many of whom she'd grown up with. Her two older children rejoined their classes, but the school district said that Seth was now classified as a GNETS student. He would have to take a bus to a GNETS school called Pathways, in Bainbridge, thirty minutes away.

Latoya's sister Sonja, who lived in Bainbridge, occasionally stopped by Pathways in the middle of the day. She described the school as a kind of ghost town. The front office was empty—the secretary and the coördinator had left, and the positions were never filled—and there was no full-time nurse, social worker, resource officer, or behavioral specialist. (The district's superintendent said that off-site staff provided support to the school.) Sonja said, of the first time she came to the school, "I walked down the hallway hollering, 'Hello? Hello? Anybody here?'" She looked in Seth's classroom and saw him sleeping on the floor, alone. His teacher was in another room.

There are roughly a hundred students at Pathways, which has three sites in the region, and all of the students are classified by the state as "economically disadvantaged." In Bainbridge, there was only one other student in the elementary-school class: MaKenzie Phillips, a petite thirteen-year-old white girl who immediately warmed to Seth, calling him her baby. MaKenzie took antidepressants, antipsychotics, two drugs for attention-deficit disorder, and anti-anxiety pills. She was generally calm and said, "Yes, Ma'am," when addressed, though she also interrupted conversations with vulgar words. She was in the elementary class because she had an I.Q. of 40. She spent much of the day flipping through magazines that she couldn't read. MaKenzie's mother, Erica, said that, whenever she dropped by the classroom, "there was no instruction. But I just figured I was coming at the wrong time of day."

Seth's class was led by Melissa Williams-Brown, who lived a few blocks from Latoya and had gone to her high school. She was not certified to teach elementary school, and had little knowledge of the nature of her students' disabilities. "I didn't get any specialized training," she told me. "I just winged it." The students at Pathways had bipolar disorder, schizophrenia, A.D.H.D., autism, or, as one teacher put it, "home-life issues" such as neglect, trauma, or poverty. Williams-Brown didn't understand why Seth, who was eventually given a diagnosis of autism, couldn't return to his neighborhood school, where there were more qualified teachers. "There was nothing in place for this young man," she told me. "I just felt like these students, especially the black boys, were put there, basically, because they intimidated their teachers."

THE FIRST GNETS SCHOOL, THE RUTLAND CENTER, FOUNDED IN 1970, was once housed in the former West Athens Colored School, whose principal promised to teach the "practical duties of life" to the "inferior race." The concept for GNETS was visionary. According to a report by researchers at the University of Georgia, the schools, then called psychoeducational centers, would rely on teachers trained in developmental psychology, ready to "face the assault of bizarre behavior." They were taught that they might be the "only agent for change in the life of a disturbed child." Mary Wood, a professor emerita at the University of Georgia, who developed the concept, said that she intended for each program to have a consulting psychiatrist, a social worker, a program evaluator, and a psychologist.

But as the first generation of directors retired, in the nineties, "the pieces of the mosaic dropped out," she said.

In the two-thousands, funding was cut, and the psychologists who remained seemed to be given free rein. One mother learned that a school psychologist was planning to subject her daughter, who had post-traumatic stress disorder, to fifteen hours of "experiments" devised to provoke misbehavior. "If I go to a mechanic with my car and my car is not doing the problem that I brought it there for, the mechanic can't diagnose it," the psychologist explained, at an administrative trial in 2005. "That's the same situation here." Over the years, a few parents became so suspicious of the program that they sent their children to school wearing recording devices. On one tape, as the Atlanta *Journal-Constitution* reported, a teacher could be heard giving a child what someone in the room called a "be-quiet hit." On another, teachers laughed about how they had put a student in a seclusion room because they needed a break. In 2004, a thirteen-year-old student hanged himself in a Time Out Room, an eight-by-eight concrete cell that could be locked from the outside.

Leslie Lipson, a lawyer at the Georgia Advocacy Office, a state-funded agency that represents people with disabilities, said that she first learned of the GNETs system in 2001, when a mother called to report that her son was put in a seclusion room nearly every day. "It's all little black boys at this school," the mother told her. Lipson researched the mother's claims and then rushed into her boss's office to tell him that she'd discovered an "insidious, shadow education system." She said, "I thought I was Erin Brockovich. I was, like, 'You are not going to believe this! There is an entire segregated system in Georgia! Can we shut this down immediately?' I was talking a thousand miles a minute, and my boss waited for me to take a breath. He was, like, 'Um, yeah, these schools have been around since before you were born.'"

Lipson studied the history of the schools, some of which were established in buildings that had housed schools for black children during the Jim Crow era. At a time when there was an outcry against court-ordered integration, GNETS became a mechanism for resegregating schools. "It became a way to filter out black boys, who at younger and younger ages are perceived to have behavioral disabilities," she said.

The Individuals with Disabilities Education Act (IDEA) requires that students with disabilities learn in the "least restrictive environment," a loose term that may mean different things depending on the race or the class of the student. Nirmala Erevelles, a professor of disability studies at the University of Alabama, told me that, "in general, when it comes to people of color—particularly poor people of color—we choose the most restrictive possibility," sending students to "the most segregated and punitive spaces in the public-school system." According to Beth Ferri, a disability scholar at Syracuse University, IDEA provided a kind of loophole to the 1954 Supreme Court decision in Brown v. Board of Education, which outlawed racial segregation in schools. Now racial segregation continued "under the guise of 'disability,'" she said. "You don't need to talk about any race anymore. You can just say that the kid is a slow learner, or defiant, or disrespectful." Ferri said that IDEA "treated disability as apolitical—a biological fact. It didn't think about things like racial or cultural bias."

Data obtained through records requests reveal that the percentage of students in the GNETS program who are black boys is double that of the public schools in the state. Most of the students in GNETS are classified as having an "emotional and behavioral disorder," a vague label that does not correspond to any particular medical diagnosis. A teacher who worked for five years at a GNETS program called Coastal Academy, in Brunswick, told me, "We always had a sprinkling of middle-class white kids, maybe two or three, but they didn't stay long. Everyone made sure they got out. It was the black students who were trapped there. They came in first grade and never left." Coastal Academy occupies a lot that once held an all-black school, originally called the Freedman's School, and the percentage of black males in the program is three times that of the districts that the school draws from. The teacher, who worried that she'd lose her job if she were identified, said that public schools in the area would "send the African-American kids to us for doing things like saying the word 'shit' in class or pushing a chair in really loudly. They would never, ever—never in a million years—attempt to come at a white parent with that."

The teacher said that students at Coastal Academy were routinely knocked to the floor and restrained. When they couldn't calm down, they were put in a Refocus Room. "If a student was having a bad day or hadn't taken his meds, the teacher down the hall from me would park herself in front of the room and the student would stay there all day," she said. "I heard children shrieking and screaming." (The program's director denied that students were knocked to the floor and that the room had been used for seclusion—the state banned seclusion rooms in 2010—and said that some students asked to go there.) When parents complained, the teacher said, "they were met with the same rigmarole: there is a reason why your son is here, and sometimes kids with these conditions make things up."

Suzie Dunson, the grandmother of a student in a GNETS program called the Woodall Center, in Columbus, said that, when her grandson was in first grade, she stopped by the school one day and found him sitting on the floor, handcuffed to a classroom chair. "He was six years old, and he looked like a chained animal," she told me. Her grandson routinely came home from school with a swollen face. "I'd ask him, 'How was school today?' 'Oh, I got restrained,' he'd say." According to the Woodall Center's records from the past two years, there were sixteen instances of teachers injuring students while attempting to restrain them. The reports typically blame the student: "In the process of restraining him he twisted his body and hit his head," one teacher noted. "His face must have rubbed on the ground," another wrote.

This year, when Dunson's grandson was sent to a juvenile-detention facility, at the age of eleven, he already had a friend there—a boy from his class. She describes the Woodall Center, where more than half the students are black boys, and ninety-one per cent are classified by the state as "economically disadvantaged," as a "pipeline-to-prison program." (A spokeswoman for the Woodall Center said that the school does not have documentation of Dunson's grandson being handcuffed or regularly restrained.)

It is not uncommon for students with disabilities to be placed in settings that are unnecessarily isolated, but GNETS is unusual in that this form of segregation is sponsored by the state rather than by the school district; families can't escape it by moving to a new neighborhood. Jatoyia Armour, a public-school teacher in Atlanta, said that when her five-year-old son, Jamir, was referred to GNETS, "I kept telling myself, 'This isn't a race issue. Jamir just has behavioral issues.'" She and Jamir had recently moved to an affluent suburb in northern Atlanta so that he would be zoned for a better school. He was the only black boy in his kindergarten class. He had an I.Q. of 120, but he wouldn't sit still, and had tantrums in which he threw objects. Armour said that the school called the police three times before he was transferred to a GNETS program, where the proportion of black boys to other students is nine times that of his elementary school. "When I got to the GNETS program, and it was majority black, it was glaring," Armour told me. "They wanted this little black boy out. And it hurt." She homeschooled Jamir for the rest of the year and then enrolled him in a charter school, but when the charter school reviewed his records she was told that he had to go back to GNETS. "I worked hard to move to that area to give my kid the best, and we were pushed back out," she told me. She worries that Jamir has already internalized the experience. In the past year, he has begun to introduce himself to strangers by saying, "Hi, I'm Jamir, I'm bad."

In 2016, under President Barack Obama, the Department of Education instituted the "significant disproportionality rule," which required states to more vigilantly report when students of color are disciplined and placed in special-education classes at higher rates than their peers. Black students are three times more likely to be suspended or expelled than white students, and although black students make up only nineteen per cent of students with disabilities, they make up thirty-six per cent of those who are mechanically restrained—handcuffed, strapped to a chair, tied down.

The "significant disproportionality rule" was supposed to take effect in the summer of 2017. But, when President Donald Trump directed agencies to cut federal regulations, the Department of Education said that the rule needed to be modified or rescinded, and delayed it for two years. Michael Yudin, the Assistant Secretary for Special Education and Rehabilitative Services in Obama's Department of Education, told me that he was appalled by the decision. "It flies in the face of the data, reams and reams of data, showing that the problem is massive," he said.

AFTER SETH HAD BEEN AT PATHWAYS FOR A FEW MONTHS, THE school hired a new teacher, who was properly certified. Latoya said that her son's behavior quickly improved. In her records, the teacher wrote that Seth "is affectionate with his peers and teachers (hugs). . . . He often dances and sings small phrases from the verses of song." He began to use sentences.

That summer, after Seth's first year at Pathways, Obama's Department of Justice brought a lawsuit against Georgia to "vindicate the rights of the thousands of students unnecessarily segregated in the GNETS Program." Negotiations for a settlement faltered shortly before Trump was elected. Alison Barkoff, who served as the special counsel in the Civil Rights Division of the Department of Justice under Obama, told me, "The state rolled the dice on a change in Administration and had a good roll." The new Attorney General, Jeff Sessions, had told the Senate, in 2000, that IDEA was a "big factor in accelerating the decline in civility and discipline in classrooms all over America."

In October, 2016, Seth's new teacher quit. She didn't want to talk to me or have her name printed, for fear of professional repercussions. When I showed up at her house, she wouldn't let me in. She stood on her porch and said, "What the Department of Justice is saying about GNETS is completely true. It's completely true. It's not therapeutic at all. The kids are not being educated. Not even in a social-skills way."

Melissa Williams-Brown remained in the classroom, with the help of a substitute aide who, she told me, was "just a friend of somebody who worked there. She was just a body, and that body had no educational training." Years before, Williams-Brown had learned to physically restrain middle-school students, but, she said, "I was never trained how to restrain a child as small as Seth. So I just came up with my own method." She stood behind him while folding his arms across his chest or laying his arms on a desk. Seth's doctor said that he was too young for medication, but the staff at Pathways urged Latoya to give him medication; he needed "something to keep him still," Williams-Brown said.

The middle-school aide at Pathways, Phyllis Rambo, who lived a block away from Latoya, routinely got her hair done at Latoya's house. Latoya sees some twenty clients a day in her living room. Tercel, who is out of work, sometimes assists by sitting near a power outlet, and, when she waves the cord of the blow dryer, plugging it in. Latoya's eldest sister had been a close friend of Rambo's since they were toddlers, and Latoya's best friend was Rambo's daughter Daneisha. As she weaved Rambo's hair, Latoya complained that Seth became more aggressive and defiant at school. His teachers said that he had begun cursing. "I want you to sit here and listen to how many times Seth curses here," she told Rambo. "Not one time. We do not swear in this house."

Latoya wondered if her son's condition was the cost of her behavior as a teen-ager. In her neighborhood, she had been known as a fighter, easily provoked. "I was angry for a long time about how my daddy used to treat my mama," she told me. "I thought I could change—and I did change, and that's why I named my daughter Sahrenety, to be honest—but then it came back with Seth. I felt like this was my punishment for being angry."

LAST FALL, WHEN SETH BEGAN FIRST GRADE, A NEW TEACHER, AVON-dika Cherry, was leading his classroom. Cherry, a tall, elegant black woman who was raising a daughter on her own, had been a special-education teacher for seven years in Gadsden County, Florida, where she was once named Teacher of the Year, before rising to become an administrator of the program. She took the position at Pathways because it paid slightly better than her old job. In a reference, a colleague wrote that Cherry was "a very astute, responsible, earnest, and dependable person."

Cherry had not been trained to teach students with autism; neither had her supervisor, a white woman named Jeanene Wallace, the director of all three Pathways centers, who had worked for GNETS for twenty-one years. Wallace asked a teacher who taught autistic students at another Pathways site if Cherry could observe her classroom for a few hours. "I apologize for having so little ideas, but I just don't know how to work with these students," Wallace wrote.

Cherry, who was studious and unaccustomed to wasted time, began applying for new jobs after a week. She encouraged Williams-Brown to look elsewhere, too. "I think you can do something better," she told her one day, as Seth lay on the floor on his back in a sunny spot by the window. "The way I see this place, it needs to be shut down."

The school had installed new surveillance cameras the prior year, after Georgia passed a law—named for a boy whose mother complained that he routinely came home from school bruised—allowing video monitoring equipment in special-education classrooms. A review of close to a hundred hours of classroom surveillance footage, obtained through an Open Records Act request, shows that there was usually about half an hour of instruction in Seth's class per day. Much of the day was devoted to the drama of whether or not Seth would wear his shoes. He found them uncomfortable, as many autistic children do. When he took them off, he was sent to Cool Down, a desk facing a blank wall. He went to Cool Down several times a day, for up to thirty minutes at a time, for other behaviors that stem from his disability, such as counting to ten in the wrong order, saying "no" repeatedly, or making funny noises.

MaKenzie often expressed affection for Seth when she sensed that he was being maligned. She told him several times a day that she loved him. He typically gravitated to whatever part of the room she was in. Once, after Seth took off his shoes, MaKenzie asked her teachers, "Seth is being bad, ain't he?"

"He's always bad," Cherry said.

MaKenzie, who liked to take off her shoes, too, sat on a beanbag chair, and Seth lay on the floor, curled up next to her legs. "I'm bad," she muttered to herself.

TWICE A WEEK, LATOYA TAKES HER FAMILY TO THE GATHERING PLACE, a church in a former supermarket in Donalsonville. The pastor gives his sermons in the old meat section, a large cinder-block room with L.E.D. lighting. Seth's aunts and cousins make up about a quarter of the week-night congregation. When I went with them one evening, Seth sat next to five cousins and shared a folding chair with a friend from the neighborhood, a teen-ager raised in foster care who treated Seth like a little brother. As they waited for the service to start, Seth leaned on the boy's shoulder and watched the other kids while chewing on the collar of his shirt. The pastor made announcements on a microphone, and Seth began silently weeping. He often cried when he heard loud noises. Once the congregation began singing, though, Seth stood up, closed his eyes, bowed his head, and hummed along to the melody. He danced and clapped with the other kids, but a little more vigorously.

In school, Seth was more agitated. He increasingly seemed to embody everything that his teachers resented about their jobs, and they talked about him as if he couldn't comprehend language. "You're about three grade levels behind, and you think you're going to have a career?" Williams-Brown said one day, as Seth sat in Cool Down, where he'd been sent for not listening to a story. He watched the women and whimpered.

"Turn around and be quiet," Williams-Brown said.

"I'm going to suggest he move back to day care," Cherry told her.

"If he doesn't pay attention, he's going to be locked up," Williams-Brown said.

"Ms. Williams, I love you—be nice," MaKenzie said later. "And Ms. Cherry."

"You know I'm always nice," Cherry said.

"You're lying," MaKenzie told her.

Cherry shared her frustrations with such detail and abandon that she seemed either to believe that no one cared or to wish, on some level, to be fired. When Williams-Brown missed a day of school in October and a substitute, Teresa Richardson, filled in for her, Cherry said that she felt tricked by Wallace into taking a job that no one else wanted. "You say you're the supervisor—you say you're watching the camera, then you can see the things that happen," she said. "You aren't saying nothing." She wondered if Wallace, whose office was forty minutes away, was intimidated by her, because she had so many opinions about what was wrong with the program. She was also the only black lead teacher in the building; besides Williams-Brown and Rambo, the middle-school aide, the other teachers were white.

"It's a bad situation," Richardson agreed. She was sitting on the floor next to Seth, holding his legs still, trying to coax him to take his afternoon nap. A few feet away, MaKenzie was watching "The Princess and the Frog," which was being projected onto a wall. Richardson said that her mother had heard people in town talking about how the school was "not giving them the education that's needed. It's not what it's supposed to be—you and I can see that ourselves."

Cherry shook her head. "I got to get out of here so quickly."

"I hate my life," MaKenzie blurted out.

"No, you do not," Richardson said. "Life is a wonder."

IN CHERRY'S THIRD MONTH AT PATHWAYS, SHE HIT SETH. SETH HAD taken off his shoes again. Williams-Brown shoved them back on, saying, "I ain't gonna have no mercy." Crying, Seth bolted toward Cherry, who was facing the sink, and slammed into her body. Cherry was startled, and she turned around and hit him four times on the arm and the head. He fell to the floor, and she hit him three more times. MaKenzie watched from a few feet away.

Cherry wanted to resign that night, but, with a mortgage to pay, she continued. When she arrived the next morning, Williams-Brown was chatting with Phyllis Rambo. The conversation turned to the movie "The Exorcist." The film tells the story of a twelve-year-old girl with an inexplicable disease whose severity her mother doesn't appreciate. "See, her mama was in denial," Williams-Brown said. "And that's when they got to—well, have you ever heard of an exorcism?" Williams-Brown said that the mother, after talking to a priest, "realized that there's more we have to do for this little girl than just medicating."

"So let's take our two students to the priest," Cherry said. She told Rambo how Seth had charged toward her the day before. "I thought he was the little devil or something," she said. The two aides laughed.

"That boy totally got me out of my element," she went on. "I got to reënact this." She stood up from her desk, walked to the classroom sink, and imitated herself raising her arm and striking him. "I forgot that I was in this class," Cherry told the aides. "I forgot that I was in the school here, with the camera. I forgot that this is somebody else's child. I forgot I was a teacher."

A few minutes later, Seth walked into the room. The school bus had just dropped him off.

"Your shoes—they stay on your feet today!" Williams-Brown told him. "Do you hear me?"

"Yes," he said, in a soft, hoarse voice. He sat at a table in the center of the room and ate a Pop-Tart.

The three women began to criticize Latoya for not giving him medication. "He is already, what, six years old?" Rambo said. "She should have gotten him on young."

Seth stood up from his chair and made a deep, wordless noise.

"Sit down," Williams-Brown told him. He sat down.

"I look at it like this," Williams-Brown went on. "This is his mama's fault. He is a product of his environment."

Williams-Brown added that Seth's father wasn't "bringing anything to the table." She said, "It's partly his fault for having a child like that."

"Not only is nothing happening at home, but nothing is happening here, either," Cherry said. "Because this isn't school."

SHORTLY AFTER CHERRY HIT SETH, MAKENZIE BEGAN TELLING HER teachers that she was scared. She sometimes said it more than a dozen times a day. Seth learned the words, too. Nine days after Cherry hit him, he sat at a computer, watching a music video about a tractor. "I'm scared," he told Williams-Brown.

"You ain't scared," she said.

"I'm scared," he said again.

"Look, did you become MaKenzie?" she asked him. "Don't be trying to use her antics. You ain't scared of nothing."

Later that day, Seth had refined his vocabulary. "She hit me," he said, while sitting at a table with Williams-Brown and Cherry.

"Who hit you?" Cherry asked.

"Cherry," Seth said.

Cherry seemed not to realize that he was saying her name. "Who hit you?" she asked again.

"You," he said.

That afternoon, Wallace, their supervisor, stopped by. "Hi, y'all, how are you doing?" she said brightly, from the hallway. "Good," Cherry said, without conviction. Wallace kept walking. It was the only time Wallace came to the classroom in all the surveillance footage I watched.

"You're running away," Cherry said after Wallace had passed. "Come on in and help."

AT THE END OF THE WEEK, AT WALLACE'S REQUEST, CHERRY SENT HER a chart listing nine times in two days that Seth had been sent to Cool Down, usually for the same reason: "non-compliant." Wallace was concerned about the amount of time he spent there, and she began watching footage of the classroom, taking notes as she watched. "Stop the power struggle with the shoe," she wrote. "Tone—harsh, mean." When she reviewed footage from October 10th, she saw Cherry imitating herself hitting Seth. She rewound to the previous day to watch what Cherry was reënacting.

Cherry and Williams-Brown were told to report to the office of the superintendent of the school district for a meeting the next day. The superintendent, George Kornegay, played Cherry the video of her hitting Seth, and she told him she had been asking for help since she'd been hired. Cherry and Williams-Brown agreed to resign. In an e-mail to the county board of education, Kornegay wrote, "I regret that this incident happened, but I truly don't know how it could have been foreseen or avoided." Kornegay told me that Seth's classroom was not representative of the Pathways schools.

Latoya was shown a clip of the video a few days later and wanted to pull Seth out of school. But her sister Yvette, the high-school teacher, told her, "Make them do what they are supposed to do. Make them give him his education."

Richardson, the substitute aide, filled in for Seth and MaKenzie's class with the help of rotating substitutes. After three and a half weeks, Wallace couldn't find enough teachers, so she told parents at Pathways not to send their children to school that day. "I can't continue like this," she wrote to Kornegay. "Something bad has already happened, and I am worried there might be more." Kornegay admonished her, writing, "I believe we are failing to provide FAPE"—the right to a free appropriate public education, which is guaranteed by IDEA. A month earlier, the Georgia Advocacy Office, together with the Arc of the United States, a disability-rights organization, had filed a class-action lawsuit, alleging that the state "discriminates against thousands of Georgia public school students with disabilities" by "segregating them in a network of unequal and separate institutions."

MaKenzie's mother, Erica, didn't learn that her daughter's teachers had been forced to resign, or why, until five weeks after they left. When a video of the hitting incident was played on a local news channel, MaKenzie heard the sound of Seth crying and called out, "Are they hurting my baby again?" The news program announced that Cherry had been charged with battery, assault, and cruelty to children. Williams-Brown had been charged with failing to report child abuse.

Erica decided to teach MaKenzie herself. "I'll probably continue homeschooling her all the way through, which is going to be a"—she paused, unable to find a fitting word—"a journey," she said softly. "I'd rather her be in school, but I'm scared."

CHERRY PLEADED GUILTY. BAINBRIDGE'S COURTHOUSE IS ACROSS THE street from the board of education, and both buildings overlook a small courtyard with two monuments dedicated to Confederate soldiers. At the sentencing hearing, the state solicitor general, Benjamin Harrell, a young, white attorney, played the clips of Cherry hitting Seth and reënacting the encounter the next day. "Praise the Lord for modern technology that allowed us to discover what was really going on in a school here," he said.

When Cherry testified, she sounded as if she were talking to a job supervisor. "It was definitely inappropriate," she said. "It was a mistake, and it happened, and it won't happen again."

Latoya could barely talk at the hearing, because she was crying so hard. "I no longer have a best friend, because one of those teachers was my best friend's mama," she testified. "She didn't even come tell me. These people from Donalsonville—nobody came to my house." When Harrell asked her what she thought Cherry's sentence should be, she said, "I think that Ms. Cherry should get jail time." She went on, "It's sickening that two black women—and you already know the struggle that black people have—that you would do that to your own kind."

The judge sentenced Cherry to a year in jail. Williams-Brown, who attended the hearing, said that, when she heard the sentence, "I cried and I cried and I cried and I cried and I cried." She thought that Cherry wouldn't have been punished so severely if she'd been white, but, she said, "I try not to get caught up in that." Cherry's mother, Pat Grant, told me, "I am just so discombobulated. My daughter didn't get her master's degree to babysit a child. She was on track to become a principal."

Phyllis Rambo, who had worked for the school district for nearly two decades, was fired. Williams-Brown, who also pleaded guilty, was sentenced to probation. Harrell told me, "I saw a lot of outrage that there wasn't more that could be done against them. People around here said, specifically, that all three women in the video were equally bad. They were saying that they should get life. Or even death."

In an e-mail to the superintendent, Wallace complained that Harrell was "out of control," and said that people were calling Rambo on the phone and threatening her. Rambo's daughter Daneisha told me, "It's tragic. Both parties are hurting—the guilty party and the not-guilty party."

Latoya rarely left her house. "We all live in the same community, and—ooh, it's the worst feeling I've ever felt," she said. Her sister-in-law overheard women at church saying that Latoya should be ashamed of herself for ruining her neighbors' careers. Her brother Nathan, who works at a jail, said that he heard a correction officer telling another officer, "If I were that teacher, I probably would have done the same thing."

WHEN I VISITED CHERRY IN JAIL, SHE HAD BEEN THERE THREE MONTHS, and had lost twenty-three pounds. Her mother had moved into her house to take care of her daughter, who was nine years old and growing so quickly that, Cherry said, she had "gained the weight that I lost." Her daughter visited once a week and spoke to her for an hour through a pane of glass. Williams-Brown had visited during Cherry's first week in jail, but Cherry hasn't heard from her since. "I can't mentally get myself to go," Williams-Brown told me.

I was taken aback by Cherry's beauty. She had a short pixie haircut and wore navy-blue jail scrubs. We sat at a table in a small cinder-block room, and, for three hours, she methodically narrated each disappointment at Pathways. When she got to the day that she hit Seth, she walked to the corner of the cell, telling me, "This would be the sink," and imitated herself washing her hands. "And then this force came from behind me," she said. For the second time, she reënacted hitting Seth. It was as if she were still trying to figure out what exactly she had done to him. She said that both times she'd been shown the video, in the superintendent's office and at her sentencing hearing, she hadn't been able to watch.

Cherry recounted the previous half year with almost no reference to her personal life; even when she talked about her regrets, she described them through the lens of professional development. She spoke at length about the support that she expected to be in place for teachers, and said that, without it, "I just had an immediate, instinctual reaction to Seth—it was like I had turned into his mom." When I asked her about her daughter, she said, "She's O.K. My mom does a real good job with her. Hold on." She walked out of the room, toward the bathroom. She came back with a piece of toilet paper three feet long, sat down, bent over her knees, and sobbed.

After a few minutes, she gathered herself completely. She understood that she would never get another job in education, and was contemplating working toward a counselling degree or writing a book called "From the Classroom to the Jailhouse," which would "help educators not find themselves in the same situation as me."

Every night, at nine o'clock, Cherry led five or six other inmates in prayer. They sat in a circle and held hands. Cherry said that their requests were often the same: "My prayer is that my children will not be taken away from me." All the inmates referred to one another by their first names, but they called her Ms. Cherry. She wasn't sure why, since only a few of them knew that she had been a teacher.

IN JANUARY, 2018, SHORTLY AFTER THE GEORGIA ADVOCACY OFFICE requested Seth's records, the district allowed him to return to his neighborhood school. Leslie Lipson, the lawyer with the office, said that when she becomes involved in students' cases, for possible inclusion in the class-action suit, the student is often transferred out of GNETS. (The state has filed a motion to dismiss the lawsuit. A spokesman for the attorney general said that, "as a rule of thumb, we are unable to comment on pending litigation.")

Seth entered first grade at Seminole County Elementary School. His records there describe him as "unable to perform a task for 5 minutes without engaging in physically aggressive or otherwise inappropriate behaviors." For "strengths," his records say that he "has remarkable sense of rhythm." After three weeks, he was suspended for spitting at his teacher. Latoya said that, in February, Seth pinched his teacher several times and was suspended a second time, for six days. Latoya asked MaKenzie's mother to recommend a good homeschooling curriculum, and withdrew him from school.

In the past fifteen years, the number of black families in the country choosing to homeschool their children has more than doubled. Cheryl Fields-Smith, a professor at the University of Georgia, studies why black families in Georgia increasingly make this choice. "One of the dominant themes was a desire to protect their children from being labelled a troublemaker, or having a special-education label placed on them," she told me. According to the Department of Education, students of color are roughly twice as likely to be identified as having an emotional disorder as white children and nearly three times as likely to be labelled cognitively impaired. (In 2015, four decades of research was challenged by a widely cited series of articles by Paul Morgan, a professor of education at Penn State, and George Farkas, a professor at the University of California, Irvine, who argued that if environmental factors, such as poverty and single parenthood, are taken into account, students of color are actually underrepresented in special education. But other scholars have criticized the authors for overgeneralizing and relying on variables that could be subject to racial bias.)

Chris Vance, a special-education attorney in Atlanta, said that parents who can afford a lawyer's fees are usually successful in fighting to prevent their children from going to GNETS. They will often hire a psychologist to analyze the student's behavior in class and then draft a plan that allows the student to stay in the general classroom for most of the day and work with an aide who has been trained to understand how the student's disability affects the way he learns. But, she said, "those who can't afford an attorney will often homeschool their children, and so it becomes no education."

LATOYA BEGINS SETH'S LESSONS AT EIGHT EACH MORNING WITH THE song "Jesus Loves Me," which he sings exuberantly, clapping and stomping his feet. On a recent morning, Latoya sat on the floor with a pile of frayed manila folders from Easy Peazy, an online Christian homeschooling curriculum that MaKenzie's cousin uses. Latoya's mother, who recently had a stroke, was on the sofa watching TV.

Latoya instructed Seth to recite words pictured on flash cards. Repeating the words required a vigorous windup: Seth arched his back, pumped his arms in the air, and then shouted out the words so loudly that his five-year-old cousin, Keylan, who came to the lesson uninvited, covered his ears. When Latoya told him that he'd done a good job, he clapped and yelled, "Yay, yay, yay, yay!" The celebration went on for too long. "Learn!" his sister, Sahrenety, who was on summer vacation, told him. "Do your work." She sat on the couch next to Latoya's niece, who also gave Seth pep talks.

After declaring that "I" is for igloo, Seth began rolling on the ground. Latoya called her brother Lawrence, and put him on speakerphone. He usually came over to play basketball when the lesson was over, around ten-thirty. "I won't come if you don't learn," Lawrence repeatedly warned Seth. Seth got to "K" before everyone gave up. Latoya was sweating, and her niece was snoring loudly on the couch. A few of Latoya's customers were already in the kitchen.

Latoya realizes that she cannot keep homeschooling Seth, and she plans to move back to Atlanta next month. She wants Seth to attend a public school where the day is structured and predictable and the classroom aides understand the sensory triggers for his outbursts. She doesn't mind if he's in a special-education classroom, provided he has some contact with nondisabled students during the day. She's not even opposed to the idea of eventually placing him in a school for children with autism, as long as the segregation serves a therapeutic purpose. She discovered a specialized school north of Atlanta, the Lionheart School, that she aspires to send Seth to one day, if she can afford it. The director of the school told me, "When people talk about 'behaviors,' the assumption is that the child is doing something bad, but we see behaviors as communicative. If the child is punished for screaming, then we've missed an opportunity to get to know this child and what he is telling us."

More than anything, Latoya wants to get out of Donalsonville. She told me, "I feel like everybody here is looking at me, like, Why would she do that to those teachers? She knows her son is bad."

Whenever Latoya goes to town, she must drive past Phyllis Rambo's house. Recently, when we passed it, her sister Cecelia, who was driving, became sombre. "That's Phyllis," she said, pointing to a one-story brick house. Behind the house was an old swing set where Latoya used to play with Rambo's daughter Daneisha.

Latoya had started talking to Daneisha again, after Daneisha wrote her a letter describing how important their friendship was to her. For months, friends from their neighborhood had been urging her to forgive Rambo, too, and over time Latoya had begun to soften toward her. "I think Phyllis was basically just trying to fit in," she told me. "She needed people to vent to at work." (Rambo did not want to talk to me.)

Latoya had never been close with Melissa Williams-Brown—Latoya described her as having been, in high school, part of the "fancy crowd, the kids who basically have what you call a good life"—but, as she had learned more about the GNETS system, she had begun to see Williams-Brown's mistakes in a different light.

"I'm not upset with Melissa," she told me. "I'm not even upset with Ms. Cherry. I'm just upset with the fact that, hey, if that was your"—referring to Wallace—"child, it wouldn't have happened like that." She cried quietly. "The black women got the blame. I just don't feel like it's right. You've got three teachers being slandered when they were only doing what you allowed them to do."

IN JUNE, SETH AND MAKENZIE HAD A PLAYDATE. MAKENZIE OFTEN asked for Seth, but she lived nearly an hour away, and they hadn't seen each other for seven months. When Erica parked in front of Latoya's house, MaKenzie looked up from a magazine and saw Seth sitting under the carport, beside a washing machine.

"I love you, Seth," she said, as she walked up the driveway. "I love this little boy." She combed her fingers through his dreadlocks and commented on how long they had grown. He looked away, smiling. Then he walked toward his uncle, who was mowing the lawn. MaKenzie stood still, wringing her hands. "What's wrong with you?" she said gently.

Erica apologized to Latoya in advance for the language that MaKenzie might use. "When she's nervous, her words really come out," she said. "Whatever is on Kenzie's mind she's going to tell you." It quickly became clear that one of the words that MaKenzie had difficulty controlling was the N-word. Erica was accustomed to people making comments like "That little girl needs her butt tore up." But Latoya assured her that it was fine, even when Seth began repeating the word.

In the carport, they listened to the country song "Meant to Be," by Bebe Rexha and the Florida Georgia Line. MaKenzie stood under a tree and swayed her arms in the air. Seth walked over to her and began doing the two-step, rocking his hips and shoulders from side to side. Their rhythms were familiar to each other; they had often danced together at school, while their teachers were talking. On Cherry's last day at Pathways, MaKenzie had sashayed toward

Seth, stood behind him, and begun moving his arms to the beat of a nursery song, leading him in a kind of square dance.

Throughout the afternoon, MaKenzie repeatedly told Seth that she loved him and kissed his cheek or the top of his head. Latoya took solace in believing that MaKenzie's warmth may have counteracted the harsh tone of his teachers. She was less concerned about the physical violence than about the effects of listening to them talk. "He can hear five conversations at a time and remember every word—that's one of his autistic traits," she told me. "If you call him bad, he's going to believe it. He's going to become exactly who you say he is."

THE COLOR OF BLOOD

CALVIN TRILLIN

March 3, 2008

What happened at the foot of the driveway at 40 Independence Way that hot August night in 2006 took less than three minutes. The police later managed to time it precisely, using a surveillance camera that points directly at the street from a house a couple of doors to the north. The readout on the surveillance tape said that it was 23:06:11 when two cars whizzed by going south, toward the cul-de-sac at the end of the street. At 23:09:06, the first car passed back in front of the camera, going north. A minute later, a second car passed in the same direction. In the back seat of that second car—a black Mustang Cobra convertible—was a seventeen-year-old boy named Daniel Cicciaro, Jr., known to his friends as Dano. He was unconscious and bleeding profusely. He had been shot through the cheek. A .32-calibre bullet was lodged in his head.

Normally, at that time of night, not many cars are seen on Independence Way, a quiet street in a town called Miller Place. Just east of Port Jefferson, on the North Shore of Long Island, Miller Place is in the part of Suffolk County where the commuters have begun to thin out. To the east is a large swatch of the county that doesn't seem strongly connected to the huge city in one direction or to the high-priced summer resorts and North Fork wineries in the other. The house at 40 Independence Way is part of a development, Talmadge Woods, that five or six years ago was a peach orchard; it's now a collection of substantial two-story, four-bedroom houses that the developer started offering in 2003 for about half a million dollars each. The houses vary in design, but they all have an arched front door topped by the arched glass transom known in the trade as a Palladian window—a way to bring light into the double-height entry hall. When people are asked to describe the neighborhood, they tend to say "upper middle class." The homeowner with the surveillance system is an orthodontist.

Miller Place could also be described as overwhelmingly white. According to a study released a few years ago, Long Island is the single most segregated suburban area in the United States. The residents of 40 Independence Way—John and Sonia White and their youngest son, Aaron—are African-American and so are their next-door neighbors, but the black population of Miller Place is less than one-half of one per cent. The Whites, who began married life in Brooklyn in the early seventies, had moved to Miller Place after ten years in North Babylon, which is forty minutes or so closer to the city. "You want to raise your family in a safe environment," John White, a tall, very thin man in his early fifties, has said, explaining why he was willing to spend three hours a day in his car commuting. "The educational standards are higher. You want to live a comfortable life, which is the American dream." One of the Whites' sons is married, with children of his own, and a second is in college in the South. But Aaron was able to spend his senior year at Miller Place High School, which takes pride in such statistics as how many of its students are in Advanced Placement history courses. Aaron, an erect young man who is likely to say "sir" when addressing one of his elders, graduated in June of 2005. He was one of four black students in the class.

In an area where home maintenance is a priority, 40 Independence Way could hold its own. John White is a serious gardener— a nurturer of daylilies and clematis, a planter of peel-bark birch trees—and someone who had always been proud, maybe even touchy, about his property. People who have been neighbors of the Whites tend to use the word "meticulous" in describing John White; so do people who have worked with him. He has described himself as "a doer"—someone too restless to sit around reading a book or watching television. He says that he's fished from Nova Scotia to the Bahamas. He's done a lot of hunting—a pastime he was taught by his grandfather Napoleon White, whose family's migration from Alabama apparently took place after a murderous attack by the Ku Klux Klan. At the Faith Baptist Church, in Coram, Long Island, John White sang in both the men's choir and the mixed Celebration Choir. A couple of polished-wood tables in the Whites' house were made by him. He's a broadly accomplished man, and proud of it. His wife, who was born in Panama, works as a manager in a department store and has that Caribbean accent which, maybe because it's close to the accent of West Indian nurses, conveys both competence and the firm intention to brook no nonsense. The Whites' furniture tastes lean toward Stickley, Audi. Their sons dress in a style that's preppy. Sitting in his well-appointed family room, John White could be taken for middle management.

But he doesn't have the sort of education or occupation that would seem to go along with the house he lives in. After graduating from a technical program at Samuel Gompers High School, he worked as an electrician for seven or eight years and then, during a slow time for electricians, he began working in the paving industry. For the past twenty-five years, he has worked for an asphalt company in Queens, patching the potholes left by utility repair crews. He is often described as a foreman, which he once was, but he says that, partly because of an aversion to paperwork, he didn't try to reclaim that job after it evaporated during a reduction in the workforce. ("I'm actually a laborer.") On August 9, 2006, a Wednesday, he had, as usual, awakened at three-thirty in the morning for the drive to Queens, spent the day at work, and, after a stop to pick up some bargain peony plants, returned to what he calls his "dream house" or his "castle." He retired early, so that he could do the same thing the next day. A couple of hours later, according to his testimony, he was awakened by Aaron, who, with a level of terror John

White had never heard in his son's voice, shouted, "Dad, these guys are coming here to kill me!" Instead, as it turned out, John White killed Daniel Cicciaro, Jr.

THERE HAD BEEN A BIRTHDAY PARTY THAT EVENING FOR CRAIG MARtin, Jr., a recent Miller Place High School graduate. Craig lives with his parents and his younger sister, Jennifer, in Sound Beach—a town just to the east that grew into a year-round neighborhood from what had begun as beach lots purchased in the twenties as part of a *Daily Mirror* circulation-promotion scheme. The party was mostly in the Martins' back yard, where there was an aboveground pool, a lot of cold beer, and a succession of beer-pong games. This was not the A.P.-history crowd. Craig was connected to a number of the boys at the party through an interest in cars. Some of them were members of the Blackout car club, a loose organization of teen-agers who, in good weather, gather in the parking lot of the Stop & Shop mall in Miller Place on Thursday nights for an informal car show—displaying cars whose lights and windows are likely to have been tinted in pursuit of sleekness. Dano Cicciaro (pronounced Danno Cicero) was a regular at Stop & Shop, driving a white Mustang Mach 1 with two black stripes. Dano had grown up in Selden, a blue-collar town to the south, and finished at Newfield High School there after his family moved in his senior year to one of a half-dozen houses clustered around a cul-de-sac called Old Town Estates, in Port Jefferson Station.

His father, Daniel Cicciaro, Sr., runs an automobile-repair shop in Port Jeff Station called Dano's Auto Clinic—a two-bay operation that also has some used cars parked in its lot, their prices marked on the windshields. Dano's Auto Clinic is where Dano, Jr., spent a lot of his spare time. As a boy, he had the usual range of interests, his father has recalled, but "as he turned into a teen-ager it was all cars." Even as a teen-ager, he ran a car-detailing business out of the shop, and he'd planned to keep that up when he started at Suffolk

County Community College in the fall. Dano, Jr.,'s long-term plan was to take over Dano's Auto Clinic someday and expand its services. "He did exactly as I did, in that he set goals for himself and conquered them, never sitting idle," a *Newsday* reporter was told by Daniel Cicciaro, Sr., a father who'd felt the validation of having a son who was eager to follow his calling and work by his side.

Aaron White, who had finished his first year at Suffolk County Community College, was having dinner that evening in Port Jefferson with Michael Longo, his best friend from Miller Place High School. From having attended a few of the Stop & Shop gatherings, Aaron knew some of the car crowd, and, while phoning around for something to do, he learned about the birthday party at the Martins'. Craig greeted Aaron cheerfully enough, but a few minutes later Jennifer, who was then fifteen, told her brother that, because of a past incident, she felt frightened in Aaron's presence. Dano Cicciaro was assigned to ask Aaron to leave. It isn't clear why he was given that task. It couldn't have been his size: Dano was five feet four and weighed a hundred and twenty-nine pounds. It certainly wasn't his sobriety. Dano was drunk. When his blood-alcohol content was checked later at the hospital, it was almost twice the level required to prove intoxication. Still, Dano, who thought of himself as a protective older brother to Jennifer, handled the situation smoothly, saying to Aaron something like "It's nothing personal, but you'll have to leave." Aaron later said that he was puzzled ("I never get kicked out of parties"), but he got into his car and drove back to Miller Place.

When Dano learned exactly why Jennifer felt uncomfortable around Aaron, she later testified, "he freaked out." While in an Internet chat room with a couple of other boys, Jennifer told Dano, Aaron had posted a message saying that he wanted to rape her. Obtaining Aaron's cell-phone number from Michael Longo, Dano touched off what became a series of heated calls involving several people at the party. Dano wanted to confront Aaron immediately.

It didn't matter that Aaron denied having posted the message. It didn't matter that the posting had taken place nine months before and that Jennifer's real older brother, Craig, had actually forgotten about it. In court many months later, Jennifer Martin was asked if she'd eventually learned that the offending message had not, in fact, been sent by Aaron—it had grown out of something said on a MySpace account set up in Aaron's name as a prank—and she answered in the affirmative. That didn't matter, either, because by then it was much too late. On the evening of August 9th, when Jennifer told Dano about the rape posting, there were other elements involved. A lot of beer had been consumed. It was late in the evening, a time when the teen-age penchant for melodrama tends to be in full flower. Dano was filled with what Paul Gianelli, one of John White's defense attorneys, called "a warped sense of chivalry" and Dano's godfather, Gregg Sarra, preferred to characterize as "valor, protecting a woman, honor." For whatever reason, Dano Cicciaro and four of his friends were soon heading toward the Whites' house in two beautifully painted and carefully polished cars that passed the orthodontist's surveillance camera when its readout said 23:06:11.

What happened when they got there remains a matter of sharp dispute. There is no doubt that the boys were displaying no weapons when they got out of their cars, although one of them, Joseph Serrano, had brought along a baseball bat that remained in the back seat of the Mustang. There is no doubt that John White emerged from his garage carrying a pre–Second World War Beretta pistol that he kept there—part of an inheritance from his grandfather that had also included, White later said, "rifles and shotguns and a lot of advice." Aaron was a few steps behind him, carrying a 20-gauge shotgun. There is no doubt that Dano "slapped" or "whacked" or "grabbed" the Beretta. There is no doubt that, before the shot was fired, there had been shouting and foul language from both sides. The tenor of the conversation, the defense team eventually maintained, could be surmised from the tape of a 911 line that the boys did not realize was open as they rushed their friend to a Port Jefferson hospital in the black Mustang Cobra. The 911 operator can be heard saying, "Sir . . . hello . . . hello . . . sir, pick up the phone." The boys, their muffled voices almost hysterical, can be heard shouting directions to one another and giving assurances that Dano is still breathing. The operator keeps saying, "Hello . . . sir." Then the voice of Joseph Serrano, sitting in the back seat with his bleeding friend and his baseball bat, comes through clearly: "Fucking niggers! Dano, I'll get 'em for you, Dano."

Back at 40 Independence Way, John White and his son were sitting in front of their house, hugging. Sonia White was screaming, "What happened? What happened?" In the trial testimony and police reports and newspaper accounts and grand-jury minutes dealing with what occurred in the meticulous front yard of 40 Independence Way after the cars had sped away, three statements attributed to John White stand out. One was in the testimony of Officer David Murray, the first Suffolk County policeman to reach the scene, who said that John White approached him with his arms extended, saying, "I did what I had to do. You might as well put the cuffs on me." Another is what Officer Murray said he heard John White say to his son: "I told you those friends of yours would turn on you." The third is what Sonia White testified that her husband said to her as he walked back into their castle: "We lost the house. We lost it all."

A WEEK AFTER THE DEATH OF DANIEL CICCIARO, JR., SEVERAL HUNdred people turned out for his funeral, held at St. Sylvester's Roman Catholic Church, in Medford, Long Island. The gathering was heavy with symbolism. Some of the younger mourners displayed "Dano Jr." tattoos. Dano, Jr.,'s main car was there—the white Mustang that was familiar from Stop & Shop and had won Best Mach 1 Mustang in a competition at McCarville Ford. Gregg

Sarra, a boyhood friend of Daniel Cicciaro, Sr., and a local-sports columnist for *Newsday*, gave the eulogy, praising his godson's loyalty and his diligence and his gift for friendship. After the burial, some of Dano, Jr.,'s car-club friends revved their engines and chanted, "Dan-o, Dan-o, Dan-o." As a tribute to his son, Daniel Cicciaro, Sr., attended the service in a Dano's Auto Clinic tank top. The Stop & Shop car show that Thursday, according to a *Newsday* piece, turned into a sort of vigil for Dano, Jr., with Jennifer Martin helping to light a ring of candles—red and white candles, for the colors of Newfield High—around his Mustang and his first car, a Mercedes E55 AMG.

The sadness was accompanied by a good deal of anger. John White found that understandable. "I know how I would feel if someone hurt my kid," he said in a *Times* interview some weeks later. "There wouldn't be a rock left to crawl under." Speaking to one reporter, Daniel Cicciaro, Sr., had referred to White as an "animal." For a while after the shooting, Michael Longo—the friend who had accompanied Aaron White to the birthday party and had, as it turned out, telephoned to warn him that there were plans to jump him if he returned—slept with a baseball bat next to his bed. Sonia White later testified that after some particularly menacing instant messages ("i need ur adreass you dumb nigger"), to which Aaron replied in what sounded like a suburban teenager's notion of gangster talk ("u da bitch tlaking big n bad like u gonna come down to my crib n do sumthin"), the Whites decided that he was no longer safe in the house, and they sent him to live outside the area.

The mourners who talked to reporters after the service rejected the notion, brought up by a lawyer for the White family shortly after the shooting, that Dano Cicciaro and his friends had used racial epithets during the argument in front of 40 Independence Way. Daniel Cicciaro, Sr.—a short man with a shaved head and a Fu Manchu mustache and an assertive manner and a lifelong involvement in martial arts—had called any connection of his son with racism "absurd." But by the time a grand jury met, a month or so after the shooting, even the prosecutor, who would presumably need the boys as witnesses against John White, was saying that racial epithets had indeed been used. The district attorney said, though, that if John White had simply remained in his house and dialled 911, he wouldn't be in any trouble and Daniel Cicciaro, Jr., would still be alive. The grand jury was asked to indict White for murder. Grand juries ordinarily go along with district attorneys, but this one didn't. When the trial finally began, in Riverhead, fifteen months after the shooting, the charge was second-degree manslaughter.

The grand-jury decision may have reflected public opinion in Suffolk County, where there are strong feelings about a homeowner's right to protect his property and his family. Suffolk County is a place where a good number of residents are active or retired law-enforcement officers, and where even a lot of residents who aren't own guns—a place where it is not surprising to come across a plaque that bears the picture of a pistol and the phrase "We Don't Dial 911." James Chalifoux, the assistant district attorney who was assigned to try the case against John White, apparently had that in mind when, during jury selection, he asked jurors if they would be able to distinguish between what might be considered morally right—what could cause you to say, "I might have done the same thing"—and what was permissible under the law. He asked jurors if they could put aside sympathy when they were considering the case—meaning sympathy for John White. Judging by comments posted online in response to *Newsday* articles, public opinion seemed muddled by the conflict between two underpinnings of life in Suffolk County—a devotion to the sanctity of private property, particularly one's home, and an assumption that the owner of the property is white.

Dano's mother—Joanne Cicciaro, a primary-school E.S.L. teacher who had grown up in Suffolk County—said she was extremely disappointed that the grand jury had declined to indict

John White for murder. Daniel Cicciaro, Sr., told a reporter, "Here this man points his gun at the boys and says, 'I'm going to shoot.' He says it three times. Then he shoots my son. To me, that's intentional murder." On the other hand, some of White's strongest supporters—people like Lucius Ware, the president of the Eastern Long Island branch of the N.A.A.C.P., and Marie Michel, a black attorney who joined the defense team—believed that if a white homeowner in Miller Place had been confronted late at night by five hostile black teen-agers there would have been, in Marie Michel's words, "no arrests, no indictment, and no trial." The homeowner would have been judged to have had "a well-founded fear," they thought, and if the justice system dealt with the incident in any way it would have been to charge the boys with something like breach of the peace or aggravated harassment ("What were they doing in that neighborhood at that time of night?"). For that matter, these supporters would argue, would Dano have "freaked out" if the male accused of wanting to rape Jenny Martin hadn't been black? Wouldn't teen-agers spoiling for a fight have dispersed if a white father walked out of the house, with or without a gun, and told them in no uncertain terms to go home? In other words, before a word of testimony had been heard, some people attending the trial of John White believed that in a just world he would have been on trial for murder instead of only manslaughter, and some believed that in a just world he wouldn't have been on trial at all.

THE ARTHUR M. CROMARTY COURT COMPLEX IS SET APART FROM Riverhead, the seat of Suffolk County, on a campus that seems to be mostly parking lots—a judicial version of Long Island shopping malls. Those who were there to attend John White's trial, which began just after Thanksgiving, seemed to be roughly separated by race, on opposite sides of the aisle that ran down the center of the courtroom's spectator section. That may have been partly because the room was small and on many days the prosecution's supporters, mostly Cicciaro relatives and young friends of Dano's, nearly filled half of it. Dano, Jr.,'s parents did not sit next to each other—they had separated before their son's death—but they came together as a family in hallway huddles of supporters and in speaking to the press. The people who stood out on their side of the courtroom were a couple of friends of Daniel Cicciaro, Sr., who also had shaved heads, but with modifications that included a scalp tattoo saying "Dano Jr." Although they looked menacing, both of them could be described as designers: one is a detailer, specializing in the fancy painting of motorcycles; the other does graphic design, specializing in sports uniforms.

People on the Cicciaro side might have felt some menace emanating from the phalanx of black men, all of them in suits and ties and many of them offensive-tackle size, who escorted Aaron White (wearing a bulletproof vest) through the courthouse on the first day of his testimony and then took seats across the aisle, near some women from John White's church choir. The escorts were from an organization called 100 Blacks in Law Enforcement Who Care. On that first day, their ranks were augmented by members of the Fruit of Islam, wearing their trademark bow ties, although the black leader called to mind by John White's life would probably be Booker T. Washington rather than Louis Farrakhan. As it turned out, there was no overt hostility between those on either side of the courtroom aisle, and, at the end of testimony, the Cicciaros made it clear that they would accept any decision the jury brought in—none of which, Joanne Cicciaro pointed out, would bring their son back. Talking to a *Newsday* reporter after the trial about prejudice, Daniel Cicciaro, Sr., maintained that bias existed toward what some people called skinheads. "Don't judge a book by its cover," he said.

The four boys who accompanied Dano Cicciaro to Aaron White's house that night are all car enthusiasts who now hold jobs that echo their high-school hobby. Alex Delgado does maintenance on race cars. Joseph Serrano is a motorcycle mechanic. Tom Maloney, who drove the Mustang Cobra, sells Volkswagens. Anthony Simeone works for his father's auto-salvage business. Among those who testified that they'd tried to prevent Dano from going to the Whites' house were Alex Delgado, who drove him there, and Joseph Serrano, who brought along a baseball bat. ("He's stubborn," Anthony Simeone had explained to the grand jury. "When he wants to do something, he wants to do it.") Although there had been testimony that Dano Cicciaro used the word "nigger" once or twice in the cell-phone exchange with Aaron White, his friends denied using racial slurs at 40 Independence Way. (With the jury out of the courtroom, Paul Gianelli brought up an incident that had been investigated by the police but not included in the notes and reports that they are required to turn over to the defense: according to two or three witnesses, Daniel Cicciaro had gone to Sayville Ford with a complaint a few weeks before he was shot and, when approached by a black salesman, had said, "I don't talk to niggers." The judge wouldn't admit that into evidence, but the headline of the next day's *Newsday* story was "ATTORNEY: COPS HID MILLER PLACE VICTIM'S RACISM.") The friends who'd gone with Dano, Jr., to the Whites' house that night testified that after John White's gun was slapped away, he raised it again and shot Dano in the face. As they described how Dano Cicciaro fell and how he'd been lifted from the street by Tom Maloney and rushed to the hospital, there were occasional sobs from both Joanne and Daniel Cicciaro.

Dano's friends had said that both of their cars were in the street facing north, but the Whites testified that one was in their driveway, with the lights shining up into the house—a contention that the defense bolstered by analyzing the headlight reflections on the orthodontist's mailbox in the surveillance tape. The boys testified that they'd never set foot on the Whites' property—that contention was bolstered by pictures showing Dano's blood and his cell phone in the street rather than in the driveway—but the Whites claimed that the boys had been advancing toward the house. "They came to my home as if they owned it," Sonia White said on the stand. "What gall!"

John White testified that, believing the young men had come to harm his family, he backed them off his property with Napoleon White's old pistol. In the frenzy that followed his abrupt awakening, he said, he had yelled, "Call the cops!" to his wife as he raced into the garage, but she hadn't heard him. He described Dano Cicciaro and his friends as a lynch mob shouting, among other things, "We could take that skinny nigger motherfucker." Recalling that evening, White said, "In my family history, that's how the Klan comes. They pull up to your house, blind you with their lights, burn your house down. That's how they come." In White's telling, the confrontation had seemed over and he was turning to go back into the house when Dano Cicciaro grabbed the gun, causing it to fire. "I didn't mean to shoot this young man," John White said. "This young man was another child of God." This time, it was John White who broke down, and the court had to take a recess. One of the jurors was also wiping away tears.

TO CONVICT SOMEONE OF SECOND-DEGREE MANSLAUGHTER IN THE state of New York, the prosecution has to prove that he recklessly caused the death of the victim—"recklessly" being defined as creating a risk so substantial that disregarding it constitutes "a gross deviation from the standard of conduct that a reasonable person would observe"—and that he had no justification. In its decision in the case of Bernard Goetz, the white man who in 1984 shot four young black men who had approached him on the subway demanding money, the New York Court of Appeals, the highest court in the state, ruled that justification could have a subjective as well as an objective component—fears raised by the defendant's past experiences, for instance. By bringing up the history that White's family had with the Klan, the defense team raised a subjective component of justification, along with the objective component of home protection. "We are all products of our past," Paul Gianelli said of his client during one of the breaks in the trial. "He brought to that particular evening who he is." The defense was making a case for, among other things, the power of race memory.

The racial divide is obviously less overt in John White's Long Island than it was in Napoleon White's Alabama. Tom Maloney, who'd also graduated from Miller Place High School, had apparently thought of Aaron White as a friend. Alex Delgado, who drove Dano Cicciaro to Aaron's house on August 9th, had been there before as a guest. In John White's testimony, Delgado was described as Hispanic. Joanne Cicciaro, who by name and appearance and accent might be assumed to have come from one of the many Italian-American families that moved to Suffolk County in recent decades from the boroughs, is actually Puerto Rican—a fact brought up to reporters by the Cicciaros in countering any implications of racism in Dano's upbringing. ("Our family is multicultural.") Even without those complications, the case for race memory would be harder to make to white people than to black people. White people are likely to say that times have changed: these days, after all, a real-estate agent who tried to steer John White away from buying a house in an overwhelmingly white Long Island neighborhood would be risking her license.

If times have changed, black people might ask in response, how come Long Island is still so segregated? In his summation, the prosecutor asked a series of questions as a way to illustrate how White's behavior had deviated from the behavior of a reasonable person. Two of the huge black men who had been part of Aaron White's escort were sitting in the courtroom at the time, and when the D.A. asked whether a reasonable person would really be guided partly by the memory of a Ku Klux Klan attack that happened years before he was born, they both began to nod their heads.

In that closing statement, James Chalifoux said that it wasn't until the trial began that John White started talking about a lynch mob. (It's true that in a newspaper interview in September of 2006 White seemed to downplay race, but it's also true that in his grand-jury testimony, less than a month after the shooting, he spoke about a "lynch mob.") Race, Chalifoux said, was being used to distract the jurors from the simple fact that by walking down the driveway with a loaded pistol John White, a man intimately familiar with firearms, had engaged in conduct that had recklessly caused the death of Dano Cicciaro. Matching up testimony with cell-phone logs, Chalifoux argued that the Whites had more time before the arrival of the cars than their story of a panicky few minutes implied. Chalifoux acknowledged that Dano and his friends were wrong to go to the Whites' that night, that Dano was wrong to use a racial epithet when he phoned Aaron White, and that John White had found himself "in a very bad situation that night and a situation that was not his fault." But how White responded to that situation, Chalifoux said, *was* his fault.

Chalifoux's summation followed that of Frederick K. Brewington, a black attorney, active in black causes on Long Island, who was Paul Gianelli's co-counsel. "Race has so much to do with this case, ladies and gentlemen, that it's painful," Brewington told the jury: Dano Cicciaro and his friends thought they had a right to go to John White's house and "terrorize his family with impunity and arrogance" because of "the false racial privilege they felt empowered by." In Brewington's argument, John White thought, "'Once they see I have a gun they'll back off' . . . but they did not take 'the skinny old nigger' seriously." While Chalifoux presented Joseph Serrano's slur on the 911 tape as, however deplorable, an indication that the argument at the foot of the driveway didn't include the barrage of insults that the Whites had testified to—if it had, he said, "you would have heard racial epithet after racial epithet after racial epithet"—Brewington saw it as a mirror of the boys' true feelings. "What we do under cover of darkness sometimes comes to light," he said.

Shortly after the beginning of deliberations, ten jurors, including the sole African-American, were prepared to convict John White of having recklessly caused Dano Cicciaro's death. Two jurors resisted that verdict for four days. Then they capitulated. They later told reporters that they felt bullied and pressured by jurors who were impatient to be liberated as Christmas approached. In a courtroom crowded with court officers, the jury reported that it had found John White guilty of manslaughter and a weapons charge. The Cicciaros and their supporters were ecstatic. Dano's parents seemed to take John White's conviction principally as proof that the accusations of racism against their son had been shown to be false. "My son is finally vindicated," a tearful Joanne Cicciaro said, outside the courtroom. Daniel Cicciaro, Sr., said, "Maybe now they'll stop slinging my son's name and accusing him of all this racism." Outside the courthouse, friends of Dano, Jr., honked their horns and revved their engines and chanted, "Dan-o, Dan-o, Dan-o." The next day, Sunday, the celebration continued with a sort of open house at Dano's Auto Clinic, which bore a sign saying "Thank You Jurors. Thank God. Dano Jr. Rest in Peace." In Miller Place, John White briefly spoke to the reporters who were waiting in front of his house. "I'm not inhuman," he said. "I have very deep feelings for this young man." But before that he went to the Faith Baptist Church, in Coram, and sang in the choir.

"JOHN WHITE IS A HERO," FREDERICK BREWINGTON SAID TWO WEEKS later, addressing a crowd of several hundred people, almost all of them black, who had gathered on a cold Saturday afternoon in front of the criminal-court building in Riverhead. He repeated, "John White is a hero." The guilty verdict had made White the sort of hero all too familiar in the race memory of African-Americans— someone held up as an example of the unjustly treated black man. On the podium were black officeholders, speakers from the spectrum of black organizations on Long Island, and two people who had come from Manhattan—Kevin Muhammad, of Muhammad Mosque No. 7, and Al Sharpton. A lot of N.A.A.C.P. people were in the audience, and so were a lot of people from Faith Baptist Church. Various speakers demanded a retrial, or called for the resignation of the district attorney, or pointed out the difference in how white homeowners in similar situations have been treated, or called for the young white men involved to be indicted. ("We will raise this to a level of national attention until these young men are brought to justice," Sharpton said.) There were chants like "No Justice—No Peace" and, loudest of all, "Free John White."

That chant was not meant literally. For the time being, John White is free—he addressed the rally briefly, mainly to thank his supporters—and his attorneys hope that, while an appeal is pending, he will be allowed to remain free after his sentencing, scheduled for March 19th. ("I think he should get as much time as possible," a *Post* reporter was told by Jennifer Martin, whose response to Aaron White's arrival at her house set the events of August 9th in motion. "I really do.") Until the sentencing, White is back to rising at three-thirty every morning to go into the city and patch utility holes. Everything he was quoted as saying in the aftermath of the shooting that night turned out to be true. The fatalism reflected in his statement to Officer Murray as he held out his hands to be cuffed was well founded. Aaron White accepted the fact that those friends of his had indeed turned on him. In his testimony, he said, "They have no respect for me or my family or my mother or my father. . . . They have no respect for life whatsoever. They're scum." And, of course, John White had understood the situation well when he told his wife that they had lost their dream house—a comment that, as it turned out, particularly incensed Joanne Cicciaro. (His sorrow, she said to reporters after testimony had ended, "was all for themselves—sorrow about losing their house, about their life changing. He never said, 'Oh, my God! What did I do to that boy? Oh, my God. This kid is bleeding on the driveway. What did I do to him?' He had no sympathy, no sorrow for shooting a child.") Even before the trial, 40 Independence Way was listed with a real-estate broker. Its description began, "Stately 2 year young post-modern colonial in prestigious neighborhood."

PART VII
THE UPRISING AND AFTER

THE MATTER OF BLACK LIVES

JELANI COBB

March 14, 2016

On February 18th, as part of the official recognition of Black History Month, President Obama met with a group of African-American leaders at the White House to discuss civil-rights issues. The guests—who included Representative John Lewis, of Georgia; Sherrilyn Ifill, the director-counsel of the N.A.A.C.P. Legal Defense and Educational Fund; and Wade Henderson, who heads the Leadership Conference on Civil and Human Rights—were intent on pressing the President to act decisively on criminal-justice issues during his last year in office. Their urgency, though, was tempered by a degree of sentimentality, verging on nostalgia. As Ifill later told me, "We were very much aware that this was the last Black History Month of this Presidency."

But the meeting was also billed as the "first of its kind," in that it would bring together different generations of activists. To that end, the White House had invited DeRay Mckesson, Brittany Packnett, and Aislinn Pulley, all of whom are prominent figures in Black Lives Matter, which had come into existence—amid the flash points of the George Zimmerman trial; Michael Brown's death, in Ferguson, Missouri; and the massacre at the Emanuel A.M.E. Church, in Charleston, South Carolina—during Obama's second term.

Black Lives Matter has been described as "not your grandfather's civil-rights movement," to distinguish its tactics and its philosophy from those of nineteen-sixties-style activism. Like the Occupy movement, it eschews hierarchy and centralized leadership, and its members have not infrequently been at odds with older civil-rights leaders and with the Obama Administration—as well as with one another. So it wasn't entirely surprising when Pulley, a community organizer in Chicago, declined the White House invitation, on the ground that the meeting was nothing more than a "photo opportunity" for the President. She posted a statement online in which she said that she "could not, with any integrity, participate in such a sham that would only serve to legitimize the false narrative that the government is working to end police brutality and the institutional racism that fuels it." Her skepticism was attributable, in part, to the fact that she lives and works in a city whose mayor, Rahm Emanuel, Obama's former chief of staff, is embroiled in a controversy stemming from a yearlong coverup of the fatal shooting by police of an African-American teen-ager.

Mckesson, a full-time activist, and Packnett, the executive director of Teach for America in St. Louis, did accept the invitation, and they later described the meeting as constructive. Mckesson tweeted: "Why did I go to the mtg w/ @POTUS today? B/c there are things we can do now to make folks' lives better today, tomorrow, & the day after." Two weeks earlier, Mckesson had announced that he would be a candidate in the Baltimore mayoral race, and Obama's praise, after the meeting, for his "outstanding work mobilizing in Baltimore" was, if not an endorsement, certainly politically valuable.

That split in the response to the White House, however, reflected a larger conflict: while Black Lives Matter's insistent outsider status has allowed it to shape the dialogue surrounding race and criminal justice in this country, it has also sparked a debate about the limits of protest, particularly of online activism. Meanwhile, internal disputes have raised questions about what the movement hopes to achieve, and about its prospects for success.

THE PHRASE "BLACK LIVES MATTER" WAS BORN IN JULY OF 2013, IN A Facebook post by Alicia Garza, called "a love letter to black people."

The post was intended as an affirmation for a community dis-
traught over George Zimmerman's acquittal in the shooting death
of seventeen-year-old Trayvon Martin, in Sanford, Florida. Garza,
now thirty-five, is the special-projects director in the Oakland office of the National Domestic Workers Alliance, which represents
twenty thousand caregivers and housekeepers, and lobbies for labor
legislation on their behalf. She is also an advocate for queer and
transgender rights and for anti-police-brutality campaigns.

Garza has a prodigious social-media presence, and on the day
that the Zimmerman verdict was handed down she posted, "the sad
part is, there's a section of America who is cheering and celebrating
right now. and that makes me sick to my stomach. we GOTTA get it
together y'all." Later, she added, "btw stop saying we are not surprised. that's a damn shame in itself. I continue to be surprised at
how little Black lives matter. And I will continue that. stop giving
up on black life." She ended with "black people. I love you. I love
us. Our lives matter."

Garza's friend Patrisse Cullors amended the last three words
to create a hashtag: #BlackLivesMatter. Garza sometimes writes
haiku—she admires the economy of the form—and in those four
syllables she recognized a distillation not only of the anger that
attended Zimmerman's acquittal but also of the animating principle at the core of black social movements dating back more than
a century.

Garza grew up as Alicia Schwartz, in Marin County, where she
was raised by her African-American mother and her Jewish stepfather, who run an antiques store. Her brother Joey, who works for
the family business, is almost young enough to have been Trayvon
Martin's peer. That is one reason, she says, that the Zimmerman
verdict affected her so deeply. The family was not particularly political, but Garza showed an interest in activism in middle school,
when she worked to have information about contraception made
available to students in Bay Area schools.

She went on to study anthropology and sociology at the University of California, San Diego. When she was twenty-three, she told her family that she was queer. They reacted to the news with equanimity. "I think it helped that my parents are an interracial couple," she told me. "Even if they didn't fully understand what it meant, they were supportive." For a few years, Garza held various jobs in the social-justice sector. She found the work fulfilling, but, she said, "San Francisco broke my heart over and over. White progressives would actually argue with us about their right to determine what was best for communities they never had to live in."

In 2003, she met Malachi Garza, a gregarious, twenty-four-year-old trans male activist, who ran training sessions for organizers. They married five years later. In 2009, early on the morning of New Year's Day, a transit-police officer named Johannes Mehserle fatally shot Oscar Grant, a twenty-two-year-old African-American man, in the Fruitvale BART station, in Oakland, three blocks from where the Garzas live. Alicia was involved in a fight for fair housing in San Francisco at the time, but Malachi, who was by then the director of the Community Justice Network for Youth, immersed himself in a campaign to have Mehserle brought up on murder charges. (He was eventually convicted of involuntary manslaughter, and served one year of a two-year sentence.)

Grant died nineteen days before Barack Obama's first Inauguration. (The film "Fruitvale Station," a dramatic recounting of the last day of Grant's life, contrasts his death with the national exuberance following the election.) His killing was widely seen as a kind of political counterpoint—a reminder that the grip of history would not be easily broken.

GARZA HAD MET PATRISSE CULLORS IN 2005, ON A DANCE FLOOR IN Providence, Rhode Island, where they were both attending an organizers' conference. Cullors, a native of Los Angeles, had been organizing in the L.G.B.T.Q. community since she was a teen-ager—she came out as queer when she was sixteen and was forced to leave home—and she had earned a degree in religion and philosophy at U.C.L.A. She is now a special-projects director at the Ella Baker Center for Human Rights, in Oakland, which focusses on social justice in inner cities. Garza calls Cullors her "twin." After Cullors created the Black Lives Matter hashtag, the two women began promoting it. Opal Tometi, a writer and an immigration-rights organizer in Brooklyn, whom Garza had met at a conference in 2012, offered to build a social-media platform, on Facebook and Twitter, where activists could connect with one another. The women also began thinking about how to turn the phrase into a movement.

Black Lives Matter didn't reach a wider public until the following summer, when a police officer named Darren Wilson shot and killed eighteen-year-old Michael Brown in Ferguson. Darnell Moore, a writer and an activist based in Brooklyn, who knew Cullors, coördinated "freedom rides" to Missouri from New York, Chicago, Portland, Los Angeles, Philadelphia, and Boston. Within a few weeks of Brown's death, hundreds of people who had never participated in organized protests took to the streets, and that campaign eventually exposed Ferguson as a case study of structural racism in America and a metaphor for all that had gone wrong since the end of the civil-rights movement.

DeRay Mckesson, who was twenty-nine at the time and working as an administrator in the Minneapolis public-school system, watched as responses to Brown's death rolled through his Twitter feed, and decided to drive the six hundred miles to Ferguson to witness the scene himself. Before he left, he posted a request for housing on Facebook. Teach for America's Brittany Packnett helped him find a place; before moving to Minneapolis, he had taught sixth-grade math as a T.F.A. employee in Brooklyn. Soon after his arrival, he attended a street-medic training session, where he met Johnetta Elzie, a twenty-five-year-old St. Louis native. With Packnett, they began sharing information about events and tweeting updates from demonstrations, and they quickly became the most recognizable figures associated with the movement in Ferguson. For their efforts, he and Elzie received the Howard Zinn Freedom to Write Award, in 2015, and Packnett was appointed to the President's Commission on Twenty-first Century Policing.

Yet, although the three of them are among the most identifiable names associated with the Black Lives Matter movement, none of them officially belong to a chapter of the organization. Elzie, in fact, takes issue with people referring to Garza, Cullors, and Tometi as founders. As she sees it, Ferguson is the cradle of the movement, and no chapter of the organization exists there or anywhere in the greater St. Louis area. That contentious distinction between the organization and the movement is part of the debate about what Black Lives Matter is and where it will go next.

THE CENTRAL CONTRADICTION OF THE CIVIL-RIGHTS MOVEMENT WAS that it was a quest for democracy led by organizations that frequently failed to function democratically. W. E. B. Du Bois, in his 1903 essay "The Talented Tenth," wrote that "the Negro race, like all races, is going to be saved by its exceptional men," and the traditional narrative of the battle for the rights of African-Americans has tended to read like a great-black-man theory of history. But, starting a generation ago, civil-rights historians concluded that their field had focussed too heavily on the movement's leaders. New scholarship began charting the contributions of women, local activists, and small organizations—the lesser-known elements that enabled the grand moments we associate with the civil-rights era. In particular, the career of Ella Baker, who was a director of the Southern Christian Leadership Conference, and who oversaw the founding of the Student Nonviolent Coordinating Committee, came to be seen as a counter-model to the careers of leaders like Martin Luther King, Jr. Baker was emphatically averse to the spotlight. Barbara Ransby, a professor of history and gender studies at the University of Illinois at Chicago, who wrote a biography of Baker, told me that, during the nineteen-forties, when Baker was a director of branches for the N.A.A.C.P., "she would go into small towns and say, 'Whom are you reaching out to?' And she'd tell them that if you're not reaching out to the town drunk you're not really working for the rights of black people. The folk who were getting rounded up and thrown in jail had to be included."

Cullors says, "The consequence of focussing on a leader is that you develop a necessity for that leader to be the one who's the spokesperson and the organizer, who tells the masses where to go, rather than the masses understanding that we can catalyze a movement in our own community." Or, as Garza put it, "The model of the black preacher leading people to the promised land isn't working right now." Jesse Jackson—a former aide to King and a two-time Presidential candidate, who won seven primaries and four caucuses in 1988—was booed when he tried to address young protesters in Ferguson, who saw him as an interloper. That response was seen as indicative of a generational divide. But the divide was as much philosophical as it was generational, and one that was visible half a century earlier.

Garza, Cullors, and Tometi advocate a horizontal ethic of organizing, which favors democratic inclusion at the grassroots level. Black Lives Matter emerged as a modern extension of Ella Baker's thinking—a preference for ten thousand candles rather than a single spotlight. In a way, they created the context and the movement created itself. "Really, the genesis of the organization was the people who organized in their cities for the ride to Ferguson," Garza told me in her office. Those people, she said, "pushed us to create a chapter structure. They wanted to continue to do this work together, and be connected to activists and organizers from across the country." There are now more than thirty Black Lives Matter chapters in the United States, and one in Toronto. They vary in structure and emphasis, and operate with a great deal of latitude, particularly when it comes to choosing what "actions" to stage. But prospective chapters must submit to a rigorous assessment, by a coördinator, of the kinds of activism that members have previously engaged in, and they must commit to the organization's guiding principles. These are laid out in a thirteen-point statement written by the women and Darnell Moore, which calls for, in part, an ideal of unapologetic blackness. "In affirming that black lives matter, we need not qualify our position," the statement reads.

Yet, although the movement initially addressed the killing of unarmed young black men, the women were equally committed to the rights of working people and to gender and sexual equality. So the statement also espouses inclusivity, because "to love and desire freedom and justice for ourselves is a necessary prerequisite for wanting the same for others." Garza's argument for inclusivity is informed by the fact that she—a black queer female married to a trans male—would likely have found herself marginalized not only in the society she hopes to change but also in many of the organizations that are dedicated to changing it. She also dismisses the kind of liberalism that finds honor in nonchalance. "We want to make sure that people are not saying, 'Well, whatever you are, I don't care,'" she said. "No, I want you to care. I want you to see all of me."

Black activists have organized in response to police brutality for decades, but part of the reason for the visibility of the current movement is the fact that such problems have persisted—and, from the public's perspective, at least, have seemed to escalate—during the first African-American Presidency. Obama's election was seen as the culmination of years of grassroots activism that built the political power of black Americans, but the naïve dream of a post-racial nation foundered even before he was sworn into office. As Garza put it, "Conditions have shifted, so our institutions have shifted to meet those conditions. Barack Obama comes out after Trayvon is murdered and does this weird, half-ass thing where he's, like, 'That could've been my son,' and at the same time he starts scolding young black men." In short, all this would seem to suggest, until there was a black Presidency it was impossible to conceive of the limitations of one. Obama, as a young community organizer in Chicago, determined that he could bring about change more effectively through electoral politics; Garza is of a generation of activists who have surveyed the circumstances of his Presidency and drawn the opposite conclusion.

I MET UP WITH GARZA IN DOWNTOWN SAN FRANCISCO LAST AUGUST, on an afternoon when the icy winds felt like a rebuke to summer. A lively crowd of several hundred people had gathered in United Nations Plaza for Trans Liberation Tuesday, an event that was being held in twenty cities across the country. A transgender opera singer sang "Amazing Grace." Then Janetta Johnson, a black trans activist, said, "We've been in the street for Oscar Grant, for Trayvon Martin, for Eric Garner. It's time for our community to show up for trans women."

The names of Grant, Martin, and Garner—who died in 2014, after being put in a choke hold by police on Staten Island—are now part of the canon of the wrongfully dead. The point of Trans Liberation Tuesday was to draw attention to the fact that there are others, such as Ashton O'Hara and Amber Monroe, black trans people who were killed just weeks apart in Detroit last year, whose names may not be known to the public but who are no less emblematic of a broader social concern. According to a report by the Human Rights Campaign, between 2013 and 2015 there were fifty-three known murders of transgender people; thirty-nine of the victims were African-American.

Garza addressed the crowd for just four minutes; she is not given to soaring rhetoric, but speaks with clarity and confidence. She began with a roll call of the underrepresented: "We understand that, in our communities, black trans folk, gender-nonconforming folk, black queer folk, black women, black disabled folk—we have been leading movements for a long time, but we have been erased from the official narrative." Yet, over all, her comments were more concerned with the internal dynamics of race. For Garza, the assurance that black lives matter is as much a reminder directed at black people as it is a revelation aimed at whites. The message of Trans Liberation Tuesday was that, as society at large has devalued black lives, the African-American community is guilty of devaluing lives based on gender and sexuality.

The kind of ecumenical activism that Garza espouses has deep roots in the Bay Area. In 1966, in Oakland, Huey P. Newton co-founded the Black Panther Party, which was practically defined by hyperbolic masculinity. Four years later, he made a statement whose message was, at the time, rare for the left, not to mention the broader culture. In a Party newsletter, he wrote:

> We have not said much about the homosexual at all,
> but we must relate to the homosexual movement because it
> is a real thing. And I know through reading, and through
> my life experience and observations, that homosexuals are
> not given freedom and liberty by anyone in the society.
> They might be the most oppressed people in the society.

The movement remained steadfastly masculinist, but by the nineteen-eighties Newton's words had begun to appear prescient. When I asked Garza about the most common misperception of Black Lives Matter, she pointed to a frequent social-media dig that it is "a gay movement masquerading as a black one." But the organization's fundamental point has been to challenge the assumption that those two things are mutually exclusive. In 1989, the race-theory and legal scholar Kimberlé Crenshaw introduced the principle of "intersectionality," by which multiple identities co-exist and complicate the ways in which we typically think of class, race, gender, and sexuality as social problems. "Our work is heavily influenced by Crenshaw's theory," Garza told me. "People think that we're engaged with identity politics. The truth is that we're doing what the labor movement has always done—organizing people who are at the bottom."

AS WAS THE CASE DURING THE CIVIL-RIGHTS MOVEMENT, THERE ARE no neat distinctions between the activities of formal organizations and those incited by an atmosphere of social unrest. That ambiguity can be an asset when it inspires entry-level activism among people who had never attended a protest, as happened in Ferguson. But it can be a serious liability when actions contrary to the principles of the movement are associated with it. In December, 2014, video surfaced of a march in New York City, called in response to the deaths of Eric Garner and others, where some protesters chanted that they wanted to see "dead cops." The event was part of the Millions March, which was led by a coalition of organizations, but the chant was attributed to Black Lives Matter. Several months later, the footage provoked controversy. "For four weeks, Bill O'Reilly was flashing my picture on the screen and saying we're a hate group," Garza said.

A week after the march, a troubled drifter named Ismaaiyl Brinsley fatally shot two New York City police officers, Rafael Ramos and Wenjian Liu, as they sat in their patrol car, before killing himself. Some observers argued that, although Brinsley had not identified with any group, his actions were the result of an anti-police climate created by Black Lives Matter. Last summer, not long after Dylann Roof killed nine African-Americans at the Emanuel A.M.E. Church, South Carolina's governor, Nikki Haley, implied that the movement had so intimidated police officers that they were unable to do their jobs, thereby putting more black lives at risk. All of this was accompanied by an increasing skepticism, across the political spectrum, about whether Black Lives Matter could move beyond reacting to outrages and begin proactively shaping public policy.

The current Presidential campaign has presented the movement with a crucial opportunity to address that question. Last summer, at the annual Netroots Nation conference of progressive activists, in Phoenix, Martin O'Malley made his candidacy a slightly longer shot when he responded to a comment about Black Lives Matter by asserting that all lives matter—an evasion of the specificity of black concerns, which elicited a chorus of boos. At the same event, activists interrupted Bernie Sanders. The Sanders campaign made overtures to the movement following the incident, but three weeks later, on the eve of the first anniversary of Michael Brown's death, two protesters identifying themselves as Black Lives Matter activists—Marissa Johnson and Mara Willaford—disrupted a Sanders rally in Seattle, preventing the Senator from addressing several thousand people who had gathered to hear him. The women were booed by the largely white crowd, but the dissent wasn't limited to whites. This was the kind of freestyle disruption that caused even some African-Americans to wonder how the movement was choosing its targets. At the time, it did seem odd to have gone after Sanders twice, given that he is the most progressive candidate in the race, and that none of the Republican candidates had been disrupted in their campaigns.

Garza argues that the strategy has been to leverage influence among the Democrats, since ninety per cent of African-Americans vote Democratic. She says that it will be uncomfortable for voters if "the person that you are supporting hasn't actually done what they need to be doing, in terms of addressing the real concern of people under this broad banner." She defended the Seattle action, saying that it was "part of a very localized dynamic, but an important one," and added that "without being disrupted Sanders wouldn't have released a platform on racial justice." Afterward, Sanders hired

Symone Sanders, an African-American woman, to be his national press secretary. He also released a statement on civil rights that prominently featured the names of African-American victims of police violence, and he began frequently referring to Black Lives Matter on the campaign trail. He subsequently won the support of many younger black activists, including Eric Garner's daughter.

An attempt to disrupt a Hillary Clinton rally early in the campaign, in New Hampshire, failed when the protesters arrived too late to get into the hall. But Clinton met with them privately afterward, and engaged in a debate about mass incarceration. She has met with members of the movement on other occasions, too. Clinton has the support of older generations of black leaders and activists—including Eric Garner's mother—and she decisively carried the black vote in Super Tuesday primaries across the South. But she has been repeatedly criticized by other activists for her support of President Bill Clinton's 1994 crime bill, and, particularly, for comments that she made, in the nineties, about "superpredators" and the need "to bring them to heel." Two weeks ago, Ashley Williams, a twenty-three-year-old who describes herself as an "independent organizer for the movement for black lives," interrupted a private fund-raising event in Charleston, where Clinton was speaking, to demand an apology. The next day, Clinton told the Washington *Post*, "Looking back, I shouldn't have used those words, and I wouldn't use them today."

IF BLACK LIVES MATTER HAS BEEN AN OBJECT LESSON IN THE POWER of social media, it has also revealed the medium's pitfalls. Just as the movement was enjoying newfound influence among the Democratic Presidential contenders, it was also gaining attention for a series of febrile Twitter exchanges. In one, DeRay Mckesson and Johnetta Elzie got into a dispute with Shaun King, a writer for the *Daily News*, over fund-raising for a social-justice group. The conservative Web site Breitbart ran a picture of Mckesson and

King with the headline "BLACK LIVES MATTER LEADERS JUST EX-COMMUNICATED SHAUN KING."

Last month, it was announced that Garza would speak at Webster University, in St. Louis, which prompted an acrimonious social-media response from people in the area who are caught up in the debate over the movement's origins. Elzie tweeted, "Thousands of ppl without platforms who have NO CLUE who the 'three' are, and their work/sacrifice gets erased," and said that the idea that Garza is a founder of the movement is a "lie." Garza released a statement saying that she had cancelled the event "due to threats and online attacks on our organization and us as individuals from local activists with whom we have made an effort to have meaningful dialogue." She continued, "We all lose when bullying and personal attacks become a substitute for genuine conversation and principled disagreement."

There's nothing novel about personality conflicts arising among activists, but to older organizers, who had watched as federal surveillance and infiltration programs sowed discord that all but wrecked the Black Power movement, the public airing of grievances seemed particularly amateurish. "Movements are destroyed by conflicts over money, power, and credit," Garza said, a week after the cancellation. "We have to take seriously the impact of not being able to have principled disagreement, or we're not going to be around very long."

Almost from the outset, Black Lives Matter has been compared to the Occupy movement. Occupy was similarly associated with a single issue—income inequality—which it transformed into a movement through social media. Its focus on the one per cent played a key role in the 2012 election, and it likely contributed to the unexpected support for Bernie Sanders's campaign. To the movement's critics, however, its achievements fell short of its promise. Its dissipation seemed to prove that, while the Internet can foster the creation of a new movement, it can just as easily threaten its survival.

Black Lives Matter would appear to face similar concerns, though in recent months the movement has tacked in new directions. In November, the Ella Baker Center received a five-hundred-thousand-dollar grant from Google, for Patrisse Cullors to further develop a program to help California residents monitor and respond to acts of police violence. Last year, Mckesson, with Elzie, Brittany Packnett, and Samuel Sinyangwe, a twenty-five-year-old data analyst with a degree from Stanford, launched Campaign Zero, a list of policing-policy recommendations that calls for, among other things, curtailing arrests for low-level crimes, reducing quotas for summonses and arrests, and demilitarizing police departments. To date, neither Clinton nor Sanders has endorsed the platform, but both have met with the activists to discuss it.

The announcement of Mckesson's mayoral candidacy, which he made on Twitter—he has more than three hundred thousand followers—is the most dramatic break from the movement's previous actions. (Beyoncé has more than fourteen million followers, but she follows only ten people. Mckesson is one of them.) Mckesson is a native of Baltimore and he grew up on the same side of town as Freddie Gray, whose death last year in police custody sparked protests and riots in the city—at which Mckesson was a frequent presence. His family struggled with poverty and drug addiction, but he excelled academically and went on to attend Bowdoin College, in Maine. He will be running against twenty-eight other candidates. One of them, the city councilman Nick Mosby, is married to Marilyn Mosby, the Maryland state's attorney, who is handling the prosecution of the six police officers indicted in connection with Gray's death.

In Baltimore, Mckesson told me that he is using his savings to fund his activist work. "It's totally possible to have Beyoncé follow you on Twitter and still be broke," he said. (BuzzFeed reported that a former Citibank executive would host an event at his New York City home to raise funds for Mckesson's campaign.) He wouldn't discuss his candidacy's implications for the movement, but he is very serious about running. Two weeks ago, he released a twenty-six-page report detailing his platform for reforming the city's schools, police department, and economic infrastructure. He has already been attacked for his connection to Teach for America; after he released his plan for improving Baltimore's schools, it was dismissed as a corporatist undertaking along the lines of Michael Bloomberg's and Rahm Emanuel's reforms. He rejects the idea that his lack of experience in elected office should be an obstacle. When I asked how he thought he would be able to get members of the city council and the state legislature to support his ideas, he said, "I think we build relationships. That question seems to come from a place of traditional reading of politics. That says, 'If you don't know people already, then you cannot be successful.' Politics as usual actually hasn't turned into a change in outcomes here."

GARZA IS TACTFUL WHEN SHE TALKS ABOUT MCKESSON'S CAMPAIGN. "I'm in favor of people getting in where they fit in. Wherever you feel you can make the greatest contribution, you should," she said. But she doesn't see it as her role to define the future of the movement. She told me an anecdote that illustrates the non-centrality of her role. Last month, on Martin Luther King Day, she and Malachi were driving into San Francisco, where she was scheduled to appear at a community forum, when they heard on the radio that the Bay Bridge had been shut down. Members of a coalition of organizations, including the Bay Area chapter of Black Lives Matter, had driven onto the bridge, laced chains through their car windows, and locked them to the girders, shutting down entry to the city from Oakland. Garza had known that there were plans to mark the holiday with a protest—marches and other events were called across the nation—but she was not informed of this specific activity planned in her own city. "It's not like there's a red button I push to make people turn up," she said. It would have been inconceivable for, say, the S.C.L.C. to have carried out such an ambitious action without the leadership's being aware of every detail.

In January, Garza travelled to Washington, to attend President Obama's final State of the Union address; she had been invited by Barbara Lee, her congressional representative. (Lee, who was the sole member of Congress to vote against the authorization of military force after 9/11, has a high standing among activists who are normally skeptical of elected officials.) After the speech, as Garza stood outside in the cold, trying to hail a cab, she said that she was disappointed. The President had not driven home the need for police reform. He had spoken of economic inequality and a political system rigged to benefit the few, but had scarcely touched upon the implications of that system for African-Americans specifically. From the vantage point of black progressives, his words were a kind of all-lives-matter statement of public policy.

A year from now, Barack Obama will leave office, and with him will go a particular set of expectations of racial rapprochement. So will the sense that what happened in Sanford, Ferguson, Baltimore, Charleston, and Staten Island represents a paradox. Black Lives Matter may never have more influence than it has now. The future is not knowable, but it isn't likely to be unfamiliar.

THE UPRISING

LUKE MOGELSON

June 22, 2020

On June 1st, a week after the killing of George Floyd sparked a national uprising that touched every state, convulsed major cities, activated the National Guard, and sent President Donald Trump into a secure bunker underneath the White House, Terrence Floyd, George's younger brother, visited the intersection in South Minneapolis where his sibling had died. During the previous seven days, Thirty-eighth Street and Chicago Avenue had become the site of an uninterrupted public vigil, designated by signs and banners as "sacred ground." Barricades around the four surrounding blocks impeded traffic and law enforcement. The sidewalk outside the Cup Foods grocery store—where an employee had called the police after suspecting George Floyd of using a counterfeit twenty-dollar bill—was buried under bouquets, mementos, and homemade cards. Activists delivered speeches between the gas pumps at a filling station; messages in chalk—"FIGHT BACK," "STAY WOKE"—covered the street. Volunteers passed out food and water; there was barbecue, music, tailgating. A wide ring of flowers and candles circumscribed the intersection, delineating a kind of magic circle. Later that day, within the circle, a group of indigenous women would perform the Jingle Dress Dance—a healing ritual created by members of the Ojibwe tribe during the influenza pandemic of 1918.

Terrence Floyd, who lives in New York City, arrived with a security entourage in the afternoon. As he approached the entrance to Cup Foods, guided by supporters and swarmed by an international mob of photographers and camera crews, he paused to admire a vibrant mural: his brother's face, set inside a giant sun-flower. In the background were the names of more than two dozen other black victims of police violence, including Michael Brown, Breonna Taylor, Eric Garner, and Freddie Gray. At the base of the mural, among cardboard signs, stood jugs of milk, which is used to alleviate the effects of tear gas. A couple of nights earlier, the police had conducted a raid at the site, clearing out people in violation of a citywide curfew.

Eventually, Terrence reached the curb where two officers had pinned down George's back and legs and where a third officer, Derek Chauvin, had pressed his knee into George's neck for eight min-utes and forty-six seconds while George repeated "I can't breathe" at least sixteen times before his eyes closed and his pulse stopped. Terrence sat down on the pavement where someone had painted the white silhouette of a prostrate body, its hands manacled behind its back and angelic wings spreading from its shoulders. Bowing his head, he let out an anguished cry. He remained there for several minutes, then stood to address the crowd.

"I understand y'all upset," he said, using a megaphone. "But I doubt y'all half as upset as I am. So if I'm not over here wilding out—if I'm not over here blowing up stuff, if I'm not over here mess-ing up my community—then what are y'all doing? *What are y'all do-ing?*" He went on, "Let's do this another way. Let's stop thinking that our voice don't matter, and vote. . . . That's how we're gonna hit 'em. . . . Let's switch it up, y'all. . . . Do this peacefully. *Please.*"

Terrence fell silent. Or almost silent. The megaphone amplified his exhalations. A reverend, standing at his side, rubbed Terrence's back, leaned over, and whispered in his ear, "Breathe. Breathe. Breathe. Breathe."

THE PROTESTS THAT HAVE PROLIFERATED ACROSS THE COUNTRY FOR the past two weeks have been both intimately specific and sweep-ingly ambitious, honoring a single human life while indicting a national history. In Minneapolis, they have also been about a city. The relationship between Minneapolis's law-enforcement officials and its communities of color, though always plagued, deteriorated dramatically in the five years before Floyd's death. In 2015, a white officer shot and killed a twenty-four-year-old unarmed African-American man, Jamar Clark, in North Minneapolis. (Another officer on the scene claimed that Clark had tried to take his gun; witnesses said that Clark was already in handcuffs.) Activists from Black Lives Matter camped out in front of a precinct house for eighteen days, in snow and frigid temperatures. One night, a white man opened fire on them, wounding five. His trial, which ended with his conviction, revealed that he had a history of making racist comments. The police forcibly tore down the encampment, evicting the protesters and arresting eight of them; in the end, no charges were brought against the officer who killed Clark.

A year later, in a suburb of Saint Paul, a thirty-two-year-old black man named Philando Castile was shot by a policeman during a traffic stop for a broken tail-light, after stating that he was in possession of a firearm. Castile's girlfriend, Diamond Reynolds, and her infant daughter were in the car. Reynolds live-streamed the immediate aftermath of the shooting on Facebook. In the video, Castile, who was licensed to carry, sits at the wheel, blood spreading through his T-shirt, while Reynolds cries "Stay with me" and the officer continues to aim his gun through the window. Castile died on film; Reynolds was handcuffed and detained; the officer, Jeronimo Yanez, was charged with manslaughter but acquitted.

In 2018, in North Minneapolis, Thurman Blevins, a black father of three, was killed by two white officers. A body camera worn by one of them captured Blevins running away—apparently with a gun—while calling over his shoulder, "Please, don't shoot me! Leave me alone! Leave me alone!" Blevins was shot multiple times. The county prosecutor found "no basis to issue criminal charges against either officer."

Thirty-eighth and Chicago is on the Southside of Minneapolis. African-Americans have been concentrated there and across town, on the Northside, ever since anti-black housing covenants, in the early twentieth century, prohibited them from buying homes elsewhere in the city. Subsequent infrastructure projects and redlining policies entrenched this de-facto segregation, diverting resources from the Northside and the Southside while perpetuating poverty by inhibiting African-Americans from obtaining mortgages and business loans. At the same time, predominantly white neighborhoods have grown progressively more affluent. Today, Minneapolis appears on lists of the "best places to live" even as its racial disparities rank among the worst in the country. The median annual income of black residents in the Twin Cities is less than half that of whites, and, though about seventy-five per cent of white families own their homes, only about a quarter of black families do. Unemployment is more than twice as high for black residents as it is for white residents.

Many people in Minneapolis believe that the police department both reflects and enforces these inequalities. In 1999, a law requiring officers to live within the city limits was repealed, allowing suburbanites to join the force; now most officers are white, and few live in or come from the neighborhoods they police. (Chauvin lived in Oakdale, twenty miles from where he killed Floyd.) The black community makes up about a fifth of the city's population; nevertheless, when officers there physically subdue people—for instance, by hitting or Tasing them—sixty per cent of the time the subjects are black. A 2015 investigation by the American Civil Liberties Union found that black people in Minneapolis were nearly nine times more likely than whites to be arrested for low-level offenses such as trespassing or public consumption of intoxicants. That year, the city finally did away with ordinances against "lurking" and "spitting," which had been disproportionately applied against black residents. In 2007, five high-ranking black officers sued the department, alleging pervasive institutional racism, including death threats, signed "KKK," that were sent to every black officer, through the departmental mail system. The city settled the lawsuit out of court.

Patterns of bias have been accompanied by a culture of impunity. An analysis by Reuters of nearly a decade of officer-misconduct claims in Minneapolis found that ninety per cent of them resulted in no consequences. Chauvin, the subject of at least seventeen complaints, was disciplined only once; another officer involved in Floyd's death, Tou Thao, had at least six complaints filed against him, and was sued for police brutality after he allegedly beat up a black man who was in handcuffs. (The city paid twenty-five thousand dollars to settle the case.) The only Minneapolis officer in recent memory to have been sentenced to jail for killing someone is Mohamed Noor, a black man, who shot Justine Damond, a white woman.

City officials have cited the Minneapolis police union as an obstacle to accountability. The union's president, Lieutenant Bob Kroll, was named in the 2007 discrimination suit, which claimed that he wore "a motorcycle jacket with a 'White Power' badge sewn onto it." Kroll has called Black Lives Matter a "terrorist organization" and has promoted training officers in "killology" instead of in de-escalation techniques. "I've been involved in three shootings myself, and not one of them has bothered me," he said, in April. "Maybe I'm different."

Everyone I met who lived close to Thirty-eighth and Chicago viewed the police as an alien force of constant menace and harassment. A common objection was the default belligerence of officers—their tendency to initiate physical confrontations, often under bogus pretexts. "The cops have written so many false reports on people just because they wanted to whup somebody's ass," one black resident told me. "It's pure hate. Sometimes they don't even take you to jail. They'll take you to an alley and beat the hell out of you. It's insane here, and people are sick of it." Another local, who had grown up ten minutes away from the intersection, said that any infraction, no matter how minor, risked inciting police brutality: "The way they conduct themselves for very insignificant situations is way, way beyond what's necessary. At what point do the citizens of a community say 'enough'?"

ONE OF THE PEOPLE LISTENING TO TERRENCE FLOYD SPEAK WAS SIMONE Hunter, a short nineteen-year-old with red-rinsed hair; she lived on the Northside, but had become a fixture at Thirty-eighth and Chicago since George Floyd was killed. Hunter told me that the infamous cell-phone video of the incident had filled her with anger and disgust. "I felt like I was going to throw up," she said. Until then, Hunter had never attended a large-scale protest, but two days after Floyd's death, when people gathered outside the police station in Minneapolis's Third Precinct—Chauvin's precinct—she joined them. A line of officers protected the building. Hunter, whose small stature can obscure her pugnacity, pushed her way to the front and furiously reproached them. "How would you feel if this was done to your sons and daughters?" she said. One officer pepper-sprayed her, at close range; another whacked her leg with a wooden baton, knocking her down. (The Minneapolis Police Department did not respond to requests for comment for this article.)

The next day, Hunter woke up with a large, dark bruise on her inner thigh. Her whole body burned—"Like someone dipped me in VapoRub"—but she was eager to rejoin the protesters.

"It's not just about George Floyd," she told me. "It's about all the unseen shit, where we *don't* have the video." Hunter had been removed from a difficult family situation when she was six, separated from siblings, and raised in a foster home. She had felt buffeted by an invisible, malign system her entire life, and, for her, the list of unseen shit was long. An unrelenting procession of encounters with racism had confirmed her station in a world that seemed organized against her. Recently, she said, the police had stopped and combatively interrogated her and a friend, also a black teenager, for driving with an air freshener hanging from the rearview mirror—technically a safety violation. "We're used to it, but we shouldn't be," Hunter said.

At around 9:30 P.M. on Thursday, May 28th, the night after Hunter had been pepper-sprayed and beaten, Minneapolis's mayor, Jacob Frey, ordered the beleaguered officers defending the Third Precinct to evacuate. Frey later explained that he had wanted to "prevent hand-to-hand combat." The officers fled out the back of the station, on foot and in a convoy of vehicles, while protesters hurled rocks at them. A few hours later, Hunter returned to the area and was stunned by what she found: thousands of raucous young people had congregated in the street, with no law enforcement in sight, and the station was on fire. Smoke billowed from the ground floor, and people were roaming the hazy second floor, tossing through the windows anything not bolted down: documents, folders, phones. A nearby post office was also ablaze. In the middle of the intersection, an upside-down mail truck burned. A second mail truck suddenly appeared and crashed head-on into the flaming steel. The driver jumped out, and people cheered. Cars spun doughnuts, motorcycles popped wheelies, fireworks and gunshots punctuated the mayhem; a liquor store had been broken into, then burned down, and alcohol circulated among the crowd. People in ski masks and bandannas wielded hammers and baseball bats.

Later, when I asked Hunter what it had felt like to see the Third Precinct overrun, she answered, "Like fucking therapy. It was amazing. It felt like 'Finally, we're attacking *them* instead of our own people. Finally, we're not allowing ourselves to be threatened by them.' It felt like victory. Like, *We can do this.*"

I'd arrived at the scene not long after she did. The atmosphere was an electric combination of the rage that had compelled people to battle the police and an astounded euphoria over having actually prevailed. But there was also something peculiar: some people, many of them white, seemed to be deriving an inordinate amount of pleasure from the spectacle. A white guy wearing board shorts and Apple earbuds, walking a bicycle, and sipping a bottle of malt liquor approached me to announce, in a slurred voice, "They keep giving me booze!" At a strip mall opposite the station, looters of all stripes had breached a Target, a Cub Foods supermarket, and a Dollar Tree. The Target had been nearly emptied; water from ceiling-mounted sprinklers rained down, and a fast-flowing stream carried debris into the parking lot. Several teen-agers emerged from the entrance, their pant cuffs rolled up, nude mannequins under their arms.

Hunter had graduated from high school a year ago, and had recently been working at a Target distribution center, in Woodbury, just outside Saint Paul. From 7 A.M. to 6 P.M., she had stood at a conveyor belt, packaging merchandise to be shipped to retail outlets such as this one. Though Hunter did not participate in any vandalism, it didn't bother her. In fact, she said, "it was very satisfying." She viewed corporate capitalism as an integral component of structural racism in America, and working for Target had felt as demoralizing as shopping there—a capitulation to the same rigged game whose unfair rules were upheld by the police. But now everything had changed, and, Hunter realized, her life would have to as well. She said to herself, "There's no way I can come out here and support this and be O.K. with burning shit down and also go to my job and be, like, 'This is fine. I'm cool with accepting money from these people.' No. I can't be cool with that."

The damage wasn't limited to big-box stores. Next to the Target, a charter school looked as if a bulldozer had plowed through it. Nearby, people holding metal pipes stood outside an apartment building. When a carful of young people pulled up, eying a tobacco shop on the ground floor, a thin, bearded man in reading glasses and a colorful button-down shirt told them that there was nothing to steal. "We got children here!" he yelled, waving at the upper floors.

His name was Said Maye. He was a long-haul truck driver and a refugee from Somalia. About seventy-five thousand Somalis live in Minnesota, more than anywhere else in the country. Many of them, like Maye, resettled there in the nineteen-nineties, during the Somali civil war. Maye said that more than a hundred families—some Somali, though not all—were living in Section 8 apartments above the retail spaces he was guarding. His concern was that someone might set the shops on fire, imperilling the building's tenants. Although Maye had taken his wife, his mother, and his three children to his brother's house, outside the city, he'd resolved to protect his neighbors until the tumult had subsided. When I met him, at around 2 A.M., he'd been fending off looters for fifteen hours. Another man who'd volunteered to help said of Maye, "I've watched him stand in front of people pointing guns at his head. People were waving guns in his face, and he didn't move."

Maye turned up his palms and said, "I'm from Mogadishu— what do you want from me?"

As the night wore on, the looters focussed their attention on a block of small businesses up the road from the precinct house. Midori's Floating World Café had been trashed, and a group of locals who knew the restaurant's owners salvaged potted plants amid the rubble. "They didn't deserve this," William Tully, a twenty-five-year-old outreach-and-inclusion officer for the Democratic Party, said. "What is the point of destroying the community you're protesting on behalf of?" One of Tully's friends, an immigrant from Mexico who asked to be identified only as Juan, pointed at a corner building engulfed in flames, in front of which a man posed for pictures. It had been a Latino-owned restaurant, and Juan's mother had once worked there. "These are not the real protesters," Juan said. "These are opportunists." Down the sidewalk, a white woman in a tank top and cutoff jeans used a fire extinguisher to smash the window of a barbershop.

A few minutes later, a car pulled over next to us, and a black man got out and started documenting the chaos with his cell phone. When someone in a mask told him to stop filming, the man wheeled around toward him: "This is my hood—I live here! I live fucking here!"

"I live here, too! Why you mad?"

"*Everybody's* mad right now!" the man shouted, incredulous. "We're *supposed* to be mad right now!"

TULLY AND JUAN WERE CONVINCED THAT MOST OF THE LOOTERS HAD come from outside Minneapolis for reasons having nothing to do with the killing of George Floyd. In the following days, politicians also seized on this idea. Minnesota's governor, Tim Walz, a Democrat, speculated, apparently without evidence, that eighty per cent of the people destroying property and attacking law enforcement were not residents of Minnesota. Walz attributed the rioting to "ideological extremists" pursuing a campaign of "international destabilization." Trump, for his part, blamed Antifa. In the city, rumors spread of white-supremacist infiltrators hoping to delegitimize the protests and white "accelerationists" attempting to instigate a race war.

Some people of this type do appear to have been present, and many looters unquestionably were white. On June 8th, the first arson charge for the Third Precinct fire was filed in federal court—against a twenty-three-year-old white man from Saint Paul. Of the demonstrators who have been arrested, however, none have been linked to anti-fascist groups, and few have been from out of state. Ascribing what happened in Minneapolis to murky external forces elides the profound grievances of its black community—grievances that, at least in the early days of the protests, were partly expressed through rioting. A day after the Third Precinct fell, Leslie Redmond, the president of the Minneapolis branch of the N.A.A.C.P., declared, "What you're witnessing in Minnesota is something that's been a long time coming. I can't tell you how many governors I've sat down with, how many mayors we've sat down with, and we've warned them that, if you keep murdering black people, this city will burn."

Chauvin was arrested, for third-degree murder, that same day. This appeased nobody. I was at Thirty-eighth and Chicago when the news was announced, and the reaction among the mourners there was disappointment about the charge, and indignation that the other officers involved had seemingly escaped punishment. A new chant arose: "One down, three to go!"

At dusk, throngs of people filled the street between the still smoking precinct house and the gutted Target. State troopers and National Guard units had cordoned off the area that morning but had since inexplicably withdrawn. Simone Hunter was back again. This time, she'd brought supplies: saline and milk, for treating tear gas; tampons and sanitary napkins, for packing flesh wounds. The precautions felt prudent. Trump had tweeted that the protesters were "THUGS," threatened to deploy the military to "get the job done right," and warned, "When the looting starts, the shooting starts."

Hunter was not alone in preparing for the possibility of violence. Some people arrived equipped with helmets, goggles, and sheet metal; others wore plywood shields strapped onto their forearms. A rusty van, marked with a cross of red tape, served as an ambulance—two teen-agers stood on its roof, making out. Near the station, in front of a burned Arby's, ramparts had been built with tables from Midori's Floating World Café. In the distance, the blue and red lights of squad cars flashed. The protesters faced them, crying out, "Say his name—George Floyd!" When the squad cars unexpectedly retreated, exultation gripped the crowd.

People began heading west on Lake Street, a long boulevard

leading to another station, in the Fifth Precinct. The chants grew hostile: "Fuck the police!," "Who shuts shit down? We shut shit down!," and "We want freedom, freedom! All these racist-ass pigs, we don't need 'em, need 'em!" Nevertheless, the subsequent two-and-a-half-mile march was mostly celebratory. People piled onto the hoods of slow-moving cars, and residents waved from lawn chairs on the sidewalk, as if watching a parade.

The mood changed when the crowd reached the station, as night was falling. Two perimeters made of concrete barriers topped with tall fencing surrounded the building. Officers in helmets and gas masks stood on the roof, holding rubber-bullet guns. The pro-testers pressed against the fence, taunting the officers. At a Stop-N-Shop across the street, people with crowbars had removed plywood covering the entrance, and were hurrying out with cigarettes and snacks. "This is not why we're protesting!" a young woman yelled. Another woman added, "Y'all need to fuck up the suburbs!" A middle-aged white man, wearing a motorcycle helmet with the face shield pulled down, ducked out of the store carrying bulk boxes of Advil and Tylenol.

The looting soon spread to an adjacent strip mall. For a sur-real period, the people gathered outside the precinct house chanted and gave speeches while not fifty feet away other groups ransacked an Office Depot, a Kmart, and a Dollar Tree. Several protesters pleaded, "Keep it peaceful!" Chantaveia Burnett, one of the young women who had tried to defend the Stop-N-Shop, had given up rebuking the looters, and resigned herself to collecting loose bottles of water and stacking them in a neat pile. "People are probably go-ing to need water," she explained.

By midnight, anyone looking to protest peacefully had left the scene. As a helicopter idled overhead, people taking cover behind a car wash launched bottles, bricks, and large mortar fireworks at the officers on the roof of the precinct house. Others broke into a Wells Fargo bank. In a room with overturned filing cabinets, smashed computers, and money-counting machines, two men, one white and one black, stood in front of a tall safe, arguing over a ring of keys that somebody had found. When it became clear that there was nothing inside to rob—or nothing left—a consensus rose in volume and vehemence: "Burn it down!" A black man vanished into the bank carrying a red can of gasoline; when he reappeared, the can was gone.

"We don't need money anymore!" someone shouted.

"We are the police now!" another added.

A teen-ager, wearing wraparound sunglasses with the price tag attached, stumbled past me. "Is this shit real?" he muttered. "Am I fucking dreaming?"

Ten minutes later, the flames leaping from the bank were bright enough to throw into relief the officers still standing on the precinct roof.

Simone Hunter watched the fire with what was becoming a familiar mixture of vindication and disbelief. "I can't lie—I was happy," she told me later. "If we need to make the world stop for people to pay attention to what's going on? Then we're gonna make the world stop."

Hunter's sentiment was shared by many of the protesters I met in Minneapolis. Although the vast majority of them had not committed any crimes, they recognized the political utility of such conduct. Nobody was killed, and neither law enforcement nor the military reported sustaining any injuries during the riots. Activists have argued that human life matters more than wealth and material objects, whose loss can never undermine the social compact as egregiously as the murder, by state agents, of black people. Property damage is therefore justifiable if it prevents such murders in the future. Whether or not you agree with that calculus, one thing seems indisputable: the uprising in Minneapolis has already resulted in meaningful change.

In addition to fixing the world's attention on the problems of police brutality and structural racism, the demonstrators in Minneapolis have succeeded in winning a number of concrete concessions that likely would not have been made under normal circumstances. The week after Floyd's murder, Minnesota's attorney general upgraded Derek Chauvin's charge to second-degree murder, and charged the other three officers with aiding and abetting him. Minneapolis's school board and its parks department severed ties with the police. The Minnesota Department of Human Rights launched an investigation into the police force and moved to ban its officers from using choke holds and neck restraints. Most remarkably, on June 7th, nine of the thirteen members of the City Council vowed to "begin the process of ending the Minneapolis Police Department." Although the practical import of this pledge remains vague, a radical overhaul of law enforcement in Minneapolis appears assured.

After decades of civil petitions for a reckoning with systemic racism, what finally achieved it was the issuance of an ultimatum—one with teeth. As the chant goes: no justice, no peace.

SIMONE HUNTER, LIKE MANY PROTESTERS, SEES OTHER POSITIVE CONSE-quences of the upheaval in Minneapolis. She told me that, though "there was always friction" among the city's communities of color—African-Americans, Native Americans, Latinos, various immigrant groups, and refugees—"This has broken all that down." Solidarity between the Somali-American and the African-American communities, in particular, has been galvanized by an urgent sense of common struggle that supersedes differences in history and culture. Somali-American women were ubiquitous at the protests. On June 6th, when Ilhan Omar, the Somali-born U.S. congresswoman who represents Minneapolis, spoke at a demonstration in town, she acknowledged, "I might not have been born in the United States. I might not have inherited the trauma and the tragedy that black Americans have who come from enslaved ancestry." However, she said, the ordeal of racism had initiated her into the black-American experience: "I have lived as a black person in this country. I have lived as a mother raising black children."

Nowhere has a sense of unity been more movingly on display than at Thirty-eighth and Chicago. At once a site of solemn mourning and of festive commemoration, the intersection drew more volunteers, artists, performers, and activists every day. The police had, for the most part, stayed away: buses and barriers sealed off a portion of the neighborhood, which was patrolled by residents, some armed. A medical tent was erected, and couches and lounge chairs were arranged under the canopy of the filling station opposite the Cup Foods. A stage, a d.j. table, and an industrial sound system were installed. A towering portrait of Floyd was mounted to a bus stop. Like an evolving art installation, the intersection was increasingly populated by statues and paintings. Visitors mingled, spoke, listened, danced, chanted, and prayed. Fresh bouquets piled up on top of desiccated ones. Pastors, priests, and imams gave sermons. You could sense the unprecedented extent to which Floyd's death, compared with previous police killings of African-Americans, had unsettled white Americans. Soccer moms wept openly, old hippies burned sage, and white parents kneeled with their children before the spot where Floyd was killed. Black parents brought their children as well, and it was impossible not to consider how the respective conversations would differ.

The vigil site also became the hub of an organic, citywide mutual-aid campaign. Many poorer residents had already been struggling because of lockdown measures related to COVID-19; shops that hadn't already been shuttered by the pandemic were now damaged, or covered in plywood. Nearly every business on Lake Street, the primary commercial corridor for Latinos and Native Americans, was closed. So were the bus and light-rail lines, which meant that travelling outside the area to buy groceries was impossible for those without vehicles. At Thirty-eighth and Chicago, people had set up tables loaded with canned and boxed goods, fresh produce, diapers, toilet paper, kitchen supplies, homemade face masks, and other provisions, all piled around signs that read "FREE!" and "TAKE WHAT YOU NEED!" Near Cup Foods, the headquarters of a labor-rights organization called Centro de Trabajadores Unidos en la Lucha had been converted into a food pantry, its offices swamped with donated items. A line of people snaked out the door, below the words "COMIDA GRATIS."

Other spontaneous initiatives felt less revolutionary. The day after the rioting around the Fifth Precinct, hundreds of volunteers, most of them white, descended on the neighborhood to clean it up. Although some of them found useful tasks—one group filled garbage cans with water at nearby homes, wheeled them to the smoldering ruins of a small business, and formed a bucket line to douse the flames—others seemed primarily interested in being there, or *having* been there. Most of the people I spoke to said that they had come out "to support the community." Yet it was not altogether clear whether sweeping away the wreckage left behind by the protests amounted to an endorsement or a censure of them.

This ambiguity was most palpable—and uncomfortable—at the Wells Fargo, where a broken pipe spewed water into the scorched shell of the lobby. Dozens of young women used push brooms to usher the ankle-deep water out of the building while men rescued desks and other furniture. Many of them were evangelicals from Saint Paul. "We're trying to help in any way we can," one said, a little breathlessly. The oldest person there was soaking wet and sweeping the water with visible urgency. When I asked him if he was with the church, he said, "What church?," and went on to explain that he was from Somalia. A safe-deposit box in the flooded basement contained the passports and birth certificates of his eleven children.

ALTHOUGH THERE IS A ROBUST NETWORK OF ACTIVISTS IN MINNEAPO-lis, the initial demonstrations there were improvised and leaderless, reminiscent of the Occupy movement in the U.S. and the *gilets jaunes* protests in France. Tony Williams, a member of Reclaim the Block, a local advocacy group, told me, "This uprising is not the product of any organizational strategy." He added that many local activists had not participated at all. Williams, who had been part of the eighteen-day sit-in following the killing of Jamar Clark, in 2015, said that, after the five activists were shot, "a lot of us who were there walked away with a lot of trauma." This time, rather than being physically on the ground, Williams and his colleagues focussed on channelling the public's inchoate frustration into support for specific reforms.

The absence of hierarchy, and the need for direction, thrust many previously disengaged citizens into public and political life. On May 30th, while the church members worked to salvage what they could of the Wells Fargo, Governor Walz, having declared an 8 P.M. curfew in the Twin Cities the previous day, fully mobilized the Minnesota National Guard—"An action that has never been taken," he noted. At 7:55 P.M., every cell phone in the city received an emergency alert: "Go home or to safe inside location. Avoid the outdoors. The curfew is enforceable by law." When the message went out, I was sitting with Lisa Kargou, an immigrant from Liberia, amid thousands of protesters in the intersection between the bank and the Fifth Precinct house. I asked her if she planned to stay out past curfew, and she replied, "Hell yes. I'm out here. I'm in it for good." Kargou had three sons, ages twelve, ten, and four. "I'm fighting for my kids," she said. "When they grow up to be men, I want them to be able to walk down the street without fear."

People took turns talking through a public-address system, and most of the speeches were more personal than political. If anyone was in charge, it seemed to be an African-American man in a long T-shirt with golden fringes, who had earlier scaled a street light and draped from it an enormous cloth tapestry bearing Floyd's image. When the emergency alert sent a ripple of apprehension through the crowd, the man grabbed the microphone and implored everyone to remain calm. "We gotta have some order, and we have to have decorum!" he said.

Given this projection of authority, I assumed that he was an experienced activist, or at least affiliated with an organization. In fact, it was the first protest he had ever attended. His name was Cornell Griffin, and he was thirty-nine years old; he lived with his wife in Maple Grove, northwest of the city. He'd worked as a mechanic, but for the past year and a half he had been depressed and living like a "recluse"—seldom leaving his basement and spending most of his time reading the Bible and posts on Facebook. He hadn't spoken to his extended family in months, and, when the protests began in Minneapolis, he'd felt no more desire to take part than he had after similar outrages. "I ain't gonna lie," he said. "When Trayvon Martin happened, Freddie Gray, I didn't do shit. Like, nothing." When Floyd was killed, Griffin's best friend tried to persuade him to join the protests, and for the first three days Griffin refused. Then, a few hours before I first saw him, he'd told himself, "Either I'm gonna live my life in fear, or I'm gonna try this one dang thing and see what comes of it." After Griffin offered to climb the street light, the group running the P.A. system started handing him the microphone. He found his voice, and realized that people in the crowd were looking to him for guidance.

After the emergency alert, a man on roller skates approached Griffin and told him that police officers, state troopers, and National Guard soldiers were assembling nearby: the crackdown would be violent, and the ensuing panic could cause a stampede. The man proposed that Griffin lead away as many protesters as he could. Griffin took the microphone and announced that a march was currently departing. A large group began following him toward downtown.

Not long after, a phalanx of state troopers in riot gear unleashed rubber bullets, marking pellets, stun grenades, and tear gas on the remaining protesters—more than a thousand people, including children and senior citizens, all of them peaceful—then rushed them with batons. Following behind the assault was an armored tactical vehicle; from its open hatch, a trooper aimed an assault rifle with a silencer at people. Within minutes, the intersection had been cleared. Disoriented and bleeding protesters, and some journalists, staggered through the gas. Griffin's wife, who'd stayed behind, texted him, asking where he was, and he quickly headed back. Just outside the Fifth Precinct, he came upon a woman rooted to the ground, immobilized with fear. Griffin was attempting to get her to move when he spotted a nearby officer levelling a gun at them. A rubber bullet hit his neck.

When I met up again with Griffin, a few days later, his neck was still scabbed over where the round had broken the flesh, and his voice was raspy from the trauma to his throat and vocal cords. But he was in high spirits. The protest had shifted something into focus for him. "For the last year, I've been feeling like there's something wrong with me," he said. "And then this happened. And, all of a sudden, it all made sense. It wasn't me. *My city* is hurting. *My city* is depressed. *My city* is on fire."

THE MANNER IN WHICH LAW ENFORCEMENT HAS RESPONDED TO THE demonstrations in Minneapolis has only intensified the resentment fuelling the demonstrations. Although no police officers are known to have been harmed by protesters, many protesters have been injured by the police. One man, Soren Stevenson, lost his left eye after being hit with a rubber bullet. The rioting lasted only a few days; since then, except in a few isolated instances, the main crime that protesters have committed in Minneapolis is being out past curfew. The day after Griffin led people away from the Fifth Precinct, hundreds of peaceful demonstrators gathered downtown at the U.S. Bank Stadium. As eight o'clock approached, a man with a bullhorn announced, "If anybody's confused or has questions about what's going on here, if you continue to stay in this area just know that they have been ordered to shoot to kill us."

The warning set off arguments over its credibility—surely the police couldn't use lethal rounds on protesters? Then again, hadn't the President himself threatened such violence? Tony Clark, a twenty-eight-year-old construction worker from the Southside, had no doubt. "Did you not understand what Trump said?" he asked a group huddled around him. "He said, 'We're at war now.'"

Clark had been a mainstay on the front lines—a vibrant presence, vocally and sartorially. That day, he had on a camouflage-print down vest, no shirt, and his signature adornment: a quarter-size earring gauge bearing the words "NOT TODAY SATAN." A cross was tattooed under his right eye, and a diamond under his left. The previous night, I'd walked alongside him as he'd driven slowly up Thirty-first Street, through a neighborhood of wood-frame houses with front porches and fenced-in lawns, encouraging the protesters who had fled the Fifth Precinct. At times, he'd stopped his gray sedan and climbed onto its roof to jeer at pursuing police officers. As people had gathered around his car, he had told them, "I don't give a fuck if you're Vice Lord, P. Stone, Blood, Latin Kings. We all together." Clark then waved toward the police: "*They* the gangsters. *They* the mob." Later, he'd stuck a megaphone out his window and held his phone to it while it played the video of Floyd's death. "Y'all hear George crying?" Clark had shouted. "This is why we're out here!"

Clark had known Floyd, and had looked up to him as a mentor—"My big homie," he called him. They had often talked to each other at El Nuevo Rodeo, a club where Floyd had worked as a security guard. Clark told me that Floyd had urged him to be more involved in the neighborhood, and to more consciously exercise a positive influence on its youth: "He used to tell me to use my voice—that's what he always said. Having tattoos on my face, people get the wrong impression. That's what I loved about George. He told me, 'As soon as you start talking—that's when they're gonna see you.' People don't know George. I needed those talks he gave me."

Clark had seen Floyd being arrested from afar, without realizing who it was; only later, when the video was published online, did he learn what had happened to his friend. And the protests were personal in an additional way: in 2016, Clark's brother Travis died in a car crash after being pursued by police, south of Minneapolis. "I'm also doing this for him," Clark told me. When I asked him whether his brother would have demonstrated, he said, "Travis would've led the city."

As Clark and the other remaining protesters debated whether to violate the curfew, they were joined by marchers who had walked from Thirty-eighth and Chicago, three miles away, led by a group of California activists, including Joe Collins, an African-American congressional candidate from South Los Angeles. Collins and his colleagues directed the combined groups to follow them toward Interstate 35, which had been closed to traffic. Clark stepped into the march, as did Simone Hunter.

The city was deserted, and eerily silent, and as the protesters filled a wide four-lane avenue their chants resonated between sleek office towers and high-end apartment buildings. At the front, next to Collins, a marcher with a scarf tied around his face, his hat brim pulled low, and headphones in his ears nodded and privately sang along to The-Dream: "I'm feeling real black right now, real black right now. . . ."

Reaching an on-ramp, the marchers headed onto the empty interstate, where they found themselves suddenly trapped: in both directions, a few hundred feet away, a wall of police obstructed the highway. People were clearly nervous, but one of the organizers from California—a middle-aged man, anomalously clad in a pinstriped suit with gold cufflinks—assured everyone that as long as they remained peaceful no harm would come to them. "You do not have to worry—we are not here for violence," he yelled. "They're not gonna touch you. Trust me."

Clark shook his head, unconvinced. "It's about to get dangerous," he told the man. "Y'all are playin' with fire."

As the protesters linked arms, someone handed out protective helmets from a garbage bag. "No," the man in the pin-striped suit said, snatching a helmet away. "We're not here for that." The officers, however, soon started advancing toward the protesters, firing tear gas and forcing them up a dirt embankment leading to a Mobil gas station, where they regrouped, coughing and gagging. "Everybody remain calm!" Clark urged, his face dripping with milk. State troopers and sheriff's deputies, with long batons, encircled the gas station; behind them, Joe Collins, the congressional candidate, was on his knees in a patch of tall grass, being detained. Troopers in camouflage uniforms, with Kevlar helmets, flak jackets, gas masks, and assault rifles, paced the ranks. As a sense of alarm spread, the marcher who'd been singing to himself earlier raised his voice and sang aloud: " 'Cause everywhere there's a Chicago / The only way we're getting out of here is if we hit the lotto."

Simone Hunter walked up to a row of troopers and—just as she had outside the Third Precinct, when she was beaten and peppersprayed—boldly confronted them. I had trouble hearing what she was saying: there was a lot of racket, and after five days of tireless demonstration Hunter's voice was almost gone. Still, it was obvious that she was using what little of it remained to give the troopers hell. The organizer in the pin-striped suit did not appreciate this. "Ma'am, please, can you back up?" he asked Hunter, to no avail. "Ma'am, please. Please. Please. Please."

Eventually, several other protesters steered Hunter away. She was crying. As she continued to talk, undeterred, people gathered around her, listening. "My sister has kids who live here," she said of the city. "They walk up and down these streets every day. This is our home. This is our *home* right here. We have enemies on all sides—not just on the streets. I'm tired. I'm fucking tired. I've dealt with racist shit my whole fucking life. I'm tired." Then, clutching the front of her sweatshirt, Hunter told the protesters that she was wearing a stranger's clothes and had spent the previous night in a stranger's house—a white stranger's. Later, she explained to me that she had been walking through the neighborhoods near the Fifth Precinct, after the protest there, when an S.U.V. pulled up alongside her. Inside were white men brandishing assault rifles. One of them shouted, "Go home!" Hunter sprinted down alleys and side streets, eventually encountering two white women. They invited Hunter to their place, where she slept on an air mattress in their living room. "I had never experienced anything like that before," she said. "I was, like, This is the kind of stuff that gives you hope. It was just shocking."

At the Mobil, she told the protesters, "Your neighbors got your back!" And, pointing at the troopers: "*These* people don't got your back!"

Sometime later, the troopers and police began closing in, firing stun grenades and rubber bullets, even though we were already corralled, and no one had presented any threat. The deployment of force provoked intense panic. Several protesters wept and screamed. I remember feeling that the reaction was excessive, and thinking to myself, "Come on, they're not going to kill us." Later, while reviewing photographs and videos that I'd taken, I realized that many of the protesters who had stuck around up to this point were black, and that their experience of the incident was not identical to mine. Deep down, I was not afraid of the police; on an instinctive level, I understood that there was a limit to what they could do to me. If the legitimate fear that law-enforcement officers instilled in black protesters was fundamentally unknowable to me, so was the courage that people like Hunter had to summon when standing up to them.

As the officers converged on us, Deondre Moore, a twenty-five-year-old African-American from Houston—George Floyd's home town—held his arms high and pleaded, "Don't shoot! Let us leave!" A few minutes later, a rubber bullet struck Moore squarely in the chest. He fell to the ground, writhing in pain. "I thought it was a real bullet," he later told me. The protesters were commanded to lie on their stomachs with their hands behind their backs—the same position as the silhouette painted on the pavement outside the Cup Foods. As National Guard units arrived in armored Humvees, the state troopers began zip-tying people by their wrists and leading them away. The protesters were surrounded by more than a hundred officers, troopers, deputies, and soldiers—almost all of whom were white. Hunter seemed less frightened than other protesters. Producing a Sharpie pen from her bag of supplies, she started writing the phone number of a local bail fund on people's forearms. A young police officer, crouching behind his riot shield, trained his rubber-bullet gun on her and held it there. He looked terrified.

Ultimately, around a hundred and fifty protesters were loaded onto buses and taken to jail. (Journalists were not arrested, although state troopers punctured the tires of my rental car.) After being issued citations for breaking the curfew, the demonstrators were released early the next morning. The violation, a misdemeanor, is punishable by up to a thousand-dollar fine or three months' imprisonment. Back home, Hunter brought her citation outside, held a lighter to it, and watched it burn.

A LITTLE AFTER MIDNIGHT, WHILE HUNTER WAS STILL IN JAIL, I SWUNG by Thirty-eighth and Chicago, where people were still congregating. Tony Clark was there, having slipped away from the protest moments before it was besieged. There was a palpable edge: after the past week, residents were exhausted, their emotions raw and their nerves frayed. A global uprising had emanated from the intersection, but for many locals the stresses and pressures that had defined their world before Floyd's death were no less consuming than before.

A dispute led to a fight, which gained a centripetal energy that pulled in more and more bystanders until dozens of young people were involved, weapons were pulled out, and a dire outcome looked imminent. Then, as abruptly as it had started, it was over. A tall, imposing figure with a commanding voice appeared to have single-handedly stopped the brawl. When he ordered everyone to gather around him in the intersection, nobody argued.

He was Corey Moore, a forty-four-year-old North Carolina native who had moved to Minneapolis in 2000. A veteran combat medic, he served in the Army for eight and a half years, until he was honorably discharged, in 2013, after sustaining an injury in Iraq. Moore was no fan of the Minneapolis Police Department, and he later told me that Floyd's killing had been a tragic ending to an all-too-common scenario for black Northsiders and Southsiders: "His situation went from zero to sixty, like that. That's what it's like for people out here, if you get accused of anything." But he also believed in peaceful protest. He had been at the Third Precinct house on the first day of demonstrations, and had "got into it" with a group of "Antifa-type people" spitting at the police. When Moore told an especially strident white man that he "wasn't helping our situation," the man contemptuously asked Moore for his badge number.

Now, with everyone at Thirty-eighth and Chicago sitting around the circle of candles and flowers, Moore paced in front of them, dressing down those who'd been fighting. "That's what they want!" he shouted, like a drill sergeant. "I don't give a fuck who bumps into you, who talks about your mama—that's your brother! We are not gonna entertain them with us acting like animals! We are not animals!"

"That's what's up, big bro!" someone yelled out.

"I don't know any of y'all's names, but I swear on Jesus I will die for every last one of you!" Moore went on. "We gonna do this the right way."

"Keep that peace, big bro!"

Pointing at the spot where Floyd was killed, Moore said, "This man's life will not be in vain. This is going worldwide. The entire world is hearing us." Scanning the faces of his rapt young audience, Moore continued, "Every O.G. out here knows: we failed y'all. But it won't happen another night. We got your back, come hell or high water. . . . If you an O.G., put your hand up!" Tony Clark, who'd joined Moore inside the circle, raised a fist in the air. When Moore finished, Clark offered a prayer: "Lord Jesus, I pray that we can wake up and stand still with each other."

I left not long after this, but Moore later told me that he and about twenty other people had sat there until dawn. As the night deepened, people stood one at a time to express themselves and share their stories. "You started hearing individual voices," Moore recalled. "It was awesome." There were also interludes of silence. Squad cars periodically approached the barricades, but never crossed them. The intersection, Moore said, felt like an oasis.

For the most part, he moderated and listened. He did not talk about the time, in Alabama, when he was en route to a Basic Non-commissioned Officer Course and was pulled over by white police officers, because he fit the description of a suspect. He did not re-count how he was made to get out of his vehicle, at gunpoint, even though he was in uniform, with his military orders in hand and an Army duffelbag on the back seat. Nor did he explain how, after so many similar encounters, being stopped by the police scared him more than anything he'd experienced in Iraq—especially when one of his four children was in the car. Over there, he could at least defend himself.

But Moore did try to crystallize for the white people who were at Thirty-eighth and Chicago what it felt like to be black in America. He put it this way: "It's like you're standing in this tight line that you can't get out of. And everything that's happening up ahead is horrible as hell. And you know that eventually you're going to be next."

The following afternoon, Terrence Floyd made his visit to the intersection, sat by the painted silhouette, and asked the protesters to "do this another way." Although at that point the demonstrations in Minneapolis had already become peaceful, Terrence's appeal, like Moore's the night before, arrived precisely at the moment it was needed. The mood in Minneapolis had shifted from one of fervid insurrection to fatigue—a kind of dazed astonishment at all that had happened, and tentative uncertainty about what to do now.

IF PROTESTERS ON THE GROUND WERE SUDDENLY UNSURE HOW TO PROceed, activists and organizers, who until then had been largely absent from the streets, were not. Throughout the past few years, Minneapolis's black-activist network had coalesced around an overarching policy objective that, so far, had gained little traction: defunding and disbanding the city police department. Tony Williams, the Reclaim the Block member, said that many activists in Minneapolis came to promote this solution after seeing the ineffectiveness of reform measures—such as mandated body cameras for officers—that were adopted after the Jamar Clark and Philando Castile killings. During the Obama Administration, Minneapolis was one of six cities that participated in a progressive three-year federal program intended to "increase trust between communities and the criminal justice system," and, in 2017, Medaria Arradondo, one of the African-American officers who had sued the department for racial discrimination a decade earlier, was appointed chief of police. But Williams said that such steps had been "primarily about image rather than about substance"; eventually, he and his peers concluded that "this is really a cycle, and the reforms that are a part of the cycle don't actually change the math that leads to these killings in the first place." He continued, "If we don't want to just put a Band-Aid over the bullet wound, we need to fundamentally reassess how to do public safety."

Until two weeks ago, the view that no amount of reform could fix the police department—that its essential architecture threatened people of color—was little discussed outside of activist and academic circles. "But we've seen an enormous groundswell of support since the murder of George Floyd," Williams said. As well-coördinated demonstrations have supplanted the spontaneous uprising of late May, pointed calls to disband the Minneapolis Police Department have eclipsed less programmatic and more emotional demands for justice. Notably, the majority of the people at "abolish the police" events have been white, and few of the front-line protesters I spent time with attended them.

On June 6th, Black Visions Collective, a group aligned with Reclaim the Block, organized a march that ended in Northeast Minneapolis, outside Mayor Frey's apartment. Frey, a white, thirty-eight-year-old Democrat and a civil-rights lawyer, emerged from his home and navigated the crowds to where Kandace Montgomery, the director of Black Visions Collective, stood in the bed of a truck. If Frey had planned on delivering an apologia, he was in for a surprise. Looming over the mayor, Montgomery asked into her microphone, "Yes or no—will you commit to defunding the Minneapolis Police Department?"

When, after some vacillation, Frey responded, "I do not support the full abolition of the police department," Montgomery yelled at him to "get the fuck out of here." Frey walked away, through a sea of middle fingers, shouted insults, and chants of "Shame!"

The next day, nine members of the Minneapolis City Council— a veto-proof majority—announced their pledge to dismantle the police department. The president of the council declared, "Our efforts at incremental reform have failed. Period." The historic decision has launched the city of Minneapolis into uncharted territory, and it remains unclear what, exactly, will happen if the department is indeed dissolved. (Frey remains opposed.) "We're all figuring it out in real time," Tony Williams, who is involved in discussions with the council, said. "There are a lot of questions. This has never been done before." But, Williams emphasized, "we can't build a new model from scratch without engaging with the community about what we want that to look like—that's how we ended up in this mess."

Just how broadly the community supports disbanding the police is, however, also unknown. Evidence is anecdotal. There has been no referendum, or even recent polling. On the evening of June 7th, I was at Thirty-eighth and Chicago, sitting with Tony Clark across from the Cup Foods, when reports of the council's pledge appeared on my phone. Clark looked taken aback when I told him the news. "Like, no police?" he said. It was the first time he'd heard of the idea.

Clark turned to his friend, a twenty-seven-year-old named Lavish James, who'd grown up three blocks away. "Bro, you want the cops to go home?"

James had been among the protesters arrested near the stadium, along with Hunter, and he was not shy about denouncing the racism and abusiveness of the Minneapolis police. Yet he responded without hesitation: "No. If the cops go home, we're fucking turning into Hamas."

Corey Moore is of a similar mind. Like James, he believes that violent, armed bad actors would inevitably dominate and exploit any environment free of law enforcement. It's not the institution that should be done away with, he said, but, rather, "the mentality that it's us against them."

Williams and his fellow-activists counter that Minneapolis is already dominated by violent, armed bad actors: the police.

THE DAY AFTER CORNELL GRIFFIN WAS SHOT IN THE NECK WITH A RUB-ber bullet, he went with his wife and several friends to the Third Precinct house, where the protests in Minneapolis had begun. Huge slabs of concrete sealed the entrance to the partially incinerated station. People were boarding up the Target across the street and rolling white paint over graffiti. In a corner of the parking lot, Griffin and his friends constructed a small stage from two-by-fours and plywood. A crowd gathered. Griffin mounted the structure and recited a credo: "We've decided we are not divided, because we've decided to take a stand. I don't care who you are, or your skin color, if you're with me today you're my sister or my brother."

He's been out there each day since. When people come, he asks them to repeat his refrain. Then they add their signature to the stage, which is now covered with hundreds of names. "They're held accountable from that point on," Griffin told me.

Tony Clark is considering travelling to other cities to tell protesters about what took place in Minneapolis. He is worried that the energy of the uprising is dissipating, and that the global attention it briefly attracted has already drifted elsewhere. On June 12th, he told me, "I want to keep up the fight. I want to keep the fire burning. I feel like this was just Round One."

Several weeks have passed since Floyd was killed. Simone Hunter still goes to Thirty-eighth and Chicago every day. The intersection has become a second home for her—or a first home. Recently, she joined a volunteer security detail, and now works nights, standing guard at one of the barricades from evening until sunrise. She instantly took to the role, tossing out journalists and outside visitors after dark. One morning, at the end of her shift, I gave her a ride to her friend's house. She looked exhausted. Her voice was still raw from chanting and yelling at police. Her fingers were blistered from grabbing a tear-gas cannister and throwing it at state troopers.

"I'm so tired," she said.

I asked her if she would be at the vigil site later.

"Hell yeah," Hunter said. "I'll probably walk back in an hour or two."

THE RIOT REPORT

JILL LEPORE

June 22, 2020

On February 14, 1965, back from a trip to Los Angeles, and a week before he was killed in New York, Malcolm X gave a speech in Detroit. "Brothers and sisters, let me tell you, I spend my time out there in the street with people, all kind of people, listening to what they have to say," he said. "And they're dissatisfied, they're disillusioned, they're fed up, they're getting to the point of frustration where they are beginning to feel: What do they have to lose?"

That summer, President Lyndon B. Johnson signed the Voting Rights Act. In a ceremony at the Capitol Rotunda attended by Martin Luther King, Jr., Johnson invoked the arrival of enslaved Africans in Jamestown, in 1619: "They came in darkness and they came in chains. And today we strike away the last major shackles of those fierce and ancient bonds." Five days later, Watts was swept by violence and flames, following a protest against police brutality. The authorities eventually arrested nearly four thousand people; thirty-four people died. "How is it possible, after all we've accomplished?" Johnson asked. "How could it be? Is the world topsy-turvy?"

Two years later, after thousands of police officers and National Guard troops blocked off fourteen square miles of Newark and nearly five thousand troops from the 82nd and the 101st Airborne were deployed to Detroit, where seven thousand people were arrested, Johnson convened a National Advisory Commission on Civil Disorders, chaired by Illinois's governor, Otto Kerner, Jr., and charged it with answering three questions: "What happened? Why did it happen? What can be done to prevent it from happening again and again?" Johnson wanted to know why black people were still protesting, after Congress had finally passed landmark legislation, not only the Voting Rights Act but also the Civil Rights Act of 1964, and a raft of anti-poverty programs. Or maybe he really didn't want to know why. When the Kerner Commission submitted its report, the President refused to acknowledge it.

There's a limit to the relevance of the so-called race riots of the nineteen-sixties to the protests of the moment. But the tragedy is: they're not irrelevant. Nor is the history that came before. The language changes, from "insurrection" to "uprising" to the bureaucratic "civil disorder," terms used to describe everything from organized resistance to mayhem. But, nearly always, they leave a bloody trail in the historical record, in the form of government reports. The Kerner Report followed centuries of official and generally hysterical government inquiries into black rebellion, from the unhinged "A Journal of the proceedings in the Detection of the Conspiracy formed by some White People, in conjunction with Negro and other Slaves, for burning the City of New-York in America, and murdering the Inhabitants," in 1744, to the largely fabricated "Official Report of the Trials of Sundry Negroes, charged with an attempt to raise an insurrection in the state of South-Carolina," in 1822. The white editor of the as-told-to (and highly dubious) "The Confessions of Nat Turner, the Leader of the Late Insurrection in Southampton, Va. . . . also, An Authentic Account of the Whole Insurrection, with Lists of the Whites Who Were Murdered . . . ," in 1831, wrote, "Public curiosity has been on the stretch to understand the origin and progress of this dreadful conspiracy, and the motives which influences its diabolical actors." What happened? Why did it happen? What can be done to prevent it from happening again and again?

AFTER RECONSTRUCTION, IDA B. WELLS, IN "SOUTHERN HORRORS: LYNCH Law in All Its Phases," which appeared in 1892, turned the genre on its head, offering a report on white mobs attacking black men, a litany of lynchings. "Somebody must show that the Afro-American race is more sinned against than sinning, and it seems to have fallen upon me to do so," Wells wrote in the book's preface, after a mob burned the offices of her newspaper, the *Free Speech*. White mob violence against black people and their homes and businesses was the far more common variety of race riot, from the first rising of the K.K.K., after the Civil War, through the second, in 1915. And so the earliest twentieth-century commissions charged with investigating "race riots" reported on the riots of white mobs, beginning with the massacre in East St. Louis, Illinois, in 1917, in which, following labor unrest, as many as three thousand white men roamed the city, attacking, killing, and lynching black people, and burning their homes. Wells wrote that as many as a hundred and fifty men were killed, while police officers and National Guardsmen either looked on or joined in. Similar riots took place in 1919, in twenty-six cities, and the governor of Illinois appointed an interracial commission to investigate. "This is a tribunal constituted to get the facts and interpret them and to find a way out," he said.

The Chicago Commission on Race Relations, composed of six whites and six blacks, who engaged the work of as many as twenty-two whites and fifteen blacks, heard nearly two hundred witnesses, and, in 1922, published a seven-hundred-page report, with photographs, maps, and color plates: "The Negro in Chicago: A Study of Race Relations and a Race Riot." It paid particular attention to racial antipathy: "Many white Americans, while technically recognizing Negroes as citizens, cannot bring themselves to feel that they should participate in government as freely as other citizens." Much of the report traces how the Great Migration brought large numbers of blacks from the Jim Crow South to Chicago, where they faced discrimination in housing and employment, and persecution at the hands of local police and the criminal-justice system:

The testimony of court officials before the Commission and its investigations indicate that Negroes are more commonly arrested, subjected to police identification, and convicted than white offenders, that on similar evidence they are generally held and convicted on more serious charges, and that they are given longer sentences. . . . These practices and tendencies are not only unfair to Negroes, but weaken the machinery of justice and, when taken with the greater inability of Negroes to pay fines in addition to or in lieu of terms in jail, produce misleading statistics of Negro crime.

Very little came of the report. In 1935, following riots in Harlem, yet another hardworking commission weighed in:

This sudden breach of the public order was the result of a highly emotional situation among the colored people of Harlem, due in large part to the nervous strain of years of unemployment and insecurity. To this must be added their deep sense of wrong through discrimination against their employment in stores which live chiefly upon their purchases, discrimination against them in the school system and by the police, and all the evils due to dreadful overcrowding, unfair rentals and inadequate institutional care. It is probable that their justifiable pent-up feeling, that they were and are the victims of gross injustice and prejudice, would sooner or later have brought about an explosion.

Who was to blame?

The blame belongs to a society that tolerates inadequate and often wretched housing, inadequate

THE RIOT REPORT   765

and inefficient schools and other public facilities,
unemployment, unduly high rents, the lack of recreation
grounds, discrimination in industry and public utilities
against colored people, brutality and lack of courtesy of
the police.

In Detroit in 1943, after a riot left twenty-five blacks and nine
whites dead and led to the arrest of nearly two thousand people,
Michigan's governor appointed the commissioner of police and
the attorney general to a panel that concluded, without conducting
much of an investigation, that responsibility for the riots lay with
black leaders, and defended the police, whom many had blamed for
the violence. A separate, independent commission, led by Thurgood Marshall, then chief counsel for the N.A.A.C.P., conducted
interviews, hired private detectives, and produced a report titled
"The Gestapo in Detroit." The group called for a grand jury, arguing that "much of the blood spilled in the Detroit riot is on the
hands of the Detroit police department." No further investigation
took place, and no material reforms were implemented.

That's what usually happens. In a 1977 study, "Commission
Politics: The Processing of Racial Crisis in America," Michael Lipsky and David J. Olson reported that, between 1917 and 1943, at
least twenty-one commissions were appointed to investigate race
riots, and, however sincerely their members might have been interested in structural change, none of the commissions led to any. The
point of a race-riot commission, Lipsky and Olson argue, is for
the government that appoints it to appear to be doing something,
while actually doing nothing.

THE CONVULSIONS THAT LED TO THE KERNER COMMISSION BEGAN IN
Los Angeles, in 1965. Between 1960 and 1964, the nation enjoyed
unrivalled prosperity, but in Watts, among the poorest neighborhoods of L.A., one in three men had no work. In Los Angeles, as

Mike Davis and Jon Wiener write in a new book, "Set the Night on Fire: L.A. in the Sixties," "the LAPD operated the nation's most successful negative employment scheme." Police stopped black men for little or no reason, and, if they talked back, they got arrested; left with an arrest record, they became unemployable.

On August 11, 1965, a Wednesday, a motorcycle cop pulled over a car with a driver and a passenger, two brothers, Ronald and Marquette Frye, about a block from their house, near 116th Street. Their mother, Rena, all of five feet tall, came over. Marquette resisted handcuffs—he would strike those fierce and ancient shackles. The motorcycle cop called for backup; twenty-six police vehicles raced to the scene, sirens screaming. "Does it take all these people to arrest three people?" an onlooker asked. When Rena Frye tried to stop the police from beating her sons with billy clubs, they pinned her to the hood of a patrol car and, after a crowd had gathered, arrested another of her sons and dragged away a woman in a stranglehold. "Goddam! They'd never treat a white woman like that!" someone called out. The crowd protested, and grew, and protested, and grew. What came to be known as the Watts riot lasted for six days and spread across nearly fifty square miles. On Friday night, a man said:

> I was standing in a phone booth watching. A little
> kid came by carrying a lamp he had taken out of a store.
> Maybe he was about twelve. He was with his mother. I
> remember him saying: "Don't run Mommy. They said we
> could take the stuff because they're going to burn the store
> anyway." Then, suddenly, about five police cars stopped.
> There were about 20 cops in them and they all got out.
> One came up to the booth I was standing in. The cop hit
> me on the leg with his club. "Get out of here, nigger,"
> he yelled at me. I got out of the booth. Another cop ran
> up to the boy and hit him in the head with the butt of a

shotgun. The kid dropped like a stone. The lamp crashed on the sidewalk. I ran out of the phone booth and grabbed the cop by the arm. I was trying to stop him from beating the boy. Two cops jumped on my back. Others struck the boy with their clubs. They beat that little kid's face to a bloody pulp. His mother and some others took him away. That's when I thought, white people are animals.

Johnson could barely speak about what was happening in Watts. An aide said, "He refused to look at the cable from Los Angeles describing the situation. He refused to take the calls from the generals who were requesting government planes to fly in the National Guard. . . . We needed decisions from him. But he simply wouldn't respond."

The same Friday, the National Guard arrived. "More Americans died fighting in Watts Saturday night than in Vietnam that day," an observer wrote. On Sunday, fifteen police officers fired eleven shotgun rounds into Aubrey Griffith, inside his own house, where he and his wife had been in bed while their son, on leave from the Air Force, was watching TV. The officers banged on the door, and Griffith told his wife to call the police. An inquest ruled his death—and every other death at the hands of the National Guard or the police during the days of protest—a justifiable homicide.

Martin Luther King, Jr., arrived on Tuesday. "All we want is jobs," a man said to him, at a community meeting in Watts. "We get jobs, we don't bother nobody. We don't get no jobs, we'll tear up Los Angeles, period." Later, King recalled that one man told him, "We won!" King had replied, "What do you mean, 'We won'? Thirty-some people dead, all but two are Negroes. You've destroyed your own. What do you mean, 'We won'?" The man said, "We made them pay attention to us."

Paying attention, at that point, only ever really took this form: the governor appointed a commission, this time headed by John

A. McCone, a lavishly wealthy and well-connected California industrialist who, in 1961, had been made director of the C.I.A. by President Kennedy but had resigned in April, 1965, in part because he objected to Johnson's reluctance to engage in a wider war in Vietnam. The McCone Commission report, titled "Violence in the City," celebrated the City of Angels: "A Negro in Los Angeles has long been able to sit where he wants in a bus or a movie house, to shop where he wishes, to vote, and to use public facilities without discrimination. The opportunity to succeed is probably unequaled in any other major American city." It called for the creation of fifty thousand new jobs, but, first, "attitudinal training." It blamed the riots on outside agitators and civil-rights activists: "Although the Commission received much thoughtful and constructive testimony from Negro witnesses, we also heard statements of the most extreme and emotional nature. For the most part our study fails to support—and indeed the evidence disproves—most of the statements made by the extremists." Fundamental to the McCone thesis was the claim that peaceful demonstrations produce violent riots, and should therefore be discouraged. In a devastating rebuttal, Bayard Rustin laid this argument to waste:

> It would be hard to frame a more insidiously equivocal
> statement of the Negro grievance concerning law
> enforcement during a period that included the release of
> the suspects in the murder of the three civil-rights workers
> in Mississippi, the failure to obtain convictions against
> the suspected murderers of Medgar Evers and Mrs. Violet
> Liuzzo . . . and the police violence in Selma, Alabama. . . .
> And surely it would have been more to the point to
> mention that throughout the nation Negro demonstrations
> have almost invariably been non-violent, and that the
> major influence on the Negro community of the civil-rights
> movement has been the strategy of discipline and dignity.

By the summer of 1967, when protests against police brutality had led to riots in Newark and Detroit, Johnson was facing a conservative backlash against his Great Society programs, and especially against the Fair Housing Act, which was introduced in Congress in 1966. He'd also been trying to gain passage of a Rat Extermination Act, to get rid of urban infestations; Republicans called it the Civil Rats Bill. Johnson had long since lost the right; now he was losing the left. By April, King had come out against the war in Vietnam. Beleaguered and defensive, Johnson launched an "Optimism Campaign," in an effort to convince the public that the U.S. was winning the war in Vietnam. George Romney, the Republican governor of Michigan, who was expected to run against Johnson in 1968, asked for federal troops to be sent to Detroit, which would be the first time since F.D.R. sent them in 1943. Johnson wavered. "I'm concerned about the charge that we cannot kill enough people in Vietnam so we go out and shoot civilians in Detroit," he said. In the end, he decided to authorize the troops, and to blame Romney, announcing, on television, that there was "undisputed evidence that Governor Romney of Michigan and the local officials in Detroit have been unable to bring the situation under control." Twenty-seven hundred Army paratroopers were deployed to Detroit, with Huey helicopters that most Americans had seen only in TV coverage of the war in Vietnam.

On July 27, 1967, Johnson gave a televised speech on "civil disorders," announcing his decision to form a national commission to investigate race riots. Protests had taken place, and turned violent, in more than a hundred and fifty cities that summer, and they were being televised. Were they part of a conspiracy? Johnson suspected so, even though his advisers told him that he was wrong. "I don't want to foreclose the conspiracy theory now," he said. "Keep that door open."

Johnson loved Presidential commissions: people called him, not affectionately, "the great commissioner." In the first decade after the Second World War, U.S. Presidents appointed an average of one and a half commissions a year. Johnson appointed twenty. In "Separate and Unequal: The Kerner Commission and the Unraveling of American Liberalism" (2018), Steven M. Gillon observes that "commissions became a convenient way for presidents to fill the gap between what they could deliver and what was expected of them." To his new commission, Johnson appointed a Noah's Ark of commissioners, two by two: two congressmen, one Republican, one Democrat; one business leader, one labor leader. Roy Wilkins, the executive director of the N.A.A.C.P., was, with Edward Brooke, a Republican senator from Massachusetts, one of two African-Americans. The commission included no political radicals, no protesters, and no young people. The President expected the commission to defend his legislative accomplishments and agenda, and to endorse his decision to send the National Guard to Detroit. When he called Fred Harris, the thirty-six-year-old Oklahoma senator, to discuss the appointment, he told Harris to remember that he was a "Johnson man." Otherwise, Johnson said, "I'll take out my pocket knife and cut your peter off." Nearly as soon as he convened the commission, Johnson regretted it, and pulled its funding.

OTTO KERNER, BORN IN CHICAGO IN 1908, WENT TO BROWN AND THEN Northwestern, for law school, and, in the nineteen-thirties and into the Second World War, served in the Illinois National Guard, for twenty years, retiring in 1954 with the rank of major general. Under his leadership, as Bill Barnhart and Gene Schlickman report in their biography, the Illinois guard had the nation's highest percentage of African-Americans. A former district attorney, later elected to a county judgeship, Kerner had a reputation for strict personal integrity, earning him the nickname Mr. Clean. He was elected governor of Illinois in 1960, and it is possible that his coattails delivered the state to John F. Kennedy, in one of the closest

Presidential races in American history. He had a strong record on civil rights, and was an adamant supporter of fair housing, declaring, in 1968, "Civil disorders will still be the order of the day unless we create a society of equal justice."

After Kerner got the call from Johnson, he announced, "Tomorrow, I go to Washington to help organize this group of citizens for the saddest mission that any of us in our careers have been asked to pursue—why one American assaults another, why violence is inflicted on people of our cities, why the march to an ideal America has been interrupted by bloodshed and destruction. We are being asked, in a broad sense, to probe into the soul of America."

Kerner wanted open hearings. "My concern all the time about this commission has been that at the conclusion our greatest problem is going to be to educate the whites, rather than the Negro," he said. Kerner did not prevail on this point. J. Edgar Hoover testified on the first day, to say that the F.B.I. had found no evidence of a conspiracy behind the riots, and that he thought one good remedy for violence would be better gun laws. "You have to license your dog," he said. Why not your gun? Martin Luther King, Jr., told the commission, "People who are completely devoid of hope don't riot."

Maybe the most painful testimony came from Kenneth B. Clark, the African-American psychologist, at the City College of New York, whose research on inequality had been pivotal to the Supreme Court's decision in Brown v. Board of Education. He told the commission:

> I read that report . . . of the 1919 riot in Chicago, and
> it is as if I were reading the report of the investigating
> committee on the Harlem riot of '35, the report of the
> investigating committee on the Harlem riot of '43,
> the report of the McCone Commission on the Watts
> riot. I must again in candor say to you members of this
> Commission—it is a kind of Alice in Wonderland—with

the same moving picture re-shown over and over again,
the same analysis, the same recommendations, and the
same inaction.

The historical trail is blood spilled in a deeply rutted road.

JOHN V. LINDSAY, THE HANDSOME LIBERAL MAYOR OF NEW YORK
who served as the vice-chair of the commission, got most of the
media attention. But Kerner did his work. When the commission
travelled, Kerner went out on the street to talk to people. He went
for a walk in Newark, and stopped to speak to a group around the
corner from Prince Street. They told him they had three concerns:
police brutality, unemployment, and the lack of a relocation program for displaced workers. One man told the Governor that he
hadn't had a job in eight years.

After months of hearings and meetings, the commission began
assembling its report. Kerner wanted it to be moving, and beautifully written. John Hersey was asked to write it, perhaps in the style
of "Hiroshima"; Hersey said no. (Instead, much of the report was
drafted by the commission's executive director, David Ginsburg,
who later helped write Hubert Humphrey's campaign platform.)
Toward the end of the commission's deliberations, Roy Wilkins offered emotional personal testimony that greatly informed a draft by
Lindsay, describing "two societies, one black, one white." Another
draft contained a passage that was later stricken: "Past efforts have
not carried the commitment, will or resources needed to eliminate
the attitudes and practices that have maintained racism as a major
force in our society. Only the dedication of every citizen can generate a single American identity and a single American community." Every word of the report was read aloud, and every word was
unanimously agreed on. The final draft did include this passage:
"Race prejudice has shaped our history decisively; it now threatens
to affect our future. White racism is essentially responsible for the

explosive mixture which has been accumulating in our cities since the end of World War II." In the final report, as the historian Julian Zelizer writes in an introduction to a 2016 edition, "no institution received more scrutiny than the police." That's been true of every one of these reports since 1917.

Johnson, when he got the report, was so mad that he refused to sign the letters thanking the commissioners for their service. "I'd be a hypocrite," he said. "Just file them . . . or get rid of them."

THE KERNER REPORT WAS PUBLISHED ON MARCH 1, 1968, BUT FIRST IT was leaked (probably by Ginsburg) to the Washington *Post*, which ran a story with the headline "CHIEF BLAME FOR RIOTS PUT ON WHITE RACISM." It became an overnight best-seller. It sold more copies than the Warren Commission report, three-quarters of a million copies in the first two weeks alone. Released in a paperback edition by Bantam, it was said to be the fastest-selling book since "Valley of the Dolls."

Civil-rights activists, expecting a whitewash, were stunned. "It's the first time whites have said, 'We're racists,'" the head of CORE declared. Republicans rejected it. "One of the major weaknesses of the President's commission is that it, in effect, blames everybody for the riots except the perpetrators of the riots," Nixon said from the campaign trail. "I think this talk . . . tends to divide people, to build a wall in between people." Conservatives deemed it absurd. "What caused the riots," William F. Buckley, Jr., wrote, "isn't segregation or poverty or frustration. What caused them is a psychological disorder which is tearing at the ethos of our society as a result of boredom, self-hatred, and the arrogant contention that all our shortcomings are the result of other people's aggressions upon us."

Johnson came up with his own explanation for what had happened in America during his Presidency: "I've moved the Negro from D+ to C-. He's still nowhere. He knows it. And that's why he's out in the streets. Hell, I'd be there, too." In 1969, Harry

McPherson, Johnson's chief speechwriter, tried to explain what had so bothered Johnson about the Kerner Report. "It hurt his pride," McPherson said, because it made it clear that Johnson had not, somehow, saved the Negro. But there was a bigger, sounder reason, he believed: "The only thing that held any hope for the Negro was the continuation of the coalition between labor, Negroes, intellectuals, . . . big city bosses and political machines and some of the urban poor. . . . In other words, it required keeping the Polacks who work on the line at River Rouge in the ball park and supporting Walter Reuther and the government as they try to spend money on blacks." Middle-class whites didn't give a damn, he thought, but blacks needed poor and working-class whites on their side. "Then a Presidential commission is formed and goes out and comes back, and what does it say? Who's responsible for the riots? 'The other members of the coalition. They did it. Those racists.' And thereupon, the coalition says . . . 'we'll go out and find ourselves a guy like George Wallace, or Richard Nixon.'"

That spring, Martin Luther King, Jr., was killed, and then Robert F. Kennedy. In July, five months after the release of the report, Kerner wrote his own reflections, looking back at the response to the maelstrom that had followed King's assassination, and arguing against the militarization of the police: "Armored vehicles, automatic weapons and armor-piercing machine guns are for use against an enemy, and not a lawbreaker. . . . If you come out with a show of force, you in a sense challenge the other side to meet you. Force begets force."

Still, Johnson fulfilled Kerner's wish to be appointed to the federal bench. During Kerner's confirmation hearings, he was questioned by Strom Thurmond about the conclusions of the report that bore his name:

Thurmond: Why do you say "white racism" caused these riots?

Kerner: I beg your pardon.

Thurmond: Why do you want to blame the white people . . . for this trouble?

Kerner: Because we say this has developed over a period of time, and the people in the Negro ghettos indicated that the rebellion was against the white establishment. . . .

Thurmond: . . . What does that term mean? What did you think it meant when you put it in this report or approved of it?

Kerner: I thought it meant this—that over a period of years the Negro was kept within a certain area economically and geographically and he was not allowed to come out of it.

In 1971, Kerner became involved in a scandal connected with his ownership of stock in a racetrack; he was eventually charged and convicted of mail fraud. Sentenced to three years in prison, Kerner went to the Federal Correctional Institution, a minimum-security prison in Fayette County, Kentucky, on July 29, 1974, two weeks before Nixon resigned. He insisted that his conviction was one of Nixon's "dirty tricks." "I have reason to believe I was one of the victims of this overall plan," he wrote. He suspected Nixon of punishing him for his role in Kennedy's victory in 1960. In his cell, Kerner kept a journal. "So frequently I sit here alone," he wrote, thinking thoughts that inmates have thought since the beginning of prisons:

> I wonder of what use is our prison system—as I have
> often wondered when I was seeking an alternative to this
> inhuman manner of restraining those who have violated
> the law. The waste of man power—both by the restrainers
> and the one restrained. Removing the individual from
> the outside world really accomplishes nothing of a

positive nature. The restraint builds up frustrations and a smothering of the will. It kills motivation and completely removes decision ability.

With an ailing heart and what was soon discovered to be lung cancer, Kerner was paroled after serving seven months. He spent what time he had left urging prison reform. He died in 1976. Not long before his death, asked about the Kerner Report, he said, "The basis for the report, I think, is as valid today as the day we sent it to the government printing office."

ON JUNE 1ST, IN WASHINGTON, D.C., POLICE IN RIOT GEAR CLEARED LA-fayette Square of peaceful protesters, by force. ("Take off the riot gear, I don't see no riot here," protesters chanted.) The purpose was to allow President Trump to stride to St. John's Church, accompanied by the Attorney General and the chairman of the Joint Chiefs of Staff, and be photographed holding a Bible. The next day, Ohio's Republican senator, Rob Portman, called for a national commission on race relations. "It would not be a commission to restate the problem but to focus on solutions and send a strong moral message that America must live up to the ideal that God created all of us as equal," Portman said. He suggested that it might be co-chaired by the former Presidents Barack Obama and George W. Bush.

The United States does not need one more commission, or one more report. A strong moral message? That message is being delivered by protesters every day, on street after street after street across the nation. *Stop killing us.* One day, these reports will lie archived, forgotten, irrelevant. Meanwhile, they pile up, an indictment, the stacked evidence of inertia. In the summer of 1968, the civil-rights leader Whitney Young published an essay titled "The Report That Died," writing, "The report is still there, it still reads well, but practically nothing is being done to follow its recommendations." It was as it had ever been. It is time for it to be something else.

HOW DO WE CHANGE AMERICA?

KEEANGA-YAMAHTTA TAYLOR

June 8, 2020

The national uprising in response to the brutal murder of George Floyd, a forty-six-year-old black man, by four Minneapolis police officers, has been met with shock, elation, concern, fear, and gestures of solidarity. Its sheer scale has been surprising. Across the United States, in cities large and small, streets have filled with young, multiracial crowds who have had enough. In the largest uprisings since the Los Angeles rebellion of 1992, anger and bitterness at racist and unrestrained police violence, abuse, and even murder have finally spilled over in every corner of the United States.

More than seventeen thousand National Guard troops have been deployed—more soldiers than are currently occupying Iraq and Afghanistan—to put down the rebellion. More than ten thousand people have been arrested; more than twelve people, mostly African-American men, have been killed. Curfews were imposed in at least thirty cities, including New York, Chicago, Philadelphia, Omaha, and Sioux City. Solidarity demonstrations have been organized from Accra to Dublin—in Berlin, Paris, London, and beyond. And, most surprisingly, two weeks after Floyd's death, the protests have not ended. Last Saturday saw the largest protests so far, as tens of thousands of people gathered on the National Mall and marched down the streets of Brooklyn and Philadelphia.

The relentless fury and pace of rebellion has forced states to shrug off their stumbling efforts to subdue the novel coronavirus that continues to sicken thousands in the United States. State leaders have been much more adept in calling up the National Guard and coördinating police actions to confront marchers than they were in any of their efforts to curtail the virus. In a show of both cowardice and authoritarianism, Donald Trump threatened to call up the U.S. military to occupy American cities. "Crisis" does not begin to describe the political maelstrom that has been unleashed.

There have been planned demonstrations, and there have also been violent and explosive outbursts that can only be described as a revolt or an uprising. Riots are not only the voice of the unheard, as Dr. Martin Luther King, Jr., famously said; they are the rowdy entry of the oppressed into the political realm. They become a stage of political theatre where joy, revulsion, sadness, anger, and excitement clash wildly in a cathartic dance. They are a festival of the oppressed.

For once in their lives, many of the participants can be seen, heard, and felt in public. People are pulled from the margins into a powerful force that can no longer be ignored, beaten, or easily discarded. Offering the first tastes of real freedom, when the police are for once afraid of the crowd, the riot can be destructive, unruly, violent, and unpredictable. But within that contradictory tangle emerge demands and aspirations for a society different from the one in which we live. Not only do the rebels express their own dismay but they also showcase our entire social dilemma. As King said, of the uprisings in the late nineteen-sixties, "I am not sad that Black Americans are rebelling; this was not only inevitable but eminently desirable. Without this magnificent ferment among Negroes, the old evasions and procrastinations would have continued indefinitely. Black men have slammed the door shut on a past of deadening passivity. Except for the Reconstruction years, they have never in their long history on American soil struggled with such creativity and courage for their freedom. These are our bright years of emergence; though they are painful ones, they cannot be avoided."

King continued, "The black revolution is much more than a struggle for the rights of Negroes. It is forcing America to face all its interrelated flaws—racism, poverty, militarism, and materialism. It is exposing the evils that are rooted deeply in the whole structure of our society. It reveals systemic rather than superficial flaws and suggests that radical reconstruction of society itself is the real issue to be faced."

By now, it should be clear what the demands of young black people are: an end to racism, police abuse, and violence; and the right to be free of the economic coercion of poverty and inequality.

THE QUESTION IS: HOW DO WE CHANGE THIS COUNTRY? IT'S NOT A new question; for African-Americans, it's a question as old as the nation itself. A large part of the reason that rebels swell the streets with clenched fists and expressive eyes is the refusal or inability of this society to engage that question in a satisfying way. Instead, those asking the question are patronized with sweet-sounding speeches, made with alliterative apologia, often interspersed with recitations about the meaning of America, and ultimately in defense of the status quo. There is a palpable poverty of intellect, a lack of imagination, and a banality of ideas pervading mainstream politics today. Old and failed propositions are recycled, but proclaimed as new, reviving cynicism and dismay.

Take the recent comments of the former President Barack Obama. On Twitter, Obama counselled that "Real change requires protest to highlight a problem, and politics to implement practical solutions and laws." He continued to say that "there are specific evidence-based reforms that would build trust, save lives, and lead to a decrease in crime, too," including the policy proposals of his Task Force on 21st Century Policing, convened in 2015. Such a simple, plain-stated plan fails to answer the most basic question: Why do police reforms continue to fail? African-Americans have been demonstrating against police abuse and violence since the Chicago riots of 1919. The first riot directly in response to police abuse occurred in 1935, in Harlem. In 1951, a contingent of African-American activists, armed with a petition titled "We Charge Genocide," tried to persuade the United Nations to decry the U.S. government's murder of black people. Their petition read:

> Once the classic method of lynching was the rope.
> Now it is the policeman's bullet. To many an American
> the police are the government, certainly its most visible
> representative. We submit that the evidence suggests that
> the killing of Negroes has become police policy in the
> United States and that police policy is the most practical
> expression of government policy.

It has been the lack of response, and a lack of "practical solutions" to beatings, harassment, and murder, that has led people into the streets, to challenge the typical dominance of police in black communities.

Many have compared the national revolt today to the urban rebellions of the nineteen-sixties, but it is more immediately shaped by the Los Angeles rebellion of 1992 and the protests it unleashed across the country. The 1992 uprising grew out of the frustrated mix of growing poverty, violence generated by the drug war, and widening unemployment. By 1992, official black unemployment had reached a high of fourteen per cent, more than double that of white Americans. In South Central Los Angeles, where the uprising took hold, more than half of people over the age of sixteen were unemployed or out of the labor force. A combination of police brutality and state-sanctioned accommodation of violence against a black child ultimately lit the fuse.

We remember that, on March 3, 1991, Rodney King, a black motorist, was beaten by four L.A. police officers by the side of the freeway. But it is also true that, two weeks later, a fifteen-year-old black girl, Latasha Harlins, was shot in the head by a convenience-store owner, Soon Ja Du, after a confrontation about whether Harlins intended to pay for a bottle of orange juice. A jury found Du guilty of manslaughter and recommended the maximum sentence, but the judge in the case disagreed and sentenced Du to five years probation, community service, and a five-hundred-dollar fine. The L.A. rebellion began on April 29, 1992, when the officers who had beaten King were unexpectedly acquitted, but it was also fuelled by the fact that, a week earlier, an appeals court had upheld the lesser sentence for Du.

In the immediate aftermath of the verdict, a multiracial throng of protesters gathered outside the headquarters of the Los Angeles Police Department, chanting, "No justice, no peace!" and "Guilty!" As people began to gather in South Central, the police arrived and attempted to arrest them, before realizing that they were over-matched and deserting the scene. At one point, the L.A. *Times* recounted, at Seventy-first and Normandie streets, two hundred people "lined the intersection, many with raised fists. Chunks of asphalt and concrete were thrown at cars. Some yelled, 'It's a black thing.' Others shouted, 'This is for Rodney King.'" By the end of the day, more than three hundred fires burned across the city, at police headquarters and city hall, downtown, and in the white neighborhoods of Fairfax and Westwood. In Atlanta, hundreds of black young people chanted "Rodney King" as they smashed through store windows in the business district of the city. In Northern California, seven hundred students from Berkeley High School walked out of their classes in protest. In a short span of five days, the L.A. uprising emerged as the largest and most destructive riot in U.S. history, with sixty-three dead, a billion dollars in property damage, nearly twenty-four hundred injured, and seventeen thousand arrested. President George H. W. Bush invoked the Insurrection Act, to mobilize units from the U.S. Marines and Army to put down the rebellion. A black man named Terry Adams spoke to the L.A. *Times*, and captured the motivation and the mood. "Our people are in pain," he said. "Why should we draw a line against violence? The judicial system doesn't."

The uprising in L.A. shared with the rebellions of the nineteen-sixties an igniting spark of police abuse, widespread violence, and the fury of the rebels. But, in the nineteen-sixties, the flush economy and the still-intact notion of the social contract meant that President Lyndon B. Johnson could attempt to drown the civil-rights movement and the Black Power radicalization with enormous social spending and government-program expansion, including the passage of the Housing and Urban Development Act of 1968, which produced the first government-backed, low-income homeownership opportunities directed at African-Americans.

By the late nineteen-eighties and early nineties, the economy was in recession and the social contract had been ripped to shreds. The rebellions of the nineteen-sixties and the enormous social spending intended to bring them under control were wielded by the right to generate a backlash against the expanded welfare state. Political conservatives argued that the market, not government intervention, could create efficiencies and innovation in the delivery of public services. This rhetoric was coupled with virulent racist characterizations of African-Americans, who relied disproportionately on welfare programs. Ronald Reagan mastered the art of color-blind racism in the post-civil-rights era with his invocations of "welfare queens." Not only did these distortions pave the way for undermining the welfare state, they reinforced racist delusions about the state of black America that legitimized deprivation and marginalization.

The Los Angeles uprising not only exposed the police state that African-Americans were subjected to but also uncovered the hollowed-out core of the U.S. economy after the supposed economic genius of the Reagan Revolution. The rebellions of the nineteen-sixties were disparaged as race riots because they were confined almost exclusively to segregated black communities. The L.A. rebellion spread rapidly across the city: fifty-one per cent of those arrested were Latino, and only thirty-six per cent were black. A smaller number of whites were also arrested. Public officials had used racism as a crowbar to dismantle the welfare state, but the effects were felt across the board. Though African-Americans were disproportionate recipients of welfare, whites made up the majority, and they suffered, too, when cuts were imposed. As Willie Brown, who was then the speaker of the California Assembly, wrote, in the San Francisco *Examiner*, days after the uprising, "For the first time in American history, many of the demonstrations and much of the violence and crime, especially the looting, was multiracial—blacks, whites, Hispanics, and Asians were all involved." Though typically segregated from each other socially, each group found ways to express their overlapping grievances in the furious revolt against the L.A.P.D.

The period after the L.A. rebellion didn't usher in new initiatives to improve the quality of the lives of people who had revolted. To the contrary, the Bush White House spokesman Marlin Fitzwater blamed the uprising on the social-welfare programs of previous administrations, saying, "We believe that many of the root problems that have resulted in inner-city difficulties were started in the sixties and seventies and that they have failed." The nineteen-nineties became a moment of convergence for the political right and the Democratic Party, as the Democrats cemented their turn toward a similar agenda of harsh budget cuts to social programs and an insistence that African-American hardship was the result of non-normative family structures. In May, 1992, Bill Clinton interrupted his normal campaign activities to travel to South Central Los Angeles, where he offered his analysis of what had gone so wrong. People were looting, he said, "because they are not part of the system at all anymore. They do not share our values, and their children are growing up in a culture alien from ours, without family, without neighborhood, without church, without support."

Democrats responded to the 1992 Los Angeles rebellion by pushing the country further down the road of punishment and retribution in its criminal-justice system. Joe Biden, the current Democratic Presidential front-runner, emerged from the fire last time brandishing a new "crime bill" that pledged to put a hundred thousand more police on the street, called for mandatory prison sentences for certain crimes, increased funding for policing and prisons, and expanded the use of the death penalty. The Democrats' new emphasis on law and order was coupled with a relentless assault on the right to welfare assistance. By 1996, Clinton had followed through on his pledge to "end welfare as we know it." Biden supported the legislation, arguing that "the culture of welfare must be replaced with the culture of work. The culture of dependence must be replaced with the culture of self-sufficiency and personal responsibility. And the culture of permanence must no longer be a way of life."

The 1994 crime bill was a pillar in the phenomenon of mass incarceration and public tolerance for aggressive policing and punishment directed at African-American neighborhoods. It helped to build the world that young black people are rebelling against today. But the unyielding assaults on welfare and food stamps have also marked this latest revolt. These cuts are a large part of the reason that the coronavirus pandemic has landed so hard in the U.S., particularly in black America. These are the reasons that we do not have a viable safety net in this country, including food stamps and cash payments during hard times. The weakness of the U.S. social-welfare state has deep roots, but it was irreversibly torn when Democrats were at the helm.

THE CURRENT CLIMATE CAN HARDLY BE REDUCED TO THE POLITICAL lessons of the past, but the legacy of the nineties dominates the political thinking of elected officials today. When Republicans insist on tying work requirements to food stamps in the midst of a pandemic, with unemployment at more than thirteen per cent, they are conjuring the punitive spirit of the policies shaped by Clinton, Biden, and other leading Democrats throughout the nineteen-nineties. So, though Biden desperately wants us to believe that he is a harbinger of change, his long record of public service says otherwise. He has claimed that Barack Obama's selection of him as his running mate was a kind of absolution for Biden's dealings in the Democrats' race-baiting politics of the nineteen-nineties. But, from the excesses of the criminal-justice system and the absence of a welfare state to the inequality rooted in an unbridled, rapacious market economy, Biden has shaped much of the world that this generation has inherited and is revolting against.

More important, the ideas honed in the nineteen-eighties and nineties continue to beat at the center of Biden's political agenda. His campaign advisers include Larry Summers, who, as Clinton's Treasury Secretary, was an enthusiastic supporter of deregulation, and, as Obama's chief economic adviser during the recession, endorsed the Wall Street bailout while allowing millions of Americans to default on their mortgages. They also include Rahm Emanuel, whose tenure as the mayor of Chicago ended in disgrace, when it was revealed that his administration covered up the police murder of the seventeen-year-old Laquan McDonald, who was shot sixteen times by a white police officer. But Emanuel's damage to Chicago ran much deeper than his defense of a particularly racist and abusive police force. He also carried out the largest single closure of public schools in U.S. history—nearly fifty in one fell swoop, in 2013. After two terms, he left the city in the same broken condition he found it, with forty-five per cent of young black men in Chicago both out of school and unemployed.

This points to the importance of expanding our national discussion about what ails the country, beyond the racism and brutality of the police. We must also discuss the conditions of economic inequality that, when they intersect with racial and gender discrimination, disadvantage African-Americans while also making them vulnerable to police violence. Otherwise, we risk reducing racism to the outrageous and intentional acts of depraved individuals, while downplaying the cumulative impact of public policies and private-sector discrimination that, regardless of personal intent, have crippled the vitality of African-American life.

When the focus narrows to the barbarism of the act that stole George Floyd's life, it allows for the likes of the former President George W. Bush to enter the conversation and claim to deplore racism. Bush wrote, in an open letter on the Floyd killing, that "it remains a shocking failure that many African Americans, especially young African American men, are harassed and threatened in their own country." This would be laughable if George W. Bush were not the grim reaper who hid beneath a shroud he described as "compassionate conservatism." As the governor of Texas, he oversaw a rampant and racist death-penalty system, personally signing off on the execution of a hundred and fifty-two incarcerated people, a disproportionate number of them African-American. As President, Bush oversaw the stunningly incompetent government response to Hurricane Katrina, which contributed to the deaths of nearly two thousand people and displaced tens of thousands of African-American residents of New Orleans. That Bush is able to sanctimoniously enter into a discussion about American racism while ignoring his own role in its perpetuation and sustenance speaks to the superficiality of the conversation. Although many are becoming comfortable spurting out phrases like "systemic racism," the solutions proposed remain mired in the system that is being critiqued. The result is that the roots of oppression and inequality that constitute what many activists refer to as "racial capitalism" are left in place.

Joe Biden, in a recent, rare public appearance, came to Philadelphia to describe the leadership necessary to emerge from this current moment. His speech sounded as if it could have been made at any time in the last twenty years. He promulgated a proposal to end choke holds—even though many police departments have done that already, at least on paper. The New York Police Department is one of them, though this did not prevent Daniel Pantaleo from choking Eric Garner to death, nor did it cause Pantaleo to be sent to jail for it. Biden called for accountability, oversight, and community policing. These proposals for curbing racist policing are as old as the first declarations for reform that came out of the Kerner Commission, in 1967. Then, too, as the nation's cities combusted into a frenzy of uprisings, federal reformers enumerated changes to police policy such as these, and, more than fifty years later, the police remain impervious to reform and often in arrogant refusal to heel. It is simply astounding that Joe Biden has not a single meaningful or new idea to offer about controlling the police.

Barack Obama, in an essay that he posted on Medium, describes voting as the road to making "real change," although he also writes that "if we want to bring about real change, then the choice isn't between protest and politics. We have to do both. We have to mobilize to raise awareness, and we have to organize and cast our ballots to make sure that we elect candidates who will act on reform." Obama has developed a tendency to intervene in political debates as if he were a curious and detached observer, rather than a former officeholder of the most powerful position in the world. The Black Lives Matter movement bloomed during the final years of Obama's Presidency. At each stage of its development, Obama seemed unable to curb the police abuses that were fuelling its development. It is easy to get bogged down in the intricacies of federalism and the constraints on executive power, given that police abuse is such a local issue. But Obama did, after all, convene a national task force aimed at providing guidance and leadership on police accountability, and we can consider its effectiveness from the standpoint of today.

Obama's Task Force on 21st Century Policing delivered sixty-three recommendations, including ending "racial profiling" and

extending "community policing" efforts. It called for "better training" and revamping the entire criminal-justice system. But they
were no more than suggestions; there was no mechanism to make
the country's eighteen thousand different law-enforcement agencies
comply. The Task Force's interim report was released on March 2,
2015. That month, police across the country killed another hundred and thirteen people, thirty more than in the previous month.
On April 4th, Walter Scott, an unarmed black man running away
from a white cop, Michael Slager, in North Charleston, South Carolina, was shot five times from behind. Eight days later, Freddie
Gray was picked up by Baltimore police, placed in a van with no
restraints, and driven recklessly around the city. When he emerged
from the van, his spine was eighty-per-cent severed at his neck. He
died seven days later. Baltimore exploded in rage. And Baltimore
was not like Ferguson, Missouri, which was run by a white political
establishment and patrolled by a white police force. From Mayor
Stephanie Rawlings-Blake to a multiracial police force, Baltimore
was a black-led city.

Even as the wanton violence of law enforcement has come into
sharper focus in the last five years, there has been almost no consequence in terms of municipal budget allocations. Police continue
to absorb absurd portions of local operating budgets—even in departments that are sources of embarrassment and abuse lawsuits. In
Los Angeles, with its homelessness crisis and out-of-control rents,
the police absorb an astounding fifty-three per cent of the city's
general fund. Chicago, a city with a notoriously corrupt and abusive police force, spent thirty-nine per cent of its budget on police.
Philadelphia's operating budget needed to be recalibrated because
of the collapse of tax collections due to the coronavirus pandemic;
the only agency that will not suffer any budget cuts is the police
department. While public schools, affordable housing, violence-
prevention programming, and the police-oversight board prepare
for three hundred and seventy million dollars in budget cuts, the

Philadelphia Police Department, which already garners sixteen per cent of the city's funds, is slated to receive a twenty-three-million-dollar increase.

Throughout the Obama and Trump Administrations, the failures to rein in racist policing practices have been compounded by the economic stagnation in African-American communities, measured by stalled rates of homeownership and a widening racial wealth gap. Are these failures of governance and politics all Obama's fault? Of course not, but, when you run on big promises of change and end up overseeing a brutal status quo, people draw dim conclusions from the experiment. For many poor and working-class African-Americans, who still have enormous pride in the first black President and his spouse, Michelle Obama, the conclusion is that electing the nation's first black President was never going to change America. One might even interpret the failures of the Obama Administration as some of the small kindling that has set the nation ablaze.

WE CANNOT INSIST ON "REAL CHANGE" IN THE UNITED STATES BY CONtinuing to use the same methods, arguments, and failed political strategies that have brought us to this moment. We cannot allow the current momentum to be stalled by a narrow discussion about reforming the police. In Obama's essay, he wrote, "I saw an elderly black woman being interviewed today in tears because the only grocery store in her neighborhood had been trashed. If history is any guide, that store may take years to come back. So let's not excuse violence, or rationalize it, or participate in it." If we are thinking of these problems in big and broad strokes, or in a systemic way, we might ask: Why is there only a single grocery store in this woman's neighborhood? That might lead to a discussion about the history of residential segregation in that neighborhood, or job discrimination or under-resourced schools in the area, which might, in turn, provide deeper insights into an alienation that is so profound in its intensity that it compels people to fight with the intensity of a riot to demand things change. And this is where the trouble actually begins. Our society cannot end these conditions without *massive* expenditure.

In 1968, King, in the weeks before he was assassinated, said, "In a sense, I guess you could say, we are engaged in the class struggle." He was speaking to the costs of the programs that would be necessary to lift black people out of poverty and inequality, which were, in and of themselves, emblems of racist subjugation. Ending segregation in the South, then, was cheap compared with the huge costs necessary to end the kinds of discrimination that kept blacks locked out of the advantages of U.S. society, from well-paying jobs to well-resourced schools, good housing, and a comfortable retirement. The price of the ticket is quite steep, but, if we are to have a real conversation about how we change America, it must begin with an honest assessment of the scope of the deprivation involved. Racist and corrupt policing is the tip of the iceberg.

We have to make space for new politics, new ideas, new formations, and new people. The election of Biden may stop the misery of another Trump term, but it won't stop the underlying issues that have brought about more than a hundred thousand COVID-19 deaths or continuous protests against police abuse and violence. Will the federal government intervene to stop the looming crisis of evictions that will disproportionately impact black women? Will it use its power and authority to punish police, and to empty prisons and jails, which not only bring about social death but are now also sites of rampant COVID-19 infection? Will it end the war on food stamps and allow African-Americans and other residents of this country to eat in the midst of the worst economic crisis since the Great Depression? Will it finance the health-care needs of tens of millions of African-Americans who have become susceptible to the worst effects of the coronavirus, and are dying as a result? Will it provide the resources to depleted public schools, allowing black children the opportunity to learn in peace? Will it redistribute the hundreds of billions of dollars necessary to rebuild devastated working-class communities? Will there be free day care and transportation?

If we are serious about ending racism and fundamentally changing the United States, we must begin with a real and serious assessment of the problems. We diminish the task by continuing to call upon the agents and actors who fuelled the crisis when they had opportunities to help solve it. But, more importantly, the quest to transform this country cannot be limited to challenging its brutal police alone. It must conquer the logic that finances police and jails at the expense of public schools and hospitals. Police should not be armed with expensive artillery intended to maim and murder civilians while nurses tie garbage sacks around their bodies and reuse masks in a futile effort to keep the coronavirus at bay.

We have the resources to remake the United States, but it will have to come at the expense of the plutocrats and the plunderers, and therein lies the three-hundred-year-old conundrum: America's professed values of life, liberty, and the pursuit of happiness, continually undone by the reality of debt, despair, and the human degradation of racism and inequality.

THE UNFOLDING REVOLT IN THE U.S. TODAY HOLDS THE REAL PROMISE to change this country. While it reflects the history and failures of past endeavors to confront racism and police brutality, these protests cannot be reduced to them. Unlike the uprising in Los Angeles, where Korean businesses were targeted and some white bystanders were beaten, or the rebellions of the nineteen-sixties, which were confined to black neighborhoods, today's protests are stunning in their racial solidarity. The whitest states in the country, including Maine and Idaho, have had protests involving thousands of people. And it's not just students or activists; the demands for an end to this racist violence have mobilized a broad range of ordinary people who are fed up.

The protests are building on the incredible groundwork of a previous iteration of the Black Lives Matter movement. Today, young white people are compelled to protest not only because of their anxieties about the instability of this country and their compromised futures in it but also because of a revulsion against white supremacy and the rot of racism. Their outlooks have been shaped during the past several years by the anti-racist politics of the B.L.M. movement, which move beyond seeing racism as interpersonal or attitudinal, to understanding that it is deeply rooted in the country's institutions and organizations.

This may account, in part, for the firm political foundation that this round of struggle has begun upon. It explains why activists and organizers have so quickly been able to gather support for demands to defund police, and in some cases introduce ideas about ending policing altogether. They have been able to quickly link bloated police budgets to the attacks on other aspects of the public sector, and to the limits on cities' abilities to attend to the social crises that have been exposed by the COVID-19 pandemic. They have built upon the vivid memories of previous failures, and refuse to submit to empty or rhetoric-driven calls for change. This is evidence again of how struggles build upon one another and are not just recycled events from the past.

THE TRAYVON GENERATION

ELIZABETH ALEXANDER

June 22, 2020

This one was shot in his grandmother's yard. This one was carrying a bag of Skittles. This one was playing with a toy gun in front of a gazebo. Black girl in bright bikini. Black boy holding cell phone. This one danced like a marionette as he was shot down in a Chicago intersection. The words, the names: Trayvon, Laquan, bikini, gazebo, loosies, Skittles, two seconds, I can't breathe, traffic stop, dashboard cam, sixteen times. His dead body lay in the street in the August heat for four hours.

He was jogging, was hunted down, cornered by a pickup truck, and shot three times. One of the men who murdered him leaned over his dead body and was heard to say, "Fucking nigger."

I can't breathe, again. Eight minutes and forty-six seconds of a knee and full weight on his neck. "I can't breathe" and, then, "Mama!" George Floyd cried. George Floyd cried, "Mama . . . I'm through!"

His mother had been dead for two years when George Floyd called out for her as he was being lynched. Lynching is defined as a killing committed by a mob. I call the four police officers who arrested him a mob.

THE KIDS GOT SHOT AND THE GROWNUPS GOT SHOT. WHICH IS TO SAY, the kids watched their peers shot down and their parents' generation get gunned down and beat down and terrorized as well. The agglomerating spectacle continues. Here are a few we know less well: Danny Ray Thomas. Johnnie Jermaine Rush. Nandi Cain.

Dejuan Hall. Atatiana Jefferson. Demetrius Bryan Hollins. Jacqueline Craig and her children. And then the iconic: Alton Sterling. Eric Garner. Sandra Bland. Walter Scott. Breonna Taylor. Philando Castile.

Sandra Bland filmed the prelude to her death. The policeman thrust a stun gun in her face and said, "I will light you *up*."

I CALL THE YOUNG PEOPLE WHO GREW UP IN THE PAST TWENTY-FIVE years the Trayvon Generation. They always knew these stories. These stories formed their world view. These stories helped instruct young African-Americans about their embodiment and their vulnerability. The stories were primers in fear and futility. The stories were the ground soil of their rage. These stories instructed them that anti-black hatred and violence were never far.

They watched these violations up close and on their cell phones, so many times over. They watched them in near-real time. They watched them crisscrossed and concentrated. They watched them on the school bus. They watched them under the covers at night. They watched them often outside of the presence of adults who loved them and were charged with keeping them safe in body and soul.

This is the generation of my sons, now twenty-two and twenty years old, and their friends who are also children to me, and the university students I have taught and mentored and loved. And this is also the generation of Darnella Frazier, the seventeen-year-old Minneapolis girl who came upon George Floyd's murder in progress while on an everyday run to the corner store on May 25th, filmed it on her phone, and posted it to her Facebook page at 1:46 A.M., with the caption "They killed him right in front of cup foods over south on 38th and Chicago!! No type of sympathy </3 </3 #POLICEBRUTALITY." When insideMPD.com (in an article that is no longer up) wrote, "Man Dies After Medical Incident During Police Interaction," Frazier posted at 3:10 A.M., "Medical

incident??? Watch outtt they killed him and the proof is clearlyyyy there!!"

Darnella Frazier, seventeen years old, witnessing a murder in close proximity, making a record that would have worldwide impact, returned the following day to the scene of the crime. She possessed the language to say, precisely, through tears, "It's so traumatizing."

In Toni Morrison's "Sula," which is set across the bleak black stretch of Ohio after the First World War, the character Hannah plaintively asks her mother, Eva Peace, "Mamma, did you ever love us?" To paraphrase Eva Peace's reply: *Love you? Love you? I kept you alive.*

I believed I could keep my sons alive by loving them, believed in the magical powers of complete adoration and a love ethic that would permeate their lives. My love was armor when they were small. My love was armor when their father died of a heart attack when they were twelve and thirteen. "They think black men only die when they get shot," my older son said in the aftermath. My love was armor when that same year our community's block watch sent e-mails warning residents about "two black kids on bikes" and praising neighbors who had called the police on them. My love for my children said, *Move.* My love said, *Follow your sons,* when they ran into the dark streets of New York to join protesters after Eric Garner's killer was acquitted. When my sons were in high school and pictures of Philando Castile were on the front page of the *Times,* I wanted to burn all the newspapers so they would not see the gun coming in the window, the blood on Castile's T-shirt, the terror in his partner's face, and the eyes of his witnessing baby girl. But I was too late, too late generationally, because they were not looking at the newspaper; they were looking at their phones, where the image was a house of mirrors straight to Hell.

My love was both rational and fantastical. Can I protect my sons from being demonized? Can I keep them from moving free?

But they must be able to move as free as wind! If I listen to their fears, will I comfort them? If I share my fears, will I frighten them? Will racism and fear disable them? If we ignore it all, will it go away? Will dealing with race fill their minds like stones and block them from thinking of a million other things? Let's be clear about what motherhood is. A being comes onto this earth and you are charged with keeping it alive. It dies if you do not tend it. It is as simple as that. No matter how intellectual and multicolored motherhood becomes as children grow older, the part that says *My purpose on earth is to keep you alive* has never totally dissipated. Magical thinking on all sides.

I want my children—all of them—to thrive, to be fully alive. How do we measure what that means? What does it mean for our young people to be "black alive and looking back at you," as June Jordan puts it in her poem "Who Look at Me"? How to access the sources of strength that transcend this American nightmare of racism and racist violence? What does it mean to be a lucky mother, when so many of my sisters have had their children taken from them by this hatred? The painter Titus Kaphar's recent *Time* magazine cover portrays a black mother cradling what should be her child across the middle of her body, but the child is literally cut out of the canvas and cut out of the mother, leaving a gaping wound for an unending grief that has made a sisterhood of countless black women for generations.

My sons were both a little shy outside of our home when they were growing up. They were quiet and observant, like their father, who had come to this country as a refugee from Eritrea: African observant, immigrant observant, missing nothing. I've watched them over the years with their friends, doing dances now outmoded with names I persist in loving—Nae Nae, Hit Dem Folks—and talking about things I didn't teach them and reading books I haven't read and taking positions I don't necessarily hold, and I marvel. They are grown young men. With their friends, they talk about the pressure to succeed, to have a strong public face, to excel. They talk their big talk, they talk their hilarity, and they talk their fear. When I am with them, I truly believe the kids are all right and will save us.

But I worry about this generation of young black people and depression. I have a keen eye—what Gwendolyn Brooks called "gobbling mother-eye"—for these young people, sons and friends and students whom I love and encourage and welcome into my home, keep in touch with and check in on. How are you, how are you, how are you. How are you, baby, how are you. I am interested in the vision of television shows like "Atlanta" and "Insecure," about which I have been asking every young person who will listen, "Don't you think they're about low-grade, undiagnosed depression and not black hipster ennui?" Why, in fact, did Earn drop out of Princeton? Why does Van get high before a drug test? Why does Issa keep blowing up her life? This season, "Insecure" deals directly with the question of young black people and mental-health issues: Molly is in and out of therapy, and we learn that Nathan, a.k.a. LyftBae, who was ghosting Issa, has been dealing with bipolar disorder. The work of the creative icon of their generation often brings me to the question: Why is Kendrick so sad? He has been frank about his depression and suicidal thoughts. It isn't just the spectre of race-based violence and death that hangs over these young people. It's that compounded with the constant display of inequity that has most recently been laid bare in the COVID-19 pandemic, with racial health disparities that are shocking even to those of us inured to our disproportionate suffering.

BLACK CREATIVITY EMERGES FROM LONG LINES OF INNOVATIVE RE-sponses to the death and violence that plague our communities. "Not a house in the country ain't packed to its rafters with some dead Negro's grief," Toni Morrison wrote in "Beloved," and I am interested in creative emergences from that ineluctable fact.

There are so many visual artists responding to this changing same: Henry Taylor, Michael Rakowitz, Ja'Tovia Gary, Carrie Mae Weems, lauren woods, Alexandra Bell, Black Women Artists for Black Lives Matter, Steffani Jemison, Kerry James Marshall, Titus Kaphar. To pause at one work: Dread Scott's "A Man Was Lynched by Police Yesterday," which he made in the wake of the police shooting of Walter Scott, in 2015, echoes the flag reading "A man was lynched yesterday" that the N.A.A.C.P. flew outside its New York headquarters between 1920 and 1938 to mark the lynchings of black people in the United States.

I want to turn to three short films that address the Trayvon Generation with particular power: Flying Lotus's "Until the Quiet Comes" (2012); his "Never Catch Me," with Kendrick Lamar (2014); and Lamar's "Alright" (2015).

In "Until the Quiet Comes," the director, Kahlil Joseph, moves us through black Los Angeles—Watts, to be specific. In the fiction of the video, a boy stands in an empty swimming pool, pointing his finger as a gun and shooting. The bullet ricochets off the wall of the pool and he drops as it appears to hit him. The boy lies in a wide-arced swath of his blood, a portrait in the empty pool. He is another black boy down, another body of the traumatized community.

In an eerie twilight, we move into the densely populated Nickerson Gardens, where a young man, played by the dancer Storyboard P, lies dead. Then he rises, and begins a startling dance of resurrection, perhaps coming back to life. The community seems numb, oblivious of his rebirth. That rebirth is brief; he gets into a low-rider car, that L.A. icon. The car drives off after his final death dance, taking him from this life to the other side. His death is consecrated by his performance, a ritual that the sudden dead are not afforded. The car becomes a hearse, a space of ritual transport into the next life. But the young man is still gone.

What does it mean to be able to bring together the naturalistic and the visionary, to imagine community as capable of reanimating even its most hopeless and anesthetized members? What does it mean for a presumably murdered black body to come to life in his community in a dance idiom that is uniquely part of black culture and youth culture, all of that power channelled into a lifting?

A sibling to Joseph's work is Hiro Murai's video for Flying Lotus's "Never Catch Me." It opens at a funeral for two children, a black boy and girl, who lie heartbreak-beautiful in their open caskets. Their community grieves inconsolably in the church. The scene is one of profound mourning.

And then the children open their eyes and climb out of their caskets. They dance explosively in front of the pulpit before running down the aisle and out of the church. The mourners cannot see this resurrection, for it is a fantasia. The kids dance another dance of black L.A., the force of black bodily creativity, that expressive life source born of violence and violation that have upturned the world for generations. The resurrected babies dance with a pumping force. But the community's grief is unmitigated, because, once again, this is a dreamscape. The children spring out into the light and climb into a car—no, it is a hearse—and, smiling with the joy of mischievous escapees, drive away. Kids are not allowed to drive; kids are not allowed to die.

WHAT DOES IT MEAN FOR A BLACK BOY TO FLY, TO DREAM OF FLYING and transcending? To imagine his vincible body all-powerful, a body that in this society is so often consumed as a money-maker and an object of perverse desire, perceived to have superhuman and thus threatening powers? In the video for Kendrick Lamar's "Alright," directed by Colin Tilley, Lamar flies through the California city streets, above sidewalks and empty lots, alongside wire fences.

"Alright" has been the anthem of many protests against racism and police violence and unjust treatment. Lamar embodies the energy and the message of the resonant phrase "black lives matter," which Patrice Cullors, Alicia Garza, and Opal Tometi catapulted into circulation when, in 2013, they founded the movement. The phrase was apt then and now. Its coinage feels both ancestral in its knowledge and prophetic in its ongoing necessity. I know now with certainty that there will never be a moment when we will not need to say it, not in my lifetime, and not in the lifetime of the Trayvon Generation.

The young black man flying in Lamar's video is joyful and defiant, rising above the streets that might claim him, his body liberated and autonomous. At the end of the video, a police officer raises a finger to the young man in the sky and mimes pulling the trigger. The wounded young man falls, slowly—another brother down—and lands. The gun was a finger; the flying young man appears safe. He does not get up. But in the final image of this dream he opens his eyes and smiles. For a moment, he has not been killed.

Black celebration is a village practice that has brought us together in protest and ecstasy around the globe and across time. Community is a mighty life force for self-care and survival. But it does not protect against murder. Dance itself will not free us. We continue to struggle against hatred and violence. I believe that this generation is more vulnerable, and more traumatized, than the last. I think of Frederick Douglass's words upon hearing slaves singing their sorrow songs in the fields. He laid waste to the nascent myth of the happy darky: "Slaves sing most when they are most unhappy." Our dancing is our pleasure but perhaps it is also our sorrow song.

My sons love to dance. I have raised them to young adulthood. They are beautiful. They are funny. They are strong. They are fascinating. They are kind. They are joyful in friendship and community. They are righteous and smart in their politics. They are learning. They are loving. They are mighty and alive.

I RECALL MANY SWEATY SUMMER PARTIES WITH FAMILY FRIENDS where the grownups regularly acted up on the dance floor and the kids d.j.'d to see how quickly they could make their old-school parents and play-uncles and aunties holler "Aaaaayyyy! That's my jam!" They watched us with deep amusement. But they would dance, too. One of the aunties glimpsed my sons around the corner in the next room and said, "Oh, my God, they can dance! They've been holding out on us, acting all shy!"

When I told a sister-friend that my older son, during his freshman year in college, was often the one controlling the aux cord, dancing and dancing and dancing, she said, "Remember, people dance when they are joyful."

Yes, I am saying I measure my success as a mother of black boys in part by the fact that I have sons who love to dance, who dance in community, who dance till their powerful bodies sweat, who dance and laugh, who dance and shout. Who are able—in the midst of their studying and organizing, their fear, their rage, their protesting, their vulnerability, their missteps and triumphs, their knowledge that they must fight the hydra-headed monster of racism and racial violence that we were not able to cauterize—to find the joy and the power of communal self-expression.

This essay is not a celebration, nor is it an elegy.

We are no longer enslaved. Langston Hughes wrote that we must stand atop the racial mountain, "free within ourselves," and I pray that those words have meaning for our young people. But our freedom must be seized and reasserted every day.

People dance to say, *I am alive and in my body.*
I am black alive and looking back at you.

HOMECOMING

HILTON ALS

June 29, 2020

By the late summer of 1967, when I turned seven, we'd been living in the house for six years. By "we," I mean my mother, two of my four older sisters, and my little brother. And although we shared the place with a rotating cast of other relatives, including my mother's mother and an aunt and her two children, I always considered it my mother's home. The house was in the Brownsville section of Brooklyn. Like all the moves my mother engineered or helped to engineer for our family, this one was aspirational. Despite the fact that Brownsville had begun its slow decline into drugs, poverty, and ghettoization years before, my mother's house—the only one in her life that, after years of work and planning, she would even partly own—symbolized a break with everything we had known before, including an apartment in Crown Heights, with a shared bathroom near the stairwell, where, on Sunday nights, my mother would line her daughters up with freshly laundered towels so that they could take their weekly bath.

Privacy was something my sisters had to get used to. Our new house had doors and a proper sitting room, which sometimes served as a makeshift bedroom for visiting Bajan relatives. (My mother's family was from Barbados.) The sister I was closest to, a poetry-writing star who wore pencil skirts to play handball with the guys, composed her verse amid drifts and piles of clothes and kept her door closed. My brother and I shared a smaller room and a bed. My mother had her own room, where the door was always ajar; she didn't so much sleep there as rest between walks up and down the hall to watch and listen for the safety of her children.

The Brownsville summer of 1967 was like every other Brooklyn summer I'd experienced: stultifying. Relief was sought at the nearby Betsy Head Pool, and at the fire hydrants that reckless boys opened with giant wrenches. The cold water made the black asphalt blacker in the black nights. Gossip floated down the street from our neighbors' small front porches and from stoops flanked by big concrete planters full of dusty plastic flowers. Nursing a beer or a Pepsi, the grownups discussed far-off places like Vietnam. So-and-So's son had come back from there all messed up, and now he was on the methadone. Then the conversation would shift to the kids. Every kid in our neighborhood was everyone else's kid. Prying, caring eyes were everywhere. Sometimes the conversation stopped— just for a moment—as girls in summer dresses passed. Men and women alike looked longingly at those girls, for different reasons, as they ambled down the street, pretending to pay no mind to the fine-built boys who called to them from a distance.

In short, what one saw in that place on those nights was what my mother had been searching for: community. She was a proud member of Mary McLeod Bethune's National Council of Negro Women, and had attended Martin Luther King, Jr.,'s 1963 March on Washington. When she reminisced about that march, it was with a vividness that made her children feel shy: sometime in the long ago, Ma had been part of history. Nonviolent organization, picket lines, and marches: all these strengthened our mother's conviction that inclusion worked, that civil rights worked, that the black family could work, especially if welfare officers and other professionally concerned people—journalists and sociologists, say—paid attention to what a black mother built, rather than to how she failed. ("I don't think a female running a house is a problem, a broken family," Toni Morrison said in a 1989 interview. "It's perceived as one because of the notion that a head is a man. . . . You need a whole community—everybody—to raise a child.")

If Ma failed, then we failed, and she never wanted us to feel that. Something else Ma wanted: for black people in Brooklyn, in America, not to forever be effectively refugees—stateless, homeless, without rights, confined by borders that they did not create and by a penal system that killed them before they died, all while trying to rear children who went to schools that taught them not about themselves but about what they didn't have.

And yet there was no way to save Ma's idea of community and hope when, in September, 1967, our neighborhood changed forever. Someone, or a bunch of someones, heard that a young boy, a fourteen-year-old black kid, Richard Ross, had been killed by a cop—a detective named John Rattley—in Brownsville. Apparently, Rattley believed that Ross had mugged or was mugging an old Jewish man; as Ross tried to get away, Rattley shot him in the back of the head. In those years, black boys were locked up or killed all the time; you didn't think about it much, because to think about it was to remember what a killing field New York was, and how easily you, too, could become a body in that field. The detail we hung on to in the flurry of hearsay and speculation was that Rattley was black. The activist Sonny Carson was big then; it was said that he was leading a demonstration, and it was coming our way.

Marches, protests, and the like were, we knew, a prelude to the racially motivated violence that had already cropped up in nearby Newark and other places, such as Detroit. For sure, Brownsville would get more messed up if the cops were involved; that was how demonstrations became riots. I remember that night—or was it late afternoon?—our mother walking us swiftly into the house and shutting all the doors and windows. Inside, it was lights-out. The air was close. We could hear our hearts beating. Peeking from behind one of the living-room curtains, I watched as the protesters started flinging bottles and stones at the cops, and our real world turned into a movie, a horror film in which everything we'd built together—home, hope, the illusion of citizenship—was torn to the ground. Black people, mostly men, were roaming the streets, periodically smashing car windows or overturning ashcans and torching rubbish. They were claiming what they felt to be a kind of freedom. As refugees, we knew that none of it belonged to us—not that shop, not that newly built pigeon coop—even as we knew that it did belong to us, emotionally speaking: it was all part of our community. Still, why not trash a universe that has trashed you?

Standing by my mother's living-room window, I tried, tentatively, to ask her why our world was burning, burning. She gave me a forbidding look: *Boy, be quiet so you can survive*, her eyes seemed to say. Did I want to be another Richard Ross, one of the hundred or thousand Richard Rosses out there? So many questions I could not ask—among them, had our desire for community also been reduced to rubble and ash? The chaos that night—it would last for two days before life went back to "normal"—was more vivid to my burgeoning writer's mind than what I could not see: our mother's vivid memories of King's promise of a promised land. Where was that? And was it different from—or superior to—the world my poetry-writing sister was gradually entering, through her admiration for a number of the musicians and poets associated with the Black Arts Movement? A world that promised a cataclysmic end to whiteness, if only we could carry arms and follow the teachings of early Malcolm X? Was my mother a "better" forecaster of what was to come than my sister? Martin and Malcolm, like protest marches and riots, belonged to different generations. Because I loved my sister and wanted to think as she did, I was, presumably, part of the "riot generation"; I knew about violence from the teasing, taunting black boys in my neighborhood, and Sly and the Family Stone's dark and furious album "There's a Riot Goin' On," released four years after the Brownsville uprising, stayed in my bones more than those of any weepy folksinger. But what about Ma and her dreams? I belonged to and was part of them as well.

Who would I be when the revolution finally came? A soldier for peace, or a man who might appear in "The True Import of Present Dialogue: Black vs. Negro," a poem by the activist and writer Nikki Giovanni?

> Nigger
> Can you kill
> Can you kill
> Can a nigger kill
> Can a nigger kill a honkie
> Can a nigger kill the Man
> Can you kill nigger
> Huh? nigger can you
> kill
> Do you know how to draw blood
> Can you poison
> Can you stab-a-Jew
> Can you kill huh? nigger
> Can you kill
> Can you run a protestant down with your
> '68 El Dorado
> (that's all they're good for anyway)
> Can you kill . . .
> A nigger can die
> We ain't got to prove we can die
> We got to prove we can kill . . .

But my brother and I weren't niggers. And if called upon we wouldn't have been able to protect our mother and our sisters. Whom could we rely on to protect them, let alone us? Would the young black men with bats and other weapons who were flitting down our street—they seemed to leap as they walked—come for us? Would they save us? Or destroy us, too? No door or lock could keep them out.

Ma had her girls first. I wonder what it was like for her to try to understand boys—to rear boys who were not a threat to women, who would grow up to support women's dreams and protect them. In her world, men came and went and were Something Else. My brother and I were different, and, although we were our mother's familiars, I wonder if she eyed our difference unbelievingly at times, even as she nurtured it.

WHEN WE FINALLY LEFT OUR HOUSE IN BROWNSVILLE, WE WALKED out into a changed world. Apparently, while we were inside, Lloyd Sealy, who was then the commander of Brooklyn's North Borough, had ramped up the police presence in the area. One way to control unruly, ungovernable refugees, of course, is to remind them that they are guests of a mighty police state. Every billy club that cracks open a black skull anywhere is proof of that. Once we learned that Sealy was black, too, we bent low in sorrow, or rose with arms high in grief and anger. What had civil rights wrought? Were powerful black men mere functionaries for a white administration? Did black lives not matter to them, then or ever?

Brownsville was not their home. Was it even ours? The world that Ma desired just wasn't possible yet. We were still refugees living within certain borders. We would live and die in this amount of space and no more. Emerging from our mother's house, we smelled burning tires and bedding. (Our house was relatively unharmed.) I don't remember my mother crying; I remember entering that fetid air in silence. But you could hear our community mourning the loss of itself, if you knew how to listen; mourning was our language. The world around us was not the one we had worked hard to achieve but the quiet, degraded world that our not-country said we deserved. We couldn't keep nothing, the elders said, not even ourselves.

Had the uprising been a kind of temper tantrum? Acted out by a community that was, like me, looking for a black man it could trust to protect and lead it? Rattley, Sealy, my only occasionally live-in father: there had been so many disappointments. Someone said that Sonny Carson had helped to quiet folks down. Someone said that a young Muslim man, a local youth-group leader, had also helped to calm things by serving as a liaison between the police and the crowds. Someone said that Mayor John V. Lindsay was around. And then there he was, our first celebrity, a tall white man, trailed by a group of photographers and tired-looking black people, walking through our streets, or someone's streets, surveying the damage. Lindsay also served on President Lyndon Johnson's National Advisory Commission on Civil Disorders, more commonly known as the Kerner Commission, which had been established after riots took place in Los Angeles, Chicago, and Detroit. He had access to a world beyond what we knew, and now he turned his attention to me, in this world. He took my hand. He was beautiful, like a star from a movie I had never seen. Mixed with the confusion and the vague erotics of the moment—it was a thrill to feel my small hand in his big one (was *he* my father?), though I had already learned to hide that part of myself—was my silent bewilderment over the fact that poverty and frustration could be an opportunity for a photograph, though no one asked us what it was like to lose a home or to dream of living in one.

HOPE DIES ALL THE TIME. AND YET WE NEED TO BELIEVE THAT IT WILL come back and attach itself to a new cause—a new love, a new house, something that gives us a sense of purpose, which is ultimately what hope is. Ma always had hope, because she knew that it had helped to change the world, her black world. But I had no clear examples, growing up, of what might make a difference in mine. Guns? Death? Poetry? Would any of it dismantle the economic discrepancies, for instance, that defined our de-facto underclass, that kept us scavenging for a lifeline, even if it was just a pair of sneakers snatched through a pane of broken glass? When I finally saw the National Mall, in Washington, D.C., in person, the black-and-white pictures of King's historic gathering there played in my head, but alongside memories of 1975's Human Kindness Day. Established in 1972, Human Kindness Day—a series of exhibitions, concerts, and literary events meant to inspire racial pride—was spearheaded by the National Park Service, the D.C. Recreation Department, and Compared to What?, Inc., a nonprofit organization for the advancement of the arts. Each year, a concert by a great black artist capped off the festival—Roberta Flack the first year, Nina Simone the next. But in 1975, when Stevie Wonder was the headliner, vandalism broke out. Hundreds of folks were robbed and injured. It's cited as an early example of "wildin'," but, when discussing it, people rarely mention the recession of the mid-seventies, or the way that bringing together haves and have-nots lent a stage, yet again, to the drama of inequality.

It was a drama that I saw play out, over and over again, as I was growing up. I don't remember when we moved to Bedford-Stuyvesant, but demonstrations and riots followed us there. Then, after a time, we moved to Crown Heights again; riots followed us there, too. No place was safe, because wherever we congregated was unsafe. The laws of real estate, economics, and racism made us unsafe. To cops. To landlords. To social workers, who "visited" our houses whenever they felt like it to see if our mothers were entertaining men (and, by implication, getting paid for it). To shopkeepers, who didn't understand that the deprivations of poverty were a pretty good incentive for us to take what we'd never be able to buy. To schoolteachers, who weren't paid to care. To a society that demanded our gratitude for the dried gruel at the bottom of the bowl which it tossed us after years of scarcely remunerated labor. To the black men whom we wanted to stay, but who couldn't for fear that our vulnerability would compound their own.

The question for me from Brownsville on was: How would I protect my mother and the other women in my family when the riots came again (and they always came)? Adults are supposed to protect children, yes, but when I was growing up it didn't necessarily work that way. It wasn't that your mother didn't care—you were all she had—it was just that she kept running out of time. In addition to her full-time job—and, often, a second job—there was the work that went into feeding you, listening to you, and making sure no one laughed at you or cracked you in the face because you had dreams.

As a boy in Brownsville and in Bed-Stuy, I was tormented by the question of protection, because, of course, I, too, wanted to be protected. Like any number of black boys in those neighborhoods, I grew up in a matrilineal society, where I had been taught the power—the necessity—of silence. But how could you not cry out when you couldn't save your mother because you couldn't defend yourself? Although I had this in common with other guys, something separated me from them when it came to joining those demonstrations, to leaping in the air when black bodies were threatened. My distance had to do with my queerness. The guys who took the chance to protect their families and themselves were the same guys who called me "faggot."

For a while, I thought their looting and carrying on had to do with enacting a particular form of masculinity: if white men and cops could wreak havoc in the world, why couldn't they? But, as I grew older, I realized that part of their acting out had to do with how we were brought up. They weren't trying to be men—they were already men—but in order to have the perceived *weight* of white men they had to reject, to some degree, the silence they had learned from their mothers. If they were going to die, they were going to die screaming.

The silence that I was taught as a means of survival no longer fits me, either. But I know that I wouldn't have given it up entirely—it's hard to give up, Ma—if Christian Cooper hadn't shown me another way in Central Park last month, if that fifty-seven-year-old thinker hadn't woken up next to his slumbering boyfriend, then left their shared love to look at birds, which he loved, too. By example, Cooper showed me that I was not alone. When a white woman tried to endanger him with a lying 911 call ("An African-American man is threatening my life!"), he did not run, and he did not, on a profound level, engage with his attacker's theatrics of racism. Cooper's actions that day said, Listen to yourself, not to your accuser, because your accusers are always listening to their own panic about your presence. And if what they are saying—or shouting— threatens your personal safety, protect yourself by any means necessary. If you can protect yourself, you'll be around to love and take care of more people, and be loved and taken care of in return.

I DON'T ENTIRELY AGREE WITH THE GREAT RALPH ELLISON WHEN HE says, in his 1989 essay "On Being the Target of Discrimination,"

> It isn't necessarily through acts of physical violence—
> lynching, mob attacks, or slaps to the face, whether
> experienced firsthand or by word of mouth—that a child is
> initiated into the contradictions of segregated democracy.
> Rather, it is through brief impersonal encounters, stares,
> vocal inflections, hostile laughter, or public reversals of
> private expectations that occur at the age when children
> are most perceptive to the world and all its wonders.

The truth is that nothing is impersonal when it comes to racism, or the will to subjugate. Every act of racism is a deeply personal act with an end result: the unmooring diminishment of the person who is its target. If you have suffered that kind of erasure, you are less likely to know who you are or where you live. My brother has suggested that we moved so much when we were kids because our mother kept looking for safety. I don't remember exactly how many times we moved; in those days, my focus was on trying to win people over, the better to protect my family, or—silently—trying to fend off homophobia, the better to protect myself. My being a "faggot" was one way for other people to feel better about themselves. My being a "faggot" let cops know what they weren't.

At present, I live in a predominantly white neighborhood in Manhattan. For a number of reasons, I was stuck at home when the demonstrations started downtown last month. Panic set in when I heard the helicopters flying low and the police sirens going. I was convinced that the cops would run across my roof and, on seeing my black ass sitting in an apartment in a neighborhood where I had no business being, would shoot me dead. I asked a white male friend to come and be with me.

What I felt during that first wave of panic was a muscle memory of riots and rootlessness; the thought of those cops took away my feeling of being at home in my home. The real-as-hell feelings I had in my apartment that evening before my friend got there were also a metaphor, but I don't know for what kind of story— and if it is all a story where do I put Richard Ross? Where do I put George Floyd, whose murder by a white police officer in Minneapolis launched those demonstrations? Where do I put Tony McDade, the black trans man who was killed by a police officer in Tallahassee on May 27th? Or Breonna Taylor, shot to death in her bed by Louisville police in March? Or Robert Fuller, whose death by hanging, in Palmdale, California, this month may have been a suicide or may have been a lynching, and how horrible it is that either is possible, in a world hellbent on a certain kind of extinction? And why are these stories becoming conflated? That is, why have they become one story in the media's mind—a story of black death and black uprising and black hope and regeneration? Inevitably, we are losing sight of the individual stories, because it takes too long to consider them one by one. The rope around Robert Fuller's neck becomes Billie Holiday trying to breathe out the choking words as she sings:

> Here is a fruit for the crows to pluck
> For the rain to gather, for the wind to suck
> For the sun to rot, for the trees to drop
> Here is a strange and bitter crop.

Are we a strange crop, constantly provoking strange responses—which are now out in the open, because, truth to tell, black people are also an important revenue stream, and Hulu wants to show us that, by streaming the "black stories" in its archives? Hulu is only one of any number of media outlets that are rushing blindly to show their solidarity with the cause, without mentioning the financial and political benefits that may accrue to them. We all hurt, but some of us want to continue to be paid. And what will the world look like after this period becomes just another moment in history (and it will). Will there be a backlash? Will culture become tired of his blackness and her difference and revert to what it's always reverted to—Andrew Wyeth–tinted dreams, impatience, or downright amnesia once black lives mattering doesn't pay, in all senses of the word? Is this all one story?

I keep looking for the loneliness inherent in black life, our refugee status dressed up in self-protective decorum, because if you can get to your loneliness and articulate it you can also begin to talk about community, and why it is needed in life, too. My community is my memory, which includes the image of my late best friend—he died of AIDS thirty years ago now—who was white and Catholic, being beaten up outside a gay Asian club he was exiting, and me asking later, when he showed up with blood on his jacket, if he'd called the police, and him staring me dead in the eye and saying, "Why bother?" I looked at him and heard the terrifying sound of him being punched in the head because he was interested not only in his own queerness but in Something Else, a gay world where he was not looking in a mirror but was a guest in someone else's home.

IS THIS ALL ONE STORY? AS A WRITER, I INHABIT A WORLD OR WORLDS where the prevalent ethos is presumed to be liberal, but I can't remember a time when the publishing industry, like other institutions devoted to the arts—museums, Broadway—didn't come down on the side of fashion and power. At meetings and parties, one spends a great deal of time with people I call the collaborators—functionaries in service to power—who'll step on your neck to get to the next fashionable Negro who can explain just what is happening and why. When white America asks black artists in particular to speak about race, it's almost always from the vantage point of its being a sort of condition, or plight, and, if those collaborators can actually listen, what they want to hear is, Who are *we* in relation to *you*? In his powerful essay "Within the Context of No-Context," published in this magazine in 1980, George W. S. Trow described that phenomenon further:

> During the nineteen-sixties, a young black man in
> a university class described the Dutch painters of the
> seventeenth century as "belonging" to the white students
> in the room, and not to him. This idea was seized on by
> white members of the class. They acknowledged that they
> were at one with Rembrandt. They acknowledged their
> dominance. They offered to discuss, at any length, their
> inherited power to oppress. It was thought at the time
> that reactions of this type had to do with "white guilt"
> or "white masochism." No. No. It was white euphoria.
> Many, many white children of that day felt the power of
> their inheritance for the first time in the act of rejecting
> it, and they insisted on rejecting it . . . so that they might
> continue to feel the power of that connection. Had the

young black man asked, "Who is this man to you?" the
pleasure they felt would have vanished in embarrassment
and resentment.

Why embarrassment and resentment? Because what passes for
intellectual inquiry at cocktail parties and in many contemporary
institutions is a way of masking the continued and seemingly endless grip that the cultural status quo has on blacks and whites alike.
And, if you confront your white interlocutor with that truth, he has
to confront why he thinks that he and his culture are better than
yours. You may have blackness, but we have Rembrandt. Or, in the
words of Saul Bellow, "Who is the Tolstoy of the Zulus? The Proust
of the Papuans? I'd be happy to read them."

Who will tell this story? Many of us and none of us. Because
the "exceptional" black artists who are asked to sit around the fire
and explain why riots, why death, or why a child has a mother and
not a father, have a built-in expiration date: they function as translators of events and rarely as translators of their own stories, their
own loneliness in a given place and time. As my friend sat with
me earlier this month to help ease the terror I felt on hearing the
helicopters, I thought about what certain other writers might have
made of this place and time if life and our segregated society hadn't
exhausted them long ago: Richard Wright, dead at fifty-two. Nella
Larsen, prematurely silenced. Zora Neale Hurston, broke and forgotten by the time she was sixty. Wallace Thurman, drunk and
disgraced, dead at thirty-two, and, of course, James Baldwin, fa-
tigued and lonesome, dead at sixty-three. Imagine all the things
they didn't say because they couldn't say them. All those journeys
abroad, all the shutting themselves off from the world.

Was it worth it, Ma? (You yourself died at sixty-two.) Was it
worth Richard Wright spending so long on his book-length essay,
"White Man, Listen!" (1957), in which he wrote about racism and
his hopes for African nationalism, with all the sense and confusion

that was in him? Racism can break your heart, break your body. Did Wright, Baldwin, Chester Himes, W. E. B. Du Bois, and so many others forgive their country before the end or did they die screaming? They were my parents, too. Are destruction and hope my only models? Ma, tell me where to begin this story, which will have to include your fear of my death—I'm sorry. Because we are all dying. Shall I begin by showing the collaborators the wounds I've suffered on the auction block of gay and black life and culture? Or should I shut up and learn forgiveness on top of forgiveness?

O.K., Ma, maybe forgiveness is the way, because I love you. But can I forgive myself for forgiving? For the temerity of wanting to be an artist and eating shit to support that impulse? An impulse, Ma, that you supported from the very beginning by writing your comments on the stories I shared with you ("Very good. Mommy"), just as you supported all those poems my sister wrote in her bedroom with the door closed in Brownsville. I've lived with forgiveness for so long—surely there is another language, a different weight on the soul?

Ma, can I forgive the white movie executive who thought it might be "fun" to tell our black host at a luncheon that he'd confused him with another black man? Can I forgive the white Dutch director who asked me to step in for a black actor—to play the character of an old family retainer—since I was, you know, black myself? Can I forgive the self-consciously "queer" white academic at a prestigious Eastern university who made disparaging remarks about my body in front of his class—I was his guest speaker—because he wanted to make a point about one of my "texts"? Can I forgive the white editors who ask me who the next James Baldwin might be, so that they can stay on top of the whole black thing? Can I forgive the white female patron of the arts who, after I'd given a lecture in Miami, at a dinner that was ostensibly in my honor, turned the party against me because I hadn't paid more attention in my speech to an artist whose work she collected? Can I forgive the white former fashion-magazine editor who promised me a job but then discovered that his superiors would never hire a black man? Can I forgive the white magazine writer who, a day or two after I was hired by this magazine, yelled at me in front of friends—with whom I was celebrating the occasion—that I had been hired only because I was black? Can I forgive the white musician who "accidentally" faxed me a racist drawing that her child had made in school, which she thought was funny and his teacher saw no reason to criticize? Can I forgive the white couple who, at a memorial for a friend, made it a point to tell me they'd had no idea that I was so big and so black? Can I forgive the white book editor who said on a first date that his family had had some financial interest in Haiti, where they had owned people "just like you"? Can I forgive the white arts benefactress in Boston who, at another dinner after another lecture, told the table how much she'd loved spirituals as a child, and said, rhetorically, "Who doesn't love Negro spirituals?" Can I forgive the white woman who sat next to me at a Chinese restaurant while I was enjoying a quiet dinner by myself and leaned over to ask if I was a cast member of "Porgy and Bess," which was playing across the street? Can I forgive the white curator who shapes much of the city's, if not the world's, understanding of modern art, who, exhausted by the whole question of inclusion and apropos of an exhibition at her institution, said, "I'm just not into Chinese art"? Can I forgive the white editor who invited me to lunch and during the course of the meal defended his use of the word "nigger" in one of his predominantly white college classes with the Lenny Bruce argument that the only way to defuse the word is to take its power away by speaking it, and added that, besides, one heard it used all up and down Lenox Avenue, in Harlem, and what about that? The old model—Ma's model—was not to give up too much of your power by letting your oppressor know how you felt. But, Ma, I was dying anyway, in all that silence.

You get it only when the shit happens to you, too; we all know that. And now the effects of our segregated democracy are happening to you. And now you can see or understand that, all along, I've been trying to get along, just like you. The way Ma taught me. To be independent and help my chosen family. I've tried to make a living at something I love and to explore the intricacies of love, just like you. I've lost friends and forgotten to pay a credit-card bill, just like you. But I wasn't allowed to be like you. And now my "other" is happening to you. Now degradation and moral compromise and your body breaking down are happening to you. Because Donald Trump has happened to you. Oxycontin has happened to you. Broken families have happened to you. Gun violence—in schools, in supermarkets, in movie theatres, at concerts—has happened to you, along with riots, and frustration, and cops who can't pass up an opportunity to flash their guns and their batons in your presence, even as you search for home, even as the dream comes tumbling, tumbling, tumbling down.

ACKNOWLEDGMENTS

We're grateful to our friends at Ecco, who contributed their wisdom and judgment to this anthology: Dan Halpern, Denise Oswald, Helen Atsma, Norma Barksdale, Martin Wilson, Miriam Parker, Meghan Deans, and John Jusino. We owe thanks to our ever-ready matchmaker Eric Simonoff and to his deft aide, Jessica Spitz; to the photographer Devin Allen, for his startling image on the cover; to our colleagues at *The New Yorker*, particularly Henry Finder, Hilton Als, Vinson Cunningham, Erin Overbey, Fabio Bertoni, Daniel Zalewski, Deirdre Foley-Mendelssohn, Pam McCarthy, Natalie Raabe, Risa Leibowitz, Clare Sestanovich, Nicholas Blechman, Joanna Milter, Leily Kleinbard, Jessica Henderson, Toni Burdick, and so many more who provided words of advice and encouragement along the way. Special thanks to Mengfei Chen, who did so much excellent editorial work on this anthology; to all the editors and fact-checkers who helped bring these pieces to print; to our families; and, above all, to the writers of *The New Yorker*.

CONTRIBUTORS

CHIMAMANDA NGOZI ADICHIE is the author of three novels, "Purple Hibiscus," "Half of a Yellow Sun," and "Americanah"; a story collection, "The Thing Around Your Neck"; and the essays "We Should All Be Feminists," "Dear Ijeawele, or A Feminist Manifesto in Fifteen Suggestions," and "Notes on Grief." She divides her time between Nigeria and the United States.

RENATA ADLER became a staff writer at *The New Yorker* in 1963 and, except for a year as the chief film critic of the New York *Times*, remained at *The New Yorker* for the next four decades. Her books include "A Year in the Dark: A Year in the Life of a Film Critic 1968–1969," "Canaries in the Mineshaft: Essays on Politics and Media," and the novels "Speedboat" and "Pitch Dark."

ELIZABETH ALEXANDER, a poet, a scholar, and a cultural critic, most recently published the memoir "The Light of the World." She is the president of the Andrew W. Mellon Foundation.

DANIELLE ALLEN, a political theorist, is the James Bryant Conant University Professor at Harvard. Her books include "Cuz: The Life and Times of Michael A" and the forthcoming "Democracy in the Time of Coronavirus," which will be out in December 2021.

HILTON ALS, a staff writer at *The New Yorker*, won the 2017 Pulitzer Prize for criticism. He is the author of "The Women," "White Girls," and "Alice Neel: Uptown." He is also an associate professor of writing at Columbia University.

JERVIS ANDERSON, who died in 1999, was a staff writer for *The New Yorker* for three decades. He was the author of several books, including the biographies of A. Philip Randolph and Bayard Rustin.

RACHEL AVIV, who joined *The New Yorker* as a staff writer in 2013, has received a Rona Jaffe Foundation Writers' Award and the Scripps Howard Award, for her reporting about police violence. She won a 2020 Whiting Nonfiction Grant for her book in progress about mental illness.

JAMES BALDWIN, a novelist, an essayist, a poet, and a playwright, died in 1987. His works include "Go Tell It on the Mountain," "Giovanni's Room," and "The Fire Next Time."

SARAH M. BROOM grew up in New Orleans and lives in New York. She won the 2019 National Book Award for Nonfiction for her book "The Yellow House."

TA-NEHISI COATES has published "The Beautiful Struggle," "We Were Eight Years in Power," "Between the World and Me," which won the 2015 National Book Award, and the novel "The Water Dancer."

JELANI COBB, a staff writer at *The New Yorker*, teaches in the journalism program at Columbia University. He is the author of "The Substance of Hope: Barack Obama and the Paradox of Progress" and the co-editor of "The Essential Kerner Commission Report: The Landmark Study on Race, Inequality, and Police Violence."

STANLEY CROUCH, who died in 2020, was the author of numerous books, including "Always in Pursuit," "The All-American Skin Game, or, the Decoy of Race," "Don't the Moon Look Lonesome," and "Notes of a Hanging Judge."

VINSON CUNNINGHAM joined *The New Yorker* as a staff writer in 2016. Since 2019, he has served as a theatre critic for the magazine. His debut novel will be released in 2022.

EDWIDGE DANTICAT has published many books, including, "Krik? Krak!," "Brother, I'm Dying," and "Everything Inside: Stories."

CHARLAYNE HUNTER-GAULT is the author of "In My Place," "New News Out of Africa: Uncovering Africa's Renaissance," "To the Mountaintop: My Journey Through the Civil Rights Movement," and "Corrective Rape."

HENRY LOUIS GATES, JR., an Emmy Award–winning documentary filmmaker, is the author or co-author of over twenty books, including "The Black Church: This Is Our Story, This Is Our Song."

MALCOLM GLADWELL, a staff writer for *The New Yorker* since 1996, won the 2001 National Magazine Award for profiles. His books include "The Tipping Point: How Little Things Can Make a Big Difference," "Outliers: The Story of Success," and "The Bomber Mafia: A Dream, a Temptation, and the Longest Night of the Second World War." He is the host of the podcast "Revisionist History."

JENNIFER GONNERMAN joined *The New Yorker* as a staff writer in 2015. She is the author of "Life on the Outside: The Prison Odyssey of Elaine Bartlett."

JAMAICA KINCAID has written numerous books, including "See Now Then," "A Small Place," and "My Brother." A professor of African and African-American studies at Harvard University, she was elected to the American Academy of Arts and Letters in 2004.

ANDREA LEE, a longtime contributor to *The New Yorker*, is the author of five books, including the memoir "Russian Journal," the story collection "Interesting Women," and the novels "Sarah Phillips," "Lost Hearts in Italy," and "Red Island House."

JILL LEPORE, a staff writer at *The New Yorker*, is a professor of history at Harvard and the author of fourteen books, including "The Secret History of Wonder Woman," "These Truths: A

History of the United States," and "If Then: How the Simulmatics Corporation Invented the Future." She is the host of the podcast "The Last Archive."

LUKE MOGELSON, a contributor to *The New Yorker* since 2013, has published the short story collection "These Heroic, Happy Dead." He won the 2020 Polk Award for National Reporting.

TONI MORRISON was the author of eleven novels, including "The Bluest Eye," "Song of Solomon," and "Beloved." Among her books of nonfiction are "Playing in the Dark: Whiteness and the Literary Imagination," "The Origin of Others," a collection drawn from her Charles Eliot Norton lectures, and "The Source of Self-Regard: Selected Essays, Speeches, and Meditations." She received the Nobel Prize in Literature in 1993.

EMILY NUSSBAUM won the Pulitzer Prize for criticism in 2016. Her book, "I Like to Watch: Arguing My Way Through the TV Revolution," came out in 2019.

ALEXIS OKEOWO, a staff writer at *The New Yorker*, received the 2018 PEN Open Book Award for "A Moonless, Starless Sky: Ordinary Women and Men Fighting Extremism in Africa." In 2020, they were named journalist of the year by the Newswomen's Club of New York.

ALEX ROSS has been *The New Yorker's* music critic since 1996. He is the author of "The Rest Is Noise: Listening to the Twentieth Century," "Listen to This," and "Wagnerism: Art and Politics in the Shadow of Music."

CLAUDIA ROTH PIERPONT has contributed to *The New Yorker* since 1990 and became a staff writer in 2004. Her books include "American Rhapsody: Writers, Musicians, Movie Stars, and One Great Building," "Roth Unbound: A Writer and His Books," and "Passionate Minds: Women Rewriting the World."

KELEFA SANNEH has been a staff writer at *The New Yorker* since 2008. He is also a contributor to "CBS Sunday Morning."

KATHRYN SCHULZ, a staff writer at *The New Yorker* since 2015, won the 2016 Pulitzer Prize for Feature Writing. She is the author of "Being Wrong: Adventures in the Margin of Error," and "Lost & Found," which is due out in 2022.

ZADIE SMITH has published the novels "White Teeth," "The Autograph Man," "On Beauty," "NW," and "Swing Time," as well as three collections of essays, "Changing My Mind," "Feel Free," and "Intimations." She is a professor of creative writing at New York University.

DOREEN ST. FÉLIX has been a staff writer at *The New Yorker* since 2017 and was named the magazine's television critic in 2019. In 2019, she won a National Magazine Award for Columns and Commentary.

KEEANGA-YAMAHTTA TAYLOR is a contributing writer at *The New Yorker*. She is a professor of African-American studies at Princeton University and the author of several books, including "Race for Profit: How Banks and the Real Estate Industry Undermined Black Homeownership," which was a 2020 finalist for the Pulitzer Prize for History.

CALVIN TOMKINS has been a staff writer for *The New Yorker* since 1960. He has published more than a dozen books, including "The Bride and the Bachelors: Five Masters of the Avant-garde," "Merchants and Masterpieces: The Story of the Metropolitan Museum of Art," and "Duchamp: A Biography." "The Lives of Artists," a six-volume anthology of his artist profiles, was released in 2019.

CALVIN TRILLIN, a staff writer, has contributed to *The New Yorker* since 1963. His books include "Jackson, 1964: And Other

Dispatches from Fifty Years of Reporting on Race in America"
and "About Alice."

REBECCA WEST, who died in 1983, was a novelist, a biographer, a
journalist, and a critic. She published numerous books, including
"Black Lamb and Grey Falcon," "The Meaning of Treason," and
eight novels.